BEN NEVIS

Britain's Highest Mountain

FOR AYSEL & CHRISTINE

'A seder ci ponemmo ivi ambedui
volti a levante ond' eravam saliti,
che suole a riguardar giovare altrui'

And here we both sat down to face the east,
to rest, as we surveyed all we had climbed –
a backward glance can often lift the heart.

Dante: 'Purgatorio', Canto IV, 52.

BEN NEVIS

Britain's Highest Mountain

KEN CROCKET
SIMON RICHARDSON

SCOTTISH MOUNTAINEERING TRUST

ISBN 978-1-907233-10-4
A catalogue record for this book is available from the British Library

This book is published by the Scottish Mountaineering Trust, a charitable trust registered in Scotland. Revenue from all books published by the Trust is used for the continuation of its publishing programme and for charitable purposes associated with Scottish mountains and mountaineering. Visit <www.smc.org.uk/trust/trust.htm> for more information

Front cover:
Main picture, Orion Face and Tower Ridge *Andy Nisbet*.
Below from left, Harold Raeburn *SMC Archive*, Point Five Gully *Con Higgins*, Charles Inglis Clark Memorial Hut and Càrn Dearg Buttress *Cubby Images*, Andy Turner on the first ascent of The Secret *Viv Scott*

Frontispiece: Charles Inglis Clark Memorial Hut, January 1984 *Ken Crocket*

Designed and produced by Tom Prentice for Scottish Mountaineering Trust (Publications) Ltd
Page design and typesetting: Ken Crocket
Colour scanning: Core Image, East Kilbride, Scotland
Printed and bound in Thailand by Kyodo Printing Co

Distributed by Cordee Ltd, Leicester, United Kingdom
(t) 0116 254 3579, (w) www.cordee.co.uk

Contents

Acknowledgments

Many have aided in the preparation of this book, whether in lending photographs, providing information and/or advice, or reading part or all of the MS. I am deeply grateful to all for their generosity. In no particular order they are: Ian Sykes, for pushing me into starting; Tom Weir, for providing a Foreword, for editing the MS and for encouragement; Bill Murray, for comments on Ch.6; Jimmy Marshall, for comments on Ch.9; John Lackie, for constructive comments on the MS; Adam Curtis, for word processing facilities; Andy Hart, for excellent work in the darkroom; Colin Stead and Bob Lawford, Librarians of the Scottish Mountaineering Club and The Alpine Club respectively; Graham Tiso, for trusting me once again with selections from the A.E.Robertson Photographic Collection; Karuna, for material on her husband, the late J.H.B.Bell; the late Bill Peascod, for material in Ch.7; Miss Marjory Roy, Superintendent Meteorological Office (Edinburgh), for unpublished and other material in Ch.3; Bill Brooker, Editor SMC Journal, for permission to borrow heavily from his Journals; Rab Carrington, for permission to use material first published in *Mountain* magazine; Jim Perrin, for an extract from a revised article in *On And Off The Rocks*; Alan Rouse, for an extract of an essay first published in *Cold Climbs*; the Secretaries and other office-bearers of the SMC, AC, FRCC, YRC, EUMC, GUMC, The Wayfarers' Club, The Rucksack Club and any other club who helped; Mr Alex Ross, Secretary Ben Nevis Race Association and Manager of the Ben Nevis Distillery, for his help and Highland hospitality; Nat Allen of The Rock & Ice; Julian Dow, for the analysis of Kellett's handwriting; Miss Archibald, Curator West Highland Museum, Fort William; Mr Adrian Hope, Engineer, Fort William Aluminium Smelter; Archie Hendry, for material; Hamish MacInnes and Alex Gillespie, for photographic material; The University Library of Aberdeen, for permission to use a print from the Wilson Collection in Ch.1; the Scottish Mountaineering Trust, who published this book, for financial assistance; Len Lovat, for comments on the MS; Jim MacLeod, for help with Dante's Purgatorio; botanists Rose Scott and John Mitchell of the Nature Conservancy Council, for pointing out my botanical inadequacies; Graham Wylie, who designed the book; Seonag MacDonald and Mary MacLeod, native speakers both, for help with the Gaelic appendix; W.A.Mozart & J.S.Bach, whose music helped on many a night ascent to the CIC Hut; Derek Pyper, SMC Slide Custodian; Jim Renny, for figures; Peter Hodgkiss, for information and other help, Evelyn Soutar, Alastair Walker, Ken Smith, Rab Anderson, Peter Birrell, Norrie Muir, Arthur Paul, John MacInnes, Alec Small.

The debt that all climbers owe to the members of the rescue teams, civilian and RAF, is only too obvious. Climbers themselves, we must be thankful that they enjoy this difficult and often hazardous aspect of the mountains. Some photographic materials have come to me by circuitous routes, but I have tried to acknowledge their source in the captions. Any photograph not so acknowledged is probably from the Author's collection. I apologise in advance for any errors or omissions and also to anyone else whom I may have overlooked.

In addition to those listed above, I gratefully acknowledge the following for permission to use copyrighted material: MacMillan & Co., for lines from *The Last Enemy* by Richard Hillary, in Ch.2; Heinemann, for Material from *Don Whillans: Portrait of a Mountaineer* by Don Whillans and Alick Ormerod, in Ch.8; John Farquharson Limited, agents for the literary estate of the late Dougal Haston, for material from *In High Places* by Dougal Haston, published by Cassell, in Chs. 8 & 9; Long John International, for material based on *The Romance of Long John* by Jack House, in Ch.10.

The authors would also like to thank the following who have helped or contributed to the second edition. Photographers are credited where known.

Jimmy Marshall for his Foreword and photographs, Ian Parnell, for his Foreword, MS review and extracts from his writings in *Climb*, *Climber* and *Alpinist* magazines and his blog; Andy Perkins for an extract from his heartfelt obituary for Mal Duff; Jim Blyth for his stories about climbing with Godefroy Perroux; Es Tresidder, Blair Fyffe, Roger Everett, James Edwards, Nick Bullock, Rick Campbell, Con Higgins, Colin Moody, Andy Tibbs for first hand accounts that bring the book alive; John Ashbridge and Brian Davison for extracts from articles in the SMC Journal; Robin Campbell, SMC Hon Archivist for a quote from an essay first published in *Cold Climbs* and other help; Iain Small and Graham Dudley for personal reminiscences; Chris Cartwright for company on Simon's finest adventures on Ben Nevis and an extract from his article on Darth Vader in *Alpinist* magazine; Dave Cuthbertson for a quote from his blog; Dave MacLeod for extracts from his writings in *Climb* magazine and from his blog; Colin Wells for his quote from *On The Edge* magazine and MS comments; Andy Nisbet for MS comments and recounting the development of mixed climbing on the Trident Buttresses; Guy Robertson for extracts from his winter season reviews in *Scottish Mountaineer* magazine; Raphael Slawinski for extracts from the American and Canadian Alpine Journals; Ed Douglas for permission to quote from his profile of Stevie Haston in *Climber* magazine; Sean Isaac, for an extract from his book *Mixed Climbing* and a quote from his blog; Rob Jarvis for a comment that appeared on the *Alpinist* website; Andy Turner for extracts from his article on The Secret in *Climb* magazine; Francois Damilano for recovering historic Ben Nevis first ascent photos from the estate of Godefroy Perroux; Ken Wilson for permission to reproduce the covers of *Cold Climbs* and assistance with photographs; Highland Libraries and the Am Baile website <www.ambaile.org.uk> for the illustration of Alexander MacDonald of Keppoch; Rab Anderson, Roger Webb, Duncan Tunstall, Harold Gillespie, Bruce Goodlad, Jimmy Jardine, Hugh Dan MacLennan, Gary Latter, Viv Scott, John Hepburn (Nevisprint Ltd), Steven Gordon, Stephen Venables, Kate Burke (Editor, *Climber*), for their help sourcing photos and other advice.

An extract from Alasdair Steven's obituary of Godefroy Perroux in The Scotsman is also acknowledged. Peter Adamson for information on Clement Wragge, Ken Smith for Kellett photos and David Stephenson and Graham Leslie of BGS for help with the geology. Tom Prentice co-designed the book, produced original illustrations, and steered us through its production with tact and consummate skill.

Foreword to the First Edition

Two inportant events in the late 19th Century made Britain's highest summit easy for anyone possessed of time and money. The first was the building of a pony track from Glen Nevis to Britain's only mountain-top Observatory, while the second was the opening of the West Highland Railway in 1894. Before these momentous events the climbing of Ben Nevis by a casual tourist would have been regarded as something of a feat. In May 1880 a trio of climbers who came to it on hearing that the giant had not been scaled since the previous autumn decided that they would make the snow-dome theirs. They didn't expect however to meet real winter conditions when they were only half way up.

The lochan at that height was still partly covered with ice, while above the snow was almost continuous and disappearing into the clouds. Resolving to wait on the chance of the weather clearing at mid-day they amused themselves in the snow, then after two hours when nothing seemed to be happening, they took a compass bearing finding the snow getting harder and harder until they were kicking strenuously to make steps. But as they came on to the summit plateau they were floundering in deep powder snow up to the knees.

W.W.Naismith's party was keeping a sharp look out in the white-out world of the summit plateau, steering for where they thought the top must be. They knew that the flattish top sheered away in a sudden plunge of tremendous cliffs. He wrote:

> ...with appalling suddenness we found ourselves upon the brink of a yawning gulf, walking straight for it. The black rocks were capped by heavy folds of snow many feet thick, which overhung the abyss in a grand cornice festooned with colossal icicles.

The summit cairn was,

> ...almost entirely covered with only a stone or two and a pole projecting; and it was only by discovering a bottle with names inside that we felt sure we had reached the actual summit, and realised there was nothing above us nearer than Norway.

They were shortly to get another shock of surprise when they plunged down the snow for 1500 feet out of white gloom into a world of sea and mountains,

> Loch Eil with the sun shining on it; while beyond on either side, were the mountains of Morven and Knoidart, of Mull and Skye, *unto the utmost sea*.

They were back in Fort William by six-o'clock discovering their feat had been daring enough to be reported in the local newspaper as the *First Ascent of Ben Nevis – without guides*.

W.W.Naismith was an example of a new breed of adventurist tourist, mountaineers looking for challenging routes, and the great cliffs where winter lingers into mid-summer was their target. One was Professor Norman Collie, of whom you will read more. His party were able to refresh themselves inside the summit observatory after their first complete ascent of Tower Ridge in 1894. I knew nothing of the historical background to Nevis on my first heavy-pack-carrying ascent in 1931, after a cold night in a blanket on the floor of the mouldering half-way hut built in 1883. Nor did my odd companion Ritchie who was 26 and ten years older than me.

Ritchie was odd in that he liked to travel continuously over mountains carrying all his gear rather than go up and down lightly laden. His plan was to go over Nevis and on over Aonach Beag. That morning we had the top of Ben Nevis to ourselves in thick mist, and like Naismith we were on the edge of the cliffs before we expected them. Route-finding on Nevis is tricky. On finding the edge of the ground falling away rockily in front of us we should have retired. We continued down the rocks and I was soon in a state of anxiety clinging above a ferocious drop with the weight of my rucksack feeling it would unbalance me and drag me down. Far below the cliff I could see boulders, and remember letting out a wail for help. With assistance from Ritchie I was able to work a way to safety, and keeping together we managed to traverse out. Ben Nevis had taught me a very frightening first lesson, and at the same time given me a taste of the unknown that was to draw me back to this gigantic face of cliff whose complications are so difficult to get to know, even with the help of Scottish Mountaineering Club literature. Stormy weather and obscuring mist will see to that.

On my next visit to Nevis I came to climb the Tower Ridge, and would have been a bolder 17 year-old with a like-minded companion and a length of Alpine Club rope. As before I had slept out on the mountain and took fright as I watched with apprehension curling mists swirling round the snow-patched pinnacled crags which seemed to get bigger and bigger as I looked. Their hugeness daunted me, yet I had just come from two weeks rock climbing in Skye. Nevis looked much more savage. I turned away, feeling inadequate. I was intimidated, fearing I might lose the route, get stuck or fall off.

Third time was lucky however, when on an April day and on Army leave I set off with a member of the Scottish Mountaineering Club from Fort William to try the Observatory Ridge, which in his opinion was the most elegant of the three great Nevis ridges. Contouring into the coire he pointed out to me the main architectural features of the great cathedral of rock rising over 2000 feet above us, naming each buttress, gully, chimney and ridge. When I asked him if he thought the narrow icy blade of ridge we were intending to try was really possible in these conditions, he replied,

It's for you to decide, for you are going to have the honour of leading it.

I did, and treasure the memory of working a way up its soaring edge, step-cutting, clearing rocks of snow to feel the friction of tricouni nails, revelling in the exposure to the increasingly big drop below our heels. Then the final arete and we were up and looking to the Cuillins of Skye and the peaks of Rum, silhouetted against the gold of the declining sun. North, south and east all the distant peaks stood clear, and we enjoyed ourselves walking within safety of the snow-cornices overhanging the big cliff edges and dropping into the depths of the Allt a' Mhuilinn over 2000 feet below.

A more chilling memory is of a January day of wet falling snow which soaked us on the northern cliffs, and as we descended our clothes froze on us and put a skin of ice on the rocks making it such slow work that I doubt if I have ever been so near being a victim of hypothermia. I was under-clad, unlike my companion. I suffered for it and had to wear a flannel round my kidneys for a year, which was another lesson from Nevis I am not likely to forget.

However my memories of Ben Nevis are slight in comparison with those of the author of this book, who puts Ben Nevis in perspective as one of the great climbing mountains of the world, with a seriousness out of all proportion to its height in metres above sea-level. Ken Crocket is a modern mountaineer who in the wintriest conditions of snow and ice has pioneered new ways on the steepest crags of the north-east face.

But it is about the whole mountain and its history he writes. Mountaineers have their own guidebooks, and climbers can find out all they need to know about routes from descriptions in the excellent works published by the Scottish Mountaineering Trust. Ken Crocket looks at every aspect of Ben Nevis. For me it has been a great privilege to go over the work with him before publication. His is an absorbing story and he tells it well.

Tom Weir, May 1986

Forewords to the Second Edition

It is hard to believe the first edition of this book is over 20 years-old, moreover it's now three times that since I first climbed the winter cliffs of the Ben, alas, *tempus fugit*.

Dumped from a JMCS bus into the dark blustery night, up to ten of us finally piled into the tin shed by the dam, jammed in like herrings in a barrel. Multiple brews, endless jokes and music kept us merry, as blizzards battered the doss late into the night until belatedly we all dozed off into fitful sleep.

Awakening to a fine clear dawn with the Ben looking like a Christmas cake, we hurriedly stuffed our breakfast down then partner Bill and I were off, tearing up the hill, inspired by the sensational looking Tower Ridge. We ploughed through deep drifts to get onto the ridge, all corniced and alpine looking but half way to the Tower the blizzards resumed; soon blinded and frozen we made an epic retreat, battle enough for one day and were even happy to resume our squalid life style, glad once more to be warm.

Two hours later a great alpenglow pulled us out to see the Tower Ridge bathed in roseate light, looking absolutely invulnerable and seemingly taunting us to try again.

In the post war years, just getting to the Ben was difficult, so however fickle the weather, we learned to make the most of our trips. Icy, wet, or occasionally dry, skills were called up to make one think and we were ultimately rewarded by the cumulative experience of success or failure, to enjoy an awareness of real mountaineering

On a later trip, as students we hitched from Edinburgh mid-week, to return by meet bus. It was fine, spring like weather, and in our ignorance we expected to enjoy rock climbs in Glen Nevis or Alpine style climbs on the big ridges. A fabulous sunny arrival induced a change of mind and we found ourselves toiling up the tourist track, thinking the weather would allow a doss in the Observatory ruins but as we got higher the snow got deeper. It was very exhausting and occasionally I'd fall face down in the snow, pinned by a bulky sac. Bill, always stronger, would haul me to my feet as the need arose, till we reached the top.

There was such an accumulation of snow, we couldn't find the Observatory so we dug about where we thought the old Tower would be but it was obvious burrowing down with ice axes was pointless labour. Our tent was only meant for grass and we were contemplating descent when we noticed skis and a tent nearby, whence anguished curses wafted into the superb arctic evening sky. It transpired that the occupant, Jimmy Ness, had frozen feet, but couldn't give them due attention, as cramp attacks in the legs denied all his efforts, so we cuckooed in and rubbed some life into his feet. Due to further risk, Jimmy decided to ski back down and generously left us to use his tent for the night. On getting organised, I found my socks were frozen into my boots but no frostbite, and we enjoyed a comfortable night.

We woke to the morning light and got the stove going, the paraffin had lumps in the tank, presumably ice, and the shells of our eggs had split longitudinally. When passed over the stove the internal content could be handled before committing them to the pan, so it must have been extremely cold. But it was the morning view that greeted us, absolutely still and fabulous, no moisture in the air and sharp clear views to the horizons. It seemed we could almost touch the Cuillins and every nearer summit stood out in startling clarity

We meant to glissade Number Three Gully, climb Tower Ridge, then enjoy lunch in our new doss but the ridge looked hard and Number Three Gully intimidating so we went via the Càrn Mòr Dearg arete and round to Number Three Gully, this gave us a good climb, having to surmount several stacked cornices. The highlight was Bill's discomfiture on sticking his nose over the cornice – the windblown spume stuck to his glasses, now two white discs and for him no vision. The weather showed signs of deterioration, so we packed our bags and moved down to the Alt a' Mhuillin to enjoy grass and running water, sadly we soon had more than wanted as the warm winds moved in and the deluge began.

In the morning we joined the meet party in the CIC, then went into Observatory Gully to investigate endless thumping noises emanating from the mists above. We were climbing the first rocks of Tower Ridge to see what was going on, when out of the mists a great wall of jumbled icy blocks up to 20 feet high appeared, creaking, grinding, and tumbling along, a slow but majestic sight, a mini glacier moving inexorably forward.

This was the source of all the noise, the marvelous cornices of yesterday were collapsing in the wet thaw, we had to scramble higher to avoid its passage, but all raised a great cheer on its terminal end in the Alt a' Mhuillin.

Back then we were clad in ex-army anoraks, baggy camouflaged breeks and ordinary army boots with clinkers, hemp ropes and the odd karabiner for belays; runner technology hadn't arrived so it was long leads and little information, fortunately we were unaware of these refinements so it didn't matter. We could only manage the Ben about four weekends a year but they were long holiday weekends and could be quite productive climbing, nigh on every trodden bit of rock, almost to the exclusion of making any of our own. I even came to enjoy wandering up greasy rocks, socks over gym shoes, struggling up the more frightening, rattling gullies of which there's no shortage on Ben Nevis.

These early days gave me a profound respect and interest in the mountain and ultimately led to a decision to update the Macphee guide. I spent a leisurely six years' of enjoyable and fascinating research into the intricacies of the mountain, only to be left with considerable doubt as to the wisdom of such a task, for it seemed a betrayal of the wonderfully naive nature of climbing there as we knew it.

The fascination of winter climbing is that each ascent is virtually original and climbers can to a large extent enjoy major variations of cover or condition. I like to think of the artist's blank canvas; he or she can make a painting but not be satisfied, so blanks it over. On the winter cliffs, nature blanks it over and over again, and we can all make an original work to our satisfaction.

Finally I note, though there is a fascinating chapter on the tunnels of Loch Treig, there is no record of the misuse of the bogies along the associated light railway. So-called friends of mine had discovered the thrill of riding the rails boarding the bogies (wheeled buckets) high on the Loch Treig line and competing as to how long they could be kept on track. This was much more harrowing than the weekend's climbing. One either chickened out between 20/30mph (my level), or stayed riveted to the bogie till it flew off the tracks (conveniently close to the old CIC path). That there were no serious accidents was certainly only down to luck for there was very little means of control.

Interestingly this ploy could be considered as a precursor of the current mountain bike usage of these same slopes.

Jimmy Marshall, August 2008

If you were to ask climbers to dream up their very own ultimate mountain, what would it be like? Surely they'd want it to be the highest in their country; we climbers always want more. And no doubt we'd carve into this imaginary peak line after line of compelling features. Great soaring ridges, steep imposing buttresses and faces that looked so blank as to be unclimbable, but by some miracle for the patient and well aquainted their secrets of ascent could be revealed.

Of course our dream mountain will have the longest and most beautiful routes in the land, with classics of every grade from ideal introductions to terminal testpieces both for summer and winter climbing. The more fevered imagination might even conjure up a perfect summit plateau onto which all these great climbs would rise above the clouds to finish. Some Alpine dreamers might even go so far as to believe that this mountain might even somehow have its own micro climate that created ideal climbing conditions far longer than other hills. Their crazed minds envisioning ice climbing conditions stretching into early summer. Surely such a peak couldn't exist?

Well as Britons perhaps we are the luckiest climbing nation alive because, in Ben Nevis, we do have that ultimate mountain. At 1334 metres Ben Nevis would probably go unnoticed in most major alpine ranges, but what it lacks in sheer altitude it makes up for with character. 'The Ben' is the sort of mountain that leaves a huge impression and once visited many return again and again to build their own relationship with this special peak.

Amongst those return visitors were some of the finest climbers from successive generations of British mountaineering, each of them taken in by the Ben's spell and adding their own stamp on Nevis's growing history. This book records in enthralling detail each twist of that history. From the pioneering efforts of Collie and Naismith through to the technical advances of first Raeburn and then Bell and Kellett. Some of that history stands out as extraordinary in stature on even a world level, such as Smith and Marshall's unique route-bagging week in 1959.

On a personal level I've been lucky to develop my own little love affair with the Ben, from my first ascent of the track aged seven through to my new routes on the great North Face. I've been privileged enough to climb on some the world's most renowned mountains but often they struggle to compare. I remember repeating a famous testpiece in the Alps provocatively called 'Scotch on the Rocks' and couldn't help thinking that McKenzie and Spence's audacious winter ascent of Centurion on the Ben would have been at least as hard but climbed a decade earlier. Similarly I couldn't help but contrast the feelings of euphoria that Olly Metherell and I shared on the first winter ascent of Sioux Wall alone on the Ben on a New Year's Day, with queuing the same year for the summit of Everest.

It's been 23 years since Ken Crocket's first edition and if anything those two decades have reinforced the Ben's importance in British and even World climbing. Simon Richardson's extensive knowledge has brought these modern developments to vivid life with seven new chapters for this new edition. Capturing Nevis's growing global stature through the International Winter Meets organised by the British Mountaineering Council which introduced climbers from countries as diverse as Iran to Latvia to 'the big bad Ben'. Detailing the wonderful impression the mountain made on the French icefall legend Godefroy Perroux who after many years of visits even went on to publish his own Nevis guidebook. This new edition concludes with the most recent efforts of Dave MacLeod who's pushed Ben Nevis once more into the global limelight with two astonishing routes which hold claim to be amongst the very hardest traditional climbs in summer and winter respectively.

A peak as impressive as the Ben will continue to inspire and offer new possibilities for future generations to make their mark. One's mind does boggle on what stories the third edition of this book might hold. For now, though, sit back and enjoy Ken and Simon's great tale of this Ultimate Mountain thus far.

Ian Parnell, October 2008

Introduction to the First Edition

This offering of mine on Ben Nevis concerns itself mainly with man's interaction with the mountain which is not only the highest in Britain but one of the most ferocious in Europe for weather changes. Yet on the huge cliffs of its northern face standards of climbing and technique have evolved to lead the climbing world.

I think I can claim to have run almost the full gamut of experiences good and bad that this big mountain can offer; frozen and frightened to a point of near despair, committed on an icy overhang with only two options open, climb or fall off; or soaked and shivering in a cloudburst with water foaming down the steep rocks on to which I was clinging; and the joyous good days, moving up confidently on small holds on warm rock.

The memory floods with other days on Nevis. Days when an overcast, drizzly start in Fort William gave no warning of the cloud sea visible from the summit, realised only when cutting the last steps through a gully cornice. To see only the tops of the surrounding mountains piercing a silent layer of cloud meant staying on top for the sunset – never mind that the long descent by Coire Leis was a purgatory of ice-glazed boulders.

For true suffering there is always the dreaded Allt a'Mhuilinn path, its seemingly endless inclines and elusive tracks through acres of black, quaking bog the only route not in the guidebook. The old start up the mountain lay through the Distillery and over a boggy morass known to climbers, with a grim sense of humour, as *The Everglades*. Tales of lurking alligators helped lighten the apprehension of the dour trudge ahead. Strong men have wept on that route.

> This Mount is not like others: at the start
> it is most difficult to climb, but then,
> the more one climbs the easier it becomes;

Dante: *Purgatorio, IV, 88.*

A sense of history began to creep in at the edges one night in the CIC Hut when, as a young lad of about 22, I started adding up the accumulated years of mountaineering experience visible in the hut. Some 300 years of living history was distilled there, crammed into a wooden cigar-box of a hut, itself now beyond the half-century. We were from disparate backgrounds and had travelled by different routes, but there was a common purpose, enjoyment of the mountain.

We were testing ourselves as all who come to this steep side of Ben Nevis in summer and winter do. My own pleasure was intensified by reading tales of adventure on Ben Nevis in the pages of the Scottish Mountaineering Club Journal by some of the mountain's greatest explorers. It was the genesis of this book which I hope you will enjoy.

Ken Crocket
Glasgow 1986

Introduction to the Second Edition

Since the first edition of this book there have been many improvements and changes to both access and equipment. These include a new car park and footpath leading to near Intake No.11 on the Allt a' Mhuilinn, and a vastly improved path leading to the CIC Hut. The ownership of the mountain's summit and surrounding area has changed, with the wild land charity the John Muir Trust now charged with its protection. The JMT has begun a slow process of cleansing their area, including the removal of many of the man-made cairns and other items deemed an eyesore on the summit plateau. The redundent emergency shelters in Coire Leis and on Càrn Dearg have been removed.

With equipment improvements, climbing can be a much safer game. This also allows harder routes to be climbed, with recent advances in winter climbing especially spectacular. This has kept Ben Nevis in the forefront of world mountaineering, to the extent that on a good day in winter the cliffs can be ringing with many different languages, as climbers from many countries arrive in search of some adventure.

The extensive use of the internet has allowed the rapid dissemination of information, both on route conditions and the weather, permitting the savvy climber to go where the climbing is at short notice. With a GPS unit and satellite communication, it's easy to know one's exact position at any time. The downside of all of this is that it can be common to have to queue at the foot of a hard winter classic, which in past decades might go for months at a time with no ascents.

For the second edition we have been fortunate in being able to enlist the expertise of Simon Richardson. Not only is he the current author of the Scottish Mountaineering Club Climbers' Guide to this mountain, he is one of a number of activists responsible for many of the recent first ascents and has unparalleled knowledge of this superb mountain.

The earlier chapters have benefited too from modern technology; it's painful to recall that the first edition was done without the internet, digital photography, or the increasingly easy access to old records. New information has been found and added to the story. Colour throughout the book has added a new dimension, and the authors are grateful to the unfailing generosity of climbers who have made their photographs and experiences available for use.

Both authors started out as climbers seeking adventure on Ben Nevis. With time, a growing sense of its history became all too pervasive, adding to our enjoyment of its climbing riches. We hope we have succeeded in passing on some of this enjoyment of this unique mountain.

Ken Crocket
Menstrie 2009

Simon Richardson
Aberdeen 2009

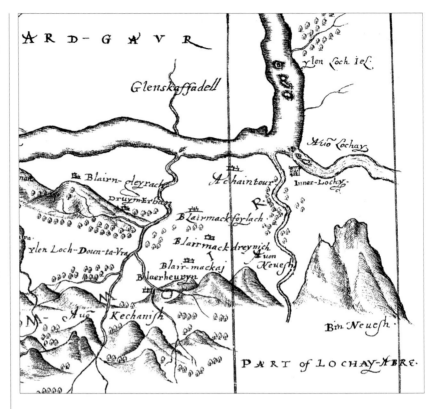

Detail from Pont's original manuscript map showing a sketch of Ben Nevis (Bin Nevesh), possibly drawn from one of The Mamores.
The map is oriented with North to the right. Loch Linnhe is in a horizontal position at the top of the map and Loch Eil vertical. Flowing in from the right is the River Lochy with present day Inverlochy at its foot. Glen Nevis and the River Nevis (Avon Nevesh) are central, separating Ben Nevis from the lower northern end of The Mamores. The River Kaichnish and the present day settlement of Blairmachfoldach, possibly Blairmackfoylach on Pont's map are present. Achaintour lies in the vicinity of the future Fort William, perhaps close to Achintore at the south end of the present town

Image: National Library of Scotland (NLS)

1: Early Travellers (1585 – 1865)

THE ORIGIN OF THE NAME *Nevis* is just as difficult to pin down as are early ascents. In his *History of the Celtic Place-names of Scotland*, the late Professor Watson suggests an Old Irish word *neamhaise*, meaning *terrible*, and also a Gaelic word *ni-mhaise*, meaning *no beauty*. W.C.MacKenzie, writing in his book on *Scottish Place-Names*, has made an attempt to associate the Irish *neamhaise* with the Scottish *uamhais*, or *dread*, thus drawing in the two mountains Nevis and Wyvis. The word *neamh* in Gaelic means a *raw and bitingly keen atmosphere*, and is sometimes confused with the gaelic word *neimh*, meaning *poison, bitterness, and malice*.

To any mountaineer who has endured a day of bad weather on the frozen north face of Nevis, or indeed to anyone who has walked to the summit in poor conditions, there will be a familiar ring to any of the above names. There is no shortage of possibilities as to the origin of the mountain's name.[1-4] (See also Gaelic Place Names, page 378.)

The year 1585 as a starting point for this history is partly conjectural, though it seems likely that it marks the beginning of a period during which a certain Timothy Pont (1565 – 1614) was responsible for the first topographical survey of Scotland. Pont's difficult and self-imposed task is of interest to us for two reasons. Firstly, it indicates the difficulties and dangers of travel in Scotland at the close of the 16th Century, and secondly it led to the publication in 1654 of the Scottish edition of maps by Blaeu of Amsterdam, showing for the first time Scotland's highest mountain as a *Bin Novesh*. In Johann (or Joan) Blaueu's *Le Grand Atlas*, the map of Scotland marks a Bin Novesh, a Glen Nevish and, flowing down that Glen, the Avon Nevish. There is no Fort William of course, as that garrison was not built until 1650 and was in any case named otherwise. There is an Achiontoir (Achaintour on Pont's manuscript map), about where Achintore is sited.[5]

Strangely enough, although it is reasonably certain that Pont travelled through the Cairngorms, there is no recording on his maps of either Ben Macdui, Braeriach or Cairn Toul.

Of Pont and his arduous journey over Scotland we have little first-hand information, the only original reference being found in a letter from Sir Robert Gordon of Straloch (1580 – 1661) to Sir John Scott of Scotstarvet (1585 – 1670), dated 1648. Pont, a Scot and son of the Minister at Dunnet, Caithness, graduated from St Andrews in 1583 and there exists a map of Clydesdale by him, dated 1596. He died without seeing his work published and indeed the manuscript maps would have rotted away in the royal archives of King James VI but for their rescue by Sir John Scot. It was the latter who arranged both for Robert Gordon of Aberdeenshire to revise and complete the maps, and for Blaeu of Amsterdam to print them in his monumental *Atlas of The World*. Gordon's revisions in effect made Pont's manuscript sketches more map-like, and included some slight changes in spellings of settlements and other features, including Ben Nevis. Later work would include the addition of some colour.

Of Pont's task we have the following excerpt, taken from the 1648 letter by Gordon.[6] The translation is by Caleb.G.Cash, utilising both Latin and French versions.

> ...For, with small means and no favouring patron, he undertook the whole of this task forty years ago; he travelled on foot right through the whole of this kingdom, as no one before him had done; he visited all the islands, occupied for the most part by inhabitants hostile and uncivilised, (and with a language different from our own); being often stripped, as he told me, by the fierce robbers, and suffering not seldom all the hardships of the dangerous journey, nevertheless at no time was he overcome by the difficulties, nor was he disheartened. But when, having returned, he prepared to publish the results of his labours, he was defeated by the greed of printers and booksellers (who refused to supply the necessary funds), and so could not reach his goal. While awaiting better times, untimely death took him away (in the flower of his age)...[7]

In his book *Scotland's Mountains before the Mountaineers*[8], Ian R. Mitchell, examining Pont's sketch of Ben Nevis, makes the interesting suggestion that it was made from a position some way up a nearby mountain on the Mamore ridge. The sketch shown opposite in Pont's original manuscript map (as distinct from the maps printed following Robert Gordon's editing), shows the summit plateau, the lower Càrn Dearg summit, and between them what could be the Allt Coire Eoghain corrie. The Timothy Pont website of The National Map Library of Scotland

...he [Pont] travelled on foot right through the whole of this kingdom, as no one before him had done; he visited all the islands, occupied for the most part by inhabitants hostile and uncivilised, (and with a language different from our own); being often stripped, as he told me, by the fierce robbers, and suffering not seldom all the hardships of the dangerous journey...

(Edinburgh) is an excellent source for further information.[9]

The growth of the present town of Fort William, situated near the head of Loch Linnhe and at the southern end of the Caledonian Canal, can be said to have properly begun in 1650. It was then, during Cromwell's protectorate, that General Monk erected a fortress. Two weeks later Cameron of Lochiel attacked the fort, which was built mainly of earth, many of the garrison being either killed or drowned. This first garrison, which had been named the Garrison of Inverlochy, was rebuilt by General MacKay in 1690, in the reign of William III. To that date, the village which had grown alongside the garrison had been known as Gordonsburgh, the land then being the property of the Gordon family. With the building of the more substantial fort in 1690 the village was renamed Maryburgh, while the garrison became Fort William.

About this time in clan history occurs one of the earliest references to Ben Nevis. Of the origins of the Camerons we know little, other than several mentions of them starting in the 11th Century, when one Angus married Marion, daughter of the Thane of Lochaber. Going forward to about 1647, Allan, the sixteenth chief, was succeeded by his grandson, Sir Ewen Dubh. When Ewen was 12 years old he was sent to the Earl of Argyll for his education. He returned to his clan when he was 18 and soon showed himself to be a strong and capable leader.

When the young chief heard that Monk was cutting down large quantities of wood for his newly built garrison he attacked, killing a large number of soldiers. Such was his character however, that he and Monk eventually settled their differences, developing a strong friendship. We have the early reference to Ben Nevis from the *Memoirs* of Sir Ewen Cameron of Lochiel, written by John Drummond of Balhaldy in about 1737. Drummond was a Jacobite agent.

> Behind the fort there arises a huge mountain, of prodigious hight, called Beniviss, at that time adorned with a variety of trees and bushes, and now with a beautiful green. Its ascent is pretty steep, though smooth. The top or summit is plain, covered with perpetual snow, and darkened with thick clouds.[10]

This early description of Ben Nevis would suggest that by the early 18th Century ascents of the mountains were not unheard of, but were very rare until about the mid-18th Century. Before then the prevailing attitude to mountains in general was one of repugnance and distaste, feelings very evident in the travel writings of the period. The native Highlanders had little use for the summits, cattle and game being confined mainly to the corries and lower slopes where there was grazing.

That local inhabitants visited the northern corries of the Ben before the 18th Century is very likely. An old legend, one shared with some other Scottish mountains, has it that should all the snow vanish from Ben Nevis then the land shall be forfeit. To prevent this Cameron of Lochiel, in a summer when it looked as if the last of the snow might melt away, is said to have sent locals up the mountain with straw, to protect the remaining snow patches.

There are two recorded occasions when snow could not be found on Nevis; in 1933, and in 1935. In the Scottish Mountaineering Club Journal (SMCJ), G.Graham Macphee, who was then writing the first climbing guide to Nevis, wrote that –

> ...on 28th September 1935 he visited the places on Ben Nevis where snow usually lies all the year round. He found no trace of snow anywhere. About midday a snowstorm commenced, and, by the time a climb was completed, snow was lying on the summit plateau to a depth of nearly 1 inch...The entire mountain was thus free from 'perpetual snow' for only the second time within living memory, or within the memory of a deceased local resident who was born in 1840.[11]

Macphee concluded that this supported the belief that there was a trend to a warmer climate on Nevis, supported by a study of old photographs. With recent, solid data which confirms this warming trend[12], it is noteworthy that in early October 2006 there were also reports that no snow was visible on the mountain.

Following the 1715 Rebellion, Major-General George Wade was instructed by King George I to proceed to the Highlands, 'to report on the situation and to suggest such remedies as would conduce to the settlement of that part of the kingdom.' General Wade's report was presented in the autumn of 1724, and on Christmas Day of that year he was appointed *Commander-in-Chief of all His Majesty's Forces in North Britain*. The end results of Wade's work in Scotland (and also of the much-underrated William Caulfeild, who was responsible for more miles of new road and became Inspector of Roads before retiring as a Lieutenant-Colonel) are well-enough known, being a programme of road and bridge building which radically changed communications in Scotland.

Of pertinence to our story of Ben Nevis is a certain Edward Burt, who accompanied Wade to Scotland. Captain Burt's position in Scotland, from about 1725 to 1740, was that of the receiver and collector of rents on such of the estates still remaining unsold after the 1715 Rebellion, the so-called *Forfeited Estates*.

Edward Burt was the author of *The Letters from a Gentleman in the North of Scotland*. This was published in 1754[13], but the letters, some 26 in all, were written to a friend in London about the years 1727 – 1728. With the sole exception of the last letter, which was written eight

...the prevailing attitude to mountains in general was one of repugnance and distaste, feelings very evident in the travel writings of the period

Fort William is surrounded by vast mountains, which occasion almost torrential rain: the loftiest are on the South side; Benevish soars above the rest, and ends, as I was told, in a point, (at this time concealed in mist) whose height from the sea is said to be 1450 yards. As an ancient Briton, I lament the disgrace of Snowdon; once esteemed the highest hill in the island, but now must yield the palm to a Caledonian mountain

years after the others, the letters were sent from Inverness at fortnightly intervals. They provide a fascinating glimpse into a world far distant from the present one – or even to the outside world at that time.

Burt himself was no lover of the hills, which he described as *'monstrous excrescences'*, but we are fortunate in that he left an account of an early attempt to climb Ben Nevis.

> Some English officers took it in their Fancy to go to the Top, but could not attain it for Bogs and huge Perpendicular Rocks...This wild Expedition, in ascending round and round the Hills; in finding accessible Places, helping one another up the Rocks, in Disappointments, and their returning to the Foot of the Mountain took them up a whole Summer's Day from five in the Morning.

The account went on to comment on how fortunate the officers were in having a cloud-free day. A second, early description of Ben Nevis follows from the tours of Scotland made by Thomas Pennant in 1769 and 1772. Of Ben Nevis Pennant writes –

> Fort William is surrounded by vast mountains, which occasion almost torrential rain: the loftiest are on the South side; Benevish soars above the rest, and ends, as I was told, in a point, (at this time concealed in mist) whose height from the sea is said to be 1450 yards. As an ancient Briton, I lament the disgrace of Snowdon; once esteemed the highest hill in the island, but now must yield the palm to a Caledonian mountain.[14]

Pennant was a leisured and cultured English squire with an interest in natural history. His journeys were made through a land virtually unknown to the average Englishman.

The earliest recorded visits to Nevis were for scientific purposes. Professor John Hope of Edinburgh records *Veronica alpina* as having been collected on Ben Nevis in 1767, by Dr de la Roche and Fabricius, Edinburgh medical students. Twelve years later George Don of Forfar, author of *Herbarium Britanicum* (1804), began his excursions into the Highlands. On Ben Nevis Don collected the alpine form of *Sagina maritima*, the Sea Pearlwort, (though later research has argued that this solitary native record from the inland montane site of Ben Nevis is erroneous.[15]) and the rare grass *Poa flexuosa*.

For five summers the botanist James Robertson collected specimens in Scotland for the College Museum in Edinburgh. In 1771, along with eight other first recorded ascents, he made an ascent of Ben Nevis. Unfortunately he left few details of the actual ascent.[16] A letter published in the Philosophical Transactions of the Royal Society in 1769 tells us a little more of Robertson's travels.

> A letter from John Hope, M.D., F.R.S., Professor of Physic and Botany in the University of Edinburgh, to William Watson, M.D., F.R.S. on a rare plant found in the Isle of Skye. (The plant) was found, September 1768, in a small lake in the island of Skye, by James Robertson, whom I sent there in search of new or rare plants. Mr James Robertson is an élève of mine, and has been employed by the commissioners of the annexed estates to make a botanical survey of the distant parts of Scotland.[17]

Robertson subsequently went to Calcutta, gaining employment with the East India Company.[18] Three years later, in 1774, the second recorded ascent was made by John Williams, a Welshman. The ascent on this occasion was prompted by the possibility of commercial gain, as Williams had been instructed by the Commissioners of the Forfeited Estates to 'examine the different sorts of stones particularly on the tops of high hills.' Williams later published a book on minerals, the second edition of which includes a character sketch of Williams by James Millar (Editor of *Encylopaedia Edinensis*).

> ...he seems to have been a man of acute observation and nice discernment, of great activity, and ardour of mind; and, what is not unusual in such characters, the warmth of his enthusiasm, on the peculiar subjects of his contemplation, seems at times to have led him too far into visionary speculations.

Visionary speculations apart, Williams includes a description of Ben Nevis in Chapter 4 of his book, where he describes the *Natural History of Mountains*.

> Ben Nevis is about a mile in perpendicular height...More than two thirds of the height of this mountain are composed of an elegant red granite...the summit of it is, nevertheless, regularly stratified with a different stone, to about one fourth of the whole height...the hardest rocks in this mountain are the highest...There is a deep gulph at the bottom of a frightful precipice, about five hundred yards on the north-east side of this mountain...The precipice...exhibits a magnificent section of the internal structure of that mountain, in which we distinctly see where the uniform mass of granite ends, and the stratified rock begins above it. We also see, that the strata of different rocks dips towards the south-east with an easy declivity.[19]

Fortunately for the following generations of mountaineers John Williams found no rocks of commercial interest on the summit of Nevis, and the mountain fell back into a brief respite, to be broken by the arrival of a new type of mountaineer – the tourist.

In 1787, some 13 years after the ascent by Williams the Welshman, an expedition of 11 set out from Glen Nevis. The instigator of the climb was a Lieutenant Walker who was stationed at Fort William; his chief companion was the Rev. James Bailey, vicar of Otley, in Yorkshire. The party left the Glen at 6am, accompanied by three Highland guides, two sergeants and three privates of the Royal Fusiliers, the soldiers acting as porters for the liquors and provisions. A Mr Kayne was also in the party.

Military training had obviously influenced the preparations for this trip, for the party was equipped with a rope and grappling iron; used on a series of rocky shelves. Throughout the ascent, which took seven hours, difficulties were encountered, and at several points combined tactics were employed. One of the soldiers collapsed just before the summit, but the strong smell of rum indicated an over-enthusiastic use of the liquor supply and he soon recovered.

The successful summit party celebrated in the age-old sport of *trundling*, the reckless heaving of boulders from cliff tops, before turning their attention to the descent. This was accomplished in six hours, and though it was described as being '...*rapid, though excessively fatiguing, for we were, for the most part, obliged to slide upon our haunches*', by modern standards it was a slow descent.[20]

The successful summit party celebrated in the age-old sport of trundling, the reckless heaving of boulders from cliff tops, before turning their attention to the descent

Another ascent in 1787 was that of a certain Thomas Wilkinson, a neighbour of the poet Wordsworth, who accompanied John Pemberton, an American Quaker, on a preaching tour of the Highlands and other parts of Scotland. Wordsworth described Wilkinson in a letter to a friend as *'An amiable inoffensive man and a little of a poet too.'*

Reaching Fort William, probably in late summer or early autumn, Wilkinson determined to climb Nevis, but being unable to find a willing guide he set off alone. He found himself on the wrong side of the River Nevis which he succeeded in fording, burning his boats by throwing his shoes to the far bank. His ascent details are almost non-existent, but the following extract from his account is worth quoting.

> The base of Ben Nevis is covered with soil; grass, shrubs, and trees climb up its sides to a considerable height, but its lofty summit is composed of grey rocks that seem to leave vegetation below. The north side of the mountain may be said to be hung with terrors. Perpendicular and projecting rocks, gulphy glens and awful precipices, gloomy and tremendous caverns, the vast repositories of snow from age to age; these, with blue mists gauzing the grey rocks of the mountain, and terrible cataracts thundering from Ben Nevis, made altogether a scene sublimely dreadful.[21]

Though these ascents in 1787 were the third and fourth recorded so far, there must have been others since the ore-hunting trip of Williams, for Lieutenant Walker's party found more than 30 small stone

cairns on the summit plateau, erected by previous visitors.

In 1796 the Hon Mrs Murray Aust of Kensington made a thorough and energetic tour of Scotland. Arising from that tour was a descriptive guide – *A Companion and Useful Guide to the Beauties of Scotland, and the Hebrides*. While Mrs Aust did not herself climb Ben Nevis, she did describe in her interesting book the surrounding countryside. Her tour began on May 28, and finished about October. She travelled down from Inverness about the beginning of August, describing the scene on the road from Spean Bridge to Fort William.

Through the vast moor before me, there was nothing but the road to be seen, except a few scattered huts; some of them in such bogs, that it seemed impossible for any human being to exist in such places...The eight miles from High Bridge to Fort William, is the most dreary, though not the ugliest, space I had travelled in Scotland...The huts on this moor are very small and low, are soon erected, and must very soon fall down. They consist of four stakes of birch, forked at the top, driven into the ground; on these they lay four other birch poles, and then form a gavel at each end by putting up more birch sticks, and crossing them sufficiently to support the clods with which they plaster this skeleton of a hut all over, except a small hole in the side for a window, a small door to creep in and and (sic) out at, and a hole in the roof, stuck round with sticks, patched up with turf, for a vent, as they call a chimney...

In these huts they make a fire upon the ground...At night they rake out the

fire, and put their beds of heath and blankets (which they have in abundance) on the ground, where the fire had been, and thus keep themselves warm during the night.

Continuing on to Fort William, Mrs Aust was lucky enough to gain a view of the mountain.

In its shape there is beauty, mixed with the sublime and terrific. In front a soft verdant sloping hill; behind which is a hollow, and a lofty crescent rising from it, with its high pointed horns; joining to one of which are towers of huge rocks, furrowed by continual torrents; with hollows and chasms filled with snow, forming a rare contrast in summer, with the black and grey rocks of the crescent, and other huge masses adjoining...The summit, however, of Ben Nivis, I am told, is a bed of white pebbles, some of them beautiful.

Finally, Mrs Aust retold an amusing story connected with Ben Nevis.

I learnt, in those parts, another instance of the great love a Highland man has for whisky. A lady of fashion, having conquered that ascent, before she quitted it, left on purpose a bottle of whisky on the summit: when she returned to the fort, she laughingly mentioned that circumstance before some Highland men, as a piece of carelessness; one of whom slipped away, and mounted to the pinnacle of 4,370 feet, above the level of the fort, to gain the prize of the bottle of whisky, and brought it down in triumph.[22]

I learnt, in those parts, another instance of the great love a Highland man has for whisky

The poet John Keats made a grand tour of Scotland with his friend Charles Brown, in 1818. On August 2 he made an ascent of Nevis with Brown and a local guide. The ascent was described in a four-page letter to his brother Tom, which also included an imaginary dialogue between a Mrs Cameron and Ben Nevis; running to 74 lines. It seems that this Mrs Cameron had the dubious honour of being the fattest woman in all Inverness-shire, who at the age of 50 had nonetheless succeeded in climbing Nevis, some years before Keats. The Keats party set out at 5am and soon arrived at the first slopes, '*...after much fag and tug and a rest and a glass of whiskey apiece we gained the top of the first rise.*'

Before long, the party entered a mist, in which they walked to the very top.

> The whole immense head of the Mountain is composed of large loose stones – thousands of acres – Before we had got half way up we passed large patches of snow and near the top there is a chasm some hundred feet deep completely glutted with it – Talking of chasms they are the finest wonder of the whole – they appear great rents in the very heart of the mountain though they are not, being at the side of it, but other huge crags arising round it give the appearance to Nevis of a shattered heart or core in itself.

Keats went on to describe the cloud effects and glimpses of other mountains through '*cloudy loop holes*', before climbing a cairn built by some climbers. '*It was not so cold as I expected – yet cold enough for a glass of Whiskey now and then.*' The descent was not to his liking. '*I felt it horribly. Twas the most vile descent – shook me all to pieces.*' In the letter to his brother was a Sonnet Keats wrote at the summit of Nevis:

> Read me a Lesson, muse, and speak it loud
> Upon the top of Nevis blind in Mist!
> I look into the Chasms and a Shroud
> Vaprous doth hide them; just so much I wist
> Mankind do know of Hell: I look o'erhead
> And there is sullen mist; even so much
> Mankind can tell of Heaven: Mist is spread
> Before the Earth beneath me – even such
> Even so vague is Man's sight of himself.
> Here are the craggy Stones beneath my feet;
> Thus much I know, that a poor witless elf
> I tread on them; that all my eye doth meet
> Is mist and Crag – not only on this height,
> But in the world of thought and mental might.[23]

After his 1818 ascent of Ben Nevis, the poet John Keates recalled: 'It was not so cold as I expected – yet cold enough for a glass of Whiskey now and then'

Several factors help explain the rapid growth of tourism in Scotland at the end of the 18th and beginning of the 19th Centuries. The improved road networks of Wade and Caulfeild made travel easier. Also the Napoleonic Wars, by cutting off the Continent, redirected adventurous tourists north to Scotland. Many of these early travellers were inspired by recently written travel books; of a type containing a new enthusiasm for the countryside. It should be borne in mind that that great catalyst of travel, the railway, did not reach Fort William until the autumn of 1894, an absence which greatly delayed the exploration of Ben Nevis. Sir John Carr described a tour through Scotland undertaken in 1807; his description of Fort William as it was then is probably a fair and accurate one.

> Fort William is situate on Lochaber, bordering on the Western Ocean, yet within the shire of Inverness...the town was erected into a borough in honour of Queen Mary: it is a long street of indifferent houses, stuccoed white, and is chiefly inhabited by fishermen, who carry on a considerable fishery in the lake. The inn is rather destitute of accommodation. Nothing can be shabbier, as a fortification, than Fort William; it has neither strength, space, nor neatness...The

Rain, which continues in this neighbourhood for nine or ten weeks together, is called by the natives by the gentle name of a shower

farce of shutting the gate at the hour usual in fortified towns is still preserved in this travesty of a fortification.

I was now in the region of rain, which descended with little intermission, during my stay at Maryborough, with a copiousness which I have not often beheld. Rain, which continues in this neighbourhood for nine or ten weeks together, is called by the natives by the gentle name of a shower.

When I first saw (Ben Nevis), the atmosphere was tolerably clear, and it then appeared to be as ugly in shape as it is in size. In some of its chasms in its northern side, the whiteness of eternal snows singularly contrasted with its vast masses of black and grey rocks.[24]

Another travel book written at that time was *The Highlands and Western Isles of Scotland*, by John Macculloch. Published in 1824 this described an ascent of Ben Nevis, in which Macculloch only too clearly turns out to be the hero. It also describes a summit blizzard and the shortcomings of the professional guides then available.

A critical riposte to Macculloch. In 1825, obviously incensed with the writing in Macculloch's book, a James Browne had printed in Edinburgh a book entitled 'A Critical Examination of Dr Macculloch's work...' Browne provided the following example

'As we have occasion to give a flat contradiction to so many of this man's stories, it may be proper to take one at random, and leave it to speak for itself. A robust young Highlander had accompanied him as a guide to Ben Nevis, and during the excursion they were involved in a little snow-drift...A Highlander blubbering and 'greeting for his mammy,' because he found himself in a snow-shower!'

(Edinburgh, John Brewster, 1825, p72)

...on the 20th of August, as I looked out of the window of the inn at Balahulish, at six o'clock in the morning, it was a fine day...I stole my own horse, saddled him, roused the ferryman, launched the ferry-boat, rode off to Fort William, breakfasted, and by one o'clock was on top of the mountain...

Doubtless, the ascent of Ben Nevis is considered a mighty deed; and, in consequence, there are various names inscribed on the cairn within the plain; while some had been written on scraps of paper, and enclosed in bottles which had been drained of their whisky by the valiant who had reached this perilous point of honour....

But the summit itself is utterly bare, and presents a most extraordinary and unexpected sight...It is an extensive & flat plain, strewed with loose rocks, tumbled together in fragments of all sizes, and, generally, covering the solid foundation to a considerable depth...I had not time, however, to walk round the whole plain before there came on as dense & bitter a storm of snow as I ever experienced...I was not, however, alone, since I had with me what is commonly called a guide; a lad who had volunteered his services...I had gained too much experience in guides not to know that...they were, generally, either useless or mischievous...when my guide found himself in a whirlwind of fog and snow, so thick that we could scarcely see each other...he began to cry...the unhappy animal...vowed that if he ever lived to get home, he would never guide a gentleman again. He would even surrender his five shillings, if I would show him the way down the hill...There was but one way down from this wide plain...I had observed the bearing of this path at first, and therefore, taking out the compass, walked boldly on.

By the time his kilt was thoroughly cooled, and that he had vowed never to wear one again, the storm cleared away, and we returned by the road of Glen Nevis. The descent from Ben Nevis by the glen is not inconvenient, and it is wild and romantic. It is said that Cameron of Glen Nevis holds his lands by the tenure of an unfailing snow-ball when demanded.[25]

Another early tourist was the Rev C. Lesingham Smith, who had been a lecturer in mathematics at Christ's College, Cambridge. He made two tours of Scotland, in 1835 and 1836, taking in Ben Nevis during the first. He went on to publish a book detailing his trips, containing one of the very earliest of illustrations showing the north-east face.[26]

On August 31st he walked up Ben Nevis with two companions recently

Day & Haghe Lith.ᵗˢ to the King.

CRAGS OF BEN NEVIS.

Illustration from Lesingham Smith's book, published in 1837. The lithograph was by Louis Haghe of Day & Haghe ('Lithographers to the King'). Smith himself sketched as he went, and in all probability this lithograph was made from one of Smith's sketches. (It exhibits all the usual exaggerations of Victorian mountain drawings.) The view is looking down one of the major gullies; probably Number Three or Number Four

Illustration courtesy The Mitchell Library, Glasgow

The modern photo above looks down Number Four Gully, from a position part way down the gully. The Douglas Boulder is prominent in both illustrations, just below centre

Photo: Andrew Hunter

met and a guide. He was very impressed with the cliffs as seen from the summit plateau– 'Yet who can look down from the crags of Ben Nevis without a shudder...'

From the early 1830s until the late 1860s a small salmon-curing factory used a storeroom belonging to the Caledonian Canal. This cured salmon caught locally in Loch Eil and Loch Linnhe, the cured fish then being taken south in sailing smacks. At Corpach was an ice-house, used for storing the fish before they were processed. The ice was usually taken from a nearby millpond during winter cold spells, but there is a

reference to the collection of snow from the north face of Ben Nevis in two seasons when the supply of ice must have run out, presumably in the summer or autumn. The following account was written in 1835 by the parish minister.

> The deep clefts on the north-east side of Ben Nevis are never without snow. For two seasons when ice failed, the snow gathered and condensed into ice in these clefts and was of great service to the salmon curers. The country peasants with their small hardy horses carried it down in panniers on horseback.[27]

As to the actual site of ice collection there is no description, though a study of the mountain in early summer shows that one possible site accessible to horses is the gorge lying below the Secondary Tower Ridge. Failing this, ice collectors would probably have had to climb up to one of the large snow patches which linger on to mid or late summer, such as the one below Zero Gully.

Mountaineering for the sake of Science continued on into the 19th Century, the geologists following upon the heels of the botanists. Born in 1809 of an ancient Scots family, James David Forbes (1809 – 1868) was elected (in competition against Sir David Brewster) to the Professorship of Natural Philosophy in the University of Edinburgh in 1833. He was then not quite 24 years of age. This early ability was despite, or perhaps because of, an absence of formal schooling. Though primarily a physicist, his keen powers of observation coupled with a love of the mountains led him naturally to a secondary interest in geology, culminating in his classic study on glaciation, *Travels Through The Alps*.[28]

C.E.Mathews, in the Badminton Book of Mountaineering, describes Forbes as being

> ...pale, thin, and had indifferent health, but his expression was singularly sweet and winning, and he had the beautiful and refined manners of the old school.[29]

Portrait of James David Forbes (c. 1833)

Frontispiece from 'Travels Through The Alps', first published in 1843 (Author's Collection)

Scottish professors at this time had the option of giving all of their annual lectures in any space of six consecutive months; allowing much time for research or holidays. Forbes made several extended rambles across Scotland during his long holidays, and in 1847 climbed Schiehallion and visited Ben Nevis, *'hoping to write a book on the group.'* In 1848 he made a survey of Ben Nevis, walking round the mountain in three days with a guide, but carrying his own provisions. In 1851 his health broke down and his climbing days were over. Despite this, in 1855 he wrote that he was *'still crazy about the Alps, and loved the Scottish hills the better for their snow.'*

During the 1848 trip of Forbes we have the first record of step-cutting on Ben Nevis (though not in Scotland, for in 1812 a Colonel Peter Hawker cut steps on Ben Lomond).

As we approached the head of the glen, we got only glimpses of snow fields and broken rocks above us; and at length we were immersed in the fog, which fortunately was not very deep. We kept on the rocks as long as we could, and at length found that there only intervened between us and the ridge a short steep ascent of drifted snow, most truly Alpine. It was too late to think of receding, and it was not far; so assuming my new mahogany tripod as an Alpine stock, I proceeded foremost to make steps in the most approved Swiss fashion, to the no small edification of my companion, who had never seen such an operation before. The upper few yards were so steep that I actually could not get one foot stuck into the snow before the other, and had to get along sideways.[30]

After the scientists came the measurers, the Ordnance Survey. There is an amusing reference to these map-makers in a book by John Hill Burton, published in 1864. (Burton was an advocate. In 1867 he was appointed H.M. Historiographer for Scotland.) Climbing Ben Nevis by the tourist route, Burton gained the summit plateau, where slowly thinning mist revealed a strange sight,

It was neither more nor less than a crowd of soldiers, occupying nearly the whole table-land of the summit! Yes, there they were, British troops, with their red coats, dark-grey trousers, and fatigue caps...The party were occupied in erecting a sort of dwelling for themselves – half tent, half hut. Though in fatigue dresses, and far from being very trim, it was easy to see that they were not common soldiers. They belong, we believe, to the educated corps of sappers and miners; and a short conversation with them showed that the reputation of intelligence and civility long enjoyed by that distinguished body has not been unjustly earned.[31]

It seemed, as Burton soon learned, that the Survey had already conducted some surveys on Ben Macdui, and were now beginning to do the same work on Ben Nevis, so as to decide which of these two mountains had the honour of being the highest in the United Kingdom. At this time, Burton was told, the Cairngorm mountain was 'leading' by some 20 feet, subsequently he was informed that Ben Nevis had it by a few feet.

With slow, timid steps, one individual at a time, a new direction towards the hills was beginning to take shape – the climbing of mountains for fun. Ben Nevis had a few years respite left in the middle of the 19th Century, but the day of the climber was fast approaching.

References

1. **Watson**, William J., *The History of the Celtic Place-names of Scotland*. (Edinburgh: Blackwood, 1926.)

2. **Mackenzie**, W.C., *Scottish Place Names*. (London: Kegan Paul, Trench, Trubner & Co., 1931.)

3. **Johnston**, J.B., *Place Names of Scotland*. (London: John Murray, 1934.)

4. **MacMillan**, Somerled, *Bygone Lochaber*. (Glasgow: Printed privately, K. & R. Davidson, 1971.)

5. **Blaeu**, Johan, *Le Grand Atlas Ou Cosmographie Blaviane*. (Amsterdam: 1663). Facsimile edition in 12 volumes (Amsterdam: Treatium Orbis Terrarum Ltd, 1967.)

6. **Gordon**, Sir Robert, *Unpublished letters to Sir John Scot of Scotstarvet*. NLS, Adv. MS, 1719.

7. **Cash**, Caleb.G., *The first topographical survey of Scotland*. Scottish Geographical Magazine XVII, 399 – 413, 1901.

8. **Mitchell**, Ian R., *Scotland's Mountains before the Mountaineers*. (Edinburgh: Luath Press, 1998.)

9. The National Map Library of Scotland (Edinburgh) www.nls.uk/pont/

10. **Drummond**, John, *Memoirs of Sir Ewen Cameron of Locheil*. (Edinburgh: Abbotsford Club, 1842.)

11. **Macphee**, G.G., *Snow on Ben Nevis*. SMCJ 20, p451. 1935.

12. Climatic Research Unit. *www.cru.uea.ac.uk/*

13. **Burt**, Edward, *Letters from a Gentleman in the North of Scotland*. (London: 1754). (Edinburgh: John Donald Publishers Ltd., 1974 – Facsimile reprint of 5th edition, London: s.n., 1818.)

14. **Pennant**, Thomas, *A Tour in Scotland, 1769*. (Warrington: Printed by W. Eyres, 1774, 3rd edition.)

15. **Corner**, R.W.M., The enigma of montane *Sagina maritima* Don. Watsonia 24: 215 – 217, 2002.

16. **Robertson**, James, *MS Journals in the NLS* (1767 and 1771).

17. **Hope**, John, *Letter to William Watson, dated 10 April, 1769*. Philos. Trans. R. Soc., 59, 241 – 242, 1769.

18. **Fletcher**, H.R., *Exploration of the Scottish Flora*. Trans. Bot. Soc. Edin., 38, 30 – 47, 1959.

19. **Williams**, John, *The Natural History of the Mineral Kingdom*. In 2 Vols. (Edinburgh: Bell & Bradfute, 1810, 2nd edition.)

20. **Bailey**, James, *Diary of Scottish Tour*. National Library of Scotland.

21. **Wilkinson**, Thomas, *Tours to the British Mountains, with the Descriptive Poems of Lowther and Emont Vale*. (London: Taylor & Hessey, 1824.)

22. **Aust**, Mrs Murray, *A Companion and Useful Guide to the Beauties of Scotland, and the Hebrides*. (London: 1799, sold by George Nicol.)

23. **Garden**, William, *Keats And Ben Nevis*. SMCJ 21, 407 – 413, 1938.

24. **Carr**, Sir John, *Caledonian sketches or a Tour Through Scotland in 1807*. (London: Mathews & Leigh, 1809.)

25. **Smith**, C. Lesingham, *Excursions through the Highlands and Isles of Scotland in 1835 and1836*. (London: Simpkin, Marshall & Co., 1837.)

26. **Macculloch**, John, *The Highlands and Western Isles of Scotland*. (London: Longman, Hurst, Rees, Orme, Brown, and Green, 1824.)

27. *The New Statistical Account of Scotland*. (Edinburgh & London: William Blackwood & Sons, 1845.)

28. **Forbes**, J.D., *Travels Through the Alps*. (London: Adam & Charles Black. Revised and annotated by W.A.B. Coolidge, 3rd Edition, 1900.)

29. **Dent**, C.T., *Mountaineering*. (London: Longmans, Green and Co. 2nd edition, 1892.)

30. **Adam Smith**, Professor George, *Rise And Progress of Mountaineering in Scotland – V. The Works of Professor James D. Forbes*. SMCJ 3, 309 – 315, 1895.

31. **Burton**, John Hill, *The Cairngorm Mountains*. (Edinburgh & London: William Blackwood & Sons, 1864.)

Sketch of J.D.Forbes in later years

From: The Badminton Book of Mountaineering, edited by C.T. Dent, 1892 (Author's Collection)

Joseph Gibson Stott (1861 – 1938) First Editor of the SMC Journal – shown here reclining on Cruach Ardrain with an alpenstock. This was a long pole with a metal spike at its foot – a forerunner of the ice axe.

Stott was responsible for the SMC song, sung at the annual dinner; he later left for New Zealand, perhaps voluntarily. (The song is full of Victorian sentiment and bathos, leading to the suspicion that he may have been banished...)

Photo: A.E.Robertson

2: The First Climbers (1866 – 1896)

THE MIDDLE of the 19th Century saw a new phenomenon – the outdoor club. Originally social and walking groups, they gradually evolved into something like the climbing clubs we know today. One of the earliest Scottish clubs to show a specialisation towards climbing was the Cobbler Club, formed in Glasgow in 1866. For the main part, however, the Scottish hills were still regarded as a training ground for the Alps. There was a nucleus of Alpine Club members living and working in Scotland. These climbers, some of whom began exploring in Scotland, were to function as a catalyst, in bringing about an awareness of what Scotland could provide as a climbing ground in its own right.

Though further south than the Isle of Skye, Ben Nevis in the 1880s was less accessible. From 1870 a train from Inverness could meet the Skye ferry at Strome. By contrast, when travelling from the south the Oban Line stopped at Tyndrum, leaving a wild stretch of rough road to Glen Coe and Fort William. It was probably not only on picturesque grounds that Glen Coe was often approached by boat up Loch Etive; it was easier to travel by water. The old road to Glen Coe took a higher route than the modern route and was often blocked in winter by drifting snow. So it was that as late as 1880, an ascent of Nevis by the tourist path could excite the national newspapers to print an account.

The 16 years beginning in 1880 saw the development of Ben Nevis as a climbing ground. More than that, it saw Scottish mountaineering develop as an entity, distinct in character and style from Alpinism. It is perhaps appropriate to begin with an account of the first ascent of the season of Ben Nevis, in 1880, by a man who stands amongst the giants of Scottish mountaineering pioneers – William Wilson Naismith (1856 – 1935).

Born to parents who were fond of the hills, Willie Naismith received his schooling at Gilbertfield House School, Hamilton, where he had Andrew Bonar Law as an almost exact contemporary. Hamiltonians remembered Naismith, to put it mildly, as a rather careless, pleasure-loving young man. He became, however, as his obituary in a local newspaper stated, *'a conspicuous example of the transforming power of the Gospel'*, and was, as his tribute from the pulpit read, *'one of the "twice born".'*

Naismith began walking from an early age, and remembers being taken up a hill of over 300m when six or seven, and Ben Lomond when about nine.[1] Always a prodigious walker, in 1879 at the age of 23 he walked from his home in Hamilton to the summit of Tinto and back – a distance of 90km. At the age of 60, in July 1916, he walked from Glasgow to the summit of Ben Lomond and back again; 100km in 20 hours, including stops. When asked by his young nephew John Fergus what food he carried on this expedition, Naismith replied that he found a bag of raisins in his pocket quite good. His favourite low-level hills appeared to have been the Campsies; the boggy, basaltic hills which protect Glasgow from the worst of the northerly winds. In his small pocket note-book from 1873 to 1919 he kept a brief record of his ascents; including a note of 313 visits to the Campsies, reaching Crichton's Cairn 139 times, and Earl's Seat on 85 occasions.[2]

On leaving school Naismith took classes at Glasgow University, eventually qualifying as a chartered accountant. In 1872 George Ramsay, Professor of Humanity at Glasgow University and a member of the Alpine Club, gave his Junior Latin Class a lecture on Alpine Climbing, along with a demonstration on the use of an ice axe. Naismith was fascinated, and when he came across a copy of Whymper's *Scrambles in The Alps* he devoured it with the most intense delight.

Growing up as he did into a man of deep religious convictions, Naismith eventually avoided Sunday climbing, though never passed judgment on those whose love of the hills surpassed their desire for a hard bench and a long sermon. For 27 years he was an elder in Kelvinside (Botanic Gardens) Church, Glasgow. Professionally busy as a chartered accountant and insurance manager, he found time for activities in addition to mountaineering. These included skating; once on a frozen Loch Lomond as far as Rowardennan (during the great freeze of 1895), and a balloon ascent over Glasgow on September 2, 1901, reaching an altitude of 1,630m.

Lord Mackay (a Court of Session Judge, member of the SMC and the AC) described Naismith as,

> ...a human being of the finest steel, modest and self-effacing. He was physically compact and of small build, with corresponding small hands and feet, which seemed made to go into or on the tiniest holds.[3]

Naismith's friends considered him to be a confirmed bachelor, but at the age of 70 he surprised them by marrying the daughter of an Aberdeenshire minister. He died in Strathpeffer aged 79, while attending an Evangelical meeting, and is buried in Bent Cemetery, Hamilton.

Other than eponymous routes, Naismith will be remembered for his

Always a prodigious walker, in 1879 at the age of 23 he [Naismith] walked from his home in Hamilton to the summit of Tinto and back – a distance of 90km. At the age of 60, in July 1916, he walked from Glasgow to the summit of Ben Lomond and back again; 100km in 20 hours, including stops

*Other than epony-
mous routes,
Naismith will be
remembered for his
formulation of
what came to be
called Naismith's
Rule, first described
by him in the
SMC Journal of
September 1892*

*...a simple formula,
that may be found
useful in estimating
what time men in
fair condition
should allow for
easy expeditions,
namely, an hour
for every three
miles on the map,
with an additional
hour for every
2,000 feet of
ascent*

*...It is not too
fanciful to surmise
that Naismith's
training in accoun-
tancy had led to
his calculations of
walking times*

formulation of what came to be called Naismith's Rule, first described by him in the SMC Journal of September 1892. This was, in his own words,

> ...a simple formula, that may be found useful in estimating what time men in fair condition should allow for easy expeditions, namely, an hour for every three miles on the map, with an additional hour for every 2,000 feet of ascent.[4]

It is not too fanciful to surmise that Naismith's training in accountancy had led to his calculations of walking times. These rules continue to fascinate, and there have been several modifications to Naismith's Rule since the original. (The metric equivalent is usually given as 1.2 minutes per 100m distance, and one minute per 10m of height gained. Descending a steep slope requires about the same time as ascent, while an easy descent approaches speed on the flat. All these times, of course, will vary depending on fitness, weather, terrain and so on.)

On the evening of May 1, 1880, Naismith and two clerical friends arrived in Fort William, after a tedious if charming voyage down the Caledonian Canal in the ancient steamtub *Plover*. There they learned that Ben Nevis had not been climbed since the previous autumn, and the next day, despite a layer of cloud covering the summit, they set off after 9am to attempt the hill.

After gaining the north ridge of Meall an t-Suidhe and passing the lochan, the party climbed above the snowline and into the cloud. Hoping for a clearing, they amused themselves for two hours attempting to glissade; sliding upright down the snow with the aid of stout walking sticks. This almost ended in tragedy when one of the party began to accelerate down a gully packed with hard snow, but fortunately a rock stopped the descent in time.

Finally they decided to recommence the ascent, mist or not, floundering along on the broad summit plateau up to their knees in deep snow. After finding themselves at one point walking straight towards the cliff edge, they corrected their course and continued to the top using a compass bearing. The summit cairn was almost completely covered, and it was only by discovering a bottle with names inside that they could be certain of their ascent. A hasty lunch during a sleet shower and an uneventful descent saw them back at Fort William at 6pm.

On their return they were interviewed by the local newspaper reporter (probably, Naismith thought, at the instigation of the landlord of the Alexandra Hotel), with the result that a report headlined *First Ascent of Ben Nevis – Without Guides* was published in the national press. They had in fact attempted to find a guide that morning, but were provided instead with a compass and an 'indifferent map.'[5] To help put this period into perspective, a glance through the *Glasgow Herald* for May 12, 1880 would find such current matters as the Afghan War, the continuing Inquest into the Tay Bridge Disaster, and a note that, 'last night, St. Enoch Railway Station was lit by electric light.'

This ascent was three years before the summit observatory and its good bridle path were built, and the year before Clement Wragge began his daily summer ascents; making meteorological observations at the summit and at intermediate points. (The story of the Observatory is told in Chapter 3.) Surprisingly, it was to be another 12 years before the first

Willie Naismith waiting for a train. Date unknown but probably 1880s

SMC Archives

rock climb on the north face of Ben Nevis was put up, and then by a team from the north of England. There is good evidence, however, that at least one of the easy snow gullies received an ascent during the 1880s.

The Summit Meteorological Observatory was built in 1883, and from a book written by W.T.Kilgour, who was a relief observer for a period at the Observatory, we have the following interesting account of what must have been one of the first climbs.

> One bracing afternoon in winter, not long after the Observatory had been opened, a member of staff who had gone out for a walk on the snow was more than amazed on looking over a precipice to see, about 1500 feet down, two dark objects laboriously scaling the ice-covered and snow-clad face of the declivity...Roped together, and cutting foot and handholds with their ice axes, slowly but surely those two venturesome climbers made the top by a route which had never, within mortal ken, been previously attempted.[6]

This description, written round about the mid-1880s, is of one of the earliest snow and ice routes put up in Scotland, and most likely refers to an ascent of Number Three or Number Four Gully, by climbers unnamed. Unfortunately, there is no reference to this ascent in the Observatory Logbook. From the floor of Coire na Ciste, the upper section of Number Four Gully is concealed, while Number Three Gully is plainly visible directly above, making it likely that Number Three would have received early attention. In his 1902 Ben Nevis Guide, W.Inglis Clark notes that,

> there can be no doubt that this gully was one of the earliest climbed, the writer's knowledge of it going back to 1870.[7]

This statement might be taken as indicating an ascent, in which case it dates the first known route on the north-east face of Ben Nevis.

In March 1884, a solo ascent of a very icy Ben More, equipped only with an alpenstock (a long, metal-tipped pole), convinced Naismith that in winter and spring the higher Scottish mountains ought to be treated as seriously as Alpine peaks – using the same equipment; axes and a rope. The chief difficulty, as Naismith admitted, and other individuals were experiencing, was in finding someone else with whom to climb.

To provide an idea of the growing popularity of walking up Ben Nevis, an article in *The Scotsman* for September 8, 1886 described in good detail the route up the Bridle path. The article also provided the astonishing information that in the summers of 1884 and 1885, a total of 6,800 visitors made the ascent. The route described eventually reaches the summit, with, on the left and close to the path a, '*...deep chasm in which snow lies all the year round.*' [Gardyloo Gully].

> Right in front is seen a low wooden structure, with large letters painted along its side, 'Observatory Hotel', and having over the door the Gaelic inscription 'Aoidheachd.' This word – though altogether unpronounceable to the person who is not accustomed to using his nasal organ as a speaking-trumpet – means in English that strangers are entertained within. Not a few English tourists, however, pronounce the word 'Oddheight', and believe it to be the name of the proprietor. Inside the hotel, while the cook is preparing refreshments, the eye of the visitor easily spotted a prominent notice which advertised 'dry stockings for wet feet.'

This last notice, apparently, cheered up most visitors. It belonged to a small hotel built apart from the Meterological Observatory. (See Chapter Three for their story.)

Although Scotland in the late 1880s had a growing number of mountaineers, contact between them was almost nonexistent, and consequently information about mountains, routes, techniques and so on difficult to come by. On January 10, 1889, a letter appeared in the *Glasgow Herald*, proposing a '*Scottish Alpine Club*'. The writer was Naismith, and in spirited tones he described mountain climbing as '*one of the most manly as well as healthful and fascinating forms of exercise.*' Naismith also declared that it was –

> ...almost a disgrace to any Scotsman whose heart and lungs are in proper order if he is not more or less of a mountaineer, seeing that he belongs to one of the most mountainous countries in the world.

Naismith's letter was answered on January 14 by *Cairn*, the pen-name, as it turned out, of Gilbert Thomson and D.A.Archie. These two, while in favour of the formation of a club, objected to any Alpine reference, pointing out that height was no test of difficulty. Naismith replied favourably on January 18, and the following day Ernest Maylard wrote suggesting the name *Scottish Mountaineering Club*.

In 1866 Professor George Ramsay, along with Professor Veitch and Mr Campbell Colquhoun of Clathick had founded the Cobbler Club. Since then, wrote Ramsay in a journal article,

> ...with the notable exception of (Professor Veitch) I had never, outside the limits of my own family, met with a single Scotsman who cared seriously to practise the art of mountaineering.[8]

Consequently, on a gloomy, foggy morning in the last week of January 1889, Ramsay was delighted to receive a visit from Maylard and a friend,

To provide an idea of the growing popularity of walking up Ben Nevis, an article in The Scotsman for September 8, 1886 described in good detail the route up the Bridle path. The article also provided the astonishing information that in the summers of 1884 and 1885, a total of 6,800 visitors made the ascent

who wished to discuss the formation of a club. As a result of that meeting, Maylard organised a meeting for any gentleman (and, as a point of fact, lady), who might be interested.

The first meeting took place in the Christian Institute, Bath Street, Glasgow, on February 11, 1889, with Professor Ramsay in the chair. About 40 were present and a provisional committee was formed to set up a constitution. The Scottish Mountaineering Club was formally set up in Glasgow one month later, on March 11, 1889, with a membership of 94. Of these original members, 14 were already members of the Alpine Club, 17 came from Edinburgh, 13 from various other areas in the east and 12 from England; the remaining 38 living in and around Glasgow. It would seem that no ladies were present at this first meeting; they were soon to found The Ladies' Scottish Climbing Club.

Although the Cairngorm Club had been founded in 1887, the SMC became the driving force in Scottish mountaineering. Its first journal appeared in January 1890, with Stott as Editor. (Stott was responsible for the SMC Club Song, sung once a year at the Annual Dinner. Work duties took him first to New Zealand, then Australia. His letters to Willie Douglas are full of nostalgia and the desire to return to Scotland, but he married and settled in Australia.) The first full committee included: Maylard, who was then a surgeon at the Victoria Infirmary, Glasgow, as Secretary, Thomson as Librarian. Naismith, characteristically refusing all attempts to elect him President, became Treasurer, while Ramsay became the first President.

With the publication of the SMC Journal, originally thrice yearly, and a succession of mountain guidebooks, the SMC became a mine of information; many of its members already being experienced Alpinists able to pass on knowledge and techniques. Ben Nevis and Glen Coe were still difficult of access, but the golden age of Scottish mountaineering was about to unfold.

In 1894 Edward Whymper wrote of the north face of Ben Nevis –

> This great face is one of the finest pieces of crag in our country, and it has never been climbed, though every now and then adventurous ones go and look at it with wistful eyes.[9]

Unfortunately Whymper, in common it seems with everyone else, had no knowledge of the highly successful visit in September 1892 by a family from the north of England – the Hopkinsons, three brothers and a son. Ironically, Whymper himself had spent a week ascending Nevis – not to put up any climbs – but to conduct experiments with aneroids for a manufacturer, comparing readings taken top and bottom. This was just one month before the visit by the Hopkinsons.[10] The Hopkinson family from Manchester was a Victorian example of progress through hard work. The father began as a mill mechanic and later rose to become Mayor of Manchester. All five of his sons were academically gifted and became experienced alpinists. The noted alpinist W.C.Slingsby was a cousin. The eldest son and natural leader was John (1849 – 1898). John's son Bertram (1874 – 1918) joined his father for the trip to Ben Nevis. The other brothers were Alfred (1851 – 1939), Charles (1854 – 1920), Edward (1859 – 1921) and Albert (1863 – 1949). Following a climbing disaster in the Alps in 1898 in which John, two

George Gilbert Ramsay (1839 – 1921). First President of the SMC, Ramsay took up the Chair of Humanity at Glasgow University in 1863, aged 24. He became a member of the Alpine Club in 1876. Unlike his friend Munro, he had a strong sense of humour, and his 'friendly wrangles with Hugh Munro were a source of pure delight'

Photo: SMC Archives

The North-East Face of Ben Nevis. Tower Ridge is the prominent buttress left of centre. North-East Buttress is the larger buttress forming the left-hand edge of the face

Photo: Alex Gillespie

daughters, and his son Jack were killed on a traverse of the Petit Dent de Veisivi, the surviving brothers ceased climbing completely.

On Saturday September 3, 1892, John, Edward, and the 18-year old Bertram walked up under the north face of Ben Nevis. They were confronted with a bewildering succession of steep aretes, ridges, pinnacles and gullies; extending for a total frontage of 3.2km of cliffs. Three immense rock features formed prominent landmarks; North-East Buttress and Càrn Dearg Buttress on the left and right flanks, and the great central feature of Tower Ridge. None had been climbed or named. That day the barometer was rising briskly; there were squally N and NE winds with showers of snow throughout the day. It would have been excusable had the Hopkinsons been content with a lesser route – instead they chose the major feature of Tower Ridge. Starting at an elevation of about 730m, Tower Ridge rises boldly to form a shapely pinnacle 213m high. A climb in its own right, this is the Douglas Boulder. Crossing the Douglas Gap behind the Boulder, the ridge narrows and leads, at a moderate angle, to a rock step in the ridge called the Little Tower, which presents the first real difficulties of the ridge.

Above the Little Tower the ridge leads without complication to the uncompromising bulk of the Great Tower, leading steeply in a 30m rise to its cairn at 1,285m. (This raises an interesting question, as the cairn was already present when the Hopkinsons approached Ben Nevis. Someone, perhaps climbers, perhaps Observatory staff, had presumably descended from the summit plateau using ropes and built the cairn. It

could even have been the Hopkinsons during an earlier attempt, but no record has been found.) As far as the foot of the Great Tower the route is straightforward but here the climber is obliged to find a way up the tower. On that Saturday in 1892, Edward, John and his son Bertram climbed the ridge as far as the Great Tower. We have little details of the ascent; they almost certainly avoided the Douglas Boulder and started instead up the gully to the east. On reaching the Great Tower they traversed rightwards on to the west face and climbed a narrow chimney. They were then defeated by a steep pitch. Presumably they then reversed back down to their starting point and so down to Fort William.

The weather was poor for the next two days, being very cold on the Sunday as the Hopkinsons returned. Charles joined the original three in walking to the top. There was mist or fog around until 4pm, after which the summit was frequently clear. The temperature remained low all day, with slight showers of snow falling in the forenoon. This time the four Hopkinsons descended from the summit plateau to gain the Great Tower from above. They then reversed this by a route on the west face, probably by a Very Difficult variation now known as the Recess Route. After an exposed traverse, they regained their high point of Saturday and completed the descent, thus completing, albeit it in descent, the first recorded rock climb on Ben Nevis.

On Tuesday September 6, the Hopkinsons returned for further exploration. Again there was mist or fog until the afternoon, followed by occasional sunny intervals. The three brothers and Bertram walked

further up the Allt a' Mhuilinn to the biggest challenge visible on the skyline – the North-East Buttress, the eastern of the three ridges. They described the climbing on this as interesting, but much easier than on the centre ridge. Finally, on Thursday September 8, they climbed the introductory pinnacle at the foot of Tower Ridge, now known as the Douglas Boulder. Their route cannot be identified with any certainty, though they '*descended it on the north face.*' In the current guide, Tower Ridge in summer is a 600m Difficult, given four stars for quality.

The Hopkinsons had enjoyed exciting and doubtless satisfying climbing on two of the major features on Ben Nevis – and for the first time at that – but despite this they chose not to report their ascents until August 1895, when a short note appeared in the Alpine Journal under the title *Alpine Notes – Ben Nevis*.[11] In all probability they regarded their ascents as training for the Alps, and had little or no conception of their significance in the early days of Scottish climbing. In the interim however, the growing activity of the recently formed SMC was soon to provide its own impetus. The interest of that club, and one of its members in particular, was about to switch its focus to Ben Nevis. That member was Doctor, later Professor, Collie.

John Norman Collie (1859 – 1942) was born on September 10, 1859 at Alderley Edge, Manchester. '*It might be fairly claimed that he was a Scot*', stated his obituary notice[12], as his grandfather, George Collie, was tenant of the farm of Wantonwells at Insch, Aberdeenshire, and his father John Collie lived for several years at Glassel on Deeside, before moving to Bristol. It was at Glassel that Collie ascended his first hill, the modest Hill of Fare, at the age of eight. In a long scientific career which spanned over 40 years, his original researches in Chemistry won him many honours, as did his outstanding endeavours as an explorer and mountaineer. At University College, London, he had succeeded Sir

John Lackie descending into Tower Gap. Crampon-scratched rocks show up lighter, while Glover's Chimney drops away on the left

Photo: Ken Crocket

William Ramsay in 1902 as Professor of Organic Chemistry and in 1913 as Director of the chemical laboratories. He took the first X-ray in the U.K. of a human subject for medical purposes, of a lady who had a needle fragment embedded in her thumb, and there is a strong argument that he, and not Ramsay, should be credited with the discovery of the rare gas Neon.

Collie joined the SMC in 1891 and the Alpine Club two years later, serving on the committees of both clubs and becoming President of the Alpine Club in 1920. His travels and climbs were widespread; from the Alps and the Canadian Rockies, to the Himalayas, and the Isle of Skye, which eventually became his chosen home and final resting place. In Canada he made six expeditions, which accounted for 21 first ascents of peaks. Mount Collie, 3,116m, in British Columbia was named after him. His long partnership, and indeed deep friendship with the local Skye guide John Mackenzie was responsible for many successful ascents on that island. When Mackenzie died in 1933, Collie made a lone ascent of Am Bhasteir, stating that it was his last climb – and so it was. In 1939, with the outbreak of war, he left London and settled down at Sligachan Hotel, facing out over the moors to his beloved Cuillin.

There is a poignant reference to Collie's last years at Sligachan, when a trainee fighter pilot, Richard Hillary, and his companion decided to spend their four days of leave on Skye. This was in the spring of 1940. A bus advert prompted them to seek out the Sligachan Hotel.

1896 X-rays showing steel needle embedded in lady's thumb

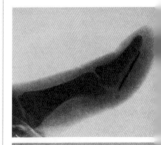

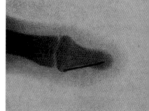

> We were alone in the inn save for one old man who had returned there to die. His hair was white, but his face and bearing were still those of a mountaineer, though he must have been of a great age. He never spoke, but appeared regularly at meals to take his place at a table tight-pressed against the window, alone with his wine and his memories. We thought him rather fine.

The next day the two pilots set off early to climb Bruach na Frithe. After a successful ascent they decided to follow a stream which led back

The famous SMC meet at Easter 1894, at the Inveroran Inn. It was from this meet that Collie moved onto Fort William and, in company with his friends Godfrey Solly and Joseph Collier, made the first ascent of Tower Ridge, on March 30, 1894. Solly is in the centre back, wearing a deerstalker hat, Collie with pipe second from right, Collier at rear, in doorway (with hat)

Left to Right: James Maclay, Willie Douglas, D.A. Forbes, Dr Joseph Collier, G.G. Ramsay, T. Fraser, S. Campbell, Godfrey A. Solly, L.W. Hinxman, Charles C.B. Moss, J. Rennie, F.O. Bower, W. Ramsay (sitting), J. Norman Collie and H.C. Boyd

Photo: SMC Archives

to the hotel, a rather cold and wet decision, as it turned out. Over dinner they described their exploits to the landlord.

His sole comment was 'Humph', but the old man at the window turned and smiled at us. I think he approved.

Hillary returned to the Battle of Britain in which he was shot down and badly burned. During a long period of convalescence he wrote *The Last Enemy*[13], containing the above description of Collie. He was killed in active service in 1943. Collie died in November 1942. Fishing in Loch Storr, he had managed to find a spot sheltered from a strong wind and pulled in a good number of trout. Regaining the bank the wind blew him back into the loch and following the cold soaking he succumbed to pneumonia. He was buried according to his wish beside his old companion and friend John Mackenzie, in the little graveyard at Struan. Here, where sheep come in through a gap in the drystane dyke and crop the green turf, an unpolished piece of gabbro from the Black Cuillin rests on the grave as a headstone. (As this book was being revised, there were plans to design and erect a statue to Collie and Mackenzie, on a site at Sligachan.)

The SMC had early begun to organise club meets at several centres, notably at Inveroran Inn at the west end of Loch Tulla. At this time the nearest railway station was 16km south, at Tyndrum. On the first of January, 1894, Collie wrote to Willie Douglas, the Editor of the SMC Journal.

If I possibly can allure a few friends I shall be up in Glencoe next Easter so we may meet there, there is a splendid climb straight up Aonach Dhu on Stob Corrie an Lochan from Loch Triochtan about 2400 feet of precipice which I once did years ago – and which I should'nt mind doing again. I have been away from Scotland too long.[14]

Collie attended the Easter Meet of 1894, based at Inveroran. He had

The High Street, Fort William, in the 1890s, with the Palace Hotel centre

Photo: from old postcard (Author's Collection)

with him two guests from the Lakes; Godfrey Solly (1858 – 1942), a solicitor, and Joseph Collier (1855 – 1905), a Manchester surgeon. After a night in the crowded Inn the three moved on to Glen Coe, where they recorded several new routes before moving on again, this time to Fort William.

On Friday, March 30, Collie and his two friends decided to attempt Tower Ridge. There is no evidence that they were aware of the Hopkinson descent 18 months earlier, and it is certain that there was no knowledge of the ascent of North-East Buttress as late as May, 1895 – even by W.C.Slingsby, a cousin of the Hopkinsons. Ben Nevis was in full winter condition as they bypassed the Douglas Boulder on its eastern flank to gain the ridge just above the Douglas Gap. That fruitful combination of the right party, route and conditions was about to culminate in a magnificent ascent.

Those seeking precise details of the first ascent of Tower Ridge may be disappointed, for the account which Collie left in the SMC Journal of September 1894 is in a somewhat unusual form. In a letter to Douglas, dated June 27, 1894, and accompanying his account, Collie wrote that,

> I send an attempt – written largely of experiment – laborious I fear – a pseudo Rabelaisian alchemistic etc attempts – which I commend to your Editorial clemency. Deal gently with it – but don't scruple to say if you don't want it – I go to Switzerland to be dragged over the mountains by Mummery and Hastings in about a month. Yours in haste, Norman Collie.[15]

Douglas of course accepted Collie's article, and with great efficiency had it ready for publication shortly after, as a letter from Collie confirms.

> Kensington W. 11 July, 1894. Dear Douglas. I return the proof sheets corrected – + hope that when they appear in the S.M.J. the select band you mention may find some interest in their perusal – but 'I hae ma doots.' I have put my signature in the form of an anagram at the end of the paper. P.S. would'nt the title look better in italics?[16]

A very early photograph taken at Tower Gap. Newbigging on the left is looking down Glover's Chimney, while his companion Morrison holds the rope (c. 1890s)

Photo: A.E.Robertson

Collie's article for the SMC Journal was signed by *Orlamon Linecus*, the expedition setting out from a *Castrum Guillelmi*.

> Nor did they issue forth unprepared, for they bore with them the proper, peculiar, fit, exact, and lawful insignia of the brotherhood, a flaxen rope coiled even as the mystic serpent, likewise staves curiously shapen did they take in their hands...

Very early on in the ascent, Collie's party came across the nail scratches left by the Hopkinsons, for having gained the ridge the party pressed on,

> ...and by inspection were they aware how others had travelled on the same way, for on the stones and rocks were there certain petrographical scrapings and curious markings deeply graven, and very evident.

The Little Tower does not receive a mention by Collie, the climbers continuing on up the ridge until they came,

> ...to a great rock, a majestic tower; here were they perforce compelled to depart to the right hand, placing themselves in steep and perilous positions on slopes of ice.

Today, this way of climbing the Great Tower in winter, by the West face, is rarely attempted. One competent team who climbed this way in the 1970s described it later as *desperate*. Tower Ridge is currently graded IV,3, with the Western Traverse graded IV,4. Collie continued –

> Still all things have an end at last, – good Wine, Pinnacles, Spires, cabalistic

Emblems, and oromaniacal Wanderings...So did the three find the perilous passage across the headlong steep finish. Then did they pass onwards to the Labyrinth, the rocky Chaos, and greatly did they marvel at the exceeding steepness thereof; so that only by great perseverance, turning now to the right and now to the left, were they able to break themselves free from the bonds and entanglements, and climb sagaciously upwards to the summit of the great tower.

Looking down from its top the party saw –

Behind, and far below, imprinted in the snow were the steps by which they had mounted upwards, winding now this way now that, looking like scarce seen veins in finest marble.

Now the party of three had to negotiate Tower Gap to reach the final slope leading to the summit plateau and the safe haven of the Observatory.

Thither therefore did their footsteps trend. First did they pass along the narrow Way, treading with exceeding care and exactness, for there was but foothold for one alone, the path being no broader than a man's hand. Next did they descend into the Cleft...But now before them stretched the white Slope, which lay beneath the topmost summit, and steeper became the path, going upwards with a great steepness.

Collie's party was beginning to feel despair, as the top part of the Ridge does indeed look very steep from below, when –

...lo! from out of the clouds a rope descended, and a voice was heard:- 'Fear not, now have ye attained to the Consummation, enter into the mystagorical, quintessential, and delectable pleasure-house of devout Oromaniacs.' And what joy, think ye, did they feel after the exceedingly long and troublous ascent? – after scrambling, slipping, pulling, pushing, lifting, gasping, looking, hoping, despairing, climbing, holding on, falling off, trying, puffing, loosing, gathering, talking, stepping, grumbling, anathematising, scraping, hacking, bumping, jogging, overturning, hunting, straddling, – for know you that by these methods alone are the most divine mysteries of the Quest reached.[17]

Climbers approaching Tower Gap from the top of the Great Tower
Photo: John Trudgill

The three happy climbers had taken five hours for the first complete, and first winter ascent of a major route, climbing in nailed boots with long, wooden-shafted ice axes and short lengths of manila rope. Their time would be regarded as good by a modern party, on a long route whose difficulties increase with height and which in most winters sees a number of slow parties and late starters benighted. The Observatory logbook for March 30, 1894 reads –

Today Mr McIntyre postmaster Fort William and Mr Wallace Post Office surveyor visited the observatory. Three other gentlemen also came up; climbing the cliff up the buttress at point beyond second gorge and having to cut steps almost the whole way in the ice.

Collie thought that it *'resembled the Italian side of the Matterhorn, and was the best climb he had ever had in Scotland.'* He certainly must have been very pleased with the route, for the Observatory log for the next day stated,

Today two strangers climbed Ben Nevis and the cliff the same way as before, one of them being one of the previous party.

The sketch drawn by Naismith on the reverse of a letter and sent to Willie Douglas on April 25, 1895. Naismith had made the first ascent of Castle Ridge on April 12, while attending the Easter Meet at Fort William. His companions were Collie, Thomson and Travers. Later annotations were made to the sketch, e.g. in May Tough and Brown climbed the North-East Buttress, Naismith (not yet aware of the Hopkinson ascent) having marked it originally as 'unclimbed'

Photo: Ken Crocket

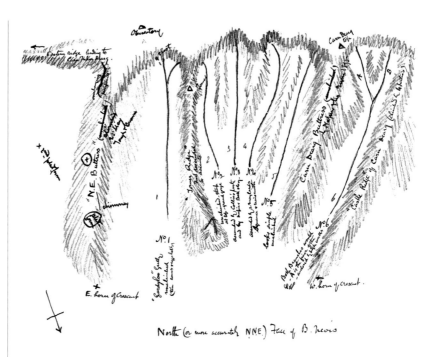

North (or more accurately NNE) Face of B. Nevis

Collie no doubt is 'a pure Scotsman' (tho' perhaps in a Gladstonian sense) but his 3 pals tho' all very nice chaps are undoubted undiluted specimens of the genus pock-pudding. This is truly a sad day for auld Scotland. Let us hope that the hotel keepers at Ft.Wm. took a good few bawbees off the Englishers

Collie's partner on this second ascent was Geoffrey Hastings. On hearing of Collie's ascent Naismith sent a rueful letter to Douglas.

Hamilton, Saturday night. My Dear Douglas, Just got yours enclosing Collie's which I return with many thanks. The Sassenachs have indeed taken the wind out of our sails maist notoriously I wull say that. However I suppose we must make a virtue of necessity & try to look pleasant about it. Those beggars were more wide-awake than we – in skimming the cream off Glencoe & Ben Nevis the year before the railway opened, while we in our innocence were still planning what we should do after that event.

Collie no doubt is 'a pure Scotsman' (tho' perhaps in a Gladstonian sense) but his 3 pals tho' all very nice chaps are undoubted undiluted specimens of the genus pock-pudden. This is truly a sad day for auld Scotland. Let us hope that the hotel keepers at Ft.Wm. took a good few bawbees off the Englishers. Flodden or even Culloden was nothing to this...[18]

In 1894, Englishman and four times Prime Minister William Gladstone was then resident at Fasque, near Fettercairn. Always the gentleman however, Naismith wrote to Collie congratulating him on his ascent, as a letter from Collie to Douglas confirms –

16 Campdengrove, Kensington W., 20.4.94. ...I had a letter the other day from Naismith in which he congratulated me in the most delightful manner on my Easter climbs. After I had read your letter I felt as if I had rather been poaching on your ground on Ben Nevis, but I assure you it is many years ago since I made up my mind that on the first possible opportunity when I could get another man I would have a try at the old Ben...[19]

For the next decade or so the defences of the ridge, particularly around the Great Tower, were probed and tested, and variations and escape routes recorded. The ridge had its third ascent on September 27, 1894, by Willie Naismith and Gilbert Thomson. Informing Douglas by letter from Fort William, Naismith suggested the name Tower Ridge, and so it has been ever since. Naismith's letter is interesting in showing the standard of proficiency so early gained by those pioneers.

> Fort William, Friday morning. My dear Douglas, As my telegram y'day would announce Thomson and I got up the North face of B. Nevis all right. We followed Collie's route exactly except I think that while we got on the rocks of the ridge near the foot Collie seems to have kept up a gully to the left (E) for some distance & joined the ridge higher up.
>
> The climb at present is quite easy – the only bit that requires care being 10 feet 'a.p.' [absolutely perpendicular] on the side of the big tower, but when the first man is up there is no difficulty for those following...Excepting the tower and the cleft the only places where one would like to be roped are one or two short chimneys in the lower portion of the ridge...The whole N. face is bare rock and snow and very grand. There are several easy gullies most of them still full of snow so one had better take an axe even in Sept. unless he means to stick to 'the Tower Ridge'. How w? that name do for Collie's climb?
>
> The climb I want to look at when I come back is by the great eastern ridge or buttress due E of the Observatory and next to Collie's ridge on the left as you face the Ben. On most views of the hill from Banavie or Corpach this Eastern buttress is seen on the skyline. It is a.p. at the end but might I think be reached higher up.[20]

Willie Naismith cutting steps
Photo: A.E.Robertson

In the autumn of 1894 the West Highland Railway finally opened, and the SMC switched their 1895 Easter Meet to Fort William. That April, some 27 members and their guests assembled at the *Alexandra Hotel*. Norman Collie was present, as were other figures such as Douglas, Maclay, Mayland, Munro, Naismith, and the Rev. A.E.Robertson, first person recorded as having completed all the Munros. Several gullies were climbed by the *Axe-men*, including a winter ascent of Number Three Gully by Collie and Travers, and also by J.H.Bell, Napier and party, Number Four Gully by Naismith, A.E. and M.W.Mayland, and Squance. Number Five Gully was still unclimbed at this date, as mentioned in an SMC Journal article by Lionel Hinxman. On a sketch of the NE Face described below, Naismith also marked Number Five Gully as unclimbed, though he thought it would be straightforward. A new ridge leading to the top of Càrn Dearg was climbed by three parties; the first being composed of Collie, Naismith, Thomson and M.W.Travers. The new ridge was christened the Castle Ridge, after the huge castellated rock mass which towers over it. The two great ridges however, Tower Ridge and the North-East Buttress, were pronounced impracticable, due to the thick plastering of snow and ice which hung in great white blossoms from the rocks.

Naismith wrote a letter to Willie Douglas following this Meet, dated the 25th April. On the reverse of the letter he had drawn a rough sketch of the NE Face, marking the six gullies then numbered from one to six. The diagram and letter is a fascinating document, as it has the North-East Buttress marked as unclimbed; this is scored out and the words 'climbed 25 May Tough & Brown' written under. Likewise, Càrn Dearg Buttress is marked as being unclimbed, this is also scored out and the words 'by Napier & Co. June 1895' are written down. This ascent referred

to the first ascent of Ledge Route, now a very popular scrambling route at a grade of Easy in summer, and Grade II in winter. The later writing appears to be by Naismith, and he presumably added these updates to the sketch at some later date. It is clearly evident, however, that even as late as the end of April 1895, the ascent of North-East Buttress by the Hopkinsons in 1892 was indeed unknown to Scottish climbers. On the same sketch, Number Six Gully is now the North and South Castle Gullies.

There are several other morsels in this letter of interest to the mountain historian. Referring to [Gilbert] Thomson's photographs of the north face, Naismith remarks that

'From that high standpoint the whole face looks perfectly awful. As Fraser Campbell w[d] say 'it is a mercy any of us are spared to tell the tale! I wonder whether one of the Carn Dearg views w[d] stand reproduction. It would show the Sassenachs what we can do up here in the steep way.'[21]

During the Easter Meet of 1895, the North-East Buttress became –

...the object of ambition to a large circle of climbers, the chief topic of the smokeroom at nights, and the focus of many critical glances during the day. It would also have been climbed had the ice upon the rocks not forbade the attempt.

So William Brown began his delightful account of a later successful ascent – the second – of the buttress, along with his friend William Tough (pronounced *Tooch*).

The new railway was to be used in approaching Fort William, with the Queen's Birthday as the date, but the two could not find a suitable train. They accordingly worked out an original

'...programme which, as Tough remarked, would have been utterly repulsive as applied to anything else but the N.E. Buttress.'

They therefore arranged to travel to Kingussie by the night express on Friday, May 24, cycle to Fort William, climb their route on arrival, cycle back to Kingussie the same day, and return to Edinburgh by train, reaching the city on the Sunday evening. There was, wrote Brown,

...a certain gloomy satisfaction that we were doing something quite out of the common, which deepened in gloom as our arrangements waxed in originality.

It was, predictably enough, very grey and miserable when Kingussie was reached at 3.50am on Saturday morning. '*Rain was falling dismally, and underwheel the roads were a fell compound of mud and newly-laid metal.*' Cycling past Laggan Bridge, the two intrepid travellers had just topped a stiff brae when,

...a sudden report, resembling the simultaneous opening of six bottles of 'Bouvier', was followed by Tough's despairing cry, 'Your tyre's punctured'.

Pushing the cycle 4km to the Laggan Hotel, in the expectation of finding a horse and trap, they found nothing zoological other than midges, and were then faced with a 21km walk to Inverlair.

Tough mounted the remaining bicycle, with a pyramid of ropes, axes, and

An SMC party tackles a massive cornice in 1894. An earlier thaw had obviously cause a partial collapse. What is of interest here is that the leading climber is wielding an alpenstock, the precursor to the ice axe (see the photo of Stott at the start of this chapter)

SMC Archives

rucksacks piled up on his shoulders, while his fellow-traveller half-walked, half-trotted alongside. In this order, with an occasional change of parts, when the pedestrian became (or said he was) exhausted, we straggled to Inverlair, and completed the rest of the journey comfortably by train.

The weather had remained fairly clear if dull, until the two climbers swung past Meall an t-Suidhe and descended into the valley of the Allt a' Mhuilinn. Then,

> ...the blackness that had been lying on the horizon rose high towards the zenith and threatened to cover it. The Red Mountains were still clear & sunny, but round the flanks of Càrn Dearg the mist came stealing, – at first in mere wisps of vapour, then in great smoke-like masses, which mounted to the topmost crag, and blotted out nearly the whole mountain. In ten minutes there was scarce anything to be seen but the scree slope on which we stood, and a black swirling mass straight ahead, where the storm clouds were eddying round the crags of the four great ridges.

The well-travelled pair eventually reached the foot of the buttress at 5.30pm As to the weather,

> Even a native might have praised it. For ten minutes the rain descended with a straightness that would have been creditable in furrows at a ploughing match...Crouching behind a stone we saw our visible world fade away into a murky circumference of twenty feet broad...Early in the day there had been some awful penalties laid upon the man who should breathe even the word 'retreat', but now we shamelessly discussed it in all its bearings.

Suddenly it cleared as they approached the rocks from the east. There was by now a respectable waterfall coming off the ridge, with innumerable

This engraving, from the 'Badminton Book of Mountaineering', illustrates rather graphically the state of belaying in the 1890s; the rope was thrown round any convenient flake of rock while climbers understood that 'they must not fall'

(Second edition, 1892)

smaller ones. They gained the first platform and roped up at 6.15pm.
Following a succession of small chimneys and gullies they gained a tiny
platform, more of a small cup scooped out of the ridge. This they called
the second platform, above which they found the really interesting work
began.

> There are little towers up which the leader had to scramble with such gentle
> impetus as could be derived from the pressure of his hobnails upon his
> companion's head...A sloping slab we found too, where the union of porphyry
> and Harris tweed interposed the most slender obstacle to an airy slide into
> the valley.

The SMC travelling by train, probably to one of the Fort William Meets. Naismith is at the rear, standing, William Inglis Clark centre, wearing spectacles.
(The figure third from the left bears an uncanny resemblance to Lenin, which might make this his return to Russia by train to lead the Revolution there, but the definite presence of Clark and Naismith would tend to negate this fancy)

Photo: A.E.Robertson

The climb then went steadily until they reached a point when they judged they were within a hundred metres or so of the top. In the thickening mist, they had come up against a small problem, made difficult by water. Then they tried the slabby rocks on the left, but these turned out to be *'the man-trap of the ridge.'* This feature is an innocuous-looking, smooth-faced piece of steep rock, about 3m in height, and placed right on the line of the ridge. To the left are steep rocks, to the right a step down into a corner. It is known as the Man-Trap, and its name can strike fear into many a toughened climber. Tough amused himself for three-quarters of an hour there but,

> Judging by the movements of the rope, and the vigorous adjectives that reached my ears, the game was more energetic than amusing.

Tough admitted defeat and came back to join Brown. By this time – it was 9.45pm – daylight was almost gone, and the two climbers were facing a bivouac.

> Over the gaunt grey rocks the darkness of night had settled down, rendering our position inexpressibly weird and eerie. To me it seemed that the only alternative was to bivouac where we stood; but the chief guide, while frankly admitting that two inches of nose represented his own limit of vision, drove me at the point of his axe to explore the rocks on the right. They *'went'* quite easily. Up a short gully we raced and panted to the foot of a steep smooth corner about 40 feet high, formed by the junction of two rock slabs. Here, when I mildly suggested the absence of reliable holds, the inexorable guide gave me the choice of going up at the point of his ice-axe, or by pure traction at the end of the rope, along with the luggage. I chose the former.[22]

The hard-pressed pair reached the Observatory at 10.05pm, and were welcomed by the staff there. After an hour of sleep they began the descent and the weary journey back to Edinburgh; regaining that city

The SMC Dinner Menu for December 1896 showing the umbrella stand in the Alexandra Hotel during the Easter Meet of that year; it was likened to the entrance hall at some Alpine resort. SMC archives include a photograph from which the drawing on the menu was made

SMC Archives

early on Sunday evening, after 45 hours of continuous travelling. They were met at the station by the Club Editor Willie Douglas. A telegraph sent from the Ben Nevis Observatory at 9.05am on Sunday to Douglas read: *'Climbed our ridge reaching top 10.5 Saturday extremely difficult and sensational Brown.'*

After Brown had written his account the Alpine Journal came out with the short note of the Hopkinson climbs. These came as a complete surprise to the members of the SMC, and in an appended note to his article, Brown is at pains to make it clear that they knew nothing of the earlier ascent. A letter from Gilbert Thomson to Douglas shows some of the nationalistic spirit that was running high then.

75 Bath St. Glasgow, 27th May, 1895. Brown and Tough will be prood prood men over their buttress. I have studied its photograph pretty much, and W.W.N. and I thought it looked as if it might go. Next to the pleasure of being one of the pioneering party, at the loss of which I must confess a little disappointment, there is the satisfaction of having it done by two men who are so thoroughly identified with the S.M.C. and not by what N. would call glaikit Englishers.[23]

Today, an ascent of the 300m-high North-East Buttress in summer is considered to be a classic Scottish mountaineering outing and graded Very Difficult.

A Meet of the Club will take place at the Alexandra Hotel, Fort-William, from Thursday 2nd April, to Tuesday 7th...A special Saloon Carriage, reserved for Club members & their friends, will leave Queen St (High Level), Glasgow, at 3.50 p.m. on Thursday, 2nd April and Fort-William on Tuesday, at 7.35 a.m.[24]

Thus was the SMC Easter Meet of 1896 advertised, the second to take place at Fort William. The 1896 meet was beset by wet weather, but despite this, Tower Ridge received five ascents; one before the actual meet, and four during it. Of the 32 members and guests present perhaps the most infamous name was that of Aleister Crowley (he was later to dabble in black magic) , while amongst the guests there appeared a name destined to take Scottish mountaineering to levels of ability and skill which remained unmatched for over a quarter of a century. The name was Raeburn, of whom more later, but the 1896 Easter Meet is now remembered for one of Naismith's finest climbs – the first winter ascent of North-East Buttress.

As regards information on the winter ascent, Naismith's modesty is again a major obstacle, as it was not until 1925, in a retrospective article on early winter climbing, that he gave a few lines of detail of the ascent. In the contemporary report of that 1896 Meet by William Brown, a few highlights of this major ascent are mentioned.

The N.E. buttress was only ascended by one party. It held a good deal of ice, and was reported to be in rather difficult condition. The gully above the first platform was paved with blue ice, and had to be left severely alone. Higher up also, below the last "peeler," the summer route (by the forty foot corner) was impracticable for the same reason, and a new line had to be struck out up the rocks on the left.[25]

The party of five consisted of: Naismith, then 40 years of age; W.Brunskill;

SMC meet at Fort William, Easter 1896. Raeburn was a guest at this meet, and is sitting, cross-legged, front right. Naismith is the central figure sitting atop the left-hand gate post

Photo: A.E.Robertson

A.B.W.Kennedy; William Wickham King (1862 – 1959); and Frances Conradi Squance. The date was Friday, April 3. In his 1925 article Naismith wrote of the ascent:

> This was a long day, for we were on the buttress for nearly seven hours. The party was a jolly one, but rather large for speed. The rocks were plastered with snow and ice and distinctly difficult. At one or two places the route followed by the first climbers was impossible, and had to be varied. [Here Naismith seems to be referring to Brown and Tough, though by April 1896 he must have known of the Hopkinson's ascent though not of its details]. Until we actually reached the summit, there was a slight doubt as to whether the top would '*go*' or not, for a pitch that Brown had climbed with difficulty was now found to be iced and hopeless; but by crossing to the left side of the buttress, we followed a narrow gully, at first hard ice but afterwards good snow, which led us past the last obstacle. It was pitch dark long before we arrived at the Alexandra Hotel.[1]

North-East Buttress in winter is now a classic, IV,4. Like Tower Ridge the major difficulties are high on the mountain and in most winters both routes see their share of epic ascents, with retreats, benightments (the Man-Trap!) and other character-building occasions. There are some who consider the Man-Trap technically 5, if climbed without help or aid, and it is probably safe to say that most who climb it in winter quite happily pull up or stand on anything they can find on this short but brutal rock barrier. Further up, the '*forty foot corner*' can also be awkward, with several difficult moves and minimal protection.

Elsewhere on the mountain other climbers on this Meet were busy. Both of the easy, if avalanche prone, Castle Gullies were climbed. Naismith climbed the Original Route on The Castle, now a III, along with Brown, Maclay and Thomson. Late on Good Friday morning, William Cecil Slingsby, Geoffrey Hastings and Dr. Collier left for the north face of Nevis. After some indecision they decided to attempt a

Collie's party, almost certainly in Fort William during the SMC Easter Meet of 1896. Collie and some seven other members of the Alpine Club were not staying at the Alexandra Hotel and did not appear in the group meet photo, above and left. Personnel definitely identified are Collie (with rope), Solly behind Collie's left shoulder. Sitting on the steps with the hat, is William Cecil Slingsby, an alpinist and cousin of the Hopkinsons

Photo: Alpine Club

Raeburn et al were about to usher in new standards of climbing, standards which would take mountaineering on the rocks and winter slopes of Nevis to new heights

steep and narrow snow gully visible high above, even though it was by now after 3.30pm. The top of the gully, now named Number Two Gully, was invisible to the climbers as they broke steps in the soft snow leading towards the gully. At the foot of the gully was a frozen boss of ice, a useful landmark in misty conditions.

The three climbers proceeded up the gully; its average angle of about 40 degrees increasing to about 60 degrees nearer the top. To the great dismay of Slingsby, the finish of the gully was blocked by a cornice some 3 – 4m in height, overhanging in places, with its lower half of ice. It was now 5.30pm, and the party had *'partly frost-bitten fingers and toes.'* Collier volunteered to attempt an escape on the left; traversing to where the snow seemed to abut on to a snow ridge. Reaching the foot of the cornice again, Collier belayed on to a cone of hard-frozen snow (a belay known as a snow bollard, which when correctly applied is much superior to an ice axe belay) and decided to bring Slingsby up. With the backing of Slingsby, Collier was able to overcome the final few metres, and soon Hastings was able to join them, puffing up behind with his 6kg camera and two rucksacks. On gaining the summit plateau they found two men in kilts, not climbers, one of whom complained that he had eaten all his food, half of his companion's, and had drunk all of his flask of whisky, and that he was still dying for want of food. The three climbers fled.[26]

It seems fitting somehow to end this section with a preliminary glimpse of a major character in the story of Ben Nevis. Harold Raeburn was a guest at this 1896 Easter Meet of the SMC in Fort William. During the meet he began his list of climbs on Nevis with the first ascent of Direct Route on the Douglas Boulder. The other three on the climb were William Brown, who led the crux, Lionel Hinxman and Willie Douglas, the affable Editor of the SMC Journal. All 215m of the *Boulder* was irreverently named after Douglas. Currently graded Very Difficult, Direct Route was climbed in hail showers and with a cutting wind.

As early as 1896 then, with routes such as these and a core of skilled and energetic mountaineers, Ben Nevis had been established in no uncertain terms as a major British climbing ground. It was also, no less significantly, *the* major winter climbing area. And as we will shortly see, Raeburn *et al* were about to usher in new standards of climbing, standards which would take mountaineering on the rocks and winter slopes of Nevis to new heights.

References

1. **Naismith**, W.W., *Early Winter Climbing*. SMCJ 17, 124 – 132, 1925.
2. **Naismith**, W.W., *Diary of Ascents*. National Library of Scotland (NLS).
3. **Mackay**, Lord, *Vignettes of Earlier Climbers*. SMCJ 24, 169 – 180, 1950.
4. **Naismith**, W.W., *Notes and Queries*. SMCJ 2, p136, 1892.
5. **Naismith**, W.W., *Ben Nevis in 1880 and 1889*. SMCJ 1, 215 – 221, 1891.
6. **Kilgour**, W.T., *Twenty Years on Ben Nevis*. (Paisley: Alexander Gardner, 1905. Glasgow: The Ernest Press, reprint, 1985.)
7. **Clark**, W.I., *Scottish Mountaineering Club Guide to Ben Nevis*. SMCJ 7, 134 – 176.

Glen Nevis (c. 1880s)

Photo: 'from Ben Nevis and Vicinity', a photo album published by Archibald MacIntyre, Fort William (Author's Collection)

8. **Ramsay**, Professor G.G., *The Formation of the Scottish Mountaineering Club*. SMCJ 4, 73 – 91, 1896.

9. **Whymper**, E., *On the Top of Ben Nevis*. Leisure Hour, September 1894.

10. *Logbook of Ben Nevis Observatory*, Vol.4, 1891 – 1894, entry for August 7, 1892. Archives Scottish Meteorological Office, Edinburgh.

11. *Alpine Notes* – Ben Nevis. Alpine Journal 17, 520 – 521, 1895.

12. **Garden**, William, *Norman Collie. Obituary Notice*. SMCJ 23, 95 – 97, 1943.

13. **Hillary**, Richard, *The Last Enemy*. (London: MacMillan, 1942.)

14. **Collie**, N., *Letter to W. Douglas*, 1/1/1894. NLS.

15. Ibid., 27/6/1894. NLS.

16. Ibid., 11/7/1894. NLS.

17. **Collie**, N., *Divine Mysteries of the Oromaniacal Quest, by Orlamon Linecus*. SMCJ 3, 151 – 157, 1894.

18. **Naismith**, W.W., *Letter to Douglas* (undated). NLS.

19. **Collie**, N., *Letter to W. Douglas*, 20/4/1894. NLS.

20. **Naismith**, W.W,. *Letter to W. Douglas*, 28/9/1894. NLS.

21. Ibid., 25/4/1895. Letter missing, photograph copy used.

22. **Brown**, W., *Ascent of Ben Nevis by The N.E. Buttress*. SMCJ 3, 323– 331, 1895.

23. **Thomson**, Gilbert, *Letter to W. Douglas*, 27/5/1895. NLS.

24. *Notice to Club Members*, 1896. Club Scrap Book, NLS.

25. **Brown**, W., *Proceedings of the Club*. SMCJ 4, 129 – 132, 1896.

26. **Slingsby**, W.C., *An Easter Holiday in the Scottish Highland*. The Yorkshire Ramblers' Club Journal 1, 173 – 187, 1902.

*A temperature
inversion from the
Ben Nevis summit
plateau, looking
south to distant Ben
Cruachan over the
Mamore Ridge, the
Aonach Eagach Ridge
and the Bidean nam
Bian massif*
Photo: Ken Crocket

3: The Observatory (1883 – 1904)

TO THE WALKER or climber who gains the summit plateau of Ben Nevis on a summer's day, the two most prominent features will be the cairn and trigonometrical point at the actual summit, and the spartan emergency shelter; both raised to stay above the level of the winter snows. But there is a much older structure. Stretching away to the west of the summit will be seen the remains of what was once home for several hardy Victorian gentlemen scientists – amateur meteorologists who conceived and built a remarkable observatory on Britain's highest summit – and manned it continuously for 21 years.

The English and Scottish Meteorological Societies were founded in 1850 and 1855 respectively. These Societies were run by enthusiastic amateur meteorologists who maintained their own weather stations and collected and analysed data on rainfall, hours of sunshine, cloud cover, wind speed and direction and so on. The unpaid observers, as they were known, were for the main part schoolteachers, ministers, doctors and those of a curious bent who had both the time and facility for such work. The Secretary of the Scottish Meteorological Society (SMS) from 1860 to 1907 was Alexander Buchan (1829 – 1907), and in filling this salaried position he played a leading role in the development of meteorology both nationally and internationally.

Buchan was also Librarian of the Royal Society of Edinburgh. In 1867 he identified six cold spells and three warm spells for that year in Scotland. His first cold spell occurred from February 7 – 14. Examining data over a number of years he concluded that these spells happened at approximately the same date from year to year, with rare exceptions. In 1928 a Parliamentary Bill fixing the date of Easter foundered, because the proposed date, April 11-14, coincided with Buchan's Second Cold Spell. This latter term became fixed in weather lore.

*Alexander Buchan,
Secretary of the
Scottish Meteorological
Society*

Photo: Courtesy Royal
Meteorological Society
(RMS)

SMS members may have been meteorological amateurs, but they had some very talented members in their lists, including many professors from the Scottish Universities such as Tait, Crum Brown, Chrystal, Geikie the geologist, McKendrick, and Lord Kelvin. The Honorary Secretary of the SMS in 1877 was Thomas Stevenson, father of Robert Louis and designer of lighthouses and inventor of the Stevenson thermometer screen. They were therefore quick to rise to the challenge laid down in the summer of 1877, when the President of their English counterpart suggested the establishment of *'mountain observatories on isolated peaks.'*

The opinion of the Scottish Society was that Ben Nevis was the obvious candidate for such an observatory; being the highest summit and lying close to the main track of incoming Atlantic depressions. Any observations which could be made at the summit, it was thought, would be of prime importance in the preparation of weather forecasts and, more importantly perhaps, in the accumulation of useful data which could then lead to a better understanding of weather processes in the Atlantic Seaboard area. They were thinking in four dimensions – including the vertical. At this time the mechanism of frontal systems was not understood; had it been, it would have been seen that the logic behind such an Observatory was flawed. A similar observatory placed on one of the Outer Hebrides could have been just as useful at indicating fronts, but nonetheless the observations have special value as a detailed record of mountain weather.

Clement Wragge
Photo: Courtesy RMS

The fund raising by the Scottish public, the building of the bridle path, the erection of the summit Observatory, and its continuous manning for 21 years was nothing short of a magnificent achievement of both the SMS and the generosity of the Scottish public. Stevenson drew up plans in 1879 and based on his calculations the Society ascertained that a sum of £1,000 (£192,000) would be sufficient to build an observatory and that annual maintenance, including the salaries of the observers, would come to about £300 (£58,000). (Note. Figures in parentheses are given for approximate equivalent values in 2008.)[1] The Society felt that if using money gathered from individuals and Scottish firms they could build the summit station, then it would not be asking too much from the Government to take on the annual running costs. On approaching the Government for funding however, they were disappointed to learn that no money could be made available, and there the plans for the observatory halted.

At this point an interesting character popped up. His name was Clement Lindley Wragge. Hearing of the Society's plans he volunteered his services for a preliminary series of observations. In a letter to Alexander Buchan, the Secretary of the SMS, he offered to climb Ben Nevis daily during the summer of 1881, making observations along the way and at the summit. The Society would pay Wragge's expenses. Wragge himself was a 'tall, lanky, gawky, red-headed man with big feet always encased in Blücher boots.'[2] (Blücher Boots were a leather half-boot, named after L. von Blücher [1742 – 1819)], a Prussian general.)

From June 1 until October 13, 1881, Wragge ensured the daily observations on Nevis, accompanied by his faithful, though no doubt occasionally bemused Newfoundland dog *'Robin Renzo.'* Wragge was additionally assisted by William Whyte, who usually relieved Wragge

Wragge himself was a 'tall, lanky, gawky, red-headed man with big feet always encased in Blücher boots'

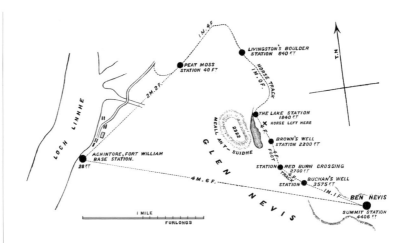

Wragge's route as taken in 1881 and 1882. There were 8 furlongs to the mile, with one furlong equal to 220 yards or 201.2 metres. Wragge's route as indicated on this map was 7 miles and 3 furlongs each way (11.79km), with the horse taking the first 5 miles (8km); his daily total would be about 19km.

Wragge was then living at Achintore (now Ach' an Todhair on the current OS map), at the south end of Fort William. His base station was on the lochside opposite to the house

Illustration from 'Nature', 22nd March, 1883

two days per week. The route Wragge took is now mostly redundant, though it was the way often taken by the first climbers. Wragge used a pony as far as 640m above sea level. Starting from Banavie at an unearthly 4.40am, his route was by the north flank of Meall an t-Suidhe, to reach its lochan in time for a 7am set of readings. His observations included the obvious ones such as temperature, humidity and barometric pressure, as well as the wind direction and strength and comments on clouds and any other phenomenon he found of interest. Buchan's Well, a spring at a height of 1,029m was the site of the next halt at 8.30am, followed by the summit itself, where readings were taken every 30 minutes from 9.00 to 11.00am Readings were again taken on the descent, sea level being regained at 3.30pm Meanwhile, Wragge's wife, who had the splendid full name of Leonore Eulalie Florence d'Eresby (neé Thornton), was making simultaneous observations at sea level, 20 in all, between 5am and 6pm All of these times, naturally, were at the

Mr. Wragge's Hut on the Summit of Ben Nevis. (From a Photo. by P. Macfarlane, Fort William.)

Wragge at the door of his temporary summit shelter. His dog, Robin Renzo, is visible, a large black Newfoundland bitch with a white chest blaze

Engraving in the 'Good Words' article, from a photograph by P.McFarlane

The remains of the Observatory and Wragge's instrument cage on the summit
Photo: Alex Gillespie

Robert Traill Omond, first Superintendent of the Ben Nevis Observatory, and presumably a keen golfer!
Photo: Courtesy RMS

mercy of the weather. Leonore had eight children with Clement.

On numerous occasions Wragge, quickly nicknamed *'the inclement rag'*, was so cold and stiff on reaching the summit that he was unable to unlock the instrument cage there until a small fire was lit to thaw out his fingers, all the while crouching under a miserable shelter of stone walls and tarpaulin. In late August of that year, a reporter from the *London Times* was unlucky enough to accompany Wragge on one of his trips. Sleet was falling in a Force 11 gale, and the journey across the plateau had to be made on all fours. The reporter was suitably impressed both by the conditions and Wragge's work and a glowing article followed.

On October 14 a severe storm ripped off the canvas roof of Wragge's temporary summit shelter, greatly adding to his difficulties and preventing readings for the first time since they began in June. A week later, on the 21st, he encountered heavy icing on the summit, as an excerpt from his letter to *The Scotsman* dated October 21, 1881 shows.

> The canvas roof of my hut having been carried away during the late storm, I have now no shelter, and winter has set in with extreme severity. This morning at nine o'clock I found the rough agglomerates and felstone lavas of the summit heavily covered with ice, and ice incrustations on the thermometer cage, notice-board, &c., measured from 5 to 12 inches in depth. The barometer cairn has already been built up for the winter. I much regret that the observations must now be discontinued...

Wragge had indeed been hard at work in 1881, as he had succeeded in obtaining summit observations every morning from the 1st June to the 13th October, a trained assistant generally relieving Wragge about twice per week. Wragge finished his letter with a postscript, suggesting that a pony track to the summit was much needed. The Society presented a gold medal to Wragge on March 22, 1882; for his great services of the previous summer. The summer of 1882 again saw Wragge making the

The [Observatory] appeal was a great success, £4,000 (£640,000) plus being raised within a few months, most of the donations coming from the Scottish public, though there were some donations from further afield, including one from Queen Victoria for £50 (£8,000). For some reason, the Worshipful Company of Fishmongers, London, also made a donation, of some 25 guineas (£4,200)

daily climb, this time assisted by Angus Rankin and John McDougall; making additional observations at six intermediate stations. Angus Rankin would later stay on to work at the observatory for the entire duration; he ended up in the post of assistant to the Superintendent. For the two summers' work, Wragge and his assistants received £450 (£72,000). The distance from Wragge's home at Banavie to the summit of Nevis was just under 12kms. Assuming that Wragge shared out the £450 equally over the two summers, which is unlikely, the reward per trip would have been about £1.15s. This of course would have had to cover wages, equipment and expenses

Clement Wragge did not stay to work on at the observatory; there are suggestions that he was not a popular figure, and significantly perhaps, he was not present at the opening. He went on to other, even higher offices, becoming Government Meteorologist in Queensland, Australia. His efforts over the two summers however were the subject of great public interest, and stimulated by this an appeal for funds was launched early in 1883. At a meeting of the Directors of the Ben Nevis Observatory held on September 6, 1883, the post of Superintendent was discussed. An advertisement placed in *The Scotsman*, *Glasgow Herald*, and the scientific journal *Nature*, attracted 19 applicants including Wragge and Robert Traill Omond, both of whom had written in earlier. Omond had worked in Professor Tait's laboratory, and though not a graduate he had attended classes at Edinburgh University. In the end, Omond, who obtained the position, turned out to be an ideal choice.

The appeal was a great success, £4,000 (£640,000) plus being raised within a few months, most of the donations coming from the Scottish public, though there were some donations from further afield, including one from Queen Victoria for £50 (£8,000). For some reason, the Worshipful Company of Fishmongers, London, also made a donation, of some 25 guineas (£4,200). Work began almost immediately, both on the summit stonework and on the construction of the bridle path. The designer of this path was the local schoolmaster, Colin Livingstone. He was one of the last of the old parochial schoolmasters, dying in Fort William on January 10, 1916, at the grand age of 89.

Modern ascenders now follow the route taken by the path; from the farm of Achintee in Glen Nevis across the south flank of Meall an t-Suidhe, up through Coire na h-Urchaire to the lochan, and then by long zig-zags up a tiresome slope to gain the plateau. The bridle path was built by local labour in an amazing four months, and nowhere in its 7.35km length does it exceed a gradient of one in five. Many years were to pass before major repairs were deemed necessary, raging burns having long since washed away portions of the track. A more direct start is often taken now, beginning from the Youth Hostel in Glen Nevis, though the original start from Achintee Farm is well-maintained and more pleasant.

As the path was steadily nearing the summit the observatory was taking shape, the contractor being a James McLean of Fort William. (The final rise before the summit plateau is named after him as 'McLean's Steep'.) The local masons employed were, naturally enough, using the rock at hand – the dark volcanic rock known as andesite – named after its original type rock first described in the Andes Mountains in South America. At first the observatory consisted of one room about three

A Road Permit ticket, c. 1913

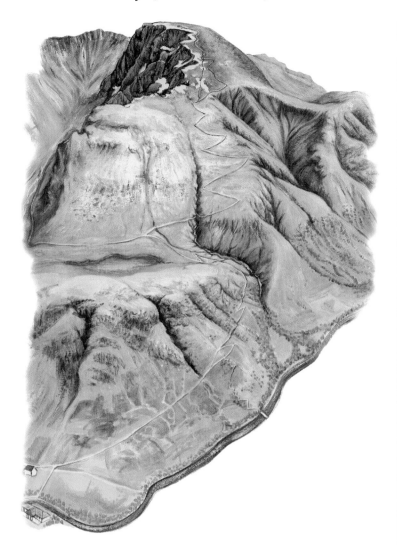

A bird's-eye view of Ben Nevis showing the modern mountain path starting from Glen Nevis, either from Achintee at bottom left, or opposite the Youth Hostel further up the glen. The topography of the summit indicates the perils of poor navigation in descent. Stray too far west and you hit the edge of the NE Face; too far east and you descend into Five Finger Gully

Illustration by Felicity Nightingale. Courtesy: The Nevis Partnership

square metres, off which opened three small sleeping bunks at one end, and a coal-cellar and storeroom at the other. The building was built following the double skin practice; an interior wooden core consisting of a double wall of wood filled with felt, the inner wall being further covered with linoleum, and an outer shell of stone walls, built to with-stand the shrieking violence of a sou'easter.

The stone walls at their bases varied from 1.2 – 3m thick, this last below the tower. The roof was sheeted in lead covered by snow board-ing, and the windows were double-glazed. The architect was a Mr Sydney Mitchell, son of Sir Arthur Mitchell, who worked on the Council of the SMS from 1860 until his death in 1909. To provide the observatory with communications, an armoured telegraph cable, originally a marine cable laid on the bed of the Atlantic Ocean, was laid from Fort William to the observatory, the Post Office collecting an annual fee of £357 (£57,120). The telegraph was replaced by a telephone in July 1897.

The Half-Way Station Hut, overlooking Lochan Meall an t-Suidhe. (See Chapter Five for the part this hut played in the origins of the CIC Hut)

Photo: RMS

The formal opening of the Ben Nevis Observatory took place on Wednesday, October 17, 1883... The path, from its newness and the amount of rain which had recently fallen, was a perfect quagmire, and most of the party, which included nine ladies, took to the slopes to the side of the path...For the last 300m the ascent was particularly tedious on account of the snow, and the party were much refreshed when the pipes struck up with 'The Campbells are coming'

The cost of construction for the summit observatory, including equipment, came to £1237.15s.2d., (£198,000) while the bridle path costs amounted to £793.6s.3d. (£12,693). To help defray the cost of maintaining the path a permit system was brought into use. Those going up the mountain on foot bought a ticket for one shilling (£8), while three shillings (£24), later raised to five (£40), was charged for those going up by pony. A small guidebook, priced one shilling, was also available. However, as one commentator stated later, many of those reaching the summit must have by-passed the toll-gate, as takings never matched the number of tourists.

The formal opening of the Ben Nevis Observatory took place on Wednesday, October 17, 1883. A reporter from *The Scotsman* was there to record the ascent by the opening party.[3] At 7am the rain was descending in torrents, but by 8am it had miraculously stopped. The procession met at the *Alexandra Hotel* and punctually at 9am set off, headed by a piper playing the march *Lochiel's away to France*. Mrs Cameron Campbell of Monzie, on whose ground the observatory had been built, had agreed to perform the opening ceremony.

The path, from its newness and the amount of rain which had recently fallen, was a perfect quagmire, and most of the party, which included nine ladies, took to the slopes to the side of the path for the first part. Higher up, the snow gradually thickened, being eventually about 30cm in depth. For the last 300m the ascent was particularly tedious on account of the snow, and the party were much refreshed when the pipes struck up with 'The Campbells are coming'. The leaders of the party reached the observatory just past noon, and were met by Mitchell (the architect), R.T. Omond, Mr Omond (of Oxford), W.M. Whyte (the current observer) and Mr Haig, the Inspector of Works, these gentlemen having ascended the hill earlier in the morning.

Mr Mitchell handed the key of the doorway to Mrs Cameron Campbell and the party wasted no time in entering the *'living room'*. A fire was blazing, around which the ladies speedily clustered, and in a few minutes cups of coffee and tea were being gratefully received, along with

The summit Observatory in 1885. A modern photograph from almost exactly the same spot can be seen on page 263

Photo: from a contemporary postcard by Valentine & Sons, Courtesy R.N.Campbell

sandwiches. Only then did the official opening ceremony take place. John Murray (later Sir John Murray of the *Challenger* expedition office) was present on behalf of the Scottish Meteorological Society, and in a speech in reply to Mrs Cameron Campbell, he prophesied that in future years thousands would ascend Ben Nevis.

The observatory was not complete that first winter; the observing tower being deliberately left until the following year. The first winter's observations, taken by Omond and his assistant Angus Rankin, were intended to be mainly eye observations, after which the Council would have a good idea of what instruments the observatory should be equipped with. Observations did not start from the summit station until November; until then readings were taken in the same fashion as had Wragge. Angus Rankin experienced no little difficulty the day after the observatory had been officially opened, as the following extract from the Logbook indicates.

> Fort William 4am (A.R.) 2,000 ft., 6.15am Did not reach the top! Reached about 200 ft. above Buchan's Well at about 8.30am But could not untie my coat to make a note or look at my watch (hail drift) all along from 2,500 ft. but at Buchan's Well it became so thick and blinding that I could not see anything. I stood for some time (I could not sit, nor walk easily, my clothes were one solid mass) but the drift and hail became worse and worse, till it became quite impossible to ascend, and almost so to descend – my own tracks being filled up. Reached the lake at 9.30am.[4]

Regular observations commenced on November 28, 1883, the observatory being manned by a crew of three; two observers and a cook. On occasion there would be an extra observer or scientist in residence, and in summer a telegraphist was provided by the telegraph office in Fort William. For the first seven years, the observers stayed at the observatory for 10 months; when the low-level observatory was built in Fort William this was changed to a duty spell of three months, observers rotating between stations. Apparently, the luckless cook stayed for an 11 months' tour of duty!

The summit observatory in summer. The 'conning tower' structure behind the observer allowed access when the building was snowed in. The small object on top of the 'cairn' is the glass globe which focused the sun's rays on either a curved strip of wood, or a strip of heat-sensitive paper, thereby recording any sunshine. This was an invention of John Francis Campbell (Iain Og Ile, 1821 – 1885). Campbell was brought up on the island of Islay and was a polymath, being interested in the collection of Gaelic folklore, the sciences and natural history. His practical sunshine recorder was invented in 1853 and was later improved by Sir George Stokes. It is now known as the Campbell-Stokes Sunshine Recorder. Although now being replaced by electronic recorders, it is still being manufactured. The recording material is designed to char, and not burn.

See page 66 for another photograph

Photo: RMS

Hourly readings of instruments had to be made manually, due to the often hostile conditions, and so a shift system was devised; eight hours at night and four hours during the day. The first heavy snows of the winter soon highlighted design flaws, as drifting snows quickly enveloped the observatory. As snow accumulated, the observers had to tunnel their way through to the surface, and eventually the tunnel extended to over 9m in length, with a rise in level of some 3.7m. Thereafter, the entrance became very difficult to keep clear, and although the

The ponies supplying the Observatory made the journey three or four times weekly. It was also possible to hire a pony for the ascent. The collie in the foreground is sensibly wary of flying hooves
SMC Archives

observers were very snug while inside their cocooned shelter under snow, readings were becoming more and more difficult to make.

The summer of 1884 saw modifications to the summit observatory, including a slightly larger extra room for use as an office and laboratory, two more bedrooms, a visitor's room and, to overcome the snow problem, the 9m high tower, the final effect reminiscent of a conning tower of an old submarine.

The wooden frame of the new tower was put together in Edinburgh, dismantled, and brought to Fort William. It vibrated in a strong wind but its construction was sound and it performed sterling duty every winter, acting as a high level door when snow was covering the main structure. Windows in the tower permitted a view of conditions, before venturing outside to read instruments, and in addition anemometers were attached.

As may be imagined, life on the summit of Ben Nevis was one of extremes, from the indescribable fury of a winter storm, to the paradisiacal beauty of a temperature inversion, when only the highest peaks rose out of a flat sea of cloud, the summit basking in calm sunshine. The observatory was provisioned by pony, and as a precaution against bad weather preventing the roadman reaching the observers, stores for nine months were kept. Tinned foods in the larder included; beef, mutton, tongue, salmon, turnips, peas, peaches, prunes, tomatoes, milk. Other staple food included bread, potatoes, rice, tea etc.

Observers at the summit accepted the poor working conditions simply because they came to appreciate the strange and beautiful isolation of the summit. The log books are crammed with descriptions of sunrises, sunsets, haloes, auroras and electrical phenomena such as St. Elmo's Fire, when all projecting objects including the observer's hair emitted a hissing sound, a glow being visible if at night. R.T.Omond, the first Superintendent, received £100 (£16,000) per annum. It was often more

The system of grading the wind strength had as its unofficial top grade, the disappearance of the observatory. Fortunately this was never realised – though a remarkably accurate method of estimation of wind force employed the angle at which an observer had to lean into the wind

Duncan at the sunshine recorder
Photo: RMS

difficult to find a cook prepared to stay for the duration.

W.T.Kilgour, author of a book on the observatory, seems to have worked at the summit for two holidays as a relief observer, probably for a month at a time. He ran a typing and shorthand business in Fort William. He graphically described typical winter weather.

> Here, in the day-time there was always the same blank whiteness. Above, below and around, with not a single particle the eye could rest on, and at night an awful pitch darkness which might be felt. There was the terrible boom of the gale on the sides of the hill, the rattle and groaning of the chimney pipes, the constant vibration of the tower and the ever-present feeling that the rest of the universe was tearing past at double the speed of an express train.[5]

High wind was one of the most difficult conditions the observers had to contend with, and on many occasions they were knocked off their feet while attempting the hourly readings. In the worst gales they roped together, and found that crawling on all fours was the easiest and safest method of progression. For the very worst of weather, an emergency system was employed, using thermometers whose bulbs projected through holes in a screen attached to the tower.

They calibrated their wind force estimates against the Robinson anemometer, when that was working in the summer, but had no direct calibration observations for the highest speeds, since those had occurred in the winter, when the anemometer was iced up. The system of grading the wind strength had as its unofficial top grade, the disappearance of the observatory. Fortunately this was never realised – though a remarkably accurate method of estimation of wind force employed the angle at which an observer had to lean into the wind. Another part-time observer, Alexander Drysdale, later presented lectures illustrating life at the summit. He describes the readings made during a typical storm, which, perhaps surprisingly, were almost welcomed by the observers, as being a relief from days of dull, misty weather.

> Soon the main door...was blocked with drift, and the use of the tower door was necessary. The one appalling moment was when the tower door was opened and the 100 mile per hour gale roared past, sucking the air from the building...Out, nevertheless, on to the roof he went closing the snow-choked door with difficulty behind him, steadied himself against the gale and waited for a lull to tack over to the guiding rope to the thermometers. The rope attained he slipped his arm round it, and struggled blindly forward, with lantern carefully shielded...Last hour, perhaps, the snow lay level with the roof, now a broad channel had been swept out by the wind. Into that he stumbled. A yard or two further on an immense snowdrift had been formed. Into that he next blindly dived, and so on until at last after a much longer 30 yards than you would imagine...the thermometer screen was reached.[6]

The thermometer screen was fixed to a vertical ladder, up which it would be raised step by step as the depth of snow increased. The luckless observer on a bad night would find his lantern blown out at the wrong moment, necessitating a retreat to the observatory and a start all over again. To read the rain gauge in such weather was, of course, nonsensical. A few days of such weather was more than enough to alleviate the observers' boredom, then they were ready to welcome back

The Summit Observatory in winter, 1893. The main door in deep snow conditions was accessed by the ladder next to the figure, descending into a trench dug by the observers. When even this became too difficult, the 'conning tower' on the right became invaluable
Photo: SMC Archives

the formerly hated monotonous, calm foggy weather.

In summer, ponies made three or four journeys a week with a load of 102kg each towards the winter supplies. In winter, the roadman, as mail carrier, climbed the Ben nominally once a week. This obviously depended upon the weather, and up to six weeks elapsed between visits to the observatory. This six weeks' isolation is alluded to in an article by the alpinist C.D.Cunningham. On February 11, 1884, Cunningham made an ascent of the Ben by the bridle track in company with Emile Rey, the Courmayeur guide, and John Cameron, a local guide from Fort William. They were the third party of visitors to climb the mountain since the observatory opened.

> The three observers had had no communications for about six weeks apart from telegraph, so we offered to bring fresh fruit and milk, newspapers, mail etc. The snow on the ground was hard and crisp & much sooner than we expected we reached the final slopes before gaining the summit.

Cunningham noted that,

> ...there is no physical reason why the observers should not go down to Fort William whenever they feel disposed to do so, if for no other reason than for health and exercise. 'Had you come here on the Lord's Day', said the head observer, 'you would not have gained admittance.' This gentleman's dread of Sabbath breaking was evidently greater than his fear of alcoholic '*steemulants*', as he accepted, with apparent satisfaction, a quart bottle of whisky which we brought.[7]

On the descent Cunningham and Rey were able to glissade for some distance, a mode of descent which Cameron evidently saw for the first time. Cameron showed his appreciation of an ice axe versus cromach (shepherd's crook) by taking Cunningham's axe to the local blacksmith's to be copied.

The one fatality suffered by Observatory staff was that of a telephone clerk, Duncan Macgillivray. The observatory had a telephone installed in 1897. He had descended to Fort William on Friday, September 9, 1898, to take part in an annual shooting competition the following day. On the Sunday evening he began the ascent back to the observatory, which

In the worst gales they roped together, and found that crawling on all fours was the easiest and safest method of progression

he never reached. A visitor to the summit found his body on Monday morning, lying just off the path and close to the top of Gardyloo Gully, within shouting distance of the summit. He had cuts to his hands and face and had presumably died of exposure some time in the hours of darkness. The observer on duty that night was badly affected by this tragedy, as they had been semi-expecting Macgillivray to return that day. Unfortunately, no one had thought to actually confirm by telephone that he was walking up on that Sunday, otherwise a deliberate lookout would have been set up.[8]

A later member of staff at the Observatory was a Glasgow University student, Ewen McKinnon, who for two summer periods took vacation work as the Sub-Postmaster, in 1903 and 1904. The wage was ten shillings (£80) per week, which covered board, washing and lodgings. McKinnon eventually ended up as the headmaster of East Keppoch in Glasgow. Writing a short article in 1966, at the age of 84, he stated that he was the last surviving member of any of its staff. McKinnon reached the Observatory on June 30, 1903.

> The observatory was covered by drift snow about 8 feet deep, so that only part of the funnel and tower appeared above it. There was a passage cut down to the kitchen door. Inside there was a fine luncheon set for us hungry men. The room was lit by a paraffin lamp and heated, over heated by a coke fire. There were two observers and a house steward in permanent residence – and a cat...
>
> By the dim light of an observer's lantern I was shown my office, an annexe to the main building, the whole interior covered with dew or damp, which could be swept off the walls by the palm of the hand; the telegram forms a soggy mass; the copying ink pencils colouring the whole damp place. As the office had to be opened the next day, I had to go out and dig an entrance through the snow; then dry and clean the interior. There was no heater of any kind. The door was left open to air the place.[9]

Recreation for the observatory staff during off-duty hours was not difficult to improvise; in winter tobogganing was a great favourite, and it seems a miracle that no serious accident took place, considering the proximity of the great cliffs. Skating and curling was also possible on a frozen Lochan Meall an t-Suidhe. The ability to play a musical instrument was valued, and on one occasion they arranged a gramophone recital by telephone from Fort William. Playing table tennis on a prepared table of hard snow was another unique form of recreation.

Summer tourists provided another form of amusement. Many of these made use of the telegraph office to send messages to relatives and friends, though, as Kilgour noted rather wearily, most of the messages were of a mediocre standard, about 75 per cent. being along the lines of '*Missed the view but viewed the mist*'. Climbing visitors, particularly during the winter months, were made very welcome, and many a late night knock at the observatory door was the result of a hard ascent under poor conditions. The observers themselves had little opportunity or perhaps inclination to climb, though a note in the log for September 8, 1889 records an ascent of Number Three or Number Four Gully by observers Turnbull, Gray and Miller, the party having first descended via the Càrn Mòr Dearg arete.

Animal life on Ben Nevis, as recorded by the observers, seems little different from the present; bird life commonly included the raven and snow bunting, with lower down the mountain ptarmigan. Eagles were a rare sight. On a smaller scale insects were often found in large numbers, particularly following autumn storms, when they would be carried up by wind. A family of stoats was usually present, taking up residence near or in the observatory stable. These were often chased but seldom caught; two which were caught, suffered the fate of being stuffed. The observers reported that the stoats on Ben Nevis retained their ermine-white coats throughout the year, presumably an effect of the low annual temperatures at that altitude. Weasels and field voles, rats and mice were also seen, while a fox made its presence known only by its prints in the snow. Plant life at the summit was virtually absent amongst the volcanic rocks.

At Edinburgh University, those who had graduated with Honours in Mathematics and Natural Philosophy were given the opportunity to work at the summit for one of the summer months, in order to allow the regular observers to take a holiday. In September 1896, two students availed themselves of this chance, one of them being a John S.Begg. He was so taken with his month at the summit station that he volunteered to return again in the middle of October, taking up an ordinary observer's duties until Christmas.

Fortunately, Begg kept a diary of his experiences, to be published in the Cairngorm Club Journal in 1897. The latter half of Begg's article is taken up with his personal observations, and paints some of the details of observatory life and the scenes that they witnessed while working there. The middle fortnight of November 1896, wrote Begg,

> ...was one of the most disagreeable, as regards weather, one could imagine. With the exception of one day throughout that fortnight we never saw more than ten yards in front of us; thick, soaking mist; with the temperature mostly above freezing point; heavy showers of rain and sleet, and occasional gales from the S.E. reaching one day a velocity of 100 miles per hour. The house too leaked badly and the floors both of office and kitchen were pretty much

A male snow bunting (Plectrophenax nivalis) on the ruins of the Observatory. This popular bird is a true arctic species, found in Greenland, Iceland and Scandanavia. It winters in Scotland though a small number stay on to breed in the Scottish summer

Photo: Alex Gillespie

Up this, with ropes, ice axes, and all the other para- phernalia of the Alpine climber, came three members of the English Alpine Club. It certainly seemed a rash and foolhardy experiment, but their coolness and courage were rewarded after six hours' hard work by their reaching the summit in safety, when the four of us greeted them with a hearty cheer and all-round hand-shaking, and finished up with a merry meal in the observatory kitchen

covered with basins, pails, etc, to catch the water...However, about the 23rd, the mist rolled away, and once more we revelled in the sunshine. Such a revolution, in fact, did this delightful change in the weather work in our spirits that we got quite excited, threw sea boots at each other, and ended by dancing on the roof the Highland Fling.

The two weeks' bad weather ended with that most beautiful of mountain weather phenomena; a temperature inversion or cloud sea, when only the tops of hills rise above the clouds. These conditions, as Begg experienced, sometimes last for several days, and while an observer at sea level is experiencing raw, cold and overcast conditions with occasional drizzle, the summits above the cloud are in brilliant sunshine, with air so dry that any snow would sublime, or pass into water vapour without first turning into water. Begg described one particular scene during November 1896.

I had just taken the 7pm observation and the air was so delightful that I took a constitutional up and down the observatory roof. The lightest of southerly airs blew gently and caressingly, and prevented the stillness of the whole scene from becoming oppressive. Above, the sky was cloudless; below, the clouds were sinking like great white lakes into the hollows between the hills. From the bosom of one of these lakes to eastward rose the moon, and while it was rising the upper half was as gold, while the half still in the cloud was red as blood. But not till it had risen quite above its white bed and shone with all its pale splendour in the opal sky did one feel the full charm of the scene. Over all the clear blue island mountain tops around it seemed to cast a fairy-like shimmer; and in that calm and impressive stillness, far, far above the noise and feverishness, the sin and misery of man, cut off from it all by those white sheets of cloud, amid the everlasting hills, bathed in the soft ethereal moonlight, one's spirit felt linked to the eternal and at rest.

ON BEN NEVIS : A MEMORY
My heart the beauties of the night enthral,
A dream of tenderness and pure delight;
Round me below the fog-lakes slowly fall,
Yet linger in the valleys, pure and white.

Calmly the moon in her pale splendour shines,
And casts o'er all her opalescent shroud;
Mountain and hill stand forth in softest lines,
Peeping like myriad islands through the cloud.

Blest is my soul to know this tranquil hour,
Earth with its sin and strife is far away;
Love seems the essence of the eternal power,
Life is no riddle but a harmony.

On the morning of Sunday, November 29, Begg was startled by a tap at the window. He went out to find two men shivering in the pre-dawn chill; they had been drinking in Fort William the previous evening, and while in their cups had laid a wager with their cronies that they would climb the Ben.

The unfortunate narrator had frequently to break off his story and leave the room as his drinking, combined with the excessive exercise of climbing, had

Climbers in Tower Gully

Photo: Henning Wackerhage

sadly upset him, otherwise I have no doubt he would have fallen asleep too like his now snoring companion.

In April, 1897, Begg returned to the summit for a few weeks, and while there witnessed the first ascent of Tower Gully, on the 25th.

> Up this, with ropes, ice axes, and all the other paraphernalia of the Alpine climber, came three members of the English Alpine Club. It certainly seemed a rash and foolhardy experiment, but their coolness and courage were rewarded after six hours' hard work by their reaching the summit in safety, when the four of us greeted them with a hearty cheer and all-round hand-shaking, and finished up with a merry meal in the observatory kitchen. The most intrepid members of the Scottish Mountaineering Club had declared this feat to be impossible, so it must have been with considerable chagrin that they read in the papers next day of the success of their English friends.[10]

This delightful sketch was captioned 'Now then, don't fall over both at once.' The gentlemen were of course engaged in 'bucket drill', a potentially hazardous task

Source: The Graphic (London), Saturday, January 12th, 1884, Issue 737

The three climbers were Geoffrey Hastings and the two Haskett-Smiths; on the 26th they made the first ascent of Gardyloo Gully. The ascent of Tower Gully had been complicated by a huge cornice overhanging the finish; through which the party had tunneled. The SMC Easter Meet in 1897 was at Tyndrum, and also from a yacht; some of the SMC must have felt some emotion at the snatching of two obvious routes in their absence.

In summer the water supply was Wragge's Well near the observatory, as well as roof drainage, though before the erection of a large water tank at Wragge's Well – a relic of Wolseley's campaign in the Sudan apparently – a drought necessitated a pony lift of water from the Red Burn. The other necessary routine at the summit station was bucket drill, the dumping of accumulated rubbish etc over the cliff edge. The gully into which much of the rubbish accumulated was originally named 'Tin-can Gully'; it is now known as Gardyloo Gully, from the old Edinburgh cry

as rubbish was about to be heaved out of a householder's window into the street below.

The dumping of rubbish in winter was made more exciting by the weather and the occasionally overhanging snowy edge of the cliff; accordingly we find an interesting early reference to a prototype snow anchor or belay. The disposal party would be roped to a log fixed under a pile of stones. In one incident the observers discovered how difficult it was to pull a man over a snow cornice, when an observer had been lowered to recover a snow-shoe. His companions were beginning to despair of getting him up when reinforcements arrived in a party of mountaineers.

The building was warmed by an open cooking stove in the kitchen and also by a closed stove in the office. The usual fuel was paraffin coke; light to transport and burning with a clear hot flame and little ash. Only during the worst of storms did the temperature of the office fall much below 16°C. Fires then had to be kept low, as the flow of air up the chimneys heated them to red-heat. The coldest conditions were obtained indoors during storms in late autumn or early winter, before snow had a chance to build up an insulating cover. Temperatures then could fall below freezing point inside the observatory. Another necessary duty of the observers was to adjust the chimney when a change of wind began to blow back smoke and fumes into the office. Drysdale gives an account of this perilous operation; usually required during bad weather.

> The roof was gained by means of a narrow outside ladder whose rungs had to be cleared of ice...The top attained, the adventurer made a grab at the lightning rod, dropped on his knees; hacked off the masses of ice encrusting what was now by a change of wind the lee side of the chimney cowl; and then proceeded to tie the canvas firmly round the windward side; – shielding his face the while from the icy chunks that pervaded the air and giving an occasional shake to his half-frozen fingers; whilst not forgetting to keep his head clear of the rotating anemometer or the wildly-swinging wind-vane.[6]

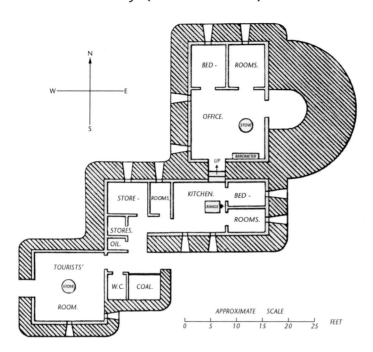

BED - ROOMS.

OFFICE.

STOVE

BAROMETER

UP

N
W——E
S

STORE - ROOMS. KITCHEN. BED -

RANGE

ROOMS.

STORES.

OIL.

TOURISTS'

STOVE

W.C. COAL.

ROOM.

APPROXIMATE   SCALE

0   5   10   15   20   25   FEET

Plan of the summit Observatory. This shows a later modification – the addition of a room for tourists

With living conditions such as described, it is perhaps hardly surprising that the observers seemingly felt no pressing need to add mountaineering to their already exciting and periodically uncomfortable lives.

Another hazard of the weather was that of electrical storm. These were rare but unpleasant, as an observer was occasionally knocked down when near the office stove. On June 19, 1895 a lightning strike caused some damage. Two of the observers were eating in the small hotel adjacent to the observatory, while a third was in the office. Shortly before 3pm a great flash filled the hotel, accompanied by a terrific crash. In the observatory there was an even more vivid flash and deafening report. The telegraph apparatus emitted a cloud of smoke as did the stove, the office being soon filled with dense smoke. Kitchen items were hurled across the room while parts of the telegraph were fused. The casing which screwed on and retained the bone button of the electric bell in the visitors' room was burst and with the button was also thrown across the room. Smoke and flame appeared from behind the wainscot between the kitchen and office doors, but was soon under control. No one was injured during this strike, which was the closest call the observatory suffered.

Each hour the office barometer was read. The observer on watch then made the outside readings of the thermometers in the screen, changed the rain gauge, and made cloud and wind notes. At certain other times other observations were made; depth of snow, atmospheric dust, ozone, rain band, earth currents, duration of sunshine, earthquake records. One effect of the wind was to create a partial vacuum in the building, an effect well known to the staff. (On another Scottish summit in a high wind, Ken Crocket once had a compass sucked out of a jacket pocket.)

The sunshine recorder used an ingenious system still in use today and based on a crystal ball; as the sun's rays were focussed through the

Shortly before 3pm a great flash filled the hotel, accompanied by a terrific crash. In the observatory there was an even more vivid flash and deafening report. The telegraph apparatus emitted a cloud of smoke as did the stove, the office being soon filled with dense smoke. Kitchen items were hurled across the room while parts of the telegraph were fused

Hours with windspeed exceeding 43 knots (22.12m/s, 49.48mph) on the summit of Ben Nevis, 1884 – 1896

Data Courtesy Marjory Roy

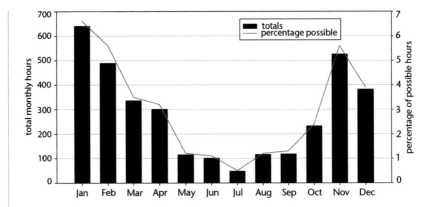

glass they burned a line on a prepared strip of card. The observers had a problem with a certain class of tourist who enjoyed showing how the recorder could also light a pipe. For measuring the wind speed a Robinson hemispherical cup anemometer was mounted above the tower. This could, however, only be used when the temperature was above freezing point as ice built up rapidly during conditions of freezing fog. Throughout the year the direction and force of the wind was recorded by the observers, standing on the observatory roof. This estimate was then compared with the anemometer readings made during the summer months.

The Observatory eventually used a unique Ben Nevis wind scale where the speeds for a given force were much greater than the Beaufort Scale. It is not clear from the information in the Transactions of the Royal

Average minimum and maximum temperature variations at the Ben Nevis Observatory, 1884 – 1903

Data Courtesy Marjory Roy

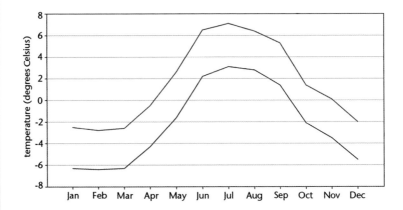

Society of Edinburgh if the observers had originally intended to use the Beaufort scale, but had none of the normal reference indicators on land (movements of trees, falling chimneypots etc) to assist in their estimations, or whether they wanted to use a 12 point scale like Beaufort, but because of the much stronger winds they had been obliged to adjust the limits of each force so as to have the complete range covered. On calibrating wind force with the anemometer readings, it was found that

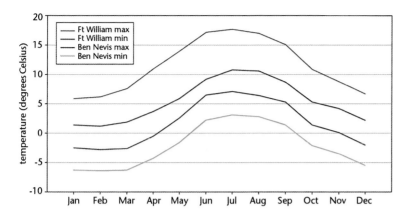

Average monthly minimum and maximum temperature variations at the Ben Nevis Observatory and the Fort William Base Station, 1884 – 1903

Data Courtesy Marjory Roy

on the Ben Nevis scale a given wind force had a considerably higher mean wind speed equivalent. For example, Force 8 on the Beaufort scale normally meant a mean wind speed of 37 knots; on the Ben Nevis scale it was 63 knots. A gale is defined as having a mean wind speed of 34 knots or over.

In a 1903 paper Angus Rankin provided statistics on the number of gales with mean speeds over 43 knots observed in the 13 year period 1884 – 1896. Rankin's data show, not surprisingly, that January was the worst month for gales, with a total for the 13 year period of 640 hours

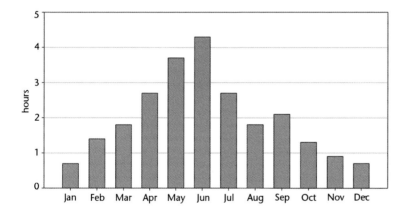

Average daily sunshine recorded at the Ben Nevis Observatory 1884 – 1903

Data Courtesy Marjory Roy

of gales, 6.6 per cent. of the possible time. This was in comparison with the *'quietest'* month July, which had only 48 hours of gales. The frequency maxima occurred around midnight and 9am, and most of the gales were from the southern half of the compass, with the strongest being from the south-east. The observers noted that northerly winds struck the cliffs and were then deflected upwards, passing over the top of the observatory without attaining high mean speeds at Observatory level. This is a feature of micro-climate well known to most mountaineers.[11]

A comparison of the wind frequencies at Ben Nevis made with later data from Stornoway radiosonde ascents show significant differences. Assuming that wind directions are fairly similar to those from

*Average monthly
rainfall at the Ben
Nevis Observatory
1885 – 1903*

Data Courtesy Marjory Roy

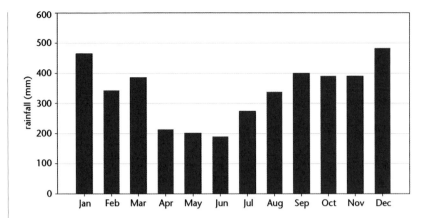

*Average monthly
rainfall at the Ben
Nevis Observatory
1885 – 1903*

Data Courtesy Marjory Roy

observatory years, the conclusion is that the wind speed and directions on Ben Nevis are very site-specific. It is likely, for example, that winds from the west or north-west are deflected around Càrn Dearg and appear as very gusty northerlies at the summit. South-westerly winds may be backed to a more southerly direction, while south-easterlies are accelerated up the relatively gradual slope.[12]

The average annual temperature for the summit of Ben Nevis was minus 0.3°C for the period 1884 – 1903. At Fort William it was 8.4°C over the period 1891 – 1903. An interesting feature of the temperature averages was the low value for March, reflecting the strongly maritime influence on temperature. The average temperature differences between the Fort William and Ben Nevis Observatories (difference in height 1,331m) was at a maximum in April and at a minimum in December, the average difference for the whole year being 8.5°C. This is equal to 0.64°C per 100m height difference. This temperature difference should be carefully noted by those intending to walk to the summit. It could be a reasonable 8°C in Glen Nevis and just below freezing on the summit, in addition to which a fresh breeze of say, 25 knots would give a wind-chill equivalent of about minus 11°C.

Temperature inversions were associated with anticyclones centred close to the area, and were often accompanied by very low humidity at the summit. Frequently the top of the inversion layer lay between Fort William and the summit, the temperature increasing with height between Fort William and the top of the inversion, and then decreasing up to the summit observatory. The largest negative temperature difference observed was 9.8°C at 9am on February 19, 1895; i.e. the summit of Ben Nevis was 9.8°C warmer than Fort William.

The lowest air temperature observed on Nevis is surprisingly high to those unfamiliar with the data, the lowest temperature actually observed being -17.4°C on January 6, 1894. Weather conditions which give very low temperatures at valley sites in Scotland are those in which a marked inversion is likely to occur. The mean daily variation of temperature is also surprising, being very small. For July it is 2.2°C, while in winter it was only 0.3°C.

The staff frequently noted the rapid changes in temperature, pressure, wind speed and direction, and precipitation which occurred. These rapid changes are of obvious importance to mountaineers. The mean temperature ranged from about -5°C in February, to 5°C in July, being below freezing point from the beginning of October to early May. These figures apply to the summit, however, and conditions at the foot of the cliffs can be quite different, as some climbers have found to their cost.

During the 21 years of summit observations, Ben Nevis was in sunshine for only about one-sixth of the possible time; the summit was clear for about one hour in five in December to one hour in two in June. The diurnal variation in the occurrence of mist or fog was small; it rarely pays, therefore, to wait in the hope of a clearing. The sunniest month was June 1888, with an average of 8.3 hours per day, while December 1893 will probably go down on record as one of the gloomiest, with a total of 1.1 hours of sunshine for the entire month.

Since temperatures on Nevis are close to freezing point for most of the year, the additional factors of saturated conditions and moderate to high wind speeds combined with a temperature of slightly below freezing point often give a rapid build-up of rime ice, whiskery crystals of ice building up on any projecting features, including a climber's beard, eyebrows, eyelashes, and the rocks of the cliffs. The log book describes a post of cross-section 10cm^2 which in less than a week grew a crystalline growth of about 152cm by 30cm.

The observers had, as mentioned earlier, great difficulty in measuring precipitation. The rain gauge would often be filled with drifting snow, for example, even although no snow was falling. On average the late spring and early summer gives the driest parts of the year, like the rest of Scotland. The wettest year was 1898, which had just over twice the rainfall of 1895, the driest year. The nature of the rainfall on Nevis is indicated by the data for 1898, when daily falls of 25mm or over accounted for 58% of the total rainfall, and falls of less than 12.5mm only accounted for 18%. The mean annual rainfall of Ben Nevis was 4.08 metres.

Much of the snow which falls on the summit plateau of Nevis is subsequently thawed or is blown elsewhere. The depth of snow was measured at a post on a flat part of the plateau, over 18m from any obstruction. Maximum snow depths were normally reached in April, but in 1903 the maximum depth of 3.17m occurred on May 18. The greatest depth recorded was 3.61m on April 3, 1885.

Somewhat ironically, although weather was the prime area of research at the Ben Nevis Observatory, perhaps one of its most outstanding, if indirect contributions to science was to come from the realms of particle physics. During the summer months, young physicists sometimes acted as relief observers. One of these was Charles Thomson Rees Wilson, who at the age of 25, two years after taking his degree at Cambridge, spent a fortnight at the summit in September, 1894. Wilson (1869 – 1959), was a Scot, born in Glencorse, just south of Edinburgh. During his stay at the observatory, the various cloud and optical effects, along with later experiences of electrical storms on Nevis, all made a great impression on him. The following year he began experiments at the Cavendish Laboratory which led to his development of the Wilson Cloud Chamber.

Wilson's original intent was to study experimentally the optical phenomena of coronas and glories and Brocken Spectres. These are the rainbow-like coloured rings and human-shaped shadows that you can

During the 21 years of summit observations, Ben Nevis was in sunshine for only about one-sixth of the possible time; the summit was clear for about one hour in five in December to one hour in two in June. The sunniest month was June 1888, with an average of 8.3 hours per day, while December 1893 will probably go down on record as one of the gloomiest, with a total of 1.1 hours of sunshine for the entire month

Digging a snow profile on Ben Nevis; top to bottom – A.N.O., Angus Rankin, and the Observatory cook! What can be clearly seen in the snow are bands due to precipitated material. At this time the industrial Central Valley of Scotland was heavily industrialised. The observers often noticed that with a southerly wind the surface of the snow would quickly become dirty. A change of wind direction and fresh snow would provide a clean surface again

Photo: RMS

see thrown onto a bank of mist by strong, low sunlight. Almost immediately however, he found that his apparatus would allow him to make visible the tracks made by individual ions and to study their behaviour.

> In September 1894 I had spent the fortnight working at the Observatory on Ben Nevis which was to lead both to my cloud chamber work and to my life-long interest in atmospheric electricity. Now I began to make experiments on clouds, made by the expansion of moist air, attempting to reproduce the beautiful optical phenomenon of the coronas and glories I had seen on the mountain top...I found that within a certain range of expansion there was rain-like condensation at each expansion showing the existence of nuclei of a particular kind always being reproduced. With greater expansions the condensation became cloud-like, the number of droplets increasing at an enormous rate with increasing expansion. By May 1895 these experiments were sufficiently advanced for me to read a paper before the Cambridge Philosophical Society.[13]

By a happy coincidence, in the autumn of that year (1895) Röntgen discovered X-rays, and in 1911 Wilson finally succeeded in producing the first photographs of the tracks of ionizing particles. For this he was awarded the Nobel Prize in 1927.

On July 27, 1969, Miss Rosamund Wilson, his daughter, unveiled a commemorative plaque on the summit of Ben Nevis. The plaque, affixed to the south-east wall of the observatory ruins, identifies the ruins and tells briefly of the connection between Professor Wilson and the Observatory.

Other scientific and well-known personages visited and worked at the observatory in its time. In July 1885, Professor Vernon and his assistant performed experiments on the intensity of light from flames at low pressure. During 1890 – 1891, John Aitken tested his dust counter at the observatory. Captain Scott received permission to test equipment for his Antarctic expedition but was unable to go himself, two of his officers spending the winter of 1900 instead; Michael Barne for magnetic observations and Charles Rawson Royds for meteorology. The cook of the *Discovery* also stayed at the observatory.

W.S.Bruce, who had been temporary superintendent of the observatory from 1895 – 1896 was later to mount the *Scotia* voyage to the South Orkney islands and Weddell Sea. Two of the *Scotia*'s scientific staff, D.W.Wilton and R.C.Mossman had also worked on Nevis.

By the end of the 19th Century, the running costs of the observatory were about £1,000 (£160,000) per annum. Many private individuals were exceptionally generous in supporting the cause, but could hardly be expected to continue thus for much longer. In 1902 the Meteorological Council announced that the annual grant of £250 (£40,000) for the low-level observatory would cease after that year. The Prime Minister was led to appoint a Committee of Enquiry, before which eminent scientists gave evidence; some of which, unfortunately, was conflicting.

Lord Kelvin, on the Committee, was supportive, whereas Professor, later Sir Arthur, Schuster, felt that it had served its purpose. The Treasury offered an annual grant of £350 (£56,000), the same total as before, as the summit observatory was then receiving an annual grant of £100

The Summit Hotel, built by a Fort William hotelier and separate from the Observatory. It remained open until about 1916 and was used by some climbing teams as a base for exploration. The two ladies shown would have been those running day to day operations

Photo: from an old postcard, courtesy Granite House, Fort William

(£16,000). As the necessary income was £950 (£152,000) per annum the outcome was inevitable, and the Directors of the Management Committee had no real choice but to close down the observatory. A caustic letter to *The Scotsman* newspaper in October 1905 compared a list of grants which had been made to English bodies and their Scottish equivalents. The Meteorological Council (of England) £15,300 per annum, the Scottish Meteorological Council £100; The Royal Society of England £9,000, The Royal Society of Edinburgh £300; The Royal Academy and College of Music (of England) £1,000; the Royal Irish Academy of Music, £300; Scotland, nil. And on, and on, and on the list went. It may have been that the Scots lacked quality support from their parliamentary members in Westminster, or that there was a genuine awareness that the Nevis Observatory had passed its sell by date. There were certainly words in Parliament, but to no avail. Whatever the cause, there was an atmosphere that it was Culloden all over again.

The last entry in the log was that of October 1, 1904. Snow was falling and mist enveloped the summit. A week later, the equipment having been dismantled and removed, the staff turned the key to lock the door and went down the mountain for the last time. The sum cost of the entire venture during its remarkable 21 years' life had been just over £30,000 (£4.8 million). The Government had contributed a little over £5,000 (£800,000) of that amount.

One of the rooms at the summit observatory was opened during the summer months for the refreshment of visitors. This continued until 1916, with a previous observer, James Miller, acting as keeper. Miller had served at the observatory from 1884 until its closure, and when the possibility of a reopening was examined in 1930, in conjunction with an International Polar Year Commission, he immediately volunteered, though he must have been about 70 years of age. The observatory was never reopened however, and the ravages of time, weather and careless visitors to the summit all took their inevitable toll. An accidental fire in 1932 caused some damage, and the attentions of climbers seeking shelter did little to help matters. Perhaps the final nail in the coffin

In 1887 Robert Omond reported in the scientific journal Nature what may have been the first use of the term 'Green Flash'. This is normally seen when the sun sets over a sea horizon, with a green flash of light seen as the sun disappears. Omond saw this phenomenon from Ben Nevis, as the last portion of the sun's disk disappeared into the sea. The distant sea horizon from the summit of Ben Nevis is just over 112km

From: A Green Light at Sunset', Nature 35, 391 (1887)

Theosophy is a doctrine of religious philosophy and metaphysics originating with Helena Petrovna Blavatsky. In this context, theosophy holds that all religions are attempts by the 'Spiritual Hierarchy' to help humanity in evolving to greater perfection, and that each religion therefore has a portion of the truth. Together with Henry Steel Olcott, William Quan Judge, and others, Blavatsky founded the Theosophical Society in 1875

occurred just before Easter 1950, when a party of climbers was seen stripping the valuable roof lead with the skill of practised craftsmen, the booty of coiled lead being rolled down the mountain for removal by lorry.

The observations made at the Ben Nevis and Fort William observatories were extensively studied at the time, notably by Alexander Buchan, Robert Omond, Angus Rankin and R.C. Mossman, and many papers were published. The actual data were published *in extenso* in the *Proceedings of the Royal Society of Edinburgh* ; they are available there to all for further study. Summary tables were also published.[14] In her publication *The Weathermen of Ben Nevis*, Marjory Roy comments that there is much that could still be learned from the data, especially considering the growth in mountains as an area for enjoyment and sporting activities.[15]

It is worth a note on the later years also of that eccentric weatherman Clement Wragge, especially as so much written about him is erroneous. His first wife Leonore had helped in his two summers' observations. Disappointed at not obtaining the job on Ben Nevis, he returned to Australia by 1884, where he arranged regular observations on the summit of Mt Lofty for the purpose of comparing mountain and sea level observations, a natural continuation of his work on Nevis. He was appointed Government Meteorologist in Queensland in 1887, and by 1893 had established many weather stations. The use of personal names for storms appears to have its roots with Wragge. Ivan R.Tannehill's 1938 book *Hurricanes* says Wragge began giving women's names to tropical storms before the end of the l9th Century. Unfortunately, he also appears to have continued his practice of upsetting people, by naming storms after people he took a dislike to, particularly politicians! On a positive note, he was attached enough to his faithful dog *Robin Renzo* that he took it with him when he emigrated.

In another parallel to his Ben Nevis intentions, Wragge in 1897 established a high level observatory at Mt Kosciusko, the highest peak in Australia, with the object of comparing those observations with observations at Merimbula on the adjacent coast. In 1898 he left Leonore, claiming that her jealousy was driving him mad, and while in India met the Anglo-Indian and keen Theosophist, Louise Emeline Horne, who agreed to be his unmarried companion. His weather bureau closed in 1903 through lack of funds and when he failed to get the head job at the newly established Commonwealth service, he left to set up an observatory in New Zealand. After several years' travelling he came to Dunedin, but it was 1910 before he finally settled in Birkenhead, bringing with him Louise. Meanwhile, his wife Leonore, who was obviously made of strong material, refused to give Wragge a divorce, and issued a huge writ against him for maintenance. The amount demanded was too great for Wragge to afford, and this effectively prevented him from returning to Australia.

In Birkenhead, he founded the Wragge Institute & Museum, also the Waiata tropical gardens, in which he grew tamarisks and ginger, bananas and forty varieties of palms. Dressing in Indian clothing, and wearing a turban, Wragge took up theosophy and yoga. An enthusiastic lecturer, he began to attract tourists to the otherwise quiet and conservative Birkenhead. He never divorced Leonore, and never married Louise. There are now two Wragge families; one in Australia, and one in New Zealand, the latter descended from his son through Louise, Kismet.

Through lectures and newspaper articles, Wragge expounded his theosophical beliefs and displayed extensive scientific knowledge and inventiveness. He suffered a stroke and died on 10 December 1922 at the age of 70. He was working on a publication on the petroglyphs of Easter Island, on which he was, as with so many other subjects, an authority. His son through Louise, Kismet Kent Wragge, *'First Officer'* of the Institute, stayed on to keep the house and gardens open. Wragge is buried in the old Birkenhead cemetery.

Angus Rankin, by all accounts a very popular man, had eventually taken over the post of Superintendant, as Omond had become unable to carry out the summit duties from about 1895 onwards due to illness. Following the closure, Rankin was offered a position with the Meteorological Office of Argentina. He was posted to the South Orkneys initially, following the return of the *Scotia* from its Scottish Antarctic Expedition of 1902 (several of whose members had served some time at the Ben Nevis Observatory). From there he went to Buenos Aires, eventually becoming the chief weather forecaster for the whole of the Argentine. He retired in 1925 and moved to live in the hills of Cordoba, where he died on 30th June, 1929.

The summit Observatory continues to inspire. On October 2, 2004, a ceremony was held in the West Highland Museum, Fort William and witnessed by members of the Highland Council, the John Muir Trust, the Royal Meteorological Society, representatives from Alta in Northern Norway, and a number of people from the Lochaber area. The occasion was to mark the twinning of the Ben Nevis Observatory with Haldde Observatory (Northern Norway), and also to celebrate and connect the lives of two scientists who found inspiration at these mountain sites in the late 1800s. C.T.R.Wilson, a young Scottish researcher, was stationed at Ben Nevis in 1894, and Kristian Birkeland, a Norwegian physicist, was responsible for building the northern lights observatory on Haldde Mountain in Northern Norway in 1899.

Kristian Birkeland (1867 – 1917) was one of Norway's most prominent scientists. He published the first realistic theory of the northern lights, the main point being that electrically charged particles ejected from the sun are captured by Earth's magnetic field and directed towards the polar atmosphere. To prove his theory, he performed his famous *'Terella'* experiment, in which he artificially created the aurora.

This chapter cannot close without brief mention of another act of private enterprise – the hotel on the summit, close to but independent of the observatory. This was a small wooden structure built by Mr Robert Whyte, owner of the Imperial Hotel, Fort William in 1885, two years after the building of the observatory. It was open during the summer months right through to the middle of World War I, and was run by two ladies, Mrs Rodger and Sarah Cameron, who were frequently indignant at being awakened at all hours by visitors coming up to view the sunrise. Board and lodgings, of a rough sort, were available; lunch for three shillings, or tea, bed and breakfast for ten shillings. There were three rooms; the reception room (doubling as a bedroom), a small ladies' room, and a kitchen. Alcohol was not served, it being a temperance hotel. One of the ex-cooks from the Observatory, James Miller, latterly

An atmospheric phenomenon also seen from Ben Nevis was the little understood appearance of noctilucent clouds. These are formed at extremely high altitudes, between about 85 and 95 km, well above normal cloud levels. They are composed mainly of water ice and are most commonly observed in the months of June and July after sunset or before sunrise and at latitudes of between 50° and 70° north and south of the equator. This makes Scotland a good country from which to see them. As they are at very high altitudes, during twilight they catch the sun which is below the horizon at ground level. They are often a beautiful milky blue in hue

http://en.wikipedia.org/wiki/ Noctilucent_clouds

The reception room of the summit hotel on Ben Nevis, looking towards the entrance door. The seats round the wall doubled as beds. This room measured 18 x 12 feet (5.49 x 3.66m). The walls were triple in parts, to avoid damp, with the outer wall painted white, which must have made finding the hotel fun in certain conditions!

Photo: from an old postcard, courtesy Granite House, Fort William

helped to run it. It closed in 1916. As will be seen shortly, this hotel had a role in some explorations on Ben Nevis.

References

1. House of Commons Library: *Research paper 02/44*, 11th July 2002. Inflation: the value of the pound 1750 – 2001. See also Lawrence H. Officer, *Purchasing Power of British Pounds from 1264 to 2007. Measuring Worth*, 2008.

2. **Humble**, B.H., *An Epic of Ben Nevis*. Chamber's Journal, January, 1936.

3. The Scotsman, October 18, 1883. *Opening of the Ben Nevis Observatory – Interesting Ceremony.*

4. *Observatory Log*: Meteorological Office Archives, Edinburgh.

5. **Kilgour**, W.T., *Twenty Years on Ben Nevis*. (Paisley: Alexander Gardner, 1905. Glasgow: The Ernest Press, reprint, 1985.)

6. **Drysdale**, Alexander, *Life at Ben Nevis Observatory*. Unpublished Lecture Notes.

7. **Cunningham**, C.D., *Hill Climbing in Scotland*. Alpine Journal, 12, 502 – 509, 1884.

8. The Scotsman, 13th September 1898. *Sad Death of a Young Man on Ben Nevis.*

9. **McKinnon**, Ewan, *The Highest Sub-Postmaster Ever in Britain*. The Sub-Postmaster. May 1966

10. **Begg**, John S., *Life And Work at Ben Nevis Observatory*. Cairngorm Club Journal 2, 253 – 270, 1898. Reprinted in SMC Journals for 1984 and 1985.

11. **Rankin**, A., *Note on the number of gales observed at the Ben Nevis Observatory*. Journal of the Scottish Meteorological Society 10, 20 – 22, 1903.

12. **Roy**, Marjory, *The Ben Nevis Observatory 1883 – 1904*. (Unpublished.)

13. **Wilson**, C.T.R., *Ben Nevis Sixty Years Ago*. In: Weather 9, 309 – 311, 1954.

14. *Transactions of the Royal Society of Edinburgh* Vols. 34, 42, 43, and 44 (Parts 1 & 2).

15. **Roy**, Marjory, *The Weathermen of Ben Nevis – 1883 – 1904* (Fort William: The Royal Meteorological Society, 2004, ISBN 0948090243.)

Other Useful Works

Paton, James, *Ben Nevis Observatory 1883-1904*. Weather 9, 291 – 308, 1954.

Gatty, Victor H., *The Glacial Aspect of Ben Nevis*. Geographical Journal 27, 487 – 492, 1906.

Duncan, C.N. and **Weston**, K.J., *Ben Nevis Observatory, 1883 – 1983*. Weather 38, 298 – 303, 1983.

Wragge, Clement, *Ascending Ben Nevis in Winter*. Chamber's Journal 19, No.957, Saturday, 29 April, 1882.

Wragge, C.L., *Resumption of the Ben Nevis Meteorological Observations, 1882*. Symons's Monthly Meteorological Magazine 17, July 1882.

Wragge, C.L., *Ben Nevis Observatory*. Nature, 487 – 491, 22 March, 1883.

Omond, R.T., *Zoological Notes from the Log-Book of the Ben Nevis Observatory*. The Annals of Scottish Natural History, July, 1905.

Barton, Jim and **Roy**, Marjory, *A Monument to Mountain Meteorology*. New Scientist, 804 – 805, 16 June, 1983.

Gilchrist, Bruce & **Joelson**, Jo (Eds.), *Little Earth*. (London: London Field works Ltd, 2005.) Published in conjunction with the exhibition of Little Earth, a fictional narrative using the parallel stories of C.T.R.Wilson and Kristian Birkeland.

Roy, Marjory (Ed.), *The Life, Achievement and Legacy of Alexander Buchan MA LLD FRSE (1829 – 1907)*. Extended abstracts from a commemorative meeting at Heriot-Watt University, Edinburgh on 7 September 2007.

Sunrise over Aonach Mòr from Ben Nevis
Photo: Alex Gillespie

4: Raeburn and Company (1896 – 1926)

EACH YEAR, USUALLY ON THE FIRST SATURDAY in December, the Scottish Mountaineering Club holds its Dinner. Every second year the retiring President steps down and without ceremony, indeed it goes unnoticed by some, hands over to the incoming President his seals of office. The first is a club badge in gold, to distinguish it from the usual bronze, but the second pays a singular honour to one of Britain's most accomplished mountaineers of the past. It is a long, wooden-shafted ice axe once owned by Harold Raeburn (1865 – 1926).

An all-round mountaineer, Raeburn had both a burning passion for the mountains and the natural ability that sets apart so many of the great. A native of Edinburgh and, (other than a short spell in Partick, Glasgow) resident there for most of his life, Raeburn belonged not to the professional classes which continued to dominate climbing at the turn of the century, but to the new and fast-expanding middle classes, his career being that of a brewer. A bachelor all his life, Raeburn devoted his considerable energies to mountaineering, with yachting and ornithology as secondary recreations. His diaries on the Birds of Shetland arc lodged in the National Library of Scotland.

A measure of Raeburn's climbing activity can be judged by the fact that of the 30 new routes on Nevis from 1896 to 1921, his name appears on exactly half. In 1902, he made the second ascent of Crowberry Ridge Direct on the Buachaille Etive Mòr, at that time dismissed by the Scottish establishment as unjustifiably difficult. Of more significance perhaps were his ascents of Raeburn's Arete on Nevis, that same year, and his earlier lead, in July 1898, of Flake Route, Very Difficult, on Church Door Buttress of Bidean nam Bian. A contemporary described Raeburn thus,

> Few have had a wider knowledge, or a more intense love of Nature in all its aspects – birds and beasts, flowers and rocks, the natural features of the countryside – all attracted his keen observation, and to a nature such as his the call of the mountain was irresistible...Light, wiry and active, with supple limbs and a beautiful balance, he added to his physical gifts an indomitable will, a sound judgment as to routes and possibilities, and a fearless self- reliance.[1]

Lord Mackay, a keen judge of men, made a terse description of Raeburn.

> Physically and mentally hard as nails, trained by solitary sea-cliff climbing after birds' haunts, he was certain, unyielding and concise in every movement, both mental and physical.

It seemed that Raeburn had his own peculiar climbing style, one borne out by photographs of him climbing.

> He could keep his lithe body closer to, and in almost complete contact with any rock he had to deal with. And he had a capacity of grip that was astonishing. He was possessed of strong muscular fingers that could press firmly and in a straight downward contact upon the very smallest hold.

Of Raeburn's character, Mackay makes what is clearly an honest appraisal.

> In controversies as to routes or as to times required, he was a stern opponent. His notes of recorded times in every climb achieved, and his constant comparisons by small seconds with the time of to-day, were often anathema to me, who preferred to enjoy the hopes and the passing incidents at large, without being checked by the watch...Something, I sometimes thought, of Stalin was in his make-up. Even you could see his mind, acting as Molotov's, as it came back and back to his original assertions. And yet he was ultimately fair in debate.

Lord Mackay finished his portrait of Raeburn with a revealing anecdote. Raeburn, Lawson and Mackay had had a long, tiring but successful day on Arran, and were descending Glen Rosa. Raeburn hated being

Physically and mentally hard as nails, trained by solitary sea-cliff climbing after birds' haunts, he was certain, unyielding and concise in every movement, both mental and physical

forced to a pace that was beyond his liking and Lawson walked at a tremendous pace.

> Harold suddenly sat down and refused to go another inch unless the pace moderated. Lawson did not agree. So he said, 'Just go on, I'll wait.' Lawson went on and, if anything, increased his pace. I (torn between) lengthened my step and kept up with Lawson. In due time and in complete darkness we arrived in the square of light before the door of Corrie Inn. We turned to one another to wonder what had become of Raeburn, and looked round casually. There he was, just at our backs, on the edge of the same square of light from the inn door. That again, I think, is a bit typical of his pertinacity and endurance.[2]

In the autumn of 1896 Raeburn applied to join the SMC, proposed by Willie Douglas and seconded by Naismith. On December 2 his application was passed. Within the club hierarchy, he rose to become Vice-President from 1909 – 1911, ultimately turning down the Presidency itself, just as Naismith had done before him, through modesty. Indeed, as a letter from Naismith to Douglas in 1896 indicates, Naismith also refused the post of Secretary, writing that,

> I have no ambition whatever for any more important post in the Club – Indeed I should prefer either now or soon to retire into private membership [3]

The first climbers on the Ben had quickly reached a high standard in mixed climbing in winter – snow, ice and rock – on routes such as Tower Ridge and the North-East Buttress. Raeburn was to push back the known frontiers of possibility and extend this expertise into the pure snow and ice of the gullies, in addition to which he brought to Scotland the rock climbing standards already in vogue further south.

A prominent Edinburgh man had joined the SMC the year before Raeburn. The two would make many ascents together in the coming years. William Inglis Clark (1856 – 1932) was born in Bombay, where his father was minister of the Scots Church (confusingly, in Scotland, Inglis is pronounced Ingils). His mother died of cholera when he was about a year old, when he and his elder brother came to Edinburgh. When he was nine the two brothers made a night ascent of Goat Fell on Arran, to watch the sunrise. Clark's interest in Ben Nevis was probably kindled by an uncle, Charles Simson Clark, who had climbed the mountain some 45 times. When one day William made an ascent of Nevis with a friend, by way of Glen Nevis and the Càrn Mòr Dearg arete, he was fortunate to find a temperature inversion at the level of the arete. There he also met Professor Heddle and Colin Philip.

Foster Heddle, Professor of Chemistry at St Andrews, held that chair for 23 years. His great interest in geology is marked now by the Heddle Collection of Scottish minerals. Heddle was one of the first Honorary Members of the SMC and attended the opening ceremony of the Ben Nevis Observatory. Colin Philip was an accomplished watercolour artist and member of the SMC, designing and drawing at least one of that club's early dinner menus. Both Heddle and Philip accompanied Clark and his friend to the summit of Nevis.

Clark, who later went on to become President of the SMC, was just as interesting a personage outside of mountaineering. At Edinburgh University, studying chemistry, he became assistant to Professor Crum

William Inglis Clark enjoys a brief rest
SMC Archives c. 1900

The SMC Easter Meet of 1901 in Fort William. What is obvious is the athletic confidence exhibited by Raeburn – standing happily in balance on the left gatepost, hands in pockets. Contrast this with Willie Douglas, nervously teetering on the right gatepost, clutching the hand of Glover!

SMC Archives

Brown, gaining his D.Sc. before he was 21. He had to wait until that age to be formally capped. In order to be independent he then went to work in the lab of Messrs Duncan Flockhart & Co, where he later became a partner. While in that firm Clark was the first to have the idea of putting unpleasant tasting drugs into capsules, inventing and designing the necessary machinery for the entire process. Clark in 1879 submitted to the Edinburgh University a thesis entitled *An Attempt to Place the Manufacture of Ink on a Scientific Basis*. His introduction of blue-black ink and his deductions and research on the necessary dyes are recognised in a standard book on ink as being of the greatest possible value judged from a scientific standpoint.[4]

Becoming a wealthy Edinburgh chemist, he owned that city's first car, with the registration S1. Passing this on to Lord Kingsburgh (First President of the Automobile Association), he kept the registration S2 for his own use, running an Arrol-Johnston '*dog-cart*'. The Clarks were early advocates of the use of the car for mountaineering transport. As one of the first car drivers in Switzerland, they were stopped and fined for driving at the alarming velocity of 9 mph (14.5km/hr). He was also an enthusiastic and expert photographer, in the days when a camera was built of mahogany and brass and could weigh over 6kg. His early experiments in colour photography were published in the SMC Journal for 1909.[5]

For the next two years the easier gullies were explored, April 1897 seeing ascents of Tower Gully (I), and Gardyloo Gully (II), by Hastings and the Haskett-Smiths. Moonlight Gully, next to Number Five Gully, was climbed on January 3, 1898 by William Inglis Clark and Tom Gibson. Moonlight Gully (II), as the name would suggest, was finished under the light of the moon, and gave the party nine hours of constant step cutting. Staircase Climb, Very Difficult, was climbed on July 12, 1898, by J.H.Bell, J.Maclay and Willie Naismith. On September 11 of that year, Raeburn and Gibson made the first summer ascent of the Original Route on The Castle, a Very Difficult rock climb.

Becoming a wealthy Edinburgh chemist, he [William Inglis Clark] owned that city's first car, with the registration S1...The Clarks were early advocates of the use of the car for mountaineering transport. As one of the first car drivers in Switzerland, they were stopped and fined for driving at the alarming velocity of 9 mph (14.5km/hr)

Until 1900, any climber going up or down Tower Ridge climbed the Great Tower by any of the variations to the west; none of which were particularly easy in summer, and all of them serious undertakings under snow or ice. On September 6 of that year Naismith and the Rev. Archibald Aeneas Robertson discovered a narrow ledge leading out onto the eastern face of the Great Tower. This exposed traverse led through a tunnel formed by a fallen block, then climbed directly up to the summit of the Great Tower. As it was easier than the western variations it almost immediately became the favoured route, and is now followed by virtually every climber doing Tower Ridge.[6]

During the SMC Easter Meet of 1901, held from April 4 – 9, a very strong team consisting of Raeburn, Douglas, Rennie and Willie Ling attempted Observatory Buttress, the wall-like buttress facing Tower Ridge across Observatory Gully. Snow was pouring down over ice-sheeted rocks, and after a gain in height of between 60 – 90m they decided to retreat. As Ling wrote later,

> The steepness was such that in places handholds as well as footholds had to be cut in the ice. Such climbing may not be very difficult, but it becomes a question of time and endurance, and the party decided that neither commodity would hold out.[7]

As it was, the party ran into a blizzard crossing the plateau, reaching Fort William just before midnight.

That Ling should remark on the climbing in such terms is indicative of their abilities, as Observatory Buttress in winter is now Grade V,4. [Raeburn climbed guideless in the Alps from 1902 onwards. With his closest friend Willie Ling, he climbed the North face of Monte Disgrazia in 1910, now graded at TD.] During the retreat that day, the party's eyes, and those of Raeburn in particular, must have rested often on the next ridge to the east, Observatory Ridge, which was to be the scene of a remarkable solo ascent two months later.

Dr Inglis Clark and his wife Jane decided to spend several nights in the small summit hotel on Nevis, and on June 21, 1901 walked up to the summit, having first sent a wire to Raeburn in Edinburgh. Raeburn caught the 4.30am train the next day, arriving in Fort William by 10am, but unable to form a rope at such short notice he continued alone, walking up through a cloud burst to gain the foot of Observatory Ridge.

Of his solo ascent Raeburn wrote,

> I remember three distinctly good bits on it. First the slabby rocks near the foot. Then a few hundred feet up an excellent hand traverse presents itself. It is begun by getting the hands into a first-rate crack on the left, then toe-scraping along a wall till the body can be hoisted on to a narrow overhung ledge above. This does not permit of standing up, but a short crawl to the right finishes the difficulty...The third difficulty, and the one which cost the most time, is rather more than half-way up, where a very steep tower spans the ridge. I tried directly up the face, but judged it somewhat risky, and prospecting to the right, discovered a route which after a little pressure 'went'.[8]

Raeburn's solo ascent had taken three hours. Sitting in the sun at the top of the route, Raeburn heard for the first time in summer a snow bunting (usually, though not always, a winter visitor), and he finished

High on Observatory Ridge, first soloed by Harold Raeburn in June 1901. Tower Ridge and Càrn Dearg Buttress in the background

Photo: Noel Williams

Aysel Crocket leads
the tunnel pitch
on Eastern Traverse,
Tower Ridge
(Difficult). In winter
this is often filled
with snow and the
chockstone is then not
obvious

Photo: Ken Crocket

*Sitting in the sun
at the top of the
route, Raeburn
heard for the first
time in summer a
snow bunting
(usually, though
not always, a
winter visitor), and
he finished his
account of the
climb by admitting
that if asked to
choose between the
climb and the
song, he would be
tempted to choose
the latter*

his account of the climb by admitting that if asked to choose between the climb and the song, he would be tempted to choose the latter; fortunately, he concluded, the snow bunting's song was a bonus to a most enjoyable scramble. The next day, with the Inglis Clarks, he again attempted Observatory Buttress, but heavy rain forced them down and they finished up North-East Buttress. Climbing just left of Slingsby's Chimney, they gained the First Platform by a new route, Raeburn's 18-Minute Route.

In 1902 Dr Inglis Clark was convalescing from an illness. Towards the end of June he decided to climb on Nevis, and stay at the summit hotel. In company with his wife and George Glover a start was made on Thursday, June 26 with the second ascent of Staircase Climb, a Very Difficult route on the west flank of Càrn Dearg Buttress.

Jane Inglis Clark was a highly competent climber and wife of William Inglis Clark. She was on the first ascent of Raeburn's Arete in June 1902 along with her husband and Raeburn. She was one of three women climbers who founded The Ladies Scottish Climbing Club in 1908, at a boulder near the Lix Toll in Perthshire

SMC Archives

'What a spot for middle-aged folks to be in!' wrote Clark, having gained the crux, an overhung recess in an exposed position.

> No thought of business or secretarial duties...but a steady stand with muscles braced and a side hold in the crack, were the prelude to the contact of fierce hobnailers with but lightly protected shoulder blades.[9]

The Clarks had arranged a rendezvous with Raeburn, who was in a yachting race in the Firth of Forth; due to poor winds Raeburn would arrive later on the Saturday, and meet the party at 2pm at the foot of Observatory Buttress. The Clarks, with Glover, now turned their attention to the west flank of Tower Ridge, and Friday evening saw a successful summer ascent of Glover's Chimney, a wet Very Difficult now neglected in summer, but popular as a winter route, leading to Tower Gap.

Saturday morning dawned as clear as the previous days, and Clark and Glover decided to tackle another line while waiting for Raeburn. They chose the Pinnacle Buttress of The Tower, which lies immediately left of Glover's Chimney. A late start, due to the midnight finish of the previous day, saw them gaining the Great Tower at 4.15pm from where, wrote Dr Clark,

> ...eagerly looking down we espied a moving speck on the rocks of the Observatory Buttress. It was that solitary climber, who amid the great immensities of the place seemed to traverse invisible ledges, and to climb where foot and hand holds could not be seen. Our chance of a share in his great enterprise was gone, and the reproachful glance of my wife who had waited for us two and a half hours at the 'Gap' was such as to make us hasten aloft...

That *'solitary climber'* was of course Raeburn, who had given up the wait and decided to solo the buttress. In a remarkably understated essay by Raeburn the climbing is confined to just 34 words.

> Below, was the fast flowing shadowtide; above, the blaze of sunlight, and oh, blessed thought, perhaps afternoon tea. It was enough, I went up, and, fifteen hours from the Sea, stood upon the Summit.[10]

Observatory Buttress, Original Route, is a 340m Very Difficult, steeper and more compact than earlier routes. Drinking his afternoon tea on the summit, Raeburn described the climbing to his friends, telling them of the *'pulling in holds'* which made the steep climbing possible. It was Raeburn's third attempt on the route and the fourth day of a heatwave, the shade temperature at the summit on that day reaching a record 22.7°C.

Glover now left the party, leaving Raeburn and the Clarks. On the Sunday, the fourth day of the Clarks' stay, they climbed the South Trident Buttress, called by them Pinnacle Buttress. The difficult pitch on this was the steepest ever experienced by Clark, and at several points, he noticed, the rope hung parallel to the rocks. The 1902 team avoided the lowest tier of the Buttress, which seemed impossibly steep; indeed, it was not climbed until 1934, by G.Graham Macphee.

Not content with one route, Raeburn and the Clarks now turned their attention to The Comb, the fierce buttress which is the most prominent feature in Coire na Ciste between the Tower Ridge and Number Three Gully. They succeeded in climbing the easy sloping ledges at the foot

The original title of this photograph was 'Breakfast in Blankets', and it has the Clarks sitting in the Summit Hotel enjoying just that. They made several exploratory trips using the Hotel as a base. The lady with the tea pot may well be Mrs Rodger, who ran the Hotel along with Sarah Cameron

Photo: W.I.Clark, SMC Archives

of the buttress and the rightward slanting rakes; these led to the buttress edge overlooking a gully (the future Green Gully). Here Raeburn declined to try the *'rotten chimney'*, but instead traversed rightwards into the gully, which they then followed for 100 feet.

As they had been forced off The Comb proper, Raeburn's party, not liking the look of the rest of the gully came back some distance and traversed rightwards across the face. They eventually found a way up the cliffs overlooking Number Three Gully, following ledges and rocks of what is now known as Number Three Gully Buttress, a popular winter route. This was on the fourth day of the week and was the fifth first ascent.

Pinnacle Buttress, South Trident Buttress (now known as Pinnacle Arete), climbed by Raeburn and the Clarks in June 1902

Photo: A.E.Robertson (c. 1902)

The first successful and complete ascent of The Comb was not to be made until 1921, when A.S.Pigott and J.Wilding, leading climbers from the south, succeeded in finding a way through the band of steep rock above the slanting rakes. They followed the sloping ledges – which are of rotten and loose rock in many places – much as had Raeburn 19 years earlier, and then forced the *'rotten chimney'* rejected by Raeburn. The chimney proved to be the crux of the route, graded Severe.

But if Raeburn had failed on The Comb that sunny Sunday, he succeeded brilliantly on the Monday with his best and hardest route of the week – the futuristic Raeburn's Arete on the First Platform, North-East Buttress. This excellent Severe lies on the same buttress as Raeburn's 18-Minute Route, recorded the previous June. The arete looks down the Allt a' Mhuilinn, and consists of a parallel series of steep, narrow ramps. Raeburn gave no details of his ascent with the Clarks, beyond a straight route description, though he did comment that –

> From a climbing point of view this ranks among the steepest on Ben Nevis, and would be impossible but for the magnificent nature of the rock.[11]

There is a mention of Raeburn's Arete elsewhere by Clark, which describes Raeburn soloing besides the Clarks, but it is not clear whether

Raeburn's Arete (Severe), First Platform of North-East Buttress. A climber dressed in yellow can just be seen on the crest of the lower third of the arete, where the background scree goes into the shade

Photo: Noel Williams

The Rev Archibald Eneas Robertson, c. 1906. He has a claim to be the first person to have ascended all the Munros, though there is some dispute over this point. He was certainly an energetic and highly competent photographer, leaving many excellent glass slides

SMC Archives

this was on the first ascent or on one made later. From Raeburn's performance that sunny June it was probably the first ascent, and he was indeed soloing alongside his friends.

Outside of that week's climbing, the only other new route on Nevis that year was a Very Difficult climb by W.C.Newbigging and a Swiss companion, on August 21. This was Newbigging's 80-Minute Route, some distance left of Raeburn's Arete, and from its name we might detect a little poke at Raeburn's obsessive regard to time-keeping for ascents. After that superb week of climbing, Ben Nevis was not to see another such burst of concentrated activity by one party for more than half a century.

No first ascents were recorded in 1903; the SMC held their Easter Meet at Inveroran and on Skye, Raeburn attending the latter. On the first day of 1904, however, a strong party climbed the North Trident Buttress. The rope of four was Maclay, Raeburn, and two cousins from Dundee, Harry and Charles Walker. The route is now a III. On the first ascent the Ben was in a not untypical January condition, with little snow, and thin ice lining the cracks and chimneys.

Raeburn returned to the Trident Buttresses in April 1904, when with Jane Inglis Clark and her son Charles he completed his trilogy of ascents here with the Central Gully, South Trident Buttress (III), more of a gully than a buttress on this snowy ascent. Elsewhere on the mountain, the Walkers found a rock climb on the North Wall of Carn Dearg – Cousins' Buttress, Very Difficult, climbed on June 11, while a Moderate route was found up the south-west ridge of the Douglas Boulder. The first thundering wave of exploration on Nevis had broken. There were to be no routes in 1905, Raeburn *et al* had untouched rocks to explore on other mountains.

As an indication of the dangers of descent from the summit, A.E.Robertson had a very lucky escape in April 1905. An account was published in *The Scotsman* newspaper. He was descending the mountain and was about 150m below the summit in a blizzard, with mist and driving snow. This had forced him further south than he had intended, to avoid the summit cliffs. He remembers his ice axe hissing and sparking, due to an electrical build-up in the atmosphere, then he recalled nothing until he regained consciousness *'well over one thousand feet lower.'* He had lost his cap and ice axe, and was bleeding from a head wound. Despite this, he managed to struggle off the mountain and walked, unaided, to his Fort William hotel.

Robertson required stitches for his wound and believed that there had been a lightning strike either directly onto his ice axe, or very close to him. If he was about 150m below the summit he may have just passed above the entrant to Five Finger Gully, which has seen many bad accidents in the years since. He was certainly very lucky to survive. The report commented on his experience, stating that he had ascended Ben Nevis some 23 times prior to this fall. He required over a month for full recovery from his escapade.

In 1906, Raeburn was fast approaching the peak of his form, and recorded two outstanding routes before the Great War broke out. The first of these was to be the only route recorded in 1906. It may have been the only route that year on Ben Nevis, but it was a winter ascent which stretched both Raeburn and his meagre equipment to the limit – Green Gully.

Raeburn had attempted to climb The Comb during the summer heatwave of 1902. His party then had gone a little way up the gully on the right of the Comb, but had not persevered and had retreated. Raeburn was unstoppable however and on Sunday, April 22 of 1906 he met the Rev. Robertson in Fort William, for another attempt on the Comb. Gales had been hammering Nevis for several weeks, and Raeburn reached Fort William in rain and snow to find that Robertson was unable to climb, due to a *'slight indisposition.'*

Raeburn was saved from the necessity of soloing, fortunately, as Robertson introduced him to a gentleman from Geneva, a member of the Swiss Alpine Club, Monsieur Eberhard Phildius, who was staying in Fort William. Phildius was deeply involved in a Youth Christian Movement, and was probably in Scotland to meet Robertson, due to this interest. He seems to have had a reputation as a competent Alpinist,

Step cutting as it was. This climber is making a difficult descending line, made easier by the long axes then in use

Illustration taken from the 'Badminton Book of Mountaineering', published 1895 though it is difficult to find any information on this. As the two climbers passed Càrn Dearg Buttress, the wind, which had changed overnight from a wet southwest to a cold northeast, blew flurries of powder snow about the ice-covered rocks.

Raeburn's target was the rocks of The Comb, and his plan was to climb Green Gully until it was possible to gain access to the buttress rocks on the left, but the climbers found even the approach difficult, with one or two feet of soft snow covering harder, icy stuff. These potential avalanche conditions prompted them to clear the soft snow away and cut steps in the hard layer underneath. Raeburn described the ascent in a now classic essay.

> Now we found ourselves looking up, so far as the mist and the descending cataracts of snow dust would permit, the steep gully which should give access to the ridge. Then began the real struggle. Keen frost reigned, and a biting wind moaned among the icy battlements...we two, stormers of one of the salient towers, felt the blast strike us now and again as it swept round the angle of the Comb.

A great problem, then, as now, was the choking clouds of spindrift, the seemingly innocuous, tiny crystals of snow blown by the wind.

> From above one could, to a certain extent, take cover beneath the shield of our cone-pointed, brim-turned-down felt hats, but occasionally the snow that fell mixed with the seldom ceasing stream that poured down the gully, was caught by the powerful ascending eddy and rushed up, thus taking us behind our defences. The pain of a stream of icy snow in the face is so great that work must stop, and the face covered till breath is regained.

Raeburn and Phildius found the gully rising, initially, in two steep sections; with an average angle of probably 70 to 75 degrees, small portions approaching 90 degrees. While climbing ice, as many a leader has discovered to his dismay, an angle of 75 degrees feels like 90 degrees, or vertical, with anything steeper feeling overhanging. The conditions underfoot that day in the gully were fortunately excellent, snow-ice allowing Raeburn to cut firm handholds as well as footholds. Raeburn continued, with a prophetic vision.

> Ice work of this kind is, however, particularly cramping and exhausting, and progress was slow. To hang on with one hand, while that long two-handed weapon, the modern ice axe, is wielded in the other, is calculated to produce severe cramps in course of time, and did so now...I suggest for climbs such as this our going back to the original Swiss icemens' tools, the iron-shod straight *baton*, and the light tomahawk-like hatchet stuck in the belt when not in use.

In advocating the use of a shorter ice tool Raeburn was decades ahead of his time. However, he seems to have retreated somewhat from this point of view a few years later, as in his book, published in 1920, he criticises the fashion for very short axes. The two introductory ice pitches were led by Raeburn, the second pitch taking three attempts before a tired leader cut his way up to an easier section of the gully. Here Phildius took over, the two deciding to continue up the gully, as the buttress to the left, though now accessible, was fringed and crowned with unstable-

Harold Raeburn dressed for winter climbing on Liathach

Photo: A.E.Robertson

Brian Dunn on the headwall of Green Gully (IV,3). The drooping cornice lip on the right illustrates the plastic tendency of snow under earlier thaw conditions

Photo: Con Higgins

looking cornices of ice and snow.

The finish to the gully was blocked by a huge cornice, almost 4m high. This is fairly large by Nevis standards, obviously having been built up by the gales of the preceding weeks. The climbers decided that their only chance at this point was to traverse out right, where a rib of ice-covered rock ran up to meet the cornice, reducing its height by half. At this point also, the cornice was only slightly overhanging. Raeburn described the hair-raising finish.

> This way eventually 'went', but the Comb was game to the last, and I must confess to a feeling of helplessness for a moment as I stood on my ice-axe, driven horizontally into the vertical snow wall, some hundreds of feet of little less than vertical ice-plastered rocks stretching away down into the depths of the mist beneath, while my fingers slid helplessly from the glassy surface of the cornice nevé, in the vain endeavour to find or make a hold by which I might haul myself up. The problem was solved by a retreat, until Phildius was able to pass me up his axe. Then the ice-plating was quickly shattered, and with fingers well crooked in the tough nevé, a steady drag landed the body over the cornice lip, and Phildius soon followed.[12]

Ironically, Raeburn himself may have helped to consign this fine climb to its long period of obscurity. In his essay he apologised for the climb, admitting that they were never once on the exact arete. But he was defiant in stating that this did not matter, as he and Phildius went out for a climb and got one, both of them being pleased by the ascent, in as icy conditions as Raeburn had ever seen Ben Nevis. In the 1919 edition of the Nevis Guide, an updated edition of the 1902 publication, the gully is dismissed in a few sparse lines.

> Raeburn made an icy ascent on 22nd April, 1906, which, although not on the arete, yet led to the summit of the Comb. The climb was, however, almost entirely on snow and ice.[13]

Ice work of this kind is, however, particularly cramping and exhausting, and progress was slow. To hang on with one hand, while that long two-handed weapon, the modern ice axe, is wielded in the other, is calculated to produce severe cramps in course of time, and did so now...

The dotted line indicates the route followed from the foot of the Tower to the cornice.

Raeburn's ascent of Green Gully (IV,3) rapidly faded into the pages of the SMC Journal, as no one seemed willing or able to follow such a masterly lead. (The route suffered the exact same fate as another classic route of Raeburn's – Crowberry Gully in Glen Coe – a later party making what they thought was a first ascent.) On April 4, 1937, 31 years later, J.H.B.Bell recorded a winter ascent of the Nevis gully, naming it Green Gully. Raeburn's ascent was still unrecognised on the publication dates of subsequent climbing guides to Ben Nevis – in 1936[14], and even 1969[15], and it has taken until the 1970s for a growing awareness of Raeburn's achievements to surface.[17]

In 1906, Green Gully was easily the hardest ice climb in Scotland, if not the world. Simon Richardson has made the observation that it was probably some 20 years before it was surpassed in difficulty, with ascents in the Alps by Welzenbach.

Not all ascents made during this period went smoothly, though fatalities were, for a long time unknown, because leader falls were likewise unknown. The consequences of a leader fall were so obviously serious, given the minimal equipment used then, that no leader dare fall. The early mountaineers were well aware of the low breaking strain of their hemp ropes, and climbed accordingly. In Raeburn's book, *Mountaineering Art*, published in 1920 (though written just before World War I), he has several hair-raising stories which illustrate early rope technology. On one occasion he was showing a friend sea birds' sites on a 60m cliff. The friend decided he wanted some guillemot eggs, so Raeburn prepared a descent by putting a walking-stick into the turf and looping the rope round it. In fixing the rope he bent it sharply, when it at once broke half-way through. It was thoroughly rotten, having been put away wet by another climber, though on handling it felt and appeared dry. On another occasion in the Alps, a plaited rope snapped following a fall of a few feet by the leader. But poor conditions and lack of experience were just as awkward then as they are now, and the following account was not the last grand epic to be experienced on Nevis.

The 1907 New Year Meet of the SMC was based at the Alexandra Hotel, Fort William. The first three arrivals on the Friday, December 27, were J.H.A.MacIntyre, Thomas E.Goodeve, and Charles Inglis Clark, the 18-year old son of Dr and Mrs Inglis Clark. On the Saturday the trio decided to attempt Tower Ridge, a first for all three, as the ridge did not seem to have as much snow on it as the North-East Buttress. They had with them two ropes; one 24m and one 18m. They tied on to the shorter rope, their first error, as the necessary shorter pitches inevitably meant greater delays.

The party started up the West Gully of the Douglas Gap at 10am, Goodeve leading, as he did throughout the entire episode. Considerable effort was needed to gain the ridge itself by noon, which should have warned the party of the limited daylight remaining, but they pressed on, their second error, and reached the Great Tower at 4pm. Darkness was now setting in and they decided to take the variation now known as the Eastern Traverse, first climbed six years earlier. Unfortunately, as Clark wrote later,

> We had a hazy impression that an easy ledge ran round the west side, enabling one to reach the Gap, without climbing the Tower itself.

This was a serious error to make, one which was to land the party in difficulties. They began to traverse the Great Tower on its western face, encountering difficult route finding. After 'a couple of hours' they reached a snow gully, which they could follow visually about halfway down to Coire na Ciste. This they began descending, easily at first, then with step cutting, until finally, after lowering the last man down an ice step, the other two joining him using steps, they found themselves at the top of an overhanging pitch. The gully, they finally realised to their horror, was Glover's Chimney, first climbed in summer by G.T.Glover and Charles' father. Further descent was impossible. Abseil slings were not used then, even given a belay, ropes were of inadequate length, and the foot of the pitch an unknown distance away in the dark, hidden by an overhang.

The three were now fairly exhausted, but began to climb up to the ridge again, using the rocks on the right of the gully. By 8pm they had regained their former level, opposite the western traverse under the Great Tower. To this point there had been a little starlight, but now clouds rolled in, and with no lanterns, their visibility was very limited. This fact may have been an advantage, as their position would have been a frightening one in daylight. On the other hand, in daylight they would have seen the lower, easy snow ledges leading up and under the summit cliffs, now taken by Raeburn's Easy Route.

Not far below the summit cornice, a 6m rib of steep rock was encountered. Goodeve and Clark succeeded in climbing it, though not without difficulty, and then it was MacIntyre's turn.

Major Thomas E. Goodeve was the leader of the epic ascent of Tower Ridge in December 1907. He was a railway engineer who died in 1919 while serving with the Royal Engineers in Palestine, killed in a train accident

SMC Archives

A 30m rope was shared between the three, Raeburn leading, Goggs second and Mounsey, the heaviest, being third man. This was a conscious decision, belays and protection often being non-existent at this time

As my frantic struggles had effectually removed every trace of snow for the last man to get a foothold on, there was nothing for it but to lift him bodily by the rope. Goodeve and I sat stridelegs on the ice-arete...and at a shout from below, with all the speed our tired muscles would allow, brought MacIntyre up, struggling and kicking like a fish...Half an hour of step-cutting up a terribly steep ice-slope brought us to the cornice[17]

Fortunately the cornice was straightforward, and some time after midnight the plateau was gained. As they were unable to take a compass bearing, a gale blowing out their light, they wandered off route into Glen Nevis, missing the search parties organised by the rest of the Meet. One party, however, found their steps on top. Finally, Raeburn found them at 9am on Sunday morning, and led them back to Fort William, 30 hours after they had set out. Two of them had frostbitten hands, and Goodeve a head cut from a slip during the descent, but otherwise their remarkable display of endurance says much for their general level of fitness.

MacIntyre, in his report of the Meet in the SMC Journal, ended with the following apology.

Some of the members present offered an opinion which might profitably be enlarged to the following:- It is a courtesy due from every party to their fellow-members to make sure before leaving the hotel, either that some one connected with the hotel, or that some of their fellow-members, then resident, are conversant with their intentions for the day.[18]

As a post-script to this episode, The White Line (III) was recorded in the winter of 1971, on the right side of Glover's Chimney. A careful reading of Clark's original Journal account, including a sketch of the cliff, appears to approximate his ascent with the upper section of this later climb . Goodeve's party certainly climbed the buttress right of Glover's Chimney, and as a tribute to this expedition, the buttress was named Goodeve's Buttress in the 2002 guidebook.

If one regards the diagram published along with the original account as being accurate, there seems little doubt that an impressive piece of climbing had been forced upon the 1907 team. The diagram was drawn by Clark's mother, Jane, presumably with help from Charles, and would seem to be very clear. Additionally, in the second edition of the Ben Nevis Guide, written after the First World War, William Inglis Clark, makes the comment that –

It would have been possible by continuing the traverse...to have reached easy ledges and slopes...whence either the corrie near Number 2 Gully or the summit plateau could have been reached without difficulty.

Clark refers here to another diagram and a photograph, which indicate that the *'easy ledges and slopes'* belong to what is now known as Raeburn's Easy Route. Goodeve, who served in the Royal Engineers and was a railway specialist, died while serving in Palestine in 1919, accidentally run over by a train and killed immediately. He had been mentioned in Despatches and had reached the rank of Major.

The pace of exploration had slowed by 1905 and was about to cease completely. On September 28, 1908, Raeburn climbed the fine buttress which now bears his name, in Castle Coire. His companions were Harry

MacRobert and D.S.Arthur, and the Very Difficult route was finished despite heavy rain. Raeburn's Buttress is now a fine winter route, though its arete section is enjoyable in summer. Raeburn did little new in the next few years, partly due to an accident on Stuc a' Chroin in the Southern Highlands. He had been climbing, roped, with a party of ladies, when one of them fell, pulling Raeburn off his stance. He had a broken rib and other injuries and managed to descend to the nearest farmhouse with some difficulty.

On September 28, 1911, he climbed Raeburn's Easy Route, an elegantly easy way up the cliffs left of The Comb. In 1914 the First World War broke out, almost completely putting a halt to climbing. Those not away fighting were working to near exhaustion on the home front, while economic measures in any case reinforced a voluntary ban on luxuries such as unnecessary travelling. The strictures of war also hit publishing, delaying the second edition of the Nevis Guide and preventing Raeburn from publishing his book, then in manuscript.

Raeburn, now 49, was too old to be accepted for the Royal Flying Corps despite all his efforts. Instead he threw himself into 15 and 16 hour days in an aeroplane factory. Younger men enlisted and some of them died in the fighting, including Charles Inglis Clark. Serving in what is now Iraq, he was killed by a sniper's bullet in 1919, and was buried in a military graveyard in Baghdad. By 1920 however, the strict economic conditions had eased somewhat, and in April of that year Raeburn made a return visit to Nevis for his last major ascent on that mountain – the first winter ascent of one of his own routes, Observatory Ridge.

The Easter, 1920 Meet of the SMC at Fort William was the first to be held there since 1914. Enthusiasm was raised by the new guide to Ben Nevis, an update of the original. On Tuesday morning of the Meet, Raeburn, W.A.Mounsey and Frank Sidney Goggs set off from Achintee. A small amount of new snow had fallen overnight and the party decided to try Observatory Ridge, a first winter ascent being especially tempting. A 30m rope was shared between the three, Raeburn leading, Goggs second and Mounsey, the heaviest, being third man. This was a conscious decision, belays and protection often being non-existent at this time.

The good memory of the leader facilitated the route-finding in the lower, steep section. Higher up, stamina and experience were to be demanded, as snow began to fall again and conditions became steadily worse. High up the ridge, steep, glazed rocks formed a barrier, as Raeburn attempted a traverse to gain an easier gully line. Goggs described the ascent –

Observatory Ridge, centre and Observatory Buttress above and to the right

Photo: Hamish MacInnes

> Once again Raeburn went to the left, saying, 'It's got to go.' I stood at the rock spike with Mounsey a yard or two away, Raeburn disappeared round the corner, and for the next quarter of an hour we saw nothing of him, but heard and saw hard snow and ice hurtling down. The rope went out very slowly, but it went, and that was the chief thing.

Raeburn's party now found themselves in a broad, open, snow gully. The snow was hard, and at two small ice falls steps were cut; but otherwise Raeburn scraped and kicked footholds in order to save time.

> Raeburn ran out length after length of rope, only one man moved at a time, and rarely was our leader able to say that he had his ice axe well in.

The steep lower section of Observatory Ridge (IV,4) – technically the hardest of all the Nevis ridges in summer and winter

Photo: Rab Anderson

Our conversation seemed to consist in the following repetition :- Goggs to Raeburn, 'Last six feet.' Raeburn to Goggs, 'You must come: I have no hitch.'

In his article Goggs conveys the epic nature of such ascents, with the physical and mental discomforts accepted by the climbers as being intrinsic to a good day on the hill.

> The only thing I feared was cramp: the steps were perforce small, the angle steep, the ice axe could rarely be depended on to give a satisfying sense of security, the leader had to take his time, and occasionally we had to wait, not at the most convenient stances, but just where we happened to be at the moment: the strain on our leg muscles (after five war years) was therefore considerable. As under the conditions described, physical failure on the part of any of us would have been distinctly unpleasant, I eased my position as much as possible, but from start to finish, the climb was remarkable for its lack of comfortable stopping places.[19]

Finally, just under six hours from the foot of the ridge, the successful party gained the plateau. The sun, which had been threatening to break through the scurrying clouds, bathed them in a triumphant glow as they finished the climb. It had been a remarkable exhibition of sustained, mixed climbing. Raeburn, who had led the entire route, was 55. The winter ascent of Observatory Ridge by Raeburn's party was the most significant Scottish winter ascent of the decade, and was not equalled until the 1930s. Today, the route is grade IV,4, and deserves respect. Indeed, in lean, mixed conditions, some consider the ridge to present more of a challenge than the classic Nevis Grade V ice routes.

The second edition of the Ben Nevis Guide, sub-edited by Harry MacRobert and published in December 1919, had been put out of date by Raeburn's ascent of Observatory Ridge. One thousand copies were published, some 600 selling in the first year, most of them to non-members of the SMC.

During the same Easter Meet an unnamed SMC party made a winter ascent of Raeburn's Easy Route, the pleasant, zig-zagging line weaving up through the cliffs at the head of Coire na Ciste. In September, 1920, a Dr E.Lüscher on holiday in Scotland soloed both the North-East Buttress, and a new route on the North Wall of Càrn Dearg. Subsequent parties and guide book authors however have found it impossible to define the latter line with any certainty.

Most parties of climbers from the south were at this time heading for The Cuillins of Skye, but in September 1921 A.S.Pigott and J.Wilding spent two days exploring Ben Nevis. On the 23rd they put up a variation on the Great Tower, a Very Difficult corner and slab rising up from the start of the Eastern Traverse. The next day they succeeded in climbing the steep rocks of The Comb, following the path of Raeburn for the initial section of slabby rocks, then climbing a Severe and loose flake-chimney which Raeburn had declined to attempt in 1903.

> This crack proved loose and rotten, and after ascending for about fifteen feet the leader was glad to traverse to the left on small and sound holds.[20]

In 1920 Raeburn's *Mountaineering Art* was published[21], dedicated to his friend Willie Ling, *'climbing colleague in the solution of some severe problems of mountaineering art.'* Raeburn was on an expedition to Kanchenjunga in 1920, and in 1921 he was made leader of a mountaineering party on the Everest Reconnaissance. Overwork while ill with influenza, and a bad bout of dysentery in Tibet put him into hospital for two months. On recovering he set off cross-country to rejoin the expedition, eventually reaching 6,700m by sheer will-power. Returning home he suffered a complete breakdown of his health and gradually weakened, dying four years later, on December 21, 1926.

With Raeburn's death, the art of Scottish winter climbing went into a decline. During the next decade winter ascents of Castle Ridge and the easy gullies would be made, but little else, for there was no one of Raeburn's stature to continue the exploration. These winters were also lacking in good snow and ice conditions. The few routes made after Observatory Ridge were ripples in the otherwise still waters following the maelstrom of the Great War. Raeburn himself had been an anomaly; a prodigy even in age, while the next generation was still learning to walk.

Harold Raeburn in action on Salisbury Crags above Edinburgh. The only real tactic the belayer could employ was to try and run the rope behind or over a flake of rock, as slings were not yet used in climbing. Falling off was not an option. The second man here was J.Gall Inglis

SMC Archives

References

1. **Ling**, W.N., *In Memoriam, Harold Raeburn*. SMCJ, 18, 26 – 31, 1927.

2. **Mackay**, Lord, *Vignettes of Earlier Climbers*. SMCJ, 24, 169 – 180, 1950.

3. **Naismith**, W.W., *Letter to W. Douglas*, November 17, 1896. NLS.

4. **Carvalho**, David N., *Forty Centuries of Ink, or a Chronological Narrative Concerning Ink and Its Background*. (New York: Banks Law Publishing Co., New York, 1904.) Also available as a paperback and in e-texts. Kessinger Publishing, 2004, ISBN: 1419120395.)

5. **Clark**, W.I., *Photography in Colour for Mountaineers*. SMCJ 10, 294 – 306, 1909.

6. **Naismith**, W.W., *Ben Nevis, Tower Ridge*. SMCJ, 6, 131, 1901.

7. **Ling**, W.N., *A Blizzard on Ben Nevis*. SMCJ 6, 213 – 217, 1901.

8. **Raeburn**, H., *The Observatory Ridge, Ben Nevis*. SMCJ 6, 249 – 250, 1901.

9. **Clark**, W.I., *New Climbs on Ben Nevis*. SMCJ 7, 199 – 211, 1903.

10. **Raeburn**, H., *From Sea To Summit*. SMCJ 7, 194 – 198, 1903.

11. **Raeburn**, H., In: *Ben Nevis Guide*, edited by W.I.Clark. (Edinburgh: Scottish Mountaineering Club, 1903.)

12. **Raeburn**, H., *A Scottish Ice Climb*. SMCJ 9, 153 – 158, 1907.

13. *Scottish Mountaineering Club Guide to Ben Nevis*, edited by H. MacRobert (Edinburgh: Scottish Mountaineering Club, 1919.)

14. **Macphee**, G.G., *Ben Nevis*. (Edinburgh: Scottish Mountaineering Club, 1936.)

15. **Marshall**, J.R., *Climbers' Guide to Ben Nevis*. (Edinburgh: Scottish Mountaineering Club, 1969.)

16. **Campbell**, R.N., *The First Scottish Ice Climbers*. SMCJ 30, 48 – 57, 1972.

17. **Clark**, C.I., *Thirty Hours on Ben Nevis*. SMCJ 10, 73 – 81, 1908.

18. **MacIntyre**, J.H.A., *Proceedings of The Club*. SMCJ 10, 112 – 119, 1908.

19. **Goggs**, F.S., *Ben Nevis: Observatory Ridge'*. SMCJ 15, 310-318, 1920.

20. **Pigott**, A.S., *Notes on some Scottish Climbs*. Rucksack Club Journal 4, p193, 1921.

21. **Raeburn**, H., *Mountaineering Art*. (London: T. Fisher Unwin Ltd., 1920.)

The evening sun in summer enters the CIC Hut through a window in the uphill gable end, lighting up the Climbs Book. Like its companion volumes, this record of mountaineering made by climbers based in the CIC Hut, is now lodged in the National Library Scotland

Photo: Ken Crocket

Charles Inglis Clark in his military uniform. He attained the rank of Captain in the RASC, maintaining transport. Serving in what is now Iraq, he was killed by a sniper's bullet in 1919, and was buried in a military graveyard for Allied forces in Baghdad

Photo: SMC Archives

5: A New Hut, New Clubs (1924 – 1933)

THE SUMMIT Observatory had closed in 1904; the small hotel was to follow suit in 1916. Both had afforded shelter and hospitality to many climbers and walkers reaching the wind-swept summit, perhaps fatigued after an arduous winter ascent. In 1925, most climbing on the Ben was undertaken, as before, on a daily basis from a Fort William hotel, a strenuous exercise at the best of times, more so if for several days in a row.

Two SMC members attending the Club's Easter Meet in 1925, A.J.Rusk and R.N.Rutherford,

> ...disdained the flesh pots of Fort William, and camped out in the palatial Rest House, halfway up the Ben, the comforts of which they shared together with a number of unusually active rats.[1]

The '*palatial* Rest House' was the refuge on the bridle path; the old half-way station of the Observatory, now falling into disrepair. As chance would have it, also attending the Meet was A.E.Maylard, one of the original members of the SMC, and indeed one of its founders. Alfred Ernest Maylard (1855 – 1947) was a physically tall man, the proud owner of a beard which, wrote an observer, '*was so carefully tended that it seemed as if he couldn't be the man himself if you took and shaved him.*'[2] He was somewhat reserved in character, a consultant surgeon at the Victoria Hospital, Glasgow. He died at his home in Peebles, in his 93rd year.

Walking up the old path to the summit Maylard came up to the refuge.

> On arriving at the half-way refuge I found it occupied by two junior members of the Club who were away at the time, but had left all their belongings for a day and a night's lodgings. The rotten wooden building was in a wretched condition, absolutely unfitted be occupied by any human beings. As a medical man I could not but admire the enthusiasm of these two junior mountaineers, that they were willing to undergo such discomforts in the pursuit of their pleasure; but at the same time I recognised the risk they were

running in damaging their health for future days by sleeping in such a hovel with wet and wind creeping through innumerable crevices.[3]

During dinner in Fort William, at the Alexandra Hotel, Maylard spoke to those seated nearby about the need for a properly constructed hut. Sang, the Club Secretary, was also present, and seated next to him was his guest, the factor for the Ben Nevis Estates. The factor was amenable to the idea of a hut and promised to give as much assistance as possible. The next problem was in financing the project. Maylard thought that the hut should be built as a war memorial, and recollected the loss of one of the Club's most popular younger members, Charles Inglis Clark, son of William and Jane Inglis Clark. Maylard then wrote to Clark explaining his idea, and to his great joy Clark replied almost at once that he and his wife would gladly erect a hut to the memory of their son.

Negotiations commenced regarding the lease, Sang playing a major role. Permission to go ahead was received on July 28, 1927. Negotiations were greatly delayed because the Club's application for a site coincided with the transference of ground around Ben Nevis from the Abinger Trustees to the North British Aluminium Co. Ltd. (In the early 19th century, the lands of Inverlochy were bought by Sir James Scarlett, the first Lord Abinger, who later built a new Castle of Inverlochy, now a hotel.)

That year, a small group consisting of Sang, Alexander (Sandy) Harrison, owners, architect and builder walked up the Allt a' Mhuilinn, and after some deliberation chose the site for the hut. These worthies have often been (unfairly) the object of much nocturnal abuse, as tired climbers staggered up through the energy-sapping and demoralising bogs of the Allt a' Mhuilinn path on dark, stormy nights. In fact the hut, at a height of 680m, is placed on a small spur just above the spot where one turns up from the Allt a' Mhuilinn to enter Coire na Ciste. In all probability its position could not be bettered.

The architects were Mears and Carns-Wilson of Edinburgh, and the builders W.T.Gibson & Co. of Glasgow. Initially, plans were drawn up for a hut built to accommodate 20, but the cost would have been excessive and the hut was scaled down to sleep eight, in the comparatively luxurious comfort and spacing then employed. The builder, T.J.Gibson, was a member of the SMC, and lived at the site for six weeks as foreman. The first load of materials went up by Katie the pony on May 7, 1928, and by June the massive stone foundations had been laid and most of the woodwork delivered to the site. The workers were meanwhile living in bothies at the construction site. The building was finished by October 8, attention then switching to the interior furnishings.

The dimensions of the hut, in its original form, were 7.9 by 7.3m, with a 2.9m ceiling. The walls are 76cm thick, of local stone. An inspection will show both andesite and granite in the walls; the hut actually sitting on andesite, with granite boulders having tumbled down from Càrn Mòr Dearg, the boundary between the two rock types being nearby, approximately following the course of the Allt a' Mhuilinn burn which runs just behind the hut.

As with the summit Observatory, the hut is really a double; a wooden hut sitting inside a stone shell, separated by an air space. There is a small attic reached by ladder, used for storing hut spares. The original entrance

Alfred Ernest Maylard (1855 – 1947), one of the founder members of the SMC, and its first Secretary. He was a consultant surgeon in Glasgow

SMC Archives

A workman with 'Katie' at the CIC Hut

SMC Archives

door faced the cliffs, and opened into a tiny hallway with an inner door beyond. Excess snow could then be shaken off before entering the hut itself, though in winter the floor never really dried out. Later, a small annexe with a drying-room was added, allowing storage of rucksacks outside of the main living and sleeping area. The Charles Inglis Clark Memorial Hut, to give its full name, is unique in Britain.

Originally eight teak bunks with wire mattresses were installed; each bunk having bedding, air-pillow, and a fold-down front. The original stove was for cooking as well as heat, and of course used coal. The possibility of delivering the coal by air was looked into at first, this being the age of the aeroplane, but it was quickly deemed impracticable. Instead, coal was brought up by pony.

Since then the hut has been converted to propane gas for cooking and heating; and the gas cylinders are replaced every year with the aid of a helicopter, though for a number of years tracked vehicles managed to carry cylinders to a site just below the hut, from where they completed their journey by man-powered stretcher. The helicopter lift affords an exciting hour or two of hard work, as empty, and full, gas cylinders are swung in a cargo net above the hut site.

Original furniture still present in the hut includes a wooden table, made and presented by the Rev A.E.Robertson, and a small bookcase from the Ladies Scottish Climbing Club. A bronze memorial plaque to Charles Inglis Clark hangs on the wall.

The opening ceremony was set for Monday, April 1, 1929, at 3pm, and in preparation for this the Inglis Clarks went up by pony on the Sunday. As the occupants were finishing dinner on Sunday evening, the inner door of the hut was violently thrust open and two climbers lurched in, covered in snow and near exhaustion. In a story all too familiar, it transpired that they had fallen down Gardyloo Gully, and had gone down 180m or more. After rest and refreshment they were able to continue down the hill. So even before its official opening, the CIC hut had justified its presence as an emergency shelter – given that someone is in residence.[4]

The possibility of delivering the coal by air was looked into at first, this being the age of the aeroplane, but it was quickly deemed impracticable

The opening party at the hut included the President – Col. G.T.Glover, Vice-Presidents A.E.Robertson and Harry MacRobert, past Presidents Maylard, Ling and Goggs, the first Custodian of the hut – Robert Elton, and of course the Clarks. With a healthy and typical irreverence, there had been pre-opening visitors, *'members of the baser sort'*, whose names on the first page of the Visitor's Book were pointedly ignored,

> ...in the hope that the Hon. Custodian would thereafter cut it [the page] out and consign it to the Allt a' Mhuilinn.[5]

At 2.55pm punctually the hut was emptied and the door locked. President Glover opened the proceedings with a few words about the steps leading to the building of the hut. This was followed by a prayer of Dedication by the Rev. Robertson. Dr. Inglis Clark formally presented the hut to the SMC and amid cheers and *'the ticking of amateur cinemas'*, Mrs Inglis Clark unlocked the hut. All then entered for tea – at one point nearly 100 were actually inside, a record which even subsequent University Club Meets have failed to surpass. Some 400 cups of tea were consumed. The afternoon's proceedings were followed by a Dinner in Fort William. The *'amateur cinemas'* were early models of cine camera, and in fact an original film of the opening has been saved and transferred to video and digital disk.

Fifty years on, in 1979, the CIC Hut celebrated its Jubilee. Obviously there had been changes since 1929, including the building of the annexe in 1974. Inside, the coal stove and paraffin lamps have long gone, as have the original bunks. Now the hut uses low voltage lights for lighting and gas and wind power for heating. Rebuilt sleeping accommodation (mostly under the supervision of the then custodian, Ian Clough), along the lines used in Alpine huts, allows sleeping space for 20, though now and again some unfortunate on the outside berth of a top bunk crashes to the floor or lands on top of a table while turning over in mid-sleep.

Jane Inglis Clark at the CIC Hut opening

Photo: from film taken of opening

The opening ceremony of the CIC Hut; William Inglis Clark, George T.Glover and the Rev A.E.Robertson. The day was cold and windy and one can see Clark's coat tails swirling around in the breeze. This still is from the cine film of the opening, taken by Harry MacRobert and George Sang. Clark would have been in his 72nd year

Photo: from film taken of opening

*This photograph was
captioned 'the first
occupants of the CIC
Hut', and it is
certainly taken from
the door of the Hut. It
is uncertain, however,
whether the gentle-
men shown were the
'members of the baser
sort' referred to
earlier, who had
'crashed' the hut
months before the
official opening.
(Macpherson,
C.W.Parry, P. Donald
& Hanning. 12th
November, 1928 –
Armistice Weekend)*

Photo: Percy Donald,
SMC Archives

For the Jubilee celebrations on May 12, 1979, the SMC used modern transport and engaged a helicopter to fly up several of the senior non-mountaineering guests. These included Charles F.Inglis Clark, the son of Charles Inglis Clark, and some of the Jeffrey family, related to Mabel Inglis Jeffrey, daughter of the Clarks. Robert Elton, the first custodian, was also present. A plaque was unveiled by Mr Clark, between 60 and 70 visitors being present, despite poor weather. Echoing proceedings in 1929, a Dinner in Fort William followed the opening.[6]

As with any other hut privately built, owned and run, the CIC Hut has come in for its share of abuse over the years; both verbal and physical. The hut was originally built for the use of the SMC and their guests. This was fine when climbers were much fewer in number and perhaps less aggressive in character than now. With an annual usage upwards of 2,000 bed nights, it is now difficult for non-members to gain winter access without booking well in advance. To be as fair as possible, bookings with the custodian are not accepted more than a year in advance. The CIC Hut is available to members of any mountaineering club, booked through that club's secretary.

On a busy day on Nevis at the peak of the winter climbing season, several hundred climbers may pass the hut, many with expectations of being able to use its facilities as a casual shelter, patently a demand impossible to accept. Additionally, there is the sad fact of a tiny criminal element who now roam the hills with an eye to stealing any valuable equipment left unattended. Ironically, one victim who lost a rope from the unlocked hut had been an advocate of the *open hut philosophy*. Any genuinely needy persons, of course, can expect help from the hut's occupants, who, it should be remembered, are climbers themselves, and who, being in the *front line*, have on very many occasions effected rescues from the hut. A stretcher is kept in an unlocked annexe along with the police radio for just such events.

During the 1990s, it became necessary to improve the CIC Hut and its immediate environment. Toilet facilities had been lacking for decades, the red propane gas cylinders stored outside the hut were an eyesore, and replacing them, even every two years, was expensive. Alternative sources of energy were researched, including hydropower, solar energy, and wind power. The first was rejected for several reasons; it would have been expensive, and flash floods bringing down boulders would have been a problem. In winter, freezing conditions would drastically reduce water flow in the burn. It would also have added visible works. Solar energy was a virtual non-starter, given the limited amount of sunshine the Ben enjoys. That left wind power.

The small brick annexe, containing the rescue equipment, has on its roof a 75-watt wind generator. This charges the radio battery and also runs two low-voltage lights in the hut. (Incidentally, the brick annexe appeared overnight, with no warning, coming as a surprise to the SMC. Permission would not have been a problem, and might have resulted in something easier on the eye, however, this is not so much water under the bridge, as wind over the hut.)

The SMC, after much research, found that a robust wind generator of turbine type (i.e. it does not require a steering vane) was manufactured in Scotland. This is the Proven WT2.5 of 2.5Kw power rating. This

Work in progress on the upgrading of the CIC Hut during summer 2008

Photo: Noel Williams

has three flexible polypropylene blades which continue to deliver power at high wind speeds, unlike the auto-steering types which drop power drastically when they yaw out at high wind speeds. The turbine is mounted on a 6.5m column and the blade diameter gives an overall maximum height of 8.25m. At a cost of about £8,000 (£3,200 per Kw), this has the lowest capital/power ratio of any of the renewable energy sources.

A number of these generators have been installed in remote locations in Scotland (e.g. Corrour railway station, Glen Affric Youth Hostel) and others are used for domestic supplies (e.g. Lealt on Jura). They are also widely used by the Irish Lighthouses Board. The power available from such an installation would give reliable supplies for the radio, lights, the auxiliary heater for a proposed composting toilet and would also power up to an additional 2Kw of space heating when the batteries were fully charged. While most of the environmental impact around the hut is caused by day visitors to the mountain, at least the SMC was working towards reducing the hut's *footprint*.

A mock up of the turbine was made, erecting a *flagpole*, and after some digital photography editing, photographs showing the hut before and after the installation of just such a turbine were published on the club web site, and public consultation was invited. There was one objection to the turbine from a member of the public. There was probably more resistance to the plan from members within the SMC, but after several interesting meetings, the plan was accepted and the turbine put in place. Its installation has enabled the SMC to reduce the number of gas cylinders (they are still required for cooking), which have also been placed in a wood-lined pit dug close to the hut so as to further reduce their visual impact. Gas cylinders will now be replaced by helicopter, in smaller numbers, on an annual basis. A new annexe, containing internal hut toilets and updatedcooking and dining facilities, began construction in 2008.

The upgrading of the CIC Hut, finished during the spring of 2009, was the most radical since its creation in 1929. The fabric of the hut was showing its age, and an increasing awareness of the need to protect the environment both conspired to force the issue. Hut toilets are self-composting, obviating the necessity of a trudge across the moor wielding

A montage of the CIC Hut interior, shortly after completion. Made from two photographs, even allowing for unavoidable distortion of perspective it gives some indication of what it would have looked like during the 1930s, with a large coal-fired stove taking pride of place. The unpainted wood would have meant a dark interior. Facing south-east, door to the right

Original Photos:
A.E.Robertson,
Montage: Ken Crocket

a pickaxe. Regrettably, these cannot be open to the public, as there is no permanent hut guardian. This opportunity was not used to significantly increase the number of bed spaces; rather, it has reduced the internal squalor found throughout the winter seasons. As all hut users are obliged to carry down their own refuse following a stay, the onus is now on non-hut users to demonstrate a knowledge of environmental awareness and so help keep the mountain clean.

Members of the SMC work hard on several work parties every year, as do other clubs on their own huts. The CIC Hut suffers because of its isolated, and valued position. However, most contemporary climbing on Nevis is done by day visitors who walk up from the road, and when one reads some entries in the CIC Log Book, it is debatable whether on some occasions the hut has been an advantage or a liability.

> 24th November, 1973. People without the key arrived at 3.15am after a really foul walk-in...found hut locked and empty. Party of seven spent night in radio shack. Party with key failed to find hut...spent night on some God-forsaken scree slope in poly bag (100 yards from hut).

> Dec. 1973. We hereby claim a record. Distillery to CIC in 22 hours – one bivouac.

This last unfortunate, indeed, could not find the hut during his second day's wanderings in the Allt a' Mhuilinn glen, and was about to settle down for a second bivouac when he was found by another party going up to the hut.[7]

The opening of the CIC Hut in 1929 acted as a powerful stimulus to exploration on Nevis. The increasing numbers of younger, active and less wealthy mountaineers had little in common with their elders; many of them simply could not afford the cost of hotels. Hotels in any case were less enthusiastic, and less well staffed after the 1914 – 1918 War, with the days of the *call at 5.30 for breakfast at 6* fast disappearing.

In July 1924, R.N.Rutherford, Archie Hutchison and Arthur Rusk, all SMC members, enjoyed a climbing holiday in the Bernese Oberland. Rusk told the others of his idea for a new mountaineering club – one in which younger, inexperienced climbers could learn the basics of mountaineering with kindred spirits. The SMC at this juncture was, to be brutally honest, in some danger of becoming a fossil institution; the

The SMC at this juncture [1924] was, to be brutally honest, in some danger of becoming a fossil institution; the 1914 – 1918 War, a generation gap, and the SMC's self-limiting qualification rules, modest though they were, all conspired to prevent a necessary growth in membership

1914 – 1918 War, a generation gap, and the SMC's self-limiting qualification rules, modest though they were, had all conspired to prevent
a necessary growth in membership.

In 1924 the three main Scottish clubs were the SMC, the Cairngorm
Club, and the Ladies Scottish Climbing Club. The SMC held two meets
a year, based at hotels, and had no indoor meets other than its Annual
Dinner. There were no slide shows or other informal meetings outside
these venues, at which information and advice could be gleaned, and
partnerships struck up. The growing number of new climbers were
becoming increasingly frustrated. In essence, the SMC had regressed
since the War.

During a stormbound day in the Mutthorn Hut in the Lauterbrun-
nen Valley, the three climbers mentioned above worked out a
constitution and penned a name for the new club – The Junior Mountaineering Club of Scotland. The first meet of the JMCS was held at the
Narnain Boulder below The Cobbler, Arrochar. The weather was bad,
and Rusk was still in his sleeping bag under the boulder when the first
section of the Club, the Glasgow section, was officially inaugurated.
There were 13 present; five of whom were already members of the SMC.
Shortly after, the Edinburgh section was begun.[9].

Qualifications for entry to the JMCS were refreshingly minimal; one
had to be at least 17 years of age. The constitution further stated that
its intentions were to provide a training ground for men taking up mountaineering and a source of new members for the SMC. Within ten years
the Glasgow section alone numbered 72; in later years it would grow
to over 200. During these ten years, its members helped to re-establish
rock climbing standards; meanwhile winter climbing, all but neglected
since the First World War, was about to recommence, thanks to inspiring examples from a handful of SMC members.

A now classic article exists describing the early JMCS Bus Meets. This

*A helicopter gas-
lift at the CIC Hut
June 1985. The
daring panache of
the climber is hair-
raising, while the
skill of the pilot was
a must. (SMC
member Iain Hyslop)*

Photo: Ken Crocket

was written anonymously in the form of a letter to the Editor of the SMC Journal. The letter describes in hilarious and obviously scathingly accurate detail many of the characters and activities of the 1950s – but the atmosphere was little different then from what it was in the early days and a few short excerpts will paint the picture.

> Youth Hostels we never liked much; they were like trains but slower and wanted their wardens sweeping out. Ritchie's loud genealogical salute to the four-eyed one at Crianlarich who liked dancing still warms up Old Men...Marshall was there, a wee laddie and polite; Haig, Hood, Cole, Rodgie, Scott, Millar, Bulbous and more, sundry musicians on mouth-organs, combs, jugs and alimentary tracts, a varied horde, and when all these were emptied on to a stricken land-scape together they drained into the night at once, like swill down a gutter, tentless ones trotting helpful and effusive and friendly, gloomy grubhunters like Dutton furtive behind, undeterred by stones; these parasites, clutching dogsbowls for alms, wandered from tent to tent suitably undernourished, then crawled into dubious heaps of their own for the night. And all this time the driver was backing his 32 seats alone in the dark down a 10 ft. Highland water-way with no lights and 32 dead lemonade bottles clanking behind him.[10]

The JMCS was not the only club to be formed during this period of social change, though as regards climbing on Nevis its influence was initially to be the most important. Between 1920 and 1933 at least six other Scottish clubs were formed: Dundee University Rucksack Club (1923); the Grampian Club (1927); the Ptarmigan Club (1929); the Tricouni M.C. (1930); the Creagh Dhu Club (1930); the Lomond M.C. (1933). These were to be followed shortly by several University clubs, whose more liberal outlook allowed women easier access to the hills.

There was now a hut on Ben Nevis, and new clubs with young, enthu-siastic climbers. Conditions were suitable, given a catalyst, for the next wave of exploration on the mountain.

References

1. Proceedings of the Club, *Easter Meet, 1925 – Fort William*. SMCJ 17, 206 – 214, 1925.

2. **Mackay**, Lord, *Vignettes of Earlier Climbers*. SMCJ 24, 169 – 180, 1950.

3. **Maylard**, A. Ernest, *The Club In Retrospect I. – Its Origins and Growth*. SMCJ 22, 6 – 13, 1939.

4. **Clark**, W.I., *The Charles Inglis Clark Memorial Hut*. SMCJ 18, 325 – 335, 1929.

5. Proceedings of the Club. *The Official Opening of the Charles Inglis Clark Memorial Hut*. SMCJ 18, 365 – 369, 1929.

6. **Richardson**, R.T., *The C.I.C. Hut – Jubilee Celebrations*. SMCJ 31, 342 – 344, 1979.

7. *C.I.C. Log Book*, Vol.5, 1971 – 1980. NLS.

8. **Rutherford**, R.N., *Five Nights in the Scottish Hut*. SMCJ 17, 117 – 122, 1925.

9. **Hutchison**, A.G., *The Formation of the JMCS (i) The Beginning of the JMCS*. SMCJ 30, 309 – 310, 1975.

10. **Anon.**, *Those J.M.C.S. Bus Meets*. Letters to the Editor. SMCJ 27, 153 – 156, 1961.

CIC Hut and Càrn Dearg Buttress. This recent shot shows the wind turbine uphill of the hut and a re-located, sunken storage area for gas cylinders, to help reduce their visual impact

Photo: Cubby Images

*Bill MacKenzie,
Archie MacAlpine
and Bill Murray after
the third ascent of
Rubicon Wall
(Severe), August 1,
1937. Murray
declared later that it
was the hardest rock
climb he knew on
Nevis*

Photo: Douglas Scott

6: The 1930s (1930 – 1939)

THE 1920S IN SCOTLAND found the hills at their quietest and mountaineering on them at a low ebb; the 1914 – 1918 War had caused many
changes. But a new regime was about to emerge, not from the SMC,
though it was to provide some leadership, but from a host of new and
energetic young club members –

> ...those vagrant hordes unwashed, unshaven and chip-eating, sleepers in
> howffs and travellers in fish-lorries, those who – in their unselfconscious days
> – are the salt of the sport.[1]

They were to play a major role in the coming revolution in Scottish
mountaineering. If those 'vagrant hordes', mostly belonging to the fast-
expanding ranks of the JMCS, were the foot-soldiers of the revolution
(at least as regards Nevis), then the SMC provided two senior generals in
the shapes of Bell and Macphee. These two were very different characters, and of great influence in the exploration of Nevis during the 1930s.

James Horst Brunnemann Bell (1896 – 1975) was born in Auchter-
muchty, Fife. The son of a Scottish minister and a German mother, he
began his mountain adventures when he was about 14, setting out for
the hills by bicycle with his sister Ilse. He walked up Nevis when he
was 16, having cycled the 75km from Newtonmore in the teeth of a
gale. This was in 1913, when the summit hotel was still open and one
shilling (five pence) was charged for the use of the track. Bell joined
the SMC in 1922, and his steady development as a mountaineer, both
in the Alps and at home, was to establish him finally as one of the most
able and influential of Scottish mountaineers between 1930 and 1950.

By profession he was an industrial chemist specialising in papermak-
ing, gaining a D.Sc. from Edinburgh in 1932. Like most of the employed
in the 1930s, he usually had to work on Saturdays, and had only a few

week's annual leave, and yet his output of routes was steady for 20 years or so, apart from three war years. Not only did he inspire young climbers by example, he made a point of finding and climbing with the most active of those around, male or female, his generosity of mind and spirit encompassing all.

His well-documented enthusiasm, or at least tolerance of bad rock, *'any fool can climb good rock. It takes craft and cunning to get up vegetatious schist and granite'*, led to some routes which are now rarely climbed, such as Hesperides Ledge on The Comb.

> It is a steeply inclined, curving shelf and is a perfect garden of mossy and lush vegetation...there are several exceedingly delicate corners to negotiate with a most precipitous drop on the right. The vegetation is loosely anchored, the rocks are rather loose, and there are practically no positive holds...

In this description by Bell, the obvious enthusiasm rings through loudly. Alex Small later recalled how,

> ...often in the company of Sandy Wedderburn we would, after attending a concert by the Scottish Orchestra, compress ourselves into the redoubtable Austin Seven and head out for Glen Coe, Jim driving with his legs wrapped in a travelling rug against the cold and invariably taking his logically direct route over the Anniesland roundabout, discoursing the while, – Marx, dialectical materialism, Engels, Russell, Mozart, the Aonach Dubh buttresses, handmade pitons, Forfar bridies, civil rights, Cambridge, and more supporting proof of his theory that there had to be three concurrent factors to induce a major accident. Kingshouse would appear out of the dark; and stiffly we entered.[2]

Bell's most significant new routes on Ben Nevis were to be the series of seven routes on the west face of the North-East Buttress. These lay below and above the Basin, midway between Zero and Minus One Gullies. Their pattern, when traced out, led the cliff to be named the Orion Face, after the winter constellation in northern skies. As the editor of the SMC Journal for a record 24 years (1936 – 1959), he was influential in a wider sense. W.H.Murray wrote of this aspect,

> His editorship of the Journal coincided most fortunately with a period of revolution in Scotland. He made the various new climbing forces known to each other, and linked them by airing their ideas. He kept all abreast of events, at the time presenting articles that related Scottish conditions and practice to those of the world's greatest ranges. In short, he tried to keep us all in balance, and succeeded.[3]

Of very different appearance to Bell was George Graham Macphee (1898 – 1963). Born and educated in Glasgow, Macphee graduated in Medicine then moved to Dentistry. Settling finally in Liverpool he had two lucrative private practices and a University post. As President of the University Club, Macphee was conscientious, helping young climbers find their feet in the sport. Where Bell was small and sturdy, with a broad Fife accent, Macphee was big and broad. Bell's lack of concern over his weekend dress was obvious, whereas Macphee took more care. Macphee was a somewhat reticent man; when he did speak it was slowly and quietly, with, as his daughter Hermione recalled, *'an enchanting Scottish burr'*.[4] In the Lake District he made the first descent of Moss Ghyll

...those vagrant hordes unwashed, unshaven and chip-eating, sleepers in howffs and travellers in fish-lorries, those who – in their unselfconscious days – are the salt of the sport

A key figure in the history of Ben Nevis, George Graham Macphee was one of a handful of climbers who helped restore Scottish winter climbing to its former heights. His first ascent of Glover's Chimney was to be particularly important. He was the author of the Ben Nevis Climbers' Guide in 1936 and 1954 (February 1956)

Photo: Douglas Scott

Grooves, ostensibly so as to be able to write in the hut book, *M.G.G.G.G.M.*

A very real antipathy arose between the two, a situation not unknown in a sport which has its fair share of strong personalities. Apparently, this situation began during a visit to the Alps, when Bell, Frank Smythe, Macphee and a fourth set out to do a route. It seems that the fourth man, who was climbing with Macphee, dropped his axe and was obliged to retreat. Macphee should have gone down with him but instead left it to Bell. On Nevis in particular a great rivalry existed between them; they climbed together at least once there but thereafter they had to go their own ways. Occasionally this rivalry spilled over on to the pages of the CIC Hut Log Book, as the following exchange of entries indicate.

> April 14th, 1938. G. Graham Macphee. Arrived from Liverpool (Glasgow-Fort William 2 hrs 29 mins) Left Hut 4.30 p.m. Up Tower Gully, Down No.3 Gully.

> This book is for *climbs* – Time of reaching first hairpin, first bog – time taken to boil kettle etc are equally irrelevant!

> April 6th, 1939. G. Graham Macphee. Arrived from Liverpool; Glasgow-Fort William 2 hrs 28 and a half minutes.[5]

On New Year's Day, 1929, Bell made a solo first ascent of Number Four Gully Buttress (II), on easy ground just right of Number Four Gully. Though not in itself a particularly worthy route, it was the first new route on the Ben since Pigott's visit in 1921. The route was recorded as having been climbed in company with Robert Elton, first custodian of the CIC Hut, but Bell's personal logbook makes it quite clear that Elton had gone down the hill, leaving Bell to solo the route. Four other first ascents followed that year; one by Bell, a Very Difficult variation on the north face of the Great Tower.

In 1931 Macphee, who had first reached the summit of Nevis at the tender age of eight, returned as a climber to spend a June holiday in the CIC Hut, along with his guests A.T.Hargreaves and H.V.Hughes, both excellent climbers in the Fell & Rock C.C. Hargreaves especially was an active climber on gritstone and sandstone outcrops, and was to write the 1936 Climbing Guide to Scafell. In 1930 Hargreaves and Macphee had climbed The Crack on Deer Bield Crag in the Lake District, origi-nally graded at Severe, later upgraded to HVS (and considered by many to be E1, and a route capable of defeating strong parties. (In 1997, the route suffered a major rockfall. After a period allowing the buttress to stabilise, a new climb at XS was made in 2005.) Hargreaves had a repu-tation of being an impatient man, probably born of a desire to fill every available minute of the day on the hills. His idea of a day's climbing was an early walk to the crags, a good day on the rocks, and a good walk home – whatever the weather.

On June 14 the three climbers were joined by Mrs Mabel Inglis Jeffrey, the daughter of William Inglis Clark, for a wet and miserable ascent of the Douglas Boulder Direct. Two days later Hargreaves, Hughes and Macphee made the second ascent of a direct variation to Observatory Ridge. This had first been done in August 1930, by George C. Williams, J.Logan Aikman, A.R.Lillie and A.N.Rutherford. The first ascent party had needed to use combined tactics and considered the climb a magnif-icent expedition at a grade of Severe. Macphee's party recorded their ascent with the short comment that *'combined tactics were not employed'*.

From the hut door however, they had spotted an unclimbed line on the Great Buttress of Càrn Dearg. This magnificent 180m buttress presents rock architecture on a scale almost unequalled in Britain; its great series of overlapping slabs, steep corners and chimneys offer many of the longest and finest routes in the country. By 1931 no route had attacked the steep face of the buttress, though several had taken the easier, broken rocks on its northern flanks. On the left flank of Càrn Dearg Buttress, as it is now called, Macphee's party noticed a smaller, curving buttress, up which Hargreaves forced a route.

The rocks were wet from morning rain, and vegetation gave the pioneers some extra work. The crux on the day was an exposed slab just over halfway up the route. Small holds on the slab had to be dug out from beneath turf and slimy earth moistened by incessant drips from the overhanging right wall. This pitch gave the party no little difficulty. But the buttress had been breached, even if by a flanking route. The route was finished in rain, snow and mist, and when the trio arrived at the top of Number Three Gully, then a favourite descent route, it looked too fearsome to tackle without axes. They then made a long trudge over the summit and back to the hut via the Càrn Mòr Dearg arete. This probably pleased Macphee, as one more ascent to add to the tally he kept of summit visits to Nevis throughout his climbing career.

To this date many new climbs had been named after the leader. Fashions were changing however, and Hargreaves gave this route the logical if dull name of Route I. The grade was Severe and the date was June 17. The current climbers' guide to Ben Nevis introduces this climb thus –

Colin Stead on Observatory Ridge (Very Difficult), (1980)

Photo: Ken Crocket

> One of the finest chimney climbs on Ben Nevis, calling for determined use of an armoury of bridging and back and foot techniques, with the crux right at the top.[6]

The following day it rained heavily and they rested, *'and even Hargreaves was quite resigned to a day's inactivity'*.[5]. The next day, having read in the Climbs Book of an attempt on Observatory Buttress by Williams and Aikman in September 1930, they set off to 'have a look at it'.

The climb they were to succeed on was to the left of Raeburn's Original Route and took a more direct line. The leader was again Hargreaves, and it is interesting to note that rope techniques had not changed much from the previous decade, 24m of rope for the leader, pitches no more than 18m in length, rope being required both for attachment round the climber's waist and for belaying. When Bill Murray began climbing in 1935, the only authority he had to go on was the General Guide published by the SMC, and a section therein by Raeburn. The article by Raeburn recommended 24m of rope between three climbers. It was immediately obvious to Murray that this was insufficient, and they began climbing using first 18m between climbers, then 24m. By 1936 they were using 30m for the leader, and 37m for the longer winter leads. During the 1930s, a gradual change was made from the full-weight hemp rope to a thinner line; 2.5cm or 3.2cm circumference (8 or 10mm diameter, similar to modern rope sizes). This permitted a longer rope to be carried and longer run-outs by the leader, especially in winter. Nailed boots were commonly used, though the use of plimsolls or rubbers

The Direct Start to Route I. Added in 1941, this offers a more delicate approach to the tough chimneys of the original route, but retains the Severe standard

Photo: Cubby Images

Raeburn's Arete (Severe) considered by Macphee to be one of the finest climbs on Ben Nevis

Photo: Cubby Images

A bowline on a bight. This knot was commonly used to tie in the middle climber on a rope of three

Source: 'Badminton Book of Mountaineering'

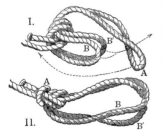

for the harder rock climbs was on the increase.

High on Observatory Buttress a snow shower halted proceedings, Macphee's party reversing a pitch to wait it out at a safe belay. After lunch the snow stopped and the route was continued. An early example of a chockstone belay, using a rock, on a Scottish climb is mentioned here, when Macphee described a *'removable chockstone found in a hole, which was used as a belay'*.

The difficulties on Route I had been graded at Severe, mainly due to the first ascent problems of vegetation and wet. Route I is still a Severe, while Macphee's Direct Route on Observatory Buttress is now a Very Difficult. Standards on Ben Nevis had not yet risen above those of Raeburn, but the whiff of exploration was in the air. On Sunday, June 20, Hargreaves had to leave, but first they rose early and made an ascent of Raeburn's Arete. This was probably the third or fourth ascent, and certainly a very early one, Macphee finding the route to be one of the best on Nevis. (Pigott & Wilding had made an ascent in September, 1921.)

> This climb must be one of the finest on Nevis. We were fortunate to get it done on the only occasion during a whole week when the weather conditions made it justifiable. The rain held off until we were past the difficult parts. Reasonably good conditions are essential. 120 feet of rope was found inadequate between 2 climbers if satisfactory belays were to be used. Shortage of rope occasioned much loss of time on the climb.[7]

In fact Hargreaves inadvertently made a variation; being forced on one pitch to make a run-out of 40m to gain a belay. There was still no use of intermediate runners for protection, though on rare occasions a leader had been known to untie and thread his end of the rope behind a chockstone, before tying on again and continuing.

The lack of an up-to-date Guide Book told on the Monday, as they made what they thought was a new route on The Comb. In fact, as they discovered later, they had followed Pigott's Route of 1921. Later that year, 1931, Macphee was given the task of editing a new edition of the Ben Nevis Guide, the current version being the 1919 revision edited by MacRobert. In writing his guidebook Macphee had taken on quite a task. He was living in Liverpool, which meant a round trip of about 1,030km, and the holiday allowance of that period was not generous. However he owned a comfortable Bentley , in which he would drive to Glasgow on a Friday evening and pick up a climbing partner, who would then drive the remaining distance to Fort William.

At this point it should be recalled that the new Glen Coe road was still four years in the future. The old road, (now followed by a section of the West Highland Way), had been made following the 1745 Rebellion, and was virtually unchanged from that period. The part over the Black Mount was particularly prone to drifting snow in winter, while the road surface was usually noticeable by its absence; potholes being numerous. Most climbers had no car; the members of the new clubs especially being unable to afford such a luxury. This, and the long working hours, or unemployment with a corresponding real poverty, helped explain the continuing domination of Nevis climbing by the SMC, JMCS, and a handful of visiting English climbers.

The rising tide of young people enjoying the countryside did not go unnoticed. At the SMC Dinner in Glasgow in 1931, the Rev. George McLeod, in an impromptu speech, told,

> ...of a rising movement in his parish of young men who had not the opportunity of the gentlemen present, but who satisfied a genuine craving for beauty by 'hiking'. This desire, he was convinced, could be extended into a proper appreciation of mountains, if guided in the proper way.[8]

The nation, of course, was then enduring an economic depression.

On September 13, 1933, Alan Hargreaves returned to make another first ascent on Observatory Buttress. Rubicon Wall, as it was named, lay on the left flank of the buttress, and we may deduce from its name that the party found it a difficult and committing climb. Hargreaves' companions were Frank and Ruth Heap. Belays were difficult to find on the climb's slabby rocks, and the party wore plimsolls due to the delicate climbing encountered. The route became known as the hardest rock climb on Ben Nevis, being graded then Very Severe. It is now a Severe.

The second ascent was probably in September 1936, by Bell, Colin Allan and E.A.M. (Sandy) Wedderburn. Bell described the climb as being sound, steep and difficult, but also recommended it highly to a strong party, noting in passing that there must be considerable scope for variations. On August 1, 1937, a strong JMCS party assembled below Observatory Buttress in a heat-wave. The climbers were Bill MacKenzie, Bill Murray, Archie MacAlpine and Douglas Scott, and they were intent on climbing Rubicon Wall. Like Hargreave's party, MacKenzie's team changed into plimsolls when the difficulty increased, stowing their heavy, nailed boots in their rucksacks. At one point the JMCS party attempted to climb more directly a short traverse which Hargreaves had been obliged to make; they failed, and MacKenzie had to retreat by abseil.

The lack of good protective equipment such as chockstones, which modern climbers take for granted, was becoming a serious limiting factor by the 1930s. Climbs such as Rubicon Wall highlighted this shortage, as MacKenzie's party found only two good natural rock belays during the entire 310m climb. But a new style of climbing was beginning to emerge; by balance and the occasional friction move, and with the ascent of Rubicon Wall by Hargreaves in 1933, standards on Ben Nevis were again on the rise.

The JMCS were active elsewhere on Nevis in 1933, as M.S.Cumming, E.J.A.Leslie and Pat Baird (JMCS and President of the Cambridge University MC) made the first ascent of Green Hollow Route, a Very Difficult line just right of Raeburn's Arete, on April 6. Baird, who died in Ottawa on New Year's Day, 1984, went on to complete 50 years' membership of the SMC. He was also one of the leaders of the winter climbing renaissance that was about to unfold in Scotland, making the first winter ascent of S.C.Gully in Glen Coe in 1934.

By 1934, Macphee was deeply engaged with research for the Ben Nevis Guide. His task could be compared to running on a treadmill, for as fast as he climbed one route, a new one would rise up to taunt him. His old rival Bell was active in this respect, though as Bell's climbing was geographically more widespread than Macphee's (who through necessity had to concentrate on Ben Nevis), the latter made more first ascents on Nevis.

A rare winter route was recorded in March 1934, when H.W.Turnbull

The lack of good protective equipment such as chockstones, which modern climbers take for granted, was becoming a serious limiting factor by the 1930s. Climbs such as Rubicon Wall highlighted this shortage, as MacKenzie's party found only two good natural rock belays during the entire 310m climb

The north-east face from Càrn Dearg Buttress to Castle Ridge. From right to left the first distinct buttress is Castle Ridge (III). Left again is the downward tapering buttress of The Castle (III), with North Castle Gully (II) to its right and South Castle Gully (II) to its left. To the left lie Raeburn's Buttres and Cousins' Buttress, then the black bulk of Càrn Dearg Buttress. This is defined on its right side by the prominent right-curving line of Waterfall Gully (IV,4)

Photo: Cubby Images

South Castle Gully (II), location of Maurice Linnell's fatal accident in 1934

Photo: John Trudgill

and J.Y.Macdonald climbed North Gully (II). This was the first route to find a way up Creag Coire na Ciste, left of Number Four Gully, and it opened the door for several other short but enjoyable winter lines. The description of the first ascent indicates the state of winter climbing in the early 1930s.

> The difficulties were encountered in the lower pitch...This pitch required a full run out of 80 feet rope up a steep ice wall, over an ice bulge at the narrowest point, & thereafter up a further steep ice wall where the gully widens. This pitch was not overcome until 2 hours had been spent in clearing loose sloshy snow (one foot thick) and in step cutting...four attempts were made on the lower slope before the bulge was reached and successfully climbed... Crampons were used by one of the party.[5]

Easter 1934 saw a fatal accident on Nevis, one which robbed Britain of one of its most promising climbers. Maurice Linnell and Colin Fletcher Kirkus left Kendal on Linnell's motor bike, just after midnight on Good Friday. They camped on the slopes of the mountain and at 8am on the Saturday, March 31, set off to climb the Castle, the slabby buttress lying between the two Castle Gullies.

At 1pm that same day, Kirkus was found wandering alone on the shoulder of the Ben. His face was badly damaged and covered in blood, but he managed to gasp out *'He's in Castle Gully. I think he's dead. He's hanging from the rope by the neck'*. The three climbers who had come upon him, Alistair Borthwick, Bill Thomson and Colin Petrie, covered Kirkus with all spare clothing, while a fourth climber descended to Fort William for medical help. Borthwick and his friends retraced Kirkus's steps, having no trouble deciding which steps to follow as bloodstains had pattered a gruesome trail from the cornice edge.

The bloodstains led to the top of the South Castle Gully, up which they could see erratic steps. For 150m the gully was bounded by the impressive walls of the Castles. It was from a point round an edge below the Castles that the steps had come. Using a 30m length of rope Borthwick was lowered over the cornice to look. He found the surface to be very dangerous – soft snow on top of ice. At the slightest touch this snow would slip away, revealing the bare ice.

It seems that Kirkus had slipped when only 60m or so from the finish of the route. Linnell was belayed 30m below on an ice axe driven into the snow. Kirkus accelerated down in a cloud of falling snow, passing Linnell. The axe snapped, Linnell was dragged from his stance and both climbers fell about 100m, falling over small rock cliffs. Somehow the rope snagged, bringing the two climbers to a halt. Kirkus hung unconscious, while Linnell, his neck broken in the fall, was dead. When Kirkus came to he dragged himself over to his friend and tried to carry him down the 45 degrees slope. When this proved impossible he tried to drag him upwards.

Finding that he was unable to move Linnell's body, Kirkus set off up the gully, bleeding badly and concussed, using a broken ice axe to cut steps. The slope steepened above to an angle of 70 degrees, blocked at the top by an overhanging cornice. Ben Nevis this Easter of 1934 was in exceptionally heavy snow condition. The cornice overhung by 90cm and was over a metre thick. Borthwick described the finish of Kirkus's ordeal.

> Three feet below it were two steps chipped in the ice. They were about 3 inches deep by 4 inches wide. On these two tiny ledges, Kirkus must have stood for close on an hour while he hacked his way through the cornice. And he did it all with only half an ice axe...Kirkus' climb is one of the finest mountaineering feats I know.[9]

More climbers were enlisted into the rescue effort, Kirkus being put into the small tent he had shared with Linnell for one night. Over a dozen mountaineers eventually gathered at the cornice edge. Four of the most experienced were lowered on 150m of rope, tied together from several climbing lengths. They cut their way down the other Castle Gully, finding that the gully Kirkus had climbed was too dangerous. At 8pm the four had run out all the rope and were still 90m short of Linnell. His body lay at the same level but separating them were 90m of icy slope. The four unroped and began cutting their way across. After 45m however, clouds obscured the moon, making their already dangerous task virtually impossible. They then descended to the CIC Hut using two torches, reaching that haven at midnight.

The next morning a party from the Hut cut their way up to Linnell. He was, as they feared, dead. They brought him down, a party of 30 taking turns to carry the stretcher. Kirkus himself had endured the often bumpy descent without a murmur.

Kirkus recovered and climbed again, later writing an instructional climbing book. He was never to regain his full powers as a climber however. He was killed in action during the Second World War, flying over Germany. Linnell is buried in the small graveyard in Glen Nevis. Their accident is only one of a series of fatal episodes in this area of Ben Nevis, parties being avalanched either while approaching or while climbing The Castle or the Castle Gullies. The slabby rocks hereabouts can only just hold snow, an avalanche being easily triggered by the

Colin Kirkus (c. 1932 – 33). Kirkus survived a serious accident in which Linnell was killed, only to die in action during World War II

Photo: Bâton Wicks Archives

Maurice Linnell's grave in Glen Nevis

Photo: Noel Williams

Near the top of Slav Route (Severe), with the CIC Hut and the start of Tower Ridge below (1985)

Photo: Peter Hodgkiss

In the various articles which have been written about her climbs she has been likened – or rather her method of climbing has – to a squirrel and to a spider. Clad as she was in someone else's trousers, her movements were as striking as they were skilled....

unwary or unlucky climber. Borthwick made the following comment on the accident.

> The outside risk in this case was soft snow on top of ice. The snow had a hard crust on it. Even to the expert eye it looked as it would hold. It did not. It gave when weight was put on it.[9]

In September of that year, two visiting Yugoslavian climbers were introduced to Sandy Wedderburn, who arranged to accompany them on some climbs. The visitors were Edo Derzaj and Marko Debelak, and as they were accustomed to climbing on the steep limestone of the Eastern Alps, they accepted the use of pegs for protection and belays as being normal. Wedderburn approached Bell and asked him to suggest a line, as *'none of the known routes were difficult enough to give them a due impression of the majesty of the Ben'*.[10] Zero Gully was suggested, but on arriving at its foot on September 16, it was neither dry nor filled with snow, so they took to the rocks on the left.

Wedderburn described the first ascent of what was to be called Slav Route, made on September 16.

> The fun began at once. After a lead out of over 50 feet up a delicate slab the rock provided no belay. A sound as of hammering came from above, but...I held my peace. Then Marko climbed the pitch. In the various articles which have been written about her climbs she has been likened – or rather her method of climbing has – to a squirrel and to a spider. Clad as she was in someone else's trousers, her movements were as striking as they were skilled....

After a further two pitches the rain started and the fourth pitch, an easy chimney ending at an overhang with no belay, demanded another peg. Starting up the fifth pitch heavy rain began washing rocks down on the unprotected climbers, who were forced to retreat some distance to find shelter.

> At last the rain slackened and the eye of faith was able to discern a diminution in the water supply. The pitch above was climbed again. 'What would you like most now?' Edo called down. I shivered: 'A hot bath.' 'All right.' A movement to the right, and before I could even pull at the rope Edo was plunging through a large waterfall which joined the main gully just below.

The climbing after the waterfall was interesting but not difficult, and the three soon reached the summit to meet up with Bell. Slav Route, at 420m, is now graded Severe. Wedderburn was well aware of the then current antagonism against pegs, a feeling echoed by later generations.

> On our first pitch we had a choice of three courses: we could have descended and abandoned our route; we could have continued up the difficult and unknown rock without any belay for the second man; we could drive in a piton to be used as a belay. One must distinguish between two entirely separate ways of using pitons: as direct aids to climbing...or as safeguards where the natural rock provides no belay...I have been able to satisfy myself that the use of pitons...purely to safeguard, is, on new climbs at least, unexceptionable.[10]

As for Jim Bell, he was delighted that the party had used pegs – probably because he knew that it would annoy Macphee. The second ascent, under mixed conditions, was that by Bell and Colin Allan on April 5, 1936. (See later this chapter.) The summer ended with an ascent of Platforms Rib by Bell, Allan and M.B.Stewart on 30 September, climbing a rib on the left of Minus Three Gully.

In the early 1930s winter climbing in Scotland was still moribund. Nothing of great import had been climbed in the 14 years since Observatory Ridge; even that route was still awaiting a second ascent. There were tentative moves towards some of the gullies, but with rare exceptions the peak of difficulty on Nevis at this time seems to have been the short ice pitch in Gardyloo Gully. The ten winters that had followed 1920, it must be admitted, had been lean ones for snow, even had there been climbers willing and able enough to extend the known limits of difficulty. By 1935 Raeburn's thoughts and deeds had, as if with the snows, all but disappeared; dusty notes in journals held by old men, unread or misunderstood by young climbers. A demonstration of the Scottish winter potential was badly needed, and there was none better to provide it than Macphee.

He was reaching the peak of work on his Nevis guide, visiting the mountain at least monthly. Despite bad weather he was repeating old routes and putting up new ones. In March 1935 he was rewarded with better weather, staying at the CIC Hut with his frequent companions, George Williams, and Drummond Henderson (JMCS). The intention was a winter ascent of the Tower Gap West Chimney, better known as Glover's Chimney, which descends into Coire na Ciste from the Tower Gap. It was this gully that Goodeve's party had partly descended on their epic night out. The route is now graded III,4.

Macphee's party was slow to start on March 17, reaching the foot of the gully after midday. The first pitch, in typical good condition, was a steep icefall, some 35m in length and overhanging at one point. The

By 1935 Raeburn's thoughts and deeds had, as if with the snows, all but disappeared; dusty notes in journals held by old men...

*Pinnacle Buttress of
the Tower and
Glover's Chimney
leading up to Tower
Gap on Tower Ridge*

Photo: Ken Crocket

*Andy Nelson exiting
Glover's Chimney
(III,4) at Tower Gap*

Photo: Cubby Images

three climbers tied onto a 60m length of line as Macphee set off up the big pitch. Williams described the climbing later in what was to be for some an inspirational journal article.

> After a preliminary reconnaissance, Macphee started cutting up the wall. Owing to the excessive inclination of the pitch, handholds had also to be cut, and all the cutting had to be done with one hand, whilst the other preserved the balance. It was obviously extremely exhausting work, and after 40 feet or so the leader descended for a short rest.

Macphee set off again and ran out 30m of rope, at which point Williams had to unrope to give the leader more rope. After two hour's step-cutting and a 40m run-out he gained a stance and brought up the other two. They then traversed left over iced slabs to enter the gully proper, continuing up over two smaller ice-falls. Stopping for lunch, the tension was temporarily released when it was discovered that Macphee had packed away the hut firelighters in place of the sandwiches.

They continued up the gully in worsening snow conditions. Macphee had to clear away 45cm of loose snow to cut steps in the underlying ice, with the other two in the direct line of fire below. This was years before crampons became common-place of course, and although nailed boots could work well with small steps, they did need these steps. By the time Macphee reached the foot of the final chimney it was 8pm and virtually dark. He continued up the chimney, climbing a chockstone pitch which proved almost impossible.

> I could now but dimly see him as he moved slowly and steadily upwards. Now and then, when in cleaning holds of ice his ice-axe struck the bare rock, I could see sparks fly out. Above the chockstone the conditions, instead of easing off, became harder. The entire chimney was sheeted with ice and there was no place where the leader could take a proper rest, much less to which he could bring me up. It was a thrilling experience for the second and third, straining their eyes in the darkness watching the leader's figure dimly silhouetted against the sky as he got nearer to the Tower Gap. By superb climbing he reached the Gap and announced his arrival there in no uncertain manner.[12]

Ice sheeted the rocks on the last 9m of the chimney, the second and third man using a loop of rope let down by Macphee to facilitate their ascent. Even then difficulties continued, with more than a hundred steps having to be cut before the summit plateau was reached. Macphee and his two companions finished up on the plateau at 10pm, where Macphee with his characteristic thoroughness walked across to tick off another visit to the summit cairn. His companions considered that they were quite satisfied with the exertions of the day, however, and coiled the rope instead. Later that night, Macphee made an uncharacteristic confession in the Hut Log,

> Under the existing conditions, this magnificent climb was one of the most arduous & exacting expeditions the present leader has ever accomplished.[5]

Williams' article on the ascent was published in November 1935. It was the long-overdue seed crystal; from then on a growing number of climbers began to regard any route as a winter possibility, given a good coating of snow and ice. Continuously steep or overhanging ice would have to wait until new techniques and better equipment made these accessible to a greater number of climbers, but with increasing confidence a new impetus had been gained.

In April 1935 Macphee, Williams and G.F.Todd made an icy ascent on Cousins' Buttress, the rounded pinnacle just left of Raeburn's Buttress. From the description by Williams, there seems little doubt that they made the first winter ascent, in thawing conditions, of at least the lower section of the Ordinary Route. Macphee chose not to record this ascent however and it was for some years credited to C.H.C.Brunton and Jim Clarkson, on February 14, 1957. At a standard of III, the route includes a spectacular traverse over the chimney of Harrison's Climb.

1935 might safely be called '*Macphee's Year*', for he climbed no less than 11 first ascents, summer and winter. Among these were: Glover's Chimney (III,4), the unrecorded Cousins' Buttress (III), a Direct Start to the North Trident Buttress, Severe, a Very Difficult on the Central Trident Buttress (Jubilee Climb), two Very Difficults on the First Platform to the right of Raeburn's Arete (Bayonet Route and Ruddy Rocks), and a Severe on the east face of the North-East Buttress. (The Eastern Climb). Ruddy Rocks was named from the presence of some small vermilion protuberances about half-way up the climb.

On August 5, along with R.C.Frost, he made the first summer ascent of Gardyloo Gully. In his guidebook to Ben Nevis[13], published in 1936, he wrote that it was one of the hardest rock climbs on Ben Nevis, and graded it at Very Severe. Interestingly, he also stated that Raeburn had prospected the upper rock pitch in summer, and '*considered that the prospect of ascending it when free from snow was slender*'. Near the overhang pitch, Macphee came across a narrow stratum of soft white caseous rock, which could be broken by hand. The route is Severe, 4a in the current guide and is probably rarely climbed in summer, remaining as a popular winter route. Perhaps the greatest impact of Macphee's routes lay in their acting as an example; encouraging young climbers to follow his lead and find their own way on the under-utilised rocks and icy gullies of Ben Nevis.

Jim Bell, meanwhile, was plotting an audacious project, one that would take him five years to complete. The steepest large rock feature on Nevis is Càrn Dearg Buttress, but the largest by far and easily the longest is the west face of North-East Buttress, now known as the Orion Face. This huge slabby face overlooks Observatory Ridge, and dominates the view up the Allt a' Mhuilinn glen. Just below the centre of the face is the Basin, a depression where snow lingers late in the season, and a good landmark.

In June 1932 Bell was at the CIC Hut in poor weather with his friend Frank Smythe. They formulated a plan to make an ascent of the face, starting at the bottom right near the foot of Zero Gully and climbing to the Basin. From here, Bell was confident that he could find a finish to the plateau. Over two years passed, and in September 1934 Bell pointed Wedderburn and his two Yugoslavian guests to the general area, resulting in Slav Route. But the face was still inviolate. Wedderburn advised Bell that access to the Basin from the lower part of Slav Route looked impracticable, and in July 1935 Bell attacked the face from a point further left.

G.G.Macphee, leading the first pitch of Glover's Chimney (III,4), during the first winter ascent, March 1935

Photo: Drummond Henderson

The rock structure determined the general line of Bell's route. Seen from a distance, the face consists of huge ribs, running up and leftwards at an angle of about 20 degrees from the vertical. Bell and his companion, Miss Violet Roy of the Grampian Club, decided to follow the rib which passes to the left of the Basin. The features of the face, as Bell discovered, were seen clearly on rare occasions; either very early or late on a mid-summer's day, when the glancing rays of the sun threw up highlights and shadows.

Bell realised that plimsolls, especially the tatty, aged pair that he possessed, were of no use on the smooth, slabby ribs – socks were used instead. The two climbers found the lower section of the climb to be the hardest, with very few belays on a slabby rib of excellent rock. A little higher up difficulties eased somewhat and nailed boots were donned. From the Basin two well-defined routes seemed possible; the left and right-hand rims of the Basin, with the right appearing the more broken and the left developing into a true arete, finally terminating in a very short ridge abutting on the crest of the North-East Buttress.

Bell and Roy decided to continue up the left rib, which gave easy climbing until it steepened into an overhanging nose. To climb this on the left seemed impossible, so Bell moved rightwards on very small holds then back left and up. It had been a hard section, and to lessen the risk of Roy hurting herself in a swinging fall she climbed up more directly. Roy, who had been unhappy on the lower section using the unfamiliar technique of climbing in socks, came on the rope at one point, but this was at the last difficult part of the route and the climb was soon successfully completed. The face had been opened up, though to Bell it had many unsolved problems. (Their route was later named Variation Zeta, as part of Bell's complete ascent of The Long Climb.) Bell was still intent on climbing a direct route from the Basin to the summit of the North-East Buttress, though that particular wish had to wait until 1940 for fulfilment.

A small but interesting event occurred in 1935: on June 23, a large block in the Tower Gap which had become very unstable finally crashed down Glover's Chimney, fortunately with injuries to no one. The block had been stepped on by hundreds of climbers crossing the Gap; with its disappearance the Gap was now safer, if a little more difficult. A note in the Hut Log for June 18 by Macphee had noted its instability. On June 23 Macphee and Williams aided the erosions of time and sent the block crashing into Coire na Ciste. (Another large block departed the Gap, some time in 2000.)

The second event in 1935 was the complete absence of snow on Ben Nevis for only the second time in living memory; or at least within the memory of a deceased local resident who had been born in 1840. On September 28, Macphee visited the places on Nevis where patches of snow were usually to be found, and there were none. The one other occasion when a complete absence of snow was recorded was in 1933.

(In 2006, local guide Mick Tighe could find no snow on Ben Nevis on 13 September. Across in the east, the well-known patch of snow in the remote Garbh Choire Mòr of Braeriach had disappeared by early October. There was thus probably no snow left on any Scottish mountain in 2006. March, 2006 had been a snowy month, but the winter as a whole had less than usual snow.[13])

In 1936 Jim Bell began his 24-year reign as Editor of the SMC Journal, a position in which he had considerable influence on the course of Scottish mountaineering. It should be remembered that there were no glossy climbing magazines then in print – information was spread by word of mouth or more slowly by club journals. In the same year Bell's old rival Macphee had his Nevis Guide published, containing 110 pages of text and 35 illustrations[14] The Guide was reviewed generously by Bell, though not without one or two errors being highlighted, one of which was a premature summer ascent of Green Gully, wrongly attributed in the Guide to Bell. One other error was Macphee's description of Goodeve's Route, where in a poor diagram of the West Face of Tower Ridge he has the line continuing the traverse along Raeburn's Easy Route, and not climbing up steeper ground above as in two previous diagrams. As with most guidebooks, its compilation had promoted an increase in exploration on Nevis; admittedly much of it by Macphee.

The two great gullies which flank Observatory Ridge – Zero and Point Five – had interested Bell since 1925. They were so prone to avalanche, and so often inundated by continuous spindrift, however, that Bell doubted their feasibility, though Zero looked the more possible of the two. Its name had been suggested by Bell, who admitted that though it was not a good name, they had yet to hear of a better one. The principal gullies on Nevis were numbered, beginning with Number Five Gully on the left flank of Càrn Dearg Buttress. Moving leftwards across the NE Face of Nevis, and counting down, what is now called Tower Gully should in fact be Number One Gully. The next one on the left to be named, logically enough, was Zero Gully, running up the left side of Observatory Ridge.

Zero Gully received a partial ascent on April 5, 1936, by Bell and Colin Allan. It was a partial ascent as the gully was abandoned after 30m when they ran out of good snow, the rocks of Slav Route on the left then being followed for several pitches before re-entering the gully and cutting steps the remainder of the way. The two climbers had left the hut complete with ice axes, a couple of pitons and a hatchet. Their plan was to attempt the gully and if the lower part proved impossible, to traverse right under Observatory Ridge and attempt the gully right of that (what would become Point Five!). This second gully, Bell remarked, was shorter but looked pretty awful with a cascade of ice halfway up.

The day was a glorious one as Bell and Allan worked their way up the snow at the foot of Zero Gully. All went well up to the bergschrund below the almost vertical section of the gully. On the right side was a cascade of icicles while ahead were waterworn and frozen moss-covered slabs, quite impossible. Bell and Allan took to the rocks on the left, bypassing this section by some difficult slabby climbing. Finally they gained the easier ground in the snow-filled gully and cut steps to the summit plateau. Descending by Number Three Gully, Bell suffered what could have easily been a fatal fall.

> Then it came to me by carelessness. Allan said that I started down with a grin on my face. I myself don't remember just where it struck me that things were not just right. He said I slipped into an avalanche runnel of polished ice. In

Macphee's 1936 guide to Ben Nevis, complete with dust wrapper. Under this is the familiar red cloth cover. It was a 110 page, large format book, 218 by 146mm, and not designed for carrying in a breeches' pocket. What it did include however, were five pull-out panoramic photographs of the cliffs, assorted other summer and winter cliff photographs, one photo-diagram, five line drawings and James Shearer's 1895 drawing of the 360 degree view from the summit, in four pull-out panoramas

His [Bell's] partial ascent of Zero Gully, like all other winter climbing to this date in Scotland, had been done in nailed boots... and the lack of suitable crampons would become a barrier to further developments

any case all my efforts at braking were useless. I shot off with extreme rapidity, was flung onto my back and continued accelerating. I was past the portals of No.3 now. There was a little cleft below, an embryo bergschrund of which I struck the lower lip and was promptly tossed up into the air. Then I rattled down on to a pile of hard avalanche debris, was tossed into the air again and came down with another bump still on my back.

Bell had almost come to a halt when he began to pick up speed again. He finally came to rest about 60m above Lochan Coire na Ciste. It had been an amazing escape for Bell, who suffered only scratches and a strained ankle.

In any case Allan and I both declared that never had we enjoyed such a magnificent, hard winter climb...The old Ben is a grand opponent but even No.3 gully in such circumstances exacts respect.[15]

There is an amusing postscript to this escape, illustrating the Fife origins of Bell. The year after Bell's fall, Dick Morsley (of whom more later), had a similar unplanned and rapid descent down the gully,

...which he described in the Horse Shoe Bar [in Glasgow] with his usual exuberance. When he'd finished Jim turned to him asking 'When you slid oot on to the Lochan did ye see onything o' a wee silver watch I lost there?'[16]

Of interest are the various angles of slope in Zero Gully as measured by Bell's clinometer. The gradient of the gully for a long way above the steepest section was 55 degrees, higher up it continued at a uniform 51 degrees[17]. These figures might suggest fairly easy angles to a non-climber, but on a slope of snow and ice every angle feels steeper, with 80 degrees for example feeling vertical. The weather remained fine for a week after Bell and Allen's ascent, and on April 11 Macphee and Williams followed Bell's footsteps. Macphee made it clear in the Hut Climbs Book that he considered the ascent to have followed Slav Route for the main part.

Set out to do the climb described by Bell...We found traces of Bell's steps leading up to the highest part of the snow cone at the foot of the gully. Here the steps led on to the rocks on the left, and from Bell's description and the recent scratches on the rock it was clear that he followed the Slav Route...We saw where the footsteps re-entered the gully, after climbing the Slav Route for about 700 feet The two icefalls mentioned by Bell were surmounted just before a blizzard suddenly started to blow. In a short time new snow began to pour down the gully, and the final and fortunately now short portion was negotiated with difficulty to reach the summit at a late hour.[5]

Nailed boots in action, as they were until the 1940s. With careful placing, the nail edges allowed small holds and rugosities to be used

Photo: SMC Archives

Bell considered the ascent the hardest winter climb that he and Allan had ever done, though he admitted that it was not a 100 per cent. pure ascent. His partial ascent of Zero Gully, like all other winter climbing to this date in Scotland, had been done in nailed boots. Ten point crampons, with no front points, were available, though very rarely used. On iced rocks, nails still retained a definite advantage, allowing for delicate climbing. This often suited the terrain found, say, in the Southern Highlands and in Glen Coe, but most of the major winter climbs on Nevis contain a high proportion of snow and ice, and the lack of suitable crampons would become a barrier to further developments. The ice axe was becoming shorter, though at some 80cm long it remained heavy and clumsy, particularly for the overhead, one-armed cutting which steep bulges required. Despite this, winter climbing was slowly emerging from the dark ages.

On April 10, 1936, Macphee soloed South Gully, Creag Coire na Ciste. This very enjoyable, if short, III begins with an exposed traverse out from the foot of Number Three Gully, then climbs up steeply via a narrow gully. Macphee experienced great difficulty at the cornice. This was a bold ascent to make in 1936, given the equipment of the day. The only other routes of note in 1936 were both by Bell. The North-West Face Route on the Douglas Boulder, climbed on May 10 with W.G.McClymont, is a Difficult, with good rock and climbing. A far tougher proposition was made on September 13, when Bell was joined by Allan and Wedderburn for an ascent of Left Edge Route, a Severe on Observatory Buttress. This climb starts up the right-bounding rib of Point Five Gully.

At first the three climbers attempted the wall on the left of Point Five Gully, but it proved impossible, with holdless slabs and sections of overhanging rock. They then turned their attentions to the edge of rock at the extreme left of Observatory Buttress.

> The first 100 ft. were easy, then we roped up, Wedderburn being on the lead. There followed 60 feet of pretty severe stuff, slabby, finally trending a bit to the right to a good stance.

The whole climb was on good rock, wet in places, taking four and a half hours climbing time. The leaders, Wedderburn and Allan, thought the route Severe.

If one were to analyse ascents on Nevis in the mid-30s, the prevalence of the SMC and JMCS would continue to be apparent. The newer clubs such as the Glasgow-based Creagh Dhu, partly by choice and partly by circumstances, concentrated on hills nearer to home – the Arrochar hills and latterly Glen Coe. By 1936 the JMCS was about 200 strong and growing. For an annual fee of 7s.6d. [37p], wrote one Club historian,

> ...each member obtains the joy of attending Club Meets (often including a lift to the hills), comradeship on the hills, and, where necessary, the advice and leadership of experienced members (JMCS or SMC), two issues of the SMC Journal (which would cost 2s.6d. [12p] each if bought in a shop), the privilege of using the CIC Hut at reduced terms, the right to attend six winter lectures (with a free tea thrown in) ...

In 1936 the SMC membership numbered 303, and of 11 applications for membership, six were declined, having insufficient mountaineering qualifications. The official qualification deemed necessary then was 40 ascents with each ascent either a 3,000 foot mountain or a climb involving some little difficulty. (This was an increase over the original 1896 necessity of a minimum of 12 climbs, at least six of them in Scotland.) There were signs of friction developing between the two clubs, as the top climbers in the junior club climbed ever steeper and smoother walls while the old guard in the SMC stayed firmly and happily rooted in the past (Bell, Macphee, Williams and a handful of others excepted). The JMCS, however, were supplying the SMC with about two-thirds of their new members, and an uneasy truce ruled, one perhaps best exemplified by the following extract from the CIC Log.

Jim Bell leading the first difficult pitch in Green Gully (IV,3), during the second winter ascent in April 1937. Poking out of the top of the belayer's rucsac can be seen what are almost certainly several carpet rods, with which Bell was experimenting as protection on snow and ice pitches

Photo: J.H.B.Bell Collection

April 4th, 1937. W.M. MacKenzie, W.H. Murray, A.M. MacAlpine. Gardyloo Gully + arete to Carn Mor Dearg. The gully was found to be ridiculously easy and is not at present recommended to other than complete novices in snow-climbing.

(This party should try the climb again when there is less or, better still, no snow in the gully. GGM). (The above party has every intention of climbing the gully again under better conditions. They are not unaware that gully climbs vary enormously in winter. On 4/4/37 Gardyloo Gully was easy. WHM)[5]

Bell was again active in 1937, and on April 4 made what he assumed was the first ascent of Green Gully. Raeburn's ascent in 1908 had been overlooked or forgotten, partly due to the reticence of Raeburn himself – besides which, ran current thought, no one could possibly have climbed such a route in 1908. Bell's companions were a good team from

England. Dick Morsley, heavily bearded and the spokesman, Jack Henson, tall and quieter, and Percy Small, the expert rock climber. Bill Murray later described the breakfast scene in the CIC Hut, providing further insights into Bell's character.

> I watched Bell make breakfast for his own party. Porridge, sausage, and kippers were all stirred into the one pot. As a practical chemist, he was imbued with the truth that a meal was a fuel-intake, therefore its separation into 'courses' was an auld wife's nicety, and not for climbers. He later persuaded me to share his burnt toast, on the grounds that charcoal was a bodily need. He expounded equations of chemical change, and showed how charcoal absorbed the troublesome gases of stomach and gut, to our mutual benefit. Bell when cook could talk one into eating almost anything. But not even that toughest of characters, Dick Morsley, had a palate tough enough for Bell's porridge. After one spoonful, he strode to the door and flung his plateful out onto the snow. The hut for me was a school of further education.[18]

Bell's opinion of this breakfast was of course somewhat partisan,

> We arose at 8 a.m. & cooking commenced. Our first course was a magnificent collation of porridge, tomato soup, peas & beans. One had to acquire the taste...Sausages were partaken alongside & then smokies & finally tea, cheese etc.[15]

The four climbers were soon to need the energy devoured at breakfast, as Ben Nevis provided the climbers with a grand epic. Bell began soloing the first easy section of Green Gully. On reaching the first steep pitch they roped up.

> The pitch started from the lower right hand corner & led obliquely upwards to the left over a bulge of very hard ice which took much hard cutting to fashion steps. Twenty feet up there was a prospect of rock holds, but when I got there the first big rock came away...

Bell stayed on and finished the first pitch, bringing up Morsley to the belay. Above was another bulge of ice which Bell had to climb directly. This was dangerous as the ice was wet and none too compact. Bell found it necessary to drive in the pick of the axe well above his head, using the wooden shaft as a steadying hold. Bell continued leading above this pitch, several pitches taking them to the upper basin of the route and the second big pitch. This pitch gave the four climbers as severe a test as any they had experienced on a mountain.

> The ice wall was nearly vertical. In the right hand corner & straight up was a possibility as some rocks with tiny ledges promised a way up. But that was about vertical too at the start and the falling drops of water from the overhanging right wall fell out in a most discouraging manner. I should have realised that I was getting tired...

Bell was defeated on the steep ice and came down to discuss the situation with his friends. They decided to try the arete on the right, first Henson and then Bell failing before the best rock climber in the group, Percy Small, had a try.

> We all fixed ourselves securely with our ice axes in the somewhat loose snow & let him start. With a magnificent effort using the smallest holds he got on

I watched Bell make breakfast for his own party. Porridge, sausage, and kippers were all stirred into the one pot. As a practical chemist, he was imbued with the truth that a meal was a fuel-intake, therefore its separation into 'courses' was an auld wife's nicety, and not for climbers

to the arete & turned the corner. We cheered, but there was no heartening reply.

Small had got himself into a desperate position. Rock holds were very poor or non-existent and his balance was precarious. He decided to reverse the pitch before he became tired.

Soon he reappeared on the edge. He had to descend quickly as his strength was ebbing away. With a final warning that he might come off any minute he started to descend, imploring us for advice where to put his feet. About a quarter of the way he held on, then he came off & fell clear of rock into the gully bed. I felt a tremendous strain on my axe & it was jerked right out. But the second axe held tight & he was brought up on the snow unhurt but a little shaken. A party of two could not have taken this risk.

It was now almost 5pm with the climbers in a perilous situation. The mist had descended, shuttering them into the icy confines of the gully. The wind gusted down coldly, swirling the mist about and hurling down loose snow to fill up their hard-won steps below. The prospect of a night out was not inviting and in any case would solve nothing. There were about two hours of light remaining and a descent, sacrificing an axe as a belay above the first big pitch, would take longer than that. Even climbing the pitch above would guarantee nothing.

They finally agreed to allow Henson another attempt, this time trying the inside right route. They gave him exactly 30 minutes, by which time he must have shown reasonable grounds for ultimate success. Henson soon attacked the pitch in the corner and after a retreat for a rest got lodged on some rock footholds.

At intervals we shouted up enquiries. Henson was a tall, quiet fellow. His replies were always quiet and deliberate – 'I think it ought to go' – 'I think I can do it' – and then after a long period of hacking with little apparent progress – 'I know I can make it go!'. Morsley turned to me in triumph. 'You leave it to Henson. He doesn't say much, but he means what he says...[15]

At last Henson reached snow above and straightened up to his full height. The relieved climbers below gave out a loud cheer as he disappeared over the top of the pitch. A uniform slope of hard snow lay above, leading into the gloomy twilight. The cornice was reached and Henson took the lead again. A careful break in the last snow wall and he was on the plateau in the last glimmer of daylight. Bell said farewell to his new friends at Achintee, with mutual expressions of friendship and respect and the promise to climb together again. He had only met them two days earlier. As a footnote to this meeting, they did climb together again, meeting in Glen Coe a few months after their epic ascent of Green Gully.

One intriguing point may be spotted in the photograph taken on this ascent. Poking out of the top of the belayer's rucsac there appears to be a collection of what could be carpet rods, metal sticks which keep a carpet in place on a set of steps. Bell had carried these on steep winter routes, intending to try them out as runners in the snow or ice. Bill Murray writes of meeting Bell for an attempt on the Centre Post of Coire Ardair, on Creag Meagaidh. Bell had brought a sac full of brass curtain rods, of which he had ringed the tops and filed the bottoms. He had found that tubular pegs were better for ice.[19]

Bell's summer route of 1937 was with J.F.(*Hamish*) Hamilton, who a

Stuart Smith soloing Green Gully (IV,3). His position on the first pitch is similar to that of Bell on the previous page. Some spindrift is coming down the gully (April 1979)

Photo: Ken Crocket

Bell had brought a sac full of brass curtain rods, of which he had ringed the tops and filed the bottoms. He had found that tubular pegs were better for ice

Climbers approaching The Comb and Number Three Gully Buttress. Green Gully (IV,3) is the obvious gully separating the left-hand rock mass of The Comb from the rest of the buttress

Photo: John Trudgill

year before had led the first ascent of Agag's Groove on Glen Coe's Buachaille Etive Mòr. In the autumn of 1936 the same two had made an abortive attempt on the slabby rocks left of Point Five Gully, in bad weather. On July 11, 1937, a repeat attempt found the slabs to be too difficult, so they chose to go some distance left. The route taken followed the left edge of the slabs by an intricately weaving line round overhangs and up grooves. After climbing for a hundred metres or so, Bell and Hamilton were faced with a vertical wall, broken by a steep chimney. Bell described this difficult section.

> The entry into the chimney involved difficult progress up smooth, sloping ledges. From a niche in the chimney it was quite obvious that direct upward progress was hopeless, as the chimney was roofed by steep, holdless slabs. An escape seemed to be possible on the left, but the position was so precarious that the leader was compelled to drive in a ring-spike and pass the rope through a spring-hook before moving upwards to the left on to a small jutting corner of rock. For the next 4 feet of traverse boots and socks were removed, and a delicate friction glide on a smooth slab led to assured safety.[20]

Bell's route, now named the West Face, Upper Route, was graded at Severe. Although not of high quality, it was yet again the opening up of a new face by the old master. This face is now taken by several excellent winter routes, while the difficult slabs further right were not to be climbed until the two Marshall brothers effected a Very Severe up them in 1966.

Membership of the JMCS by 1938 had risen to almost 400, a piece of news ill-received by the SMC. Bill Murray, who was Secretary of the younger club at that time remembers having to pass on this news –

> A brass hat fixed me with a steely eye and barked, 'We don't want climbing gorillas in this club!'

Murray told this senior member of the Club why he (and others) were not particularly enthusiastic about joining the SMC. The main points of the argument by Murray and his contemporaries were the lack of

Bill Murray, who was Secretary of the younger club at that time remembers having to pass on this news –

'A brass hat fixed me with a steely eye and barked, 'We don't want climbing gorillas in this club!'

Comb Gully (IV,4) with heavy snow cover. The crux section is just above the start of the narrowing, while Tower Finish to The Comb, Left Flank (IV,4), climbs the prominent tower high above and to the right

Photo: Brian Findlay

monthly meets and indoor meets such as slide shows. However a possibly awkward situation between the two clubs was soon to be averted, with the onset of another World War in a year's time. Since then, relations between the clubs have been amicable.

The different generations of climbers were also going their own way as regards equipment. In a 1936 article on Snow and Ice, Macphee advised that the modern tendency to have a very short ice axe was, like many modern tendencies, carried to absurd extremes. *'A shaft about the length of an ordinary walking-stick is probably best'*, he wrote, though he did recommend longer ropes, moving away at last from the 24m length of Raeburn's time.[21]

Meanwhile, Douglas Scott in 1936 had a very short axe made for him by a blacksmith. This short axe facilitated the third winter ascent of Crowberry Gully that same year (Raeburn, of course, had made the first ascent, while Bill MacKenzie, using a long axe, had made the second a week before Scott). On hearing of Scott's axe, Murray immediately went to an ironmonger's shop and bought a 36cm slater's hammer. With its side-claw removed, this ultra-short ice tool allowed steep pitches to be cut with greater ease, reducing route times dramatically. Tricouni-nailed boots were still worn, however.

Learning from a hard lesson on the Buachaille at the end of 1936, Murray and his friends also took to carrying battery head-torches, to enable them to climb up or down after dark and reduce the fear of benightment. Archie MacAlpine, who was a dentist, used a dental head-torch to great effect. This ability was soon to be needed when, in February 1938, the second winter ascent of Observatory Ridge was made.

When MacKenzie, Murray and MacAlpine stepped on to the start of Observatory Ridge at 9.30am, they soon discovered that conditions were not good; 5cm of wind-slab covering sugar-like snow. The steep, bottom section of the ridge took more than four hours, with even worse snow and the most dangerous section of the day's climbing. Finally, Zero Gully was gained, only to find loose snow covering hard ice. By now it was dark, head-torches were donned and steps were cut all the way. Fortunately the weather was good, with a star-studded sky above as the party thankfully gained the plateau and hurried to shelter in the old Observatory. It was just before midnight, 14 hours from the start, and 18 years after Raeburn's ascent.[22]

The winter discovery of 1938 was Comb Gully, running up the left flank of The Comb. This fell to a strong party from England, F.Gardner Stangle, Dick Morsley and Percy Small, the latter two having been on the second ascent of Green Gully with Bell the previous year. On April 12 they headed towards Comb Gully, with the climbers' familiar intention of *having a look at it*. Stangle was to be the acknowledged leader of what was probably the hardest gully at that time on Nevis, Green Gully being the only other contender. Owing to a period of very mild weather and a wet March, the gully contained much ice and little snow. Normally a section of steep snow leads up towards a rock outcrop, where the gully narrows and becomes more chimney-like. Typical of Nevis, it is difficult to find a good rock belay here, as hopeful-looking cracks turn out to be disappointing. On the first ascent Stangle found the short length of his modified slater's hammer invaluable on the steep ice and

Bill Murray at home on Loch Goil. His modified slater's pick allowed harder and steeper ice to be climbed in the 1930s (1990)

Photo: Ken Crocket

he used the pick of this tool on all the ice pitches. The ice cave at the foot of the crux ice pitch was eventually gained, and again no rock belay was found, but as the snow was good and hard an axe belay was taken. Stangle set off up the ice.

> The gully now curled to the right…Water falling over a chockstone had frozen into a solid column for 20 feet, the upper reaches of which had partially thawed suggesting a stance under the chockstone. There was no possible way of continuing save up this pillar. After much cutting, hand-holds were made through the column and after several descents for rest, the diminishing thickness of the ice contained natural holds less satisfying. The lip made a good stance and much demolition of icicles hanging from the rock roof revealed a thread belay. A lot of ice had to be removed before a landing on the right wall could be effected. This was disconcertingly free from ice or footholds.[23]

The crux ice pitch leads on to steep snow, with perhaps a tiny bulge to overcome before the final snow slope. The climb had taken Stangle and his rope over eight hours, most of which had been spent on the ice pitches. Today, Comb Gully is a fine and justly popular route, a IV,4 route of 125m. Its companion gully on the other side of the Comb, Green Gully, is 180m and a IV,3. Comb Gully will often provide a steeper crux section and perhaps more technical climbing, while Green Gully is usually more sustained. But to directly compare two such good routes is a fruitless exercise.

The summer of 1938 produced several rock climbs. Two were on the First Platform and other than a few remaining variations they completed the obvious routes on this face of the North-East Buttress. The first of these was by Leslie and Baird on June 19. Lying between Newbigging's 80-Minute Route and Raeburn's Arete, this new Severe was christened with the clumsy title of Newbigging's 80-Minute Route (Right-Hand Variation). Three weeks later, four members of the Ladies Scottish Climbing Club arrived to tackle Raeburn's Arete. Nancy Ridyard and Annette Smith

The final section of Good Friday Climb (III). (December 1984). Climbers Bob Richardson and Alastair Walker

Photo: Ken Crocket

formed the first rope, with Nancy Forsyth and Janet Smith as the second.

The four ladies started about 9m too far to the left; a fortuitous mistake, as they ended up doing a fine, independent line. Their Severe route followed grooves parallel to Raeburn's Arete and finished close to the original line of Newbigging, thereby being tagged with the name of Newbigging's 80-Minute Route (Far Right Variation). (Sadly, Forsyth, an excellent climber, was to be killed six years later elsewhere on the mountain.)

Baird and Leslie found another route in June, 1938, with the pleasant 90m Baird's Buttress, Very Difficult, just left of Raeburn's Buttress. The last route to be recorded in 1938 was a short Difficult in June, by a team who had figured prominently during this period – Leslie, Murray, Wedderburn and Bell. Their route, the North-West Face, lay on the right-hand side of Observatory Buttress.

Meanwhile, Macphee had finished his Nevis Guide in 1936, and perhaps understandably had reduced the frequency of his tedious 1,030km drives from Liverpool. But he returned to make one more ascent before war broke out in 1939. On April 7, 1939, Good Friday, Macphee and three others traversed left from the foot of Gardyloo Buttress under the steep rocks of Indicator Wall. This compact face – the highest on Nevis, and consequently in Britain, is named after a viewpoint indicator which the SMC erected on the plateau above, in 1927. (The indicator was destroyed by vandals in 1942.)

Macphee, R.W.Lovel, H.R.Shepherd and D.Edwards completed their exposed traverse and reached the end of Indicator Wall, where a gully leads upwards. This gully gave what Macphee described as *'a magnificent climb'*, a 150m III, and often a fairly hard one at that, depending, as always, on the conditions prevailing. The traverse out from Observatory Gully to gain the foot of the climb is exciting in poor conditions, while the climb itself – Good Friday Climb – is a short but interesting route, twisting up a series of short gullies and through rocky steps to gain the plateau. The best belay at the top is often the summit trig point, as the climb finishes opposite the highest point in the land.

With the winter ascent of Good Friday Climb, the inter-war exploration of Ben Nevis was at an end. Unlike the First World War however, climbing did not come to such a grinding halt, but continued, albeit at a reduced level, throughout most of the war years. The leaders were to be Jim Bell and G.G.Macphee as before, with the addition of a new name on Nevis – Brian Kellett.

References

1. **Dutton**, G.J., *J.H.B. Bell as Editor*. SMCJ 31, 85 – 88, 1977.

2. **Small**, A.C.D., *J.H.B. Bell as Companion*. SMCJ 31, 83 – 84, 1977.

3. **Murray**, W.H., *J.H.B. Bell as Climber*. SMCJ 31, 80 – 82, 1977.

4. **Fletcher**, Hermione (née Macphee), *Personal communication, February 1987*.

5. CIC Hut Log Book, *Vol.1. 12 November, 1928 – 5 July, 1949*. NLS.

6. **Richardson**, Simon, *Ben Nevis Rock & Ice Climbs* (Glasgow: Scottish Mountaineering Trust, 2002, ISBN 0907521738.)

7. **Macphee**, G.G., *Twelve Days in the Hut*. SMCJ 19, 229 – 237, 1931.

8. **McLeod**, Rev. George, *Proceedings of the Club*. SMCJ 19, 348, 1932.

9. **Borthwick**, A.C., *Epic Story Behind The Ben Nevis Tragedy*. Glasgow Weekly Herald, April 7, 1934.

10. **Bell**, J.H.B., *A Ben Nevis Constellation of Climbs*. SMCJ 22, 367 – 376, 1941.

11. **Wedderburn**, E.A.M., *A Climb on Ben Nevis*. SMCJ 20, 233 – 237, 1934.

12. **Williams**, G.C., *Days on Ben Nevis*. SMCJ 20, 394 – 400, 1935.

13. **Watson**, A., *No Snow Survives*. SMCJ 40, p628, 2007.

14. **Macphee**, G.G., *Ben Nevis*. (Edinburgh: Scottish Mountaineering Club, 1936.)

15. **Bell**, J.H.B., *Personal Log Book – Vol 4*.

16. **Small**, Alex, *Personal communication, January 1987*.

17. **Bell**, J.H.B., *New Climbs – Zero Gully, Ben Nevis*. SMCJ 21, 200 – 201, 1937.

18. **Murray**, W.H., *The C.I.C. Hut – 1930's*. SMCJ 31, 334 – 336, 1979.

19. **Murray**, W.H., *The Evidence of Things Not Seen*. (London: Bâton Wicks, 2002, ISBN 1898573247.)

20. **Bell**, J.H.B., *The West Face of Observatory Ridge – Ben Nevis*. SMCJ 21, 352 – 354, 1938.

21. **Macphee**, G.G., *Scottish Mountaineering and its Relation to Mountaineering Abroad. II – Remarks on Snow and Ice Conditions*. SMCJ 21, 85 – 92, 1936.

22. **MacKenzie**, W.M., *Fourteen Hours on the Observatory Ridge*. SMCJ 21, 337 – 338, 1938.

23. **Stangle**, F.G., *New Climbs – Comb Gully, Ben Nevis*. SMCJ 22, 65 – 66, 1939.

Additional Reading

Dean, Steve, *Hands of a Climber, A Life of Colin Kirkus* (Glasgow: The Ernest Press, 1993, ISBN 0948153210.)

Douglas Laidlaw, Bill Murray and Jim Bell outside the CIC Hut, (June 1940)

Photo: James MacEwen

7: Constellations (1940 – 1949)

THE EFFECTS of the Second World War on Scottish climbing were less severe than those of the 1914 – 1918 War. Although travelling was restricted, the island of Skye and areas north of the Great Glen being out of bounds to most, more servicemen were stationed in Britain. It was possible, with much determination, to climb during leave periods. The summer of 1940 was to be remembered throughout Britain as one of the best for weather and by the end of May even Nevis was sweltering under a blue sky.

In July 1935 Jim Bell and Violet Roy had opened up the possibilities of the great face left of Zero Gully, climbing the rib system left of the Basin. But Bell had ambitions of a direct ascent from the Basin to the summit of the North-East Buttress. He expressed surprise in 1940 that nothing had been done here during the intervening years, and certainly it seems a strange neglect, as there were by now many fine young climbers doing great things elsewhere – The Rannoch Wall, Raven's Gully and Clachaig Gully were all climbed during that period.

On June 10 a JMCS/SMC group assembled at the CIC Hut. W.H.Murray, Douglas Laidlaw and W.Redman of the JMCS, and J.H.B.Bell and James E.McEwen of the SMC. Bell's log book described the day's activities.

> McEwen & I went up Slav Route to the final easy terrace, where he photographed Murray posed at the foot of the great slab rib on the Basin route. Actually Murray & Co did not climb this rib, although it was part of the 1935 route. I could not, at the time, positively say to him whether this

The summer of 1940 was to be remembered throughout Britain as one of the best for weather and by the end of May even Nevis was sweltering under a blue sky

was so, or not, so his party climbed up the open slab corner on the other side of it (from us) & re-emerged above it...He got good photos of Murray on Rib Slab below Basin.

Murray had been climbing with Laidlaw and Redman. Laidlaw was then 18. (Two years later Laidlaw was killed over Germany when his bomber was shot down, the rest of the crew having bailed out at his command. Once they were clear of the bomber he tried to head the aircraft westwards, but never made it. Redman, also in the RAF, was also killed in the war.) On June 14, Bell returned with John Wilson of the Perth JMCS and at last succeeded in making his direct route from the Basin. They left their boots at the foot of the rocks and followed the original route to the Basin, climbing in plimsolls and, for the main part, in socks. (The best plimsolls for this task, apparently, were sold by Woolworth's, who stocked the thinnest.) One hundred and fifty metres or so of climbing took them to the Basin, where Bell stopped for lunch.

Bell described the crucial, upper stretch of his direct route.

> After lunch we ascended a moderate buttress for 120 feet to an easy terrace. Then the difficulties recommenced and continued for about 600 feet. The crux is at and just above a remarkable, prominent, steep slab overhung by a wall on the right. This main feature is well seen from the Hut and so is the second great slab. One follows an oblique, upward line to the left towards this double slab, which is about 200 feet in height. There is a short, bad traverse above it, some easier rocks, and then a final steep wall with knobs of quartzite for holds. Above the difficulty we gained the crest of the N.E. Buttress above the Mantrap and reached the cairn on the top of the Buttress after 215 feet of easier climbing....We are both convinced that this 'Long Climb' of 1,480 feet is the longest and finest route of sustained difficulty on the Ben.[1]

Bell thought there were now two problems remaining on the face. One was to climb the original route more directly up the inclined rib of rock above the Basin. Murray and Laidlaw had climbed the rib by a more difficult way, Redman having climbed up first by the original route, but they had included a right traverse and the truly direct line was still waiting. In August 1940, George Dwyer arrived, fresh from hard exploits on Clogwyn du'r Arddu, Wales. On the 4th they launched themselves at the rib of the original route. Proceeding up the left rocky rim of the Basin they reached the overhang where the route traversed to the right. Here they took to a tenuous groove just left of the crest instead, negotiated a severe pitch, then broke through the difficulties by entering a smooth scoop. The holds in this were just sufficient, easier rocks being gained above.

The second problem Bell wished to solve was an entry to the Basin from the large ledge low down on Slav Route, known as the First Platform of Slav Route. An easy traverse into the Basin from higher up Slav Route had been made in July 1938 by Alex Small, J.Wood and A.Anderson, but Bell wanted a more direct entry. Again Dwyer and Bell left their boots behind and climbed in socks, Dwyer leading the crux pitch. Even with the rope above for comfort and in socks, Bell found the first few moves to be about at the limit of faith and friction. A short traverse above to avoid an overhang then allowed access to the Basin. From the Basin, Bell and Dwyer made a relatively easy traverse leftwards, finally emerging

Bill Murray at foot of The Great Slab Rib, (June 1940)

Photo: James MacEwen

on to the crest of the North-East Buttress at the Second Platform. This traverse gives access to the Basin from North-East Buttress, starting at a conspicuous V-notch. Bell was to use this knowledge in his plans for a complete Girdle Traverse of the cliffs.

There now remained the difficulty in naming the routes. The climber or climbers who first climb a route have the privilege of giving it a name, and until about the mid-1930s route names tended to be rather dry; Central Buttress, Route 1, and so on. With the influx of new clubs and young climbers on to the scene, and latterly with the sometimes heated imaginations of student climbers, route names became more interesting. Perhaps the ideal course, as Bell was eventually to take, was to find some feature of the climb or crag, and find a name which was in accord with the feature.

After Wilson and Bell had finished the direct or *Long Climb*, they had long discussions as to its name. Wilson suggested calling it the *Fall of Paris* climb, not realising (according to Bell's log) on that perfect climbing day how tragically appropriate that casual suggestion was. Soldiers of the Third Reich occupied Paris that very day, June 14.

That winter Bell went on a solitary ramble on some low hills and came up with the solution to his route-naming problem. No doubt the sky was clear and starry as he walked home that night, with the winter constellation Orion rising before him. He would name the routes based on the principal stars of that constellation – Orion the Hunter, whose fancied similarity to the figure of a man with upraised arm, belt and sword was described in antiquity.

The Basin would occupy the position of the three stars of the belt, while from each of these rose one of the upper routes. The straightened out original climb led to the giant red star Betelgeuse, forming the right arm of Orion. This was the brightest star in the constellation and was accordingly given by astronomers the Greek letter Alpha, and so that climb was Alpha Route. The original route above the Basin would be Zeta; in the middle would be Epsilon Chimney; while to the right would be Delta Route, forming the upper half of the Long Climb, and leading to Orion's head.

Below the belt of Orion is a vertical line of stars representing his sword. This agreed with the Great Slab Rib of the original route. The bright star Rigel was at the start of both Slav Route and the direct entry to the Basin, hence Beta Route. Through the passage of time and the rise and fall of favoured routes, Bell's *Long Climb* has, ironically, been firmly fixed as the title of his best route, a long climb indeed at 420m, and a classic and popular Very Severe, despite some loose rock. The variations Alpha, Zeta, Beta, and the Epsilon Chimney retain his original names.

Bell had looked leftward across this giant of a face – now known to climbers across the world as the Orion Face – and pronounced that it seemed very unlikely that any climb could be done between Platforms Rib on the left and Bell's Alpha Route. Most of the great ribs of rock on this section, he noticed, were severely undercut in their lowest sections. As will be seen shortly, Bell was soon to be proved wrong; this area of the face was breached in 1944 by two routes.

Elsewhere on Nevis that fine June in 1940, other routes were being discovered, no less than five by one man – Henry Iain Ogilvy. A Scot

The winter constellation Orion, described in Greek mythology as a mighty hunter. The principal stars are denoted by the Greek alphabet, brightest first

Jim Bell climbing in his socks, on the first ascent of The Long Climb (VS), (June 1940)

Photo: John 'Jock' Wilson

who was President of the Cambridge University M.C. from 1939 – 1940, Ogilvy was one of the new breed of rock climbers, shaking the established groups with his ascents of the first Very Severe wall routes on the Rannoch Wall of Buachaille Etive Mòr – Red Slab Route and Satan's Slit, both climbed in 1939. The history of Scottish mountaineering would almost certainly have looked very different had Ogilvy not been killed in a climbing accident in September 1940, along with his girl-friend, Lucy Robson, in the Cairngorms.

Quisling has become a derogatory name and is taken after the Norwegian politician Vidkun Quisling, who assisted Nazi Germany to conquer his own country. It is usually employed to describe traitors and collaborationists

Ogilvy's explorations on the Ben began on June 19, climbing with C.F.Rolland and making an ascent of the big, right-hand wall of Càrn Dearg Buttress. Evening Wall, a 210m Very Difficult, overlooks Waterfall Gully, its name suggested by the pleasing exposure to the setting sun. Two days later they climbed Compression Crack, a 230m Very Difficult on the right flank of Raeburn's Buttress. The latter route starts up a clean water-worn chimney corner, providing strenuous and progressively more difficult climbing. On June 22, Ogilvy and Rolland, along with J.R.Hewit, climbed the Tower Face of The Comb, a Very Difficult line taking in some dubious rock. In fact, as Ogilvy commented in the CIC Log, *'Owing to the nature of the rock & moss encountered we suggest Quisling Wall as a name.'* [2]

Two variations on either side of the Great Tower completed Ogilvy's list of first ascents on Nevis, climbed in one busy week. But this was not his last visit to Ben Nevis during his tragically short climbing career. On July 25 he attempted Gardyloo Buttress with N.P.Piercy. This steep little buttress stands imperiously at the head of Observatory Gully. Its name is by association with Gardyloo Gully on the left, into which the Observatory staff used to dump refuse.

(The word Gardyloo is probably a corruption of the French *gardez l'eau*, from the warning cry of Edinburgh householders as they were about to pitch domestic refuse, and worse, into the public street below. This was usually done at 10pm each evening to the beat of the town drum; woe betide any passer-by who was either not nimble of foot or quick to shout *'Haud yer han!'*.) The buttress has two edges. Ogilvy attempted to follow the clean-cut left edge, and wearing socks made considerable progress before the rain came on. He then abseiled into Gardyloo Gully, leaving behind three rope slings and two karabiners.

Another attempted route was that of the complete girdle traverse of the Ben Nevis cliffs, a Bell inspiration. Girdles, the climbing of a cliff across its width, rather than the more normal bottom to top, were in fashion at this time. Although seldom repeated in later years, they certainly provided the pioneers with much entertainment at the time, often landing them in positions and situations otherwise never reached. In August 1940, Bell and Dwyer made a start on the grand girdle, beginning on the valley side of Castle Ridge. Their attempt fizzled out four hours later, in dense mist on The Comb, the two climbers finishing up Pigott's Route to complete their holiday.

Bell was back on September 21, 1941, with J.D.B.Wilson. Starting at the Càrn Mòr Dearg arete, they roped up on reaching the North-East Buttress and reversed the V-traverse to gain the Basin. Exciting times were had crossing the great, and then unclimbed gully of Point Five and also on a section of rock right of Glover's Chimney. They crossed The Comb on their grand tour by means of Hesperides Ledge, first climbed by Bell and Wilson the previous June. At this point Wilson made it quite clear that he *'hated the very sight of the beautiful plants on Hesperides Ledge and considered that he had done enough for the day'.*[1]

They crossed The Comb on their grand tour by means of Hesperides Ledge, first climbed by Bell and Wilson the previous June. At this point Wilson made it quite clear that he 'hated the very sight of the beautiful plants on Hesperides Ledge and considered that he had done enough for the day'

Bell continued alone, taking less than an hour to go from Number Four Gully to South Castle Gully.

...an easy rise took me to the Carn Dearg Buttress Cairn...There I halloed and

Looking up Observatory Gully. Gardyloo Buttress is catching the late sun, with Kellett's Route (HVS) starting at the buttress foot near the shadow terminator and climbing directly up

Photo: Dave MacLeod

danced a war dance, seen by Wilson from the corrie below.

The Girdle Traverse was complete.

June 1941 on Nevis saw attacks, both by climbers on Gardyloo Buttress, and by a German bomber on the vital installation that was so valuable a target – the Fort William aluminium factory. The Dundonian team of Syd Scroggie, John S.Ferguson and Graham S.Ritchie were in residence at the CIC Hut; Ritchie described both of these attacks in an entertaining essay. At two o'clock in the morning the hut residents heard the drone of an aircraft.

> Steaming mugs of tea in hand, we moved out into the night where the great cliffs of the Ben towered jet-black against a dark sky. No sound came to us save a soft rustle of wind. Yet we lingered expectantly. Then lazily, so lazily, converging streams of red tracer-shells rose from behind Càrn Dearg and mounted the sky. Two great flashes lit the horizon and the hills stood revealed for an instant. But not a sound was heard. It was all rather eerie and exciting, yet peaceful and strangely beautiful.

The audacious German bombing run came to nothing strategically; one bomb exploded in a tinker's encampment, but of the two bombs which were direct hits neither went off. One landed next to the water pipe where it comes out of Meall an-t-Suidhe, while the other crashed through the roof to land in the very centre of the factory floor, surprising the workers at their benches. Later that day the climbers left the CIC Hut and approached Gardyloo Buttress. By the time the first rocks were gained it was 6pm (Double Summer Time would then be in force).

> Sydney led off from the bergschrund below the rocks, leaving John and myself contemplating a litter of Observatory rubbish, prominent among which were

unmistakeable portions of a certain china article which caused quite dispro-
portionate mirth, as such things do on such occasions. Our leader meantime
was not on difficult looking rock; yet, after a paltry 30 feet, there he was calling for ironmongery, and in particular for a variety referred to as 'wee beauties'.
'John,' I said, 'nip up and give Syd a hand; he's off form.' After 'nipping up'
some 10 feet he descended precipitately upon me, lit a cigarette and commented
shortly, 'Syd's doing O.K.' Thereafter we both sobered up considerably.

At the top of the slabby first section, all three removed boots and
continued in socks. The buttress had little in the way of natural protection and only two rock belays were found by the climbers. Eventually
they gathered on a ledge below two thin chimneys, at the top of which
were some insecure-looking blocks. They decided that the gully wall
offered the best chance for future advance, and after placing a piton
roped down and returned to the Hut via Tower Ridge, first leaving an
ice axe high up on the Little Tower, *'just to ensure that we did return
on the morrow'*.

The next day saw the three back on the buttress at their previous high
point. From there Scroggie set out to climb on the gully wall. After some
12m he moved back onto the true ridge, throwing down a huge unstable block. This weaved its way down the snow in Observatory Gully,
finally coming to rest by the Allt a' Mhuilinn. Another 9m of steep but
delightful rock led to a small ledge, and there all three perched, *'feet
dangling in the void, for all the world like the Three Wise Monkeys'*.

Ritchie was to spend hours on this ledge, while the other two
attempted what was plainly the crux of the route.

> Time passed swiftly and inexorably. The evening shadows began to lengthen
> in the corrie. Then a glorious light flooded down Gardyloo Gully, suffusing
> the rocks with an unbelievable purple glow which slowly paled and suddenly
> was gone....An hour fled by while the ropes moved spasmodically upwards,
> never more than a few feet at a time. The tension never relaxed, but rather
> grew...No verbal communication was possible...and when, at length, the ropes
> began to swing down like the cables of a lift I could only assume that our
> attempt had failed.[3]

The two leaders told of steep holdless grooves and ribs and continuous exposure and had continued until further direct progress was
doubtful and a traverse right to the central snow patch out of the question. A deeply rusted karabiner and a weather-faded belay loop were
produced – evidence that they had passed Ogilvy's high point of July
1940. Scroggie and Ferguson were convinced that the only chink of weakness in the buttress armour lay further right, a good prediction, as it
turned out.

The line attempted by Ogilvy and Piercy and by the Dundonians in
1940 and 1941 respectively, was finally climbed in June 1962, by the
brothers Marshall and George Ritchie. At a grade of Scottish Very Severe
4c, it is described in the current guide book as a superb route with fine
situations – Left Edge Route. The prefix of *Scottish* also implies that not
enough is known about the route to be entirely certain of its grade!

Speaking in 1984 of the attempt by the Dundee team, Jimmy Marshall
was of the opinion that had they traversed right then the route would
have fallen and the buttress would have been climbed, but climbing is

*A blind Syd Scroggie,
left, in the
Cairngorms in the
early 1950s*

From 'The Cairngorms Seen
and Unseen' (1998)

a sport permeated with such fascinating *ifs*, and to the climbers on the spot at the time an outcome is often not visible and sometimes highly risky. By 1941 then, Gardyloo Buttress was both unclimbed, and growing in reputation. Scroggie was to serve as a Lieutenant in the Lovat Scouts, fighting his way up Italy. Two weeks before the end of the war he stepped on an anti-personnel mine and lost a leg and his eyesight. Undeterred, this amazing man continued to climb and walk, writing a book on the Cairngorms. He taught himself Greek in Braille, so as to better understand the classics, and was awarded an Honorary Doctorate in Law by Dundee University in 2001. He died on September 9th, 2006.

Other than Bell's Girdle of the North Face, there were three new climbs and a variation in 1941. The first route to breach the steep Indicator Wall was climbed by J.F.Scott, J.T.Austin and W.Moore, on July 11. A Very Difficult, it climbs grooves and a wall near the left end. The previous day, M.W.Erlebach and Edward Pyatt had climbed a Difficult on Creag Coire na Ciste – Central Rib, while on September 23, S. and B.P.Thompson climbed the Difficult Thompson's Route on Number Three Gully Buttress. All three of these routes now provide excellent winter climbing, though it was not until 2004 that Central Rib was followed in its entirety in winter to give Central Rib Direct VI,7. Finally, on the last day of August, Route I received a Direct Start by Robin Plackett and W.W.Campbell, at a standard of Severe .

By 1942, the setbacks of the war in Europe and the consequent economic stringencies were beginning to tell; very little climbing was done, and on Ben Nevis only one new climb was recorded. That sole route however saw a new name on the mountain, a climber whose short-lived but intense climbing career was to fascinate later generations of climbers – Brian Pinder Kellett (1914 – 1944).

The lone route of 1942 was the first summer ascent of Number Two Gully. Several prominent climbers had previously failed on this. In September 1911 Raeburn attempted a relatively snow-free second ascent, but high in the gully there was a considerable quantity of fresh snow. At one wet and slimy pitch not far from the top a large amount of snow came down upon the leader and retreat seemed sensible. Twenty-four years later Macphee had a try at climbing the gully; he too was stopped, this time by the great volume of water coming down the major difficulty – the Great Pitch.

On August 30, Kellett and J.A.Dunster entered the gully. It had been dry for a week, though this often makes little difference in a wet gully. The scree in the upper parts was so unstable that Dunster unroped and sheltered at the foot of a subsidiary gully. Kellett graphically described the crux section, a 10m stretch of very thin climbing -

Brian Kellett, (1942). In two summers, Kellett recorded an astonishing 32 new routes and repeated most of the existing lines on Ben Nevis

Photo: Lorna Kellett

> There was a good spike belay very high up on the right wall, over which the rope was thrown. But the small holds on the right wall were rotten and worthless and the ascent was finally effected by the back on this wall with the side pressure of the foot on small vertical holds in the gully bed. These latter holds sloped badly and were water-worn and wet, so great difficulty was experienced. Near the top one could face inwards and reach good holds at the top of the steep part...[4]

With the possible exception of Point Five, Number Two Gully remains

*To indicate the
level of Kellett's
activity in the
summer of 1943,
he climbed 91
routes or variations
on Nevis, out of the
existing total given
of 106...17 were
first ascents, 14 of
them solo*

the hardest of the summer gullies on the north face of Nevis, being at
least Very Severe. Kellett however was not to commence the main thrust
of his Nevis explorations until 1943, when he arrived in Torlundy below
the Ben to work in the Forestry Commission. He was a pacifist who had
determined not to fight; after a spell in prison he volunteered for the
Forestry, hoping at first to work on Skye, then settling for Torlundy and
Ben Nevis.

Kellett's brief but illuminating period on Ben Nevis lasted two years,
essentially the summers of 1943 and 1944. As regards first ascents in
1943, Kellett's climbing began on May 22 and finished on August 11.
His climbing on Ben Nevis took a systematic approach, with a view to
climbing and checking all the known routes. We are very fortunate
indeed that he kept a series of three personal notebooks, into which
were entered detailed notes on the routes.[5] Into these small, maroon-
coloured books, entries were made in a neat and concise hand, dark blue
ink for descriptions, red for route names. A handwriting expert, analysing
Kellett's writing, has made the comment that by nature the writer was,

> methodical rather than brilliant, a highly controlled and physically strong
> individual who was nonetheless occasionally prone to making mistakes.[6]

In the April 1944 number of the SMC Journal was an article by Kellett
titled, *Recent Rock Climbs on Ben Nevis*, stating that the article was
intended to serve as a supplement to the 1936 Macphee edition of the
Ben Nevis Guide. At the end of his article, which contains descriptions
of many routes, was a classified list of climbs, including routes graded
as Very Severe. To indicate the level of Kellett's activity in the summer
of 1943, he climbed 91 routes or variations on Nevis, out of the existing total given of 106. Many of these he was obliged to solo, sometimes
climbing midweek after a hard day's Forestry work. He would also take
the odd day off when the weather was settled, to the annoyance of his
employers. For training, Kellett would hire a bike and climb on the
Polldubh crags in the evenings.

Where Kellett's notebook mentioned photographs for illustrating cliff
features, he often gave Cartesian coordinates; e.g., (Photo. J. 22, 327, 3.8,
3.3); the last two numbers given being horizontal and vertical coordinates
in inches, measured from the bottom left-hand corner of the photograph.
The first two numbers were, of course, the source and page number.

Over Kellett himself there hovers an almost inevitable air of mystery.
At school he was competent in several sports and an excellent chess player.
(He played chess after work with the blacksmith at Torlundy, and was
Lancashire county champion for 1938-39.) Powerfully built, he had begun
to solo routes while working in the Lake District – though not in accoun-
tancy, in which he had qualified – but in the Forestry in Ennerdale.

Of the 91 routes climbed by Kellett in 1943, 17 were first ascents, 14
of them solo. From these bare statistics we have to picture a solitary
climber steadily working his way through the lines on Ben Nevis, existing or future, with a methodical determination. Not that his days on
the hill were without incident; on Nevis he suffered three falls, before
the one that ended his life. In January 1943, while on a solo ascent of
the Secondary Tower Ridge, he fell while crossing the Tower Gap, shooting down the entire length of Glover's Chimney and over the ice pitch

*Kellett engaged in
Forestry work at
Torlundy, (1943)*

Photo: Lorna Kellett

at the foot of the route to land in snow. When he got back down to the hut after this fall, miraculously unhurt, he pinned a note on the door asking for help in recovering his axe, lost during the fall.

But Kellett's standing as a climber, in a technical sense at least, should be judged by the routes he left. On May 22 he made a Hard Severe variation to Bayonet Route, climbing alone above the overhang bypassed by Macphee on the first ascent. Leading Bayonet Route in 1985, roped, with a V.Diff second, Ken Crocket declined to take Kellett's variation at the overhang, instead moving up the overhang at its left end. To follow Kellett's variation involves a bold and committing move using a friction hold, with no certainty of the outcome.

Two weeks later on June 9, Kellett made a lone examination of the upper reaches of a line to the right of Route I. There was a St. Andrews University Club meet in the CIC Hut that day when Kellett appeared looking for a partner. Arnot Russell agreed to go along with him. The two made the first ascent of Route II, a Severe which started up Route I then broke out right to traverse across the great buttress below the overhangs. It is a remarkably fine climb with breathtaking situations, climbed on the first ascent in socks, in order to overcome damp and vegetation. Kellett's note in the CIC Log makes the following comment on Route II.

> Conditions good as far as Green Ledge, where light rain started. This gives a good face climb mainly on rough slabs with good, small holds. It is very exposed, but not unduly difficult in rubbers. Severe...[2]

Following the ascent Russell and Kellett descended via Route I then to round off a good day climbed the Direct Start to the North Trident Buttress.

On July 2, Kellett escaped death for the second time, on a solo ascent of Route A on the North Wall of Càrn Dearg. While attempting to identify this old route he fell on a chimney pitch, possibly due to loose rock. Kellett gave the route a grade of Very Severe, the hardest of the routes he climbed that year. A slightly easier solo climb that month was the first ascent of Italian Climb at Severe. This chimney-gully line on the west flank of Tower Ridge is now a popular III in winter, and was climbed on the eighth day of perfect weather. The initial chimney proved to be the hardest pitch, mossy and still wet. Above this Kellett made a strange discovery. Moving up the next section he reached a small cave at the back of the cleft.

> ...a walk then led to the cave...where a piton and a sort of ladder, formed by a strong pole, with nails on both sides was found.[2]

Higher up Italian Climb, Kellett inspected the overhanging Left-Hand Branch, but judged it impossible. The ownership of the home-made ladder found in the cave will probably never come to light. In March 1940 J.Y.Macdonald and H.W.Turnbull had attempted the route, but found the second pitch to be in bad condition. No doubt other parties attempted the route as well. Italian Climb Left Branch was eventually climbed in February 2006 by Dave MacLeod, an SMC member, at VIII,9.

The following day, Sunday, July 25, Kellett made no less than three new routes, two at Very Difficult and one at Severe, the last a solo ascent of 1943 Route on the bottom tier of the South Trident Buttress. Climbing

Brian Kellet on South Trident Buttress, (c. 1944)

Photo: Geoff Curtis

Nancy shouted to me to grasp & try to stop the rope. It was, of course, utterly impossible. The thing was running down fast & jerking about. Then it stopped, Nancy was drawn up sharp against the belay in a strained position & there was silence

Brian Kellett on Route II (Severe), Càrn Dearg Buttress (probably 1943)

Photo: Geoff Curtis

with E.M.Hanlon and Gordon Scott, Kellett made an ascent of Evening Wall, possibly the second, then made the first descent of Route II. Scott took up the position of last man, the most responsible position on descent. The original finish of Route II was up the right-hand of two grooves mentioned by Ogilvy. In order to give Route II a separate finish from Evening Wall, Kellett descended the left-hand groove. The green ledge on Route II, visible from the hut,

> ...was carpeted with yellow, white, and pink flowers. Those who wish to perfect their turf technique are recommended to visit this airy garden.[2]

The second ascent of Route II was that by Kellett and B.P.Thompson on April 10, 1944. The two were almost benighted on this occasion, descending by Ledge Route. Of the last pitch of 1943 Route Macphee, in his 1936 Guide, stated that the final groove was the obvious route but that it looked almost impossible. Kellett was now beginning to look unstoppable.

Route B, on August 11, was the scene of a near tragedy. Kellett was climbing with Jim Bell and Nancy Forsyth on the North Wall of Càrn Dearg. There are several explanations for the attraction this face seems to have held for Kellett. Firstly there were several vague routes, the clarification of which had eluded Macphee. Secondly, this area of impressively steep walls was one of the lowest on Nevis, a point of some convenience to Kellett who on occasion climbed in the evening.

Bell gives an account of this third fall by Kellett.

> K. started off, N.F. belayed round belay near foot of chimney. I was unroped as I was coiling up the 100-ft line which was no longer necessary. A rumble from above & I just caught sight of Kellett flying downward past me. At the same time I felt a blow on the head, not sharp but dull & my head began to feel all warm – with flowing blood. Nancy shouted to me to grasp & try to stop the rope. It was, of course, utterly impossible. The thing was running down fast & jerking about. Then it stopped, Nancy was drawn up sharp against the belay in a strained position & there was silence. The rope to Kellett was taut. It held.

Bell looked down to the edge where the rope disappeared, about 21 or 24m below. Then he heard Kellett shouting. He was unhurt apart from numb hands, hanging with just a faint pressure on the rocks and no real hand holds. After some time Bell succeeded in getting the end of the 30m line to Kellett, who then tied on to that. With both Bell and Forsyth pulling, Kellett appeared above the edge, shaken. After a rest he climbed up until level with the other two but 10m to the right. As he had doubts about making the traverse, the other two climbed over to join him. Bell had a profusely bleeding scalp wound, while Forsyth, who had belayed Kellett with the rope running behind her body, suffered from a badly lacerated hand, a result of braking Kellett's fall with her bare hands.

Kellett admitted that Forsyth had been very successful in slowing his fall; she had probably saved his life. Slowly, the shaken but grateful trio made their way down easy terraces leading to the usual staircase-gully approach to Raeburn's Buttress. This was very wet. Bell was last, with Kellett letting Forsyth down on the rope. Bell missed what happened next, but a hold broke off while Kellett was descending, pitching him down about 2m or so. Ironically, this tiny fall severely damaged his left knee and his right hand. As he insisted that he could make his way down the other two soon drew ahead, reaching the hut just before 7pm. An hour later, with supper ready, Kellett was still not in sight, so Bell went up to look for him.

> I soon met him going very slowly but past the worst of the descent. He had to keep the injured leg & knee joint straight all the time. For this he had arranged a loop on a bit of line, the loop under the instep & rope in his hand.

The next day, Kellett's knee had swollen to twice normal size. The fall had taken place on the Wednesday; on the following Monday Kellett slowly hobbled down to Fort William, using a hut broom as a crutch. There it was found that he had fractured a patella and a finger. Bell also went down on the Monday, soloing up Tower Ridge and returning to Fort William via Glen Nevis. As to the cause of the fall, it seems that Kellett had been relying on a chockstone placed by him on a previous ascent. When pulling up on this it came out and Kellett fell with it.

Route B was also the last first ascent Bell made on Nevis. He continued to edit the SMC Journal until his last issue, in 1959. He died on October 11, 1975, with his ashes scattered over the summit of Ben Lomond, overlooking some of his favourite areas of Scotland.

By the time Kellett recovered fully, summer had finished, the first of the two summers he lived to the full climbing on Nevis. Route B (a Severe) along with a Direct Start climbed by the Placketts the following June, an introductory chimney pitch, and Route A, are now climbed in combination, fittingly called Kellett's North Wall Route, a 180m Severe.

Bell climbed with Kellett on one occasion only, described above. Following Kellett's last and fatal fall, he remarked that it had come as no surprise to him. This remark may well have been coloured by the frightening experience on Route B, and it was no help that Bell, who was a personal friend of Nancy Forsyth, had introduced her to Kellett. After that fall on Route B, Bell warned Forsyth about climbing with Kellett. However, she did climb with him again. The point remains however, that the sensible codes of the day decreed that the leader must not fall.

Apart from Kellett on Nevis, no other climber was making first ascents in 1943. Over a third of those using the CIC Hut were troops, a party of whom climbed Tower Ridge fully equipped, including rifles. The army group comprised one officer and 14 other ranks of the Lincolnshire Regiment, who climbed the Ridge in full battle order, carrying rifles and wearing army boots (excepting the C.O.). The party moved in five ropes of three and despite wind and rain climbed the ridge in under six hours. All but the leader were virtual novices with only scrambling experience.

One wet day some soldiers staggered into the CIC Hut where they accepted the hospitality of the climbers resident there, who included Bell. The soldiers began complaining about their C.O., referring to him as a *'bloody mountain goat'*. When Bell enquired as to his name, he was highly amused on learning that it was Sandy Wedderburn. Bill Murray was now a prisoner of war, as were others. Wedderburn himself would die during the war, knocked down by a truck. If the war was to bring any benefits to mountaineering, it would be in the form of better equipment – nylon ropes, better karabiners, vibram-soled boots – though the

Kellett at the crux of Route B (Severe) on the North Wall of Càrn Dearg, during the first ascent (August 1943)

Photo: J.H.B.Bell

majority of climbers had to wait several years to see any of these. On October 25, the JMCS approved Kellett's membership application, thus allowing him easier access to the CIC Hut.

The summer of 1944 was to see another one-man campaign by Kellett, a total of 15 first ascents; 11 solo. He opened his last summer with a variation to Bell's Beta Route on the Orion Face, climbing wet and mossy slabs in socks to gain the Basin by a more direct line. This was on June 17, but perhaps of more interest was his climb of June 20, one of his best discoveries on Ben Nevis – Left-Hand Route on the Minus Face.

East of the Orion Face the rock has a leftward tilt and is seamed by a series of buttresses and gullies, three of the latter being particularly prominent. Bell had already named the steep gully on the left flank of Observatory Ridge Zero Gully. The broad and easy Tower Gully to the left of Tower Ridge was originally named Number One Gully. This nomenclature overlooked the narrow rift full of overhung pitches, lying between Observatory Buttress and the steep slabby rocks on the right-hand edge of the west face of Observatory Ridge. This steep gully, Kellett decided, should be called Point Five Gully, while the three gullies left of Zero, again by analogy, he named Minus One, Two and Three Gullies respectively.[8]

The narrow buttress between Minus One and Two Gullies was named Minus One Buttress, while the broad buttress between Minus Two and Three Gullies became Minus Two Buttress. It was on this last buttress that Kellett was to record two routes, the Left- and Right-Hand Routes, both Very Severe. The first to be climbed was the Left-Hand Route, climbed on June 20 in company with Robin and Carol Plackett. Three days earlier, Kellett had spent three or four hours examining this face, deciding that there were at least three routes to be found.

The route followed cracked slabs to a stance below and right of the prominent overhanging nose on this face, then took to a steep bulging slab on the left. The slab was the crux of the route. Each of the three climbers took their own line on the crux pitch, the leader wearing socks for a wet slimy crack, traversed above a bulge. Thereafter plimsolls were worn, with 18m of rope found to be just adequate.

The second ascent of Kellett's Left-Hand Route was on July 9, 1949 by J.H.Swallow and Arnot Russell. Ten years after the first ascent, a strong team from Cambridge University made the first of a series of summer raids on Scotland. Two ropes approached the foot of Minus Two Buttress in the summer of 1954, the first composed of Mike O'Hara and Eric Langmuir, the second of John Peacock and Arthur Muirhead. Conditions were wet and greasy and a late start ensured that it was afternoon before the rocks were gained. O'Hara set off and at the top of the first pitch, a smooth and greasy slab, belayed to a peg. Langmuir described the second, crux pitch, in an essay written for his club journal.

> Mike was overflowing with confidence and could hardly be restrained from dashing off before I was properly belayed. When he was unleashed he disappeared over the edge with a grin. 'Hold tight.' I gave what I hoped was a reassuring 'Aye'. I still retain a vivid picture of his massive frame moving slowly upwards on invisible holds and can recall the prickly sensation at the back of my neck as I caught a glimpse of daylight between the uppers and vibram sole of one boot. A fierce looking mantelshelf on to a tiny ledge on the edge of space came as a fitting climax to this splendid pitch.[9]

The Minus Face. The slender Minus One Buttress starts directly above the snow, while Minus Two Buttress spreads left from the snow to the deeply shadowed Minus Three Gully

Photo: Andy Nisbet

*Bill Duncan
approaching the crux
slabs of Left-Hand
Route (VS) on Minus
Two Buttress, one of
the more popular of
Kellett's climbs*

Photo: Colin Stead

Today, Left-Hand Route is a deservedly popular climb, only just Very Severe and taking in a fine series of steep slabs and corners. It requires a few days to dry out, as do most of the routes on this face.

The day following the first ascent of Left-Hand Route, June 21 1944, Kellett made an unsuccessful attempt on a major line on Càrn Dearg Buttress. The line he had been thinking of since the previous summer was the long, conspicuous chimney near the right-hand edge of the buttress – now the classic route Sassenach. The chimney does not reach to the ground and is seemingly impossible to reach from directly below, but like other climbers who were to follow, and possibly even earlier climbers unknown, Kellett hoped to gain the foot of the chimney by traversing in from the left.

To gain this traverse Kellett climbed a steep 15m wall on a little subsidiary buttress. This deceptive pitch is now the start of another great classic route – Centurion. Kellett and Robin Plackett gained the ledge left of the start of the impressive Centurion corner and decided that the gangway traverse looked feasible. A direct entry to the gangway was prevented by a serious-looking steep and smooth mantelshelf and an attempt was then made to traverse right at a higher level by climbing the chimney of Centurion. This was successfully followed for 9 or 12m to a spike belay where an old rope sling was found. An unknown team, it seems, had attempted the formidable line of Centurion some time ago.

Further upward progress, noted Kellett,

> ...was not inviting, nor was the projected traverse right across a very smooth slab, so we had to come down.[2]

Frustrated, that same evening Kellett soloed an easy route on the Douglas Boulder, the Left-Hand Chimney, recording it as a poor climb. Sassenach was to have several other attempts made on it before finally succumbing to the power climbing of Whillans and Brown in 1954.

The good weather of June 1944 left, being replaced by a familiarly wet July. Kellett was indefatigable however, and on the first day of July attempted the prominent gully which drains the lower part of Secondary Tower Ridge. This last feature is a curious slanting shelf, running parallel to the main Tower Ridge, and some distance below its crest on the west side. Secondary Tower Ridge had first been climbed in the early 1930s by J.Y.Macdonald and H.W.Turnbull. The prominent gully attempted by Kellett was one of two mentioned by Macdonald and Turnbull, who climbed the left-hand one. Kellett climbed the lower shallow section of the gully, but half-way up ran into a formidably steep pitch of 18 to 21m. This was also wet and Kellett descended slightly before escaping by a rightward traverse.

The gully was named Vanishing Gully by Kellett, no doubt due to the fact that as it nears the ground it narrows to a crack and finally vanishes altogether. Macdonald and Turnbull had rather diffidently named it as being a *'Trouser-Leg Gully'*. Vanishing Gully is now a popular winter route, a Grade V,5 climb high on many climber's list.

One week later in the afternoon and evening of July 8, Kellett explored the west face of Observatory Ridge, where Bell and Hamilton had already pioneered a route in 1937. The Very Difficult line Kellett found lies to the left of Bell's route and he suggested that it be called the Lower Route to distinguish it from the original (upper) route. Kellett's West Face Lower Route is now a neglected gem, graced with the less clumsy title of Hadrian's Wall. These winter ascents, however, were some years in the future and had to wait for the changes that were still to affect Scottish winter climbing, changes that were going to see standards increase by an order of magnitude.

The last two weeks of July 1944 were to be Kellett's finest, climbing alone on another seven routes. On July 20 he made use of the fourth day of a spell of dry weather and climbed Minus Two Buttress by the Right-Hand Route, Very Severe. We will never have full knowledge of such ascents – there were so few climbers about during the war years especially that there was rarely anyone who could witness such events – but from descriptions of contemporaries, we know that Kellett was very methodical in his explorations; carefully examining a possible route from as many angles as possible before deciding whether to attempt it or not. As to his climbing technique when soloing we again have little knowledge, though in addition to his powerful physique we know that he had the high degree of self-control necessary when soloing routes of a high calibre in uncharted areas. His climbing style has been described by a contemporary as excellent, a pleasure to watch.

When Kellett considered a route of sufficient difficulty, he carried a rope. Equipment then was very limited and unless good spikes and blocks were evident on the route then protection would always have been minimal. Once started on his lone ascent of Right-Hand Route, Kellett was, to all practical purposes, committed to finding a way up the cliff.

Right-Hand Route is 275m in length; giving delicate and exposed climbing with more sustained difficulties than its companion route. Kellett noted the absence of belays, remarking that very long run-outs would probably be necessary. Following the difficult lower section, 165m of easier climbing leads to the Second Platform on North-East Buttress.

climb. Once preparations were completed. the right hand was shifted from a flat press- (rather unsatisfactory) hold to a much higher hold, and then the left hand unwillingly left the beautiful spike for another hold, also much higher; this was really the hardest movement, as both feet were on very poor holds, and body was being pushed off left all the time by the overhang. Once both these higher handholds had been reached, there was no further difficulty in stepping up on to the large flat hold previously used by the right hand, and then climbing the remaining few feet of the corner.

The ascent of Right-Hand Route owes itself to a strange quirk of fate. On the walk up the weather was so hot that Kellett decided to shed his shorts and other unnecessary clothing, placing these garments on top of his rucksack. On gaining the Hut he found the clothing missing, having fallen off somewhere on the path. His intended route that day was Gardyloo Buttress, but he thought that the sight of him arriving at the summit almost naked would not have amused the tourists on top, so instead he chose to attempt the line on Minus Two Buttress. Right-Hand Route then became perhaps the only new route on Nevis to be climbed trouserless.

The second ascent was in June 1955, by the Cambridge team of Langmuir, O'Hara and Downes. They considered it to be a route of high quality, *'another daring performance by Kellett.'*[8] Comparing the two routes of Kellett's on Minus Two Buttress is invidious, but Left-Hand Route, though easier, is the more interesting route.

But Kellett's eyes were returning again and again to the little buttress which dominates the head of Observatory Gully – Gardyloo Buttress. On Sunday July 16, he made a reconnaissance of the buttress, climbing the short, Moderate crack up slabs on the Tower Face of the buttress. Gardyloo Buttress had been attempted at least twice in the past; by Ogilvy in 1940, and by Scroggie in 1941. Both of these failures had been on the clean-cut, left edge of the steep buttress face, looking down the full length of Observatory Gully. Kellett, with his highly developed instinct for a line spotted an alternative on the right wall of the left edge.

The section of Kellet's notebook describing the crux moves on Kellett's Route, Gardyloo Buttress

The text reads: '...Once preparations were completed, the right hand was shifted from a flat press-hold to a much higher hold, (rather unsatisfactory) and then the left hand unwillingly left the beautiful spike for another hold, also much higher; this was really the hardest movement, as both feet were on very poor holds, and body was being pushed off left all the time by the overhang. Once both these higher handholds had been reached, there was no further difficulty in stepping up on to the large flat hold previously used by the right hand, and then climbing the remaining few feet of the corner'

Photo: Ken Crocket

The Slab Climb, (Severe), on the middle tier of South Trident Buttress, was climbed by Kellett on the same day as the 1944 Route (Severe) on the lower tier

Photo: Gary Latter

July 22 was to see Kellett's boldest solo yet, as he started up the band of easy angled rocks at the foot of Gardyloo Buttress. Serious climbing started for Kellett as he climbed up twin cracks on the steep wall above, traversing right beneath an overhang then directly over a smaller overhang to gain a very small stance in a recess. Kellett recommended that it would be better not to bring up a second to this point, as the only belays were small, insecure-looking blocks on the floor of the recess. The 5m corner that followed was to prove to be the crux of the route and in some ways Kellett's finest moment on Nevis.

Kellett, significantly, described this section of the route in great detail, as he spent almost an hour in a strenuous position, cleaning holds and working out a solution, all the while conscious of a horrible and very final drop to the gully boulders below.

> The left wall is perpendicular, the right wall slightly overhanging; handholds on the left wall, though well placed for climbing straight up it, are not well adapted for preventing the body being pushed off to the left by the overhanging right wall. The key to the pitch is the large spike handhold facing horizontally left; this was used by the left hand and had to take most of the weight of the body, while the mossy holds above were cleaned and tidied with the right hand. The higher holds had to be groped for as they could not be seen from below.... Once preparations were completed the right hand was shifted from a flat press hold to a much higher hold (rather unsatisfactory) and then the left hand unwillingly left the beautiful spike for another hold, also much higher. This was really the hardest movement as both feet were on very poor holds and the body was being pushed off left all the time by the overhang.[8]

Once Kellett had gained the upper handholds he was able to step up on to his previous right hand hold and finish the corner. Some strenuous yet delicate climbing remained to be overcome before the wet and mossy final gully was gained. The route had been climbed solo in three hours, wearing plimsolls, with the crux corner alone taking one hour. It was, obviously enough, Very Severe.

The second ascent of Kellett's Route was made in damp conditions in June 1955, by the ubiquitous Downes and O'Hara. There was snow at the top of the buttress, which is at a height of about 1,220m, with melt water trickling down the rocks. The two Cambridge climbers found the 5m corner reminiscent of the corner on Pigott's Climb on Clogwyn du'r Arddu, though steeper and more exposed. Kellett's *'beautiful spike'*, so necessary at the crux, was found to be unsound, wet rock additionally precluding the required pull-up. The corner was eventually climbed with the aid of a foot-loop hung delicately from the *'flat press-hold'*, no apology being felt necessary, considering conditions.[10]

Several other routes fell to Kellett during the remainder of July, including a Very Severe on the lower tier of the South Trident Buttress and a Very Difficult – The Slab Climb, now graded Severe – on the middle tier of the same buttress. The Very Severe is now graded at Severe, giving what the current guide describes as a '...*good climb, which can be combined with Pinnacle Arete on the middle tier to give a fine combination'*.[11] This 1944 Route, as it is called, climbs the right-hand of four large and conspicuous grooves. The rock was very wet when climbed by Kellett, which may account for his uncharacteristic overgrading.

On August 20 Kellett recorded his last route on Nevis – a direct ascent of Cousins' Buttress, the subsidiary buttress abutting the North Wall of Carn Dearg Buttress. This Severe route took the buttress directly, Kellett in his description referring several times to loose rock, noting that it required careful treatment throughout. This particular area of Ben Nevis, as has been noted above, was one of Kellett's favourites; he was to return here for one last, fatal climb.

The weekend of September 1 was a holiday weekend and Nancy Forsyth travelled from Dumfries to Fort William to spend a weekend climbing with Kellett, based at the CIC Hut. When Forsyth had not returned home by the Monday evening her sister contacted the Fort William police. They sent a man up to the hut on Tuesday afternoon. He reported that their belongings were in the hut, but that there was no note of their whereabouts. A search party numbering 18 was organised to go up on Wednesday. By 9pm on Wednesday Bell heard that nothing had been found.

The weather on the Saturday had been showery and much worse on the Sunday. Bell arranged to join Miss Forsyth on the Thursday, meeting her on the Oban train at Dunblane. At Fort William they picked up Nancy Ridyard, all three walking up through heavy rain to reach the CIC Hut at 7pm. Just after midnight they were joined by Archie Hendry's party, including Geoff Curtis and G.H.Townend. The search was organised for Friday by Bell and Hendry, the latter and four others going up to Castle Coire.

The likeliest location, Bell argued, would be the base of Cousins' Buttress, as (a) Kellett had just done a new route there and (b) Kellett was unhappy with Macphee's guide description of the original route. Hendry decided to climb the Castle himself. A recall signal had been arranged, beating an empty oil drum with ice axe shafts. Bell and Ridyard were in Number Two Gully when the dull booming of the oil drum was heard. Hendry had spotted two bodies from below the rocky base of the Castle and had shouted the news to his party. Everyone now gathered at the hut, joined by Harrison and Fletcher who had come up from Fort William with the SMC stretcher. Twelve men went up to the site of the accident.

The two bodies were severely injured, particularly Kellett's. Forsyth was lower down, near the foot of the stepped gully between Cousins' Buttress pinnacle and the foot of Raeburn's Buttress. Kellett was some 5m higher up the gully. Above them was the almost 60m-high pinnacle of Cousins' Buttress. Forsyth had most of Kellett's full-weight climbing rope coiled regularly over her left shoulder and lying over her right hip. She lay on her left side and was wearing an oilskin hood. Both climbers were tied on by waist loops in the usual fashion. The stretcher party took Forsyth down first then after a rest and some food went up again for Kellett. Thereafter a party consisting of naval and police personnel took over, carrying the bodies down to Fort William.

Bell was wary of arriving at a cause of the accident given the flimsy evidence available. He thought that it had probably occurred on Saturday, September 2, as they had been up in the hut on the Friday evening. Forsyth had left her oilskin cape in the hut and the Sunday had been wet all day. To judge from the arrangement of the rope, the

Nancy Forsyth (lower left), climbing with fellow LSCC members Nancy Ridyard (top) and May Green (Suilven, Easter 1939).
Margaret Martha (Nancy) Forsyth was 37 when she died. A schoolteacher in Dumfries, her obituary by her fellow member in the LSCC and friend Nancy Ridyard described her as being 'a fine climber and a splendid companion on the hills, very tall, with a swinging stride and beautiful balance.' (FRCCJ., 39, 1945)

Photo: Ilse Bell, courtesy Ladies Scottish Climbing Club

two had probably been on easy ground, with Kellett leading. Bell thought also that it had not been a slip by Forsyth, as the top coil of rope carried by her had not been drawn up tight. It was perfectly possible, of course, that Kellett had been struck by a rock and had then pulled Forsyth off. Whatever the cause, death was obviously instantaneous. Bell later wrote .

> A brilliant rock climber, he seemed to be devoid of fear on the rocks. Hence, it may be that his margin of safety was really smaller than if he had a touch of fear in his constitution.... I had a sub-conscious feeling since 11/8/43 that K. was not altogether safe. Also, I warned him by mouth & letter later on. On the other hand K. had given up the idea of 2 desperate new climbs which he had formerly contemplated [Sassenach and Point Five Gully]. Also K. was meticulous about his belays.[12]

That Friday night Bell and Hendry stayed at the hut. Understandably, it was not a pleasant evening and the two slept but little. Also present were J.A.Dunster and B.P.Taylor who were up for a week's holiday. They were, according to Hendry, not very competent, and did not propose to climb anything exceeding Very Difficult in standard. (This was the same Dunster who had seconded Kellett on the first summer ascent of Number Two Gully.) Taylor spoke little and Dunster discussed routes with Bell and Hendry. Bell remembered warning Dunster that Observatory Buttress, though not especially difficult if on the correct line, was likely to give problems if one went off route. Two days later Taylor was killed on Observatory Buttress, the two climbers being unroped at the time.

Dunster and Taylor has completed Observatory Buttress as far as the start of the 90m of easy scrambling which leads to the summit. The two set off up this unroped. After about 60m Taylor traversed below a small buttress which Dunster tackled direct. When Dunster was about 15m up this he heard a considerable rockfall and could get no reply from his friend. He descended and traversed to where rock scars were evident. Only a coil of rope was visible in a small gully below. Taylor was lying dead at the foot of the buttress. The next day, Saturday, Hendry went down to Fort William. The weather was now glorious, and Bell wished to leave the mountain with some of his gloom dissipated.

> So I left early & alone with my pack & reached Tower Ridge below first steep bit beyond the Douglas Boulder Gap. There was a good deal of new snow higher up & not a little verglas in places, I remember difficulty at a place on Little Tower, little or none at Eastern Traverse Great Tower, some considerable trouble at Tower Gap & at final exit above. But what was more impressive was the glorious aspect of Gardy Loo Buttress, a stupendous fairy castle, glistening white in the sun which had just pierced the mists on the crest of the Ben.[12]

Kellett was gone, killed while doing what he loved the best. It would be difficult, if not impossible, to suppose where Kellett's climbing might have led. In more normal times – with no war, regular climbing partners and improved footwear and equipment – it is difficult to imagine many routes on Nevis proving too difficult for a climber of Kellett's abilities. At the time of his death he was 30 years of age. In his two summers on Ben Nevis he had lived on a wave of exploration never seen before or since. He was buried in Glen Nevis, looking over to the southern slopes of the mountain he made the last two years of his life. His other monuments remain on the north face of Nevis, including the fairy castle that is Gardyloo Buttress, first climbed by him to give Kellett's Route, and as seen by Bell, *'glistening white in the sun…'*

Kellett's death left a vacuum in climbing on Ben Nevis which was not to be filled until activity picked up again in the 1950s. By the mid-1940s, members of the established clubs were too involved with the war effort. The membership of the SMC, some 307 at the outbreak of war, was down to 276 in 1944. Of 310 CIC bed-nights that year, four SMC members accounted for 17. Between the wars the number of small clubs had risen amazingly, especially in Glasgow, Dundee and Aberdeen. That the SMC was not yet fully aware of this latent force may have been evident in 1945, when a review of Scottish Climbing Clubs by Jim Bell referred to a Dundee Rambling club as a *training Club for the SMC*.[13] To be fair to Bell, many members of this particular club had in fact gone on to join the SMC, while Bell in particular was well aware of the *'democratising effects'* of those new clubs.

The University clubs in Scotland had been active in varying degrees since about 1920 but it was only following the Second World War that their contributions to mountaineering became more tangible. The Scottish clubs for a long time never approached the size and activity of the Oxbridge clubs; almost certainly the chronically impecunious condition of the average Scottish undergraduate was a major cause.

The Ptarmigan Club founded by Jock Nimlin and W.C.Dougan in 1929 was no longer active as a club. There had been 16 original members and no others were admitted, a certain way towards corporate suicide. The Creagh Dhu were 22 strong at December 1945, the club's limit on membership being 30. This limitation, along with a six month's *apprenticeship*, maintained a friendly and close-knit atmosphere in the years following the war, even if it did lead to an ironic elitism, a state normally tacked on to the established clubs. It also led to a fierce standard of climbing, and the Creagh Dhu, especially in Arrochar and Glen Coe, were soon to be responsible for some remarkable ascents.

The Lomond Mountaineering Club had been founded by John Harvey in 1933. From the start it was a well-organised mixed club, having around 70 members at the end of the war. The exploits of the Lomond Bus which carted members round all the major climbing centres – and twice to Switzerland – have gone down into history.

Other clubs were now hiring buses, and with a flood of cheaper and better equipment – thanks to the war – an increase in the number of climbers was not far off. Unfortunately this also meant an increase in the number of accidents on Scottish hills. Between 1925 and 1945 there were 45 deaths, eight on Ben Nevis. In the pre-war years, a call for help following an accident usually meant organising a rescue party put together by the SMC in Glasgow and Edinburgh. An accident would invariably be followed by letters of censure in the press, condemning climbing as too dangerous, suggesting that Ben Nevis be put off limits during the winter. Following the war, a more rational argument began to be heard, especially as statistics showed that a healthy, fit and properly equipped competent climber was much safer on a mountain than while crossing a busy road.

Brian Kellett's headstone in Glen Nevis. When his sister Lorna realised how much he had done on Ben Nevis and its significance to him, she had this headstone erected, and took the opportunity of adding their father's name. Richard Kellett had been lost at sea during World War I, being the commander of the small destroyer HMS Flirt, and so until this point had no personal memorial

*In Memory of
Brian Pinder Kellett
Rock Climber
Died on Ben Nevis
1944
son of
Lt.Richard Pinder Kellett.
R.N.
Commanding Officer
H.M.S. Flirt
Killed in action 1916
and Dorothy
C.E.Kellett
of Iver, Bucks
Died 1974 aged 84*

Photo: Ken Crocket

Arnold Carsten. His battle with The Crack on Raeburn's Buttress provided yet another fine route on the mountain

Photo: Bâton Wicks Archives

This incident prompted the often-quoted remark that if a man could climb safely on Ben Nevis, he could climb safely anywhere. It also brought about the story that Nevis had something against members of the Alpine Club

By 1945 the number of climbers living in and around Fort William prompted the formation of the Lochaber section of the JMCS. This club was later to become independent; its contributions to mountaineering and mountain rescue on Ben Nevis have always been high. In particular Dr Donald Duff, who settled at the Belford Hospital, Fort William, became deeply involved in the treatment of accident victims.

On February 22, 1946, the Himalayan climber and explorer H.W.Tilman of the Alpine Club and J.Cortlandt-Simpson of the JMCS were involved in an accident. They had finished a route, arriving at the summit in mist. From there they chose to descend via the Càrn Mòr Dearg arete, taking a compass bearing in order to find the correct line of descent. Unfortunately the two were soon heading, as have many others, too far leftwards, towards the line of cliffs known as the Little Brenva Face.

Seeing a gully, Tilman started to descend, but slipping on powder snow covering ice he fell over a hundred metres, injuring though not breaking a leg. Cortlandt-Simpson, seeing so experienced a leader apparently descending under control, leapt after him, to discover to his horror that he too was falling. By some miracle no major injuries were incurred, the two continuing their descent to the hut rather shakily. This incident prompted the often-quoted remark that if a man could climb safely on Ben Nevis, he could climb safely anywhere. It also brought about the story that Nevis had something against members of the Alpine Club.

Climbing on Nevis following the war had to wait until those in the armed forces were released to civilian life, though before 1950 there were some isolated but significant ascents. June 16, 1946 saw one such route when The Crack, a 250m Hard Very Severe on Raeburn's Buttress was climbed. The party on this occasion were H.A.Carsten of the Climber's Club and Tommy McGuinness, a good climber in the Lomond MC. The crack taken by this fine, if neglected route is the most striking feature on the slender pinnacle on the front face of the buttress. The Crack is about 90m long and strenuous, with a series of overhangs.

At Whitsuntide Carsten and Macphee went up to the CIC Hut. On the walk up Carsten's attention was fixed by a feature not mentioned in any of the books he had read. It was also, Macphee assured him, unclimbed. The feature was the straight and vertical crack cleaving Raeburn's Buttress. That evening the two climbed Tower Ridge, but the next evening, following an ascent on the North Wall of Càrn Dearg, Carsten made a short visual inspection of the line, while Macphee went down to the hut to prepare dinner.

The upper section of the crack, Carsten knew, had been climbed by Raeburn on the first ascent of the buttress, gaining it from the gully on the left. Remaining unclimbed was the steep lower section. Carsten thought that the approach rocks looked practicable, with the crack itself a formidable problem. In a slight drizzle and in the rapidly deepening dusk he went down to the hut, the line now a major objective for his holiday.

Three days went by before Carsten could approach the buttress again. After a solo ascent of Route II he decided that there was just enough time to attempt the approach rocks. The result, as Carsten put it

...was one of those dogged fights into which a climber can plunge quite unintentionally, and which he has no desire to repeat.[14]

Carsten found that the approach rocks made a staircase of about half a dozen steps. The steps were, however, deceptive. Each step concealed a rounded top and an overhang. At 9m he found a crack and banged in a peg, resting from a sling while he recovered his nerves. He was trailing a length of line behind him and fed this through the peg and sling as a purely psychological running belay. Finally his curiosity got the better of him again and he moved on, finding the next moves to be harder still, with little chance of reversal.

> The next few feet had to go and I gave them no chance of standing upon the order of their going, so they went. With a strange feeling, a blend of triumph, respect and some surprise I reached and stood on the ledge beneath the crack itself.

Carsten realised that it was quite out of the question to continue alone. Looking around the ledge for a belay he found it to be loose and rotten, but a traverse found some perched blocks, suitable for an abseil anchor. The abseil was the most awkward he had ever done, as to go straight down would have left him suspended in space and he was obliged to make a diagonal descent, hoping he would neither swing off the line of descent, nor bring down the perched blocks and fall to the bottom. As luck would have it he made it to the precise spot as planned. Tucking away the free end of the rope under an overhang he descended to the hut to join Macphee.

It was to be another three days before Carsten could return to his route. Macphee went down the hill pleading a sore leg, leaving Carsten alone in his tent, awaiting Dr Duff who had promised to come up the hill and help recover the rope. Until then Carsten soloed several routes, and on his last day on the hill he was pleased to see Duff, with Tommy McGuinness. Carsten's spirits rose as saw another chance at attempting the Crack. Duff stayed at the bottom to watch the battle.

Repeating the first pitch, Carsten was surprised how difficult it was, despite his prior knowledge and the presence of the fixed rope as a safety factor. On the ledge below the crack the two were soon sorting out the 80m of line, their sum total of rope. The drizzle had now started as Carsten launched himself at the crack. At first it was wide enough to admit his entire body, narrowing and forcing him partly on to the face. 15m above the ledge he abandoned the crack and took to an overhang. The holds were good, allowing him to reach a ledge on the right, not visible from below. Here a peg belay permitted him to bring up McGuinness.

The two climbers were now assembled below the biggest bulge on the face, the crack, little more than a few centimetres wide, and the crux of the route. As the rest of the face was smooth, it was the only way up.

> However, a chockstone immediately below the overhang provided encouragement. I went up to examine its stability and returned temporarily exhausted by the effort. After a short rest I again ascended and before my strength faded away I managed to whip a sling round it and clip in a karabiner. Then down I went like a sack of potatoes. After a short rest my strength again returned and with it came determination. I tackled the third ascent with some energy, pulled up to the chockstone, jammed arms and fists into the Crack and stepped up minute holds on the left wall, hoping my feet would stay put as the tricounis in my boots were worn down to the plates.

Carsten had hoped that there would be a ledge at the level of the overhang, but it turned out to be sloping. His arms were beginning to weaken as he was forced to continue jamming up the crack.

> This proved a little too wide for secure jamming but the closeness of the goal provided power for a few more energetic movements until I found myself firmly wedged in the now widening Crack, gasping for breath. The bulge had gone.

The Crack had been climbed, though there was still one good, steep pitch remaining above the climbers' heads. A third ledge below this provided a good belay for the pair, as the drizzle hardened into a steady rain. Despite the rain, the climbers and the rock remained dry, thanks to the overhang above. Good holds on this made it enjoyable though, and Carsten could look down past his feet to enjoy the rock scenery below.

> The rain beat into our faces but we hardly felt it. Our spirits were above the clouds for we had won the day and made a climb which promised to be comparable in quality with the other good routes of Ben Nevis and was possibly harder than any of them.[14]

Commenting on the crux pitch, Carsten thought that it had not been excessively severe, merely strenuous and a problem similar to Holly Tree Wall on Cwm Idwall, the whole beautifully clean and reasonably safe. McGuinness had thought that the first pitch was the worst. Ten years later The Crack had an eventful ascent when in September 1956 an 18-year old student from Edinburgh University decided to attempt the route. The student's name was Robin Smith, who was to feature largely in the near future, but on this ascent events were not to go so smoothly. Smith succeeded in gaining the ledge above the crux, and was bringing up his second, whose,

> ...hands were above the bulge, one hand in the crack, and one hand on the slab, he was very nearly there with only one more move to make, but there he came off. He was on a tight rope, but with the stretch of the nylon he went down about 2 ft and swung away from the overhang. His fingers were too tired to pull him back, he was hanging on the rope, slowly spinning, with nothing below him for about 150 ft.

There was no other option but to lower his swinging second to the ground. Smith was now marooned at the foot of the last crack pitch in the fast gathering darkness, the very stuff of epics. He decided to attempt a solo ascent, thinking he could hide inside the crack and wiggle his way up with some security. Unfortunately, just before the end of the overhang the recess was blocked by a roof.

> So from under the roof I had to wriggle sideways to the edge of the Crack, and leaning out, fumble for the guidebook's good holds over the overhang, then swing out of the Crack, and swarm over the top...I set off on the wriggle, at first facing the recess, but I went too high and my head got stuck, so I came back and I thought, if I face the recess then I can't see where I'm going. I set off again, facing space, and I got to the end of the wriggle and finished up leaning out of the Crack. From here I began to fumble and before long I found the good holds, but I thought, rot the guidebook, these are obviously

Surgeon's Gully (Scottish VS or V,5) on the Glen Nevis face of Ben Nevis; named after Dr Donald Duff

Photo: Noel Williams

poor. I had no qualms about the swing, it was just that having swung I might not make the swarm, and I might not manage to swing back.[15]

Smith somehow managed to reverse back to the ledge, where he spent a miserable night. At dawn, as his would-be rescuers were pounding up the hill, he noticed a line of weakness crossing the face to the right. This traverse turned out to lead fairly easily to easy ground above the bulge, and so to the terrace below the final arete.

There were only two new routes in 1947: Number Two Gully Buttress, Very Difficult, on August 2 by J.D.B.Wilson and G.A.Collie, and Surgeon's Gully. The former climb is now a pleasant winter route, lying just left of Number Two Gully at the head of Coire na Ciste. Surgeon's Gully, originally called the Strawberry Chasm, is of a very different nature from any of the routes normally climbed on Ben Nevis: it is formed, not from the usual dark volcanic rock which forms the summit mass and cliffs of Nevis, but from the reddish Outer Granite; on the Glen Nevis flank of the mountain.

There are seven main gullies facing Glen Nevis, most of which were explored by 1946 and 1947. Perhaps the one person most closely involved in these explorations was Dr Donald G.Duff, after whom Surgeon's Gully was named. A Scottish Very Severe route of some 450m, this is one of the major gullies in Scotland; as late as the 1970s it still awaited a complete ascent of the introductory, middle and upper central branch. It was first climbed by D.H.Haworth and G.J.Ritchie on August 15, 1947. The guide book describes 21 pitches of varying lengths, taking a climber as far as the finishing point of the original ascent. Above lie

*The previous eight
years' of clothing
rationing were not
helping to equip
enthusiastic
climbers wanting
to tackle winter
routes... All this
helped explain the
quiet note with
which the 1940s
were ending; no
routes in 1948, two
variations and one
route in 1949*

the final three branches of the gully, only the leftmost, easy branch having been recorded.

The winter of 1947 – 48 went down as being one of the coldest of the century, with a major pandemic of influenza scything through the population. The previous eight years' of clothing rationing were not helping to equip enthusiastic climbers wanting to tackle winter routes; food was rationed to about 110gm of meat per week, with 25 or 50gm of cheese as additional protein. All this helped explain the quiet note with which the 1940s were ending; no routes in 1948, two variations and one route in 1949.

The route in 1949 was a winter ascent of Tower Cleft, the unusual deeply-cut chimney at the right-hand side of the small crag lying under Tower Gully. On January 22 J.Francis and G.Pratt attempted what they thought was Gardyloo Gully, but owing to bad visibility they in fact had entered the deeply-cut chimney. They retreated in the face of a 9m ice pitch. Francis and Pratt returned on February 13; on this occasion they turned back on coming up to a 6m ice wall. Finally, on February 19, their determination paid off with a successful ascent. As they emerged on to the snow slope below Tower Gully they discovered that a sudden thaw had made snow conditions very dangerous. Rather than continue upwards or traverse left under Gardyloo Buttress they abseiled back down their new route.

In the summer of 1949 Bill Peascod made his first trip to Nevis. He had been climbing with Macphee since 1945, putting up several first ascents with Macphee in the Lakes. Peascod's first impression of the cliffs of Ben Nevis was a fairly typical one – amazement at the size and scope of the great north face. He recognised almost immediately that the normal Lake District pitch-by-pitch route description was not easily applied on Nevis, which had a more Alpine atmosphere.

Macphee and Peascod climbed, in addition to other routes, Rubicon Wall and The Long Climb, in order that these routes be checked out for a new edition of the guide, written by Macphee. Rubicon Wall was climbed without much difficulty, though it was found to be delicate. The Long Climb, however, provided a problem at one point, due to a lack of suitable belays.

Macphee at this time was climbing with 60m of lightweight rope, known as abseil line, and of about 8 mm in diameter. This long rope saved the day, as Peascod found himself almost 30m up with no belay, the climbers using the rope doubled. His two slings had already fallen off small spikes lower down. With difficulty, hanging on to handholds, he managed to retie the rope into one long length, and with this rather doubtful security just gained a niche higher up where he fastened a belay round a dubious spike.

When Macphee gained the belay, he frightened the life out of Peascod by putting his full weight on to the spike belay – an *all or nothing test*. Nine hours after starting the route, and still maintaining the full length of Macphee's abseil line between them, the two climbers reached the top. Peascod, who died of natural causes at the foot of Clogwyn du'r Arddu in May 1985, tells of his long and interesting climbing life in his autobiography, published just before his death at the age of 65.[16]

The relatively slow pace of climbing at the end of the 1940s was to be much shorter-lived than that following the First World War. Clothing and equipment were improving, as ex-W.D. gear became available. Jim Bell was delighted with his first pair of rubber soled boots, bought in 1948 and first tried out in Skye, in May of that year.

> I was highly delighted with my boots shod with Itshide moulded rubber soles & heels. They proved excellent for Cuillin rock dry, wet or even with hail on it. They were perfectly good on trap. They did wear down a bit at the toes in the course of a week involving quite a number of descents on sharp scree.[12]

A small flood of mountaineering books was entering the bookshops: Bill Murray's *Mountaineering in Scotland*, published in 1947[17] was to have a significant influence on young climbers, as did Bell's *A Progress in Mountaineering*, published in 1950.[18] There were other good books of the time of course, but these two included chapters on climbing on Ben Nevis. Another milestone had been reached in the course of mountaineering.

References

1. **Bell**, J.H.B., *A Ben Nevis Constellation of Climbs*. SMCJ 22, 367 – 376, 1941.

2. *CIC Hut Log Book, Vol.1. 12 November, 1928 – July 5, 1949*. NLS.

3. **Ritchie**, Graham S., *Third on the Rope*. SMCJ 25, 137 – 142, 1953.

4. *New Climbs and Notes – Ben Nevis; No.2 Gully*. SMCJ 23, 109 – 110, 1943.

5. **Kellet**, B.P., *Personal notebooks – Climbs on Ben Nevis, Vols. 1 – 3*. NLS.

6. **Dow**, J.A.T., *Personal communication 1984*.

7. **Kellett**, B.P., *Recent Rock Climbs on Ben Nevis*. SMCJ 23, 139 – 152, 1944.

8. **Kellett**, B.P., *A Record of Ben Nevis Climbs*. SMCJ 23, 333 – 340, 1946.

9. **Langmuir**, Eric D.G., *Nothing Venture*. Cambridge Mountaineering, 18 – 21, 1955.

10. *Scotland 1955 – Ben Nevis*. Cambridge Mountaineering, 61 – 65, 1956.

11. **Richardson**, Simon, *Ben Nevis Rock & Ice Climbs* (Glasgow: Scottish Mountaineering Trust, 2002, ISBN 0907521738.)

12. **Bell**, J.H.B., *Climbing Log, Vol.6, p.41, September 1944*.

13. **Bell**, J.H.B., *Scottish Climbing Clubs: A Survey. I*. SMCJ 23, 252 – 260, 1945.

14. **Carsten**, H.A., *The Crack*. Wayfarer's Journal No.8, 44 – 47, 1947.

15. **Smith**, R., *Twenty-four Hours*. Edinburgh University M.C. Journal, 1957. (Reprinted in SMCJ, 29, 341 – 346, 1971.)

16. **Peascod**, W., *Journey After Dawn*. An Autobiography. (Milnthorpe: Cicerone Press, 1985.)

17. **Murray**, W.H., *Mountaineering in Scotland*. (London: J.M. Dent & Sons Ltd, 1947.)

18. **Bell**, J.H.B., *A Progress in Mountaineering*. (Edinburgh & London: Oliver & Boyd, 1950.)

Other Reading

Scroggie, Sydney, *Cairngorms Scene and Unseen*. (Out of print; e-book available from the SMC website, www.smc.org.uk, ISBN 0907521258.)

Graham Macphee (standing) and Allan McNicol in the CIC Hut (c. 1951). The coal stove could be coaxed to red-heat on cold winter evenings. It also provided space for one or two cooking pots or kettles, which meant that in a crowded hut paraffin stoves had to be used. The atmosphere in damp conditions was often full of character. Fashion note: Allan McNicol, who later joined the SMC following in his brother Ian's foot-steps, is wearing a string vest. These became very popular in the 1950s, having been invented in 1933 by a comman-dant in the Norwegian Army, Henrik Brun, who had based the design on fishing nets. They allowed sweat to escape easily while if covered by another layer of clothing they trapped warm air and provided better insulation. They have now all but disappeared

Photo: Tom Weir

8: Renaissance (1950 – 1958)

BETWEEN THE START of 1950 and the end of 1955 just ten routes were recorded on Ben Nevis. Several of these, however, were of great signif-icance. Macphee's guide to Ben Nevis had been published in 1936 and was due for revision. It's format was in any case unsuited for a climber's breeches pocket – it measured an unwieldy 220mm x 145mm in the familiar SMC red cloth binding.

Towards the end of August 1950 Macphee arranged a week's climb-ing based at the CIC Hut. Bill Peascod and Brian Dodson hitched their way up from the Lakes to join him. On August 28, Peascod spotted a likely-looking buttress route just left of Number Three Gully, which they were descending at the time. Macphee, C.H.Peckett and J.Renwick had been climbing Observatory Ridge, and they followed Peascod and Dodson up the new buttress route. It was raining during their ascent, which probably accounts for their grading of Severe, Very Severe in bad weather. They named the route Gargoyle Wall, after a projecting rock seen on the skyline of the buttress. It is still graded Severe.

When the Lakes climbers had arrived at the CIC Hut, Macphee had explained his method of maximising the amount of climbing. This included minimising the amount of time spent in washing up after a meal. Instead, each climber would stick to his own set of cutlery and would save half a slice of bread for the end of each meal. With the bread, cutlery could be cleaned as its owner saw fit.

The day after Gargoyle Wall, Macphee, Peascod and Dodson set off to attempt Minus Two Gully. At this time, 1950, none of the Minus Gullies had been climbed, summer or winter. They roped up with Peas-cod in the lead and Macphee as third man. Peascod climbed the first 30m or so fairly easily in one run-out then brought up Dodson before continuing up the second pitch of 24m to a cave belay. While taking in the slack rope between him and Dodson a small stone was dislodged, and headed for Macphee, nearly 60m below, bouncing off the rocks to strike Macphee on the side of his head.

No safety helmets were used by British climbers at this time. Macphee collapsed on the stance, blood streaming from his wound. Peascod and Dodson prepared to descend when to their great relief Macphee slowly levered himself upright. After a few moments, and holding a handkerchief to his head, Macphee decided that he was fit enough to descend to the Hut; the other two must continue. As he seemed perfectly coherent, they reluctantly carried on, noting Macphee's deliberate descent to the CIC Hut.

In the prevailing damp and greasy conditions the gully proved awkward at several points, with the crux on pitch five involving a hard move round a bulging edge. With Macphee's accident and these conditions, it took the climbers seven hours in total to climb the route. Minus Two Gully, like its two sister gullies, is now a much sought-after winter climb, while in summer it rates as one of the hardest Severes. On their return to the Hut, Macphee was found to be fully recovered, the remainder of the week's holiday continuing as enjoyably as the start.

The sole discovery of 1951 on Ben Nevis was the Severe Continuation Wall, climbed on October 7 by Tom Weir and the brothers Ian and Allan McNicol. This route took the *'repulsive wall'* left of Raeburn's Buttress. The day was a wet one and Weir (later a well-known writer and television personality) was obliged to climb in socks. The wall was also very loose, and is perhaps a safer route in winter, following its ascent by Con Higgins and Dougie MacArthur, who continued up from the Girdle Ledge to complete Boomer's Requiem in February 1973. It then provides an icy V,5 in this quiet corner of Nevis.

The early 1950s saw the fast growth of the University Mountaineering Clubs, with Cambridge and Edinburgh prominent on Nevis from about 1954 onwards. Astonishingly, since Comb Gully in 1938, there had been no winter first ascents on Nevis until March 23 1952, a spell of 14 years. That day marked the first winter ascent of Observatory Buttress, when Dan Stewart and W.H.Foster of Edinburgh University climbed the Direct Route. On their ascent, which took just under six hours, they encountered a considerable quantity of ice.

Direct Route is a rarely-repeated IV which, despite its name, is somewhat confusingly not as direct a winter line as the Ordinary Route to its right, which it crosses. Nonetheless, Direct Route was a fine piece of climbing and a harbinger of the new age soon to arrive on Nevis; an age already arrived at further south, where the Creagh Dhu and others were busy climbing the rough lava walls and icy chimneys and gullies of Glen Coe.

The two ascents recorded in 1953 – one route and one variation – introduced several names that were to influence Scottish climbing for more than 20 years to come. On an Edinburgh JMCS meet in September of that year were Jimmy Marshall and Charles Donaldson, staying at the CIC Hut. It had been wet for days when on September 23 the two climbers recorded Fives Wall, a Severe on the south face of Number Five Gully Buttress. The climb was wet and socks were worn. The following day, as the hut log book cryptically records, the weather was good, and a line was attempted on Càrn Dearg Buttress, 27m being climbed before descending. The two climbers then made a damp ascent of The Long Climb.

While taking in the slack rope...a small stone was dislodged, and headed for Macphee, nearly 60m below, bouncing off the rocks to strike Macphee on the side of his head. Macphee collapsed on the stance, blood streaming from his wound. Peascod and Dodson prepared to descend when to their great relief Macphee slowly levered himself upright

Càrn Dearg Buttress.
Centurion (HVS)
climbs the shadowed
corner on the left,
Sassenach (E1/E3) the
corner on the right

Photo: Gary Latter

Ritchie for some
reason had a very
awkward time
entering the corner,
and with his
confidence seeping
away persuaded
Marshall to give up
the attempt. A
great opportunity
had been lost to
the Scots

The line attempted by Marshall is now the great chimney of Sassenach. On the first look at the line, Marshall worked out a traverse line, crossing the slabs right of the corner, before retiring to the hut. The next day, in company with George Ritchie, a serious attempt was made, but the lack of protection on the overlaps became only too obvious. They then decided to try the huge corner above, known to them as the *great book corner*. Marshall stepped right from the belay ledge and followed the corner to take a belay where it steepened. Ritchie for some reason had a very awkward time entering the corner, and with his confidence seeping away persuaded Marshall to give up the attempt. A great opportunity had been lost to the Scots. That summer in the Alps, Marshall met Joe Brown and Don Whillans in Chamonix and mentioned the chimneys and corners waiting to be climbed on the right of the great buttress. '*There was no great sense of urgency regarding lines*', remembers Marshall.

1953 saw another notable failure on Sassenach, when on October 7 the lure of its dank chimneys attracted a strong Aberdonian team. Over on one of their rare forays to Nevis were Tom Patey, Mike Taylor and Bill Brooker, then students at Aberdeen University. They followed previous attempts and tried an entry from the left; starting up the small, subsidiary buttress taken by the first pitch of Centurion.

Brooker recollects that with a youthful romanticism they had already named the big buttress the *Wall of the Winds*. So far apart were they in technique from events further south, he also confessed, that it never entered their heads for a moment that a direct entry to the Sassenach chimney might be possible. They started up the first pitch in what was their usual order of climbing – Patey first, Taylor in the middle, and Brooker as third man. Patey had just that summer in the Alps bought his first pair of vibram-soled boots, an over-tight pair of 'Frendo' boots. It seems from a photograph of this attempt, however, that Patey was wearing plimsolls while trying the difficult traverse. Reaching the first stance he brought up Taylor.

Belayed by Taylor, Patey crossed the overlapping slabs right of the great corner of the future Centurion, placing a peg runner halfway. He was unable to turn the edge, however, handicapped by his footwear. When it became obvious that they had no hope of gaining the chimney system from the left they retreated by abseil, just as Kellett had been obliged to do nine years earlier. Undaunted, the three climbers moved to the right flank of Càrn Dearg Buttress and attacked the rocks at a new point.

The Aberdonians gained the foot of the prominent chimney by a 45m traverse from the right, from the grass section above the lower part of Evening Wall. The traverse itself was not without interest, starting with a 12m abseil and continuing with a very hard move across an overhanging wall to gain some exposed ledges on the very edge of the buttress. This point was some 30m above the ground. An 18m Severe traverse then led round to the foot of the chimney.

Patey led up the chimney, coming up hard against a massive chockstone at 12m. This rock, he realised, could not be dislodged without wiping out his second. The chockstone moved when touched, unnerving Patey. There was just over an hour of light left, thanks to the earlier manoeuvrings of the day, so a tactical withdrawal was decided on. The overhang below was so great that their 30m abseil rope hung free without reaching the ground, forcing the tired climbers to reverse the last part of their traverse. In the general rush to get off the rocks before night fell three pegs were left behind. To add to the gloom of the party, their first abseil rope remained firmly jammed, though the thrifty trio returned two days later to recover that item.

Before any Scottish party could return to the chimney line on Càrn Dearg Buttress, the long and wet autumn nights had arrived, to be followed by winter. Scottish climbers up until then did next to no rock climbing through the winter, waiting instead until about late April before putting down the axe and taking to rock again.

One impressive day's mountaineering was the April 1954 outing by Len Lovat and Tom Weir, during which they climbed all three major ridges on the north face of Ben Nevis in winter condition. From their tent in Glen Nevis they made an early start, reaching the CIC Hut before its occupants were up. Their first route was Observatory Ridge. Descending Tower Ridge, they passed a party from Inverness. Crossing the foot

Tom Patey in fairly typical conditions! This tough Aberdonian was a major driving force for over two decades, initially based in Aberdeen and latterly on the west coast. He was killed in an abseiling accident in May 1970, following the first ascent of the easternmost of The Maiden sea stacks off Whiten Head near Durness (1957)

Photo: Douglas Scott

One of Britain's most outstanding climbers in the 1950s, Brown was almost killed attempting Point Five Gully in 1956

Photo: Nat Allen

The Scottish climbing fraternity, or in reality its West, East and North-East cells, received this ascent as they would a national disaster. 'English Bastards!' was the immediate reaction by Ritchie. This unorthodox message of congratulations immediately suggested the route name Sassenach to Whillans and Brown

of Observatory Gully, they went up Slingsby's Chimney and climbed the North-East Buttress, passing the top of Tower Ridge to greet the same Inverness party finishing their ascent.

The ascent of Sassenach in April 1954 came as a bad surprise for Scottish climbers. The successful party was the Mancunian team of Joe Brown and Don Whillans. Joe Brown has been described as the greatest household name in British climbing since Whymper and certainly his productive rock climbing career, often in partnership with Don Whillans, was responsible for advances in techniques and standards during the 1950s. For six winters of that decade Brown and his fellow members of the Manchester-based Rock and Ice Club climbed on Ben Nevis. At this time, Point Five Gully was unclimbed in either summer or winter, Brown joining the select group of climbers who had, or were, attempting it.

At Christmas 1954 Brown visited the Ben with his girlfriend Val. Nat Allen remembers seeing her for the first time on the platform at Fort William. *'Who the hell's that?'* he said to Brown, *'Hi!'* Val said. *'Well, she can't stay in the Hut, it's men only'* Allen stated. So Nip Underwood and Allen stayed in the CIC Hut while Val and Joe camped outside for five days until the tent collapsed, forcing them into the hut to join the rest of the party. In fact, while SMC membership at that time was all-male, it did not exclude mixed parties from the CIC Hut, which indeed used to have a small corner set aside by a curtain as the *married quarters*. Allen's misapprehension may have arisen from the situation at Lagangarbh, the SMC hut in Glen Coe, where a condition of the original lease excluded mixed parties and was outwith SMC control.

In April 1954 the Rock and Ice were again on Nevis. Brown and Ron Moseley were planning another attempt on Point Five, having gone as far as having Moseley's mother make a two-man bivouac tent out of old barrage balloon material. The tent was to be pitched close to the foot of the gully so as to ensure an early start. The mountain, oblivious to such human follies produced a gale. Point Five Gully was also in uncompromising mood, waves of loose powder snow pouring down its narrow confines. After two days of fruitless gully watching Brown and Moseley gave up. On Saturday April 17, Brown went over to Càrn Dearg Buttress, where Don Whillans was working on a new route.

Donald Desbrow Whillans (1933 – 1985) would be rated by most climbers as one of the best mountaineers Britain has produced, with ascents of many classic rock climbs in Britain and in the Alps. Later in his bold climbing career he took part in a series of expeditions to the bigger ranges, including Everest and the successful ascent of the South Face of Annapurna in 1970. His name continued to live not only in his routes, but through the Whillans climbing harness and Whillans Box, the latter a metal-framed rectangular tent for expedition work. He died of heart failure in the summer of 1985.

Whillans had been working on a direct entry to the great chimney system on the buttress, trying to find a way through the steep lower band of rock which defends the chimney. Nat Allen had been his second throughout these attempts. On Good Friday Whillans and Allen had attempted one steep groove then climbed the first pitch before abseiling down. On Saturday they were back on the route with Brown, who suggested an alternative line. Traversing right, Brown came across an old sling, left, thought Whillans, by John Cunningham of the Creagh Dhu MC on an earlier attempt. Whillans joined him at the stance from which they surveyed the next section; a vertical wall leading to a massive overhang. About 3m up a crack was a smaller overhang, above which was the base of the main roof.

Brown jammed a couple of stones into the crack and using slings on these pulled up to the big roof. A large chockstone loomed out above. Moving slowly, Brown managed to reach this and place a sling on it. Whillans was certain the pitch was now secure, but to his surprise Brown began to retreat, saying he had nearly fallen off, that it was too strenuous. It had taken an incredible amount of strength to thread the sling in freezing conditions, and darkness was now falling, so they agreed to return next day. Brown thought that the overhang was too strenuous for one man to climb in one go so they decided that Whillans would replace the slings removed by Brown during his retreat.

On the Sunday morning Whillans led direct from the ground to the belay beneath the overhang. Continuing on up to the chockstone, he found that through careful climbing he still had plenty of strength, so Brown suggested that he continue. Whillans later described the crux section.

> I moved out and round the edge of the overhang. Straight away I knew why Joe had said it wouldn't go...the only holds were small, slanting grooves leaning awkwardly to the left. I got my right foot jammed in the crack, foot tapping against the chockstone and levered myself so that I could see the rock above. Stretching my right hand, I gripped the top of a V-shaped block. I was just preparing to put my full weight on it, when I felt it move. Like lightning, I jammed my leg even further into the crack. Carefully I tested the block again. It was either that or nothing. I decided it probably wouldn't pull out any further and, before I could have any second thoughts, I put my weight on it. A couple of moves to the left on the sloping holds and the pitch was finished.[1]

The barrier pitch to the chimneys above had finally capitulated. The chimney itself gave 60m feet of classic climbing, followed by grooves for 90m. The route had been snatched from under Scottish noses. Nat Allen had left the attempt to Brown and Whillans on the Sunday, watching Whillans powering over the roof. Allen then joined up with Don Cowan and climbed The Castle, descending Càrn Dearg Buttress to the top of the difficult climbing carrying the nailed boots belonging to the successful pair (who were climbing in pumps). The party then descended Number Five Gully, to be shouted at by George Ritchie who was soloing Jubilee Gully with his weekend sack. The Scottish climbing fraternity, or in reality its West, East and North-East cells, received this ascent as they would a national disaster. *'English Bastards!'* was the immediate reaction by Ritchie. This unorthodox message of congratulations immediately suggested the route name Sassenach to Whillans and Brown.

Any thoughts the Rock and Ice may have had for celebration were rudely interrupted that evening, when a climber rushed into the encampment with the news that a woman had fallen from the Great Tower and was hanging on the rope. A rescue party set out into the night, formed of Rock and Ice, Creagh Dhu, who were camping nearby, and SMC members from the hut. Brown and Whillans reached the Great Tower from

Don Whillans, Cwm Glas, Snowdonia (1983). Erstwhile climbing partner of Joe Brown, Whillans went on to make many major ascents in higher mountains, including Annapurna by a difficult new route. He died of a heart attack in 1985, aged 52

Photo: Joe Brown

above, and reversing the line of Eastern Traverse reached the tied-off rope to which the victim was attached. The two climbers pulled on the thin, icy rope until their hands were bloody, but it remained firmly fixed. The woman had fallen about 12m while climbing the Great Tower and though held by her woman companion, had hit her head during the fall.

Archie Hendry and Allen pulled the stretcher up Observatory Gully. Hope, who had been arguing with Hendry all evening about some missing coal had the First-aid sack, so he went on with Don Cowan and Ray Greenall to join Whillans and Brown. With all five pulling on the rope it remained stubbornly fixed. Although there was little doubt in the climbers' minds that the woman was dead, Brown was lowered down to her. By now it was about 1am. Her rope had frozen to the rock where it made contact, explaining its immobility. The woman was dead. Even had she survived the head injuries and the cold, the rope would have slowly asphyxiated her; climbing harnesses were a long way in the future and 30 to 40 minute's constriction from a simple waist attachment would kill. The exhausted climbers had risked their own lives on a dangerous rescue attempt. The climbers waiting on the summit plateau were also in danger, from exposure to the biting wind. All were much cheered by the arrival of the RAF Mountain Rescue team just before dawn.

Sassenach set a new pattern in Nevis climbing, being both long, at 270m, as well as difficult and steep – the first of the modern 'classics'. Kellett's ascent of Gardyloo Buttress had been difficult if short, while Bell's Orion Face routes were long but not difficult. The route is now graded E1 if aid is used to enter the chimney, E3 6a if climbed free, technically straightforward for the modern hard climber, though in nature a grand mountaineering route of character. The following summer Len Lovat and Tom Patey arrived, armed with a letter from Brown describing the route. The first pitch went easily for Lovat and he brought up Patey to look at the second pitch. Patey's eyes opened wide as he examined the overhangs and realised that he would never be able to hang on, let alone climb the pitch. The two climbers doffed their hats and retreated.

Some of the character of the route may be gleaned from the account of the second ascent on June 13, 1956, by Bob Downes and Mike O'Hara, two very competent climbers of the Cambridge University MC. Downes and O'Hara were wearing PAs by 1956, the rock climbing boots designed by Pierre Allain in France. These enabled another leap in rock climbing standards. The boots had smooth rubber soles, flexible along their length but stiffer across the sole, allowing both friction climbing and small edging holds to be used. Manufactured nuts, or chockstones, were still some years away however, jammed knots or slings being used on Sassenach for protection.

On the crux second pitch, noted the Cambridge climbers, some of the rock required delicate handling, while the leftward grooves above the overhang were found to be more technical and strenuous than the roof itself. This pitch occupied the team for four hours.

> The chimney itself is very strenuous, characterised by loose chocks and green slime. The security itself is sufficient, but owing to the width of the chimney it is a mistake to carry a rucksack...The pitches above are not easy...it's difficult to think of a route which has the character of Sassenach, or its grande envergure. Although the hard pitch is only half the length of Cenotaph Corner,

SMC member Rick Allen wrestles with the Sassenach chimney

Photo: Noel Williams

to this party at least, it seemed more tiring, more precarious, certainly more baffling than that climb.[2]

In describing their 11-hour battle on Sassenach, Downes was demonstrating a characteristic modesty, as his remarkable determination had been tested by a prolonged hailstorm during their ascent, causing some delay. Mike O'Hara, later Professor of Geology at Aberystwyth, remembers,

> ...coming off with a whole ledge while leading up to the base of the big chimney, and being stopped on the lip of the overhang. Also a fantastic moment having followed Bob up the first pitch of the chimney, carefully avoiding the huge jammed (loose) flakes and putting my knee onto the jammed boulder stance which Bob had been using – which promptly exited downwards and cleared the loose flakes from the chimney, and swept the whole area. Heard all over the mountain![3]

The loose flakes of the Sassenach chimney were to give to give other climbers shaky moments. A well-known and infamous rotating chockstone finally parted company with the mountain about 1970. At the time the Edinburgh climber John Porteous was hanging on to it. As a later souvenir he would produce a somewhat distorted karabiner which had been part of his protection at that point.

The first free ascent of Sassenach is credited to Steve Wilson, in August 1969. During a week of superb weather, most of the big routes on Nevis were repeated. The 18-year old Wilson had already repeated routes such as Shibboleth, The Bat, and The Crack. Tragically, in November 1969 he was badly injured abseiling and was subsequently paralysed.

In 1954 then, Sassenach was one of the greatest mountaineering routes in Britain – continuously difficult and strenuous for 270m, an Alpine line. Its ascent stunned the Scots; complacency had been revealed. All that could be found elsewhere on Nevis that year was a Difficult by Malcolm Slesser and party, a short route right of, and parallel to, the upper part of Glover's Chimney. The Gutter, as it was christened, was climbed in heavy rain. Even that route may have been in part a summer ascent of the winter ascent taken by Goodeve's party in 1907, on their epic 30-hour travail on Tower Ridge.

As if to add insult to injury, the first new route the following year was by the energetic Cambridge Club, on their second summer visit to Nevis. Downes and O'Hara spent five perfect days in June 1955, camping under the cliffs. Included in the list of routes by the Cambridge team were second ascents of Kellett's Route on Gardyloo Buttress, and Right Hand Route on the Minus Face. New ground was also broken, with the first ascent of North Eastern Grooves, a possibility of which they had first noticed during a visit the previous New Year.

North Eastern Grooves climbs Minus One Buttress – that *'elegant court companion'* to the Orion Face, which it defines on the left. The Buttress starts off as little more than a broad rib, its foot often masked by the last of the winter's snow. It then swells to its maximum breadth at half-height before tapering spectacularly to a finish at a giant flake, reluctantly connected to the main mass of the North-East Buttress by a rickety arete. The original intention of Downes and O'Hara had been to follow a crack line on the buttress, running from bottom right to top left. However, at just over one third height a belt of overhangs crosses

Bob Downes was on three major first ascents in 1956, including Centurion, Minus One Buttress, and The Shield. Tragically, in July 1957, he was to die from pneumonia, during an expedition to Masherbrum with Joe Brown and Don Whillans

Photo: Mike O'Hara

Mike O'Hara (1954).
One of a band of
Cambridge climbers,
O'Hara was to pick
off many plum routes
on Ben Nevis and
Scotland, including
Minus One Buttress

Photo: Mike O'Hara

Eric Langmuir (1931
– 2005) was born in
Glasgow and became
influential in outdoor
education

Photo: Mike O'Hara

the face, forcing the two Cambridge climbers off to the left on the fourth pitch. After an excursion across Minus Two Gully and up by its left edge, a right traverse allowed Minus One Buttress to be regained. The continuation of the lower crack line, in the form of a deep groove, was then followed for a short distance to reach the buttress crest at a spacious terrace. A giant 12m flake, the crest of the ridge and the final arete saw the finish of the route, abutting on to the North-East Buttress.

Downes and O'Hara had pioneered the first part of the route on June 17; on June 21 they finished the climb, joined by Eric Langmuir. It was, they admitted, artificial in its upper section, though the climbing was good and the position excellent.

There were two other first ascents in 1955 – both made in the same weekend on a rare visitation by the Creagh Dhu. Perhaps one of the most succinct descriptions of that renowned Glasgow club comes from the pen of Jimmy Marshall, often associated with the Creagh Dhu, and an honorary member. Writing in a retrospective journal article, Marshall describes a youthful summer ascent of Raven's Gully, when he and his friend had been *'taken'* by Bill Smith (i.e. taken up, and taken in!)

> ...it came to me that we had partaken of the height and depth of experience, but more significantly, had been shown the way and the light by Glasgow's Ullyssean crew, to a new and vital life style waiting to be enjoyed in our Scottish mountains.[4]

It must be left to some other place and time to tell the story of the Creagh Dhu. Suffice it to say that in life they are as large as the legend. One point which must be examined is their relative neglect of Ben Nevis during the 1950s. Most of the Club could and did have weekends in the Lakes and in Wales, travelling by motor bike. One of their members, Charlie Vigano, has explained this neglect of Nevis.

> The Ben was too far for even a club bus at the week-ends because you had to get back to Glasgow early enough on a Sunday night to allow people who lived out of town to catch their last buses home. This meant leaving Fort William at 5.00pm. Motor-bikes in winter were alright occasionally for Glen Coe because you made for and left from proper huts. A couple of wasted and wet trips to the Ben would soon kill the urge: it really needed four-wheeled transport.[5]

Had the Creagh Dhu been as active on Ben Nevis during the 1950s as they were in Glen Coe, the guidebook would read very differently.

On Saturday, August 27, 1955, Zero Gully finally received its first ascent. The three Creagh Dhu climbers were Bill Smith, George McIntosh and Mick Noon. Wearing vibrams they soloed the first 60m or so before roping up. Then followed 90 to 120m of climbing with poor belays. The crux was about half-way up the gully, requiring a run-out of about 43m. The 300m route was graded a Hard Severe and had occupied them for three and a half hours.

On the Sunday Noon and McIntosh entered Point Five Gully, switching to nailed boots. This is harder than Zero Gully, summer or winter, and provided eleven pitches of climbing before easing off higher up. The grading of Point Five Gully is now given as Scottish Very Severe. Neither gully is likely to receive many summer ascents. Indeed, both gullies had been the object of a winter ascent since at least the 1930s, the only factor preventing a strong attempt on them by MacKenzie and Murray's group being the heavy snow and ice conditions of that decade. Marshall, who has climbed Point Five in summer, probably making the second ascent, rates it as a good and worthwhile climb, though some care has to be taken over the rock, the typical small flakes found in Nevis gullies being on occasion suspect.

The increasing use of the comfortable and light rubber-soled boots with Vibram or Commando soles was being paralleled by the number of winter accidents. These were usually caused by a slip on hard snow or ice, or by a loss of control when glissading. It was not yet fully understood, particularly by impecunious young climbers, that vibrams in winter could be lethal unless used in conjunction with crampons. This was in contrast to nailed boots, which in effect carried their own built-in crampons.

In the May 1954 issue of the SMCJ there was a note by Dr Donald Duff, containing a warning about icy conditions on Ben Nevis and inadequate footwear. This warning was to be highlighted by a shocking accident on December 19 of that year, when five naval cadets lost their lives by sliding off the descent slope towards the Càrn Mòr Dearg arete, falling on to the rocks of Coire Leis.

A climber reaching the summit plateau of Nevis in winter has three common routes of descent to choose from. If returning to Glen Nevis then the route used is the bridle path. If descending to the Allt a' Mhuilinn then the choice is either via the Càrn Mòr Dearg arete to the south-east, or by Number Three or Number Four Gully, usually the latter. This gully is just over 1.6km from the summit as a climber would have to walk, avoiding the cliff edge and the potential threat of cornices above the gullies en route. In bad weather at an altitude of over 1,200m, 1.6km can be an impossible distance to cover, particularly as a south-west gale would be forcing one directly towards the cliffs.

The alternative descent route, should a climber reject Number Four Gully, lies south-east, down the relatively short slopes to gain the start of the Càrn Mòr Dearg arete and the head of Coire Leis. This route has two great dangers, however, and its deceptively easy slope has been the site of several tragic accidents, including that of the unfortunate naval cadets mentioned above. In clear weather the descent is a pleasant one with super views over the surrounding hills. In wintry conditions, two factors can combine to make this route a death-trap to the inexperienced or unready.

On either side of the descent is a steep slope; that to the north-east drops 380m into Coire Leis, that to the south-west drops 457m to Coire Eòghainn. The descent route receives any sunlight direct. After many cycles of alternate thawing and freezing a particularly hard surface of ice can build up, coating the slope and any projecting boulders with a smooth and dangerous surface. This is the first factor in the equation. The second factor follows from the subtle topography of the descent. In going down from the summit the general direction for the arete is to the south-east, but the plateau leads one in a more easterly direction, towards the finish of the North-East Buttress. If a climber continues to be drawn this way for too long, a deceptive, convex slope will be reached. This leads, imperceptibly at first, into a gently sloping scoop, followed by a slide into the top of a gully and the last steep fatal slope

The final knife-edged arete of North-Eastern Grooves (VS) – also utilised by Minus One Direct (E1)

Photo: Ken Crocket

over the Little Brenva Face to drop into Coire Leis.

Lower down the descent slope the angle eases, and the descending climber must face in a more southerly direction. A slip here can land one on the boulders of Coire Eòghainn. This necessary change of direction on the descent to the arete complicates an apparently straightforward route. The obvious surface feature near the summit of Ben Nevis in winter is the emergency bivouac shelter a few metres from the summit; built on the ruins of the Observatory and on the spot where the Observatory tower used to stand. This shelter is like an ice-box in winter, though it continues to save lives from the crippling effects of the wind.

To find the arete in bad conditions, steer 130 degrees (true) from the shelter for 365m, descending meanwhile, then turn east to reach the arete and the head of Coire Leis. From the arete a slightly steeper but uncomplicated slope leads down into the floor of Coire Leis. Following a fatal accident on Nevis, Dr Duff oversaw the erection of direction posts indicating the safe descent route to the arete. Duff's original pair of three-foot wooden posts were later added to, but only after the terrible accident involving the cadets.

On a more positive note for 1954, Macphee, then President of the SMC, celebrated his completion of the Munros (with a completion number of 20), his 100th ascent of Ben Nevis, and his 100th night in the CIC Hut. To complete these personal achievements, the new Climbers' Guide to Ben Nevis was published, written by Macphee and containing, as a last-minute addition, descriptions of Sassenach and Fives Wall. The guide book marked a change in format by the SMC in being pocket-sized at 158mm by 110mm, in the dimpled cover of red board which was to become a familiar sight on Scottish crags for over twenty years.

Summer climbing in 1956 opened on Nevis on All Fool's Day, with Tom Patey and Jerry Smith climbing the 215m Severe Rogue's Rib on the west flank of Tower Ridge. At that early stage in the season, the gully immediately right of the rib, the Italian Climb, was filled with snow and ice. The Aberdonians, climbing in nailed boots, were forced by slabby rock to climb the ice pitch in the gully. They then moved on to the steep and exposed rib which they followed to the upper section. Not long after, Kenneth Bryan and N.Harthill made a complete ascent, climbing the lower rocks in their entirety.

Even better things were to appear during this summer of 1956. Cambridge University MC were again up on their post-exam spree. The previous summer Minus One Buttress had been climbed, if somewhat indirectly, by North Eastern Grooves. On June 10 Downes and O'Hara, camping under the stars, were joined by Mike Prestige. O'Hara had been dreaming all winter of a direct route up Minus One Buttress, one which would avoid the left traverse into Minus Two Gully. The next day all three headed for the Minus Face.

Minus One Direct, for the Cambridge students, took a corkscrewing line up the buttress, following the earlier North Eastern Grooves for the first three pitches. On the second pitch they eliminated an aid sling which had been used on the first ascent. The fourth pitch, led by Downes, was the crux. From a large block belay a step right is made on to an exposed rib, jutting out over an overhang. Above is a ledge

The 1954 Guide to Ben Nevis by Macphee. For the first time the book was published in a pocket-sized edition, suitable for carrying on the hill. The dimpled, red card binding was to be a familiar sight on SMC guidebooks for decades to come. 110x158mm, 156pp, 14 diagrams

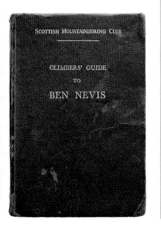

Alastair Walker leading the first pitch of Minus One Direct (E1). The arete is visible high above on the left, with the crux overhang of Minus One Gully seen on the right of the photograph

Photo: Ken Crocket

leading rightwards to an undercut groove. The groove requires a committing step up. This leads to another committing move and a third beyond that before difficulties ease off. The rock is perfect, though cracks are blind and handholds scarce.

O'Hara, leading through with Downes, climbed the fine crack above, leading into a regrettable section in the summer looseness of Minus One Gully. A pitch and a half in the gully, climbing up its left corner, then O'Hara traversed left into a cosy if somewhat shattered niche on the buttress. From the niche a fine step left on to the buttress crest is made, where cracked slabs and a small but puzzling overlap lead to the great terrace. This is the reunion with North Eastern Grooves. The giant, 12m flake leads on familiar ground to the final, flimsy arete and the North East Buttress.

Since the first ascent of Minus One Direct there have been several variations to the route, two of which have been made inadvertently by parties climbing without guidebooks. The second ascent of the route was probably made by a party from the energetic Cambridge club in 1957, when Mike O'Hara, Ted Maden, David Fagan and Bill Turrall were camped opposite Càrn Dearg Buttress. Maden described the three days of perfect weather enjoyed by the party in a Climbers' Club Journal article.[6]

Ten years later, in 1967, the first of the variations was made when Ian Rowe and Peter MacDonald climbed without guidebook. (This was two years before the Marshall guide was published.) At the time they were not fully aware that there were two routes up the buttress, North Eastern Grooves being the original. From the plinth stance at the start of the fourth pitch they moved left as for North Eastern Grooves, realised they were moving off the buttress proper, then made a rising traverse back right above the crux groove, to regain the original line of Minus One Direct below the undercut crack. This is now called the Plinth Variation.

Five years further on, in August 1972, Ken Crocket and Ian Fulton made a second variation, again climbing without a guidebook. On this occasion the original line was followed through the crux to the

Minus One Buttress. The original route climbs the crack line on the right-hand side of the face

Photo: Noel Williams

Noel Williams on the summit of Ben Nevis after climbing the Arete Variation to Minus One Direct, (August 1983)

Photo: Steve Abbott

Alastair Walker starting out on the Serendipity Variation, Minus One Direct

Photo: Ken Crocket

undercut crack. Here it was felt that the crack was leading the climbers off the buttress proper and into the gully, so a rising traverse left was made to regain what was instinctively felt to be the true line of the buttress. Two excellent pitches led to the great terrace and the original finish up the flake and arete.

A later ascent by Crocket in 1976, following the original line with a guidebook, gave a belated realisation of the accidental discovery of the 1972 variation. The variation was named The Serendipity Line, after the Princes of Serendip, characters in a Walpole novel who were always making discoveries of things they were not in search of.

Finally, on August 28 1983, Noel Williams and Steve Abbott found a variation on the upper part of the route, climbing the first part of The Serendipity Line then breaking out left by a tension move on a peg to climb the Arete Variation, at Hard Very Severe. This finishes at the great terrace as for North Eastern Grooves. Williams, a local school teacher, had noticed the possibility of this variation on an earlier ascent, on August 13, and had determined to return. On Saturday 27 the second pitch was still damp and they retreated to climb elsewhere. They were up the next day with more success, as the diary entry of Noel Williams relates –

> Back up to try MOD with Stevie Abbott. I led the Arête Variation, but took a tiny tug on the rope to cross the initial slab. I could easily have reversed it and done without. (Stevie said I was too honest when I reported it!) We knocked a big block off the second pitch of the Arête Variation, and nearly wiped out a party on the scree at the bottom. Fortunately they were all looking up at us at the time and they scattered in all directions. It was a relief when we saw that no-one was hurt.[7]

Annoyed by the tension move, Williams returned to the route on Sunday July 8, 1984, and repeated his Arete variation free with Willie Jeffrey. Whichever variation is taken, Minus One Direct will give a magnificent day's climbing – through and up an Alpine environment on what many mountaineers would accord to be the best summer route on Ben Nevis. The route overall, if taken by the original first four pitches then the Serendipity and Arete Variations, is an E1. The current guide says of this climb –

> An outstanding climb, and one of the finest of its grade in the country. It combines superb rock with interesting route finding, and has a distinct alpine feel.[8]

Three more routes were found on Nevis in the summer of 1956. A Severe on the East Wall of Tower Ridge and two Very Severes on Càrn Dearg Buttress. The Severe was Echo Traverse, by Len Lovat of the SMC and two JMCS members, Ken Bryan (killed in a car accident in Canada in the 1970s) and Norman Harthill. Lovat later went on to write the second Climbers' Guide to Glen Coe. Echo Traverse, a neglected route in summer, was later climbed in winter at III by the Marshall brothers. Its position on a thus far obscure face has contributed to a continued neglect.

The summer of 1956, however, will be remembered for the ascent of a major classic line on Càrn Dearg Buttress. Mike O'Hara recalls how, in August of that year, he was a first-year research student whose work was beginning to fall behind due to too much climbing. He was at that

Keith Milne moving
through the overhangs
on the penultimate
pitch of Centurion
(HVS)

Photo: Tom Prentice

Càrn Dearg Buttress.
The nature of this
huge buttress is very
obvious here, with
overlapping walls and
steep slabs of near-
perfect rock. The
climber is on the
first hard pitch of
Centurion (pitch 2)

Photo: Ian Fulton

time in the Department of Mineralogy and Petrology in Cambridge, and was in the middle of a big programme of analyses when Bob Downes and Don Whillans called in. They had a motorcycle-sidecar combination with room to spare, but, *'Like a fool I said no...'* O'Hara later regretted that decision, because Whillans and Downes went up Nevis to make the first ascent of the major corner line on the buttress on August 30. The line is now known as Centurion.

Centurion had been attempted several times in the past. The first pitch had been climbed by Kellett in June 1944, on which occasion he had come across an old sling, 9 to 12m up the big corner on pitch two. Jimmy Marshall had made a commendable attempt in 1953. Leading a party from Edinburgh which included Archie Hendry and George Ritchie, Marshall attempted to gain the chimney of Sassenach from the left. Failing, as had Kellett, they then turned their eyes on the corner of Centurion. Marshall almost had the crux moves in his hand when demands from his second forced him to retreat.

The first pitch of Centurion takes the small flying buttress, with its deceptive 15m wall. A step right then leads into the main feature of the route and the first of its two hardest pitches, the corner of pitch two. This central corner takes a direct line up Càrn Dearg Buttress, midway between Route I and Sassenach. The groove is flanked on its right by smooth overlapping slabs - their appearance brought to mind the battle armour of a Roman centurion.

Whillans, who led all but one of the pitches (Downes led the masterly penultimate pitch), had taken a long time on the second pitch, the groove. This is a fairly open corner, with steep slabs on the right and a vertical, left retaining wall. The line follows the crack between the slabs and the wall until one can break left across the wall then up a rib on its outside edge to a ledge vertically above the start.

On the first ascent Whillans had climbed from the belay at the top

Little Brenva Face above Coire Leis. Cresta (III) runs up the face centrally while on the right the upper rocks of North-East Buttress catch the sun

Photo: Patrick Roman

Approaching the icefall first climbed by Malcom Slesser and Norman Tennent on the second ascent of Cresta

Photo: Ian Fulton

of the groove up a vicious crack in the left wall, to gain the retaining rib high up. Downes spotted a more subtle horizontal traverse across the vertical wall, gaining the rib lower down. This is the way now followed by parties bent on survival. Above this point the route relents somewhat in angle and difficulty, climbing gradually slabbier rock to cross the traverse line of Route II. From here, Downes led the penultimate pitch starting up the intimidatingly steep headwall, and the second of the two hard pitches on the route (both now graded 5a).

In 1973 Centurion was the scene of a fatal accident. A well-known American climber, Rocky Keeler, was leading pitch 4 but had strayed on to a direct exit from the diedre, instead of taking the normal way out to the left. He slipped, his single rope cutting on a flake and he fell to his death at the foot of the buttress. His partner, having only a short length of rope, was stranded on the cliff and refused to be lowered, a helicopter dropping a rope to him so as to enable him to abseil to safety. American climbing techniques are often based on the use of a single rope, many of their routes having a more straightforward layout than British routes

The final two pitches of Centurion, almost unbelievably, continue the direct line of the route through the huge overhangs above. Downes's contribution to the climb was his masterly route finding on pitch seven, the second crux of the route. This finds its way through the overhangs by a series of jinking traverses on narrow, gangway-like steps, set sideways to the buttress face. One last pitch with (to a tired leader) a strenuous little rib, then the route finishes as abruptly as it begins, at a small ledge.

The ascent of Centurion was a second Sassenach, a national disaster. To make matters worse, the next day Whillans and Downes went out again and climbed The Shield, another Very Severe on the Great Buttress. Above Waterfall Gully, on the north face of the buttress, an enormous flake forms a chimney, the line of the route. On the first ascent on September 1, wet conditions caused the pioneers some difficulty and they gave the route the grade of Very Severe with some misgivings. Both routes however are graded Hard Very Severe in the current guide.[8] Sadly, less than one year later, in July 1957, Bob Downes was to die from pneumonia, during an attempt on Masherbrum. In his memory, the R.O. Downes Memorial Hut was opened in Froggat, Derbyshire, on April 29, 1961, under the auspices of the Climbers Club.

It was to be three years before outraged Scots could reply with a route of their own on Càrn Dearg Buttress, but by 1956 the long-awaited revival of winter climbing on Nevis had begun. In this year we see an inflexion in the curve of Scottish winter ascents. One solitary route and a variation was made during this winter. The route was Neptune Gully, a III on the North Trident Buttress. This was by Arthur Bennet and Jim Clarkson and was the second winter route to be made since Good Friday Climb in 1939 – a period of 17 years. The variation was also on the Trident Buttresses, on March 11, when Ken Bryan and Len Lovat, climbing Central Gully, took the icefall direct. This variation is now a III. Hereafter, the curve rose sharply. The revival in winter climbing can be dated precisely to February 1957, as an examination of the record will bear out. In the seventeen winter seasons since 1939 two routes had been recorded. In February 1957 there were five. On the 14th, C.H.C.Brunton and Jim Clarkson recorded a III on Cousins' Buttress, climbing the Ordinary Route. Much of this had been previously climbed by Macphee, Todd and Williams in April 1935 under thaw conditions, probably the reason why Macphee chose not to record the ascent.[9]

Two days later, on February 16, the first route was recorded on the South-East face of the North-East Buttress, overlooking the Càrn Mòr Dearg arete above Coire Leis. Cresta, III, was climbed by Tom Patey, Len Lovat and Graeme Nicol. It followed a line on this alpine-style face first suggested by Bill Murray, who had reconnoitred this area in the winter of 1947. Like the potentially dangerous slopes above, this face receives any sunlight going and readily builds up ice, particularly on the left section of the face.

The main feature of Cresta is a shallow couloir about 180m long, beginning above and left of a 90m rock spur. The couloir leads to the exit cliffs, which include a prominent and steep ice pitch. This pitch was avoided by the first ascent party who traversed right beneath it to break out on to easier ground. The Little Brenva Face, as it is now known (through a supposed likeness to the Alpine face), can be climbed virtually anywhere, and though later routes have been recorded, there seems little point in having more than about three recorded routes on this pleasantly sunny area of Ben Nevis. Further right however, steeper rocks form the top flank of the North-East Buttress, looking over to Coire Leis. Harder routes with complex route-finding would be found here in future years.

The mountain was in superb condition during that week in February 1957, and those who were staying at the hut made the most of it. On the 18th, Slesser and Norman Tennent made the second ascent of Cresta, finishing by a slightly more direct line through the exit cliffs. Also that day, Lovat and Donald Bennet climbed Number Three Gully Buttress, a highly popular III in later years and a route recommended for its relatively secure but nonetheless exciting positions. As elsewhere on the mountain, good snow-ice made step cutting a delight. But the plum of the day, the week, and the year, was the ascent of the much-sought after Zero Gully.

The news of good conditions had attracted some of the best Scottish climbers from both ends of the country, principally from Glasgow and Aberdeen. The main attraction was Point Five Gully, with Zero a close second. These two gullies were, in effect, the great problem routes of the post-war years. Of the two, Point Five looked to be technically the harder. In addition to their obvious steepness and length, a major stumbling block to an ascent of either gully was spindrift. Even in a day of complete calm, both gullies could be rendered unclimbable by reason of vast icy waves of fine snow pouring down their narrow confines.

That weekend a dozen good climbers had gathered at the hut. From Aberdeen Patey and Nicol had arrived, followed the next day by climbers from the Glasgow area, including Slesser, Bennet, Douglas Scott and Tennent. On February 16 a strong south-west wind was shifting snow down the major gullies, forcing Lovat, Patey and Nicol on to Cresta. The other four took to the North-East Buttress. The events that followed were chronicled by the late Tom Patey, in a long and entertaining journal article.

When Patey's party returned to the CIC Hut they found visitors,

...two climbers, whose characteristic patois, coupled with a distinct air of authority, stamped them as members of the Creagh Dhu Club.

Graeme Nicol c. 1952, climbing at Souter Head on the Aberdeenshire coast

Photo: David Grieve

Climbers in the upper reaches of Zero Gully (V,4)

Photo: Viv Scott

*John Cunningham
(1957). This Creagh
Dhu climber was an
innovator in front-
pointing techniques*

Photo: Douglas Scott

*Hamish MacInnes
(1957). Inventor of
the Terrordactyl ice
tool, MacInnes was to
be influential in
mountain rescue
developments.*

Photo: Douglas Scott

The two were John Cunningham and Mick Noon, who announced
that they intended to climb Zero Gully the next day, much to the
discomfiture of Patey and his friends. Shortly afterwards another character entered stage left, as Hamish MacInnes burst into the hut. On
hearing of the competition building up for Zero Gully he had set off
from Steall Hut in Glen Nevis to cross the Càrn Mòr Dearg arete.

> It was impossible to remain indifferent towards such a man: his appearance
> alone invited controversy. A great rent extending the whole length of one
> trouser leg had been repaired unsuccessfully with string. In his hand was the
> famous all-steel hammer-pick, named affectionately by the club 'The Message'.

MacInnes immediately settled the terms with Cunningham; these two,
along with Noon, would attempt Zero the next day. Meanwhile, in the
small hours of the morning, just as a reluctant search party was beginning to organise itself, the foursome from the North-East Buttress
staggered in, *mumbling excuses about 'Two feet of ice on the Man Trap'.*
The next day MacInnes and the two Creagh Dhu climbers were defeated
by avalanches and deteriorating weather. Cunningham and Noon
decided to return to Glasgow that night. Suddenly the die was cast –
MacInnes teamed up with Patey and Nicol and an early rise was fixed
for the next morning. The gully, to judge from Cunningham's distress,
was in excellent condition, apart from spindrift. All that was required
now was good weather.

Zero Gully, by 1957, had been attempted several times. On March
15, 1951, two students from Oxford University MC had a narrow escape.
Hamish Nicol and Anthony Rawlinson were near the top of the difficult
section when the leader fell, ripping out several ice pegs and pulling his
second down with him. Through great fortune both survived the 120m
fall. Hamish Nicol admitted that the traditional rivalry between the two
University Clubs, Oxford and Cambridge, was uppermost in his mind.
He was utterly determined to beat Cambridge to an ascent of the gully.

Early in the morning Patey, MacInnes and Graham Nicol gathered
at the foot of Zero. The steep gully was in perfect condition – surfaced
with snow ice, that magic material intermediate in consistency
between snow and water ice which can be carved, cut or moulded and
which, when present, allows virtually any route to be climbed. A shallow trough ran up and left for 30m to below an overhang. A line of steps
ended abruptly at a height of 12m, the point at which Cunningham
had been hit by a warning rattle of ice, recommending a retreat.

Patey set off up the first pitch, climbing in nails as was Nicol.
MacInnes was wearing crampons.

> I straddled the side walls of the trough, unable to resist a morbid satisfaction
> in noting that the rope hung absolutely free from my waist to the two at the
> bottom. They seemed strangely remote and not very interested in my progress,
> though Hamish would occasionally stir himself to shout 'Straight on up' when-
> ever I stopped for a rest.

Patey gained a small stance at a piece of nylon cord sticking out of
the snow. This marked a previous attempt by MacInnes (his sixth!) and
Bob Hope, the cord being attached to Hope's frozen-in ice axe which
had been used as an abseil point on their retreat the previous month.

The second pitch lay up the overhang, which Patey climbed using tension from inserted ice pegs. Present day climbers use ice screws or drive-ins, but these were unknown in the mid-1950s and quite often the long poker belonging to the hut stove was seen to grace an ice pitch for protection. The technique used by Patey – a rather delicate one in winter – was to rely on rope tension through an ice peg placed as high as possible until the next few holds had been cut. The next peg was placed higher still while hanging on with one hand, and when that was in place tension was taken from that and the lower peg removed to be used again later. The long, flat ice pegs then in use (they were to be seen as late as 1970) had virtually no holding power if pulled in an outward direction.

Above the overhang Patey belayed to a driven-in ice axe, unable to excavate MacInnes's buried ice peg, another souvenir of the MacInnes-Hope retreat during a snow-storm. Thus far, the three climbers had taken less than two hours. The route now led rightwards towards the gully proper, taking an exposed traverse between two overhangs. At the end of the traverse Patey stepped round an edge into the gully chute, to gaze up at a gigantic ice pitch rearing up ahead. Patey and Nicol belayed below the steep ice wall and brought up MacInnes for a shot at the lead.

> In went the first ice-piton, and with a violent heave Hamish got a crampon level with where his nose had been. The only indication of his passage was a large bucket hold every 6 feet. The urgency of his climbing indicated that this pitch was to be a vindication of the use of crampons for the benefit of the tricouni-favouring Aberdonians... More and more snow came down as the minutes ticked past. Hamish was now out of sight, and we wondered if he was tunnelling the overhang. Every now and then we heard a gasp, 'Thank God for a piton,' but that was all. Two hours elapsed before the signal came to follow on.

The way was now clear to the final cornice. The party, as Patey commented,

> ...moved together, the pace of the party (contrary to the textbook) dictated by the fastest member. Nicol was the most exhausted; he carried the pitons.

Five hours after entering the gully they collapsed on the plateau rim in a triumphant heap. Zero Gully (currently V,4) had been climbed.[10]

The state of Scottish climbing in 1957 was somewhat bitterly summed up by the streetwise Haston in a later autobiography.

> Scottish climbing was a mess of mediocrity and pettiness. It was full of mountaineers who considered their average talents to be exceptional. The main things in their lives seemed to be club rules, correct committee meetings and good etiquette in huts. These things are fine but climbing should have a place somewhere.[11]

Haston continued to state that arrogant and uncouth as he and his companions were, their climbing ideals were unimpeachable; they wanted only to climb as hard and as well as they could to advance the state of Scottish climbing. In his own brilliant fashion, Haston certainly went on to make history on higher hills, before his death in a lone skiing accident in 1977. To balance his own view, it must be said here that

Bob Ross on the 'Wall Pitch' of Zero Gully (V,4), a steep pitch just above the start of the gully (April 1996)

Photo: Brian Findlay

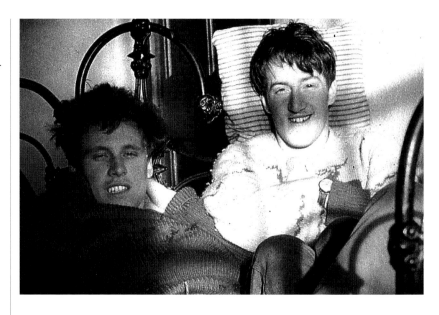

Dougal Haston and his sometime climbing partner James Stenhouse were two of the Edinburgh 'enfants terrible' who nonetheless injected some fresh air into Scottish mountaineering in the late 1950s

Photo: Jimmy Marshall

Scottish climbing was a mess of mediocrity and pettiness. It was full of mountaineers who considered their average talents to be exceptional. The main things in their lives seemed to be club rules, correct committee meetings and good etiquette in huts

with the exception of one or two friends, Haston was not popular when a youth. He went out of his way, contemporaries recall, to offend many decent people. Following an unfortunate motoring accident in Glen Coe, which resulted in the death of a hillwalker, Haston left Scotland to live in Switzerland. Here he became Director of the International School of Mountaineering, going on to make several great ascents in the bigger mountain ranges of the world, including Everest, the hard way.

In 1957 Haston met Marshall and, later in the year, Robin Smith. Marshall had joined the SMC in September 1955, his proposer Dick Brown describing him in a covering letter as a *'very competent mountaineer'*.[12] In a letter supporting Marshall's application, Len Lovat described him in terms which suggested that the spirit of Raeburn had risen again. Marshall's winter climbing career had begun shortly after his rock climbing, with Central Gully on Bidean in December 1949. By December 1952 he was climbing Crowberry Ridge Direct on the Buachaille. At the time he joined he was a 26-year old architect who, according to Haston, recognised the poor state of Scottish climbing, and in Haston, Smith *et al* saw the chance of better days to come. Glen Coe and Ben Nevis were to be their proving grounds and, ultimately, the salvation of Scottish mountaineering.

One of the major players in this second Golden Age was to be Robin Clark Smith (1938 – 1962). Born in Calcutta, Smith was sent back to Scotland aged eight, to be educated, initially in Crieff, then from 12 onwards at George Watson's Boys' College in Edinburgh. He rapidly showed an independent character and competence at his studies. One of the masters at the school was SMC member Archie Hendry. His non-participative direction acted as a catalyst for the young Smith, who rapidly found that in mountaineering he had found a passion both absorbing and fulfilling. Hendry himself had character in plenty, commuting to school by motor cycle, and being known as a *'mountaineer of no mean ability'*.

Smith's string of first ascents span from 1957 to 1962: many of these are still regarded as classic routes, often recognised for their fine line and *must-dos* by young climbers. Ken Crocket recollects leading a fairly early ascent of Glueless Groove on the Cobbler, in April 1974, first climbed by Smith in June 1957 and then probably unseconded. The crux of this lesser-known route is a steep wall of schist, moving between tiny quartz ripples, with no protection. It is a serious and bold piece of climbing, currently graded at E2 and for a 19-year old in 1958 an auspicious route. The following brief summary by Jimmy Marshall gives the kernel of what was Smith.

> Whilst others (e.g. the Creagh Dhu) were climbing at least equal in difficulty to Smith, it was the consistent aesthetic of line in which he surpassed and from 1957 till his death in the Pamirs, he more or less at will plucked some of the finest rock and ice lines in the country, e.g. Shibboleth, winter Orion Face, Yo Yo, The Bat, Big Top etc. Remarkably, he had no consistent climbing partner but chose anyone available from contemporary, talented associates.
>
> Furthermore he rarely exhibited much concern as to footwear, frequently making serious ascents in battered old walking boots. His fairly short thick-set physique, coupled with a finely developed sense of balance, seemed to enable him to hang about on difficult sections for hours, e.g. three hours on the entry pitch of Shibboleth, and four hours on the Barrier Pitch of the Aonach Dubh Girdle.
>
> These aspects were expressions of an awareness to the corrosive nature of protection, aid, and gear, and wherever possible he would maintain a minimal use, 'to give the mountain a chance', as he was wont to say.[13]

Smith's first climbing partner, while still at school, was Jimmy Cruik-shank, who in 2005 published an exhaustive biography of Smith.[14] Meanwhile, the increase in the number of new climbs being recorded on Nevis continued in 1958. Of a total of thirteen routes that year, ten were due to one man, a 21-year old native of Bradford called Ian Stewart Clough (1937 – 1970). National Service with the RAF took him to Scotland, where his love of climbing led to Kinloss and the Mountain Rescue. At this time too he was a pupil on a Mountaineering Association winter course with Hamish MacInnes. Although he was to be heavily criticised for the style of several of his early Scottish ascents, he also came to be accepted by those who knew him as one of the kindest and least selfish characters in the climbing world.

Dougal Haston, who in his later years was to enjoy several fine routes with Clough, recollected that in the late 1950s,

> We also didn't have very much time for the routes he [Clough] was doing in winter on Nevis. Later, we found out that they were usually fine and not difficult lines, but at that time we were very intolerant and also suspicious of any Englishman who thought he could climb ice.

At that time, continued Haston, it was genuinely believed that only Scotsmen could climb ice. Clough was an accomplished mountaineer, with many alpine routes under his belt including five of the six north faces. These included the Eiger, the first ascent of the Central Pillar of Frêney and a successful expedition to Patagonia. He was killed by a falling serac while on the successful Annapurna South face expedition in 1970.

The first route of 1958 was a January 2 ascent of Italian Climb, III, by Marshall, A.McCorquodale and George Ritchie. Starting as a narrow gully, the upper section fans out to the right, where snow slopes lead to the crest of Tower Ridge under the Little Tower. A steep ice pitch which forms low down on the right wall of the gully was first recorded by Steve Belk and Ian Fulton in 1973. This is now Italian Right-Hand, IV,4. In 2001, it was so popular that fixed Abalakovs could be used to abseil the line.[15] (An Abalakov is a method of belaying on ice using ice screws to thread a sling through the ice, devised by the Russian climber of the same name.) Right-Hand rejoins the original line higher up.

Italian Climb was the scene of a tragic accident in January 1970, when three experienced climbers were swept to their deaths by a slab avalanche from above. By one of those chances of fate the fourth member of the party survived. John Grieve, a teacher from Kinlochleven and an active member of the Glen Coe Rescue Team, had set out to do the route with Jim MacArtney, Fergus Mitchell, and Mary Ann Hudson. Above the steep lower section Grieve, last on the rope, found his rope badly snagged and released it from his karabiner to shake it free. At that point a huge slab avalanche was triggered, probably by one of the leading climbers, and the rope was pulled out of Grieve's hands, leaving him trapped on a ledge.

Twelve years later Grieve described the accident in an SMC Journal article, written about mountain rescue in general.

> When I returned from The Italian Climb the sole survivor of a rope of four, victims of one of Nevis's murderous avalanches, I was summoned to the Police Office in Kinlochleven and suffered an intense grilling lasting for hours by two detectives...They asked the same, to me stupid, questions time after time. I now know that Tom Patey, highly distraught with the death of Jim MacArt-ney, contacted the Procurator Fiscal at Fort William and suggested that more than a simple accident had taken place. Tom could not accept that I had survived and Jim had not...What Tom really thought had taken place I do not know...The reason for relating this episode is to help illustrate a common reaction shown by survivors of fatal climbing accidents. Part of what Tom could not stomach was witnessing my return to the CIC hut in what...might have been construed as good spirits.

John Grieve was in fact, in his own words, *'bloody well glad to be alive'*.[16]

One other climb was recorded in the CIC Hut Log for Jan 2, an ascent by two JMCS members of Staircase Climb on the rocks flanking Water-fall Gully. Staircase Climb is now a IV,5 and though a neglected route, when in condition it provides a technically difficult ascent on mixed ground. The two JMCS members were Dougal Haston and James Sten-house, both of whom would return again to make their mark on Nevis, in the august company of Jimmy Marshall.

On March 23, Jimmy Marshall climbed Number Two Gully Buttress III, with Lovat and Hendry. In addition there were five easy winter routes by Clough and his friends, while in April Clough found a rising line up the Little Brenva Face of the North-East Buttress with his ascent of Frostbite, III. On this ascent the five climbers found great difficulty in overcoming the dreaded Man-Trap, attempting to climb the seemingly innocuous 3m nose of rock by forming a human pyramid.

As if to remind climbers of the narrow safety margins involved in winter climbing, Zero Gully was the scene of a triple fatality on April 9, when three experienced alpinists attempted the gully in poor conditions. They had no ice pitons and were belaying on ice axes. The outcome when the leader fell from the third pitch was inevitable, the two wooden ice axes snapping like matchsticks and all three falling to their death.

Clough returned to Nevis in the summer, making three first summer ascents of gullies. Comb Gully with John Alexander at the end of June, Minus One Gully and Green Gully with Don Pipes on July 5 and 6 respectively. Green Gully had defeated several notable climbers in the past, mainly due to the appalling quality of the rock. Minus One Gully had two short sections requiring the use of aid by Clough, and is graded as a Scottish Very Severe.

The last ascent in 1958 was that of September 14, when Haston and Stenhouse made the third ascent of Kellett's Route on Gardyloo Buttress, making a Severe variation in the upper section by following the left rib of the final gully. Haston had just recovered from a motorcycle accident in which he had broken an arm and was shortly to show his promise as a climber. Other climbers too, were ready and waiting for Ben Nevis to come into condition. The next four years were to be remembered by later generations of climbers as perhaps the most inspiring period of climbing that Nevis, and Scotland, has seen.

References

1. **Whillans**, Don and **Ormerod**, Alick, *Don Whillans: Portrait of a Mountaineer.* (London: Heinemann, 1971).

2. **Downes**, R.O. and **O'Hara**, M.J., *Scotland 1956.* Cambridge Mountaineering, 1957.

3. **O'Hara**, Mike, *Personal communication, November 1984.*

4. **Marshall**, J.R., *The Initiation.* SMCJ 33, 1 – 3, 1984.

5. **Vigano**, Charlie, *The Creagh Dhu.* Rocksport, p9, April/May, 1972.

6. **Maden**, B.E.H., *Shirtsleeves on Ben Nevis.* Climbers' Club Journal, 192 –197, 1958.

7. **Williams**, Noel, *Personal communication, November 2007.*

8. **Richardson**, Simon, *Ben Nevis Rock & Ice Climbs* (Glasgow: Scottish Mountaineering Trust, 2002, ISBN 0907521738.)

9. **Williams**, G.C., *Days on Ben Nevis.* SMCJ 26, 394 – 400, 1935.

10. **Patey**, T.W., *The Zero Gully Affair.* SMCJ 26, 205 – 216, 1958.

11. **Haston**, Dougal, *In High Places.* (London: Cassell, 1972).

12. **Brown**, Richard, *Letter dated 30 September, 1955, to Ross Higgins.* SMC Archives.

13. **Marshall**, J.R., *Personal communication, 7 February, 2001.*

14. **Cruickshank**, Jimmy, *High Endeavours, The life and legend of Robin Smith* (Edinburgh: Canongate, 2005, ISBN 1841956589).

15. **Perroux**, Godefroy, *Ben Nevis Winter Climbs,* (Les Houches, France: Alp Impression, 2002, ISBN 2951774907.)

16. **Grieve**, John, *Nowhere To Fall But Off.* SMCJ 32, 246 – 250, 1982.

*Jimmy Marshall,
Robin Smith, James
'Elly' Moriarty and
Dougal Haston in
Glen Coe. These
climbers, all based in
Edinburgh, were to set
new levels of climbing
in the 1960s*

Photo: Jimmy Marshall

9: The Pinnacle (1959 – 1960)

ZERO GULLY had finally received a winter ascent, in February 1957. Remaining was Point Five Gully as the great winter plum on Nevis, its terrible icy cleft soaring up for 325m between Observatory Buttress and Observatory Ridge. As with Zero Gully, there had been several determined attempts on the gully, some of the suitors being violently repulsed. On January 25, 1956, a Rock and Ice party left the CIC Hut bound for Point Five. The party consisted of Joe Brown, Nat Allen and Nip Underwood. They were confident following a straightforward ascent of Green Gully – a much more benign route under average conditions.

Brown noticed that the rocks were but thinly covered in ice. In addition, the ice was showing different layers. After leading the first pitch he brought up Allen who tied on to two ice pegs, while Underwood remained belayed to a rock spike at the foot of the gully. In retrospect, this probably saved the party from annihilation. The second pitch reared up for 15m above Brown's head, culminating in the inevitable bulge. Moving up to the bulge, Brown banged in two ice pegs for protection and was making another move upwards when the front of the ice bulge fell away, throwing him backwards into space.

*...Brown banged in
two ice pegs for
protection and was
making another
move upwards
when the front of
the ice bulge fell
away, throwing
him backwards
into space. Brown
hit the ice below
Allen and bounced
out of the gully,
pulling Allen and
his two ice pegs
out after him*

Brown hit the ice below Allen and bounced out of the gully, pulling Allen and his two ice pegs out after him. The two fell some 15m apart, rebounding out of a hole in the snow at the foot of the gully, Allen badly tearing some leg ligaments. Finally Underwood, with his good spike belay, brought Allen to a halt, Brown then jerking to rest in a tangle of rope. Some strange noises from Brown warned of impending asphyxiation from coils of rope round his neck, but Allen freed him in time. Only Allen was injured, the three shaken climbers making a laborious self-rescue down to the Hut and then to the road.

Certain types of ice – particularly water ice which usually forms from freely running water, as opposed to snow ice which forms from the repeated thawing and re-freezing of snow – show an unsettling and potentially dangerous feature on being struck, known to climbers as 'dinner-plating'. This spalling or fracturing is named after the roughly dinner-plate shaped fragments of ice which break off. The old-style ice pegs which were all that was available during the 1950s were particularly liable to cause plating as they were hammered straight into the unyielding and brittle ice. Even modern tubular ice screws can be unusable with some ice, a climber then being in a potentially serious position with little or no protection.

Patey also attempted Point Five, climbing the first pitch in February 1957 before being defeated by spindrift. One month later Noon and Cunningham made the first 55m before terrible ice forced a withdrawal. Another contestant for this gully was MacInnes, who went so far as to descend the top 150m of the gully on a long length of light-weight nylon, anchored to an ice axe, before climbing back up again. At Easter 1958 Ian Clough met up with MacInnes at the CIC Hut, intent on an ascent of Point Five.

MacInnes had *The Message*, his heavy-weight ice hammer, as he and Clough started up the gully. Clough found the first pitch to be rock slabs coated with water ice, thinning with height. After 8m he retreated and allowed MacInnes into the lead. Five hours later a stance was reached, with no belay. The steady beat of MacInnes's hammer then signalled the drilling of a bolt belay. Secured with the bolt, the pair descended, leaving in place a rope.

Clough and MacInnes returned to Point Five the following day, climbing back up the fixed rope. MacInnes was suffering, not too surprisingly, from wrist-ache, and Clough took the lead above the bolt. The ice was poor and the climbers were sorely troubled by spindrift avalanches. Later in the day they were joined by Patey, who had been watching from the CIC Hut. At one point Patey thought they had been avalanched out of the gully, as the two climbers disappeared under clouds of freezing spindrift. The attack on the gully fizzled out shortly after, to be followed by a thaw and the end of winter.

The first month of 1959 saw eight new routes on Nevis, though they took a total of thirteen days climbing. Up at the CIC Hut again, '*suffering from a post-Hogmanay haze and a slight unsteadiness*', were Ian Clough and three friends: John Alexander and Don Pipes, both ex-Kinloss Mountain Rescue Team members, and Robin Shaw of Glasgow University MC.

Three easy routes were climbed during the first week, including Slalom, III, on the Little Brenva Face. On January 7 and 8 an ascent of Waterfall Gully was made, climbing the icy pitch at the start over two days. This use of 'siege tactics', with fixed ropes, was to involve Clough in a certain amount of controversy. To put this into context, on February 17, 1973, Ken Crocket and Colin Stead stepcut their way up a very icy Waterfall Gully, taking three hours for the entire route. Crocket had led the initial, hard section, some 42m of continuous ice, one of the last routes to climbed by this pair cutting steps. To be fair, Clough was to develop into an outstanding mountaineer, with many successful ascents in the Alps and

At one point Patey thought they had been avalanched out of the gully, as the two climbers disappeared under clouds of freezing spindrift

Himalaya such as the first British ascent of the North Face of the Eiger and the first ascent of the Central Pillar of Freney on Mont Blanc.

The most controversial ascent by Clough was, however, to follow shortly – his sieged ascent of the much sought-after Point Five Gully. The ascent is well-described, both by Clough himself and by Robin Shaw, the climb taking place the week after the ascent of Waterfall Gully. The style in which the two gullies were climbed, depending on aid climbing almost to the exclusion of free climbing, was to lead to Clough's application to join the SMC being rejected that year.

On Monday, January 12, Clough, Alexander, Pipes and Shaw found themselves with heavily laden sacks at the foot of Point Five. For 30m a slab reared up, covered with thin ice with the occasional bulge of snow ice. Shaw described the start of the siege, writing in a University magazine[1]

> We hesitated. 'Aw c'mon', I said hopefully, 'Let's have a bash at it', quickly tying myself on to the middle of the rope with a 'Blow you, Jack' expression. There was a scramble towards the rear but poor Dangle was not quick enough and soon found himself tied firmly on to the 300 feet of doubled three-quarter wt. rope, presented with 'Thor' our modified brickies hammer and a large bundle of ice and rock pegs, and pushed towards the pitch...Three hours later Dangle was up two thirds of the pitch and found himself a good peg crack.

Clough then descended, having fixed the rope, to join the rest in tea and sandwiches, Pipes having brought up refreshment from the Hut. Alexander then took a turn and two hours later, as darkness was falling, the bolt placed by MacInnes the previous year was gained at the top of the first pitch. The party then retired to the Hut leaving a rope hanging down the pitch and the remainder of their gear at the foot of the route. Clough described the second pitch on the Tuesday.

> John climbed the rope and brought me up. While I was having a rest after working on the second pitch for about an hour, John brought up Robin so that he could watch the proceedings. Robin Shaw's appearance was unusual; his climbing outfit seemed to consist of rags held together by no one knew how. This, with his black beard and tousled hair, gave him a Robinson Crusoeish touch.[2]

Clough continued working on the second pitch, spotting a peg high up on the left and another peg under the ice on the right.

> Soon I was standing on an etrier hanging from this peg and knocking in a further rock-peg...Next I used an etrier hanging from an ice-peg and, with another ice-peg for a hand-hold, I was over the crux. Another 25 feet up I found a place for a stance...Another day's work was at an end.

Pipes, meanwhile, had gone down the mountain and returned with yet more equipment, brought up from the party's base at Cameron's Barn. They now had some 275m of rope and about 60 assorted rock and ice pegs. They decided to operate the ascent in a shift system. The next day climbing was impossible due to continuous spindrift and a temporary halt to the climbing was called. Shaw decided that as natural belays and good peg cracks were scarce, a visit to the local blacksmith was in order, to see to the manufacture of some bolts and brackets.

> Two hours later I was in Fort Bill only to discover that the nearest blacksmith

Dougie McArthur on the 'Cave Pitch', the crux fourth pitch of Point Five Gully (V,5), (February 1973). This is a bottle-shaped chimney, narrowing towards the top which normally has a very steep, icy finish as in this photograph. In conditions of loose snow, spindrift here can be a deciding factor

Photo: Con Higgins

was 60 miles away. I was about to return to the hut when I remembered that Dangle knew a mechanic called Sammy in one of the garages. After a bit of a search I found him (a stocky, jovial chap) who devoted the rest of the afternoon to finding out exactly what I wanted and making it, occasionally mumbling, 'Och, it's lucky fur you the boss is no' in.'

Thursday morning saw Pipes and Shaw trudging up to the gully again on a beautiful clear day. It was to take them three hours of strenuous wrestling with the fixed ropes before they stood at the foot of pitch three. Pipes then spent an icy three hours and 30 minutes at his stance while Shaw nibbled away at the next section.

Robin's crampons were not very good ones and, at first, it was with mixed feelings of amusement and anxiety that Don watched his partner's crampon points curl up as he climbed the steps in the ice...The climbing was very difficult, although an ice peg or two could be kept above the leader all the while; and at the end of the day only another 30 feet had been forced.

Friday dawned clear and cold, as the next 'shift' of Clough and Alexander left for the gully. After a further seven hours' work they had reached the foot of what was their sixth pitch, the cave pitch. There they inserted an expansion bolt before sliding back down the ropes in the twilight. They were below the last major pitch in summer conditions – a steep wall of about 18m.

At 7am on Saturday morning, Pipes and Shaw left the CIC Hut. By 1.30pm, when Clough and Alexander had gained the top of pitch four, Pipes was already half-way up the steep ice of the cave pitch. This is generally reckoned to be the hardest pitch in Point Five Gully, consisting of a bottle-shaped chimney, narrowing to the inevitable bulge at the top. Pipes took three hours to lead this last difficult pitch, and by the time all four were over it night was falling. The last 180m or so involved one small steep pitch and a strenuous ice chimney before the route ended abruptly on the summit rim, gained by Clough's party at 10pm.

The first, and highly controversial ascent of Point Five Gully in winter had taken in 29 hours of actual upward climbing. There had been about 40 hours of work in total in the gully, spread out over a six day period. Shaw gamely tried to defend the ascent –

Had we chosen to climb the gully without retreating each day, this would have meant at least three bivouacs. We preferred to have our 'bivouacs' at the CIC Hut, considering it ridiculous to bivouac, for instance, at the top of pitch one.

Shaw concluded this argument with the comment that,

I have no doubt that Point Five will be climbed in less time, but a party will have to be very lucky to find it in suitable condition to climb in one day.

In September 1959 Ian Clough applied to join the SMC, proposed by Tom Patey and seconded by Jim Bell. Clough was then 22 and had been climbing for over four years. His list of ascents, including two seasons in the Alps, would normally have justified his entry, yet he was turned down. In 1962 he reapplied and gained admittance. By then Robin Smith had been killed in the Pamirs and as a letter from Clough to his proposer Patey shows, it seems that Clough felt that Smith, who

Ian Clough on the first winter ascent of Sabre Tooth (IV,5) in Glen Coe (1969)

Photo: Hamish MacInnes

was on the committee in 1959, may have let his nationalistic feelings weigh against the application. Clough wrote on hearing of Smith's fall,

> The Pamirs accident came as a great shock – I was very upset to hear of Robin's death. I wasn't at all bitter with him personally for trying to black-ball me since that was typically Robin – intensely nationalistic. Although he always seemed to regard me as a rival (why I don't know because I could never climb at anything like his standard) we always seemed to get on very well...Terry Sullivan told me...that he had spoken with Robin about bombing me out of the club and Robin excused himself by saying he was pissed at the time and having a big hate session against all Englishmen. I think this was probably true – it was a case of nationalism rather than a personal grudge.[3]

One of the reasons put forward in explanation for Clough being refused was his status as a mountaineering instructor. When he successfully joined in 1962 he was a student teacher. There is some validity in this, the SMC did not, on the whole, sit easily with professionals in their ranks. The major reason for Clough's initial rejection was the style in which several of Clough's first ascents were done. Point Five Gully and his aided ascent of Titan's Wall later that year were viewed by the committee as serious erosions of the contemporary ethic that *'pegs shouldn't replace skill or supplement a blatant lack of same.'* It was felt that as Clough and his companions could not have climbed these routes without recourse to much aid, the whole affair was in bad taste. To end this on a more positive note, Smith was not *'pissed'* at the time, nor overtly nationalistic. He was, however, obsessive about bringing Scottish rock climbing standards up to the levels of those in England.

A route of a very different nature from Point Five Gully had opened the year's climbing on January 1, 1959, when Robin Smith and Dick Holt made the first winter ascent of the Tower Face of The Comb. This superb buttress dominates the centre of Coire na Ciste, with its wedge-shaped cockscomb challenging the eye. The face looking to Tower Ridge had first been climbed by Ogilvy in 1940, giving a loose Very Difficult. In summer much of the climbable rock here is dangerously shattered. In a 10-hour day, Smith and Holt managed to fight their way up this puzzling face. A good part of their climb would have been done in the dark, as neither climber was renowned for speed and it was a moonless night.

The Tower Face of The Comb frightened off many leading climbers, and it was over 25 years before a second ascent was confirmed, by Stephen Venables and Victor Saunders in February, 1987. (Venables has always been under the impression that his was the 3rd ascent, but this is unverified.) Jimmy Marshall recorded the route in his guidebook as Very Severe, IV, probably acknowledging the hard, mixed climbing it provides. It is now a highly recommended mixed route at Grade VI,6. Smith and Holt did not even find it easy going on the buttress crest, as deep powder snow and high winds gave them much trouble.

On St Valentine's Day, 1987, Stephen Venables and Victor Saunders approached The Comb. Venables recalls the day, which included an early morning approach up the Allt a' Mhuilinn with a full moon -

> We had both been eying up the Tower Face of the Comb for some time. I remembered, years earlier, reading a piece in Mountain. Alan Rouse, I think, speculating, debating, provoking. Something along the lines that pure ice

I wasn't at all bitter with him personally for trying to black-ball me since that was typically Robin – intensely nationalistic...

Victor Saunders on pitch three of Tower Face of The Comb (IV,6). Possibly the second ascent of this Robin Smith mixed route, some 28 years after the first

Photo: Stephen Venables

had become easy, whereas mixed was the real thing. Take the Tower Face of the Comb, he had teased – only graded IV but hadn't even had a second ascent. And apparently still hadn't that February morning in 1987.

The Comb was dark and grey, dusted with icing sugar. Then we spotted a pair of bright yellow trousers edging across the top of a smooth overhanging wall. It was Simon Yates aiding his controversial way into the untouched heart of the bastion, to complete his new direct line up the Comb with Mark Miller. [Don't Die of Ignorance, VI,6,A2. In fact, they did not complete the route this day, Yates returning a couple of days later with Andy Cave for a successful ascent.]. Victor, ever garrulous, shouted encouragement to the modern pioneers as we plodded past to our more traditional target, which takes the more accessible left side of the buttress.

Venables does not recall the first two pitches as standing out, traversing in from the easier left side of the buttress, but he certainly remembers the third pitch –

> It was the kind of climbing I love – brushing, scraping, edging, hooking … searching for knobs and cracks in the frozen landscape – so much more interesting than the brutal knuckle-thwack of pure ice. I remember the satisfaction of a big solid sling draped comfortingly over a jammed block, before bridging up a steep chimney, axes clanging on their tethers, as I brushed and fingered the rock with woollen gloves. Then a slight easing, with smears of ice to take picks, and a final shuffle rightwards to a fine belay perch right on the crest of the Comb.[4]

The crest of The Comb was a satisfying alpine-style environment, with mantelshelves, steep pull-ups and tremendous views down The Comb before the final snowy crest led to the plateau.

Since the second ascent it has been climbed many times, and several variations added. Tower Face of the Comb was the first Grade VI on Ben Nevis and is now regarded as one of the greatest mixed routes on the mountain. It was decades ahead of its time, and has maintained its reputation as an absorbing and challenging climb.

Another Smith-Holt ascent in 1959 was the first winter ascent of the Orion Face, on January 25. Smith had been wanting to climb this for some time, following the line of The Long Climb. The two considered the expedition so important that they decided to go north by rail. Somewhat inevitably they missed the train, arriving in Fort William 15 hours behind their planned schedule. At the CIC Hut that Saturday evening they found Clough's party in residence and immediately regarded them as rivals for their route. Holt's article on the ascent described the scene in the hut that night.

> Robin kept up a cheerful but wary demeanour and hatched plots. To allay any fears which the opposition might have they retired early, meaning realistically, and arising just after three secured a strategic advantage. The enemy was so bewildered by these tactics that he supposed a complex double bluff and went back to sleep. Our heroes were able to creep out into the night at half past four – the earliest start that Robin had been known to make in Scotland.

An hour later at half past five, shivering in the pre-dawn gloom, Smith and Holt started climbing, running into difficulties almost immediately on the steep lower rocks below the First Slab Rib. Smith was forced to insert a poor peg on which he made a semi-tension traverse. This allowed a steep smooth rib to be turned and relatively easier ground gained at the full extent of their 45m rope.

The second pitch was little easier, with Smith attempting to gain the slabs of the summer route.

> …Robin had edged along a sloping ledge beneath a steep wall on the right which formed another rib, beyond which were the Slabs of the summer route. A 'good' runner was eventually found and following this with a moderate piton he felt sufficiently secure to announce that he would probably fall and to mind the rope. Dick, out of sight, then experienced several intermittent tugs followed by a huge jerk…

It was the kind of climbing I love – brushing, scraping, edging, hooking … searching for knobs and cracks in the frozen landscape – so much more interesting than the brutal knuckle-thwack of pure ice…

Mike Taylor on the first winter ascent of Raeburn's Buttress, original route (IV,5)

Photo: Bill Brooker

Smith had not fallen, though by drawing in the rope tightly Holt almost caused this to happen. The rope ran out when Smith was 9m short of the Slab Rib and Holt moved up to the first runner, allowing the leader to reach the corner left of the Rib. The next pitch turned out to be the crux of the day. The obvious way was up the corner for 18m, after which the finish was problematic. There was a choice between the crack in the back of the corner or the flanking wall of the Slab Rib. The crack was of knee width, overhanging near the top, while the wall was very steep but with parallel cracks.

The parallel cracks proved to be the only possible way up this section, Smith moving up the wall with wide bridging in crampons and no protection. The hardest climbing was now past as Holt led through into the Basin. It was 3.20pm with clouds gathering and the light soon to fade. At this point an escape rightward into Zero Gully was considered but rejected, the climbers deciding instead to make for the North-East Buttress by any feasible route.

On gaining a shelf below the Second Slab Rib they decided that Epsilon Chimney, a possible exit route, had been bypassed. Daylight was now going fast but Smith and Holt continued to climb upwards, finding a series of ledges which led eventually to the crest of the buttress. There remained the dreaded Man-Trap.

> Robin, removing a crampon as a gesture, stood on Dick's shoulder, took off, then after a delay, set off back down the face, accelerating under gravity, to land on a large snow padded boulder...The Man Trap was avoided.
>
> As the shelf below the last tower was reached the clouds rolled back to coat the tower in gleaming white armour, and, as they moved up this together Orion himself looked down. A fitting finish to a fine climb.[5]

From Holt's description of this ascent it would seem that their route continued above the V-traverse somewhere, perhaps even up Epsilon Chimney by a happy error. On such a vast and confusing face with darkness approaching it is remarkably easy to lose one's bearings. On the rare repeats of the Smith-Holt line difficulties have been found to be high, with the lower section probably containing harder climbing than anything on the Direct Route, which was climbed the following year. Now a V,5, it was the first winter route on this vast face.

Clough also returned to Nevis at the end of January, two weeks after his controversial ascent of Point Five Gully. On January 27 he climbed Central Gully, III,4, on Creag Coire na Ciste, with John Alexander. This is a route often in condition and though short, at about 120m, it can be interesting, particularly if climbed by the right hand of two chimneys. This harder variation was climbed by Ian MacEacheran and Jock Knight a few years later and if followed in icy conditions the climb overall will be a Grade IV,4.

The following weekend saw the SMC on the hill in strength and four new routes. On Saturday 31, two ropes from Aberdeen climbed Raeburn's Buttress. Ronnie Sellars and Jerry Smith climbed the bottom chimneys of the buttress then finished up Intermediate Gully, the gully to the left of the upper part of the buttress, first climbed in winter by Macphee in April 1983. Following behind this pair, Bill Brooker and Mike Taylor followed Raeburn's original line, braking out right and finishing up the

arete of the buttress, plain sailing in nailed boots, taking three and a half hours in all. Raeburn's Buttress is usually reckoned a hard IV by those climbing it today. The deciding factor is probably the short but very steep wall out of the cave belay. If insufficiently iced this can prove impossible.

Elsewhere on Nevis that day the formidable if oddly matched rope of Marshall and Patey was in action. Oddly matched because true to Aberdonian conservatism, Patey was climbing in nails, while Marshall was crampon-clad. The route they had chosen was the Girdle Traverse following in part Bell's route of 1941. Starting from Observatory Gully below Gardyloo Gully, Patey and Marshall followed the snow ledges running out leftwards below Good Friday Climb. These led to Point Five Gully above the steep lower section of that route, the crossing of which proved to be the most awkward part of the day's climbing.

After crossing Point Five, thin bands of ice leading to Observatory Ridge forced a diagonal abseil. The upper part of the Basin was the next objective, gained below the Second Slab Rib and from The Basin the easy shelf leading up to North-East Buttress followed by a spiral finish round Coire Leis completed their short, five-hour crab-crawl of The Winter Girdle. The steps left by Smith and Holt a month previous were still visible.

The snow was just as hard on the Sunday as Sellars and Jerry Smith climbed the Grade IV Pinnacle Arete on the South Trident Buttress. Missing out the initial lower section, snow and ice grooves immediately right of the crest led to the easier arete above the middle section, the arete providing particularly delightful climbing. But the route of the weekend and perhaps the best known to present-day climbers was found on the West Face of Observatory Ridge by Marshall, Patey and Brooker. Hadrian's Wall, as climbed by this strong trio, followed approximately the line of a Kellett summer route, West Face, Lower Route. The climb was Patey's idea, though the original intention was to climb by what is now the icefall of Hadrian's Direct. The lack of continuous ice on this enforced a start further left. Also Patey's idea was to have been the route's name, .25!

The Aberdonians were in nailed boots, with Marshall again in crampons. On the fifth pitch, crossing thinly iced slabs, Marshall was obliged to use a peg, making a diagonal abseil to gain easier ground. Brooker, in his habitual position as third man, stood back and enjoyed watching the competition between Patey and Marshall, Aberdeen versus Edinburgh, North versus South, nails versus crampons. When Brooker himself followed the thin traverse he found no need for the peg but then, as he stated later, *'it's easy enough if you're third on the rope.'* Marshall and Patey were of course leading through on their ascent of Hadrian's

Left and Below: Tom Patey cutting steps on the FA of The Winter Girdle (IV,4), (January 1959)

Photos: Jimmy Marshall

Tom Patey sets off on the first ascent of Hadrian's Wall (West Face, Lower Route), (IV,5). Hanging from his waist loop is his favourite long ice peg, soon to be irretrieveably used by Marshall (February 1959)

Photo: Jimmy Marshall

Wall. At one point Marshall, who had earlier lost a peg through Patey, banged in to the hilt one of Patey's favourite pegs, a very long ring peg. It's rusty shards are probably there today.

Twelve years later, at Easter 1971, the prominent icefall to the right of the original Hadrian's Wall was climbed by Mike Geddes and Graham Little. Hadrian's Wall Direct (V,5), is now the line most commonly followed, it being especially suited to front-pointing techniques. The icefall gives two pitches at a fairly high angle before leading up to a small snow-field below the ice chimney, a landmark on the route.

The original Hadrian's Wall is perhaps little easier than the Direct, though of a different nature. It received its second ascent on March 12, 1972 by Ken Crocket and Colin Stead. The ascent was described in a later SMC Journal article, from which the following excerpts paint a little of the atmosphere found on a fairly major step-cutting expedition, as the two Glaswegians had not yet converted to the newly-arrived front-pointing. Crocket led the first pitch and Stead the second, taking the right-hand of two possible grooves. Crocket set off up the third pitch, cutting steps with his single wooden axe.

> The third pitch looked thin, with poorly covered slabs which had to be over-come, but adrenalin was trickling now and we were rarin' to go. Colin wanted me to traverse left, but I put my faith on a narrow tongue of snow-ice which had been caught by surprise and clamped frozen to the slab. On both sides of this tongue decaying molars of dark rock leered through thin snow, while at the top of the slab gaped a hungry chimney...Progress up the slab was deli-cate and with relief I entered the chimney, only to find it full of useless, fluffy snow. Sheathing my old axe I swam and bridged my way up...

This little chimney was at the right end of the slabby section. After they had completed the climb, the pair realised that by taking the lower section more directly they had missed out the slab traverse and the diagonal traverse of Marshall completely. The chimney led to a snowfield and the foot of the ice chimney referred to by the original party. The Direct route also leads to this ice chimney. Approaching the chimney, with Stead belayed at its foot, Crocket noticed something ominous.

> Every few seconds he would curl himself up as a silken ribbon of spindrift rushed invisibly down the chimney to explode with an angry hiss at the bottom. The entire upper basin and much of the ridge above was funnelling loose snow down through the narrows of the ice-chimney in a continuous rush.

Crocket set off up the ice-chimney, clinging on miserably to hand-holds bitterly won in the icy stream.

> At the top I had to move onto the left wall and here the spindrift was worst. I hastily chopped a few handholds, forcing myself to cut them well, and when the next lull came stepped out onto the wall. A sudden rush of snow nearly swept me off but I hung on, cursing feebly and rotating slowly on one good foothold.[6]

Once out of the spindrift in the corner the remainder of the climb went smoothly, though the two climbers were tired as they cut their way on to the summit plateau at sunset. With its mixed scenery and grand route finding, Hadrian's Wall deserves to be a popular route, but

Bill Brooker and Tom Patey at the spike belay on the FA of Hadrian's Wall. From here Marshall climbed to the right, looped a sling round a flake then made a pendulum down and right above the thinly-iced slab to gain a chimney. At the bottom of the photograph, Marshall's lead rope can just be seen at the top of the chimney

Photo: Jimmy Marshall

A young Bill Brooker
Photo: Bill Brooker

the original line is seldom, if ever, climbed. It is in condition less often than the icefall of the Direct and though providing a good mixed route, is perhaps now less attractive than the later Direct Route..

At the beginning of February 1959, Marshall, Stenhouse and Haston teamed up for a winter climbing holiday. After a 'training' weekend on Creag Meagaidh, where they had been joined by Graham Tiso, the trio moved on to Nevis, pushing into an already crowded CIC Hut. Clough and his friends were already in residence. Marshall was intent on climbing Minus Two Gully, the central of the three Minus gullies. Of the four great gullies on the Ben: Zero, Point Five, Minus One and Minus Two, only the first two had been climbed in winter; Point Five by the siege tactics of Clough.

Gerry Smith and Ian Dalley starting up the imposing line that is Minus Two Gully (V,5) in good conditions (January 1983). Tragically, Smith was killed falling from the traverse into Coire Leis after finishing the climb. On the same traverse, from the First Platform, Jimmy Marshall also slipped, but managed to stop just before the final band of cliffs

Photo: Ken Crocket

The finishing chimney of Minus Two Gully

Photo: Colin Wells

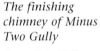

Haston later remembered the February 11 ascent of Minus Two Gully in his autobiography.

> For Stenhouse and me it was both a stunner and a mind-awakener. We were supposed to share leads, but after we had followed Jimmy over the bulge it became apparent that his experience and ability were still beyond ours. We were taking as long to second as he was to lead.[7]

Marshall's description of Minus Two Gully in the 1959 SMC Journal read,

> This was a winter ascent par excellence, the gully being barred by an impressive ice bulge which proved a bit of an impostor. Difficulties thereafter almost continuous. At the exit pitch below the final forking an étrier was used and the left fork followed to the crest of N.E. Buttress, gained at nightfall. By the feeble light of a crescent moon, stars and aurora, the Buttress was climbed. The gully took 8 hours, three pitons being used for protection, and piton belays used at each stance.

Marshall's party regained the CIC Hut at 2am, having begun the route at a traditionally late hour. The next day, February 12, they climbed Hesperides Ledge, III. This is the slanting ledge on The Comb, running up and right above the steepest section of that impressive rock feature. Hesperides Ledge must surely be safer in winter; its loose rocks bound together by ice, but its frighteningly exposed traverses deter most parties from attempting it.

Meanwhile, Clough and his friends had been busy, climbing six routes between February 10 and 12. Perhaps Clough's best discovery was the North Wall of Castle Ridge, where four routes were climbed including Nordwand (IV,3), a mixed route some 430m in length which gives interesting route finding while not being technically difficult.

It is worth remarking at this point that in 1959 winter gradings as used now were not yet in use on Ben Nevis. Climbs were described but no grade given. Climbers not in touch with those in the forefront of exploration thus suffered from a slight handicap, though they often had as a rough and ready measure of a route's difficulty the names of the first ascenders and the time taken for the ascent (this being one of the details usually recorded). Cairngorm climbers, on the other hand, had been using a numbered system for several years and the Cairngorm Climbers' Guides by Malcolm Smith were to use this system, numbering grades of difficulty on winter routes from the easiest, I, to the most difficult, V.

Only one more winter route remained to be recorded on Nevis that year – Platforms Rib (IV,4), climbed by MacInnes, Clough, Terry Sullivan and M.White, on March 8. Starting at the foot of Minus Three Gully (then unclimbed in winter), Platforms Rib follows the rib on the left until an overhang is reached. On the first ascent this was climbed using pegs for aid. Above the overhang Minus Three Gully was followed for a short distance before the rib was regained.

Throughout April and May of 1959 Clough was active, either in company with MacInnes or other friends. Several routes were recorded on the Secondary Tower Ridge, including a solo ascent of a Hard Severe, Vagabond's Rib, climbing a two-tiered slabby rib left of Vanishing Gully. The next day Clough and MacInnes compounded the Point Five controversy with a peg ascent of the magnificent wall on the right flank of Càrn Dearg Buttress. Titan's Wall, as it became, took 12 hours of climbing, 113m of the route being new. Lying between Sassenach and The Shield, this smooth, cracked wall was responsible for the glint in several climbers' eyes, though probably no one climbing in Scotland at that time had the technique to free climb it.

Attempts to free climb Titan's Wall were made since its first, aided ascent. One notable pair who tried in the late 1960s were Rab Carrington and the late John Jackson. Despite their high levels of ability, new standards and skills were required before such difficulties could be overcome. These new abilities arrived in the mid-1970s. In June 1977 the route was freed by Mick Fowler and Phil Thomas. It was graded as Extremely Severe (E4). Four days later it received a second free ascent by the Scots team of Dave 'Cubby' Cuthbertson and Murray Hamilton. They climbed it with a slight variation, finishing more directly via an awkward, 9m crack. It is now described as a brilliant route at E3.

In August, while working on a new guide, Marshall and Stenhouse made a direct start at Severe to Bayonet Route.

During the remainder of 1959 three routes were pioneered. Two of these were Very Severes on September 19, by two friends of Ian Clough; Terry Sullivan and N.Collingham. The Slant lies on Number Five Gully Buttress, right of Marshall's Fives Wall, while The Shadow is a pleasant and easy Very Severe on Càrn Dearg Buttress, parallel to and right of Route II. But the third route of 1959, also on Càrn Dearg Buttress, was to be remembered not only for its difficulties, which are tangible enough, but also for the essay its ascent inspired one of the party to write, an essay reprinted many times since. The route was The Bat, the party, Smith and Haston.

In the summer of 1959, the 19-year old Dougal Haston was waiting to enter Edinburgh University as an undergraduate. Meanwhile he

Rab Carrington leading the magnificent first pitch of Titan's Wall (E3) in the early 1970s

Photo: Ian Fulton

Haston, the painter of Lagangarbh

Photo: Jimmy Marshall

collected his weekly unemployment benefit of £2,10s and shuttled back and forth between Edinburgh and Glen Coe. As one of the *Currie Lads*, Haston set the molars of the SMC establishment grinding with rage at several of his escapades. One of these escapades involved Lagangarbh, the SMC Hut lying under the Buachaille Etive Mòr, in Glen Coe.

One of the rooms in Lagangarbh had been painted a dull green, while Glen Coe itself endured very dark and sombre weather at the time. Haston was *into* Kandinsky at the time, and as there just happened to be a stock of paint about; red, yellow, boot polish too, the outcome was colourful. Haston and Ronnie Marshall took out the paints and splashed on the brilliant reds and yellows, setting up candles all around when they had finished. The result was remembered by Jimmy Marshall.

> The room came alive – we thought it was brilliant – it was an escape from the horrible Glen Coe weather – a sunlight corner – but it so happened that a work party had just painted the place![8]

Robin Clark Smith was already at Edinburgh University, studying Philosophy. Two years older than Haston, Smith was to graduate with an Honours degree. But for his premature death in the Pamirs, Smith would have gone on to study for a doctorate in London. His application form for the SMC, in December 1958, shows a formidable list of hard ascents.

In the early summer of 1959 Smith and Dick Holt made an attempt on the unclimbed central corner on Càrn Dearg Buttress – the hanging corner in the middle of the bulging wall left of the Sassenach chimney– which was eventually to be named The Bat. Making the traditional late start and beginning via the Centurion entry, they succeeded in finding a way rightwards across the overlapping slabs, attempted in the past by Kellett, Patey, Cunningham and probably others unknown. Faced with 12m of bulging wall between them and the start of the corner proper, with daylight threatening to fade, they *retreated* by climbing up Sassenach to meet the night. The next day, wrote Smith –

> We woke...to the whine of the Death Wind fleeing down the Allt a' Mhuilinn. Fingery mists were creeping in at five windows. Great grey spirals of rain were boring into the Buttress.[9]

The two abandoned their attempts and left for Edinburgh.

Smith returned to the corner in September with Haston. The two, according to some sources, had no great liking for each other, though it may well have been that they simply preferred not to climb together. Climbing partners were scarce at that time of year however, so they teamed up in Glen Coe, making an ascent of Carnivore before moving on to Fort William on the Monday. Tuesday at 1pm saw them on the embryonic route, at Smith's previous high point. Smith was intent on climbing the corner and he offered the lead of the next, intermediate pitch to Haston. This was an ugly, overhanging groove.

Haston moved up the groove with care. To quit the groove, he had to place a sling over a small spike, which then allowed poor holds above to be reached. As he moved up the sling rolled off its spike and he barely managed to pull himself on to the ledge above. As Smith followed, more slowly than usual, Haston knew that he too had found it difficult. The big corner was now above Haston's belay, rising in two, 10m leaps, with a horizontal roof jutting out over a metre between.

Smith, who was wearing a tattered pair of kletterschuh, borrowed Haston's PAs. The impecunious pair had two full-weight ropes, but Haston's had lost almost 2m of its original 37m during an *'experiment'* on the Currie Railway Walls near Edinburgh, while Smith's, on loan from a Glaswegian friend, had been *'stretched a little'*, so that it was now 40m.

> ...and so Dougal at the bottom had quickly tied on to an end of each rope which left me with 15 feet on the one to get rid of round and round my middle to make the two ropes even.

The corner pitch up which Smith now set off looked impressive in its untouched state – a damp crack leading to the overhang, with a crack disappearing out of sight above. The pitch was mossy and vegetated and holds had to be unearthed by pulling off chunks of moss. Smith gained the overhang and as protection to this point had been poor he quickly pounded a metal peg into the crack beneath the overhang, suspended a knotted sling from the peg and stood with his right foot in the sling. Several attempts by Smith to move left and up the corner above produced only a jammed knot for a runner before his initial impetus faded and he retreated to join Haston on the belay ledge.

Changing leads necessitated much time-consuming work by the two; swapping footwear, untying ropes and exchanging ends (in order that the ropes, still running through Smith's runners in the corner, would run smoothly for Haston). Eventually Haston was back up at the black roof. Their equipment did not include artificial chockstones or nuts – these were just about to become available – but at one point in the corner-crack, just above the roof, there was a suitable widening in the crack. Here, according to Smith, Haston succeeded in hammering in a wooden wedge, used both as a runner and as a support for another foot-sling. (In Haston's account of the ascent, written 13 years later, he has it that Smith inserted the wedge, before retreating to the belay for a rest and to exchange leads.)[7]

Haston thought he could see a ledge above the roof and decided to commit himself to gaining it. In climbing as practised at this standard and time, commitment implied an all-or-nothing effort; either the climber would safely gain his objective, or he would be in considerable danger of going so far then falling off – and so it proved to be, as Haston set off upwards from the wooden wedge.

> In my overconfidence I'd hopelessly underestimated the angle of the corner. Overhanging it was, and my ledge didn't exist. I found myself with fingers stuck despairingly into a turf that was sliding.

Down below on the belay ledge, Smith was going through the worries and doubts that assail the second man on such hard, exploratory climbs, eyeing his belay points, and pulling down the sleeves of his jersey to try and protect his wrists from rope burn, should the leader fall. Not only were there no commercially available nut runners, there were no safe belay devices either. The belayer ran the rope behind his back, took one twist round the off side wrist, and hoped not to be pulled off the stance if the leader fell.

In my overconfidence I'd hopelessly underestimated the angle of the corner. Overhanging it was, and my ledge didn't exist. I found myself with fingers stuck despairingly into a turf that was sliding

*Philip 'Bish' McAra
in main corner of The
Bat (E2), (1982)*

Photo: Tom Prentice

*It began under
control as the bit
of news 'I'm off,'
but it must have
been caught in the
wind, for it grew
like a wailing siren
to a blood-curdling
scream as a black
and bat-like shape
came hurtling over
the roof...*

Then came a sort of squawk as Dougal found that his ledge was not...Rattling sounds came from his throat or nails or something...Then his fingers went to butter. It began under control as the bit of news 'I'm off,' but it must have been caught in the wind, for it grew like a wailing siren to a blood-curdling scream as a black and bat-like shape came hurtling over the roof...

The *'bat-like shape'* hurtling over the roof was to suggest the name of the route to the pair, in addition to which so much time had been spent climbing in the dark. Haston fell over the roof head-first and was brought to a shattering halt by the ropes, hanging upside down opposite a not-so-cool Smith who had been pulled off his ledge and was also suspended. The wooden wedge had done its job and was holding under the strain as both climbers scrabbled back on to the rock. By now the inevitable dusk was creeping up the rocks and the climbers were forced to retreat, first by a traverse right to Sassenach, then by an abseil down the ropes in the dark, to land in the mud at the foot of the cliff. The attempts were over for this week, as the pair returned to Edinburgh.

The following Tuesday saw Smith and Haston back under the black roof. This time Smith had a pair of PAs and as it was his turn to lead he climbed up to the roof. Threading his ropes through the peg, jammed knot and wooden wedge, he stood in a sling attached to the wedge and at full stretch he was just able to reach two small pebbles jammed in the crack above the roof. Suddenly he felt his stomach lurch as, he thought, the wedge shifted in its crack. Desperately he threaded a tiny nylon sling through the pebbles as the wedge came out and he shot into space, hanging from the jammed knot and peg about 6m below the roof.

In a rage now, Smith climbed back up to the roof, moved round it again and sat in slings depending from the two little pebbles. Moving on quickly but feeling his strength ebbing he inserted another peg about 6m above the roof, before continuing. Pulling up on this high peg it came out and Smith was once again violently precipitated into space to come to rest below the by now hated roof.

As Smith was hanging from a higher point in the overhanging corner he was suspended away from the lower corner, so Haston lowered him down to the belay. The corner pitch had occupied him for four hours, while night, once again, was flowing up the hill. But Smith's character was very strong in persistence so he made one more attempt, telling the disenchanted Haston that he was going to recover the equipment.

Robin Smith in Glen Coe

Photo: Jimmy Marshall

> So I was very sly and said we had to get the gear and climbed past the roof to the sling at the pebbles leaving all the gear in place. There I was so exhausted that I put in a piton, only it was very low, and I thought, so am I, *peccavi, peccabo*, and I put in another and rose indiscriminately until to my surprise I was past Dougal's ledge and still on the rock...

Haston followed in the twilight, leaving all the gear in the corner, then led the next pitch up a groove. At this point, although they had finally cracked the route, some 150m feet of climbing on the upper pitches of Sassenach remained before they gained the top of the buttress. Fortunately both climbers enjoyed night climbing and belaying out on the right edge they soaked up the moonlight and the alien views such light provides.

The next weekend Haston returned with Marshall while Smith was exam-bound in Edinburgh. Climbing to the end of the main Sassenach chimney they then moved left to the top of the corner of The Bat and finished by an independent line of grooves. Tied in with a pitch climbed earlier by Smith and Holt, Càrn Dearg Buttress had been gifted with a new, hard route. The fact that it had been an all-Scottish ascent probably helped salve the wounds inflicted by Centurion and Sassenach.

Robin Smith had opened 1959 with his winter ascent of The Tower Face of The Comb; he closed the year with The Bat. He was now a 21-year old, fast maturing into one of the most effective mountaineers ever to hit Ben Nevis. The following winter season, Smith and Jimmy Marshall were to climb together on Nevis, where in one week of sustained effort they were to bring to a climax the end of a decade of exciting developments in Scottish mountaineering. In one sense, they were to gain a pinnacle of achievement in step-cutting which can never be bettered.

*Comb Gully Buttress
(IV,4)*

Photo: Tom Ripley

Of the writings that Smith and Marshall left of their week, Jim Perrin made the following observation.

Robin Smith's literary persona has an attractive, if occasionally coy, ingenuousness, and there is a persuasive quality of enthusiasm & energy about his writing. Marshall's accounts are refreshingly direct...[10]

In fact, 1960 on Nevis opened not with Smith and Marshall but with Clough, who recorded three routes in January. Rogue's Rib (IV,5), climbed with G.Grandison on January 2, is a technically hard buttress climb immediately left of Italian Climb. It finds very few takers today. In addition to its low altitude, its steepness ensures that it holds little snow and ice and is consequently rarely in condition. More often accessible and a good mountaineering route of high quality is Comb Gully Buttress (IV,4), climbed with Alexander on January 8. The finish taken by Clough, a prominent, rightward curving crack, is not often in winter condition and most climbers follow the variation finish, taken by Ian Fulton and Davy Gardner in January 1971. This variation moves left to climb ice-covered rocks and a finishing chimney.

On January 29 Clough returned to Nevis, exploring Castle Coire with R.Sefton. In 1940 Rolland and Ogilvy had recorded Compression Crack, a 230m Very Difficult right of Raeburn's Buttress. Clough made what he thought was a winter ascent of this route, but Marshall later pointed out that he had climbed a completely new route, so it became Winter Chimneys (IV,4). Compression Crack itself was not to receive a winter ascent until February 1985, by Martin Hind and Chris Rice. The weather on this ascent deteriorated to such an extent that while crossing the plateau of Carn Dearg – '*The Plateau of Storms*' as Clement Wragge had accurately named it – Hind was blown 9m through the air. On the same day, while climbing on the relatively sheltered Trident Buttress area, Ken Crocket had a dead man blown off his harness.

It may be worth pointing out here that the '*easy slabs and grass ledges*', lying above the left wall of South Castle Gully, suggested as an approach route to both these routes, are by no means as straightforward as their appearance would suggest. Their awkward nature and exposed situation are potentially lethal, in addition to which in damp conditions the rock hereabouts is very greasy. In late season in recent years this wall has formed a magnificent cataract of ice that is now used to approach Compression Crack. Some climbers consider this ice approach the meat of the route, and traverse into South Castle Gully before Compression Crack itself.

Towards the end of 1959 Jimmy Marshall had suffered a series of wet weekends that made him think of giving up. '*I'm going to get married, start a business and to hell with climbing!*' At the time this seemed like a good idea, as he then missed all the wet weekends that followed. Luckily for the history of Nevis and Scottish mountaineering Marshall had second thoughts the following winter, as he described in a retrospective dinner speech.

Then I thought – I'd better do something, for there's a lot of things that I haven't done yet – that's one of the reasons why we had that great week on the Ben, Robin Smith and I, for I was getting married the month after it and

'I'm going to get married, start a business and to hell with climbing!'

Comb Gully Buttress area. Number Two Gully (II) is on the left, with its distinctive icy wall near the mouth, Comb Gully Buttress (IV,4) is central, while Comb Gully (IV,4) soars up on the right

Photo: John Trudgill

we thought – well, we'd better go out there and do something and we had great weather and a super week of climbing.[7]

Their '*super week of climbing*' began on Saturday, February 6, with an ascent of The Great Chimney on Tower Ridge. The grading of IV,5 given to it would seem too easy, as anyone who looks down the chimney and shudders would agree. (The current consensus, post 2002 guidebook, is V,6.) At its overhanging chockstone Marshall had to use a sling for aid. Smith, who all through the week seemed to have trouble with a delinquent ice axe, dropped it down the chimney, and after finishing the route abseiled back down to recover it. Sliding down the rope into the gathering darkness,

> I was right at the end of the rope...the ends were just sliding over my shoulder when I came upon my axe. The Old Man, who is very bold, went solo down the crest of the ridge and came upon terrible difficulties in the moonlight...[11]

On Sunday, February 7, the traditional late start was set back even further when Smith had to return to the hut for his forgotten ice axe. The axe worked well on the first winter ascent of Minus Three Gully however, as Smith battered and bridged his way up an icicle pitch. Marshall led through on the next pitch which turned out to be longer and harder. Eventually they emerged on to the North-East Buttress and so up to the plateau and down by moonlight, Smith pausing only long enough to lose his axe again.

Monday saw Smith hunting for the axe while Marshall waited impatiently below Gardyloo Buttress, the objective of the day. The natural winter line up this buttress lies just right of Kellett's summer line and takes in a slabby corner running up and left to a small overhang. From below the overhang the original line climbs the steep ice wall to the left. Smith having puffed his way up Observatory Gully, Marshall set off up the first pitch. Conditions, as they were all over the mountain,

*The Icicle Variation
to Smith's Route,
Gardyloo Buttress
(V,5)*

Photo: Cubby Images

*Marshall on the first
winter ascent of
Gardyloo Buttress*

Photo: Jimmy Marshall

were perfect, with much snow ice and ice, both easy to cut. Marshall led out 30m and brought up Smith.

Just above Marshall's belay in the corner was an ice-fringed cave, formed by ice drooping over an overhang at the foot of a hanging groove. Smith was all for attempting the overhang, but Marshall's judgment was for the line of least resistance and Smith continued leftwards. Marshall, with hindsight, thinks that this decision was possibly a wrong one, as Smith's higher traverses, described below, were at least as hard as the overhang, as well as being further from security.

> ...a nervous traverse left on steep ice, then a happy announcement that it's a doddle. Two hours later, hoarse with singing and groaning, I'm still watching the rope...A shout of 'Come on!' rakes me back to frigidity; it dawns on me, he's too polite, something is ugly up here besides Wheech; having lived so long for a climber and acquired a cunning commensurate with age, I point out that there is still 50 feet of rope to go; a short exchange of unpleasanteries follows, and the rope continues its neurotic advance.[12]

Smith had given up the search for his axe and was using Marshall's. The senior climber had correctly analysed Smith's politeness and realised that he was shattered and unwilling to continue past a poor belay he had arranged. But continue he did until he dropped the party's only axe.

> It stuck in the ice on top of an overhang five feet below and I crept down to pick it up in a sweating terror of kicking a bit of snow on it.

Smith now climbed up and right, across a great barrel of snow ice. The first 15cm of this were uselessly crusted and he used a long ice peg for protection, driving it in as high as he could and cutting steps up past it until it was too low, when the whole procedure was repeated. At least it was repeated until the peg was dropped at the biggest bulge and disappeared into the night. Smith's last chance of retreat was now gone. Continuing to cut steps, he lost his grip of the axe, the sign of a very tired leader,

> ...and it started somersaulting in the air with both my arms windmilling trying to grab it and my feet scarting about in crumbly holds.

Marshall meanwhile was slowly freezing on the belay ledge, as Smith fought to stay on the ice wall.

> Silhouetted against a starry sky the wee bauchle comes into sight, grunts of 'I'm nearly there' go on for another prolonged spell, then a great whoop sears the night.

Smith had reached the foot of the final gully where he belayed on his peg hammer to bring up Marshall. Even seconding this pitch impressed Marshall,

> ...feeling high and deep into the holds, a thrash with the feet for the lower steps, a quick judgment for soundness, then a queer off-balance swing for the next hole – wow! that was a false one – hands slip on the glassy ice, the footholds crunch down, I expect to come off...

Marshall stayed on and completed the pitch, then led through up the final, easy pitch leading to the plateau. Shambling down Number Four Gully Smith found his recalcitrant axe. Smith's Route on Gardyloo

Ken Crocket on the first pitch of Smith's Route, Gardyloo Buttress, February 1975, during the first ascent of the Icicle Variation. The foot of the overhanging icicle is visible above, with a poor belay in a small cave fringed by icicles. The original route goes left below the icicle to climb a steep barrel-shaped wall of ice.
Fashion Note: as perceptively spotted by Ken Wilson in his book 'Cold Climbs', the use of a hairy sweater, in this case mohair, lends increased adhesion on winter climbs

Photo: Ken Crocket Collection

Buttress, short at 125m though steep, had to wait 11 years for a second ascent in March 1971, by the Cambridge Scot Mike Geddes and Nigel Rayner, taking four and a half hours. Its third ascent came the follow-ing month when Kenny Spence from Edinburgh, then leading a party on a mountaineering course, used perfect conditions of snow ice to cut a line of pigeon-hole steps up the buttress. The grading of the route, V,5, remains inviolate, despite changes in technique. Geddes, on the

The Ordinary Route on Observatory Buttress (V,4), climbed by Marshall and Smith. The ascent was not recorded at the time because Marshall assumed Raeburn had climbed the line in winter

Photo: Cubby Images

second ascent, was using the new front-pointing technique. (See Chapter 12 for the development of this.)

In February 1975, Ken Crocket and Chris Gilmore made what was reckoned to have been the fifth ascent, climbing directly up from the ice cave, over the overhang fancied by Smith on the first ascent. Difficulties were experienced on the icy ramp above the icicle due to conditions; a damp skin of snow covering harder ice. The Icicle Variation, as it is now named, is more popular and perhaps slightly easier, than the original line.[13]

Smith was still exhausted the day after Gardyloo Buttress, but despite this they climbed the Ordinary Route on Observatory Buttress. Originally graded IV, a more realistic grading would be V,4, taking into account its length and the steep ice characteristic of the hard section of the route. This route was not recorded in the SMCJ along with the other first ascents; Marshall had assumed that Raeburn had climbed the line in winter. This also explains it being mistakenly recorded following a later ascent as The Liquidator, February 20, 1965, Grade V by I.A.MacEachran and Jim Renny. In winter it gives a superb and difficult climb with, in certain conditions, overhanging ice at the crux chimney.

Wednesday dawned wet, but as it cleared around 10am Smith and Marshall sweated up Observatory Gully towards the fierce, narrow confines of Point Five Gully, still awaiting an ascent since the five-day siege by Clough. Conditions underfoot were still perfect, with snow and ice making the climbing much more secure. Smith charged on up the third pitch,

> I pressed on up a chimney full of evil crusted snow and took an axe belay at the side of the gully. Then the spindrift started drooling down, and just as the Old Man spread himself halfway over the base of ice it grew to a hissing torrent and piled up on his great stomach and pushed him out from the ice while he clawed away for the holds and through the tips of his gloves.

Jimmy Marshall climbing in the Alps
Photo: Jimmy Marshall

The hissing stream of spindrift eventually ran dry and after one more pitch the gully eased off and Smith and Marshall finished up the gully through swirling clouds and pools of moonlight. The second ascent had taken seven hours in excellent conditions by a team at their peak; subsequent ascents by step-cutting were not always to have such smooth progress, one team being forced to bivouac on the route, finishing the next day. By 1965 Point Five Gully had seen five ascents in winter, an average of one ascent a year. Zero Gully had received four ascents up to the end of 1965.

By Thursday morning, Marshall and Smith had climbed five hard winter routes; four first ascents and the second ascent of Point Five Gully. They were plotting the biggest plum of the lot however, the direct ascent of the Orion Face, first attempted by Smith and Holt in January, 1959. Conditions then had forced an escape leftwards from the Basin; this time Smith and Marshall were determined to succeed. But first they had an *'off-day'*, as they woke on Thursday morning to mist and wind.

Crossing the Càrn Mòr Dearg arete in the teeth of the gale they climbed Aonach Beag and traversed the Grey Coires to Stob Choire Claurigh. Descending to Spean Bridge for refreshment they then took a bus to Fort William – there the fish and chip shop known to climbers as 'Hell's Kitchen' was shut so they had some more refreshment in a pub before being turned out early. Smith and Marshall were now in possession of a set of draughts from the pub and the publican, incensed at the loss of yet another set, had called in the police. It seems that Smith had played a prank, hiding the draughts in Marshall's rucsac. The climbing pair were hitching a lift back along the road when Smith, reactions slowed by the drink, thumbed the approaching police car. Despite Marshall's suggestion to heave the incriminating evidence over a wall they were consequently given a lift – back to the police station! After the statutory interrogation the two were released in time to catch the

*Even the Old man
recognised he had
had his share of
cruxes, so he
offered me the
choice and I chose
the first because
the third looked
terrible...*

last bus passing the Distillery and walked back up to the hut.

Friday, February 12, was cold, and feeling none-too-bright, Smith and Marshall had an afternoon's climb on The Comb, making a first winter ascent of Pigott's Route. Avoiding the slabby foot of the buttress, they made use of one of the long, tapering shelves of rock, running from bottom left to the right edge of The Comb overlooking Green Gully. The lead at the 'rotten chimney' fell to Marshall, thereafter long ice grooves led to the crest of the buttress. Both The Great Chimney and Pigott's Route were still awaiting second winter ascents at the end of 1985; the latter was climbed by a team from Edinburgh at the beginning of 1986. The rotten chimney of Pigott's does not seem to hold snow and ice readily and climbers have retreated on several occasions.

On Friday night the weather improved, the wind fading as quickly as it had sprung up. At last conditions were right for an attempt on the Orion Face, and at 1pm on Saturday, the pair arrived at the foot of the ice stream depending from the lip of the Basin.

> Even the Old man recognised he had had his share of cruxes, so he offered me the choice and I chose the first because the third looked terrible...[11]

Smith was mistaken, however, as the third pitch turned out to be easy and the second pitch, led by Marshall, exciting. But Smith had a little adventure at the first pitch, when at 15m,

> Wheech's tour had misled him on to a thinly iced slab, where it was obvious he would either waken up or roll back down to the hut...[14]

At the top of the second pitch the climbers were faced with the unknown, as Smith moved out left to the skyline. A series of complaints from Smith signalled arrival on to the easy ground below the Basin, Marshall leading on past to gain the right edge of the depression. A 30m ice slope followed by a 15m traverse right saw Smith belayed at the foot of the next difficult section on this classically grand mountaineering route – the Second Slab Rib of The Long Climb. In many winters this rib stands out at some distance, prominently dark against the surrounding snow and ice, as it seldom ices up. It was in this condition on the first ascent, as Marshall began the pitch.

> An exploratory traverse 10 feet round the corner disclosed a well-iced wall, shining green in the evening light and perched over the now impressive drop of the wall beneath: 130 feet higher the hunt for peg cracks failed in the gathering gloom of night and a belay in powder snow brought the sharp edges of frost and fear into the struggle...

The climbing following the Slab Traverse can give incredibly enjoyable situations, as found by later parties.

> ...sustained pitches of IV, no one move standing out as hard, no move easy enough to ignore, no protection, beautiful route finding up parallel grooves, round corners and edges, hard ice all the way and no hanging about.[15]

Reaching the snow slope beneath the terminal towers of The Orion Face, Smith and Marshall found to their dismay knee-deep, floury snow. Their original plan was to spiral up rightwards from this point, towards Zero Gully, but doubts as to the safety of a traverse in such conditions

SMC member Ronnie Richards, training for Everest, makes the awkward traverse out of the Basin and across the Second Slab Rib on Orion Direct (V,5). This pitch is often regarded as the winter crux and requires close attention, especially to footwork. The belay is good but protection scanty (March 1975)

Photo: Ken Crocket

made them consider moving left, on to the crest of North-East Buttress. But again the unconsolidated snow would have made this finish dangerous, while by now fatigue and darkness were creeping in. They decided to try straight ahead, up the final rocky ramparts of the face.

Smith belayed to rock below the last hard pitch, Marshall stopping long enough to pick up the dry gloves, reserved for the leader of each pitch. A scrabble up a cone of snow led into an icy groove. Here Marshall had to feel the angle by touch, as in the mist and gloom white fog crystals were blurring all outlines. It seemed to him that above lay an enormous cornice; more felt than seen, as he cut steps up the groove.

> About 40 feet up, the groove steepened to a bulge; finding the holds with the cramponed feet was extremely awkward at times, and often moves were made hanging from the handholds whilst the crampons scarted about in search of the 'buckets' cut below.

The bulge now forced him out on the right wall, moving along a short ledge,

French climber Francois Damilamo soloing Orion Direct (V,5) during his 'enchainement' of Sickle (V,5), Zero Gully (V,4), Point Five Gully (V,5), Orion Direct (V,5) and Smith's Route (V,5), (February 1987)

Photo: Godefroy Perroux

...then a frightening move, leaning out on an undercut ice hold, to cut holds round a rib on to the slab wall of a parallel groove. The ice here was only about an inch thick and moving into the groove was very difficult; the cat crawl up the thin ice remains imprinted in the memory, for at this 'moment of truth' strains of an awful dirge came up...from 90 feet below, 'Ah kin hear the hammer ringin' on somebody's coffin...'

Marshall finally gained a snow-filled groove, where his aching calf muscles could recover. To his side, the top of the first groove was closed over, leaving a steep, icy wall above. He resumed cutting wearily, worrying now about the amount of rope remaining as it seemed to him that he had run out more than 42m. Then suddenly there was no more ice to cut, as a gentle snow slope in front of him shone faintly in the cloud-filtered moonlight. the Orion Direct had been climbed.

As if Scots climbers were stunned by this series of routes nothing more was recorded on Nevis that winter until April 1, when Clough and some friends found a variation to Number Two Gully Buttress at III, climbing to the left of the original line. Smith, however, had another winter climb to make. On March 23, 1960, Zero Gully received its second winter ascent. Dougal Haston was now a student at Edinburgh University. Dick Holt was President of the EUMC, while Robin Smith was Editor of that Club's Journal, or *Nocturnal*, as it was wittily and aptly called that year.

I was sleeping off a scoop in the Clubrooms when Wightman came rolling in and said he wanted to go to Nevis so we spent the next night in the C.I.C. Hut.

So began Haston's article in the 1961 EUMC *Nocturnal*.[16] This account, written immediately after the event, differs in some small detail from the version in Haston's autobiography, written eleven years later[7]; as did Haston's later account of The Bat in the same book differ slightly from Smith's fresh account. In their rush from the *'foulness of the city'*, Haston and Andy Wightman had forgotten to include a rope.

> A solution was on hand, however: the Hut was full of steadfast English muttering earnestly, up Three down Four, up Two down Five, and other Nevis Gully permutations, so we waited until they had departed and went on a scavenge for rope.

They found a spare rope left behind by one of the other residents and set off at the statutory late hour for Zero Gully. The route was in fine condition, with much blue ice, but Haston's weak, out-of-condition arms ran out of strength some 24m up the first pitch and the two climbers descended to the Hut with their tails between their legs. But reinforcements were about to arrive.

> The evening was full of hateful mutterings about black rope stealing and bed thieving Scots and the Hut is fully booked. Bed had just been achieved when a grubby Smith arrived.

Smith admitted that he too had no rope, so they slept on the problem and waited to see what the next day would be like. Another late start, another *'borrowed'* rope, and the threesome arrived at the foot of Zero. Smith won the toss and set off up Haston's steps of yesterday. Two hours later he was 9m higher than Haston's high point and taking a poor belay. When Haston reached the belay, he was so shattered and icicle-like that he let Smith lead the second pitch as well. This contained an evil little bulge which turned out to be an impostor.

> ...and even Wheech using my axe because it was better than his managed to outwit it in less than half an hour. In fact he got so chuffed that he battered my axe into the ice with so much enthusiasm that the pick came flying past me...

Wightman, who as third on the rope was apparently on his second ever winter climb, was still at the foot of the route, slowly freezing. He tried to untie the rope but his hands were too cold and Haston pulled the rope in and brought him up.

> Now Andy should be called Willie the Weeper for all the moaning he does and sure enough the manky belay sent him off and I left him mumbling and grumbling to himself while I went up the bulge to curse at Wheech for breaking my axe.

Haston led the third pitch, belaying under an ice bulge. Wightman then came up to Smith's belay, while Smith went on to lead the bulge above Haston's head. Smith finished the bulge just as darkness fell completely. On the first ascent Patey, MacInnes, and Nicol had taken only an hour to climb from here to the top, as the major difficulties are concentrated in the first 270m. *'We now reckoned on half an hour as the first party were old men'*.

Stopping for a bite of chocolate they found they had one torch between the three of them as for the next few hours they wandered around in the dark, encountering bulges and rock bands. Finally they decided to go rightwards and try climbing up Observatory Ridge. While scrambling around on a snow arete, the light from their solitary torch

A solution was on hand, however: the Hut was full of steadfast English muttering earnestly, up Three down Four, up Two down Five, and other Nevis Gully permutations, so we waited until they had departed and went on a scavenge for rope

*Brian Dunn on the
penultimate pitch of
Zero Gully (V,4), with
the beckoning plateau
edge above*

Photo: Con Higgins

picked out a line of steps below and right, and with a short abseil they landed in the steps and the easiest way up to the plateau.

> It was all hell let loose up there so we quickly beetled off down Four Gully in the dim light of approaching dawn to face court martial for rope thieving by the English dayshift.[15]

The CIC log for that week has the entry, '*Zero Gully, quite hard conditions, "n" hours*'.

In May, Smith recorded his last new route on Nevis with J.Hawkshaw of the Edinburgh University MC, when he climbed Central Route. Now graded at Hard Very Severe, this climbs the raised rib between Left Hand and Right Hand Routes, on Minus Two Buttress. The Bat had a second ascent on June 26, by G.Oliver and T.Sullivan.

A jump in standards on Nevis was made on August 2 by a rope from the Creagh Dhu Club. John McLean and Bill Smith climbed the ferocious-looking line of Subtraction. The overhanging top pitch, a typical Nevis groove, slanting up and left, undercut and smooth, defeated several repeat attempts of this difficult and underrated climb.

Of Subtraction McLean has expressed puzzlement at its seeming difficulty, having found no great problems on the first ascent. The second ascent, in 1963, was by the Marshall brothers, Jimmy and Ronnie. Jimmy Marshall remembers it being very hard, while on a later ascent, by 'Big' Ian Nicolson and Dougie McArthur in 1971, the latter took a swing while seconding, which lent more weight to the route's reputation. Subsequent ascents have softened its reputation and it stands at E1.

The first winter ascent of the Orion Direct was the climax of an incredible week of mountaineering on Ben Nevis. The partnership of Smith and Marshall had joined with ideal conditions. But it was more than that. In the ten years that followed other fine and equally hard routes would be won by step cutting. But no other climbers would come near to repeating such a sustained effort, nor to writing about that week with such lasting feeling.

It is worth quoting from a letter Marshall wrote some 26 years later:

> It is somewhat disconcerting to note the significance attached to the Smith/Marshall week and I doubt it is justified by actual achievements; which though dramatic in execution, were no greater than the ascents of Patey, Grassick, Smith & I in the run up to that week.
>
> Doubtless we contributed to the myth, but when we got back to the city it was realised there was a great chance, through writing up events, to stimulate the next breed of ice men to greater effort; just as Murray's writing did for us. We certainly achieved that aim, but it was meant to illustrate the wonder world of wild winter climbing and certainly not the extreme nature of the routes or the now assumed excellence of the participants.[17]

Just as Murray had been a source of inspiration to them, so would Smith and Marshall be for those who followed. Smith would die in the summer of 1962; with Wilfred Noyce on Peak Garmo in the Russian Pamirs. Marshall would go on to record other great routes. And after an intervening decade had passed new techniques would make step cutting obsolete, fixing more firmly that week of climbing by Smith and Marshall as a remarkable and influential pinnacle in Scottish winter mountaineering history.

References

1. **Shaw**, Robin, *The Siege of Point Five*. Glasgow University MC Journal, No.4, 5 – 8, February 1959.

2. **Clough**, Ian, *Point Five, A Ben Nevis Saga*. SMCJ 26, 335 – 342, 1959.

3. **Clough**, Ian, *Letter to Tom Patey, October 1962*. SMC Archives.

4. **Venables**, Stephen, *Personal communication, November 2007*.

5. **Holt**, R.K., *The Orion Face of Ben Nevis*. Edinburgh University MC Journal, 1958 – 1959, 7 – 10.

6. **Crocket**, K.V., *Hadrian's Wall*. SMCJ 30, 147 – 151, 1972.

7. **Haston**, Dougal, *In High Places*. (London: Cassell, 1972.)

8. **Marshall**, J.R., *JMCS Dinner Speech, Bridge of Orchy, October 1984*.

9. **Smith**, Robin, *The Bat And The Wicked*. SMCJ 27, 12 – 20, 1960.

10. **Perrin**, Jim, *The Ice Climbers*, Climber & Rambler, 21, 10, 26 – 28, October 1982.

11. **Smith**, Robin, *The Old Man And The Mountains*. Edinburgh University MC Journal 1961.

12. **Marshall**, J.R., *Garde de Glace* (The Ascent of Gardyloo Buttress). SMCJ 27, 115 – 117, 1961.

13. **Crocket**, K.V., *Winter Dreams – Gardyloo*. SMCJ 31, 5 – 7, 1976.

14. **Marshall**, J.R., *The Orion Face*. SMCJ 28, 112 – 115, 1961.

15. **Crocket**, K.V., *Winter Dreams – Orion*. SMCJ 31, 3 – 5, 1976.

16. **Haston**, Dougal, *Nightshift in Zero*. EUMC Journal, 1960 – 61.

17. **Marshall**, J.R., *Personal communication, 23 March 1986*.

10: Of Whisky and Other Matters

WHISKY

UP UNTIL about the mid-1970s, most climbers began their approach to the north face of Ben Nevis by walking up from the Ben Nevis Distillery. Leaving the main road, the heavily-laden climber would walk through the distillery gate which never seemed to be closed, and which bore the crest of the Clan MacDonald, tiptoe across the courtyard, and turn a corner to gain the far side of the distillery. Here there was a large open shed containing wooden casks. These were, of course, empty, but some must have been used, as the sweet smell of whisky was always in the air. So a dark night's walk up Nevis often began with an appreciative lungful of whisky-scented air, courtesy of a long-dead Highlander named Long John MacDonald.

Long John MacDonald, who gave his name to the Long John blended whisky produced by one-time distillers, Long John International, is believed to have been born about 1798, in a house at Torgulbin in the Spean Valley. His birth date cannot be precisely known, as the Catholic records of Fort William start in 1820. He was known as Long John to distinguish him from other members of his clan – though visually his great height would have been sufficient.

The family tree shows that Long John could prove a pedigree going back to John MacDonald, Lord of the Isles in the 14th Century. John Macdonald, Lord of the Isles, lived and married royally, to Princess Margaret, daughter of Robert II, King of Scots. Margaret was also a great-granddaughter of Robert the Bruce, the Scottish monarch who so resoundingly defeated the English army at the Battle of Bannockburn in 1314, and so gained independence for Scotland.

Long John's branch of the Clan MacDonald was started by Alexander MacDonald, a son of the Lord of the Isles. He was also known as Alisdair Carrach and was the first chief of the MacDonalds of Keppoch, a branch long known for their fighting spirit. The seventh chief, Ranald Mor MacDonald of Keppoch, rebelled against the Scottish crown, paying dearly for it by being beheaded in 1547. The great-grandfather of Long John, Alexander MacDonald, had been studying at Glasgow University when the first Jacobite Rising broke out in 1715. He joined the Earl of Mar immediately, took part in the disastrous rout of Sheriffmuir and fled to France, finishing his education there and afterwards joining the French army, serving as an officer for several years before deeming it safe to return to Scotland.

By 1743 Alexander MacDonald was at work for the Jacobite cause, returning to France that year to meet with Prince Charles at the French court. The story of Prince Charles Edward's landing in Scotland to raise the clans, and the march of events leading to the invasion of England and the long retreat to Culloden is only too well known. That last battle to be fought on British soil took place in April 1746 on the wind-swept moor overlooking the cold waters of the Moray Firth. At the war council preceding the battle, Alexander MacDonald advised against a face

MAC DONALD of KEPPOCH.

London. Ackermann & C°96, Strand
Printed by C Hulf

to face confrontation with a better armed and numerically superior force. Along with other dissenting chiefs he was overruled. He died with his brother Donald, leading a futile charge against the guns of Cumberland's army.

Fifty years or so after Culloden, probably in the year 1798, Long John MacDonald was born. His father, Donald MacDonald of Torgulbin, was a farmer, as were his seven sons, with the exception of Angus who fought at Waterloo. For as long as the Highlanders could remember, the making of whisky on a small scale had gone on, the clansmen distilling their own from the raw materials readily available; barley (or some other grain), peat, and the good and plentiful Highland water. Indeed, in Gaelic

*Ben Nevis Distillery.
The traditional
route taken by
climbers going up the
mountain via the Allt
a' Mhuilinn used to
begin here*

Photo: Alex Gillespie

the name of whisky is *uisge beatha*, which translates as the *water of life*. There is no evidence that Long John or his family was in any way involved in illicit making of whisky, but it is certain that when the Government in London passed an Act of Parliament outlawing private stills, Long John applied for and was granted a Licence, building a distillery at Fort William in 1825.

His original whisky was called *Long John's Dew of Ben Nevis*, an appropriate-enough name for a drink made at the foot of Britain's highest mountain. A description of Long John – the man, not the drink, can be found in a book by Alexander Smith, published in 1864, and titled *A Summer in Skye*. Smith went to Fort William, meeting Long John and writing the following short portrait.

> When a man goes to Caprera, he, as a matter of course, brings a letter of introduction to Garibaldi – when I went to Fort William, I, equally as a matter of course, brought a letter of introduction to Long John. This gentleman, the distiller of the place, was the tallest man I ever beheld, and must in his youth been of incomparable physique. I presented my letter and was received with the hospitality and courteous grace so characteristic of the old Gael. He is gone now, the happy-hearted Hercules – gone like one of his own drams!

The Ben Nevis Distillery had been going for some 23 years when Her Majesty, Queen Victoria, paid it a visit. She was partial to *a drop of the cratur*, perhaps due to the influence of her Highland servant John Brown, and on visiting Fort William in 1848 honoured the distillery with a visit. The Illustrated London News for April, 1848, records that,

> Mr. Macdonald has presented a cask of whisky to Her Majesty, and an order has been sent to the Treasury to permit the spirits to be removed to the cellars of Buckingham Palace free of duty. The cask is not to be opened until His Royal Highness the Prince of Wales attains his majority.

The whisky would no doubt have been finely matured some 15 years later, when the Prince of Wales, later to become King Edward VII, reached his majority at the age of 21. A renowned gourmet, no doubt he enjoyed the tipple from the Royal cellars.

Long John married in 1835, having built up the family fortunes lost after Culloden. He died in 1856, at the age of 58 and was buried in the Braes of Lochaber, at the small Catholic Chapel of Killichyril, built on top of a steep hill and commanding the peaks of Roybridge and Glen Spean.

Long John's son Donald later acquired and ran the distillery his father had founded. In honour of his father, he named the single malt *Long John's Dew of Ben Nevis*. The reputation for his whisky grew considerably, and Donald P.MacDonald built a new distillery nearby, Nevis Distillery, in order to meet the growing demand for more production. The control of both distilleries stayed in the hands of the MacDonald family until 1944 when a Canadian, Joseph Hobbs gained the ownership of both Ben Nevis and Nevis Distilleries. He quickly sold the latter to the adjacent Glenlochy Distillery. The Nevis Distillery was later demolished, while only listed buildings remain of the Glenlochy Distillery, including its fine pagoda roof.

Local legend relates the story that Hobbs turned around the same day he had bought the Nevis Distillery and sold it to the adjacent Glenlochy Distillery so that they could expand their warehousing. However, sometime between the buying and selling, Hobbs had the wall and gates to Nevis dismantled, carted up the road, and installed at Ben Nevis Distillery. The gates and wall still stand at Ben Nevis today, but the gates supposedly don't quite meet when they close because they were never intended for this site. If this is true, it may help explain why climbers always found the gates open.

Hobbs had one or two ideas which went against traditional practices. He had a grain still installed next to the pot stills so that he could distil

Ben Nevis Distillery still room, showing two of the four copper stills; one pair are original patterns from 1825, the other two date from 1865 (though in situ from 1955 only). It is claimed that the shape of these stills affect the taste, with different distilleries having different shapes

Photo: Alex Gillespie

all the spirit needed to produce a blend. Additionally, he blended all of the malt whiskies and the grain whiskies together as soon as they were distilled and then filled the blends into casks for maturing, a practice he termed *'blending at birth'*. Traditionally, malt whisky and grain whisky are matured separately, then all the single malts for a blend are married together in vats for several months before the grain whisky is added. Hobbs's *'blending at birth'* resulted in inconsistent results and may be regarded as an interesting, but failed experiment.

After Hobbs died, Long John International became the owners, purchasing Ben Nevis Distillery in 1981. Until 1984, Long John used Ben Nevis only for warehousing and trial production. In 1984 they began production again, but closed it shortly afterwards in 1986 when production slowed throughout the entire whisky industry.

There is a suprisingly long association between Scotland and Japan concerning whisky production. The best known is the story of Masataka Taketsuru, who was the chairman and founder of the Nikka Distilling Company. At the end of the First World War he studied at Glasgow University and worked in the Longmorn and Hazelburn distilleries to gain experience. He returned to Japan in 1920 to build the Hokkaido distillery in 1934, having married a Scot, Rita Cowen. She never returned to Scotland, and Masataka Taketsuru died in 1979. The distillery he built, at Yoichi, Hokkaido, produces a 17-year old single malt which is highly regarded and is reputed to be the most Scottish-like of all Japanese whiskies. It is named *Taketsuru*, in honour of the founder.

This association was to be the salvation of the Ben Nevis Distillery, as in 1989 Taketsuru's adopted son returned to buy the Distillery for the Nikka Whisky Distillery Company. Nikka invested extensively in refurbishing the distillery, including the removal of concrete washbacks installed by Hobbs and building a Visitors' Centre to open the distillery to the public. The tun room now uses stainless steel washbacks, while the four original copper stills remain the heart of the distillery.

The stillman at work in the Ben Nevis Distillery. His main task is to measure the strength of the distillations and in particular to determine when to retain the 'middle cut', when a strength of 67-68 % abv is reached in the spirit safe

Photo: Alex Gillespie

Looking up the Allt a' Mhuilinn burn towards the cliffs of Ben Nevis. The water in this burn originates mainly from Coire Leis and Coire na Ciste

Photo: Alex Gillespie

Ben Nevis Distillery produces a range of blends in their 'Dew of Ben Nevis' range, using a mix of malt whiskies from various distilleries and grain whisky. They may owe at least some of their distinctive colours and tastes to the peaty Laphroaig, and much to the mysterious and, some say, magical happenings that begin when the components are married and allowed to mature in the cask. They also produce three single malts. As mentioned at the beginning of this section, the way up Nevis is now rarely begun by the Ben Nevis Distillery start, so climbers miss out on the aroma of whisky at the start of an ascent. For some, however, a good day or weekend up Ben Nevis may be toasted with a dram of this country's distinctive spirit, and for many of them the chosen brand will most appropriately be – Dew of Ben Nevis.

A 'dram' of Ben Nevis malt in a 'Skye' glass

Photo: Alex Gillespie

BEN NEVIS FOOT RACE

On the first Saturday in September each year the Ben Nevis Race is held, upwards of 500 men and women vying with each other to be the fastest to run to the summit and back to Fort William. This arduous race – the course is about 22.5km long following the bridle path, though a runner can shorten this somewhat by taking a more direct route – began to enter the record books in 1895. In September of that year, a local hairdresser, William Swan, started at 10am from the old Post Office at the far north end of the High Street. He cycled to the foot of the mountain, ran to the summit in 1.41.00, rested there for 10 minutes (while he had a cup of Bovril) then returned in 00.50.00, a return time of 2.41.00. This was the first and last race to leave from this point, as three years later the Post Office location had been moved before William McDonald from Leith made the return journey in 2.27.00 on August 2, 1898. Two months later Willie Swan regained his leadership, with a time of 2.20.00, on October 29.

The start of the 1903 Ben Nevis Foot Race. The race was begun with a shotgun wielded by Major Cameron, factor to the Lucy Cameron estate

Photo: Alex Gillespie

Two years following the 1895 ascent by Swan, a retired army officer, Lt Col Spencer Acklom, made a return trip of 2.55.00 in September 1897. He was then 53, made the run wearing his cycling shoes, and had, apparently, done no training. Having said that, he was an athlete by nature who almost certainly credited his long service in India with the Connaught Rangers, along with mountaineering and rock climbing experience as being prime factors in his feat.

These early attempts at the record were in the nature of solo runs, but on June 3 1899 the race gained a more competitive look when Mr Menzies, a local hotel proprietor, offered a gold medal to the first man to finish. The race started from the Locheil Arms Hotel, Banavie, to the sound of a shotgun and the winner was a local gamekeeper, Hugh Kennedy, in a time of two hours 41 minutes. The distance was about 1.6km longer than the course from the new Post Office. This was the first race to be run under Scottish Amateur Athletic Association rules, the starter being William Lapsley, their official timekeeper.

The summit Observatory was still running in 1899, of course, and Hugh Kennedy's arrival at the summit was relayed to the waiting public at the start by a telegram from the summit. There were nine other runners besides Kennedy, including McDonald of Leith, who came in a long way behind as second man with a time of 3.13.00. Perhaps to salve his pride, McDonald made a solo run on August 29, making his run from the new Post Office in 2.18.00.

Women were for a long time barred from entering the race, though unofficial entries were common. Their history is almost as long as that of the men and begins in 1902 with Miss Lucy Cameron of Ardechive running to the summit in 2.03.00. The previous day, it must be recorded, she had walked up Nevis to look at the route, while the day before that she had walked from Ardechive to Fort William. Later that same year, on July 19, Elizabeth Tait, the post-woman at Corrour, made the ascent in 1.59.30, a record that was to stand for seven years. Both of these ascents were made from the new Post Office.

There were two races in 1903, the first of which, for the ascent only, began at Achintee and was started with a shotgun by Major Cameron, factor to the Cameron Lucy Estate. The photograph of the start can also be seen in the second edition of W.T.Kilgour's book, *Twenty Years on Ben Nevis*. Among the seven starters was Ewan McKenzie, the Observatory roadman. The Observatory had only one more year to run at this time. Unfortunately there is no record of the race times, but at the second race, taking in the full return course starting at the Post Office, Ewan MacKenzie returned a winning time of 2.10.6, on September 28.

McKenzie, as the roadman, would not only have a unique knowledge of the route and all its variations, his daily work on the mountain, weather permitting, would keep him at a good general level of fitness. He once participated in an experiment designed to examine his work output, running from the start of the slopes to the summit in 1.08.00. This experiment, conducted by the Edinburgh physicist J.Y.Buchanan, determined that McKenzie had developed one-third horsepower over his ascent.

McKenzie was one of three running in the September race of 1903. One of the other runners, R.Dobson from Glasgow, collapsed during the race and had to be carried down. He remained unconscious for 10 hours before being brought back to life by a local doctor. The second man behind McKenzie was Hugh Kennedy of Banavie, in 2.21.00.

In October 1904 the Observatory was finally closed, the prediction on that wet and cold day being that there would be no more racing on the hill. There were certainly no more races recorded until 1937, with one exception. On September 14, 1909, on a beautiful autumn morning (there was a touch of frost), a Miss Wilson-Smith of Duns, Berwickshire made a new record for the ascent. Starting alone from the Post Office, she gained the summit in 1.51.00. Four days earlier, she had run from Achintee to the summit in three hours, but as a woman this was not recognised as a record.

In 1937, some 34 years after the last organised race, the Depute Town Clerk of Fort William revived the event. The race was held for the next ten occasions during the summer months, suitable for the spectators, but often too warm for participants, the ideal conditions being an overcast day with a cool breeze and damp underfoot, which helps bind the otherwise loose scree of the slopes. The record set by McKenzie in 1903 was finally broken in 1939, D.Mulholland of Ardeer finishing with a time of 2.3.43.

There were no races in 1940 or 1941, and in 1943 a new starting place was chosen, being the King George V Park. This resulted in a new record by D.McIntyre of Fort William, at 2.4.30. Duncan McIntyre, a local butcher, was later to serve as the Honorary President of the Race Association. The following year C.P.Wilson of Kilwinning returned his fourth win since 1937, at the ripe age of 47.

Races stopped again until 1951, since when they have been a regular event. In that year the Ben Nevis Race Association was formed, taking on the organisation necessary for an event becoming more and more popular. The starting point in 1951, as in 1943 and 1944, was the King George V Park, the change being necessitated by the growth in traffic in the High Street. The new course was about 2km shorter, and taking advantage of this Brian Kearney, a Fort William joiner, set a new time and was the first to break the tantalising two hour barrier, of 1.51.18.

A solo ascent was made in September 1955, by the 16-year old daughter of a local doctor. Kathleen Connochie was accompanied by her trainer, Duncan McIntyre, who himself had set a record in 1943. She finished in 3.02.00, having reached the summit one hour and 55 minutes after leaving the King George V Park.

The knowledge of local runners obviously played a large part in the winning lists for some years, as Fort William runners won the race for the next four years, until Pat Moy, Vale of Leven, took the title away from them in 1956 by crossing the winning line in 1.45.55.

Over the decades the number of participants has continued to increase, growing from about 100 in the early 1960s, to 200 by the late 1970s, until by the start of the 1980s it was a vast event drawing some 400 runners from all over the country. The Lochaber Mountain Rescue Team, who supervise mountain safety during the race, expressed concern in 1981 about the perils that such large numbers of people on the hill could bring, especially in poor conditions. This concern has been shown to be necessary, as a tragedy which occurred in 1957 indicates. One of the runners lost a shoe near the summit and took shelter below a rock. Despite being found by a rescue party he died of exposure on the way to hospital, his sparse clothing being inadequate for a prolonged halt on the mountain.

In 1980 the weather was deemed so severe that the race was cancelled, the first time this decision had been made. There was a fair bit of controversy over this, particularly as the runners, 400 or so, had been led to the starting line. These included 14 women, hoping to take part in the first official women's race. Meanwhile, on the mountain, a Sno-Trac broke down at the half-way point, taking up equipment and safety personnel. This delayed the start. Eventually, following consultations between medical, rescue and referee, the race was cancelled.

Many runners wanted to go anyway, while alternatives were also raised such as a race the next day, or a half-Nevis race; these were dismissed. Some runners went ahead on their own, with nine reaching the summit, including the indefatigable Eddie Campbell. There is no doubt that conditions underfoot were very slippery, and with an estimated two-thirds of the runners being inexperienced there would probably have been casualties. As the 1957 tragedy highlighted, any accident on the mountain this day leading to a runner having to stop could easily have serious results.

Women were official participants from 1982 onwards, starting at the same time as the men. The women's record, held by Kathleen Connochie since 1955 still stands, as her time of 3.02.00 is for the King George V Park start. Since 1971 the race has begun from the New Town Park and the women's record at present is the 1.43.25 held by Pauline Haworth (now Pauline Stuart) of Keswick A.C., made in 1984. The present men's record was also made in 1984 by Kenneth Stuart of Keswick A.C., at 1.25.34. He had beaten by one second the previous best, set by John Wild in 1983. Not only was he a superb runner, the entire field probably benefited from recent path improvements.

In 1985 the Ben Nevis Race broke another record with over 500 entries

A scene from the 2008 foot race with runners passing the re-entrant of Gardyloo Gully, seconds from the summit (September 6th, 2008)

Photo: Alex Gillespie

before the race started, at 2.00pm on Saturday, September 7. The winner was H.Symonds of the Kendal A.C., in a time of 1.28.00. The fastest woman was Angela Carson of the Eryri Harriers, with a time of 1.52.45. The poor weather and soggy ground, following an abysmal summer of near-continuous rain, ensured that the records of 1984 would be very hard to beat. Out of the field of 438 who completed the race was No.321, the legendary Eddie Campbell of the Lochaber A.C., who has won the race three times. The 1980 cancellation prevented Campbell from completing his 30th run in a row.

The increase in participants made the intervention of rescue helicopters almost inevitable. Two runners were lifted off by the RAF in 1983, one with injuries, one with exhaustion. It was 1988, with very bad conditions of high wind and low temperatures which really proved their value. There were 488 starters; winds were reaching 112 km per hour in freezing conditions. One runner, Hugh Symonds (winner in 1985) suffered from temporary blindness. Some were wearing shorts and singlets, despite warnings, and in the end some 16 runners were taken to hospital for observation. Had the rescue helicopters not been able to fly that day, the outcome may well have been more serious.

Following this race, safety concerns led to a tightening of race conditions, with, for example, runners being required to carry a basic survival pack. This has to contain a basic shell, e.g. light nylon trousers and top, as well as a hat and gloves. As one is running uphill, it is common to feel warm enough to continue, but extremities such as arms and head are losing much heat and the senses begin to fade in severe conditions. In 1988 for example, when each runner gained the summit they had to hand over a piece of string which had their number, as a safety factor. At least one runner was not only unable to untie the string, he was also unable to speak due to the cold, and could not explain his problem to the safety officer! In 2005 electronic keys were trialled, runners being logged in at the summit. The race also received a maximum of 500 entrants, as the

The Ford Model T at the summit in 1911. An American flag flies from the car, backed by a weather-beaten Scottish standard

Photo: from an old postcard
Courtesy: Nevisprint

numbers were beginning to impose too severe a load on safety resources.

The Centenary year of 1994 was marked by many special occasions, including an early morning run with over 70 participants. Eddie Campbell completed his 42nd official race since 1951, and Hugh Dan MacLennan wrote *The Ben Race*, a history of the event with many interesting anecdotes and illustrations. It is always fascinating to look through the recorded times and see names and times. The record of Kenneth Stuart, set back in 1984, stands, though several have come within a few minutes of bettering it. Ian Holmes of Bingley, four times winner, had a personal best in 1995 of 1.28.08. John Brooks of Lochaber recorded 1.27.24 in 1998.

One sad event in 1996 was the death of the local legendary Eddie Campbell due to cancer at the age of 64. He had completed 44 races, his last in 1995, and won three. As a special tribute both to Eddie and Ben Nevis, local man Jimmy Jardine published a book in 2005, with the title *Up The Ben wi' Eddie*. All proceeds from the book go to Cancer Research UK. The book is a wonderful collection of personal anecdotes, stories, photographs (many never seen before) both old and new, and is available from the Cancer Research shop in the High St., Fort William.

In 2007, Holmes was the 1st with a time of 1.32.57, while 1st for the Ladies was Angela Mudge (Carnethy Hill Runners) at 1.48.28. The race looks set to be as permanent a feature as the mountain it takes place on. But whether it is a runner's wish to run anonymously or carrying a club's name, the Ben Nevis Race remains an annual challenge to those who enter, one of the most demanding mountain runs in this country, one always fraught with the uncertainties of the Scottish weather on the highest mountain.

CAR ASCENTS

Another ascent of Ben Nevis was one first made in May 1911 and repeated by the same man in 1928. Henry Alexander Jnr did not make his two ascents under muscle power however, but while driving a standard production car from his family's Ford agency in Edinburgh. In 1911 Alexander was driving a 20-horsepower Ford Model T; the car with which Henry Ford revolutionised both the motor industry and factory production. The Model T was light, simple and rugged, and could be bought *'in any colour you wish – as long as it's black.'*

The 1911 ascent of Ben Nevis was a publicity stunt set up by Ford. It was a period in which the car was still proving itself superior to the horse and long-distance car runs were in vogue: the Peking-Paris Run; Paris-New York-Paris Run; trans-Australia, north to south; and other punishing runs in the Alps of Europe. Ford heard that a track existed leading to the summit of Ben Nevis and a feasibility study began.

The first section of the Observatory bridle path, leading to the old Halfway House near Lochan Meall an t- Suidhe, was quickly recognised as being impossible. Many parts on this section were too narrow for the Ford's wheelbase. The next start looked at involved leaving the road at the Ben Nevis Distillery but again it was found to be too difficult. Finally it was decided to drive the car over boggy terrain near Inverlochy, to join the present day track near where the Halfway House then stood.

As the Model T was a fairly light car parts of the boggy route would support it for long enough to allow its progress. Even so, ten days were taken in order to reconnoitre the route to the lochan, wooden planks being placed at strategic points as temporary bridges. It took three days careful driving to reach the Halfway House, the car having to be rescued three times by rope from boggy ground.

Once at the Halfway House further progress was by no means easy. There were 4.8km of rocky trail left to negotiate, the top section of which was snow-covered. Only in the latter section could the driver relax slightly, as the trail became slightly wider than the car's breadth only near the summit. On the summit plateau a path had to be cut through snow in parts, before its triumphant arrival at the now deserted Observatory and closed summit hotel, the season still some time away.

The descent was very different, taking only two and a half hours. Its arrival in Fort William, preceded by pipers, was the signal for much excitement, with a local holiday being declared and a banquet at the Caledonian Hotel. As for the real hero of the ascent, no repairs or replacements were found to be necessary, and after a slight adjustment to the brakes the Model T was driven back to Edinburgh by Alexander.

Seventeen years later, on September 13, 1928, Alexander repeated the feat, this time driving a Standard New Ford touring car – the Model A. The ascent on this second occasion took only one day, putting to good use the experience gained on the first occasion. Starting at 10.30am the Halfway Hut was reached at 1pm, where an oil change was made. By the time the summit was gained, with four passengers on board for the last 400m, darkness had fallen, and the car was left there overnight before being taken down the following day.

Three weeks later on Saturday October 6, George Simpson from Edinburgh made an ascent driving what was then Britain's smallest car, the Austin 'Baby' 7. The car on this third occasion was a standard Austin Seven tourer, with 19,312km to its credit. One passenger was carried, in addition to spares and equipment. The first-speed gear ratio was slightly lower than standard but otherwise both gearbox and back axle were standard. The car used chains on its rear wheels and assistance was given only at places where it was necessary to prevent excess wheel spin.

The Austin took seven hours and 23 minutes to reach the summit and the speedometer showed that while the distance travelled on the map was 8km, the car's wheels had revolved the equivalent of 12.9km, the difference being due to wheel spin. Despite this there was no noticeable wear on the treads. About one and a quarter hours was lost in repairing the chains at intervals, but this time was included in the total ascent time given above, as was a half hour rest at the Halfway Hut. No water was required to be added to the radiator.

After a rest at the top the descent commenced, the latter half being made in darkness. Despite this the car made it safely down in two hours and two minutes, thus having the distinction of being the first car to make the return journey in one day. The Austin's climb was monitored by George Douglas, Trials Secretary and Official Timekeeper of the Scottish Western Motor Club, who also wrote the official report of the ascent. Commenting on the condition of the Austin following the ascent, the report noted that –

> The rear mudguards were both bent owing to the chains coming adrift so often, and one spoke was broken. This was the only damage done to the whole car, and that only because when the chains went to pieces they had to be lashed to the spokes. The car was driven from Edinburgh to Fort William and also back again after the Climb without any adjustments being necessary.
>
> This speaks well for the reliability of this make of car. Only those who have seen the track to the summit can realise the gruelling that any machine with more than a single track is subjected to in making the ascent and descent, and no praise is too great for the way this small car behaved.

THE MISSING ORGAN OF BEN NEVIS

Other objects have of course been taken up Britain's highest mountain – motorbikes, bedsteads, a piano, wheelbarrows (the staff at the Observatory was once amused by a man pushing a wheelbarrow from Land's End to John O'Groats, ostensibly to *raise the wind*). The list is probably endless. The summit has been left in unusual ways as well – balloons and hang-gliders being only two methods. Some of these deeds have merit, some indeed have been done for the purpose of raising funds for charity, but all of them have taken place on the open mountainside.

In May 2006, a summit clean-up party organised by the John Muir Trust began dismantling one of the many superfluous cairns when they came across a strange metal frame. It turned out to be the remains of a piano, sans keyboard. During a period of media quiet, this soon hit the headlines. One man came forward to claim responsibility – strongman and woodcutter from Bonar Bridge, Kenny Campbell. In 1971, he confessed, he had struggled up to the summit with a 103kg organ. This was his third attempt for a cancer charity. On reaching the summit, he reported, he sat down and before a bemused group of Norwegian climbers played *Scotland the Brave*.

Campbell abandoned the organ, later returning to remove it but finding only two planks left. And so on to 2006. Under the piano, the JMT team found a biscuit wrapper dated *'best-before 1986'*. It was a piano, and not an organ, and up stepped the spokesman for a 15-man team of Dundonian removal men who, in 1986, hoping to raise money for charity, used their experience to carry the piano up the mountain. The weather was cold and they abandoned the attempt to descend with it, instead burying it under a pile of stones. Which begs the question – where is the missing organ?

For the next section we have to go underground, to learn of a remarkable tunnel through the mountain.

ALUMINIUM

A few great works are destined to remain largely hidden. One such work is the Lochaber Water Power Scheme, the first phase of which is described here. Leave Fort William going north and a factory complex will be visible on the right, lying on what was originally a boggy moor under the slopes of Meall an t-Suidhe. The factory belongs to the Canadian multinational Alcan Inc., manufacturing the metal aluminium, renowned for its light weight and great strength, when alloyed with other metals. To the climber or walker going up Ben Nevis the factory may seem just another factory, jarring perhaps against the backdrop of mountains, with its line of five massive pipes running up the north flank of Meall an t-Suidhe. What is most interesting about it however is because so much of the impressive engineering work carried out some 80 years ago is buried underground. The story of this massive Lochaber Hydro Scheme ties together the unlikely companions of rainfall and aluminium.

The British Aluminium Company was founded in 1894. Lord Kelvin joined the board four years later, taking a keen interest in the new company. It was at Foyers in Inverness-shire that aluminium was first produced in commercial quantities by the electrolytic method. This was in 1896, with an annual output of 203 tonnes. British Aluminium (B.A.) acquired the U.K. rights to two important processes. The first was the Bayer process, used for the production of alumina, or aluminium oxide, from the earthy mineral bauxite. The second was known as the Hall-Héroult process, from its two inventors, the American Hall and the Frenchman Héroult. This process reduces alumina to aluminium. With the later siting of smelters at Kinlochleven and Fort William, opened in 1909 and 1929 respectively, and a fourth smelter at Invergordon producing in 1971, Alcan is the country's largest producer of primary aluminium, and a major employer in Lochaber, producing about 40,000 tonnes of aluminium annually. British Aluminium merged with Alcan UK in 1982. Alcan is at present the world's third biggest aluminium company, with 65,000 employees in 61 countries.

Nothing is static in global big business however, and in 2007 Rio Tinto and Alcan reached a friendly takeover deal that would create the world's largest aluminum company, Rio Tinto Alcan (RTA). On October 25, 2007, the merger was completed. RTA is based in Montreal. Even this may change, as BHP Billiton, the world's largest mining company, is looking to buy Rio Tinto Alcan. In June 2009, RTA, financially weakened by the takeover, pulled out of a deal with cash-rich Aluminium Corp. of China (Chinalco), investors having demanded a rights issue.

A large supply of low-voltage electric current is necessary for the Hall-Héroult process. During the First World War increasing demand for the

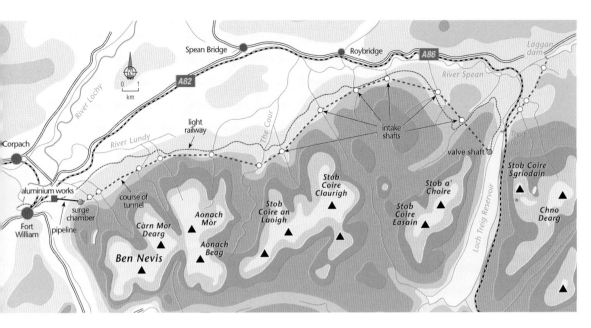

metal induced a search for more power. Water power being cheaper than steam power, the original intention was to utilise the catchment areas of Loch Laggan and Loch Treig, driving a 11.3km tunnel from Loch Treig to Kinlochleven. Here, a second powerhouse would be built. However, strong local opposition vetoed the plan.

As an alternative, a new Order was promoted, leading to an Act in 1921, allowing for the construction of a 24km tunnel from Loch Treig to the head of Loch Linnhe. Owing to poor economic conditions construction did not begin until 1924. One advantage of the second plan, offsetting the extra length of tunnel required, was the considerable amount of water available from the slopes of the Ben Nevis range of mountains. The scheme planned for a catchment area of 784km^2, extending from Loch Linnhe to the upper reaches of the River Spey. Rainfall variation is considerable in this area, with the lowest at Laggan Bridge showing an annual average of 104cm, to Ben Nevis itself, with 409cm.

Lochs Laggan and Treig form the principal reservoirs, connected by a tunnel 4.4km long and 4.57m in diameter. Loch Laggan was extended by dredging the outlet and building a dam across the Spean 7.24km below the loch, 213m long and 39.6m high. The height of the surface of Loch Laggan was to remain unchanged at 250m above sea level, while the height of Loch Treig was raised by a dam from 239m to 250m above sea level. The amount of available water from Loch Laggan, calculating on a 4.88m fall, was 41.9 million cubic metres, while Loch Treig, the larger of the two, had an available capacity of 222 million cubic metres, calculated on a drop of surface level of 37.8m maximum.

In addition to the natural catchment areas, the flood waters of the Spey in excess of 182 million litres per day are diverted across the watershed to the River Pattack by means of a dam, while a subsidiary conduit taps the River Mashie, a tributary of the Spey. From Loch Treig water runs down the very gentle gradient of 1:1100 through the 24km long horseshoe section pressure tunnel, having an equivalent mean diameter of 4.62m. Along the line of the tunnel eleven major streams are tapped by dams, their excess water entering the tunnel by vertical shafts. As the average area rainfall is high, the water collected by these intakes contributes 16% of the total power available.

Intake Number 11 is well-known to climbers going up Ben Nevis, as it taps the Allt a' Mhuilinn. From this intake, known simply to climbers as *The Dam*, the tunnel runs west to a surge chamber, situated near the top of the pipe-lines visible on the north flank of Meall an t-Suidhe. From the outlet of the tunnel through Ben Nevis, five pipes, each about 1.83m in diameter and 914m long lead to the power station. As the turbines have their nozzles at a height of 5.79m above sea level, when Loch Treig is full the maximum head of water available is c.244m.

The Lochaber Scheme was carried out in three phases. The first phase began in 1924, and comprised all the works to the west of Loch Treig. This was the largest stage and included the 24km tunnel. Completed in 1929, the first phase cost about £3 million. The Engineers were Messrs C.S.Meik and W.T., later Sir William, Halcrow of Westminster, London. Meik died in 1923, two years before main construction work had begun. Principal contractors were Messrs Balfour, Beatty & Company Ltd., while the main turbines and generators were by English Electric. The contract drawn up by British Aluminium was so tight that when costs began to mount Balfour Beatty began to suffer. It almost bankrupted them, and it was several years before they recovered financially from this project.

The second phase began in 1933, when Loch Laggan was extended by a dam to provide extra storage capacity. At the same time the capacity of Loch Treig was increased by the building of a 12.2m dam. Raising the level of the larger loch meant diverting 2.4km of the West Highland Railway Line. The third and final phase was the damming of the River Spey, the water then being fed back to Loch Laggan by a tunnel just over 3km long. This final stage was finished in 1943.

As preliminary work to the main engineering task of driving the 24km tunnel, a railway was built connecting Loch Treig to the power-house site. A temporary power plant was also necessary and was built on the River Spean to take advantage of the falls in the Monessie gorge. The power generated by this hydro-electric plant was 6 Kv, raised to 11 Kv for transmission by aluminium cables throughout the works. The total length of transmission line was eventually 40km, with 460 volts available for general use. Apart from lighting and various electrical motors, such as pumps, concrete-mixers and so on, most of the power was used for driving air-compressors for rock drilling.

The contract which was drawn up specified that a railway be built from the power-house site to Loch Treig. A clause stated that if the railway and temporary power plant be completed within nine months from the date of commencement then a large bonus would be paid, reducing week by week after the nine months was up until it became zero after 12 months. The contractors earned the bonus.

The main railway was of 91.44cm gauge and was built mainly of 13.6kg rails. Its maximum gradient was 1 in 30, the longest haul being at the west end where the line rose from 6 to 198m above sea level in about 4.8km. Numerous streams were crossed on viaducts, built mainly of timber and sometimes of steel girders. Two steam trains ran according to a time-table in each direction daily, carrying mail and stores for the camps. There were in total 41.8km of 91.44cm gauge, and 32.2km of 60.96cm.

A reinforced concrete pier was built at the head of Loch Linnhe, to be available for the handling of construction materials early in 1925. The pier was designed to carry 5.08 tonne electric portal cranes and was laid out so as to accommodate ocean-going vessels. The main road out of Fort William was diverted and regraded for a length of 102m to allow for a uniform gradient on the railway connecting the factory to the pier.

At each adit and shaft along the tunnel construction camps were set up for workmen. Sleeping huts had separate bedsteads, mess and recreation rooms, drying sheds for wet clothing, stores and canteens. A camp hospital was built near adit No.5, with a doctor in constant attendance on the scheme. At the height of construction, 3,000 men were in employment, and £75,000 was spent on camps.

The main tunnel had four working shafts and seven adits. The route of the tunnel did not take a straight line, but was chosen to afford convenient access by the vertical shafts and horizontal adits. In addition to the construction shafts, intake shafts were sunk at eight points, the depth of these ranging from 49.7m to 82.6m. The cross-sectional area of the main tunnel increases from 15.7m^2 at the beginning, to 16.8m^2 in the middle, and reaches a maximum of 17.9m^2 in the last third before the surge chamber. These increases in cross-sectional area allow for the additional water taken in from the 11 side streams. There is a 22m drop in the 24km tunnel, a gradient of 1 in 1100. The tunnel is designed to carry 45m^3 of water per second, giving a velocity in the largest section, from adit No.7 to the surge chamber, of 2.52m per second.

The velocity is lower in the initial section, from the intake at Loch Treig to adit No.3, being 2.47m per second, and intermediate in the middle section. Theoretically, an object being carried through the tunnel at a maximum velocity in all sections would travel the 24km from Loch Treig to the surge chamber at the top of the pipe-lines in a time of about two hours and 40 minutes, a speed of about 9km per hour. There are frictional losses of course, which were minimised by lining the tunnel with concrete.

The main tunnel, one of the largest of its kind in the world on its completion, passes through a wide variety of rock types. For the most part metamorphic schists had to be driven through, with Lairig schist at Loch Treig leading to Eilde flags and Leven schists and finally Ballachulish limestone near adit No.9. The schists were to cause the tunnellers great trouble. The flags were exceedingly hard, virtually quartzitic. The limestone traversed by the tunnel was impure, and where it came near the Ben Nevis granite it had been altered by heat to a hard calc-silicate hornfels. Two granite masses were tunnelled through, one near No.7 shaft and the other between a point east of No.10 adit and the portal. The rocks around Ben Nevis and its companion hills have also been intruded by numerous parallel igneous dykes, running NNE and SSW. Some of these dykes are up to 30m thick, though most are only a metre or so thick.

The tunnel was bored out from 22 faces. The usual method of drilling involved a short top heading and a bench, the heading being 3 to 4.5m

Drilling at the tunnel face in 1925. The process has, by modern standards of safety, a shaky look, with wooden planks resting on oil barrels resting on wooden planks supported by what appears to be wooden props

ahead of the bench. There were usually 22 to 30 holes drilled in the heading, 2.4 to 3m deep, with five to nine holes in the bench. In a blasting round of 26 holes in the heading there would be six cut holes, eight easers, and 12 trimming holes. The average advance gained by a blast was about 2.4m, ranging from 1.2m in the very hard hornfels, to about 3m in softer rock. The amount of gelignite used per round averaged about 82kg for a *pull* of 2.44m (about 49m^3 of rock).

Four percussive pneumatic drills were normally used in attacking the heading, bolted to vertical steel columns. At the same time one or two drills were used on a horizontal bar for drilling the bench. The drills ran off compressed air at a pressure of 550 kilopascals, or 5.63kg/cm^2. After trying various work patterns, the tunnel driving settled into a routine whereby the day was divided into two shifts of 10 and a half hours working time each. Work was arranged so as to complete a cycle of operations in 24 hours; drilling, firing, removal of spoil. The latter was, as in most tunnel work, the factor governing the rate of progress. Different mechanical methods of spoil removal were tried, but eventually most of the spoil was removed by manual labour.

The progress of the tunnel varied considerably, with a maximum advance of 27.7m in one week, or 107m in four weeks. With all 22 faces fully operational, 275 to 292m per week was achieved. It had been the original plan to begin lining the tunnel in the various sections after the excavation had been completed, but in several of the longer drives concreting began before the section was finished. Steel forms were used for the concreting, made in panels to fit the radii of the tunnel-section. The usual lengths of forms were 9.75m and 19.5m. As mentioned before, the function of the concrete lining was to reduce friction in the tunnel; the solid rock walls being sufficient support for the tunnel as a whole. Lining was done at a rate of about 30m per week when all went smoothly.

The eight intake shafts were of two sizes. The larger had a water-inlet pipe 1.5m in diameter, while the smaller had a diameter of 1.07m. In December 1929 the first tapping of aluminium was made, the water for power being obtained from the side streams until the intake was opened at Loch Treig. The surge chamber, a kind of open safety valve designed to reduce the effect of variations in water pressure, was built in solid granite to a diameter of 9.75m, 9.14m when lined in concrete. Its height is 73m. From the surge chamber two 3.66m branch tunnels connect to the pipeline, enlarging to a chamber 9.75m wide and 2.44m high, which forms the entry to the bellmouths of the pipes.

As a precursor to all this tunnelling, drilling, blasting and burrowing, a complicated triangulated survey was carried out over an area of 194km^2, using as a base-line a straight section of the railway of about 1.52km in length. As a verification of the accuracy of the survey another base-line, about 914m long and 17.7km from the first was measured. The difference between its measured and calculated lengths was 25.4mm.

One of the most fascinating features of the Lochaber scheme, and one which had not before then been carried out in Britain, was the making of an underwater intake at Loch Treig. The underwater slope of the loch at that point was found to be virtually free of debris and quite smooth, probably glacially polished, with a slope of about 1/3 to 1. Tunnelling was started from the valve shafts and moved towards the loch until within 26m of the water, at which point pilot holes 10.7m long were drilled to test for fissures. At a point 9.14m from the loch a vertical fissure was met which connected directly to Loch Treig. The crack was grouted and tunnelling continued until the wall of rock separating the tunnel from the loch was only 4.8m thick in the centre and 6m thick at the sides. The end face of the tunnel stayed remarkably dry despite being drilled with 134 holes, from 3 to 10m deep. Some sprang a leak and gave a considerable flow of water until they were plugged.

The method of constructing the underwater intake at Loch Treig, 1930

Illustration: Tom Prentice

Behind the end face a sump was excavated to contain any rock shot inwards by the blast. The holes were drilled to within 60cm of the loch. The next step was to construct a bulkhead of solid concrete 30m downstream of the valve shafts. The minimum thickness of the bulkhead was

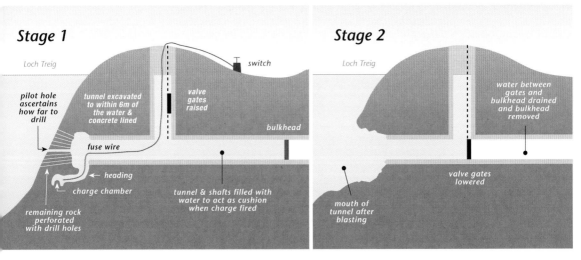

Stage 1

Loch Treig

pilot hole ascertains how far to drill

tunnel excavated to within 6m of the water & concrete lined

valve gates raised

switch

bulkhead

fuse wire

← heading

charge chamber

remaining rock perforated with drill holes

tunnel & shafts filled with water to act as cushion when charge fired

Stage 2

Loch Treig

water between gates and bulkhead drained and bulkhead removed

valve gates lowered

mouth of tunnel after blasting

The pipelines leading off the hill and down to the power-house outside Fort William. Lochs Linnhe and Eil in the background

Photo: Alex Gillespie

1.2m. When everything was ready, the drill holes were filled with 1,558kg of blasting gelatine and four separate initiators were cross-connected so that even if only one detonator functioned the whole charge would still be set off. The concrete bulkhead, which had a 122cm by 61cm safety aperture through it, had this covered with a 2.54cm thick steel plate. The tunnel was then filled with water between the bulkhead and the end face until the level in the vertical valve shafts was higher than loch level. The level of the end face was 32m below the surface of the loch.

On January 3, 1930, the charge was fired. Gases bubbled to the surface of the loch over an area of about 22m² and waves of up to 1.22m high were induced. The explosion was later shown to have removed about 2,294m³ of rock. The shot-back rock filled the sump as planned and was heaped up for more than half the tunnel's height. The steel plate over the safety opening in the bulkhead was split cleanly along both diagonals, the pieces being found later down the tunnel.

While the tunnel was being driven the pipelines and power house were also being constructed. Two pipes were built for the first phase of the scheme, the entire project requiring a final six (there are now five pipes). The total length of the pipeline is 988m. The diameter of the pipes is 1.76m for the top 374m, 1.67m for the middle 353m, and 1.6m for the final 208m. The thickness of the metal varies from 12.7mm to 28.6mm. Made of welded mild steel, the pipes were manufactured in 9.14m lengths by the South Durham Steel & Iron Company Ltd., each length being of two or three plates lap-welded. The weight of each pipe ranged from 5.58 to 11.43 tonnes. Circumferential joints were electrically welded inside and outside in situ.

Valves at the top of the pipeline control the flow of water. Perhaps surprisingly to the non-engineer, the greatest danger to the pipe system lies not in flooding, but in a pipe collapse due to a vacuum. Anti-vacuum

The powerhouse. There are 12 sets of main turbines, each driving two DC generators

Photo: Alex Gillespie

valves were built to circumvent this possibility. Should a full-area pipe-burst occur at the bottom end of the pipeline, the upper end would collapse with an excess external pressure of about 1.24 kilopascals ($1.27kg/m^2$) The anti-vacuum valves were designed to pass the maximum amount of air, about $45m^3$ per second, with an internal drop in pressure of about 24 kilopascals ($0.25kg/m^2$) below atmospheric pressure, therefore providing a safety factor of five.

The power house was excavated out of rock, and is 82.3m long by 19.2m wide. For the first stage of the scheme five turbines were installed, Pelton wheels with their nozzles 5.79m above sea level, and 243.8m below the full height of Loch Treig's surface level. Each of the five units consisted of a single runner wheel with two jets developing up to 7.46 Mw (Megawatts) and driving two DC generators. The current was then passed along aluminium conductors to electric furnaces in the adjoining factory. Below the power station a tailrace runs into the River Lochy.

The power station of the Lochaber Smelter is the largest hydro-electric power station in the UK. It now has a total installed capacity of 94 Mw. There are twelve main sets, each with a Pelton-wheel turbine turning two 3.5 Mw DC generators. In addition there are three auxiliary 1.25 Mw AC generators. The maximum electricity output achievable is about 65 Mw. This is used to run 80 electrolytic cells which run continuously, with each cell drawing 175,000 amps between 16 carbon anodes and a fixed cathode to produce 1,350 kg of metal daily. Despite the enormous current, maintenance of the cells is possible without switching off the power, as the voltage is too low for electrocution to be possible.

The actual production of aluminium is done by a reduction process at a temperature of about 1,000 degrees Centigrade. When climbers speak of a *white hell* after a trying day in winter they little realise how close they are. Aluminium oxide (alumina) is dissolved in molten cryolite (sodium aluminium fluoride) in an electrolytic cell. Direct current of high amperage is passed through the cell from the carbon anode, through the molten cryolite, to the carbon cathode. The alumina in solution decomposes, with the aluminium passing to and collecting on the cathode to form a molten pool lying under the cryolite. Oxygen released from the alumina passes to the anode, forming carbon dioxide. The anode is progressively consumed and the carbon is regularly replaced by feeding carbon paste to the top of the self-baking anodes.

The molten aluminium collects in a pool on the cathode. In simple terms this consists of a carbon-lined, thermally insulated steel box with steel bars joined to the carbon to carry the current. Metal is periodically removed by suction tapping for transfer in liquid form by a crucible. In the casting complex aluminium can be formed into ingots, rolling blocks, wire bars or extrusion billets. 2.03 tonnes of alumina are used to produce one ton of aluminium by the above process, known as the Hall-Héroult process. In doing so, 0.508 tonnes of anode carbon is consumed and 16,000 to 18,000 units of electricity used.

The bauxite used by the industry originates mainly from Australia, Guinea and Brazil, with Guinea having about 25% of the world's known resources. Alumina is produced at Britain's only alumina plant in Burntisland, Fife. Burntisland's production goes to the bauxite chemicals industries. The alumina for Invergordon comes mainly from the Caribbean area, rail and road tankers supplying the smelters at Fort William and Kinlochleven with alumina delivered at Invergordon. In addition to employing about 500 at Fort William, B.A. Highland Smelters Ltd., operates one large sheep farm and has several other properties under tenant farmers. Re-afforestation was begun in the late 1940s. Inverlochy Village was built as a direct consequence of the need for extra housing for the workers at the smelter, with almost 300 new houses.

In the 1980s, the implosion of the Soviet Union started a flood of cheaper aluminium imports. This severely inhibited aluminium production in the UK for some time, though the local product was of better quality. China is the main factor explaining the rapid increase in the price of aluminium – which has doubled in five years. They are now the world's largest producer and consumer, with a quarter of the world's production and consumption – growing at over 20% pa. Aluminium production ceased at Kinlochleven in 2000, though hydro generation continues. With increased environmental concerns, the Fort William smelter is working very hard to minimise harmful emissions and also maximise energy efficiency. Alcan has the view that offsetting the huge amount of electricity consumed in manufacture, with an unfriendly environmental image, the use of aluminium in cars has lowered their environmental footprint. The industry has reduced emissions by 70% in the last 20 years, through new technology.

The average climber is aware that much of his climbing hardware uses aluminium; its properties have made possible huge improvements in safety and weight-saving. It is perhaps ironic that the high rainfall in this area, so often complained about, has made it ideal for the Lochaber hydro-electric power scheme. The magnificent feat of the tunnel blasted through 24km of solid rock has permitted the Fort William smelter to produce much of that very same aluminium.

The summit of Ben Nevis in 2007 showing the trig point on a cairn at the left, and the Observatory ruins with the emergency shelter on the right. Compare this with the same view in 1885 on page 63

Photo: Noel Williams

CONSERVATION AND LAND MANAGEMENT

For centuries, Ben Nevis was effectively left in peace; the Gaels used some grassy slopes here and there for summer grazing – though the poor, stony slopes of the Ben were probably mostly ignored. The first real pressure was felt with the building of the summit Observatory and its concomitant Bridle Path.

A good track leading to the summit and something of real interest to visit there coincided with the rise in mountaineering. That sport, however, made very little impact on the mountain for some time. The real growth was in the numbers of people walking to the summit, often evidenced in the Observatory Logbook. Very quickly, a visitors' room had to be added to the Observatory building, where tired, wet, and no doubt often mildly distressed tourists could rest and gain enough strength for their descent to sea-level comfort.

To help pay for the maintenance of the Bridle Path, a charge was imposed on those walking up it. There were some, of course, who managed to evade this payment. One example of the then attitude to keeping the mountain clean was that of the Observatory staff, who used the climbing side of the hill as a giant landfill for their accumulated rubbish. They went so far as to build a wooden platform on the cliff edge, the easier to tip their leavings down. As late as the 1970s it would be fairly easy to come across metal junk dating from these days; battered pots and pans, bits of a chimney pipe, lying scattered over the scree in Observatory Gully.

The platform was built so that rubbish would fall into the foot of what is now known as Gardyloo Gully, 'gardyloo' being the warning call when an Edinburgh householder or serving girl was about to throw night soil out of a window and into the street below. (Gardyloo is a corruption of the French *gardez l'eau*, or watch out for the water!)

Any potential clash between climbers and Observatory rubbish tippers was avoided when the summit station closed in 1904; presumably the summit hotel, which remained open until 1916, used the same method of refuse disposal, though by then climbing had all but ceased due to the war. Gardyloo Gully was first climbed in summer on August 5, 1935, by Graham Macphee and R.C.Frost. They were amazed at the amount of Observatory rubbish found in the gully, which for many years had in fact been called Tin-Can Gully.

As tourism grew, particularly from the mid-20th Century onwards, most conservation work on Ben Nevis entailed keeping the Bridle Path open. Even without the passage of feet, natural forces of nature – frost shattering, heavy rain and so on, would have slowly obliterated the steeper sections of the path, especially so in its lower section where it rises across the flank of Meall an t-Suidhe. As the numbers using this path grew, so too did the erosion. The original wooden bridges, built at several points in order to cross burns, were on occasion washed away by floods.

Other pressures had occurred in the meantime, with grand engineering schemes being proposed – a railway to the top, permanent buildings on the summit and so on. Fortunately, none of these came to fruition. The SMC hut in the Allt a' Mhuilinn valley opened in 1929, making winter climbing especially easier and safer. It gradually became a source of frustration with some climbers, who found booking a bunk space well in advance either awkward or too much of a weather lottery. It was understandably easy to become annoyed when, on gaining the hut from the valley, it might be found to be empty and locked or under-used. Built at a natural turning point on the approach to the cliffs, it would at times become an unwarranted focus for refuse and abuse.

If the Bridle Path underwent minimal maintenance, the approach to the cliffs via the Allt a' Mhuilinn was basically ignored. The climbing side of Ben Nevis was owned by the aluminium factory, whose interest in the mountain lay solely in its powers of water catchment for their factory outside Fort William. They maintained a benign low profile, which suited the climbers, though as the numbers of mountaineers coming to the area to climb on Nevis grew, a few began to mutter about a perceived lack of interest by the local infrastructure; retailers, councillors and so on. After all, went their argument, we come here to climb and walk, we spend money in their shops, hotels and bars and we might expect a little recognition.

For years there was talk of building some sort of a hotel or respite near Half-Way Lochan, where shelter and refreshment might be found. Indeed, as the chapter on the CIC Hut outlines, the use of the disintegrating Half-Way Observatory hut by young climbers had been the catalyst for the building of the SMC hut. Even the building of some other hut near to the CIC Hut might not have been unwelcome, as at the very least it would have given the vandals some other target.

It can be somewhat depressing to learn how some other countries can maintain a system of completely open huts, stocked with food and relying on trust and honesty of users to pay for their use. Norway is a prime example. To supply a minor example for contrast, Ken Crocket was on a weekend work party at the CIC Hut when he and others went inside for a lunch break. When he came out shortly after, the hammer

Bucket drill at the Observatory. The two observers on the right are belaying the bucket tipper! A wooden platform helped deal with shifting snow and ice levels

Photo: RMS

Coire Leis headwall above Little Brenva Face. Anyone descending from the summit towards the arete but erring too far left (i.e. north) would find themselves on the convex slope heading for the steep face (in shadow)

Photo: Noel Williams

he had left on the roof had been stolen. When the new extension to the hut was built in 1976, principally for the storage of personal gear, casual visitors were often dismayed to find the outer door locked even when climbers were resident – to leave it unlocked meant losing gear to the light-fingered. This was, as you might say however, a local problem, though one which has led to some misplaced resentment against the SMC, who cannot provide casual shelter.

The inevitable question of mountain safety finally came to a head with the dreadful incident in 1954, leading to the deaths of five naval cadets. There had been deaths on the mountain before this of course, but the scale, and the fact that it involved youthful climbers was especially distressing. One who was particularly involved in safety on Nevis was Dr Donald Duff, a keen climber who was a surgeon working at the Belford Hospital in Fort William.

The topography of Ben Nevis, with its relatively narrow and elongated summit plateau, is one which in poor visibility can quite easily turn poor navigation into a serious problem. To descend from the summit trig point towards the upper zig-zags of the Bridle Path requires taking a route which is not a straight line. The first of two *legs* is the shorter one, 150m on a bearing of 231 degrees Grid. This *leg* is so as to stay away from the edge of the NE Face. The second *leg*, 800m on a bearing of 282 degrees Grid, should then lead to the upper zig-zags, avoiding the dangerous and steep slopes of Five Finger Gully.

Two other descent routes are commonly used by climbers on Nevis; Number Four Gully, leading into Coire na Ciste and so to either the CIC Hut or the Allt a' Mhuilinn path, and in the opposite direction, a descent leading to the Càrn Mòr Dearg arete and so to a descent into Coire Leis. It was while on the latter route that the cadets made the navigational error of descending the upper slopes of the Little Brenva Face, falling to their deaths on icy ground.

Following this accident, Dr Duff advocated the erection of marker posts leading down safe slopes away from the cliff edge and towards the start of the Càrn Mòr Dearg arete. From the arete, he also proposed a line of posts allowing safe abseils to be made down onto easier ground in Coire Leis. Both of these suggestions were implemented. Added to the mountain later were a small marker on a cairn at the top of Number Four Gully, and two emergency shelters, one on Càrn Dearg, and one in Coire Leis. The two shelters were placed in slightly out of the way positions, with the Càrn Dearg site being difficult to find in poor conditions, and the Coire Leis shelter being very prone to being snowed over in winter. Both were removed in 2004. The line of abseil posts did not follow the line of easiest descent into Coire Leis, probably, to be fair, due to needing to be sited on better, rocky ground. It was reasonably easy enough to descend to one side of these posts without recourse to abseiling. On the whole, climbers found the Number Four Gully marker a friendly indication, but used neither the emergency shelters nor the abseil posts.

While all this well-meaning construction work was on the go, another, less spectacular form of construction was taking place on the summit plateau and its approaches. The building of cairns, mainly by walkers, was leading to what might be described as a clutter. It was even in places becoming a dangerous clutter, as many were not marking a main path. As fast as some were kicking them over, others were building them up. In part, the cairns were also an indication of a difference in aesthetics, with most regular users of the Scottish mountains in particular being used to following ridges and slopes found in a relatively wild condition, i.e. usually with no signage or any other handiwork. These regular users, presumably, always carried a map and compass, and knew how to use them. The casual visitor, many making Ben Nevis their one and only summit, probably had no such navigational aids, and may also have brought with them an urge to mark their visit by adding a stone or two to an existing cairn. It begs the question as to why making an ascent is not enough of a personal achievement – some also have to pile up stones on top of other stones.

Removal of the Coire Leis emergency shelter in 2004

Photo: Nevis Partnership

The view down over the Ben Nevis summit plateau from McLean's Steep (August 2008). In November 2008 the John Muir Trust finished a five-year programme to clear the plateau of unsightly and excess cairns. In all, more than 120 were removed by volunteer work parties, leaving about 20 along the main path close to the summit

Photo: Sandy Maxwell

*Monitoring scree
movement on the
summit plateau*

Photo: Brian Wilshaw /
Nevis Partnership

There was worse to come. Also on the summit, and especially towards the end of the 20th Century, becoming more and more prevalent was the growing collection of memorial plaques and cairns. The summit was fast becoming to many a visually painful site in summer, to the extent that many climbers were happier to be there in winter, when the ground, and its growing collection of cairns, litter, memorial plaques etc was covered by snow.

To provide an unofficial and informal indication of just how popular the walk up Nevis was becoming, one summer weekend in the 1980s Ken Crocket and Alastair Walker were carrying up some supplies to the CIC Hut, using the Bridle Path to gain the approach via the Half-Way Lochan. At about lunch-time, and at a spot just below the Red Burn crossing, they stopped for a break and made a count of those going up the path. The estimate was 1,000 per hour. This, they admit, was on a good day at the busiest of times, but it was still a frightening picture. Many of those going up were obviously poorly equipped, especially as regards footwear. One could only guess at what clothing was being carried in the small day sacs many had on their backs.

One could almost see where this was heading; on one side we had the majority of self-contained mountaineers who, with much improved equipment and knowledge, were beginning to agonise over the increasing pressure the mountain was coming under. They were joined by the conservationists. On the other side we had the huge numbers of visitors to the area, many with no experience of any mountain, let alone Ben Nevis. All they wanted was a safe and relatively painless walk up to a glorious summit view. Mountain safety, ascetics, conservation, tourist money, all had jumbled together to provide a major headache.

The picture brightened up in June 2000, with the acquisition by the wild land charity, The John Muir Trust, of the Ben Nevis estate from Duncan Fairfax-Lucy. The estate includes the summit plateau, the upper section of the Bridle Path, with the boundary on the track at a height of about 800m, and some of the southern slopes. The area also extends eastwards taking in several of the mountains sloping down to the Water of Nevis with the Nevis Gorge.

The immediate aim of the JMT was to safeguard and enhance the wild character of this area, and restore some of the damaged habitat. Sheep were taken off upper Glen Nevis in 2002, wildlife surveys were undertaken, organised litter collections done, and the removal of redundant cairns and other artefacts discussed with interested parties. All of this immense and sensitive work was made more possible with the constitution, in 2003, of the Nevis Partnership, which has the express intent to:

> ...guide future policies and actions to safeguard, manage and where appropriate enhance the environmental qualities and opportunities for visitor enjoyment and appreciation of the Nevis area.

The Glen Nevis Site of Contemplation, opened in 2006

Photo: Nevis Partnership

The Nevis Partnership is a Scottish registered charity. It has a main board with ten representatives holding voting rights. The directorships represented at the main board include:

- The Highland Council
- Fort William Community Council
- Inverlochy and Torlundy Community Council
- Glen Nevis Residents
- The John Muir Trust
- The Mountaineering Council of Scotland
- Lochaber Mountain Access Group
- Scottish Natural Heritage

The potentially contentious issue of removal of artefacts from Ben Nevis was carefully approached by the Partnership over a five-year period. Not only cairns, but memorial plaques were to be removed, leaving for the time being at least only the original *Peace Cairn* near the summit, and a few cairns considered to be vital navigational aids. Many of the plaques had no known association with the mountain, some were downright tacky. A major campaign was nonetheless made in an effort to contact the owners, so as to avoid causing any distress. Eventually, all plaques will be removed and returned to any recognised owner. Any unclaimed plaques will be kept for five years then disposed of. Any new plaques found will similarly be removed and stored for five years.

As compensation for plaque removal, A *Site of Contemplation* was officially unveiled on Sunday, August 27, 2006, in Glen Nevis, near to the Visitor Centre and by the River Nevis. This provides a site for those who wish to contemplate on the loss of a relative or friend. The Nevis Partnership has also created a *Virtual Book of Remembrance* on the internet as part of its official website. Photographs of some of the claimed plaques can be seen there. Additionally, new memorials can be added there, in an unobtrusive and permanent manner. The mountain summit will thus be returned to an earlier, and, most would agree, better state.

The JMT decided that the best way to tackle the Observatory ruins was to *freeze them in time*, neither building, nor removing, their essence. The ruins will be maintained in a safe condition, so that visitors will see what was once the site without intrusive or dangerous structures.

Working on the path next to the Allt a' Mhuilinn. Large boulders have been winched out of the bed of the burn to be used for path repair

Photo: Alex Gillespie

Information on the mountain will be readily available, either in Glen Nevis, or on the internet.

This excerpt from the Nevis strategy outlines the partnership's position:

> Section C1,b: As the UK's highest mountain and a tourist icon, Ben Nevis should be cared for in an exemplary manner. There are major issues of degradation of the summit and high plateau, including litter, fouling, cairns and memorials. Also, the observatory ruins are un-cared for and attract wastes and litter. Fouling and gas cylinders around the CIC hut cause concern. Ben Nevis presents exceptional circumstances, with many tourists, the highly publicized path, extreme weather conditions, etc, contributing to accidents. The Ben requires some safety provision (eg emergency shelter, way marking cairns), but that these should be kept to a minimum.

> Proposal: Consolidation of the observatory ruins and removal of non-essential cairns, memorials and other artifacts.

The full strategy can be downloaded at www.nevispartnership.co.uk

An estimated 100,000 ascents of Ben Nevis are made annually, mostly by the Bridle Path. The JMT now call this the *Mountain Track*, and it will be maintained in a safe condition. Improvements to the Allt a' Mhuilinn path have also taken place, with a North Face car park near Torlundy and a vastly improved track up the Allt a' Mhuilinn itself. The ghastly quagmires of old have all but gone. The Nevis Partnership oversaw a path enhancement project starting at the upper car park and extending to approximately 300m below the CIC hut. Monies for this were donated by a host of organisations, including *The North Face* equipment & clothing company, the *Scottish Mountaineering Trust* (through guidebook sales and donations), and many others.

The enhancements were basically completed in 2006, with a late addition in 2008 bypassing the boggy section above the narrow-gauge railway. To any climber who recalls walking up in past decades, the path is now immeasurably improved, while still not spoiling the experience. It should also be noted that the SMC are involved in improving various aspects of the CIC Hut, including reducing the visual impact of the gas cylinder storage by reducing their numbers and storing them in a better position.

On February 19, 2008, *The Friends of Nevis* was setup by the Nevis Partnership (www.friendsofnevis.co.uk). The intention is to encourage individuals, families and organisations to help support and manage Ben Nevis and the surrounding Nevis area. A network of volunteers should be set up, with projects allowing their input in a wide variety of ways. One project organised by the JMT for example is the butterfly count in Coire Eoghainn. Volunteers camp high for this and look for the Mountain Ringlet (*Erebia epiphron*), Britain's only true alpine butterfly.

There is never room for any complacency however, and in addition to requiring constant funding for maintenance and improvements in the future, the JMT and others have warned, for example, about the damage and disruption caused by the Three Peaks Challenge and similar events. They urge people to consider other ways of raising funds for a charity, and to think twice about taking part. It is only with such care and thought that the wild experience that Ben Nevis and its surroundings can provide, along with the enjoyment of its natural beauty of flora and fauna, can be kept for now and ever.

References

1. **House**, Jack, *The Romance of Long John*. (Long John International Limited. 1982.)

2. **Smith**, Alexander, *A Summer in Skye*. (Edinburgh: W.P. Nimmo & Co., 2nd Edition, 1885).

3. **Halcrow**, William Thomson, *The Lochaber Water-Power Scheme*. Minutes of Proceedings of the Institution of Civil Engineers, 231, Part I, 31 – 106, 1930 – 31.

4. *The Lochaber Water Power Scheme*. Supplement to The Scots Magazine, September 1929.

5. **Paton**, T.A.L. and **Brown**, Guthrie J., *Power from Water*. (London: Leonard Hill, 1960).

6. **Howat**, Patrick, *The Lochaber Narrow Gauge Railway*. (Huddersfield: Narrow Gauge Railway Society, 1980.)

7. *Aluminium in The Highlands*. (The British Aluminium Company Ltd, 1978.)

8. **Checkland**, Olive, *Japanese Whisky, Scotch Blend: The Japanese Whisky King and his Scottish Wife* ISBN 184017004. (Edinburgh: Scottish Cultural Press, 1998.)

Other Useful Reading:

A history of the aluminium industry in Scotland *Aluminiumville: Metal, the British Government & the Scottish Highlands* will be published by Carnegie Publishing in 2009.

*Ken Crocket well up
the crux pitch of
Vanishing Gully
(V,5), (March 1974)*

Photo: Crocket Collection

11: Consolidation (1961 – 1969)

IN A GREAT LEAP forward, Scottish winter climbing had come of age.
Looking back to early days, the hills in winter had been regarded as good
training for the Alps, then interesting for themselves in a narrow sense,
before the realisation dawned that here at home could be found adventure
enough, satisfying in itself – the Alps were great, but so was Nevis
and other notable Scottish hills in true winter conditions.

Future years would see a small but significant counter-current grow,
as mountaineers from other countries began to hear of and read about
Scottish winter climbing. The gullies and buttresses of Nevis would soon
hear accents European and Transatlantic. But a few years of relative peace
remained, as the slow and hard work of step-cutting, particularly on
the more difficult routes, limited the number of aspirants.

The winter season of 1961, as in the previous year, was opened by
Clough and Grandison. The route on this occasion was Tower Scoop
(III). This lies below Gardyloo Buttress and gives a popular two-pitch
climb, variable in difficulty. The prize find came later that month
however on January 15, with the ascent of Vanishing Gully by Ronnie
Marshall (Jimmy's brother) and Graham Tiso. The route description by
the climbers was a classic in understatement. *'The climb had four ice
pitches, three of which were steep'*. In fact the crux pitch, led by Tiso, is
often overhanging for a stretch and this superb climb is generally agreed
on as being a V,5.

Vanishing Gully lies on Secondary Tower Ridge, between West Gully
and the Italian Climb. Its first summer summer was recorded by Kellett
in September 1944. In winter condition, at its foot the ice may be barely
50cm wide: it slowly widens to a shallow chimney leading to the crux
section. There will often be a cave belay here, though in exceptional
conditions this can be covered, providing a huge bulging wall of ice of
over 30m. Following the crux pitch a shorter, easier ice pitch leads to
the shelf of 1934 Route. If the shelf is followed rightwards more enjoyable
if easy climbing can be had, otherwise a more direct line on the
buttress to the left leads to Tower Ridge proper. It is probably safe to
comment that Vanishing Gully was one of the best winter routes to be
recorded in the 1960s. Interestingly, Tiso did not recollect there being
any great difficulties.

The third and last new winter route of 1961 was also in January.
George Wallace and Robin Shaw made an ascent of 1931 Route (IV,4),
some 70m right of Vanishing Gully, on January 21. This was originally
recorded as a completely new route. Marshall later reconciled it with
the older climb.

The snows finally went and the summer of 1961 arrived. With it came
Jimmy Marshall and Stenhouse, up for a weekend at the end of May.
On May 30 they climbed Càrn Dearg Buttress by one of the finest lines
in Scotland – The Bullroar. This 285m Hard Very Severe route is a masterpiece of route-finding, an initial steep section leading to a rising traverse
rightwards across the great undercut slabs of the buttress to finish up

Jimmy Marshall on the crux pitch of The Bullroar (HVS), during the first ascent

Photo: Marshall collection

Ronnie Marshall was on many eventful ascents with his elder brother Jimmy and others, including Vanishing Gully (V,5), Shield Direct (HVS), and The Knuckleduster (HVS)

Photo: Jimmy Marshall

corners and grooves parallel to The Bat finish. The crux of the route, most unusually for the buttress and indeed Nevis, is a friction move on the fourth pitch, stepping down and right in the middle of the vast slab. A fall here by the second, and it has been known, can result in a pendulum under the overlap below. The thoughtful climber seconding this pitch protects it by leaving a runner above, pulling through the rope once safety is gained.

A small but constant weep of water hits the top of the Bullroar slab. On a summer's morning the sun will keep the slab dry, but beware the climber who starts late, for as the sun moves off the slab in the early afternoon the weep gains a hold and a wet patch moves slowly down the slab to reach the traverse line. The Bullroar traverse continues across

Of all the summer routes recorded on Ben Nevis by Jimmy Marshall it is fair to consider The Bullroar as his greatest legacy. Its name derives from the aboriginal device, a wooden stick whirled in the air to produce a roaring sound during young men's' initiation rites

the buttress, crossing the line of Centurion. The section immediately after the junction with Centurion gives delightful climbing with perfect rock and good situations. Of all the summer routes recorded on Ben Nevis by Jimmy Marshall it is fair to consider The Bullroar as his greatest legacy. Its name derives from the aboriginal device, a wooden stick whirled in the air to produce a roaring sound during young men's' initiation rites.

Perhaps as an alternative to their bovine main course, Marshall and Stenhouse climbed a second route that day in May. Chicken Run, Very Severe, lies on Number Five Gully Buttress. This is right of Five's Wall, the Severe with which Marshall had first entered the lists on Nevis, in 1953. The contrast between the two routes just eight years apart, The Bullroar and Five's Wall, indicates how far Marshall had travelled as a mountaineer in the interim.

The weather continued fair for Marshall and Stenhouse and the following day another line was climbed with The Brass Monkey, Hard Very Severe. This route lies on the eastern flank of Tower Ridge and climbs the deep crack in the corner formed where Echo Wall turns out towards Observatory Gully. Across the void to the right is the deeply-cut line of The Great Chimney, the Severe first climbed by Macphee and A.G.Murray in 1935. Marshall had to use two pegs to gain the crack proper and near the top of the penultimate pitch was forced to make a move on to the right wall. The following summer McLean and W. Smith succeeded in climbing the crack in its entirety.

Ian Clough and Keith Sutcliffe were on Nevis that same sunny week-end and recorded three routes. On May 31 they made an impressive girdle traverse of Càrn Dearg Buttress. The Orgy, Hard Very Severe, all 670m of it, starts up Route I and finishes near Evening Wall. In between it descends parts of Centurion and Sassenach, crosses The Bat and Titans Wall, and follows The Shield for 90m. The next day Clough and his companion recorded two other climbs on the Great Buttress. Mourning Slab, Very Severe, climbs the slab corner on the right of Number Five Gully. Taking advantage of the dry conditions, they climbed this now rarely followed summer line. Four years later it would be climbed in winter to produce one of the busiest routes on Nevis – The Curtain. This pair's other route that day was a Severe, also on Càrn Dearg Buttress. The High Girdle starts left of Mourning Slab and crosses Route I to follow Route II to the outer edge of the buttress. Continuing to Evening Wall and past, like its lower companion girdle, this route is rarely, if ever, repeated.

Surprisingly, that weekend with its six routes by the above four marked the end of first ascents for 1961. Perhaps even more surprisingly, no routes were made the following winter, with the sole exception of an ascent of Harrison's Climb, on the North Wall of Càrn Dearg Buttress. The parentage of Harrison's Climb has been a varied one, with at least five parties having a hand in it. The route, which lies left of Cousins' Buttress, was first climbed in 1929 by Alexander 'Sandy' Harrison. Joining the SMC in 1918, Sandy Harrison was President from 1945 – 1948, and was Honorary President from 1967 – 1988. He died in December 1988, in his 99th year. Next came Macphee in 1935, with an unrecorded traverse leftwards above the chimney of Harrison's Route in thawing conditions. He was followed in 1957 by Brunton and Clarkson, who

Chris Gilmore on the main wall pitch of Harrison's Climb, during the first ascent of Harrison's Climb Direct (IV,4) in 1976. The pitch was first climbed by Norman Tennent in 1961, step cutting in nailed boots. The forbidding icicle fringes above this section of the route could be fatal during a sudden thaw

Photo: Ken Crocket

Malcolm Slesser was a major character in the SMC, driving explorations in Greenland, stravaiging across Scotland and Europe, and latterly taking up sailing. President of the SMC 1982 – 1984, he died of natural causes while hillwalking in 2007, at the age of 80

Photo: Slesser family collection

recorded their winter ascent of Cousins' Buttress. Rounding off development of this route Ken Crocket and Chris Gilmore climbed the Direct in February 1976, adding a new start and finish. In a small display of synchronicity, from the five ropes who have played a part in the development of this route, four climbers have been Presidents of the SMC; Harrison, Macphee, Slesser, and Crocket (see Chapter 12 for a description of the first ascent of Direct Route).

Early in 1962, the first complete winter ascent of Harrison's Climb by the original line was made by Norman Tennent and Malcolm Slesser. Two easy pitches on the face led to the foot of the chimney pitch, separating Cousins' Buttress from the main wall on the left. In good icy conditions a fantastic fringe of icicles builds up at the top of this impressive face, stabbing downwards at a climber approaching from below. Climbing in tricouni-nailed boots, Tennent stepped on to the foot of the 50 foot ice wall, and in a later essay revealed the leader's thoughts on an ice pitch.

Jimmy Marshall on the first ascent of The Shield Direct (HVS)

Photo: Marshall collection

Out on to the nose. The holds are all there, because you made them. Keep on cutting. You died a long time ago; now you are really living. Over the top, finish the job, give us the tools

The start often seems the worst, and this bulge is no exception. Think. Start at the bottom left, and work right, then perhaps left again. Cut as many steps as you can before you start. Move up slowly, you've all the time in the world. You can't stay on at this angle. You can; must. Keep cutting well ahead; out on to the right wall. You can't hold on to ice without a handhold. Blast! I need a step at the height of my left knee. It's no good thinking the angle eases. Keep cutting. The steps are there, even though full of snow. How can my fingers be so cold? Are burnt fingers more painful than frozen ones? That wall looks the steepest yet. Keep your distance brother, and cut with both hands. Out on to the nose. The holds are all there, because you made them. Keep on cutting. You died a long time ago; now you are really living. Over the top, finish the job, give us the tools. Why keep the head; keep the feet first. Could probably finish with fewer holds, but that would be a piece of impertinence. Taking a liberty. Technique or The Art of Love: Les Liaisons Dangereux.[1]

Above the chimney Tennent and Slesser made the exposed traverse leftwards above the big wall, with a curtain of vertical ice above them barring access to easier ground. After they had made the left traverse and were climbing upwards again an avalanche came sweeping down, obliterating the ice wall but luckily missing the two climbers who went on to finish the route. Slesser, President of the SMC 1982 – 1984, died of natural causes while hillwalking in 2007, at the age of 80.

Summer 1962 saw several easy Very Severes climbed by Clough and Grandison, including the 300m Astronomy on the left side of The Orion Face. This follows a line of cracks and grooves parallel to Minus One Gully and tends to be somewhat grassy in summer. The excellent Left Edge Route on Gardyloo Buttress was finally climbed, also in June, by the brothers Marshall and George Ritchie. Many old pegs and karabiners were found on the route, marking the sites of previous attempts; by Ogilvy in 1940 for example. Their route finished up the Direct Finish made by Haston and Stenhouse in 1958 and the route is graded as Scottish Very Severe. The summer of 1962 also saw the death of Robin Smith in the Pamirs. Smith had been roped to Wilfred Noyce, when both climbers had fallen to their deaths on Peak Garmo, one climber having slipped, pulling the other down with him. Ironically, Noyce also had some history on Ben Nevis; Alex Small recalled meeting Noyce twice on the Ben. The first time he was on a stretcher having broken a leg on the North-East Buttress, the second time he was also on a stretcher, having slid down most of Tower Gully.[2]

In June the Marshall brothers and George Ritchie recorded an important variation start to The Shield, adding several, hard pitches to the bottom section. Their direct start climbs the lower chimneys direct, these having being bypassed by Downes and Whillans in 1956. The ascent included a fall by Ritchie. Marshall considers the route to be as good as Centurion, though its position on the flank of the buttress seems to have led to a state of neglect.

Bill Smith, John McLean and James Stenhouse outside the CIC Hut

Photo: Jimmy Marshall

Another major ascent of 1962 was a hard and direct line on Càrn Dearg Buttress – Torro. John McLean, Bill Smith and Willie Gordon of the Creagh Dhu arrived on July 25. The route starts up the left side of the small subsidiary buttress taken by the first pitch of Centurion. Difficulties begin immediately upon leaving the ground, with a strenuous and gently overhanging groove to be tackled. A peg was placed here on the first ascent for protection while a sling was used for aid on pitch four, moving over an overhang. On the penultimate pitch McLean traversed hard left; most climbers at this point continue straight up. A peg, contrary to the route description published later, was not required for aid on the last pitch but was another protection placement.

Subsequent parties thought that aid pegs had been used on pitches 1, 4 and on the last pitch. In fact, according to McLean, no aid pegs were used, a sling for a hold on pitch 4 being the only point of aid on the entire route.

John Cunningham and Jimmy Gardiner were next on the route, but did not finish the climb, missing out the last pitch. The second complete ascent, climbed completely free, was accomplished by two of the 'Dumbarton Boys', 'Big' Ian Nicolson and 'Wee' Ian Fulton, in June, 1970. The two Ians were members of a small group of technically accomplished climbers who lived in and around Dumbarton, climbing skills honed to a fine edge on the exacting boulder problems of Dumbarton Rock. Other climbers from this informal group included Rab Carrington and John Jackson. Several went on to join the Creagh Dhu Club; at least two, including Fulton and Carrington, were to enter the SMC. Jackson was killed by a rockfall in the Alps. Ian Fulton described their ascent, made that beautifully sunny day.

Ian Fulton (June 1970). One of the 'Dumbarton Boys' and an SMC member, Fulton transferred skills learned on the Dumbarton Boulders to the higher hills

Photo: Ken Crocket

Ian Nicolson. Another member of the 'Dumbarton Boys' Nicolson would later settle in Glen Coe

Photo: Cubby Images

Ian started climbing and was soon performing ridiculous bridges across the bulge. My mind began working overtime as I compared my leg span with his; there would have to be another way. A few funny moves and he was up to a good resting place on the right. A couple of unusual layback moves round a jutting flake led to the foot of a smooth sweeping groove which was quickly climbed to the big comfortable belay. The rope came tight and it was time to go... I nervously fumbled my way up to the bulge and removed the protection. Think what you are going to do, don't hang on your arms, work out the moves.

Fulton worked out the alternative way round the bulge and 20 minutes after Nicolson had begun the route the two were reunited on the belay. Fulton found the slab on the second pitch troublesome due to the very dry conditions.

My feet kept slipping on the dry moss so a well timed grab was made for a big jug and I quickly hoisted myself up the short overhanging groove to the belay. An interesting pitch.

The fourth pitch was soon reached, with the aid sling waiting to be eliminated. Nicolson was determined to free this.

So up and down he went trying all the different permutations of holds until a high step up with undercut hand holds allowed him to layback round the upper overlap.

The point of aid had been eliminated. Torro then takes a long run-out up smooth water-worn slabs, topped by an overlap below the broken ground near Route II. It then breaks through the overhangs using the seventh pitch of Centurion. Nicolson set off up the last pitch.

...ridiculous bridging moves brought him up level with the decaying stumps of two old pegs, only to find progress stopped by two loose blocks. Pulling the rope out of the way he trundled them off and we watched, fascinated, as they bounded down the slabs and over the edge. Ian disappeared into the groove. Judging by the sound effects, it seemed to be strenuous but in due course he emerged on the ledge above. He smiled slyly and casually tossed down the fact that he had just done the crux.[3]

This final pitch is a shallow, vertical V-groove, undercut and with no crack in the back, the sort of problem usually found on outcrops, but the long reach and athletic physique of Nicolson had won the day. Torro is presently graded at E2,5c, with the overhang of pitch four recognised as being the crux of the route. It should perhaps be remembered that the first ascent party did not possess much in the way of today's protection equipment, such as manufactured chockstones. Their carrying and occasionally using pegs for protection was standard practice right through to the end of the 1970s. Only then with improved equipment could most leaders have the confidence to leave pegs behind in summer. What McLean's party did carry though were the first prototype chockstones – large engineering nuts with drilled out threads. For many years, one such abandoned item could be seen jammed in a crack on the first pitch of Centurion.

The poor winters which had opened the 1960s retreated slightly in 1963 and several winter ascents were made. The first of these was Wendigo, 120m IV,4 by Tom Patey and Joe Brown on February 24.

The crux overlap of Torro (E2), Càrn Dearg Buttress

Photo: Peter Hodgkiss

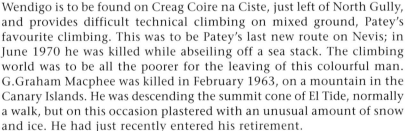

The vertical, final corner of Torro, Càrn Dearg Buttress. Climber Keith Milne

Photo: Tom Prentice

Wendigo is to be found on Creag Coire na Ciste, just left of North Gully, and provides difficult technical climbing on mixed ground, Patey's favourite climbing. This was to be Patey's last new route on Nevis; in June 1970 he was killed while abseiling off a sea stack. The climbing world was to be all the poorer for the leaving of this colourful man. G.Graham Macphee was killed in February 1963, on a mountain in the Canary Islands. He was descending the summit cone of El Tide, normally a walk, but on this occasion plastered with an unusual amount of snow and ice. He had just recently entered his retirement.

In March 1963 another well-known pair of mountaineers recorded a short but hard winter route, when Dougal Haston and Dennis Gray climbed Winter Chimney V,5. This takes the chimney, really more of a corner, lying in the back of the bay which defines the right edge of Gargoyle Wall, on No. 3 Gully Buttress. It's feasibility depends on the amount of ice to be found at the top of the chimney. Here an overhang forces one rightwards on to a steep slab and so to the top. Crocket and Fulton failed on this route in the 1970s, finding insufficient ice for the right traverse.

Peter Trudgill on the initial, steep section of Thompson's Route (IV,4) on Number Three Gully Buttress (April 2008)

Photo: John Trudgill

Summer routes in 1963 were limited to an alternative start to Left-Hand Route by Clough and friends, and a prominent line on the Douglas Boulder, Cutlass, Very Severe, by E.Cairns and Fred Harper on July 6. This 135m line takes the clean-cut corner left of the south-west arete of the Douglas Boulder, and was the first Very Severe route on the Boulder.

The brothers Marshall, along with Stenhouse, saw in the last routes of 1963 with two winter ascents in December. Thompson's Route received its first winter ascent and at IV,4 gives delightful and steep climbing, particularly in the lower section, where a narrow groove line cuts up through the buttress wall. The other winter ascent in December was the IV,4 Jubilation, weaving up through Central Trident Buttress to give Alpine-like climbing up the open slopes above. Snow conditions must be safe before considering an ascent.

As the 1960s progressed, so the number of outstanding first ascents decreased. There were obvious exceptions of course, but in the main exploratory climbing on Nevis had passed another peak and climbers were content either to slowly complete obvious gaps in the cliffs or repeat earlier lines. Jimmy Marshall was busy researching for the new edition of the Climbers' Guide to Nevis; he would go on to record more than a dozen first ascents. As Marshall's ginger group slowly declined in numbers; some moving elsewhere, some dying, some inevitably losing the momentum of their early hard days, other groups sprang up, including The Squirrels Mountaineering Club.

The Squirrels, taking their name from an Italian Alpine group, were based in and around Edinburgh. In 1964 they moved their activities from Glen Coe, where they used a renovated war-time defence bunker appropriately called 'The Drey', to Ben Nevis. Ian MacEacheran and Dave Bathgate made the third winter ascent of Point Five Gully, suffering a cold bivouac half-way up the route in the process. The winter of 1964, however, produced no more than a one-pitch variation finish to North Gully, Creag Coire na Ciste, by Bathgate, Jock Knight and Alisdair 'Bugs' McKeith.

In June 1964, Marshall climbed two routes on the South Trident Buttress, The Clanger, Severe, and the Very Severe Sidewinder. Also that June Dougal Haston made his last route on Nevis with Robin Campbell, climbing the pleasant, if grassy, rocks left of Minus Three Gully to record the Very Severe Wagroochimsla. The minimal route description left by this pair is easily augmented, once it is realised that the route name is a derivation of WAll, GROOve, CHIMney, SLAb.

In July, Marshall and George Ritchie left the CIC Hut in a downpour and made for the Minus Face and the unclimbed (in summer) Minus Three Gully. The pair splashed up the gully for some way then came to a slabby groove with a bulge. Ritchie tried this but was beaten back. Marshall took over and soon gained the high point and a stance on slings. From here two possibilities suggested themselves; a clean slab corner on the left with a couple of centimetres of surface water, or a right-forking, bulging crack. Marshall decided that the crack on the right was to be the way,

> ...with gasping warnings to the grey old man below, the crack is entered, what a thrutch! socks are thrashing about, knees rammed survivally into the crack, and gains upward secured by fingery sprags inside...Suddenly one of these wee sprags breaks, and I am leaning out backwards on knees, hands slipping green from the bowels of the crack, a backward snatch finds the cowardly provident right-wall sling, enabling the thrust back into the crack and a grunting progression to stand established in what is now a chimney.[4]

All three of the Minus Gullies had now been climbed in summer; indeed, with the ascent of Minus Three, all of the major Nevis gullies on the north face had received a summer ascent. The one outstanding winter problem remaining, at least in the classical sense, was Minus One Gully. Lack of suitable conditions for step-cutting delayed an ascent for a further ten years; it was certainly not due to a lack of suitably qualified applicants or determined attempts.

The summer of 1964 moved wetly towards the autumn and at the beginning of September wee Brian Robertson and Fred Harper sweated their way up to the Hut in uncharacteristic sunshine. Robertson had been studying the possibility of a new line on Càrn Dearg Buttress between Centurion and The Bat, skirting just right of the former line. The overhanging cracks right of the first pitch of Centurion were wet however and instead Robertson scurried his size four PAs up the first pitch of Centurion to belay at the large block.

From here, most climbers would have followed The Bat traverse before breaking away and up over the slabs and overlaps above. But Robertson was possessed with a peculiar stubbornness of purpose and instead made several difficult and devious moves. Traversing rightward from the foot of the Centurion corner, parallel to and lower than the Bat traverse, Robertson used a channel peg to gain a lower slab, before continuing to a peg belay near the end of the slab. It was now 8pm and fixing the

Suddenly one of these wee sprags breaks, and I am leaning out backwards on knees, hands slipping green from the bowels of the crack...

Brian Robertson's hard, if illogical route finding on Càrn Dearg Buttress led to the first ascent of King Kong. He now lives in Colorado, USA (2006)

Photo: Cubby Images

ropes the two climbers abseiled down from the belay.

The following day, Tuesday, Robertson and Harper repeated the previous day's climbing, ending back at the peg belay. From here Robertson followed an open corner with one peg for aid leading to the block belay on The Bat. A move down left led to a ledge near the loose block on The Bat traverse, and here Robertson belayed. All this tortuous, though no doubt difficult climbing at the start of Robertson's route is now avoided, climbers preferring the more logical course of following the second pitch of The Bat to gain the same point. Robertson now started up the futuristic fourth pitch, one which rejected several later repeat attempts. After a few moves he spotted a chockstone high up on the right.

> Being a bit on the small side, I was too wee to reach it... With my eyes firmly fixed on the sky, my teeth firmly pressed together, I prepared my body for a peel as I moved up. My forefinger managed to hook itself round the stone, then, after many miserable attempts, I threaded a baby-nylon for a runner. Groping about with my right hand, I found a crack somewhere up on the right, then I managed to get my right P.A. foot flat on the upper slab... It looked all right, so I pulled myself up on to the slab.

Robertson was now committed to climbing up the vast slab above the overhang and made for two small holds at head-height.

> As soon as I did stand on these holds ... I had the sneaky feeling that I was going to make a rapid departure from the rock. One finger, jammed in a bit of muck level with my waist, kept all my ten stone in contact with the rock, and it was failing fast. Somehow, I wangled an ace into a crack. Just as the rope was clipped in, my trusty forefinger gave up the ghost... Hanging from the peg, I suddenly felt very tired.[5]

Robertson and Harper retired once more to the CIC Hut, where the next day they were joined by two of their friends, '...*hoods from the Glasgow Etive Club – Jimmy (Weed) Graham, and Drew Campbell*'. Harper decided to withdraw from the siege at this point, so Wednesday morning saw Robertson and Graham back on the route. This time they took the more sensible course of following The Bat to gain their belay and equipment. Robertson was soon at Tuesday's high point and with further climbing gained a belay up and right. On the next pitch an overlap led to a vertical crack, near the top of which a rightward traverse led to easier ground, half-way up the buttress. More climbing lay ahead of Robertson and Graham, including a small roof overcome by using a jammed-nut and an etrier, but the major difficulties were over on this route – King Kong.

The account by Robertson of the first ascent of King Kong leaves out mention of most of the aid points given in the route description – about a dozen in total. Attempting the second ascent in 1966, John Cunningham, Con Higgins and Ian Dingwall were forced off line on the fourth pitch, finding instead, using several points of aid, a new way up the slabs right of Centurion. The second ascent, in June 1970, was by Ian Nicolson and Norrie Muir, taking the entry as for The Bat and eliminating the aid completely. The route is now Graded at E2 if the Bat entry is used, E3 if the original and often wet start is taken. King Kong is a route in the modern idiom; subtle of line, uncompromising

Rick Campbell nearing the top of the red wall on King Kong (E2)

Photo: Gary Latter

Jimmy Marshall leading the first ascent of The Chute (V,4)

Photo: Robin Campbell

in severity, sustained and at the higher end of the grade.

The decline in exploratory climbing on Nevis continued through the 1960s. During the last five years of that decade there were 17 routes and a variation made, seven by J.R.Marshall whose guide was to be published in 1969. A further four routes were by Clough who had now left the RAF Mountain Rescue Team and with Hamish MacInnes was running the Glencoe Mountaineering School.

Three winter routes in February 1965 was the sum total that winter. Jimmy Marshall and James Moriarty ('Elly', the gentle giant, and a regular partner of Dougal Haston), made the first winter ascent of Green Hollow Route on the First Platform at IV,4. This gave sustained and delicate climbing up thinly iced grooves. Also that month, Marshall teamed up with Dick Holt and a relative newcomer to Nevis, Robin Campbell. By his own confession, Campbell had chosen Edinburgh University for his undergraduate studies on the sole criterion that Smith and Marshall were climbing out of that city. Campbell later went on to edit the SMC Journal, and was President of both the Mountaineering Council of Scotland and the SMC. Elly, whose nickname followed his elegant climbing style on the rock, died in Edinburgh in 2006, following a chest infection. He had survived leukemia and was 65.

Marshall, Holt and Campbell found a tenuous winter line right of the Italian Climb, starting up the steep wall about 30m right of that route. A rising left traverse, a horizontal ledge leading right and a system of snow and ice-filled grooves above completed this hard Grade IV, Grade

*On the intial slab of
The Curtain (IV,5), in
thin conditions*

Photo: Tom Ripley

*Dave Bathgate was a
member of the
Edinburgh based
Squirrels M.C.,
responsible for much
of the activity in the
1960s, including the
first ascent of The
Curtain (2006)*

Photo: Cubby Images

V,4 if climbed directly. The second ascent is unrecorded, though later
ascents have been made under heavy cover of snow and ice. Their route,
The Chute, approximates to a disappointing summer line first climbed
on June 21, 1957 by the Cambridge University MC team of Ted Maden
and Mike O'Hara, and named by them The Ruritarian Climb.

The third winter ascent of February 1965 climbed what is easily one
of the most frequented lumps of ice on Nevis. Every winter, almost without fail, though it does fall down during a prolonged thaw, a continuous
cataract of ice forms over the wet rocks of Mourning Slab, first climbed
in summer by Clough and Sutcliffe in 1961. Named 'The Curtain' long
before it was climbed, this is a good winter route which leads nowhere
in three pitches, but gives excellent and surprisingly varied ice climbing while doing so. The first ascent in February 1965 was by two of the
Squirrels, Dave Bathgate and Jock Knight. The previous weekend
Bathgate and Ronnie Marshall had climbed 20m of the first pitch before

high winds and blowing snow forced a retreat.

The first pitch of The Curtain, a great slab at a reasonable angle, gave Knight a full run-out of 45m to a small ice-cave belay at the top of the slab. Many leaders miss the peg runner some 15m up on the right wall, though if the ice on the slab is of sufficient thickness ice screws provide adequate protection. Bathgate started up the second and crux pitch, traversing left below a bulge, up a short wall, then back right above the belay to the steepest and hardest section of the route. He tells the story in his own words.

> Twenty feet above me rose a great barrier of vertical ice, tapering and decreasing slightly in angle towards the left, where it met the rock. The intervening twenty feet of 80° ice had to be climbed before I could see if a leftward traverse to the rock was possible. Moving up into new footholds, I noticed something wrong with my right crampon. I looked down and, with the adze of my axe, just caught the front half as it slipped off. I took off the other half and clipped both pieces into a karabiner...

Bathgate managed to reverse back down to the belay, using his well-made holds. There he tied the crampon together and set off up the pitch again.

> Back on the ice and cutting up the steep section, I had to form holds that I could hang on to for as long as possible with one hand; there could be no tension assistance, for I had taken a zig-zag line. After making the normal incut hold, I chipped the sides away, leaving a mound of ice, like half a tennis ball, sticking up in the middle of the hold. Fingers could then spread and the thumb grip. Such a hold is possibly only on the hardest ice. I fixed a third screw at the beginning of the leftward traverse. I cut a handhold, then a foothold big enough for both feet; step across with the left foot, then cut another hand and foothold; bring the right foot across beside the left, then put the left foot in the last hold. Begin again. My left arm was as strong as a wet newspaper by the time I reached the rock ledge 25 feet away, with its sound rock peg.[6]

Salewa tubular ice screw. c. 1980s. Though now surpassed by later designs, at the time these ice screws provided a quantum leap upwards in security, replacing a dismal selection of thin, solid screws better suited (and often used) for pulling wine corks

Knight led through and finished the route, climbing the very steep start of the last pitch with tension from an ice screw. Equipment advances since the start of the decade had included the introduction of tubular ice screws, manufactured by the West German firm Salewa. The same company was also responsible for the introduction of the two-part, hinged crampon, adjustable in length and made from aluminium alloy. These were very quickly recognised as being excellent for mixed climbing. Until then, the favoured crampons was a heavier model made by Grivel, the Italian manufacturer based in Courmayeur.

Originally graded at V, The Curtain is a IV,5 in the current guide, due to its short length and lack of sustained high-angle ice. Protection on the climb being generally good, the ease of access and regularity of being in condition have led it to being a route which suffers a constant stream of ascents. In a busy, settled spell, so many teams can have kicked their front points up the route that a deep groove may be seen on the first pitch. Despite this indignity, and an air of being an *ice problem*, the climbing on The Curtain is to be recommended.

Another hard route was climbed that winter of 1965, and by another pair from the Squirrels. Ian MacEacheran and Jim Renny made an

Robin Campbell at the foot of Recess Route (Severe), on The Cobbler (c. 1970). A retired psychologist, Campbell has had a long and eventful membership in the SMC, at various times being Journal Editor, President, and Archivist

Photo: Campbell collection

inadvertent second ascent of the Ordinary Route on Observatory Buttress, first climbed, but not recorded, by Smith and Marshall in 1960. The Squirrels named their route The Liquidator, thinking it was a first ascent. The 340m route is very popular at V,4, with a hard icy chimney high on the climb, and slabby rocks at the foot of the buttress.

Exploration on Nevis in 1965 was completed with an August Creagh Dhu ascent of Rolling Stones, Very Severe. Climbed by John Cunningham and Con Higgins, this almost forgotten route climbs the vast wall below the Great Tower, on the East Flank of Tower Ridge. Appropriately enough, the Marshall brothers returned to this wall in February 1966, making two winter ascents. East Wall Route (III), was probably a reconnaissance for the harder Echo Traverse (III). The former route followed an old Difficult climb, traversing right to gain Tower Ridge crest, while Echo Traverse shoots upwards from the easier line, climbing exposed and sustained rocks. Great difficulty was experienced crossing a very iced slab, Marshall having to use rope tension from a rock spike.

In March 1983 the French guide Godefroy Perroux and party climbed the icefall which often forms below the initial traverse of this route. Wet Spring Start, as it is named in the guide, provides a 50m V,6 entry, and often forms late in the season. Perroux was to be responsible for many new routes, becoming a regular face in the CIC Hut and even making a film. He was killed in Les Houches, France, while attempting an icefall in thawing conditions. He was greatly liked and respected by Scottish winter climbers he met, having made several notable routes on Ben Nevis. Returning most winters, he would entertain fellow climbers in the CIC Hut, delighting them by cooking up superb crêpes. Here his memory lives on in his routes such as the steep icefall he called 'Une Journée Ordinaire dans un Enfer Quotidien'. Ken Crocket was charmed enough when Perroux and several others dropped in at his home, to allow enough clues about unclimbed lines to be extracted. Some of these were soon followed up by Perroux. Just before his death he had finished a photo-guide to the winter ice climbs of Ben Nevis, published in 2002.

Marshall continued to dominate Nevis climbing in the mid 1960s, returning in September with his younger brother Ronnie to climb two hard and excellent lines. The Knuckleduster, graded Hard Very Severe, 5a, climbs a superb line on Number Three Gully Buttress. The main bulk of this buttress forms a steep face looking down to Lochan Coire na Ciste. Gargoyle Wall lies on the right edge of this face. The Knuckleduster takes the very prominent groove towards the left side of the smooth buttress face. Fated by its altitude to be climbed infrequently, and slow to dry, this classic Marshall line received its second ascent by Ian Nicolson.

The second route by the Marshall brothers that September took a central line up the great slabby face left of Point Five Gully. This face had first been attempted by Jim Bell in 1936, in wet weather, and later by Bell and Hamish Hamilton in July 1937. They found the rocks impossible, given their footwear, and moved left to climb the West Face, Upper Route, on the left edge of the great slabs. The ascent by the Marshalls found the rocks to be Very Severe. The Knuckleduster and Pointless were climbed on the same day, September 4.

Later that month Ian Clough returned with a partner from Fife, George

Farquhar. They climbed an easy Very Severe on the left flank of Càrn Dearg Buttress, P.M., lying to the right of Clough's earlier Mourning Slab. On the following day, September 22, Clough and Farquhar recorded a girdle traverse of the Minus and Orion Faces, giving a 610m E1,5b. This monster girdle, named Marathon, included the cruxes of Right Hand Route and Minus One Direct. It continued by the Great Slab Rib of the Long Climb, finally finishing at the top of Slav Route.

New routes in 1967 opened with a near-tragedy, perhaps the closest call that Jimmy Marshall has had on Nevis. Climbing with Robin Campbell on February 25, the two had finished the first winter ascent of Newbigging's 80 Minute Route. The grading at IV,4 reflects the crux pitch, a 30m groove climbed delicately on thin ice with few positive holds. Descending from the First Platform by the traverse leftwards into Coire Leis, Marshall came off due to soft snow, but brought himself to a halt just above the cliff edge below. This same spot was the scene of a fatal accident in January 1983, and great care must be observed here, as in other spots where steep snow lies above a drop.

The only other winter ascent of 1967 was one which led to some grim amusement. Back in June 1964 Marshall and Stenhouse had been climbing on the South Trident Buttress, checking out Kellett routes for the forthcoming Nevis Guide. Looking for a groove in the middle tier they found and climbed a prominent specimen which fitted the description except for the finish. Here Kellett had mentioned a choice of routes; Marshall and Stenhouse had had to climb a vertical wall of unbelievable looseness. At the time Marshall filed the route away in his mind as a possible winter line.

Next February, Marshall and Moriarty returned to the groove, where Marshall pointed Big Elly up the big pitch. Elly climbed the 12m entrance wall, glazed and awkward, to a string runner, then moved leftward a little into the groove. Marshall tells the story of what happened next:

> Winter's worries assailed me, the axe belay was useless, the peg doubtful... Muffled mumblings and excuses filtered down the rope; brittle ice, glazed bulges, etc; the gut began to tighten ...Och, he'll be alright, he's so tall he's over most problems before they start, the happy thoughts prevail and I peer into the grim corrie below. The rope moves up, good, that's the bulge over, and then – a great rasping, rumbling, thrashing, tumbling offends my ear. I race the rope back through the string runner. Jesus Christ! there isn't a higher runner. Elly streaks out off the groove head down like a 225 lb. torpedo, my eyes are on stalks as he smashes a crater from the ledge and bounces out into orbit...[7]

Thinking of the 150m drop below, Marshall was pulled up against the belay peg which creaked alarmingly as the rope bit through the winter layers of his clothing. Amazingly, Elly's bloodstained face appeared below, as both climbers regained their footing. Other than a deep cut on the bridge of his nose Elly was unhurt, as the two shattered climbers made their way down.

Two winters later, in March, 1967, the determined Marshall returned to the groove again, this time with his brother Ronnie and Robin Campbell. The latter had now been with Jimmy Marshall on various escapades on Nevis, including the occasion when Marshall had come close to grief on the descent from the First Platform.

Ronnie Marshall belays, while Jimmy makes the first winter ascent of the prominent groove of The Clanger (IV,5). To the left lies Kellett's Slab Climb (see pages 152 and 340)

Photo: Robin Campbell

– a great rasping, rumbling, thrashing, tumbling offends my ear. I race the rope back through the string runner. Jesus Christ! there isn't a higher runner. Elly streaks out off the groove head down like a 225 lb. torpedo...

I thought ... of one day when he slipped briefly, stopping himself on the brink, and meeting my specious concern with silent seethings and a steely glare. But most of all I thought of his ungovernable rage when thwarted...[8]

Jimmy led the difficult pitch then brought up the other two. Campbell was then pushed into leading the next pitch, an open bay from which the exit was an overhanging chimney.

He leered at me, thrusting his red beak through the porridge 'On ye go, son! Up thae cracks. It's nae bother noo I've done aa the hard bits'. High above, I fumbled at a bitter overhang, bare of snow or holds. I thought he'd better hear about it. 'It won't go, Father. It's too steep'. 'Whaur's your spunk, laddie?' he bellowed. 'Do your share, ye wee bastard! Does your puir auld Faither have to dae it aa fur ye?'

Campbell tried the overhang again but to no avail. He was about to come down when a great cloud of swirling snow descended, blotting out visibility. Taking this opportunity, Campbell shuffled rightwards into an easy groove which led to a chimney.

I slotted myself in and, thus hidden, made progress to the roof, deaf to his rantings. I'll get him yet, I thought, I see a hole. So I did; deep in the chimney's frosty innards there was light.

Campbell squeezed through the narrow slot and emerged above the difficulties. When Ronnie came up he had to remove some clothing to pass through the squeeze, so they guessed that Jimmy might have difficulty with the chimney, might even stick in fact,

...and maybe for a long time at that, and it could just be that a big hoodie craw might come along and take a fancy to his wee beady eyes.

But Jimmy was very cautious,

...he stuck his head through to glare and curse, then backed off, roaring for a coil to be thrown to him. 'Throw me a rope, ye wee scut! Ye'll no lead the way again. I'll see to that, mind ye!' Uncle and I hauled him up howling with rage and beating the cold rocks in his shame. Well, that set him back a bit. He led the rest of the way, which was easy, but you could see he was livid. He took us off the buttress by a maze of floury terraces and snowy chimneys, showing off his local knowledge. Back in the stinking hut we thawed out, but he was still giving me the cold eye. 'Ah'll get ye fur that, runt. Ah'll get ma chance, ye'll see'. We left it at that. He had to wait a while; till what passes for the summer came, in fact ...[8]

As for the route, the last paragraph of this account belongs to Marshall.

Months later during a balmy spring walk around the corrie the whole scene clicked into place. Our route was not Kellett's Groove Climb after all. That climb lay tucked in a corner well to the left, a tiny little chimney, ours loomed and leered in splendid scale above, a classic Nevis joke.[7]

Named, appropriately enough, The Clanger, Marshall's route is Severe in summer and IV,5 in winter, when the description mentions a through route for thin men.

The 1960s were winding down fast. A variation to Minus One Direct

Marshall eyes up Campbell from the top of the tight chimney of The Clanger (IV,5) on the first winter ascent

Photo: Robin Campbell

Back in the stinking hut we thawed out, but he was still giving me the cold eye. 'Ah'll get ye fur that, runt. Ah'll get ma chance, ye'll see'

was made by Peter Macdonald and Ian Rowe, climbing round and above the original crux to rejoin the route above. Perhaps the best find of 1967 was the September ascent of Psychedelic Wall, Scottish Very Severe, by John Jackson and Ronnie Marshall. This is a good climb, if somewhat loose and messy. With the soon to come revolution in winter climbing it would become better known as an excellent winter route.

1968 had one solitary route recorded, Turret Cracks, Hard Very Severe, by Ian Clough and D.G.Roberts. Following a thin crack line left of the prominent line of chimneys on the vertical final tower of the Castle, this short route came too late to be included in J.R. Marshall's definitive guide, then at the mercy of the printer. The last two routes recorded in the 1960s came in 1969 with, in February, Route Major (IV,4) by Clough and MacInnes, and in September the Hard Very Severe Teufel Grooves, by Dave Bathgate and John Porteous.

Route Major is a very fine winter route, closely following in its lower part Macphee and Williams' Eastern Climb on the The Little Brenva Face. It is not a route for the inexperienced, despite its relatively easy grading, as it has some complex route finding. In the more lean winters of recent years, it has rarely been in obvious good condition. Teufel Grooves takes a good looking line of grooves on Raeburn's Buttress; right of The Crack.

In 1969 Torro had its second ascent by Nicolson and Fulton, described earlier in this chapter, while on Sassenach John Porteous had an exciting time when an infamous rotating block in the big chimney pitch decided to stop rotating and start flying. Porteous was hanging on to the block at the time, but a runner held him safely. Later he was to be seen ruefully exhibiting the mangled karabiner.

In August Sassenach was climbed free by Steve Wilson and Colin Read. There was a strong party of climbers on the mountain in superb weather, allowing many of the hard routes to be climbed. Wilson, who was only 18, showed promise, having already climbed The Bat, as well as Shibboleth, the Big Ride and other routes in Glen Coe and on the Trilleachan Slabs in Glen Etive. Tragically, in November of 1969 he was paralysed following an abseiling accident.

Another seeming lull had fallen on Ben Nevis. Talented climbers were about, though the publication of Marshall's superb guide, in its soon to be familiar blue cover, seemed to say it all. But strange hammering sounds were heard in various workshops around the world, as the conventional shape of the ice-axe was changed and bent into something new. Front-pointing was about to be sprung onto an unsuspecting public.

The first edition of Jimmy Marshall's guide to Ben Nevis, published in 1969. The cover shot is of Marshall on the first ascent of the Shield Direct

References

1. **Tennent**, Norman, *The Primitive Approach*. SMCJ 27, 228 – 233, 1962.

2. **Small**, Alex, *Personal communication, January 1987*.

3. **Fulton**, Ian, *Torro*. Glasgow University MC Journal, 1970.

4. **Marshall**, J.R., *Minus Three in Summer*. SMCJ 28, 87 – 89, 1965.

5. **Robertson**, B.W., *A Climb Called King Kong*. SMCJ 28, 103 – 108, 1965.

6. **Bathgate**, D., *The First Ascent of The Curtain*. SMCJ 28, 108 – 111, 1965.

7. **Marshall**, J.R., *In The Groove*. SMCJ 29, 378 – 382, 1971.

8. **Campbell**, R.N., *Bringing Up Father*. Edinburgh University M.C. Journal, 48 – 52, 1969.

12: Revolutions (1970 – 1985)

UNTIL 1970, winter routes were climbed in virtually the same style as they had been climbed at the turn of the century, a single, cumbersome, wooden ice axe laboriously wielded by the leader who hewed a line of hand and footholds. The early climbers had used longer axes and cut when feasible with both hands. This made it very difficult to cut steps on near-vertical ice, but the gradual shortening of the ice axe shaft made steep angles less of a strain.

Steep pitches of snow and ice were cut one-handed from about the 1930s onwards. Douglas Scott had his short axe custom-made by a blacksmith in 1936, but no British manufacturer seemed willing or able to take on such a tiny market, and long-shafted European makes continued to be the only axes available – Stubai, Aschenbrenner, Grivel, etc. A climber mail-ordered an axe, or bought an imported axe available in his local sports shop then had it shortened. This of course made the balance of the axe in the hand even worse.

Crampons came into more general use in the 1950s and helped lessen the leg-strain of standing in holds and kicking steps up easier angled slopes. Some of the early 10-point models had no upwardly projecting front-points, which greatly lessened their use. For most slopes, a climber would walk up using all crampons points, feet flat on the slope, zig-zagging up the slope, until the angle steepened, when a switch was made to kicking the front points directly into the slope, facing in. This method was fast, though good calf muscles were needed. For obvious reasons, it was called front-pointing and utilised 12-point models. Crampons initially were in two connected sections; heel section connected to a front section. These hinged models were good for general purpose climbing and hillwalking. Later models were designed with a rigid frame and were better for steep ice and harder climbs in general. Used with rigid boots they significantly lessened the strain on leg muscles as well as allowing smaller holds to be used with greater precision.

Ice daggers were used by a few climbers for balance – notably by John Cunningham who, with Bill March, climbed Zero Gully in six hours. This was in 1970, effectively the year in which front-pointing experiments first came to the notice of British climbers. Before then, direct aid from long ice pitons was the only real assistance a leader could expect to find on an ice pitch. Hamish MacInnes, the *Old Fox* of Glen Coe, had been experimenting with ice axe design since about 1965, working with metal shafts. His early designs for inclined picks did not go far enough with the angle of inclination however, his significant contributions to front-pointing coming a few years later.

In 1970 the Americans Yvon Chouinard and Doug Tompkins visited Scotland. Chouinard, long an innovator when it came to producing climbing gear, had brought out his design of rigid crampons, for use on ice. In some ways these were a refinement of the Austrian modification to Grivel's twelve point crampons, the latter first appearing in 1932. The Grivel crampons were excellent for Scottish conditions, though the metal did tend to be brittle. Salewa crampons, made from a steel alloy, were lighter, and with straight inclined front-points,

A Salewa 12-point Hard Ice Classic crampon from the 1980s. Four downward-pointing heel spikes, six downward-pointing points in the front section, and two front points angled upwards at the toes

From 'Climbing Terms & Techniques' by Ken Crocket

French climber Dominique Lewale seconding the overhanging crux of Minus One Gully (VI,6)

Photo: François Damilano

effectively took over took over the market from Grivel in the 1960s. The Salewas were hinged and of particular use on the easier buttresses, mixed climbing, and hillwalking. As their length could be adjusted, they also fitted the boot more snugly, increasing confidence. The Chouinard rigid crampons, providing a stable base, eased the strain on calf muscles when front-pointing, though were less suited for hillwalking or descent follow-ing a climb.

To accompany his crampons, Chouinard brought his curved ice

*Allen Fyffe on the
first winter ascent of
Astronomy (VI,5),
(March 197)*

Photo: Hamish MacInnes

hammers, again designed for pure ice. The two Americans climbed Raven's Gully in Glen Coe, in February 1970, making the first winter ascent of the difficult Direct Finish, now considered to be VI,6.[1] The sight of their ice hammers spurred a few observant Scottish climbers to experiment on their own. The crampon technique used by the Americans was one never taken up by British climbers, being the French style known as *pied a plat*, in which the feet are often placed flat on to the slope, including steeper angles. British climbers used the German/Austrian front-point technique, more suited to the normal terrain found on local mountains. The amusing fact about Raven's Gully is the limited amount of pure front-pointing on ice normally possible in its rocky confines.

After climbing Smith's Route wearing hinged Salewa crampons in 1975, Ken Crocket's calf muscles were painful for a week. He was so impressed with his climbing partner's Chouinard rigid crampons that he immediately switched to using these.

Like most innovations, front-pointing took a few years to become accepted. Some adventurous climbers began in 1971, with blacksmith-made axes. One of the earliest and most influential climbers to take up the new technique was Mike Geddes, a Scot from Edinburgh who went south to study chemical engineering at Cambridge University. Interested by an article in *Mountain* magazine at the end of 1970, Geddes bought a Chouinard hammer and also persuaded a blacksmith to make a copy of a Climax axe. Other climbers front-pointed using alternative equipment, such as the Salewa half-round ice screws wielded by Norrie Muir in 1970. These were never satisfactory, however, and Muir failed on The Curtain with such gear.

Even more climbers adapted to the new technique half-heartedly, testing the water, if not the ice, with cold feet, loath to buy two expensive tools when one old axe would suffice. This led to hilarious episodes with climbers trying to lead pitches with a combination of styles, which inevitably meant cutting steps. Within three years however the conversion would be complete for all but a very few. It took a considerable leap in faith to move up a steep snow or ice face without cutting holds, but once the change was made, there was no going back.

The advantages of front pointing were numerous; climbing was faster, steep snow and ice much less strenuous. The potential this new technique opened up for new advances in winter climbing was about to explode.

The 1970s opened with a conventional III in February by Norrie Muir and G.Whitten, Garadh Buttress. Possibly climbed before, this leads up the easy rocks right of Garadh Gully. March 1971 saw a new VI,5 on the Orion Face, when Kenny Spence, Allen Fyffe and Hamish MacInnes followed a line approximating to the Clough Very Severe, Astronomy. The route was sustained at a reasonable level, linking a series of snow patches by iced grooves and corners. True to MacInnes's character, the ascent was unconventional, the second and third men using jumars. Despite that time-saving technique, a late start enforced a bivouac on the North-East Buttress in bad weather, following a 10-hour ascent of the route. Soon after their March ascent, the winter fizzled out in a series of thaws.

By April 1970, the summer lines on Càrn Dearg Buttress appeared for the most part to have been either climbed or tidied up. There remained one obvious feature between Torro and The Bullroar, known as the Weep. This was a dark, wet patch which originated from the green garden on Route II, oozing water and slime down over the slabs and overlaps below, finally drying up on The Bullroar slab traverse.

Con Higgins and Rab Carrington attempted it in 1967, but were beaten by a wet slab on the second pitch. In April 1970 the Weep was dry from the winter frosts, waiting for the summer rain to begin its dribblings on the slabs below. Carrington had returned with Ian Nicolson that year to try the line again. Cowslip – for the proposed new route had already been named – began just left of Torro, following a faint groove running up leftwards to a stance below overhangs. Carrington led up the second pitch, making a hard move to gain the slab above. He found himself committed, in a poorly-protected situation.

Even more climbers adapted to the new technique half-heartedly, testing the water, if not the ice, with cold feet, loath to buy two expensive tools when one old axe would suffice. This led to hilarious episodes with climbers trying to lead pitches with a combination of styles, which inevitably meant cutting steps

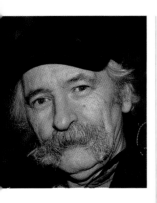

One of the 'characters' in Scottish climbing, Norrie Muir's contributions to Nevis climbing include first ascents of Left Hand Route and Strident Edge. He also opened up Central Trident Buttress rock with Heidbanger (2007)

Photo: Cubby Images

Excess energies were on occasions diverted to new and exciting ways of entering the CIC Hut without the usual paperwork – events which unsurprisingly were to lead to confrontations with the Custodian. More useful energies led to one of the best finds of the decade

With an ingenuity born through fear, I managed to wangle in a couple of tatty 5mm runners. In front of me lay the black, overhanging corner I was hoping to climb. Padding up the slab a bit, I got a mucky finger-hold in the depths of the corner. This allowed me to get my feet right up to the roof. The position was precarious: the fingers of my left hand, jammed in the corner, were holding my arching body to the rock, while my right hand was groping for a hold on the lip. One last push and my fingers curled round an edge; luckily it was good, because my feet came off almost at once, leaving me flailing in space, hanging on by my fingers. A quick heave and I landed on the ledge like some floundering porpoise.[2]

The key to the route had been found and Carrington and Nicolson soon found themselves under the final overhangs of the great buttress. Here, seemingly impossible rock forced them to traverse first right, overlooking the final pitches of Torro. Unhappy, they eventually traversed hard left under the rock to finish up the Clough/Farquhar route P.M. Cowslip is given a grade of E2 in the current guide, making it the hardest route on the buttress through the 1970s. It may be unrepeated.

June 1970 introduced the Glasgow based 'Steam Team' to Nevis. This healthily unconventional association had begun routinely enough, for some of them were members of the JMCS. Soon tiring of what was to them even that Club's polite restraints, independence was chosen by Stevie Docherty, Bobby Gorman, Norrie Muir and others. Excess energies were on occasions diverted to new and exciting ways of entering the CIC Hut without the usual paperwork – events which unsurprisingly were to lead to confrontations with the Custodian. More useful energies led to one of the best finds of the decade on Nevis, with the first routes to be recorded on the steep central wall on the front face of Central Trident Buttress.

That June of 1970 Norrie Muir and Ian Nicolson began a burst of hard climbing on Nevis. On the Saturday of their long weekend on Nevis they made the second ascent, and first free ascent, of King Kong. Sunday was reserved for the second ascent of Central Route and a free ascent, possibly the third, of Sassenach. Muir thought Sassenach was *'desperate and harder than King Kong'*.[3] On the Monday the new wall was officially breached with an ascent of Heidbanger. At E1, this excellent route climbs the centre of the crag, starting just left of a prominent crack. Muir returned seven years later with Arthur Paul to climb the true start by the prominent crack – Cranium, also E1.

The 90m or more of the new crag on the Central Trident Buttress highlighted the amazing neglect suffered by Ben Nevis in summer. The wall is steep – very steep, drops of water on a wet day falling 60m free from the top overhang – while the rock is excellent. In August 1971 Stevie Docherty returned here with Davy Gardner, to record Metamorphosis, the best line on the crag at E2. To complete summer ascents in 1970, Robin Campbell and Fred Harper recorded Gutless, Severe, on the Douglas Boulder, climbing the dirty chimney left of Cutlass.

The Nevis winter season of 1971 opened on January 3 with Davy Gardner and Ian Fulton making a logical variation finish to Ian Clough's Comb Gully Buttress. The two climbers were cutting steps, not yet being converted to front-pointing, so the crux pitch consumed several hours of hard climbing on ice. The original finish, as climbed by Clough, takes

in a rightward-curving chimney on the steep, final rocks. This is not a line which holds snow or ice well, however, and is now not often followed, climbers taking the Fulton-Gardner variation. The buttress is an enjoyable IV,4. Clough had climbed the (easier) upper half of the chimney. The complete ascent of the chimney is a difficult mixed climb at VI,6 and is called Clough's Chimney in memory of Clough.

Marshall and Campbell were back on Nevis again in February 1971, climbing a line of discontinuous chimneys on the right flank of the South Trident Buttress to record Joyful Chimneys (IV,4). Later that winter Docherty and Muir were again active. They made two attempts on the Orion Face that winter, one of them being abandoned half a pitch short of the Basin due to a sudden thaw. The two Glaswegians were using bent-down axes at this time. (Bent-down as in, give your axe to a metal-worker and have it heated and the pick given a steeper angle.) On the other attempt to repeat the Orion Direct, in March, they climbed a direct start into the Basin via steep grooves just left of Slav Route. These direct pitches are now the start of Orion Directissima, VI,5 climbed in 1994.

Another climber using home-made or *converted* equipment during the 1971 winter was Mike Geddes. Then a student at Cambridge he would make the long trip to Nevis, hitching up to Edinburgh on Friday to connect with a pre-arranged lift to Fort William. On the Sunday afternoon, using the extra time provided by the new technique, Geddes and his companion would wearily begin the tedious return to Cambridge.

On March 15 Geddes and John Higham climbed Aphrodite (IV,4). This 200m line climbed the steep mixed face between Green Gully and No. 3 Gully Buttress, beginning about the centre of the buttress and moving up and left to finish up grooves overlooking Green Gully. Three days later Geddes and Harold Gillespie, the latter in the JMCS, recorded a route right of Glover's Chimney. The White Line, a 300m III, may in part have taken

*Ian Sutherland on the
second winter ascent
of Hadrian's Direct
(V,5), March 10,
1973. Photo taken
from Point Five Gully*

Photo: Ken Crocket

the line taken by Goodeve's party, during their epic 29-hour ascent of
Tower Ridge, in 1907. (See Chapter 4 for a full account of this story).

Geddes' major contribution in 1971 came in March with the second
ascent of Smith's Route on Gardyloo Buttress and the third ascent of
Observatory Buttress, both with the Edinburgh climber, Nigel Rayner.
Their ascent of Gardyloo Buttress in four and a half hours came 11 years
after the Smith-Marshall first ascent, and sounded the beginning of the
end for step cutting.

Also climbed by Geddes was Point Five Gully. Geddes led three others
up the initial, difficult pitches, the three prusiking behind, before the
climbers continued as two ropes; Geddes and Higham first, followed by
Gillespie and Alan Rouse, the latter then a young novice. Point Five Gully
had its next front-pointed ascent in April by John Cunningham and
Bill March, whose impressive ascent of two and a half hours oddly made
note of climbing time only, belaying and so on not being included. Their
true overall time for the ascent was closer to six hours. Also in April
came the third ascent of Smith's Route, on this occasion Kenny Spence
leading a climbing course party in superb snow conditions.

The first major new route to be climbed on Ben Nevis using front-
pointing was the April ascent of Hadrian's Wall Direct by Geddes and
Graham Little. This was their third or fourth attempt on the line, each
day the two climbers starting to climb a little earlier as the daily temperature slowly rose. Little, who had just begun climbing, followed Geddes

up the hard pitches by prusiking. Hadrian's Wall Direct, originally graded at IV, begins up two very steep ice walls to enter the chimney taken by the original line. Its present grading at V,5 is probably more appropriate, given the length and nature of the climbing. It remains a firm favourite, often in condition and always exciting.

The second front-pointed ascent of Hadrian's Direct was probably that of Ian 'Sudsy' Sutherland and Ian 'Spike' Sykes, on March 10, 1973. As an interesting point, the original recording of Hadrian's Wall Direct, in the CIC Log Book, has Grade V. This has been altered to IV in a different ink, suggesting that the first ascent team were themselves unsure of the grade. (Or, just as likely, that someone else disagreed with the grade, without having actually climbed the route.)

The winter of 1971 gave way to summer and the finding of another new crag on the north face of Nevis. The North Wall of Castle Ridge is the first piece of rock seen by a climber walking round by the Lochan Meall an t-Suidhe approach. The foot of the very steep upper wall is best gained by traversing round Castle Ridge from the bay below The Castle. The first route here was found by Dave Bathgate and G.Anderson, on July 10. Plastic Max, a 150m Scottish Very Severe route, was followed in September 12 by another route, climbed by Norrie Muir and R.Schipper. Night Tripper, a 185m Scottish Very Severe, lies fairly close to Plastic Max, but as neither route have in all probability received second ascents their grades and precise locations remain in some doubt.

With ascents of a Severe on the Douglas Boulder by Klaus Schwartz, an instructor at the nearby Loch Eil Outdoor Centre, Metamorphosis by Docherty and Gardner on the Central Trident Buttress, and a Hard Very Severe, Arthur, by Schwartz and G.Webster on Number Three Gully Buttress, the summer ascents of 1971 were over – with one notable exception. In September Norrie Muir made the first solo ascent of Centurion. Muir had arrived at the foot of the buttress, intending to solo the route, when he met a pair of local climbers.

Now Muir, like many other climbers, does not like the first pitch of Centurion, the 15m deceptive wall leading to the start of the corner. He led this pitch roped, then handing over his equipment to the two climbers, soloed the remaining seven pitches of the Hard Very Severe. On arriving safely back at the foot of the buttress Muir, to satisfy his ethics and complete the route, soloed the first pitch. He then abseiled back down, the route complete. Earlier that year, in July, he had soloed Astronomy. Muir was to be one of the most active of climbers on Nevis though after marriage in 1973 he stopped climbing for several years.

January 1972 saw the Steam Team in operation again, with first winter ascents of Wagroochimsla (IV,5), by Docherty and Adam, and Left Hand Route (VI,6), by Docherty and Muir. The latter route included a tension traverse and considerable excitement on the slab pitch. Muir was leading this with a bent-down Stubai hammer and an axe. When one of his crampons fell off he was forced to cut steps to finish the pitch. The fun didn't end there, Docherty next dropping Muir's axe. Somehow the two Glaswegians managed to complete the 275m route, but due to powder snow a late finish made the logical continuation up or down North-East Buttress impossible. The two climbers then abseiled down Right Hand Route, Muir going first with the only head torch. This led to a

Mike Geddes, (Glenbeg Bothy 1985). Geddes was the first to climb a major new route on Ben Nevis using front pointing techniques

Photo: Des Rubens

*Sheila Van Lieshout
on Strident Edge (VS),
South Trident Buttress*

Photo: Gary Latter

*Rab Carrington, one
of the 'Dumbarton
Rock Boys' and
latterly an outdoor
equipment manufac-
turer, made an early
Grade VI ascent with
Kellett's Right Hand
Route*

Photo: Cubby Images

surprise for Docherty on one abseil, where Muir had come to the end
of the rope and had continued down-climbing solo for a further 9m.

In February, the triumvirate of Campbell, Carrington and Marshall
made the first winter ascent of Newbigging's Route, Far Right Variation,
a 230m IV,4. This is the natural winter line up this part of the buttress,
taking in thinly iced corners and slabby grooves. (Carrington is said to
have been so impressed by Marshall's single axe technique on this route
that he seriously considered reverting to that method). Carrington

and Marshall also teamed up that February for an ascent of Left Hand Chimney, IV,4 on the Douglas Boulder. Rab Carrington made a series of impressive ascents in the Alps, Patagonia, the Andes and the Himalayas, and later built up a successful business based on goose down; sleeping bags and duvets, with *Rab* as a trade name.

The major winter ascent during February 1972 however was the long-awaited second ascent of the Orion Face Direct V,5 – first climbed by Smith and Marshall 12 years earlier. This was made by front-pointing techniques, the climbers being Mike Geddes and Alan Rouse. Both were continuing to travel from Cambridge, making their long-distance and highly profitable trips three or four times a winter. Both climbers were also continuing to use home-made ice tools, though Rouse by now had bought a Terrordactyl. This latter was the ice tool designed by the practical MacInnes, and originally named after its supposed silhouetted resemblance to the prehistoric flying reptile the Pterodactyl. (Inevitably the ghastly name came about for marketing purposes.)

Unfortunately for Rouse, his *Terror* was one of a batch manufactured in the early years, some of which bent during use. Rouse, wearing glasses, had a hard time seconding the slab traverse, his vision obscured by snowed-up spectacles and his efficiency, unknown to him at the time, impaired by a next-to-useless Terrordactyl pick. Geddes and Rouse made the second ascent of Orion Direct harder for themselves by carrying sacks with all their weekend equipment. Finishing the route at about 9pm, they then had to head back down to Cambridge trusting to rule of thumb – hitching lifts on the road. Cambridge was not reached until late the next day. Climbers don't come much keener than that!

Kellett's Right Hand Route received its winter ascent in March, by Carrington and Rouse, at VI,6. This sustained route added to the growing concentration of long, hard winter lines on the Minus and Orion Faces. A Grade II on the North Wall of Castle Ridge and a IV immediately right of Slingsby's Chimney completed winter ascents for 1972, the last season in which winter routes of any note climbed by step cutting would be recorded.

August, 1972 marked the beginning of summer climbing on Ben Nevis, at least as regards new rock, with a variation to Minus One Direct by Crocket and Fulton (see Chapter 8). The first complete new route to be climbed however was a line on the South Trident Buttress, by the now ubiquitous Norrie Muir and D.Regan. Submitted with the suggested name of Pink Dream Maker, the Very Severe line was climbed later the same summer by Jimmy Marshall and Robin Campbell, who encountered some loose rock. Campbell now thinks that Muir's ascent went where stated, and that Muir was not, in fact, *'suffering from hallucinations'.*[4] (Campbell and Marshall had not found any obvious signs of a previous ascent). The route was named Strident Edge by Marshall and Campbell.

Other good routes from the summer of 1972 included Sioux Wall on No.3 Gully Buttress, climbed by Ian Nicolson and George Grassam. As with other excellent climbs on high crags, this Hard Very Severe route suffers an unjustified neglect. By visual inspection it would seem to provide a superb face climb, taking a rising line up the buttress right of Marshall's Knuckleduster – itself a neglected route of great appeal. Nicolson's naming of the route, after his wife Sue, was a witty attempt

A Terrordactyl axe and a Stubai ashen-shafted wooden axe. 'Terrors' came with an orange, plaited polypropylene sling which climbers quickly replaced with their own; the wooden axe here, used by Ken Crocket, weighs some 900g and is 54cm long (this after two reductions in length). The Terrordactyl, which had an aluminium alloy shaft and a steel head, weighs 760g and is 39cm in length. Electrician's tape made the shaft warmer and easier to handle. Following Marshall's example, Crocket never climbed with a sling on the Stubai, a practice best described as foolhardy. Amusingly, with current techniques, many climbers now practice leashless climbing!

to circumvent the New Routes policy of the SMC, eponymous route names being frowned upon.

The autumn of 1972 was the best for many years, with the Scottish Highlands a blaze of golden colours. The September 4 ascent of Nicolson's Sioux Wall was the first of several routes climbed in September and October. Campbell recorded two routes on the Central Trident Buttress with the delightful names of Gutbuster, Very Severe, and Nosepicker, Severe. These two routes climbed the diamond-shaped buttress between Central Gully and Jubilee Climb.

Finally came four routes from Paul Nunn. On September 30, Nunn and M.Curdy climbed Dissection, Very Severe, taking a direct but admittedly contrived line starting between The Shadow and Route II, Direct Start. On a return visit in October, Nunn and Paul 'Tut' Braithwaite recorded three short Very Severe routes on the steep upper wall of Number Five Gully Buttress. In reality, their grades were higher than Very Severe but until 1977 the SMC Journal, wherein are published new climbs done in Scotland, did not sub-divide the climbs of Very Severe standard and above. Guidebooks included graded lists, so that climbers could glean at least an indication of how hard a route was by its position on the list! In fact, the routes by Nunn and Braithwaite are Hard Very Severe (two routes) and E1.

Colin Stead in February 1972, just before taking up front pointing; wooden shafted axe, waist belt, leather boots, canvas gaiters

Photo: Ken Crocket

The superb autumn of 1972 was offset by the disappointing winter and summer of 1973. One route only was recorded for that entire year. Boomer's Requiem (V,5) by Con Higgins and Dougie McArthur. This followed a prominent icefall left of Raeburn's Buttress. In March Geddes and Rouse climbed Minus Two Gully (V,5), on what was probably the second ascent, 14 years after Marshall had led the youthful Haston and Stenhouse up the gully.

The advantages of the new winter techniques were again highlighted during that otherwise poor season of 1973, when Ian Nicolson soloed Point Five and Zero Gullies in one morning. Nicolson was climbing six days a week at this time on the Glen Coe winter courses set up by Clough and was at the peak of fitness. His partner for the day was Dave Knowles, an English émigré also living in Glen Coe. Knowles, an excitable, energetic climber, was killed several years later on the Eiger, assisting in the production of the film *The Eiger Sanction*.

Nicolson disclosed nothing of his plans that day to Knowles, as they quickly trotted up the Allt a' Mhuilinn path. On arriving at the foot of Zero Gully Knowles was quietly informed that he could come along on the route, but that Nicolson intended to solo it. Both climbers set up into the thick swirling mist, Nicolson in front using his Terrordactyls. Every so often he would stop and wait for his friend, giving confidence on the steep parts. This held him up slightly, but even so Nicolson emerged at the top of Zero one hour after entering the gully, with Knowles ten minutes behind. Descending Tower Gully, Nicolson traversed over to the foot of Point Five. Knowles declined to solo this however, teaming up with a third climber instead. Nicolson finished Point Five Gully in 50 minutes, arriving back in a Fort William pub just after 1pm, in time to polish off a well-earned pint of beer.

Most winter climbers actively engaged on Nevis had now converted to front pointing. As there was at this time very little choice in the way of ice tools, climbers decided on either the curved Chouinard gear or the straight inclined Terrordactyls, though as described earlier a few in the first wave of the new technology adapted or had made for them their own weapons. All systems worked to a degree, assuming a climber had confidence in his particular choice. The MacInnes designed Terrordactyls probably had a slight advantage in mixed conditions, though many agreed that they were not quite as good on ice.

Those climbers who started winter climbing after the equipment revolution knew no other way of course, for no one was going to revert deliberately to step cutting. To paraphrase an earlier writer, those lucky climbers who had begun in the step cutting age and then changed would always feel that they had been members of a privileged class, that they had tasted of a fabulous, yet dangerous liqueur, the recipe for which was long forgotten. Most converted climbers also felt a sense of relief at the passing of step cutting, but it was relief coloured with a little sadness.

> Strength and endurance were major factors in the years before the early seventies, when climbing ice meant hanging on with one Dachsteined hand while chopping holds in stubborn ice with the other, all with a usually ill-balanced, cut-down axe, twice as heavy as some modern tools. A good step-cutter had to be ambidextrous, to permit cutting on either side and to allow the alternate arm to recover its strength. But if the effort was high, the rewards were higher still. Each pitch was a route in itself; to be worked out and worked on. The climber on a hard route was constantly aware of the fine line between satisfied fatigue and dangerous exhaustion.[5]

Ken Crocket on Ben Nevis, 1975. Oiled cotton jacket, 'Compton Special Helmet' complete with chinstrap

Photo: Ken Crocket Collection

February 23, 1974 marked the end of an era, when the last major gully on Nevis finally received its winter ascent. Minus One Gully was climbed that day by Ken Crocket and Colin Stead to give an enjoyable VI,6 outing. The problem had lain, not so much in the actual climbing, though it is recognised as the hardest winter gully on Nevis, but in finding the key section in climbable conditions. This was the overhanging cave pitch low down the gully which had stopped all parties attempting the route to date, including an attempt by Rouse and Carrington in April, 1972. Indeed, according to a local climber, there had been over twenty attempts on the route.

Crocket and Stead soloed the first easy pitch of Minus One Gully then roped up for the cave pitch, Stead tackling the icy corner. Both climbers describe the ascent, Crocket beginning with Stead's attempts on the overhang.

> He was making no progress with the overhang and to my impatient eye seemed to be tiring. A loose suggestion to use a screw ended in technical failure as he made a soft landing on the snow-cone. Finally, caught between my impatience and the improbable left wall, he announced a tension traverse. I was impressed when he admitted it was his first ... Fascinated, I watched an apparent revolt against gravity as he teetered across from snow lump to snow lump, outlined starkly against a lowering grey sky. The climbing was obviously impossible – yet he was succeeding.[6]

Crocket managed to second this section by climbing the overhanging ice boss directly, then led through on the next pitch, a steep ice wall above an overhang.

The crux of Minus One Gully (VI,6) on the FWA. Stead fixes a tubular ice-screw runner. Eventually a series of tension moves left across the ice wall opened up the route. Crocket would climb the overhanging ice bulge in the corner direct

Photo: Ken Crocket

I traversed left under a bulge in the open gully – it was now more of a scoop – and found a steep wall of hard snow. I still had an adrenalin high from following the overhang and clumsily smashed a fingernail on a protruding lump of ice.

[A hazard commonly experienced by terrordactyl users, these axes having a limited clearance between shaft and slope due to steeply inclined picks.]

When I came to follow, wrote Stead, I found an impressively steep ice wall, which was pointed up from one resting place to another, with blood-drained arms and bruised knuckles, removing his one protection screw on the way. It was a good pitch.[7]

Both climbers were SMC members, climbing during a period which marked the beginning of a rise in that club's activities. Minus One Gully had been one of the few major ice lines unclimbed by Marshall and his contemporaries, due to its rarely being in amenable condition. With its companion routes Minus Two Gully and the Orion Direct, it completed a great trilogy of major classic winter routes, Alpine in magnitude, Scottish in nature. With hindsight, it may also have marked a cusp in winter climbing development, as increasingly, climbers began to move from pure ice routes onto harder and thinner buttresses and walls.

March 1974 brought better settled weather to Nevis and five more new lines were climbed by various parties. The Creagh Dhu were responsible for two lines, Brian Dunn and Con Higgins finding a IV,5 on March 3, with East Face, a prominent groove line starting below and right of Zero Gully and leading up the entire length of the East Face of Observatory Ridge.

Two days later, Dunn and Higgins were joined by Dougie McArthur for an ascent of Minus Two Buttress (V,5). This 275m route starts 18m left of Minus Two Gully and climbs sustained ground on the right side of the buttress to gain the crest of North East Buttress. The team managed to speed up their descent in the late afternoon by making an abseil which led to a traverse onto North-East Buttress, descending by that. McArthur and Higgins were all for naming the route Dixie Whistler, but this vetoed by Dunn so they settled for Minus Two Buttress. Some amusement was provided by the sight of Dunn wearing his balaclava over his helmet, as it would not fit inside.

On March 9 it was the turn of the SMC again, with Doug Lang and Neil Quinn making an ascent of Left Edge Route on Observatory Buttress. This 360m V,5 climb followed a Bell Severe, 120m to the Terrace running across the Buttress with another 240m leading to the plateau. The three long pitches leading to the mid-way terrace took some five and a half hours of sustained climbing by the Dundonians, a measure perhaps of its difficulty.

Quinn and Lang were one of the most consistent ropes climbing during the 1960s and 1970s. Quinn was unusual in that he did virtually no summer climbing, other than the occasional easy route – and that was sometimes done in order to make a reconnaissance for a possible attempt in winter. With several other local climbers, they were active in areas across the breadth of Scotland: Creag Meagaidh, the Cairngorms, Ben Nevis. Quinn and Lang were one of the last of the active ropes to convert to front-pointing but their abilities on snow and ice continued strongly after the technical revolution.

As a pair, the two Dundonians are physically disparate – the ectomorph and the endomorph, Laurel and Hardy, with the broad-beaming Quinn offset by the greyhound figure of Lang. Their inevitably late arrival at the CIC Hut on a Friday evening would be the signal for general hilarity, as Lang produced a great cabbage head and half a turnip for the next evening's dinner. (According to Lang, the food arrangements were usually engineered so that the actual carrying of the food fell to him.)

Quinn virtually stopped climbing in the early 1980s, taking to marathon running instead, but before then the pair made some exciting ascents, including their attempted second ascent in February 1973 of Hadrian's Wall Direct. Quinn described their epic 17 and a half hour ascent in a later Journal article. It was almost certainly the only one to have been made by cutting. (Though Crocket and Stead climbed a more

Doug Lang shakily brandishes a slightly bent Salewa drive-in screw which held him after a fall on Comb Gully Buttress. Wittily, the other screw is pointing downhill! March 1976

Photo: Ken Crocket

Brian Dunn contemplates a strategic withdrawal on Slav Route (VI,5), half a pitch from the finish

Photo: Con Higgins

Neil Quinn at the CIC Hut (March 1974). Quinn was the regular climbing partner of Doug Lang, but unusually rarely climbed in summer. An unfailingly cheerful character, he later moved onto marathon running

Photo: Ken Crocket

direct version of the original line by step cutting.) Lang led the first pitch, cutting its 45m in three hours. Quinn took over and set off up the next pitch, normally the crux in winter, with a section of near vertical ice.

> I cut holds up this final section in several sorties and at last make a move up the wall but reaching the top holds I can't let go to cut any more, not even to plant a screw or a Chouinard hammer. So down again and I put a screw just below on the right for tension. This results in dinner-plating of the right hand holds. Oh well, try the left and once again the hand holds are very effectively removed. I go back down the wall to the halfway stance to think ...

Quinn eventually succeeded in overcoming the ice bulge, but by the time both climbers were at the foot of the chimney, darkness had descended, an ever-present threat hanging over a lengthy step-cutting expedition. They continued up the chimney and ran out several rope lengths above, slowly being forced rightwards. Lang belayed below a bare wall, not far from the plateau.

> There's a bare holdless ten-foot corner on the right and an open groove leading to an overhang on the left with a practically bare wall between. Very interesting, but at midnight shattering. Lang smugly gives advice from the security of his phoney belay above. He suggests hauling the sack [the Dundonians habitually climbed with one rucksack] but we've wasted enough time so I try it with it on.[8]

Quinn managed to struggle up the wall Lang had just led and continued past the belay after leaving the rucksack again. Nine metres further on he reached an impasse with bare holdless rock. Frustratingly he could see the summit slope 6m to the right. Lang had a go at the pitch but could make no further progress, so the two climbers decided to try and sleep on the miserable belay ledge. After a short period of this, during which Quinn was frequently awakened by snow kicked down by a restless Lang, they made a move at retreat, almost immediately finding a good belay for the abseil rope. One abseil, a down-climbed pitch and a traverse left and a snow gully was gained allowing the tired climbers to struggle up to the summit. The entry in the log book for their ascent was headed *A Comedy of Errors...*

More straightforward was the Quinn and Lang ascent of Slav Route VI,5 on March 23. Theirs was the first complete ascent of this sustained route, but only just, as earlier that winter Con Higgins, Brian Dunn and Dougie McArthur had climbed all but the last 24m of the route before circumstances forced them to traverse right into the easy finish of Zero Gully. Dunn was on the last stretch but had run into poor conditions of time-consuming powder snow. McArthur was in considerable pain from sinusitis. As Con Higgins commented later –

> '...the decision was easy – we traversed into Zero above point photographed. The figure on the plateau is Dave Knowles conducting, without shouting, a conversation with me whilst Brian climbed.'[9]

For that reason Higgins decided not to record the ascent. This unselfish decision is an indication of the high ethical standards which have invariably accompanied Scottish winter mountaineering, one or two obvious exceptions notwithstanding.

From this point on, the pace of winter climbing in particular increased, with areas of Nevis opened up by front pointing unlikely to have been possible by step cutting. One such area was Indicator Wall, whose development well illustrates the jerky, irregular pace at which trends in winter mountaineering tend to advance – a result, perhaps, of the climbing conditions, equipment and individual endeavour.

Winter routes on Indicator Wall began in February 1975 with a fine ascent of the Indicator Wall ice fall by Gordon Smith and Terry King at V,4. An interval of three years then occurred, until a good spell of hard ice in January and February of 1978 saw no less than four routes. Mike Geddes and Con Higgins opened the salvo with Albatross (VI,5) on January 21, a 140m line which starts up the left corner of the central slab before breaking out left to finish up the steep grooves and chimneys on the upper wall.

The following day, Norrie Muir and Arthur Paul started at the toe of the buttress opposite the left edge of Gardyloo Buttress, climbing up

Doug Lang on pitch one, during the first winter ascent of Slav Route (VI,5) on March 23, 1974. Photo taken from Zero Gully

Photo: Ken Crocket

A busy day on Indicator Wall. From left to right, parties are on Stormy Petrel (VII,6), Rhyme of the Ancient Mariner (VII,7) and Psychedelic Wall (VI,5)

Photo: Henning Whackerage

*Ken Crocket on a
later ascent of
Harrison's Climb
Direct (IV,4). The
original line traverses
left from here*

Photo: Crocket Collection

directly to give a winter ascent of Psychedelic Wall (VI,5). Mike Geddes returned on February 11 with Alan Rouse, and after following Gardy-loo Gully for 30m or so broke out left to produce a Shot in the Dark (V,5). Finally, to complete the 1978 quartet of routes, a week later on February 18 Davy Gardner and Arthur Paul climbed a line just right of Psychedelic Wall to give Caledonia (V,5). This goes up to share the same first stance with Shot in the Dark before crossing that route and heading up and right.

Then followed a period of uncertainty, as few climbers were completely aware of either the quality of climbing on this face, or indeed of what went where. Another four years passed, until in 1982 Dave Cuthbertson and Rudi Kane broke on to the central slab, moved right under a series of undercut grooves before finally breaking out higher up on the face to record Stormy Petrel (VII,6). That confusion still existed was shown by the recording in March 1983 of a line left of Stormy Petrel. In fact this gave a fine Direct Start to Albatross, taking in a natural gully line perhaps more often in condition that the original start. Other winter ascents in March of 1975 were that of the short North West Face (V,5) on the right flank of Observatory Buttress, by Fred Craddock and Colin Stead, and the fine icy line of Two Step Corner (V,5) on Number Three Gully Buttress by D.Kirtley and D.Montgomery.

Perhaps the most interesting ascents of the 1976 winter season (there were no summer routes made until 1978) were the February 7 ascent of Harrison's Climb Direct (IV,4) by Ken Crocket and Chris Gilmore, and Astral Highway (VI,5) by Con Higgins and Alan Kimber on December 28. Harrison's Climb Direct was virtually a new route, the only pitch which had been climbed before being the ice pitch up the left flanking chimney of Cousins' Buttress. This had been climbed in 1962 by Slesser and Tennent (see Chapter 11 for Tennent's description of their ascent).

Harrison's Climb Direct took in the summer variation start which gave a superb steep ice pitch in the excellent conditions found. After climbing the chimney pitch, again heavily iced, the route took to the rocks of the Ordinary Route on Cousins' Buttress. This lies to the right of the ice wall which extends leftwards, and is started by a hidden chimney. Perhaps because some parties may have missed out the buttress section, passing the hidden chimney, the reputation of the route took some time to be established. It's now a three-star route. This section of mixed climbing maintained the interest of the route, one of the most enjoyable ascents Crocket and Gilmore made on Nevis. As with many of the best days on a mountain, its find was serendipitous, the two climbers having wandered round the foot of the buttress to *see what they could find*.

Astral Highway is a route of a very different nature, climbing the huge Orion Face. Following the Orion Direct as far as the top of the Basin,

Con Higgins. Living in Fort William for a spell, Higgins was able to make several significant ascents, including Astral Highway

Photo: Jimmy Marshall

Astral Highway (VI,6)

Photo: Viv Scott

Dave MacLeod starting the crux pitch of Titan's Wall (E3), freed by Mick Fowler and Phil Thomas in 1977

Photo: Cubby Images

[The first free ascent of Titan's Wall] brought to Nevis the new age of rock, the message learned by a new breed of climbers who treated this sport as any other serious sportsperson and trained hard for self-improvement

it then takes a groove system between Epsilon Chimney on the left and the Second Slab Rib on the right. This was an early ascent of the face for the season, made on December 28 by Higgins and Kimber.

Norrie Muir resumed his suspended climbing career in the summer of 1976. His contributions to climbing on Nevis was soon to show with four winter routes in 1977. Con Higgins was now living in Fort William, working as a maintenance fitter at the Pulp and Paper Mill. In moving to the *Fort* he was joining an increasing number of climbers stationed there, all apparently immune to the high rainfall. With Kimber, then an instructor at the Centre, Higgins climbed Lobby Dancer (VI,6), in February, approximating to the summer line of Night Tripper on the North Wall of Castle Ridge. Lobby Dancer takes the grooves right of the overhanging wall on that route.

Late in March 1977, Muir and Paul were defeated on an attempt at climbing Minus One Buttress, gaining a height of only 6m. They were back the following weekend and, like Crocket and Stead on Minus One

Gully three years earlier, they experienced conditions of excellent snow ice allowing an exciting if secure ascent of the buttress. The same pair were back on April 14, making an ascent of Rubicon Wall (V,5). Somewhat surprisingly, this seems to have been the first winter ascent of the 1933 Hargreaves route.

Though no summer lines were recorded in 1977, the first waves of the revolution taking place in rock climbing lapped at the rocks of Ben Nevis, when in June Mick Fowler and Phil Thomas made the first free ascent of Titan's Wall on Càrn Dearg Buttress. This had been an old aid route of Clough and MacInnes, first pegged in 1959. There had been attempts at free-climbing the great cracked wall, including one by Carrington, but these had petered out in the face of its great challenge. Initially graded E4, its ascent brought to Nevis the new age of rock, the message learned by a new breed of climbers who treated this sport as any other serious sportsperson and trained hard for self-improvement.

Four days later, Dave Cuthbertson and Murray Hamilton made the second free ascent, finishing by a slightly different, awkward 9m crack. Titan's Wall is currently thought to be towards the top of the E3 category and climbed free rates as one of the harder classics on Ben Nevis, nothing surprising to any innocent who has wandered under the magnificent expanse of Càrn Dearg Buttress and looked up in awe.

1977 came to an end with four winter routes, two by Muir and Paul on the face left of Hadrian's Wall. Abacus (IV,4) and Antonine Wall (V,5) both climb icy grooves to gain the crest of Observatory Ridge. Carrington and Nicolson climbed Gargoyle Wall in December, traversing in from Thompson's Route. With a later, complete ascent in 1998, this is a technically hard and demanding route, and is now graded at VI,6. Finally, an elegant line was recorded on December 29 by Mike Geddes and Brian Hall. Geddes was then living in Fort William, having moved there in 1977. Sickle (V,5), the line climbed by Geddes and Hall, lies up the slabby wall right of Hadrian's Wall Direct, climbing an attractive, steep, iced corner just parallel to Hadrian's Wall.

The winter season of 1978, as mentioned earlier, saw the development of Indicator Wall as a new winter face. That February a harbinger of the technically difficult and very serious routes that would appear with increasing frequency arrived with the ascent of The Great Glen by Paul Braithwaite and Paul Moores. This short but hard route at Grade VI,5 followed the shallow groove right of Smith's Route, Gardyloo Buttress. It is a serious route but one which is seldom in condition. On the same day, February 12, one of the best contributions by Geddes (from a long list of superlative ascents) was made with the ascent of Route II (VI,6) on Càrn Dearg Buttress, climbed with Rouse. It is one of the finest mixed routes on the mountain.

The hard winter men had been eyeing Càrn Dearg Buttress for years, waiting for conditions which never seemed to come. The great summer classics like Centurion and Sassenach never seemed to hold sufficient snow and ice to be more than uncomfortable rock climbs, and the best opportunity for a winter climb, it was felt, would have to wait for the vast central slabs to ice up. Route II had received its first ascent in June 1943, by Kellett and Arnott Russell, the latter a student plucked out of the CIC Hut for a second man. A little known winter attempt was that

Paul 'Tut' Braithwaite climbed The Great Glen in 1978 and the following year, The Shadow (VII,6) on Càrn Dearg Buttress

Photo: Cubby Images

Graeme Ettle on The Great Glen, a serious Grade VI just right of Smith's Route on Gardyloo Buttress

Photo: Pete MacPherson

Alan Rouse. His meteoric rise in mountaineering came to a tragic end on K2, succumbing to bad conditions after making the first British ascent

Photo: Leo Dickinson

Competition was raising its ugly head at this time, with so many good and active climbers living in and around Fort William

made in the early 1960s by Haston and Wightman. This ended when Wightman took a leader fall of over 30m on to a poor belay. The CIC Hut Logbook for January 21, 1961 reads:

> Attempting new stuff on Carn Dearg Buttress. Got gripped & came down after 200 ft. A. Wightman & D. Haston.

In fact, Wightman and Haston attempted Route II by the Direct Start. There is, however, a puzzle about this attempt. In the Cruickshank biography of Smith, there is an account by Robin Shaw of a chance meeting on January 22, when he came across Haston and Smith attempting Route II.[10] There is no mention of the Wightman-Haston attempt, which according to the Hut Logbook took place the day before. But then, just as with other activities, climbers dislike describing failures.

When Geddes and Rouse left the CIC Hut that February morning in 1978 the sky was clear and their intended line across the slabs of the buttress unusually white. From the bottom of the large smear of ice known as The Curtain the two climbers traversed easily right to reach the chimney of Route I. Rouse led the first pitch up the chimney then Geddes climbed through to launch himself on what proved to be the crucial traverse. Rouse described this section.

> It was obviously going to be a hard pitch. The snow would not support our weight unless, by chance, crampons bit on a rugosity beneath while sloping handholds allowed only leaning moves to clear the next few feet. It was time-consuming and strenuous on the calves. Standing on sloping footholds in crampons needs precision...[11]

Route II is a serious climb, as every move takes a climber further out across the buttress face and further away from an easy retreat in the face of difficulties. In one of these twists of fate the route received a second ascent a few days later, by Gordon Smith and Ian Sykes. This ascent began by the Direct Start, giving several hard pitches low down before joining with the normal route. Both parties, naturally enough, have strong feelings of pride in their respective lines, though Geddes felt that the ascent by the original line is the more natural winter route.

The following weekend, February 18, the partnership of Lang and Quinn made their last new route on Nevis with American Pie (V,4) on the North wall of Castle Ridge. At a length of 770m this is one of the longest routes on Nevis, and consequently Britain. It is also, due to its relatively low altitude, infrequently in condition. One wonders whether the lyrics of the song, one of Lang's favourites, prompted the route's name.

Geddes and Higgins took advantage of a late winter season with two April ascents. Burrito's Groove (IV,5) on April 8 was one of three recent routes on Number Two Gully Buttress, climbing a groove line left of the original line. It is often in condition and well recommended by its originator. The following week, on April 14, Geddes and Higgins climbed the steep slabs and grooves between Hadrian's Wall and Point Five Gully. Geddes had already attempted a climb here in February, finding that the slabs, as usual, had insufficient ice. Competition was raising its ugly head at this time, with so many good and active climbers living in and around Fort William. One of the climbers chasing lines was Gordon Smith, and when Geddes attempted a line next to Sickle in February 1978, Smith appeared a few days later and made the first winter ascent

Galactic Hitchhiker (VI,5) from Rubicon Wall during an early ascent in 1980. Two climbers are just visible mid-snowfield below the cascades.

Photo: Con Higgins

of Pointless, thinking that Geddes had failed on that line.

The climbing on both Galactic Hitchhiker (VI,5), as Geddes and Higgins named their route, and Pointless (VII,6), is of a serious mixed nature. Pointless, still a very prized route, is undoubtedly more difficult, with less protection than Galactic Hitchhiker. The latter is a better climb, and has justifiably seen more ascents. On Galactic, the original start as taken by the pioneers is hard, and has often been missed out by subsequent parties who have started up easier ground further left. Galactic Hitchhiker was a very important ascent, though under current ratings, the first grade VI on the Ben was Tower Face of the Comb. Other thin face routes such as Left-Hand Route on Minus Two Buttress pre-date Galactic, but the latter was a real venture into the unknown on the big exposed faces. Despite the passage of time it has maintained its reputation and has rightly been awarded four stars in the current guidebook.

Two months later, in June 1978, rock climbs were again being recorded on Nevis, with two hard routes on Càrn Dearg Buttress. The startling rise in rock climbing standards, first seen in England in the early 1970s, had reached Scotland by about 1976, and Nevis in 1977, with the first

*Dave (Cubby)
Cuthbertson in April
1979. Cubby has
been one of Scotland's
leading climbers for
several decades,
particularly on
rock. He lives in
Ballachulish at the
mouth of Glen Coe
and latterly has
become known for
his mountain
photography*

Photo: Ken Crocket

free ascent of Titan's Wall. The young Scottish climbers setting the pace in the north moved up from Glen Coe, where they had been busy in 1976 and 1977, to explore the cliffs of Nevis in the summer of 1978. This second climbing revolution (the first being the introduction of curved or inclinedaxes) manifested itself in two routes on the great buttress of Càrn Dearg.

On June 2, a very steep line was found up the most imposing part of Càrn Dearg Buttress. A tenuous, hanging groove to the right of Sassenach, taken in part by this line, had been known to Scots climbers for years as *the big banana groove* (see below). As with most lines that were well-known, it was also too difficult for prevailing standards. The route, christened Caligula and graded at E3, received an all-Scottish first ascent, with three young climbers from the new wave; Dave 'Cubby' Cuthbertson from Edinburgh, and Glaswegians Dougie Mullin and Willie Todd. Caligula moves across right midway up the banana groove. Cuthbertson, who lives for and by mountaineering, later joined the SMC, and continued to climb at a high standard. Latterly he has forged a name as a mountain guide and photographer, based in Ballachulish at the mouth of Glen Coe.

The other line on the Great Buttress was climbed over two days by Ken Johnstone and Willie Todd. Adrenalin Rush, at E3, is a fairly direct line taking in the slabs and roof just right of The Bullroar. Crossing the crux traverse of The Bullroar it breaks through the roof above then makes a right, rising traverse to a junction with Centurion.

Elsewhere on Nevis that summer, Con Higgins and H.Woods made a June ascent at Very Severe of the winter line East Face, on the Zero Gully face of Observatory Ridge, while on the First Platform John Mackenzie and two friends found a Severe right of Ruddy Rocks with Rain Trip. There would be no rock climbs recorded for the next two years, as a succession of wet weekends swept over the north face of Nevis, though winter routes of a high standard would continue.

From about the mid 1970s onwards there was a period during which Scottish winters were generally unspectacular. There were some good spells, naturally, but these seem to have been further and further apart and of shorter duration as the decade advanced. Whereas 1978 was a peak year for the decade on Ben Nevis, with 11 first winter ascents, all of which were Grade IV or above, the next six years, from 1979 to 1984, saw an average of only three winter lines per annum, despite the increased number of winter climbers. This decrease in winter ascents can be only partially blamed on the weather, however. Several of the active local climbers moved on, thereby lowering the competitive flame that had burned in the Fort William area for some years. Geddes was to move back to Edinburgh, recording one more route in 1979. Higgins was to move to the United States for some years. Norrie Muir, a complex Glaswegian, (a qualified fitter with a Diploma in Business Studies), was to stop winter climbing a few years later. (Rumour has it that he was the only climber ever to have wangled a pair of climbing boots out of the NHS for health reasons.)

March 15, 1979 gave the first good conditions of the year, and also the first Grade VI to be recorded as such on Ben Nevis and Scotland. (Though not climbed – that honour on Ben Nevis goes to The Tower

Face of The Comb by Smith and Holt on New Year's Day, 1959, an astonishing 20 years earlier.) The New Routes Editor of the SMC Journal had no reservations about publishing that grade for the first winter ascent of The Shield Direct, by Mick Fowler and Victor (Tony) Saunders. Even a stroll up to the foot of that route would convince the sceptical that winter climbing had taken a quantum leap upwards in difficulty. It is now graded VII,7, and is praised as an outstanding route which combines very steep ice with sustained and technical mixed climbing.

Five other hard routes were climbed in March 1979. Arthur Paul would team up with Davy 'Paraffin' Sanderson to make two ascents. The first of these was Gemini (VI,6) on March 23. This climbed a line in the vicinity of Evening Wall, which several teams had been looking at for some years, waiting for the right conditions. (The *right conditions* for some routes are often very difficult to predict, on some occasions being for a few days only, and often most inconsiderately during midweek.) Three days later they climbed the 270m line of Alchemist (VI,5) on the North Wall of Castle Ridge.

On the same day as the Alchemist received its ascent, Paul 'Tut' Braithwaite and Dave Pearce climbed The Shadow (VII,6). This followed the summer line first climbed by Terry Sullivan in 1959, starting just right of Route I and crossing the exposed slabs of Càrn Dearg Buttress by a line parallel to and lower than Route II. As with other Braithwaite lines, its low-key reporting led to it being largely overlooked. It is technically more difficult than Route II and more sustained. It has been given three stars in the current guide.

On April 8, Higgins and Geddes climbed Purgatory Wall (V,5). This was to be the last Nevis route recorded by this fruitful pair, and followed a line on the steep wall right of Lobby Dancer, on the vast, sprawling North Wall of Castle Ridge. (The route name was first submitted as *Last Day in Purgatory*, a title which sounded too pretentious to the SMCJ New Routes Editor, who at that time did not realise that Higgins was preparing to leave the country and was, in effect, saying farewell to the joys and miseries of winter climbing in particular. Higgins, like any canny Scot, bided his time and with a change of Editor corrected this oversight several years later. Climbers being climbers however, it seems that the edited name has prevailed.)

Mike Geddes, one of the most prominent winter climbers in Scotland in the 1970s, died in September 1985, after an illness. His repeat ascents of the hard Smith-Marshall routes and his early recognition of the promise of front-pointing were highly significant contributions to Scottish winter mountaineering.

The 1980s saw mountaineering on Nevis played out in a low key. Most new routes recorded have been winter ascents – despite the blazing summers of 1983 and 1984. Many of the young and active rock climbers who were climbing at high standards were not recording routes above the tree-line, and this despite the fact that there existed much untouched good rock. This does not imply laziness on their part. The nature of rock climbing near the ceiling of ability is such that potential lines often have to be inspected by abseil, offending moss or other vegetation removed and crucial sections inspected visually for holds and protection. This time-consuming procedure is often necessary before attempts

Mick Fowler climbing Zero Gully (1978). The legendary taxman with the Inland Revenue, Fowler made many daring raids up north

Photo: Fowler collection

Even a stroll up to the foot of that route would convince the sceptical that winter climbing had taken a quantum leap upwards in difficulty

One of the quiet men in Scottish climbing, Arthur Paul has an impressive list of first ascents on Nevis, including Urban Spaceman (VII,6), Psychedelic Wall (VI,5) and Gemini (VI,6)

Photo: Cubby Images

at a first ascent, some of which have required several days or even weeks of effort. All of this makes an attempt on a hard mountain line very difficult. And one has to eat.

Many climbers are loath to make the walk to the north face of Nevis two days in a row. They are even less enthusiastic about carrying camping equipment. Access to the CIC Hut remains awkward for the ordinary user, who due to the usual vagaries of weather may decide to climb on Nevis at short notice. It would be naive to maintain that some recently joined members of the SMC had not joined with the use of that Hut in mind.

Despite these drawbacks, routes continued to be found on the cliffs of Nevis, if at a reduced flow compared to the 1970s. The winter of 1980 was poor, with three routes, two of which, however, were at high standards. Journey Into Space (VII,5) marked Con Higgins' farewell to Nevis, climbed on March 8 with Alan Kimber. This was a truly Orion Face Direct route, climbing directly out of the Basin between Astral Highway and the Second Slab Rib. Its grade indicates a very serious nature to the climbing, i.e. poor protection. It received a second ascent on March 15 by Brian Sprunt and Andy Nisbet. This pair had gone off route while climbing Orion Direct, and finished with a bivouac under the sumit cornice. The route was to receive a paltry further two ascents in the next 21 years.

Interstellar Overdrive (VI,5) climbed on April 12 by Rab Anderson and Ian Kennedy, takes to the ribs and grooves between Pointless and Point Five Gully. A hard solo winter ascent was that of Slav Route by Mal Duff. Of a very different nature from these two routes was Norrie Muir's and Tam McAuley's recording of the Grade III Fawlty Towers, climbing the first icefall right of West Gully, Douglas Boulder. (McAuley was to die in 2006, drowned crossing a river in spate on the island of Rum).

Two winter routes were found in 1981, the first being the February 21 ascent by Graham Little and Bob Richardson of The Comb, Left Flank (IV,4), following a ramp and icefall out right from above the first main ice pitch of Comb Gully. In March K.Leinster, Arthur Paul and Ged Reilly climbed Augean Alley (V,5) on Gardyloo Buttress. This climbs Kellett's Route, starting midway between Left Edge Route and Smith's Route, finishing up the upper section of the buttress by following the Haston/Stenhouse summer variation to Kellett's Route which provides a superb pitch with a spectacular position. Two Very Severes by Muir and McAuley completed first ascents for 1981.

Bayonet Route received a winter ascent at Grade IV,4, on March 7 1982, by Ian Griffiths, Ed Jackson and Colin Stead. The latter also climbed the 150m Right Hand Wall Route (Slab Rib Variation) at Grade IV,4 on March 22 in company with Colin Grant. Right Hand Wall Route had first been climbed in winter by R. Ferguson and J. Higham on March 6, 1972. Stormy Petrel (VII,6) was climbed this season, as mentioned earlier in the description of the Indicator Wall routes, its ascent by Cuthbertson and Kane bringing that face further into the modern light.

Earlier in 1982, on January 28, the Edinburgh climber Mal Duff and the Aberdonian Andy Nisbet teamed up to record Venus (V,5). This follows the right-bounding arete of Green Gully for two pitches then takes to the grooves of Aphrodite on the left to finish. At the end of 1982, on December 18, the icefall on Central Trident Buttress was climbed by John Murphy and Alasdair 'Cube' Cain. Mega Route X, as it was named,

Mega Route X (V,6), Central Trident Buttress

Photo: Cubby Images

approximated to the summer line of Steam, and had been eyed by many climbers for some years, as its ice approached the ground only to crash to the ground with each thaw. At Grade V,6 and 70m it is a short hard ice exercise, well protected with ice screws, and one which is much sought after. Murphy and his partner climbed one pitch then abseiled off, returning the next day to climb up by an adjoining line before moving right and finishing up the final pitch. An ascent was made the next week, climbing the entire line in one go, by Martin Lawrence and Roger Webb. Precedence for this route has been awarded to Murphy and Cain.

The winter season of 1982/83 saw three winter routes. The first was a 140m V,5 just right of the above-mentioned Aphrodite, on Number Three Gully Buttress. This was Quickstep, climbed on March 26 by Rich Townsend and T.Bray and climbing the obvious corner to the left of Two Step Corner. Another line climbed some time that winter of 1983 was

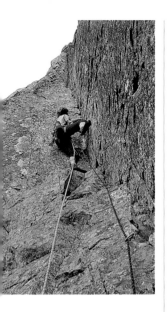

Murray Hamilton starting out on the corner of Caligula (E3), during the first ascent of The Banana Groove (E4)

Photo: Rab Anderson

With Agrippa (E5), Pete Whillance, from Carlisle, gave Ben Nevis its hardest rock climb for 18 years (1982)

Photo: Rab Anderson

Shot in The Light (V,5), climbed by Phil Thornhill and Victor Saunders and at 100m in length taking the right wall of Gardyloo Gully, left of Left Edge Route. Finally, from the winter of 1983, Arthur Paul and Dougie Hawthorn succeeded after several attempts in climbing a hard line on the Orion Face on April 12. Urban Spaceman (VII,6), all 350m of it, takes a line on the face between Astronomy and the Orion Direct in its lower section, and between Astronomy and Epsilon Chimney in its upper part. Its originator recommends it, rating it highly for length, quality and variety, though it is seldom in condition.

Moving to the summer, on August 28 Minus One Direct received a variation by Steve Abbott and Noel Williams. The Arete Variation climbed the earlier Serendipity Variation in part, then broke away to gain the arete, using a peg for tension, (later freed). Williams recalls the route being very popular that day, with a party on the Serendipity Variation, and another on the Original Route. Overall, taking in the Serendipity and Arete Variations, Minus One Direct is rated as a four-star E1, one of the best routes of its grade in Scotland. (More details of the Minus One Buttress variations are given in Chapter 8).

Just right of Sassenach lies a narrow stretch of wall, the right arete of which is the left-bounding arete of Titan's Wall. On the wall is an obvious groove line, known for years as 'the big banana groove'. This had been climbed in part by the line of Caligula, but on August 21 1983 two Edinburgh climbers, Murray Hamilton and Rab Anderson, made the first complete ascent of The Banana Groove (E4).

Perhaps the main summer event of 1983, however, was the ascent of Agrippa by Pete Whillance and Rab Anderson, on August 29. Agrippa climbs the improbable left arete of Titan's Wall, on Càrn Dearg Buttress. Whillance, an immensely strong climber from Carlisle, had been over in the Cairngorms with Anderson and two others, but deciding the weather in the west looked better moved to Nevis. On Sunday, August 28, they went up to Càrn Dearg Buttress, Whillance having designs on the arete. He decided that the easiest way to clean the route was to climb Centurion then traverse right to drop the 90m cleaning rope down the line. Whillance decided to lead Centurion using the cleaning rope, which was non-stretch and not designed for climbing. His apparently endless lead perplexed a few onlookers.

After a day spent scrubbing clean the arete and climbing the ropes, they were understandably tired. The wind had risen by now, but Whillance decided to leave the rope in case the weather improved the next day. Monday was dull and windy, and not at all promising as they trudged back up the Allt a' Mhuilinn. It was cold weather for such climbing, and the climbers went for a stroll round the crags, hoping for an improvement. After a few hours Whillance decided to abandon the route and prusiked up the rope to abseil back down the line of Titan's Wall. The ropes were coiled and the party ready to descend when Whillance suddenly changed his mind.

The second pitch of Agrippa was the crux pitch, with poor protection and the wind blowing the ropes out in a scaring fashion. Luckily there was a loose block on the arete which the climbers could rest on, wrapping both arms round it in a spectacular position. Rab Anderson describes the action.

Moves up and left gain the crux on the left side of the arete. With the wind blowing, fingers going numb and runners below his feet Pete decided to go for it. Just as he was reaching the belay ledge a gust of wind caught the rope as I was dragging it through the sticht plate and I nearly pulled Pete off![12]

Agrippa, at 85m, is graded E5, with technical pitch gradings of 5c, 6b, 5c. In a technical sense, it was the most difficult rock climb on the north face of Ben Nevis for 18 years. The second ascent was that by John 'Spider' McKenzie in the summer of 1984.

The winter season of 1983/84 began on December 17, when Arthur Paul, Colin MacLean and Dougie Hawthorn made an ascent of Right Hand Chimney on Moonlight Gully Buttress at Grade IV,4. Haston and Smith had almost certainly climbed the chimney about 1960, while the top two tiers of the buttress were climbed by Crocket and Gilmore in 1974.

There were few first winter ascents in 1984. On March 3 Cuthbertson and Calum Fraser made a True Finish to Waterfall Gully (VI,6), while the following day Mal Duff and Jon Tinker made an ascent of Point Blank. This followed the tenuous sliver of buttress between Point Five Gully and Left Edge Route. Duff noted that after the third pitch of Point Blank it was possible to keep to the edge overlooking Point Five Gully, a variation which had been done earlier by Dave Wilkinson and party. Wilkinson had started up Left Edge Route. The 1984 ascent of Point Blank was flawed because it climbed a section of Point Five. Duff remedied this with a complete ascent in 1988. The route is graded VII,6 and has yet to see a repeat (despite several determined attempts!) Duff, who was brought up in Currie, died in his sleep at Everest base camp in 1997, as he prepared to lead a team in an attempt on the world's highest peak.

It seems that only six climbers took advantage of the glorious summer of 1984 on Nevis. In May, Doug Hawthorn and John Grant recorded Orient Express on the First Platform, left of Newbigging's 80-Minute Route, a 90m E2 on excellent, rough rock, while on July 6, Noel Williams and Hawthorn had teamed up to make Steam Train, a Hard Very Severe ascent up the big corner between the above route and Newbigging's 80-Minute Route. But most of that summer's routes were done by two ropes. One of them was Norrie Muir, who in company with George Adam recorded no less than six routes, three each in July and August. Most were at an easy grade, four being Very Difficult, with two on the Douglas Boulder. A third Very Difficult, Gaslight, follows for the most part the right edge of Moonlight Gully Buttress, just right of the Right Hand Chimney, while Vanishing Glories is a 105m Very Difficult on the Coire na Ciste face of the Garadh Buttress. The latter route may have been first climbed by Robin Campbell and Jimmy Marshall in the early 1970s, but not recorded.

The Banshee, Scottish Very Severe, was climbed on August 11 by Muir and Adam, following corners and grooves between Sioux Wall and Thompson's Route on Number Three Gully Buttress. On the same day Muir and Adam climbed The Rattler, Severe, starting left of The Groove Climb on South Trident Buttress. The other pair recording routes in the blazing heat of 1984 were Arthur Paul and Dougie Hawthorn, who between them found five routes of Severe and above, climbed over four busy days.

Opening their salvo on Monday, July 2 they climbed Last Stand, 110m Hard Very Severe, on Number Three Gully Buttress, climbing the arete

SMC member Rab Anderson made his mark on Nevis with The Banana Groove (E4) and Agrippa (E5) in summer, and Interstellar Overdrive (VI,5) in winter

Photo: Cubby Images

One of the outstanding rock climbers of his generation, Murray Hamilton's contribution to Nevis was Banana Groove (E4) and the second free ascent of Titan's Wall (E3), (1980)

Photo: Rab Anderson

between Knuckleduster and Sioux Wall. On July 3 the 90m Hard Very Severe Clefthanger followed a corner system to the right of Tower Cleft, while on the same day they found The Urchin, a 60m E1 left of The Great Chimney on Tower Ridge, following the first leftward-facing corner crack. On the Wednesday Paul and Hawthorn were back on Number Three Gully Buttress, recording Chinook, 65m, at Hard Very Severe. This climbs the arete to the right of the final corner of Two Step, and when preceded by an ascent of Nicolson's Sioux Wall would make for a superb combination. The final route from Paul and Hawthorn was with a Thursday ascent of Saxifrage, a Severe on Raeburn's Buttress, following a thin groove some 9m left of The Crack. Also climbing on Nevis that summer of 1984 was Noel Williams. In the previous year he had found a variation on the upper part of Minus One Direct. Embarrassed by the use of a peg for tension he returned with Willie Jeffrey on July 8 and succeeded in climbing his Arete Variation free.

On New Year's Day, 1985, Hawthorn and Paul made a winter ascent at Grade VI,6 of Clefthanger, first climbed by them as a rock climb the previous July. On the 19th of January Mal Duff and Jon Tinker recorded Sod's Law (V,6), beginning below Route I on Càrn Dearg Buttress and taking the chimney on the left. Also apparently climbed in that January of 1985 was a mystery route, going under the name of Jazz Discharge Party Hats, by Mark Miller and Sean Smith (the name is after a Frank Zappa song, with dubious lyrics). This Grade VI route on the Orion Face climbed the crest of the buttress left of Journey Into Space. Jazz Discharge Party Hats has now been superseded by Space Invaders (2001). JDPH took the first pitch of Space Invaders and then penduled into Journey into Space.

On January 26 Martin Hind and John Christie climbed Mercury (V,5), a line between Pigott's Route and Green Gully. Their route took the first pitch of Green Gully, traversing left below the first peg belay of the gully to below an obvious chimney-crack with a chockstone. The next pitch was the crux, and according to Christie's description,

> ...consisted of climbing handsize lumps of ice some how stuck to the wall, axes occasionally jammed in cracks, tufts of moss & anything else that aided upward progress. Pitch 2 took 2 hrs to lead & was hard.[13]

Mal Duff and Jon Tinker were responsible for one other winter ascent in 1985. On February 16 they climbed Diana (V,5) on Number Three Gully Buttress. This route, to that date the hardest winter line on the crag, starts up an icefall some 12m left of Number Three Gully Buttress Original Route and trends left to grooves and corners before taking a steep icefall on the right wall of a huge corner. It is now climbed frequently when the buttress is well iced.

Martin Hind was busy in February on Nevis, making the first winter ascent of the summer route Compression Crack, first climbed by Rolland and Ogilvy in 1940. This was the route which Clough thought he was climbing in January 1960, making instead a first ascent called Winter Chimneys. Hind found the second chimney pitch particularly difficult, the route being V,5. On that day the Càrn Dearg plateau lived up to the name given to it by Clement Wragge, *The Plateau of Storms*, as Hind was blown some 10m through the air while walking towards Number Four Gully. (On the same day Crocket had a Dead Man blown off his harness by a sudden gust of wind while climbing on the relatively sheltered Central Trident Buttress.)

The summer of 1985 has gone down on record as the worst for weather for over a century. Certainly in Scotland, after the end of June there was no let up in the steady rain that fell, excepting one weekend in September. The amount of rain and lack of sun enforced a virtual ban on climbing on the north face of Ben Nevis, with no new routes being recorded that summer.

The start of the winter season of 1985/86 took place in November, with a winter ascent on Observatory Ridge left of Abacus. At V,6 and about 80m in length, this route was climbed by Paul and Hawthorn and followed a Very Difficult route first climbed by Norrie Muir and Hawthorn in May 1984 and named Observatory Wall.

The last route in 1985 took place with a winter ascent on Moonlight Gully Buttress, on Sunday, December 22, when Ken Crocket, Alastair Walker and Bob Richardson climbed the 175m Phosphorescent Grooves (III,4). This climb followed an unusual rising traverse line on the Number Five Gully wall of the buttress. Pitches three and four presented difficulties, with the line as a whole being fairly sustained. The route can be useful early in the season or if conditions are bad higher up.

The new technique of front-pointing had now been well bedded in. A virtual avalanche of new equipment, in both hardware and clothing, was available. Climbing on Ben Nevis could be extended significantly further; by expanding the weather envelope, and by finding protection where none was found before. The scene was set for a new phase in winter climbing, the exploration of thin winter face routes. There was one other significant factor in the equation; the French were coming, and the *Auld Alliance* was about to be resurrected.

Doug Hawthorn outside the CIC Hut. Several hard winter climbs in his portfolio include Urban Spaceman (VII,6) and Clefthanger (VI,6), while in summer Orient Express (E2) explored new rock on the First Platform

Photo: Cubby Images

References

1. **Chouinard**, Yvon, *Salsipuedes*. SMCJ 30, p20, 1972. [Note. Salsipuedes is Spanish for 'leave if you can'.]

2. **Carrington**, Robert, *Càrn Dearg Commentary*. Mountain 46, 26 – 37, November/December 1975.

3. **Muir**, Norrie, *Personal communication, November 2006*.

4. **Campbell**, R.N., *Ben Nevis Notes*. SMCJ 30, 185, 1973.

5. **Crocket**, K.V., *Smith's Route, Gardyloo Buttress*. Cold Climbs, 75 – 77, Ken Wilson, Dave Alcock & John Barry eds., (London: Diadem Books, 1983, ISBN 0906371163.)

6. **Crocket**, K.V., *Minus One Gully*. Cold Climbs, 41 – 43, see reference 5.

7. **Stead**, Colin, *One Below The Belt*. SMCJ 30, 221 – 223, 1974.

8. **Quinn**, Neil, *Hadrian's Wall Direct*. SMCJ 30, 224 – 226, 1974.

9. **Higgins**, Con, *Personal communication, March 2008*.

10. **Cruickshank**, Jimmy, *High Endeavours, The Life and Legend of Robin Smith*. 182 – 183 (Edinburgh: Canongate, 2005, ISBN 1841956589.)

11. **Rouse**, Alan, *Route 2, Càrn Dearg*. Cold Climbs, 102 – 105, see reference 5.

12. **Anderson**, Rab, *Personal communication, January 1985*.

13. **Christie**, John, *CIC Logbook, January 1985*.

Stormy Petrel (VII,6) on Indicator Wall. Bold and serious, the first ascent in 1983 by Dave Cuthbertson and Rudi Kane took thin face climbing to a new level. Here, Blair Fyffe and Iain Small are engrossed in a rare repeat in March 2007

Photo: Viv Scott

13: Hard Route Consolidation (1986 – 1995)

BY THE EARLY 1980S, many Ben devotees had ticked their way through the classic Smith and Marshall routes, but there was considerable reticence to try the more recent thin face climbs. A keen group of climbers based around Glasgow and Strathclyde Universities, including John Murphy, Roger Webb, Robin Clothier, Alasdair Cain, Ronnie Bruce and Alan Shand, were responsible for breaking down many of the psychological barriers.

It was soon realised that routes such as Astral Highway, Psychedelic Wall and Slav Route were quite reasonable given good conditions, although Galactic Hitchhiker only succumbed after John Murphy took a huge fall from the second pitch. He returned the following weekend to find his axes, complete with gloves in the wrist loops, still sticking out of the ice. Other routes however, such as Albatross and Pointless, retained their reputations for long run-outs and poor belays, and were left unrepeated for longer. On two occasions, Pointless repelled strong teams when the leaders fell off the crucial third pitch, and in one instance, the long fall onto the belay ripped the anchors, pulling the second to the snowfield below, although fortunately everyone survived to tell the tale.

In February 1983, the development of thin winter face routes took a step forward when Dave Cuthbertson and Rudi Kane ventured onto the steep uncharted territory to the right of Albatross on Indicator Wall to create Stormy Petrel (VII,6). This bold and committing undertaking has retained its serious reputation to this day, and has only been repeated a handful of times. The following month, Robin Clothier and Alasdair Cain climbed the Second Slab Rib above the Basin on the Orion Face to give Long Climb Finish (VI,5). Arthur Paul and Doug Hawthorn then made a true winter ascent of the lower part of The Long Climb by climbing the crest of the Great Slab Rib. Paul had made several attempts on this outstanding pitch over a number of years, before finding optimum conditions that April. They finished up the groove system to the right of Astronomy, having climbed Urban Spaceman (VII,6), one of the finest winter routes of the decade.

In general though, the development of winter climbing on Ben Nevis was beginning to stagnate. The mountain had become established as an ice climbing venue, and whilst there were still new lines to do, increasingly these required exceptional conditions. Other influences were at work too. The vast winter potential of the North-West Highlands was becoming apparent with development of the great cliffs on Beinn Eighe and Beinn Bhan, and in the Cairngorms a mixed climbing revolution was taking place with focus on harder technical climbing on shorter routes. The reverse curve picks developed in the early 1980s for ice climbing proved ideal for torquing up steep cracks, and application of the new technique culminated in the first winter ascent of The Needle, a 250m-long summer E1 climb on the Shelter Stone in the Cairngorms by Andy Nisbet and Colin MacLean in February 1985. Although it wasn't fully realised at the time, The Needle was one of the most difficult winter climbs in the world, with a technical difficulty ten years in advance of anything achieved in the Alps. Inevitably, all these developments took the spotlight away from Ben Nevis.

The situation was not helped by the guidebooks available at the time. Marshall's 1969 SMC guidebook was the definitive guide, but despite being reprinted in 1979 with a comprehensive addendum, it still felt outdated. A new selective guidebook covering Lochaber and Badenoch, written by Colin Stead and Marshall, was published by the SMC in 1981, but like many selective guides, it lacked the authority of a definitive text. Ian Clough's 1969 guidebook to Ben Nevis and Glen Coe was updated by Ed Grindley and published by Cicerone Press in 1990. This included all the winter lines, but its well-written and minimalist descriptions seemed to say it all, and it did little to encourage further exploration. For many, Ben Nevis had reached worked out status.

The most influential publication of the 1980s was not a guidebook, but *Cold Climbs,* published by Diadem Press in 1983. The brainchild of Ken Wilson and co-authored with Dave Alcock and John Barry, this large format book was illustrated with superb crag and action photos and described 70 of the best snow and ice climbs across the British Isles. Thirteen chapters were devoted to Ben Nevis, which confirmed the status of the well-known classics such as Zero and Point Five gullies and Orion Direct, but also put the spotlight on some of the more recent additions. No longer were routes such as Orion Direct and Smith's Route at the top of ambitious climber's agendas, but instead climbs such as Galactic Hitchhiker and Route II Direct were the prestigious routes to do.

Heavy snowfall in early January 1986, was followed by a stable high

The large format book Cold Climbs *published by Diadem Press in 1983, had a significant influence on British climbers. The 15 featured routes on Ben Nevis became the most sought after winter climbs on the mountain for the next 20 years*
Courtesy Bâton Wicks

The traverse on the third pitch of Centurion (VIII,8). The first winter ascent of this classic summer HVS in February 1986 was an outstanding achievement, comparable to the great mixed routes climbed in the Cairngorms during the 1980s

Photo: Pete Benson

Kenny Spence was a driving force in Scottish climbing during the 1970s and 80s. His winter ascent of Centurion set a mixed climbing standard on Ben Nevis that was not equalled for over 10 years

Photo: Rab Anderson

pressure that centred over Scandinavia and sucked in cold northerly winds. This brought the Scottish mountains into superb condition resulting in one of the best winter seasons in recent times. There was a rush to sample the newly developed winter routes in the North-West Highlands, but Ben Nevis also saw its fair share of action. Minus One Gully saw many repeats and rapidly gained classic status, and the big spotlighted Cold Climbs routes such as Galactic Hitchhiker, also began to see regular traffic. A noteworthy addition during January was the first winter ascent of Raeburn's Arete by Doug Lang and Colin Stead. This superb summer Severe is well known for being one of the cleanest rock routes on the mountain, and Lang and Stead's ascent relied on excellent ice conditions, although their line avoided the crest taken by the summer route and climbed icy grooves either side. They modestly graded the route Grade IV, although the current guidebook suggests that V,6 may be a more realistic rating.

The big event of the 1986 winter was Kenny Spence and John (Spider) McKenzie's ascent of the much-prized Centurion. The strong

Edinburgh-based pair made a planned bivouac before finishing up Route II, to create the most technically sustained undertaking on the mountain. Conditions in 1986 were exceptional, with a big weep of ice originating from the traverse line of Route II and running down the two pitches below. This focused a spindrift plume down the line of the main Centurion corner and kept the steep second and third pitches white and covered with fresh snow. One rest point was used at the top of the second pitch, although this pitch had previously been climbed free on their two previous attempts on the route.

The first winter ascent of Centurion (VIII,8) was an outstanding achievement, and was Edinburgh's answer to the Cairngorms mixed routes put up by the Aberdeen-based pair of MacLean and Nisbet. During the 1980s there was intense rivalry between climbers from the two cities, but Centurion more than equalled the difficulty of routes such as The Needle. Centurion was a quantum leap in mixed climbing standards on Ben Nevis and set a level that would not be equalled for over ten years. Unfortunately its position on the relatively low lying Càrn Dearg Buttress means that it does not come into condition as readily as several of the other 1980s Scottish Grade VIII test-pieces and as a result has seen less attention.

After a warmer March, Ben Nevis came into excellent condition once again in April, and Mick Fowler and Victor Saunders were first on the scene to make the long awaited second ascent of Pointless. Saunders took a small fall on the second pitch, which only helped to confirm the climb's serious reputation. Several good new thin face routes were added later that month. Of particular note were Riders on the Storm (VI,5) on Indicator Wall by Hawthorn and Ewen Todd, The Black Hole (VI,6) on the Orion Face by Fowler and Saunders, and Match Point (VI,5) on Observatory Buttress by Simon Richardson and Ed Hart. All these ascents showed that, given the right conditions, there were still new routes to find.

Whilst the majority were playing catch up and coming to terms with the great winter routes climbed in the late 1970s, a few individuals and teams were making their own mark. A key player in the late 1980s was Mal Duff, a larger than life figure based in Culross in Fife. He was an ex-member of the Territorial Army SAS, and in the early 1980s set up a mountaineering instructing business based out of the Clachaig Inn in Glen Coe during the winter months. Duff was a man with huge charisma and he attracted many clients together with a handful of Britain's up and coming younger mountaineers to act as instructors and guides. He had little interest in qualifications, and hired instructors on personal knowledge and climbing ability, and was the last of a great tradition to do this in an increasingly regulated sport. Duff was a good technical mixed climber but his greatest strength was his vigour and huge capacity to enthuse others, as Andy Perkins remembered.

Mal relived and enlarged every detail of the day's epic, always crediting others with the most outrageous highlights of the day, never himself. He never let the truth get in the way of a good story. The truth being that it was he who was the most outstanding, visionary and entertaining mixed climber that Scotland had, with a flair for bringing out those qualities in others. So many, Andy Cave included[1], took their first steps on snow and ice with Mal, and

Mal Duff (1953 – 1997). One of Scotland's most active winter pioneers during the 1980s, Duff's playfully tough style attracted a strong following of younger climbers

Photo: Ed Douglas

Victor Saunders on the first ascent of The Black Hole (VI,6), a direct version of Astronomy, on the Orion Face

Photo: Mick Fowler

Climbers on Diana (V,5), Number Three Gully Buttress. This sustained ice climb is one of the most popular of Mal Duff's routes

Photo: Jim Sutherland / nineonesix

many good climbers ended up seconding new Vs and VIs as part of their course.[2]

Years of working on Ben Nevis gave Mal Duff an unusual knowledge of unclimbed lines and the necessary conditions to climb them. He had a couple of good winter finds earlier in the 1980s such as Sod's Law (V,6) on Càrn Dearg and Diana (V,5) on Number Three Gully Buttress, and he continued his exploration of the mountain during the 1986 season with a string of four good new routes. He opened his account with Andy Nisbet on January 3 with an ascent of Pirate (IV,4), a varied mixed route to the right of Vanishing Gully. The slabby rocks on this part of the mountain are very smooth, and their ascent relied on a good depth of snow covering the rock and it is not known whether the climb has been repeated. At the end of the month, Duff returned to Coire na Ciste with clients M.Aldridge and J.Woods to climb the excellent line of Bydand (V,5). This fine winter line takes the steep icy corners between Italian Climb and The Chute. Again, this route is rarely in condition, but when icy, it ranks as one of the finest Nevis grooves.

The following day, Duff was on Ben Nevis again, this time climbing with Jon Tinker who was working as an instructor on one of Duff's climbing courses. Duff and Tinker started up the first two pitches of The Shadow on Càrn Dearg Buttress, and then traversed right to reach the Weep on Cowslip. This gave thin ice climbing in a very unlikely situation before finishing up the traverse of Route II Direct. Ring the Alarm (VI,5) is one of the finest mixed routes on Càrn Dearg, although exceptional conditions are required to bring it into condition. A week later, Duff and Tinker were back again, this time with visiting US climber Rick Nowack who was a regular client. Nowack spent his summer washing dishes in Highland hotels to subsidise his winter climbing in Scotland with Duff, and is perhaps best known for his ascent, naked and on a top rope, of the steep icefall of Elliot's Downfall (VI,6) in Glen Coe. Climbing with Duff, he was rewarded with the first ascent of Running Hot (V,5), a companion route to Pirate on the rib left of Vanishing Gully. Like its twin, this climb relies on good icy conditions or a heavy snow cover, and may not have seen a second ascent.

Duff's most important contribution to Ben Nevis came a couple of seasons later when he made the first ascent of the steep rib to the right of Point Five Gully. As described in Chapter 12, Duff had climbed most of the line with Jon Tinker in March 1984, but they avoided the crux groove by climbing Point Five Gully for a short way. Although they had written up the route in the SMC Journal, a comment by New Routes Editor Andy Nisbet that *'the purity of their route had been spoiled by the traverse in and out of Point Five'*[3] pricked Duff's ego, and he was determined to straighten out the line.

Duff and Tinker planned to return to the route in the winters of 1985 and 1986, but conditions were unfavourable. Conditions looked better during the 1987 season, but Duff injured his knee and was out of action for most of the winter. Instead, Tinker conscripted the very strong Aberdeen-based climber Colin MacLean to straighten out the line. The climb was going well, but when MacLean was belayed from the hanging stance at the top of the second pitch, a peg pulled out as Tinker was climbing and they both fell. Fortunately they were held by

a protection peg left from the 1984 attempt. The ever-competitive Duff admitted later that he was secretly delighted when he heard news of their failure. Finally, in February 1988, Duff returned with Rick Nowack and completed the line of Point Blank (VII,6). Twenty years on, this superlative line has yet to receive a confirmed repeat, despite a number of determined attempts. Four days later Duff and Nowack visited the North Face of Castle Ridge where they added the thin ice route Casino Royale (VI,5) with A.Bond.

Robin Clothier was another larger than life character very active on the mountain during this period. Clothier, a large and powerful man, with an athletic physique, was the manager of a large landscape gardening business and a natural ice climber. He was most interested in climbing existing lines, and throughout the late 1980s and early 1990s he was the most regular winter climber on the mountain, repeating almost all the routes and adding a number of important variations. He also plugged a number of notable gaps, such as the fine ice line of Pinnacle Buttress Direct (V,5) on the Pinnacle Buttress of the Tower, on which he shared leads with George Armstrong. Clothier formed a productive partnership with Chris Cartwright, an affable young climber from Northern Ireland who was studying at Glasgow University. Their finest

The Simond Chacal was the first tool to use a reverse curve 'banana' shaped pick. This configuration allowed better penetration into steep ice and was used by many climbers during the 1980s

Robin Clothier was the most active ice climber on Ben Nevis during the 1980s and 1990s repeating most of the existing lines. He is currently the guardian of the CIC Hut

Photo: Simon Richardson

additions were Tramp (IV,4) in 1987, the line of weakness right of Green Gully, the superb Satanic Verses (VI,5) in 1989 on Indicator Wall and Lost the Place (V,5) in 1988 on the left side of Creag Coire na Ciste.

The first ascent of Lost the Place is a good example of the serendipitous nature of climbing new routes in poor visibility. Originally graded IV, Lost the Place takes a natural line up a hidden sloping ramp and steep chockstoned chimney leading through very steep ground on the left side of the cliff just right of South Gully. The route's nondescript name meant that it went for twelve years without another ascent, and it was Cartwright himself who repeated it when he added a direct start in February 2001. Cartwright later explained:

> I wouldn't say we were exactly lost when we [first] climbed it, but it was a very poor day, and to be truthful we didn't really know where we were.[4]

Chance first ascent or not, the final chimney of Lost the Place is one of the finest gully pitches on the mountain, and the route was upgraded to V,5 in the 2002 edition of the guidebook.

Winter climbing on Ben Nevis has attracted many climbers from around the world, but few return on a regular basis. Godefroy Perroux, a French guide from Les Houches, was an exception and became a regular visitor to the mountain every March or April. Typically Perroux would book a week or two in the CIC Hut and climb with clients that had driven over with him from France. Perroux was one of the first Continental climbers to recognise the potential of climbing frozen waterfalls in the 1970s, and is remembered as one of the founding fathers of modern ice climbing. His first visit to Scotland in the winter of 1982 was a revelation. Intent on climbing Point Five Gully, Perroux and his team of four clients ended up at the foot of Observatory Ridge and decided to follow another party up this route instead. Six years later, he recounted their adventure in an article in the SMC Journal describing his Ben Nevis experiences.

> Observatory Ridge will remain as my most vivid memory of mixed climbing. According to the English party the conditions were foul, much harder than usual. Since this was a classic climb we thought there would be fixed pitons. This was not so, and for our two ropes carrying only three pitons and no nuts, the route was harrowing. We literally clung to the English. We had underestimated the Ben, darkness was falling, the length of the route was astonishing. The weather was still bad and we were worried at finding ourselves alone on the summit without a compass, map or headlamp knowing nothing of the descent. Conditions on the summit were fantastic – the violent wind and pale twilight made it all unreal, like the end of the world. Two of our party started to show signs of exhaustion. It made me think of the Pilier de Freney and the tragedy of Bonatti's party.

Perroux and his team made it down safely, and next day bought nuts, pegs, map and compass in Fort William and then climbed Point Five Gully the following day. At the end of his article, Perroux explained why Scottish winter climbing was so different to climbing in the French Alps.

> With the right frame of mind and equipment many Grade V routes are reasonable for a fit party if conditions are good. I can now understand the British

Satanic Verses (VI,5) on Indicator Wall. This popular ice climb, first climbed by Robin Clothier and Chris Cartwright, was one of the finest additions of the 1980s

Photo: Pete MacPherson

ethics which forbid bolts. I accept the custom of protection as one leads, even if nuts, pitons, Friends, Deadmen and so on amount to a lot of weight. Each ascent feels like a first ascent and when it is repeated, it is always an adventure.[5]

Not only was Perroux a superb ice climber, but his natural charm and tall athletic good looks endeared him to many Nevis regulars. Unfortunately Perroux died in 2002 when the icefall he was climbing collapsed near his home village of Les Houches in the Chamonix Valley. News of his death came as a shock to climbers throughout Scotland, and in his obituary in *The Scotsman*, Alasdair Steven wrote:

His many friends in the [CIC] Hut had the good fortune to get to know a gifted climber and a most endearing man. Of an evening, Perroux delighted in cooking for those staying overnight. Despite the cramped surroundings and the limited facilities, he served up some remarkably good food. Omelettes and crêpes were his speciality, but he was game to concoct a meal from whatever was available. Once he was introduced to a haggis – but this most courageous of men was not ashamed to admit defeat on that occasion![6]

Perroux quickly climbed the well-known classics, and his natural inquisitiveness and technical ice climbing talent soon meant he was probing new lines. In many ways his first new route on the mountain in March 1989 was his finest. Gremlins takes the thin ice streak that runs the full height of the wall just right of Thompson's Route on Number Three Gully Buttress. Although this section of the mountain does occasionally form ice, it is doubtful that this ephemeral but outstanding line has been repeated, and its grade of VI,6 in the current guidebook is little more than an educated guess. In April 1991, Perroux focused on the icefalls on the steep area of cliff above the traverse of

French climbing guide
Godefroy Perroux on
the first ascent of Le
Panthère Rose (VI,6).
A superb ice climber,
Perroux was attracted
to the steepest ice
features on the
mountain

Photo: Bruce Goodlad

Godefroy Perroux
(1957 – 2002). Tall,
good looking and
oozing Gallic charm,
Perroux's enthusiasm
for Nevis ice endeared
him to many Scottish
climbers

Photo: Perroux collection

Raeburn's Easy Route that is now known as Raeburn's Wall. Together
with Jean-Pierre Destercke, who was to become one of his regular climbing partners on the mountain, Perroux climbed The Upper Cascade (V,5),
the natural continuation of The Cascade on the lower part of the wall. The
following April, they were back again to pick off Upper Cascade Central
(V,6) and Upper Cascade Right (V,6), the prominent icefalls to the right.

The 1993 winter was a good season for ice on Ben Nevis, although
it was very stormy during Perroux's week-long stay at the CIC Hut. He
returned to Raeburn's Wall and climbed Le Panthère Rose (VI,6), a very
steep, free-hanging ice pillar on the right side of the face that is very
much in the Continental idiom. His partners that day were Robin
Clothier and Bruce Goodlad who had become good friends, together
with F.Bossier from France. Four days later, Perroux and Bossier added
Une Journée Ordinaire dans un Enfer Quotidien (V,6) to Creag Coire
na Ciste. The translation – *an ordinary journey in a daily hell* – belies the

nature of the route which takes a hidden sliver of ice just left of Central Gully, and has become a popular modern ice test-piece. '*The name of the route is an allusion to the poor weather we had during our whole week on the Ben.*' Perroux later explained.[7] Perroux also added Le Nid d'Aigle (VI,5), a superb route linking a series of thinly iced grooves to the left of Riders on the Storm on Indicator Wall. This good line had been in the sights of several Scottish climbers, and the first two pitches had been climbed by Roger Webb and Ronnie Bruce in March 1984, but they were unable to complete the route due to a rapid thaw.

The following winter, Perroux had a ten-day stay in the CIC Hut where he maintained his momentum from the previous year. His first addition was with Destercke and three other clients when they added Mega Reve (VI,6), the steep icefall to the right of Jubilation on Jubilee Buttress. Perroux then teamed up with Fort William-based climber Jim Blyth, to climb the Rien Na Va Plus (V,5) on the lower tier of South Trident Buttress. This is probably one of the most walked-past ice features on the mountain, but the thin looking ice had put off all previous suitors. Conditions were perfect that day, as Blyth later recalled:

> Godefroy had a few mishaps with his kit on the route. He got to the belay at the end of the full 50m pitch and found he had broken a crampon and a pick without realising – the ice was so good. The name literally means 'nothing works anymore' or perhaps more eloquently 'the final straw', but Godefroy led the route with his customary grace. We descended leisurely to the hut for crêpes and coffee which we ate in the sun watching the action.[8]

Perroux and Blyth were on a roll, and two days later they added the stupendous line of Place Your Bets (VI,6), the very thin hanging icefall on the right side of Creag Coire na Ciste above North Gully, with J.Breil and D.Colin. The bottom section was very thin, as Blyth explained later.

> It was detached from the rock, vibrated as I climbed and it boomed disconcertingly for the first five metres or more. I was half way up before it was worth stopping for a screw. This whole bottom section was overhanging and fairly physical. The upper half was on good quality vertical ice. The route must have formed slowly with water running down the overhanging slab [above].[9]

In 1995 Perroux was again climbing on Ben Nevis and added the fine icefall of JP is Back (IV,4) with Destercke on Number Two Gully Buttress. The key overseas addition that season however came from French ice climbing specialist Francois Damilano who added The French Connection (VII,6) on Càrn Dearg Buttress in February with Dominique Dewale. This long and demanding icy mixed route is based on a series of variations to The Shadow with a sensationally exposed finish above the traverse of Route II Direct. The two French climbers had to climb deep into the night to finish this demanding expedition and there have been no known repeats. Perroux continued to add good new routes on the mountain with the first ascent of the icy ramp line of Trop Belle pour Toi (IV,5) in 1996, on the right flank of Number Three Gully with P.Bresse, and the superb Isandhlwana (V,5) in 1999 on North-East Buttress. Perroux was delighted with the latter route, which was climbed with Robin Clothier, Jean-Francois Males and Peggy Touvet, and he wrote later that it was

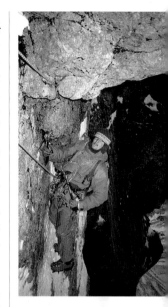

Dominique Dewale on the crux of The French Connection (VII,6) high on Càrn Dearg Buttress. This sustained route climbed with Francois Dàmilano in February 1995, is the most difficult route added to Ben Nevis by an overseas team

Photo: Francois Damilano

Climbers on The Shroud (VII,6) on the North Wall of Càrn Dearg. The route's reputation as one of the steepest ice pitches in Scotland means it receives many ascents when fully formed

Photo: Cubby Images

One of my best moments on Nevis...an incredible day, extraordinary quality of ice and a succession of great pitches in the sunshine.[10]

Until the late 1990s, few pure mixed lines had been climbed on Nevis, since it was thought that the rock does not run to protection as easily as the Cairngorms or Glen Coe. One notable exception was the first winter ascent of Gargoyle Wall by Rab Carrington and Ian Nicolson in December 1977. Although their ascent avoided the first two pitches of the summer line by traversing in from Thompson's Route and was originally graded IV, an ascent of the complete summer line is now considered to be VI,6 and one of the finest technical mixed climbs on the mountain. In 1979 Andy Nisbet and Brian Sprunt had climbed the summer HVS Central Route on Minus Two Buttress, and although they used some aid, their ascent again hinted what was possible.

In the 1980s several climbers took on the mixed challenge with winter ascents of summer routes. Notable examples were John Main and Andy Clarke's Cutlass (VI,7) in 1989, Clefthanger (VI,6) in 1985 by Doug Hawthorn and Arthur Paul, and in 1991 the serious Kellett's North Wall Route (VII,7) by Mark Charlton and Martin Burrows-Smith. Main and Clarke went on to form a strong partnership and had a superb 1993 season with the first winter ascents of The Groove Climb (V,6) on South Trident Buttress and a series of direct variations on Tower Face of the Comb that subsequently became known as Tower Face Direct (VI,6). Their finest contribution however was not a mixed route, but the broad hanging ice fang of The Shroud (VII,6) on the North Wall of Càrn Dearg. This was a much-eyed problem, but had either never formed completely, or collapsed before it had grown sufficiently to touch the ground. In 1993, the free-hanging ice fang was one metre short of connecting with the belay ledge, and the resulting ascent was a forceful and dangerous lead by Main of a long sought-after plum.

Doug Lang and Colin Stead, who had both played a pivotal role in the development of ice climbing on Ben Nevis in the 1970s with first winter ascents of several important climbs including Slav Route and Minus One Gully, formed another key partnership in the late 1980s and 1990s. In January 1988 they teamed up with CIC Hut custodian Bob Richardson to climb The Curtain Rail (IV,4) on the left edge of Càrn Dearg Buttress. This icy groove-line to the left of The Curtain was an overlooked objective that has now become very popular as an alternative for those tired of waiting in a queue for The Curtain. The following month, they made one of their finest additions to the mountain with Roaring Forties on Comb Gully Buttress. This striking V,5 line takes the sharp-cut hanging groove slicing through the right side of the headwall. It is often in condition and deserves to see more ascents. February 1993 saw the pair pick off another obvious gap with the first winter ascent of Chimney Groove (IV,6) on the east flank of Tower Ridge, which proved straightforward except for a short but fierce crux.

During the winter of 1994, Stead and Lang were active on the mountain in February and March, adding four new routes. Their best find was The Edge of Beyond (V,5) on the East Face of Tower Ridge. This exciting-looking route takes the projecting edge of Echo Wall to finish up the east face of the Little Tower. *'Like all the best routes, it was climbed by mistake!'* Lang revealed, during his presidential speech at the annual

SMC dinner later that year.[11] On North Trident Buttress they climbed the Left-Hand Ridge (IV,6), and the neighbouring Nereid Gully (III). Even closer to the hut, they enjoyed Fifties Revival (IV,6), the prominent groove on the left flank of the lower tier of Moonlight Gully Buttress.

Climbers had been attracted for years by the well-defined corner-line on the front face of The Comb to the left of Pigott's Route. It is defended at its base by a very steep wall, but there is a horizontal fault-line leading right from the start of Tower Face of the Comb into the foot of the groove. Simon Yates and Andy Cave succeeded on this line in February 1987, by aiding their way across the undercut fault to reach the corner, which gave two long pitches of sustained mixed climbing to the top. Several critics expressed surprise that a new route with an aid pitch was being added to Ben Nevis in the 1980s, but the majority were happy to accept this as an imaginative piece of exploratory climbing. The route was graded VI,6 and A2 and given the name Don't Die of Ignorance, which was a direct reference to the government AIDS campaign that was running at the time.

This mixed climbing adventure was very much a one-off experiment however, and the focus was still very much on ice. The following season, Simon Yates returned to The Comb and climbed Naïve Euphoria (V,6), the slim icy groove to the left of Mercury. In a similar vein, Bob Reid and Ian Crofton had a good find in 1987 with Beam Me Up Scotty (III), which takes a series of icy grooves on the right side of the buttress to the right of Glover's Chimney. Although relatively easy, the route finds it way through some interesting ground and pointed to the new route potential on this fine feature, now known as Goodeve's Buttress after Thomas Goodeve's 1907 route (see Chapter 4). Nine years later Reid returned to this area and added Hale Bopp Groove (III,4) with Bob Appleyard, a fine companion route to the left of the buttress crest.

The winter of 1993 revealed that Ben Nevis still had superb new ice and thin face routes to offer. It was a classic season with heavy snow-falls in January and a sequence of freeze-thaws throughout February and March, so that by the end of March the mountain was oozing ice. Roger Everett and Simon Richardson were attracted to the striking curving groove high up on the headwall of The Comb. The pair had forged an effective winter partnership resulting in a dozens of new routes across the Highlands, and Everett's wide mountaineering experience, collected from both Scotland and abroad, coupled with Richardson's enthusiasm, meant they formed a strong team. During the late 1980s and early 1990s they had been at the forefront of the development of the cliffs on the nearby Aonachs. They had never sought out new ground on Ben Nevis, but for this ascent they were well prepared, as Everett later explained.

> Simon had assembled an impressive collection of large scale photographs of all parts of the Ben. These served to determine where existing routes went, and, perhaps more importantly from Simon's point of view, where they did not. Thus was the idea of The Good Groove conceived – a blank on the map.[12]

The weather was poor, and although they couldn't see the route from below to assess the conditions, they started up regardless. From a point right of where the Hesperides Ledge leaves Comb Gully, they climbed

Goodeve's Buttress in Creag Coire na Ciste. The climbing potential on this prominent feature was first recognised by Bob Reid and Ian Crofton during their ascent of Beam Me Up Scotty (III), in 1987

Photo: Simon Richardson

a steep wall to give access to the right trending tapering groove. This was poorly protected but there was just enough ice and neve to make it climbable. Everett belayed below the crux section that reared up beyond the vertical.

> It was a day of rising freezing level and gale force sleet, a combination guaranteed to chill to the bone. Pitch three was the crux, and the scene of two simultaneous battles: Simon, with the climbing difficulties; and myself, struggling against the cold during the long belaying duty. As ever, Simon's perseverance won through and the extremely strenuous groove succumbed. As for myself, the training regime had been effective and, despite the shivers, my arms held out.[13]

The ascent of The Good Groove (VII,7), now regarded as one of the most elegant icy mixed lines on the mountain, was personally significant for both climbers. For Richardson, it was an eye-opener, and hinted at the exploratory climbing that Ben Nevis still had to offer, but for Everett it was to lead to a turning point in his climbing career.

> Although I had got through that particular battle, I was beginning to lose what might be described as the 'joy of masochism' that hard winter climbing so frequently involves. My thoughts were turning increasingly to warmer climbs, usually far from Ben Nevis.[14]

Full of enthusiasm, Richardson was back with John Ashbridge three weeks later to attempt a rising traverse across Indicator Wall, another prominent icy line. They climbed the sinuous line of grooves up the rib between Indicator Right-Hand and Riders on the Storm for two pitches, and were just starting the rising traverse, when Robin Clothier appeared through the mist below. He was climbing Riders on the Storm with Dave McGimpsey, and decided to follow Richardson and Ashbridge when he saw they were attempting a new route. Clothier and McGimpsey were the faster team, and there was a race across the face. The rivalry was friendly, but the stakes were high, for whoever reached the plateau first could lay claim the first ascent. Then as Ashbridge was starting up a section of steep bulging ice on the last pitch, disaster struck the lead team as Ashbridge described later in the SMC Journal.

> Something felt wrong. I looked down and... time just stopped: 10ft above a poor belay, 300ft up Indicator Wall, and 4000ft up Ben Nevis, my crampon had come off.[15]

Something felt wrong. I looked down and... time just stopped: 10ft above a poor belay, 300ft up Indicator Wall, and 4000ft up Ben Nevis, my crampon had come off

Fortunately, Richardson and Ashbridge were able to complete their line unchallenged and it was smiles all around at the top, because Clothier and McGimpsey found an alternative finish to the left. Flight of the Condor (VI,5) is one of the great natural lines on Indicator Wall and has seen several repeats, whilst the Mickey Mouse Finish (VI,6), one of the steepest ice pitches on the mountain, was not repeated until February 2007. The final new route of 1993 was Levitation (VI,6) by Dave Cuthbertson and Joanna George. This takes a parallel line of ice to the left of Perroux's Journée Ordinaire on Creag Coire na Ciste.

Heavy snowfalls early in 1994 resulted in superb climbing conditions throughout the Scottish mountains during February, as a cold easterly airstream stabilised the snow pack and created the best ice conditions

John Ashbridge on the first ascent of Flight of the Condor (VI,5). This rising traverse line across Indicator Wall breaks through impressively steep terrain with some remarkably straightforward climbing

Photo: Simon Richardson

since the winter of 1986. The Minus gullies and Orion Face routes proved popular, with routes such as Astronomy, which had rarely been in condition over the previous winters, seeing several ascents. The icefalls formed well, and Mega Route X was complete down to its base, eliminating the boulder problem start. Mal Duff continued to add to his Nevis scorecard with a string of new routes. He kicked off his 1994 campaign with a winter ascent of The Keep (IV,5) on The Castle with Ian Oates, before once again turning his attention to the North Face of Castle Ridge. In February 1991 Duff had made the first ascent of Le Mechant (IV,4) with Andy Perkins, and using his knowledge of this part of the mountain, he climbed Le Chat Noir (IV,4), the buttress between Casino Royale and La Petite, with D.Horrox, J.Robson and H.Ousby. Duff and Horrox then added Cherry Pickers (IV,4), the icefall to the left of American Pie with D.Potter. Further left on Fives Wall on Càrn Dearg Buttress, Duff climbed Slanting Slit (VI,6) with S. Greenhaugh, an intricate mixed climb based on the summer line of The Slant. Duff's own Casino Royale, was repeated by Robin Clothier and visiting French guide Francois Damilano in excellent conditions. Also that month across on Càrn Dearg, Simon Powell and John Wray climbed the prominent line of Wray's Rib (IV,4), which takes the right-bounding edge of Waterfall Gully.

Continued cold weather kept the snow soft and powdery throughout March 1994, which meant the higher cliffs were out of bounds, but

Roger Webb on the first ascent of The Blue Horizon (IV,4), one of the first routes to breach the steep central section of Raeburn's Wall

Photo: Simon Richardson

it allowed good ice build up at lower levels. On Càrn Dearg, The Shield Direct, Gemini and Waterfall Gully True Finish all had ascents, and on North-East Buttress, Robin Clothier and P.Pibarot, from Canada, linked together the line of steep icefalls to the right of Route Major to give The Lime Green Gaiter (V,5). Conditions became perfect in early April, when a huge snowfall was consolidated by a quick thaw followed by several days of cold weather. For the first time in many years every climb on the Minus and Orion faces was in immaculate condition, and early repeats of coveted routes such as Minus One Buttress and Urban Spaceman were there for the taking. Unfortunately by the weekend a major thaw had set in and the scores of climbers visiting the mountain were largely frustrated. On the Orion Face, Simon Richardson and Roger Webb were just early enough to climb Orion Directissima (VI,5), which links the Direct Start to Orion Direct with the prominent bow-shaped chimney right of the exit chimneys. Although their ascent covered little new ground, the route provides a worthwhile alternative to Orion Direct and Slav Route, and has seen a number of repeats when this part of the mountain is well iced.

Heavy unconsolidated snow during the 1995 season restricted activity on the mountain considerably, but after weeks of deep powder, the lower routes on the mountain briefly came into condition in late March. Mark Garthwaite and Adam Wainwright picked a major plum with the fine ascent of The Bewildabeast, a counter-diagonal to Gemini on the North Wall of Càrn Dearg. The ice smears in this area had long been considered as a possible left-hand exit to Gemini, but an independent start was found by starting some way up Waterfall Gully. Described as the most *'out there ice on the Ben'*, the VI,6 grade is probably on the modest side.

The good conditions were short-lived however, and the promise provided by the heavy snowfalls throughout the winter was broken by a major thaw at the beginning of April. Winter climbers eager to exploit the normally excellent late season conditions were disappointed to find many routes stripped, although a brief cold snap at the end of the first week prompted a couple of new routes. Roger Webb and Simon Richardson found The Blue Horizon (IV,4), a series of icy grooves to the right of Le Panthère Rose on Raeburn's Wall, and on the very right side of Indicator Wall, Neil Wilson and Jose Bermudez climbed Shot in the Foot (V,4), the short icefall to the right of Caledonia. This had possibly been climbed before, but not only does it finish on the summit of Ben Nevis, it also carries the unique distinction of starting higher than any other route in the British Isles.

An important milestone was the publication of *Ben Nevis Rock & Ice Climbs* by the SMC in April 1994. Authored by Simon Richardson, Alastair Walker and Robin Clothier, this was the first comprehensive guidebook to Ben Nevis since Jimmy Marshall's 1969 guide. It was also the first Scottish guidebook to use the two-tier winter grading system. The idea originated from an article Godefroy Perroux had written in *Montagnes* magazine in 1990, proposing a grade containing a Roman numeral alongside an Arabic number to reflect the seriousness and difficulty of French alpine routes. Perroux sent a copy of his article to Robin Clothier, who suggested to Simon Richardson that the system should be applied in Scotland. Richardson was not convinced that alpine grades were appropriate, but he saw the advantage of introducing a grading system that could adequately describe both the overall challenge and technical difficulty of Scottish winter routes. Up until that time, Scottish winter grading was a closed system with Grade VI used as the top level. As a result, many routes were undergraded, and the names of the first ascensionists often provided a more accurate indication of the likely difficulties, rather than the published grade.

Both Andy Nisbet, the New Routes Editor of the SMC Journal, and Roger Everett, the recently appointed Series Editor of the SMC guidebooks, were enthused, and a list of sample two-tier grades appeared in the 1992 SMC Journal. This list was compiled by a dozen Scottish winter activists, who agreed that Point Five Gully, as the most famous winter route in Scotland, should be the benchmark V,5 grade. Being an open-ended system, there was no need to compress routes into the Grade V and VI categories, and it was soon realised that the hardest winter routes had already reached Grade VIII in standard. The system was trialed as an appendix in the 1992 Glen Coe guide, before being formally adopted in the text in the Ben Nevis volume a couple of years later.

The 1994 edition of the Ben Nevis guidebook not only accurately described the vast array of new climbs added during the curved axe revolution, it also highlighted the huge potential for mixed climbing on Nevis. The stage was now set to look at the mountain with a fresh perspective.

The SMC 1994 guidebook to Ben Nevis by Simon Richardson, Alastair Walker and Robin Clothier, introduced a new two-tier grading system for Scottish winter climbs

References

1. Sheffield-based all-rounder Andy Cave became one of Britain's most accomplished mountaineers in the 1990s. His best known achievement was the first ascent of the North Face of Changabang in the Indian Himalayas in 1997.

2. **Perkins**, Andy, *Mal Duff – Cumha Calum*. On The Edge 69, 10 – 11, July 1997.

3. **Nisbet**, Andy, *New Climbs*, SMCJ 176, p190, 1985.

4. **Cartwright**, Chris, In: Richardson, Simon, *Forgotten Gems*. High Mountain Sports 244 , 48 – 49, Mar 2003.

5. **Perroux**, Godefroy, *Scottish Winter Climbing*. SMCJ 179, 1 – 3, 1988.

6. **Steven**, Alasdair, *Godefroy Perroux Obituary*, The Scotsman, 27 Feb 2002.

7. **Perroux**, Godefroy, *Ben Nevis Winter Climbs*, (Les Houches, France: Alp Impression, 2002, ISBN 2951774907.)

8. **Blyth**, Jim, *Personal communication, October 2006*.

9. Ibid.

10. **Perroux**, Godefroy, *Ben Nevis Winter Climbs*, see reference 7.

11. **Lang**, Douglas, In: Richardson, Simon, *Ben Nevis – Rock & Ice Climbs* (Glasgow: Scottish Mountaineering Trust, 2002, ISBN 0907521738.)

12. **Everett**, Roger, *Personal Communication, October 2007*.

13. Ibid.

14. Ibid.

15. **Ashbridge**, John, *Flight of the Condor*, SMCJ 186, 600 – 603, 1995.

14: Mixed Revolution (1996 – 2000)

THE 200 METRE-HIGH Pinnacle Buttress of the Tower lies between Broad Gully and Glover's Chimney on the left side of Coire na Ciste, and rises steeply to just below the Great Tower on Tower Ridge. It bristles with cracks and chimneys and was first climbed in the summer of 1902 by Glover and William Inglis Clark, but was ignored as a winter objective for over 90 years. The apparent reason for its winter neglect was that Donald Bennet climbed a Grade III route called Pinnacle Buttress of the Tower in 1957. It is a fine mixed expedition, but not accurately named as it completely avoids the buttress and takes a line well to the right. A more significant factor was that Ben Nevis andesite had a reputation for being smooth and crackless, and it was thought that it did not run to protection as easily as the more well known mixed climbing venues in the Cairngorms or Glen Coe. Until the mid-1990s, a handful of mixed climbs had been added over the years, but few of the first ascensionists had come back for more. With several areas of the mountain still unexplored in winter, there was clearly huge potential for adding mixed climbs for those bold enough to climb high above protection.

    The 1996 winter season was lean, with insufficient snowfall for the classic thin face routes to form. With little to lose, Chris Cartwright and Simon Richardson headed up to Ben Nevis early one Sunday in March to give Nevis mixed climbing a go. Cartwright and Richardson had forged a strong winter partnership over the previous five seasons with a series of difficult first ascents in the Cairngorms and Northern Highlands. Richardson, a petroleum engineer living in Aberdeen had two young children, and he managed the balance of family, career and mountains by opting to go climbing mainly on Sundays. Cartwright, a personnel manager based in Edinburgh, was happy to fit in with Richardson's constrained schedule, and they would meet up early most Sunday mornings through the season. Richardson's desire to look around new corners, coupled with Cartwright's determination and continuous optimism, meant they formed a strong and highly effective team.

The pair had an implicit trust in each other's judgement and had developed a systematic and tactical approach to winter climbing. After listening to the weather forecast on Saturday evening they would select a venue based on their experience of conditions the Sunday before and careful tracking of the precipitation, wind speed and temperature fluctuations during the intervening week. They always approached a cliff with primary and secondary objectives that required complementary conditions, and as a result they rarely went away empty handed.

Pinnacle Buttress of the Tower on the north-west flank of Tower Ridge. Stringfellow takes the zigzag line of weakness up the crest of the buttress

Photo: Simon Richardson

Richardson and Cartwright's plan that day was to climb the 1902 route on Pinnacle Buttress, but they almost failed before they reached the foot of the climb. As they cramponed up the rock hard neve slopes leading towards the buttress, one of Richardson's crampons came off his boot. The frame had snapped, but after some head scratching, they tied it together with cord that Cartwright used as loops for his gloves, and pressed on. The route turned out to be superb, with success in doubt until the end, as Richardson recounted several years later.

> After four pitches of sustained climbing up icy cracks and thinly plated slabs, we reached a superbly positioned platform on the very crest of the buttress topped by a vertical headwall. A steep groove cutting through the left side of the headwall was covered with bottomless rime and we ground to a halt with less than an hour before it got dark. Our options seemed exhausted. The right flank of the buttress was vertical and to our left, impossibly steep thinly iced slabs dropped down into Garadh Gully over 200 metres below. In desperation Chris peered round the right edge of the headwall and found a narrow hidden ramp that led to easier ground. In the half gloom of the approaching night, we raced up the easy connecting snow ridge to the foot of the Great Tower, scampered along the Eastern Traverse into Tower Gap and then dropped into the top of Observatory Gully. You can have a lot of fun naming routes, and by the time we reached the CIC Hut we'd come up with name of Stringfellow in honour of the short piece of cord that had saved the day.[1]

It turned out, of course, that Richardson and Cartwright were not the first climbers to have thought about climbing Pinnacle Buttress in winter. Robin Campbell had written about the possibility over 15 years earlier, in his chapter about Tower Ridge in Ken Wilson's book *Cold Climbs*, surmising that a route up the crest of Pinnacle Buttress would give –

> ...1,000ft of concentrated climbing up to the Ridge, over the Great Tower, the Gap, etc., without any of that dreadful fiddling about with coils. I don't know that anyone's actually *been* that way in winter.[2]

SMC guidebook author Simon Richardson. With Chris Cartwright he uncovered the mixed climbing potential on the mountain

Photo: Dave Hesleden

A key Ben Nevis pioneer for over 20 years, Chris Cartwright's continual optimism and focused determination was the perfect complement to Richardson's tactical approach

Photo: Simon Richardson

When Richardson spoke to Campbell after their ascent he told him a fascinating tale about Jimmy Marshall soloing the summer line one wet day in the 1960s. He was checking the line for his 1969 Ben Nevis guidebook, but he fell off the route and miraculously landed on a ledge. Richardson was intrigued when he heard the story.

> …the only ledge large enough to hold a fall was the platform below the headwall on Stringfellow. I met Jimmy a couple of years later, and asked him about the fall. Yes, he had slipped off some slime on the headwall and landed like a cat on all fours on the platform. His eyes sparkled when I told him about climbing the buttress in winter. He said he'd thought about it too and quietly mentioned several other mixed lines on the mountain that he'd picked out in the 1960s that were still unclimbed.[3]

Two weekends after Stringfellow, Richardson was back with Graham Dudley, an active climber, accomplished hill runner and oil industry colleague based in Aberdeen, to climb the fault-line slicing through the wall to the left of the buttress crest. This looked like an unlikely objective from below, but Richardson had noticed from Stringfellow that the wall was cut by a hidden slot. They reached this after two pitches and Dudley made a fine lead through intricate mixed ground up into the fault. Once he was secure at the next stance, Richardson hammered out the belay peg, and let go of the hammer expecting it to land on the end of its leash, but watched (in surprise) as it scooted down the steep mixed walls below and disappeared into Garadh Gully. It turned out that Richardson had forgotten to slip the leash through his hand, so he followed the pitch with one axe, and sheepishly asked Dudley if he could borrow his hammer to lead the next pitch. At first, Dudley didn't notice his partner's mistake.

> Simon was using the rock just like a genuine mixed climb – one tool on ice and one hand on rock. It did look like a nice technique. He got to the belay, and then I realised that he'd lost his hammer. It really surprised me, that someone of Simon's experience should drop his ice tool. 'That's a fatal error to make in the mountains,' I told him. 'I thought you were climbing with one axe to show off some fancy new mixed climbing technique![4]

Suitably scolded, Richardson continued quickly up the next pitch, which led to easy ground and the crest of Tower Ridge. As a reminder of his blunder they called the route Fatal Error and graded it IV,4, but the day ended on a high note when Dudley found the hammer at the foot of Garadh Gully on their way back to the CIC Hut.

Encouraged by their success on Stringfellow (VI,6), Cartwright and Richardson realised that other mixed possibilities were within their grasp, as Cartwright later explained in the American magazine, *Alpinist*.

> Simon and I were on a mission to rediscover Ben Nevis, and to shape it, if only fleetingly, in our own vision. Not the classic gullies and névé encrusted faces of the past - we'd done that. We wanted to add a new dimension: a Ben Nevis of hard, mixed, winter-only lines, a mountain that would challenge the limits of our abilities and, in doing so, draw out for us the essence of the Scottish winter experience. That desire distilled itself into one objective, a deep crack-line we'd name Darth Vader that cleaved an unclimbed, featureless wall high in the back of Coire na Ciste.[5]

Their attempt on the striking feature that sliced through the left end of Creag Coire na Ciste didn't start well. The weather was awful and they aborted after a brief foray onto the initial wall that barred entry to the crack itself.

> Surprised by the steepness and nervous about poor hooks in shaky flakes, I persuaded myself to back off. Still roped and racked, we scuttled left along a bulging shelf, around an arête and out of the wind to find ourselves beneath an innocuous-looking, right-facing corner. I set off up a fine crack that arched in from the right to join the corner after five metres. Thin hooks and delicate front pointing foreshadowed the riddle of the corner itself. A thread gave temporary confidence, but as I moved upward, the corner crowded me out... Soon, the moves began to resolve themselves. The walls on either side revealed hidden nooks. Sneaky knifeblades and cunning cams were bolstered by knees, elbows, shoulders, by bracing and tension, as I tested the frictional boundaries of snow, rock, steel and Goretex. I wish I could say I climbed that pitch... but I can't. I was stopped by a move that was just too difficult. I lowered off, stripped the gear and set Simon to work...[6]

Graham Dudley on the first ascent of Fatal Error (IV,4)

Photo: Simon Richardson

Cartwright had set the groundwork, and Richardson now knew the correct sequence of moves to reach his highpoint. A good nut gave him the confidence to lurch up the next few moves to a ledge that turned out to be a smooth sloping shelf, coated with loose snow. Struggling to hold on, he managed to torque an axe in a crack and step left. By standing on one foot he wasn't in balance, but at least he was able to rest his left arm. After an age he gingerly placed a wire above his axe, and then hammered home a good peg.

Richardson was now in position to consider the corner proper, which reared up to his right. Undercut at its base, it had a vertical right wall and a slightly overhanging left face. It looked hard, but the first move over the initial overlap was obvious enough. He stepped right and jammed his right boot hard into the wide crack. There was a good ice placement for his hammer and he pulled up. The corner now soared above, with blank, hoar-frosted walls on either side. The crack was parallel-sided and too wide to torque, as Richardson explained later in the SMC Journal.

> To progress any further, I needed a foothold, but there was nothing. For perhaps the first time when climbing a winter route I couldn't figure out how to climb it. Sure, I'd backed off many pitches in the past, but always I'd known it was possible for someone who was stronger or bolder than I. This corner looked impossible. I hung there with my right foot jammed beneath me and the hammer in the trickle of ice for what must have been nearly an hour. I cursed the rock. I cursed the corner. I cursed the mountain. Surely, there must be a way?

In frustration Richardson started to meticulously clear the left wall with his adze. Underneath the layer of frost he couldn't find any cracks or edges, only smooth rock. About three metres above, he could just make out a dimple under the layer of ice crystals. If only he could get that high, he thought, perhaps he could bridge across to some small holds high up on the right wall?

> I carried on scraping until at shoulder height I found a tiny chicken head.

Simon Richardson approaching the crux of Cornucopia (VII,9) on the first ascent. This short but technical route high on Creag Coire na Ciste, heralded a new phase of mixed climbing on Ben Nevis

Photo: Chris Cartwright

The knobble was perfectly formed, shallow and round, and about the size of my thumbnail. I brushed the hoar off with my glove and then used the heat of my bare hand to melt it free. It was slightly rough to the touch. Perhaps this was the key? I kept my glove off and held it between my thumb and fore-finger. It wasn't big enough to pull up on, but by leaning away to the right on my pick I could move my foot further up the crack below me. As I slowly inched up I found myself in a mantelshelf position with the chicken head pushing into the flesh on the outside of my left hand. I was about to fall, and needed something for my left foot, but the chicken head was too rounded and shallow to take a crampon point.

In desperation, Richardson had to think of something quick.

I moved my left foot above the chicken head and gently placed the vertical outside edge of the crampon frame onto it. I held my breath as I transferred my weight onto my left foot. It held! Slowly, ever so slowly, I stretched my left leg and stood up. I had to get a runner in quick. I grabbed the first piece of gear that came to hand, and pushed it into the crack. Rarely have I been so lucky. The crack was parallel-sided and slightly icy. Too icy for a Friend and not flared enough for a nut, but it was the perfect size for a Number 8 Hexcentric. A millimetre too small it wouldn't have fitted, and a millimetre too large it wouldn't have cammed. I breathed again, and continued up, one point precision front-pointing on the ripples on either side of the wall. Another first time Rock placement in an icy crack and I pulled over into an overhung shelf a few inches wide. A step right to a niche and the pitch was over.[7]

By the time Cartwright came up it had taken five hours to climb the corner. It was to take another four hours to battle up the flared cracks above, and then work out a way through the final steep walls to the top. Despite a gear tangle that resulted in a rest point low down on the second pitch, the ascent of Cornucopia (VII,9) was a landmark in the development of mixed climbing on Ben Nevis. It showed the mountain was capable of providing winter-only mixed routes of the highest difficulty and that it wasn't necessary to follow summer lines to find protection. It was comparable in difficulty with the hardest on-sight ascents being climbed elsewhere in Scotland and other parts of the world, although this wasn't realised at the time, least of all by Richardson and Cartwright who were still focused on the big Creag Coire na Ciste off-width as the major prize.

The ominous looking chimney-crack of Darth Vader became the focus of attention for the following season, as Cartwright wrote.

> Next year we were back, fearful for the sanctity of our original objective, speaking in whispers, looking over our shoulders, waiting for conditions.

Conditions in March 1997 were very icy, so they switched their attention to the unclimbed wall to the right where an impressive icy mixed line of twin stacked ramps led up to underneath an overhang breached by an impressive hanging icicle. On their first visit, Richardson and Cartwright decided the icicle was too thin, so they moved right and climbed Tinkerbell (IV,5), a right to left counter-diagonal to Wendigo. The weather throughout the following week stayed cool with fluctuating temperatures that were perfect for ice build up. They returned the following Sunday to find the cliff looking icier, but draped with fresh snow.

> Simon set off on a long tenuous lead up the ramps. The ice was barely thick enough to take his picks, but eventually he reached the foot of the icicle, and moved up to the roof to find an anchor. The only gear placement was a rather unsatisfactory sideways nut in a slot on the underside of the roof, but with no other options, he established a hanging belay and brought me up.

It was snowing heavily and there was an increasingly strong easterly wind that was shifting snow about on the upper slopes. Below, a team was avalanched out of South Gully, but they walked away in the mist, apparently unhurt. Undeterred, Cartwright confidently front pointed up the icicle. The ice was too thin to place a screw and he soon disappeared out of sight. The rope continued to pay out steadily before progress seemed to stop.

By the time Cartwright came up it had taken five hours to climb the corner. It was to take another four hours to battle up the flared cracks above, and then work out a way through the final steep walls to the top

The Simond Piranha evolved from the first generation of reverse curve tools and was very popular with British climbers in the 1990s. Note the curved shaft to allow better reach over bulges and the detachable handcuff style wrist loop

Starting the second pitch of Darth Vader (VII,8) on Creag Coire na Ciste

Photo: Viv Scott

...the slope breathed in and millions of unique wind-blown flakes of snow coalesced into a sudden whole. There was the muted thump, an interminable second as gravity took hold, and then the avalanche went off. Below me Simon waited unaware, semi-hanging off the solitary nut. A roar behind him and the sky went black. He gripped the rope, waiting for me to fly back over the roof, but I never appeared. Though the entire snow basin had avalanched, I'd driven my shafts deep into the hard layer below. With the slope now scoured, it was safe to continue to the cornice. So, this was South Sea Bubble, the crux a joyous pairing of two steep, right-to-left ramps, perched too enticingly above each other, inseparably conjoined, a teetering left-to-right umbilical its lifeline.[8]

Despite the exciting ascent and quality of the line, South Sea Bubble (VII,7) yet again felt like a consolation prize. Thoughts of attempting Darth Vader vanished as a major thaw set in, but hopes were raised when a cold spell was forecast for the Easter weekend. On March 30, the team returned for another attempt. It was an uninspiring day, misty with gentle snow, but the cliffs were white and frozen. All trace of the ice from three weeks before had gone, and the cracks were dry. Richardson led the opening pitch up to the belay ledge at the foot of the off-width, and then Cartwright set off up the vertical wall guarding entry to the off-width itself. The burden of expectation was high, but Cartwright skilfully dealt with the difficult moves low down and soon disappeared into the chimney-crack. The rope steadily ran out and after an hour Cartwright let out a whoop of delight.

Richardson was kept in suspense until he reached the belay where unbelievably the crack had opened out into a small cave. The bottom was flat and it was roofed by a giant capping chockstone with excellent belays. It was the perfect stance, and Cartwright was still grinning at their good fortune when Richardson set off up the third pitch. Pulling over the capping chockstone proved to be the crux of the route, although subsequent ascents have found that some build up here can ease the difficulty. The crack continued above, always sustained, but never too hard until the square platform common with Cornucopia was reached. From here the route continued up another tenuous off-width pitch to the plateau. Richardson and Cartwright were elated - the big objective had finally been climbed. Although in hindsight, the consolation prizes of Cornucopia and South Sea Bubble were harder and more serious undertakings, the compelling line taken by Darth Vader (VII,8) meant that it was destined for classic status.

The confidence provided by the triptych of routes on Creag Coire na Ciste was to lead to over 25 more mixed additions by the Cartwright-Richardson team over the next ten years. The following season was poor, though they made a good addition with a complete winter ascent of the summer line of Gargoyle Wall (VI,6). (The original winter ascent missed out the difficult lower two pitches by traversing in from Thompson's Route). Gargoyle Wall's position in the upper funnel of Number Three Gully means that it is exposed to north-westerlies and quickly comes into condition with the onset of cold weather. The quality of climbing and the good positions means it has become one of the most popular mixed climbs on the mountain. Later that season, the pair climbed Blockhead (V,6), the steep corner-line on the right wall of Number Three Gully up and left of Cornucopia, but in general they were disappointed not to capitalise on their 1997 successes. The 1999 season was better, with the first ascent of Hobgoblin (VI,7), the steep wall right of Gargoyle Wall, and the first winter ascent of The Banshee (V,5) on Number Three Gully Buttress. Both routes were climbed early in the season. The Banshee was climbed on New Year's Day in ferocious winds and low cloud, and they were the only team on the mountain that day. Three weeks later they battled their way up the steep smooth chimneys of the summer direct variations to Staircase Climb on Càrn Dearg to give Staircase Climb Direct (VI,7).

Chris Cartwright on the first ascent of Darth Vader

Photo: Simon Richardson

*Simon Richardson
setting off up
Hobgoblin (VI,7) on
the first ascent. This
steep mixed climb
takes the wall right of
Gargoyle Wall on
Number Three Gully
Buttress*

Photo: Chris Cartwright

Richardson and Cartwright's finest technical achievement was the first winter ascent of The Crack (VIII,8) on Raeburn's Buttress. This steep off-width splits the vertical front face of the buttress via a series of over-hanging steps and is interspersed with three horizontal ledges. Richardson had been dreaming about climbing this compelling line in winter for over ten years, but its steepness meant it caught little snow. Their big chance came in February 2000, during a rare weekend visit to the CIC Hut. A fierce storm swept in early on Friday night and dropped a metre of snow at the hut, with cover down to sea level. A reconnais-sance trip the following day resulted in the first winter ascent of Macphee's Route (V,6) on the North Wall of Càrn Dearg, and through the blizzard it was clear that The Crack was collecting snow. The storm was still raging when they left the hut at 5am next morning, but as they uncoiled their ropes at the foot of the route the skies cleared and the wind dropped. Conditions were perfect for mixed climbing, with over-hanging walls covered in a layer of hoar frost and ledges banked up with deep snow.

The first pitch of The Crack is deceptively steep and takes an impend-ing wall leading to the base of the off-width. Cartwright carefully picked his way through a puzzling maze of sloping holds interspersed with small tufts of turf and blobs of ice to a stance on the first narrow ledge squeezed under the smooth overhanging wall. To his left, the leering crack bottomed out into an overhanging left-facing chimney slot. On a surge of adrenaline, Richardson leapt up the left retaining wall of the slot and was soon teetering on a precarious mantelshelf to gain the second ledge. The stance was exposed, and the off-width split the smooth overhang-ing wall above, as if it had been cut by a knife. Cartwright was still catching his breath from following the second pitch when Richardson offered to take the lead again.

This section was clearly going to be the crux. Richardson bridged up the lower crack until he was perched below the capping off-width that overhung above his head at an angle approaching 45 degrees. He swung a large Hexcentric above his head and lodged it in the parallel-sided crack. The strain was beginning to show, and he hung off the runner to compose himself before muscling up the off-width, jamming his axe sideways across the smooth inside walls of the crack to give traction for the final heave on to another small ledge. The next pitch was still steep, but thankfully not overhanging any more. Richardson took the lead once again, but soon ground to a halt in the awkward bulging crack. Returning to the stance he stepped right along the ledge and climbed a series of overhanging walls and abruptly emerged onto easier ground below the upper section of Raeburn's Buttress.

By the time Cartwright reached the stance it was getting dark. The first four pitches had taken over ten hours, but they still had a lot of ground to cover. Swapping leads, they continued directly up the crest of the buttress, which narrowed and steepened as they gained height. They passed a final vertical blade of rock at the apex of the buttress, by climbing a steep vegetated groove situated high above the exit of Intermediate Gully.

Easy ground now led up and right into the snow bowl left of South Castle Gully, but the heavy snow that had favoured them below, and

Chris Cartwright on the deceptively steep first pitch of The Crack (VIII,8) during the first winter ascent. The crux off-width crack hangs ominously above

Photo: Simon Richardson

brought the route into condition, now conspired against them. The snow slopes were treacherously avalanche-prone so they trended up and left up snowy grooves on the right side of Baird's Buttress, digging out rock runners from deep under the snow whenever they could, and four pitches later they reached the summit of Càrn Dearg NW at midnight.

The pair were elated, and although the 11-pitch ascent was flawed with a rest point on the brutal third pitch, this did little to dampen the euphoria of pulling off such a long sought after climb. The Crack was only the second Grade VIII to be climbed on Ben Nevis, following on from the first winter ascent of Centurion climbed over fourteen years before. Rather ironically perhaps, the highpoint of the Cartwright-Richardson contribution to Ben Nevis was the first winter ascent of an established summer climb, rather than an independent winter-only line that is the distinguishing nature of the majority of their new routes.

Pinnacle Buttress of the Tower continued to play a key role in this

*Chris Cartwright
teetering up the
headwall pitch on the
first ascent of Smooth
Operator (VI,7) on
Pinnacle Buttress of
the Tower*

Photo: Simon Richardson

phase of developing mixed climbing on the Ben. Three years after the
first ascent of Stringfellow, Richardson was at the foot of Pinnacle
Buttress with CIC Hut custodian Robin Clothier, a fellow author of the
1994 SMC Ben Nevis guide. Looking at the buttress from across Coire
na Ciste the previous winter, Richardson had noticed that the steep right
flank was cut by a stepped line of chimneys, and this was the objective
for the day. Richardson and Clothier had been climbing together for
nearly 20 years, and as usual they were engaged in some energetic banter
as they geared up below the route. Richardson pulled his heavy mixed
climbing rack of battered nuts and pegs out of his pack and passed it
across to Clothier, but somehow something went wrong and it slith-
ered down the slope below them and was soon accelerating down Garadh
Gully into the mist.

It was an impressive display of incompetence, especially for two guidebook authors. Their embarrassment was compounded when they
downclimbed the upper snow slopes of Garadh Gully without a rope
and found the ice pitch wasn't banked up, so they had to climb up the
gully again and then walk the long way around the Garadh to look for
their gear. Fortunately, the first person they met was labouring under
a heavy-looking rucksack with a big grin on his face. Sure enough he
had their crucial rack of gear, so after thanking him profusely, they
headed up the slopes again and climbed the route without further incident. They named the route Butterfingers (V,6), and friends staying in
the CIC Hut that evening commented that the pair were bickering about
who dropped the rack well into the night. Clothier and Richardson made
an experienced team who added a variety of good mixed routes during

this period including Big Bad Ben (VII,7) in 1998, the steep pillar right of Roaring Forties on Comb Gully Buttress, Soft Ice Shuffle (IV,4) in 1999, the obvious mixed buttress left of Indicator Wall and in 2000 Cloudwalker (VI,6), the soaring fault-line to the right of Lost the Place on Creag Coire na Ciste.

There were two more challenges on Pinnacle Buttress to solve. The first was to climb the crest of the buttress direct, so March 2000 saw Cartwright and Richardson gearing up below the steep central section, determined to make an uneventful ascent and not break or drop any gear. The route went like clockwork, and they finished with a superb final pitch directly up the centre of the headwall. Delighted and somewhat relieved to have finally broken the Pinnacle Buttress jinx, they called the climb Smooth Operator (VI,7). Their final route was a tenser affair. Face Dancer (VI,6) teeters up the steep ice plated slabs on the left flank of the buttress that they had peered down during the first ascent of Stringfellow. Rather uniquely for Coire na Ciste, it was reminiscent of a serious thin face route high on the Orion Face, and relied on the exceptional ice conditions covering the mountain during February 2001.

With the benefit of hindsight it was fortuitous that Richardson and Cartwright's mixed explorations had taken place in Coire na Ciste. The character of the andesite on this part of Ben Nevis is dictated by its position relative to the collapsed volcano that was the origin of the mountain. Coire na Ciste, lying on the outer ring of the volcano, is comprised of more featured and cracked rock than the smooth lavas found on the Orion and Minus faces. The more amenable nature of the rock allowed the routes to be better protected than if the mixed climbing experiment had been tried on the smoother walls of Observatory Gully. Writing in a magazine article seven years after the first ascent of Cornucopia, Richardson reflected that

> ...almost by accident we had broken the spell surrounding mixed climbing on the Ben, but in truth we barely scratched the surface. A feast of possibilities awaits.[9]

With the benefit of hindsight it was fortuitous that Richardson and Cartwright's mixed explorations had taken place in Coire na Ciste...The more amenable nature of the rock allowed the routes to be better protected than if the mixed climbing experiment had been tried on the smoother walls of Observatory Gully

References

1. **Richardson**, Simon, *It's All in the Name*. High Mountain Sports 242, 22 – 23, January 2003.

2. **Campbell**, Robin, *Tower Ridge Rulebook*. Cold Climbs, 79 – 86, Ken Wilson, Dave Alcock & John Barry eds., (London: Diadem Books, 1983, ISBN 0906371163.)

3. **Richardson**, Simon, *It's All in the Name*. High Mountain Sports 242, 22 – 23, January 2003.

4. **Dudley**, Graham, *Interview, August 2007.*

5. **Cartwright**, Chris, *Darth Vader*. Alpinist 22, p38, November 2007.

6. Ibid.

7. **Richardson**, Simon, *Hooks, Torques and Chicken-Heads – Cornucopia.* SMCJ 188, 220 – 221, 1997.

8. **Cartwright**, Chris, *Darth Vader*. Alpinist 22, p38, November 2007.

9. **Richardson**, Simon, *It's All in the Name*. High Mountain Sports 242, 22 – 23, January 2003.

The immaculate rock and well-defined features of Càrn Dearg Buttress make it a magnet for rock climbers. Throughout the 1980s and 1990s, this cliff was the focus of difficult rock climbing on Ben Nevis

Photo: Tom Prentice

15: Summer Rock (1986 – 2007)

FOLLOWING THE INTENSE rock climbing developments on Càrn Dearg in the early 1980s, exploratory summer climbing on Ben Nevis went into decline for nearly 15 years. Most parties were happy to tick the classics on Càrn Dearg such as Centurion and The Bat, whilst more skilled teams tackled the harder routes such as King Kong, Caligula and Titan's Wall that were featured in the book *Extreme Rock*[1]. A series of wet summers frustrated many mountain rock climbing plans, and instead, climbers were drawn to the recently developed crags of Polldubh, or the dozens of accessible cliffs such as Reiff and Diabaig that were being explored in the Northern Highlands.

It was not just the weather that was keeping climbers away from Ben Nevis and other high mountain cliffs. Rock climbing was experiencing a rapid series of changes, and improved equipment, protection and fitness levels were leading to higher levels of technical achievement. The adoption of chalk in the early 1980s allowed climbers to keep their fingers dry and make harder moves. Chalk also made climbing well-travelled routes psychologically easier, because the white daubs on the rock often pointed the way ahead and removed route finding uncertainty. Spanish Firé boots with sticky rubber soles were introduced in the mid-1980s, pushing standards even higher, while improved protection devices such as spring loaded cams and curved nuts made it easier to protect climbs[2].

The greatest change was the wholesale adoption of specific strength training for rock climbing. In 1974, Pete Livesey, a Yorkshire-based climber with a track athletics background, demonstrated the advantages of training on a climbing wall with first ascents of Footless Crow (E5) in Borrowdale and Right Wall (E5) on Dinas Cromlech in North Wales. Livesey trained on a wall in a corridor at Leeds University. This was built by Don Robinson in 1964 and was the world's first purpose-built climbing wall. Within a year, attitudes across Britain changed, and climbers started to train seriously in gyms and on first generation climbing walls. In the mid-1970s, Very Severe was the grade that many climbers aspired to, and the hardest routes across the UK were rarely more than E3.

The new approach meant that the Extreme grade was now within reach of regular climbers. Those at the top pushed the technical envelope, and standards soared. In Scotland, a milestone was reached when Dave Cuthbertson, after extensive pre-practice, climbed Requiem at Dumbarton Rock in 1983. This was the first Scottish route to be graded E7 and one of the hardest rock climbs in the world at the time. An outstanding achievement, it took at least ten years before its significance on the world stage was fully recognised, and the route is now considered to be E8 6b. The focus on higher standards prompted climbers to climb on more easily accessible crags rather than venture into the mountains, where technical difficulty is often masked by environmental factors such as cold temperatures, wet rock and vegetation.

Ken Crocket and Alastair Walker were the only climbers to uncover new ground on Ben Nevis during the summers of 1986 and 1987. In September 1986 they climbed The Black Douglas (Severe), which finds its way up the wall of excellent grey rock to the right of the Direct Route on the Douglas Boulder. The following August they explored Garadh na Ciste, the subsidiary buttress to the right of Garadh Gully. Relatively easy climbing right of the gully led to the apex of a pyramidal mass of rock. Above the buttress steepened, but a cunning line weaving up ramps led to a spectacular breakout through some overhangs before easier ribs and corners lead to the top. They called their four pitch Very Difficult climb Blue-Nosed Baboon, and as they made their way down the short descent into Coire na Ciste they could not resist climbing the steep red wall at the right end of the wall overlooking Coire na Ciste. Cryotherapy (Very Difficult) follows the prominent corner bounding the red wall on the left, and provides a worthwhile two-pitch route, with some good positions for the grade.

The following summer, Andy Tibbs, Andy Fraser and Wills Young spent a couple of days in the CIC Hut. They warmed up with an ascent of Sassenach, and the following day they visited the line of steep crags below Càrn Dearg Buttress, that are just a short walk from the hut. Although several icefalls had been climbed on these cliffs before, they were untouched in summer. The trio climbed a cracked arete on the right side of the steepest area of rock, resulting in The Trial (E3), a superbly sustained 5c pitch. The route was led on-sight by Wills Young, a gifted rock climber, as Tibbs remembered nearly 20 years later.

> Wills is probably the most talented rock climber I've ever climbed with. He also led Organ Pipe Crack that day, another E3 at the left end of that wall which was left unseconded – the cracks looked a bit tough on the hands and if you'd ever seconded Wills on gritstone, on which he is something of an expert, you'd understand why nobody fancied following him.[3]

Wills Young making the first ascent of The Trial (E3). This steep single pitch route is situated on the line of cliffs below Càrn Dearg Buttress, just above the path from Lochan Meall an t-Suidhe

Photo: Andrew Fraser

*Guy Muhlemann on
the True Finish to
Red Rag (E2) – 'a
spectacular outing,
totally illogical but
sensationally exposed'*

Photo: Simon Richardson

Young moved to North America soon afterwards and became an active player in the US rock climbing and bouldering scene, so his impact on Scottish rock climbing was unfortunately short-lived. The difficult Boadicea (E4) was the only new route added in the summer of 1989. Willie Todd and Alasdair Cain started up Titan's Wall and then broke out right to climb the thin line of cracks to the right. Todd recalled later that the route was not quite up to the quality of Titan's Wall, but it was still a very good climb and just a little bit harder.

During the summer of 1991, Guy Muhlemann and Simon Richardson spent several weekends camping below Càrn Dearg, climbing multiple routes as training for their forthcoming alpine season. By early July, they had ticked most of the classic lines with only Titan's Wall left to do. The weather was superb, and after they had completed the route and abseiled down it was still early afternoon, so they set off up an unclimbed line they had spotted between Torro and Centurion. The first pitch took the cracked wall just left of Centurion's opening pitch and then continued up the inviting V-groove above. The crucial section above moved left onto the awkward slab on Torro's second pitch then broke right through the roofs above. Richardson traversed right into a groove and was alarmed to find a loose perched block. Gingerly avoiding this he pulled over a roof and stepped down and right into a hidden second groove on the right where he found a small belay. It was getting late as Muhlemann followed the pitch, so they decided to abseil off and complete the route the following day.

They excitedly made dinner that night in their small tent nestling in the heather under the buttress, and prayed that it wouldn't rain. The weather stayed good, and next morning they reclimbed the lower pitches and continued up the slabs above, with Muhlemann making a crucial lead through the great overlap to join the traverse of Adrenalin Rush. The way ahead was now clear up the upper slabs to reach the Route II traverse, but it was a busy day on the crag. Although most of the route was wonderfully clean on rough white rock, Richardson had to gently clear pebbles out of the crack on his lead, and stuff them into his pockets to prevent them hitting a team on The Bullroar below.

Centurion and Torro are the only routes that force their way through the upper band of overhangs above the Route II traverse, and the pair was keen to find an independent finish for their new climb. Unfortunately they ground to a halt on wet mossy rock to the left of Torro's final corner, so they backed off and finished up Centurion. As a gentle rejoinder to the dramatic-sounding route names on the buttress, they called the climb Red Rag, and graded it E2. They returned four years later and added the True Finish, which they described as – 'a spectacular outing, totally illogical but sensationally exposed.'[4]. This heel-tugging variation traverses left from where Centurion breaks through its first awkward bulge along the lip of the roofs, to finish up a steep groove left of Torro's final corner.

Later that summer, in September, Con Higgins and Tam McAuley added Prodigal Boys (HVS) to the steep buttress high up on the left side of the North Face of Castle Ridge. They returned the following June and climbed Camanachd Heroes (E1), up the left side of the wall. In common with the adjacent Very Severe climb Plastic Max climbed by Bathgate and Anderson in 1971, it is unlikely that any of these lines have seen a repeat, despite their superb position tucked under the crest of Castle Ridge. McAuley was to die in 2007, swept down a burn in spate while walking on the island of Rum. The pace slowed down even more in the following summers, though Noel Williams found three short routes below North Trident Buttress including Tuff Nut (HVS) in 1993, while Dave Jenkins and Colin Stead added Walking Through Fire (VS) in 1994 to the left of Cutlass on the Douglas Boulder.

During the 1995 summer, Colin Moody kept the rock climbing exploratory spark alive with two good new routes. On July 10 he climbed Strident Edge on South Trident Buttress with Billy Hood. They were planning to visit a lower crag later in the day, but Moody had a change of heart and persuaded Hood to do Spartacus, the neighbouring route to the right. As a result, Moody realised that the fine crack between Strident Edge and Spartacus was unclimbed, so two days later he was back with Andy Nelson to give it a go.

> Andy wanted to do it on-sight, but I talked him out of it because the route would be better after cleaning. I cleaned and did lots of trundling – the top of Strident Edge is a lot better now.

Moody was not underestimating the amount of rock he removed, because a party on Tower Ridge that day commented afterwards that the rockfall was worse than they had seen in the Alps. The effort was worth it though, and the result was Devastation, a fine two pitch E1. Appropriately, it was Moody who came up with the name. A month later, Moody was back camping by the CIC Hut with Nick Turner. They climbed King Kong, and the next day made a rare repeat of Subtraction on the Minus Face. Moody had wanted to climb this route for several

Colin Moody kept the summer exploratory spark alive on Ben Nevis with a series of good new additions in the mid 1990s

Photo: Ian Taylor

Danny Brooks on the first ascent of The Blind (VS). This direct version of Mourning Slab on the left side of Càrn Dearg Buttress is rarely dry

Photo: Colin Moody

years, and during their ascent he spotted an unclimbed line of cracks up the buttress to the right of the start. Unfortunately Turner, who found Subtraction rather disappointing, was not interested in Moody's line and went back to their camp. Rather than sit in the tent, Moody finished the day by soloing Observatory Ridge and descending Tower Ridge, but ten days later he was back with Billy Hood, and in a determined mood.

> Billy wanted to do The Pin on the Shelter Stone, so we met at Aviemore on Saturday morning, did The Pin then camped at Polldubh that night. The next day we climbed the line right of Subtraction, alternating pitches on-sight, although I had to clean a few feet of the crack with my nut key.

The appropriately named Long Division is a fine companion E1 route to the better-known Subtraction. *'Billy came up with the name,'* remembered Moody, *'I thought of Slide Rule'*. The following September, Moody and Danny Brooks added The Blind (VS), a direct version of Mourning Slab on the left side of Càrn Dearg Buttress. Moody had been considering this line for some time, but it is almost permanently wet, as he recounted later.

> I thought it would need a heat wave and a third person with a sponge and bucket at the top! Danny led the first pitch, and I wimped out of a possible second pitch which was running with water, but it might have been OK (we were climbing on-sight again), so we finished up Mourning Slab.[5]

Moody's reference to 'on-sight' in these ascents is significant because climbing styles were undergoing substantial change during the 1990s. Sport climbing, where routes are pre-protected by bolts, was developed in the 1980s on the limestone crags of Europe, particularly in France and Spain. Ten years later it had become established as a mainstream part of the sport and hundreds of sport climbs had been established in Britain, mainly in quarries and on the limestone cliffs of the Peak District. British climbers were quick to embrace the sport climbing approach as a complement to traditional climbing, and it became standard practice to take a short holiday abroad, clipping bolts in the spring as preparation for the summer season ahead.

Sport climbing allows absolute focus on the difficulty of climbing a technical crux, or linking together a sequence of difficult moves, and presents a different challenge to traditional, or *trad* climbing, where much of the difficulty comes from reading the rock, planning the moves ahead and finding protection. As the two styles became recognised as separate and distinct, various terms were used to describe the nature of different forms of ascent. *On-sight* describes an ascent where the climber has no prior knowledge of the route, either from pre-inspection or prior attempts, and *ground up* is where the route is not pre-equipped with protection from above. From a trad climber's perspective, the perfect ascent is a route climbed on-sight without pre-placing any gear.

During the 1970s it became accepted practice to abseil down potential new climbs and *clean* them to remove vegetation and loose rock. Inevitably this practice, which is essential for the creation of many modern, high standard rock climbs, allows routes to be examined, holds to be tested and moves practised. By the 1980s, the cleaning of new rock routes had become became accepted practice, and the hardest climbs

Rick Campbell on the first ascent of The Wicked (E6). With four consecutive 6b pitches, this was the most significant rock-climbing advance on Ben Nevis since Pete Whillance's Agrippa climbed 18 years before

Photo: Gary Latter

Gary Latter, a leading Scottish summer activist for more than 20 years, made hundreds of first ascents across the Highlands and Islands. His ascents of The Wicked and Trajan's Column took Ben Nevis rock climbing standards to a new level

Photo: Karen Latter

were rarely climbed without pre-knowledge. Consequently, rock climbing standards rose not just due to improved ability and equipment, but also because the ethic of establishing new climbs was softened to allow for pre-inspection. In contrast, the attitude to aid moves on rock climbs hardened considerably. Whilst it was acceptable to use a point or two of aid on a climb in the 1970s, aid points were gradually eliminated through the following decade, to the extent that many climbers would prefer to fail and retreat from a route, rather than completing the ascent by using a point of aid.

It was another five years after Moody's additions before the next summer route was added on Ben Nevis. In September 2001, accomplished Scottish rock climbers, Gary Latter and Rick Campbell completed their ascent of The Wicked, a sustained and very direct E6 line cutting through The Bat. The route had four consecutive 6b pitches, and was the most significant rock climbing advance on the mountain since Whillance's ascent of Agrippa in 1983. In contrast to the accepted practice of the day, Latter and Campbell chose to attempt the route in the most adventurous style possible – ground up and on-sight. The high technical

Rick Campbell on the first ascent of Trajan's Column (E6). This was the second important contribution to Càrn Dearg Buttress by the Campbell-Latter team

Photo: Gary Latter

Rick Campbell's fiercely traditional approach and ability to climb at his physical limit led to a series of bold and difficult new climbs across the Highlands. He is best known for his trilogy of E7s added to the Shelter Stone, Cairngorms, in the 1990s

Photo: Gary Latter

difficulty meant that the route was climbed in sections. The first three pitches were climbed in July 2000, pitches four and six added in July 2001, and the fifth pitch the following September, as Campbell described several years later.

> Gary led the two hardest pitches. Wet rock at the start of the first pitch will always be a major problem for repeat ascensionists, and this was the main factor, apart from laziness, for not re-climbing this pitch on the other two visits it took to complete the route. A certain amount of gardening on aid was required on the really steep pitches, but all pitches were then led free in a single push.

The staged style of the climb raised eyebrows at the time, and the route still awaits a single push ascent. Latter and Campbell's adventurous approach brought into sharp focus the difficulty of climbing cutting edge mountain rock routes on-sight. Writing five years after their ascent, Campbell was unrepentant about their tactics.

> I am quite satisfied with the style. I don't feel two days spent cleaning and 'inspecting' on abseil before a clean one day ascent is any improvement.[6]

The following year, Latter and Campbell returned to Càrn Dearg to attempt another difficult line based on the front face of the pillar to the right of King Kong's main pitch. After a couple of entry pitches, Campbell set off up the pillar that he later described as '*a fantastic wildly-positioned pitch, with devious wandering climbing and spaced protection*'.[7] Unfortunately he had to escape onto King Kong near the top of the pitch, but on September 7 the following year, they returned and climbed the complete route to give Trajan's Column, another outstanding E6 test-piece, and this time very much Campbell's creation.

> Whereas The Wicked was spotted from below [and only became apparent] after many visits to the crag, I fancied the buttress right of Centurion from the first time I saw the crag in 1985. Trajan's Column was my baby as I led all three new pitches. It was much more my sort of climbing, not too steep but fairly nasty (you could break your ankles on the 6b crux move) and I would say getting up ninety percent of the main pitch [on-sight] was one of my best leads ever. After climbing up to the top overlap ground-up (with a couple of big falls), I ran out of ideas and finished up the slab right of King Kong. Next year I came back and inspected it from above, did the pitch and continued to the top.

Writing in 2006, just after taking a spectacular fall whilst attempting a third new route on the crag, Campbell was sanguine about the merits of the on-sight approach compared to abseil inspection.

> This year, I was able to re-appraise the merits of the two climbing styles on the right arête of the Sassenach chimneys. The nasty bit up to the Caligula thread I abseil cleaned, which makes that sort of climbing fairly straightforward when you know there's enough gear. I then continued on-sight up the arete above with hard moves on mossy rock only to find myself laybacking up the 'precariously balanced block' left of Banana Groove...not a mistake anyone else can make now! I think the abseil approach is required herewith.[6]

In July 2005, Dave MacLeod, an outstanding young climber from Glasgow, brought Ben Nevis rock climbing standards in line with the hardest routes Scottish routes of the day, by climbing a new E8 up the overhanging front face of The Comb. MacLeod had already established a formidable reputation for climbing difficult new routes, both in summer and winter, and was becoming recognised as the finest Scottish climber of his generation. In 2006 he was to rise to worldwide prominence with his first ascent of Rhapsody (E11) at Dumbarton rock, which was hailed as the most difficult traditional rock climb in the world. By the summer of 2005, after a long apprenticeship centred on the lowland outcrops of Scotland, MacLeod was eager to leave his mark in the Scottish mountains.

> One major piece of unclimbed rock was until recently, the front face of Comb Buttress on Ben Nevis. This 200m-high pyramid-shaped face has a 1-in-3 overhanging lower barrier 60m high with no climbs on it...I had been inspired by this face since first climbing on the Ben several years ago and wondered

Rick Campbell ascending the 'fantastic wildly-positioned' crux pitch during the first ascent of Trajan's Column (E6)

Photo: Gary Latter

Dave MacLeod on the first ascent of Anubis (E8) in July 2005. This was one of the hardest rock climbs ever achieved in Scotland without the benefit of pre-practice

Photo: Cubby Images

why no one had tackled the overhanging barrier. So after a long period of doing new routes on outcrops and sea cliffs I decided to visit some mountain crags and this was top of the list.

An intermittent crack line runs up the crest of the massive ship's prow arete on the right flank of the buttress to the left of Pigott's Route, which is defended by a large barrel-shaped roof at its base. After a thorough clean on abseil, MacLeod decided to attempt the line without practising any moves.

My initial estimation of 'flashable E7' was quickly revised after my first venture on lead, which revealed the angle of the bouldery arete crux above some dubious gear and a nasty slab landing to be rather steeper than it seemed from the abseil rope. After several forays, followed by down climbs to the ground I had gained enough familiarisation to summon some bottle and make the committing crux slap and scary run out above.[8]

MacLeod graded Anubis E8 6c which meant it was a two-grade jump in difficulty from The Wicked, and one of the most difficult high mountain rock climbs in Scotland. The crux involved a powerful sequence through the initial roof, and entailed a committing five-metre run out above two suspect cams that could have left MacLeod dangerously close to the ground if they failed to hold a fall. MacLeod was particularly pleased with the style of his ascent, and commented afterwards that only Dave Cuthbertson had made first ascents of a similar difficulty in

Scotland without first practising the moves. Here MacLeod was referring to Cuthbertson's first ascents of Femme Fatale (E8 6c) in 1986, on Whale Rock in Glen Nevis and Symbiosis (E8 6b) in 1995, on Creag a' Bhancair in Glen Coe. For his part, Cuthbertson was quick to praise MacLeod's ascent, and pointed out the logistical difficulties of climbing hard rock high on Ben Nevis.

> It is worth mentioning that The Comb is no roadside crag and Dave had to endure some adventurous preparation. Those of you accustomed to doing first ascents in the Scottish mountains will appreciate the hard work involved and Dave's route is no exception. A roped solo ascent of Pigott's was made to access the line, which required cleaning but was not practised. Two trips were made and the route was flashed on an unseasonable, but not untypical, bitterly cold day.[9]

MacLeod's approach almost certainly represents the future of difficult rock climbing on Ben Nevis, and the majority of the hard lines of tomorrow will be pre-prepared, like his 2008 *tour de force* Echo Wall highlighted later. But even so, the mountain remains surprisingly neglected in summer, as MacLeod explained.

> Contrary to winter, the North Face [of Ben Nevis] is eerily quiet in summer and feels like an even bigger place than usual. Usually I'm cleaning and working on hard new routes, so I come up by myself and stay in the CIC Hut. Every time I assume that there will be some company in the hut, given the fine weather and the importance of this crag in UK climbing – but most times I have the hut to myself.[10]

Take a walk up to the CIC Hut early on a summer's day and you are confronted by three kilometres of cliffs lit up by the morning sun. The obvious mountaineering challenges were climbed long ago, and the easily accessible routes on Càrn Dearg and Trident Buttresses are frequented on good days, but many unclimbed walls and features lie untouched. The potential for exploratory rock climbing is huge, both for the adventure climber and for those like MacLeod who are pushing the technical envelope.

Contrary to winter, the North Face [of Ben Nevis] is eerily quiet in summer and feels like an even bigger place than usual...

References

1. *Extreme Rock,* Ken Wilson & Bernard Newman eds. (London: Diadem Press, 1987, ISBN 0906371368). The fourth in a series of illustrated books by Ken Wilson highlighting many of the finest summer and winter climbs across the UK.

2. *Friends* and *Rocks* manufactured by Wild Country in Sheffield were the cams and curved nuts used by the majority of British climbers in the 1980s.

3. **Tibbs**, Andy, *Personal communication, September 2007.*

4. **Muhlemann**, Guy, *New Climbs.* SMCJ 187, p95, 1996.

5. **Moody**, Colin, *Personal communication, September 2006.*

6. **Campbell**, Rick, *Personal communication, September 2006.*

7. **Campbell**, Rick, *New Climbs.* SMCJ 196, p154, 2005.

8. **MacLeod**, Dave, *Scottish Rock Report.* Climb 8, 11 – 12, October 2005.

9. *www.cubbyimages.co.uk*

10. **MacLeod**, Dave, *Stomping Grounds.* Climb 32, 32 – 37, October 2007.

16: The End of an Era (2001 – 2002)

BEN NEVIS IS RENOWNED throughout the climbing world for its thin face routes. The location of the mountain close to the western seaboard of Scotland means it is battered throughout the winter by Atlantic storms bringing snow, sleet and hail. It takes more than just bad weather to coat the mountain in climbable snow-ice however, and thin face routes are formed by a precise combination of wind direction, precipitation and temperature fluctuations. The process starts typically when cloud droplets freeze on contact with cold rock as warm air is carried on a westerly wind and uplifted over the frozen mountain. The result is a layer of rime, delicate feathery growths of ice that stick to steep slabs, vertical walls, and even under roofs as long as they are facing into the wind. With this crucial covering in place, a rapid succession of freeze-thaws consolidates the rime into more cohesive snow-ice. The resulting medium has the consistency of high-density polystyrene and is a delight to climb.

When conditions are perfect it is easy to dismiss thin face routes as soft touches. The grading of Scottish winter climbs will never be an exact science, and rating thin face routes on Ben Nevis is particularly diffi-cult. These climbs rely on a build-up of snow-ice on steep slabs and are climbable when the covering is only two or three centimetres thick. Rarely does the pattern of freeze-thaws allow the snow-ice to form thicker than this, and it only takes one big thaw to strip the routes entirely. The climbs are so sought-after and coveted, that as soon as they are climbable they receive ascents. Once committed to the route the climb-ing is rarely technically difficult, and is more a delicate game of mind control whilst balancing on tip-toe up thinly iced slabs far above protec-tion. Once every decade or so however, the ice forms more thickly and can take ice screws. The serious element of the climbs then largely disap-pears. Both the 2001 and 2002 seasons produced superb ice on the thin face routes on Ben Nevis with conditions comparable to the great winters of 1978 and 1986.

The 2001 season started with a focus on mixed routes. Dave MacLeod, a young student at Glasgow University, spent a week in January tour-ing around Scotland with Urs Stoeker, a talented Swiss climber with many difficult European mixed routes and a first ascent on Trango Tower in the Karakoram to his credit. They spent their first two days climb-ing in the Northern Corries, before moving west to Ben Nevis where they made an ascent of Tower Face of the Comb. The following day they tried Cornucopia on Creag Coire na Ciste that had recently repelled a couple of repeat attempts. Stoeker climbed up to the top of the crux corner, but the onset of a storm slowed them down, and they were forced to abseil off. They returned after a rest day to record the second ascent in better weather.

Stoeker and MacLeod are credited with the first free ascent of Cornucopia. The first ascent was made in very lean conditions with little snow in Number Three Gully (this lower section normally banks out)

Cold Climbs was reprinted in 2001 with an Addendum highlighting recent trends and developments. The book continues to inspire winter climbers to this day

Courtesy Bâton Wicks

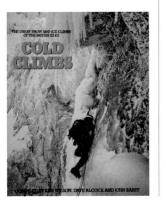

The Orion Face. Climbers can be seen on the upper snow field of Orion Direct, and at the tops of Zero Gully and Hadrian's Wall Direct. There are now 13 winter routes on this 400m-high wall

Photo: Henning Wackerhage

Improvements in ice screw design during the 1990s made ice climbing safer and more accessible. This well used example of a Black Diamond Express Ice Screw illustrates many of the features. Hard steel with razor sharp teeth and a polished tapered bore allow for rapid placements using the fold down handle

and Richardson used a rest point to free a gear tangle low on the first pitch. Stoeker rated the technical difficulty of Cornucopia M7+, which was the first time a Scottish route had been benchmarked against the new mixed grading system being developed in North America and Europe. News of MacLeod and Stoeker's success spread quickly and six days later Cornucopia saw a third ascent from the strong Aberdeen based pair of Guy Robertson and Pete Benson.

The following month, Alan Mullin, a young climber living in Strath-conon, made a remarkable two-day solo ascent of Centurion on Càrn Dearg Buttress. Mullin had rocked the climbing establishment in the late 1990s with a string of controversial but high standard mixed routes in the Cairngorms. His forthright manner made it hard for him to retain climbing partners and he began experimenting with solo climbing, often at night to add an extra challenge. Mullin's finest climb was the first

*Alan Mullin (1972 –
2007). During his
brief but highly
eventful eight-year
climbing career,
Mullin turned the
Scottish winter
climbing world upside
down with a series of
controversial and
cutting edge first
ascents*

Photo: Simon Richardson

winter ascent of The Steeple (IX,9) on the Shelter Stone Crag, which
he climbed with Steve Paget in November 1999. The climb attracted
controversy due to its early season nature. After a short, but highly eventful climbing career, Mullin retired from climbing in 2004. Tragically,
he took his own life in March 2007.

Centurion was first climbed in winter by Kenny Spence and John
(Spider) McKenzie using a rest point over two days in February 1986
and had not seen a repeat. Mullin made two attempts on the route in
bitterly cold conditions early in the 2001 season, and succeeded in reaching the top of the second pitch, eliminating the rest point recorded by
Spence and McKenzie. On his third and final attempt Mullin climbed
the route free in a single push to gain the Route II traverse. Temperatures
rose considerably during the day and he endured a miserable wet bivouac
after being soaked by a rainstorm, before continuing up Route II to the
top of Càrn Dearg the following morning.

Although Mullin's ascent clearly demanded a high level of determination and mental toughness, it was greeted with a degree of
bewilderment. In a week when nearby ice routes such as The Curtain
had collapsed due to high temperatures, many people found it hard to
believe that a steep, snowed-up rock route such as Centurion could be
in acceptable winter condition. Publicly Mullin stated that he knew his
ascent would attract criticism, but he was unconcerned as he was exploring his own limits. He had recently returned from an expedition to
Patagonia where he had made a fast attempt on the Czech Route on
the West Face of Fitz Roy. He just missed out on the summit due to the
onset of bad weather, and his horizons now stretched further afield than
Scotland. A few weeks later, Simon Richardson reported Mullin's ascent
in *High Mountain Sports* magazine and attempted to put the ascent into
context.

> Certainly as a stepping-stone towards the world's hardest alpine routes Mullin's
> ascent has validity and considerable personal significance, but within the
> Scottish context, many climbers still believe the prize of a free ascent of
> Centurion in full winter conditions is still on the table.[1]

A succession of heavy snowfalls and rapid freeze-thaws meant that
Ben Nevis was coming into superb condition by the end of February.
In the main it was the classic routes which saw the most traffic, though
on the Minus Face, Robin Clothier and George McEwan straightened
out Right-Hand Wall Route by climbing straight up out of the cave at
V,4. On Creag Coire na Ciste, Chris Cartwright repeated his own route,
Lost the Place, and added a new Direct Start (VI,6) in the process. The
mountain was shaping up for a classic season, but the onset of the Foot
and Mouth crisis in early March threatened everything. Access to the
countryside was withheld across the British Isles to prevent spread of
the disease. Prompt action by the Lochaber Mountain Access Group,
spearheaded by local guide Alan Kimber, demonstrated that climbing
on Ben Nevis posed no risk, and two weeks later the mountain was accessible again via a disinfectant point at the North Face Car Park above
Torlundy.

The Ben was eerily quiet when Cartwright and Richardson walked
up the Allt a' Mhuillin on the third Sunday of March. The CIC Hut was

Chris Cartwright on
the first ascent of
Atlantis (VI,6) on
Observatory Buttress.
'The ice was less than
a centimetre thick,
but it clung to his
frontpoints like glue'

Photo: Simon Richardson

still closed, and news that the mountain was now open had yet to spread. It was a clear morning, but there was a biting north-westerly and they sheltered in the lee of the hut to gear up. They spoke to another party who were heading for Minus Two Gully and could see a couple of teams walking up into Coire na Ciste, but otherwise they had the mountain to themselves. Richardson had a hunch that the line of grooves cutting through the Observatory Buttress headwall to the right of Rubicon Wall might be icy, so they headed up into Observatory Gully to have a look. The ski centres had stayed open throughout the crisis, and they'd heard that Ben Nevis looked to be in superb condition from Aonach Mòr. Sure enough, as they rounded the Douglas Boulder, the rumours appeared correct – the upper half of the mountain was as white and icy as a Christmas cake.

They started up the initial grooves of Observatory Buttress Direct, which were generously filled with snow-ice. Unfortunately appearances were deceptive and their tools kept pulling through the surface crust, but the angle was not too steep so they made steady progress. By the time they had left the Direct and gained the foot of the headwall, the quality of the ice had improved, but they began to get the feeling that they were following a previous ascent. There was the odd vague dimple in the snow suggesting an old footprint, and the rock had one or two

Jonathan Preston on the first ascent of Space Invaders (VI,6). Conditions on the Orion Face were excellent, and Robin Clothier and Harvey Mullen added the serious Spacewalk (VII,6), the same day

Photo: Andy Nisbet

fresh-looking scratches as though it had recently been cleared with ice tools. Their suspicions were confirmed when Richardson dug deep down into the ice to look for a belay below the crux corner and unearthed an abseil point. The gear was new and although it was buried under 20 centimetres of ice it was clear it hadn't been there for long. Cartwright came up and recognised that it belonged to CIC Hut custodian Robin Clothier, as Richardson later explained.

> It all now fell into place. We knew that Robin had climbed the Direct with George McEwan three weeks before, but we didn't realise that they'd attempted the line through the headwall. The difference was that they had ground to a halt with loose powder on rock, whilst we now had a layer of soft squeaky ice lining every groove. It looked very steep above, but when Chris stepped left onto the thinly iced left wall of the crux corner, it was immediately clear that the route was going to go. The ice was less than a centimetre thick, but it clung to his frontpoints like glue, and soon he was on the Girdle Traverse ledge wondering how we were going to explain to Robin and George that we'd climbed their line. Our ascent of Atlantis (VI,6) owed more to good luck than anything else, but the real significance of the day was the special quality of the ice. It was clear that if there was no major thaw, we were in for a very special April on the Ben.[2]

Richardson's prediction was accurate. The pace quickened over the following week with many parties enjoying the harder classics such as Rubicon Wall, Match Point, Left Edge Route and Galactic Hitchhiker. Godefroy Perroux made an ascent of the serious and much-prized Pointless, and Cartwright and Richardson returned to Observatory Buttress and added Appointment with Fear (VII,6), the serious and thinly iced groove left of Match Point.

By early April the focus shifted to the Orion Face with ascents of Orion Direct, Slav Route and Astral Highway. Robin Clothier and Harvey Mullen made the third ascent of the run out Journey into Space, which was followed swiftly by another repeat from Blair Fyffe and Es Tresidder. The previous weekend, Clothier and Andy Forsyth had added Spacewalk (VII,6), the left-trending line of thinly iced corners between Journey into Space and Long Climb Finish. Clothier recounted the tale of their ascent that night in the CIC Hut, and the climb quickly acquired the reputation as the most serious of the Orion routes.

> The belays were terrible and there were no runners. If Andy had come off the fourth pitch we'd have died.[3]

Further left, Andy Nisbet and Jonathan Preston made it a landmark day on the Orion Face, by making the first ascent of Space Invaders (VI,6), the narrow groove system to the right of Astral Highway. The first pitch had been climbed by Mark Miller and Sean Smith in January 1985 on their ascent of Jazz Discharge Party Hats, but they continued up the groove on the right and then penduled right to join Journey into Space. In contrast to Clothier and Forsyth's experience, Nisbet reported later that their route had *'good belays and a runner on each pitch which should ensure a repeat next time it gets icy.'*[2] Two major new routes on Britain's premier snow-ice face on the same day underlined the excellent conditions, although Clothier's success was no accident. It was the result of multiple ascents of Orion Direct, and a campaign spanning over ten years to repeat Journey into Space.

As the snow-ice consolidated higher up the mountain, Indicator Wall became the new playground. Psychedelic Wall, Indicator Right-Hand and Albatross saw several ascents, but the pace stepped up a gear when Jonny Baird and Mike Pescod made an early repeat of Riders on the Storm. Doug Hawthorn and Ewen Todd's 1986 line of sinuous grooves in the buttress to the right of Indicator Wall had been repeated only two or three times in the previous 15 years, but after Baird and Pescod's success it saw four more ascents over the next four days. Further right, Dave Wilkinson and Brian Davison climbed straight up the icy slabs to the right of Shot in the Dark before grinding to a halt below a monstrous cornice. Three hours later Wilkinson had tunnelled his way through to the plateau, and Shot in the Back (IV,4) was finally in the bag. Wilkinson's tunnel prompted several ascents of the neighbouring Shot in the Dark from teams eager to make use of the ready-made exit.

Over in Coire na Ciste, Andy Nisbet and Chris Dale scored a major coup when they climbed the attractive hanging groove to the right of the great corner of Don't Die of Ignorance on the front face of the buttress. Climbers had stared longingly at these grooves for decades, but they are defended by an impregnable-looking overhanging wall. In 1987 Simon Yates and Andy Cave tackled the problem by aiding right-wards across the diagonal break from the foot of Tower Face of the Comb to reach the great corner which then provided superb mixed climbing in an outstanding position. Dale and Nisbet repeated their approach, confirming the A2 Grade, and recommended that future parties take a large rack of cams. Overall, 18 points of aid were used, and the exposure was compared to the Dolomites. The excitement continued on the next pitch, as although the groove was attractively filled with blobs of ice, a short thaw the day before had left them partially detached from the rock. Inevitably, one of these blobs fell off, taking Nisbet with it, but fortunately he was unhurt. He was able to continue by mixed climbing a little to the left and continued up the appropriately named Flying Groove (VI,6) to join the final crest of the buttress.

The Comb was also the setting for the first ascent of Lost Souls (VI,6) by James Edwards and Es Tresidder. This sustained mixed route takes a line up and left of Tower Face of The Comb to gain the impressive forked chimney which cuts through the headwall, where the original route traverses right to a window. As the name suggests the route was a result of a route finding error. The pair had intended to climb Tower Face of the Comb, but they misinterpreted the guidebook description, and started too far up Comb Gully, as Edwards later explained.

> We saw a line in the mist that was just calling out to be climbed, and decided it was Tower Face of the Comb. We put the guidebook in the bag and found our own way up the buttress. At the start of the third pitch, Es asked me how I was going to get up the wall above. I told him that it looked easy, and then promptly fell off, partially opening one of my brand new 'ripper' quickdraws. It was good to know that they worked, we agreed. I tried a new sequence (it involved my knees elbows and stomach mostly), Es led through and we moved together up the remaining easy ground to the top, still not having a clue about what we'd climbed.[4]

Dave Wilkinson and Brian Davison on the first ascent of Shot in the Back (IV,4) on Indicator Wall. It took Wilkinson three hours to tunnel through the cornice above his head

Photo: Cubby Images

I told him that it looked easy, and then promptly fell off, partially opening one of my brand new 'ripper' quickdraws. It was good to know that they worked, we agreed

Ian Parnell on an early repeat of Babylon (VII,8) on Number Three Gully Buttress. The route is now one of the most popular mixed routes on the mountain

Photo: Viv Scott

Further right, Chris Cartwright and Simon Richardson succeeded on the spectacular line of Babylon (VII,8), which starts up the right edge of Number Three Gully Buttress overlooking Winter Chimney, and continues up the cracks of Gargoyle Wall before breaking right across an exposed wall to reach a prominent hanging chimney.

The Ben was busy on the last Sunday of April. There were teams on Orion Direct, Point Five Gully and Hadrian's Wall. Clothier and Richardson linked the Left-Hand Start to Tower Face of the Comb[5] with the Marshall-Stenhouse summer finish to give Quisling Wall (VI,6). On Indicator Wall there were ascents of Albatross and Psychedelic Wall, and

Nick Turner and Mike Pescod tip-toed their way up the third ascent of Stormy Petrel adding a new Direct Start in the process. Two days later a warm south-westerly came in from the Atlantic and stripped the mountain bare. The finest winter season on the Ben for 15 years was finally over.

If the 2001 season was good, then the 2002 season was to prove extraordinary. Consistently poor weather earlier in the winter laid the foundation for the finest thin face climbing on the mountain in living memory. The combination of favourable wind direction, snowfall, and short thaws during February built-up a layer of snow-ice on the high north-west facing crags that was thicker than had ever been seen before. This was followed by a long period of cold settled weather in March and April that transformed the snow-ice into longer-lasting water ice. Galactic Hitchhiker, the Mike Geddes and Con Higgins' masterpiece up the thinly iced slabs and grooves right of Hadrian's Wall, saw more ascents than it had previously seen during its entire 24-year history. The Great Slab just to its right, long lusted after by Nevis winter aficionados, was climbed by Mick Nunwick and Stephen Reid thinking it was the original route and the most obvious way to go. And so did Nick Bullock who soloed past them and Alastair Robertson and Luke Arnott who followed on behind later that day. It was only days afterwards they all discovered that they had just climbed Nemesis (VI,5), a last great problem.

This was only one example. There was so much ice on Observatory Buttress that routes like Match Point dropped two full grades, and big much-feared routes such as Pointless had almost too many ascents to count. Indicator Wall, high up below the very summit of the mountain, has probably the highest concentration of thin face routes in Scotland. These routes had big reputations until March 2002. Albatross, Riders on the Storm, Kellett's Route and Psychedelic Wall had so many ascents that they dropped out of the aspirational category to classics that could be on every winter climber's tick list.

As word got around that the Ben was the place to be, Observatory Gully was packed with teams queuing for the test-pieces of old. Not only was the ice thick enough to take screws almost on demand, grooves and corners were so well delineated with ice that it was immediately clear from the foot of a climb whether it was in condition or not. Typical Ben Nevis horror scenarios, such as discovering the good-looking icy groove you started climbing has deteriorated into centimetre-thick sugar 20 metres above your last runner, were few and far between. The predictable conditions were a soloist's dream. Several climbers had marathon days soloing multiple Grade Vs and VIs, demonstrating impressive levels of fitness by climbing well over a thousand metres of steep ice in just a few hours.

Although many climbers rushed to climb many long sought-after routes, there were some good new additions. Conditions were particularly good on Number Three Gully Buttress, which saw four new routes. Andy Nisbet teamed up with Dave McGimpsey and Mark 'Ed' Edwards to fill a prominent gap with Vulture (V,5), the line of weakness up the left side of the huge icy slab between Diana and Quickstep. They followed this ascent with the outstanding Boston Two Step (VI,5), a snaking line

Chris Cartwright on the first ascent of Babylon. Cartwright and Richardson made three attempts on the route before they were eventually successful in April 2001

Photo: Simon Richardson

*Dave Hollinger
pulling onto the
headwall on the final
pitch of Rhyme of the
Ancient Mariner
(VII,7) on Indicator
Wall*

Photo: Andy Benson

of ice up the buttress left of Two-Step Corner, but they were beaten to
Artemis (V,5), the parallel line of icy grooves to the right of Diana, by
Ed Horne and Graeme Gordon who climbed the route two weeks before
them. Andy Forsyth and Nick Harper muscled in on the action with a
bold new Left-Hand Finish (V,5) to Two-Step Corner. Further left, Chris
Cartwright and Simon Richardson made an ascent of one of the last
unclimbed gullies on the mountain. Fat Boy Slim (VI,6) starts up the
overhanging gully left of 1931 Route on Secondary Tower Ridge and
climbs a difficult mixed barrier pitch to enter the easier upper gully and
its prominent final awkward chockstone. Cartwright was unable to
squeeze behind the final chockstone, but was quick to insist that the
route name was no reflection on his physique.

Over on the Little Brenva Face, Dave McGimpsey and Hannah
Burrows-Smith solved a well known problem with the first ascent of
Super G (VI,6), the long admired icefall hanging down the headwall
above Slalom. Although this route forms consistently each season around
mid March, its existence is often short-lived as it faces the sun and can
become rotten and detached. Careful timing was the key to success with
Burrows-Smith making a fine lead of the steep undercut crux pitch. On
the West Face of Observatory Ridge, Simon Richardson and Chris
Cartwright took advantage of the exceptional ice build up to climb
Maelstrom (VI,6), the prominent groove to the left of Antonine Wall,
and Robin Clothier and Paul Thorburn succeeded on the left rib of Point
Five Gully resulting in Bombing the Pilgrims (VI,5).

High up on Raeburn's Wall to the right of Glover's Chimney, Richardson
and Cartwright climbed the icefall left of Godefroy Perroux's Le
Panthère Rose. Adieu and Farewell (V,5) was named in memory of Perroux,

who had died tragically in the French Alps that January, when the icefall he was climbing collapsed. Cartwright and Richardson also added routes either side of Glover's Chimney, with Silent Spring (V,5) a groove-line running up into the steep headwall of Pinnacle Buttress of the Tower right of the Western Traverse, and Mirror, Mirror (IV,4) the ice smear above The Gutter. They also climbed Goodytwoshoes (V,5), a steep mixed route up the front face of Goodeve's Buttress to the left of the Upper Cascade. On the other side of Coire na Ciste, Dave Cuthbertson, John Wells and Richard Murray found Nasturtium (IV,4), a good ice line based on the right-curling groove just right of Central Gully on the Trident Buttresses.

The finest ascent of the season however was Blair Fyffe's Rhyme of the Ancient Mariner (VII,7) on Indicator Wall. His first attempt with James Edwards climbed the rib right of Albatross to escape up the rising traverse of Flight of the Condor, but two weeks later he re-climbed the lower section with Es Tresidder and forced a way through the imposing headwall above. Fyffe's account captures the tension and the uncertainty of venturing onto bold new ground.

Talented all-round climber Blair Fyffe added several touchstone routes to Ben Nevis including Rhyme of the Ancient Mariner on Indicator Wall

Photo: Jenny Munro

> If anything the ice was slightly thinner this time, and the climbing was even bolder. It was Es's lead. The headwall was impending, but there seemed a possible way through directly above us. A few steep moves above the belay led to a small ledge. Es was soon up onto this, and uncovered a small hex placement, one of the best runners on the route. A few moves up and down to check it out and Es was committed. Some technical moves on rock, and then his axes were back in ice. A fall from there would have hurt. A few more moves and he was established on the ice. A fall from there and he would have hit me. He scraped about and got an ice screw in. I breathed a sigh of relief.[6]

The 2002 season will long be remembered as one of the great winters on Nevis, and the end of an era, when the reputations of the big 1970s routes were finally laid to rest. But more importantly perhaps it talks to the importance of Ben Nevis as a Scottish winter venue as the climate slowly warms. The superb ice climbing conditions that formed in the winters of 2001 and 2002 were driven by slightly warmer temperatures, providing more freeze thaw at higher elevations. Ironically, global warming is currently assisting winter climbing on Ben Nevis, but unless the trend of increasing temperatures slows down, this could just be a passing phase.

Chris Cartwright on the first ascent of Fat Boy Slim (VI,6) on Secondary Tower Ridge, one of the last gully climbs to be ascended on the mountain

Photo: Simon Richardson

References

1. **Richardson**, Simon, *Bonanza on the Ben*. High Mountain Sports 228, 14 – 15, November 2001.

2. **Richardson**, Simon, *The Finest Ice in a Generation*. High Mountain Sports 241, 24 – 25, December 2002.

3. **Clothier**, Robin, in: Richardson, Simon, *Ben Nevis Rock & Ice Climbs*. (Glasgow: Scottish Mountaineering Trust, 2002, ISBN 0907521738.)

4. **Edwards**, James, *Personal communication, September 2006.*

5. This variation was first climbed by Alan Shand and Robin Clothier in the winter of 1987.

6. **Fyffe**, Blair, *Personal communication, December 2006.*

The traverse pitch on The Slab Climb (VI,7). The first winter ascent of this Severe summer climb in November 2001 by Andy Nisbet and Jonathan Preston, established South Trident Buttress as one of the finest early season mixed venues in Scotland

Photo: Pete MacPherson

South Trident Buttress in Coire na Ciste. Spartacus and The Slab Climb start up the twin grooves to the right of the central arete that is climbed by the prominent line of Strident Edge. Right again is the snowy corner of Marshall's 1967 route, The Clanger

Photo: Simon Richardson

17: Mixed to the Future (2003 – 2006)

THE 2003 SEASON WAS HERALDED with the arrival of two new climbers' guidebooks to Ben Nevis. The SMC guide was a comprehensive re-write of the 1994 edition by Simon Richardson, while Godefroy Perroux produced a privately published photo topo guide that focused on the ice routes. Both books had different format and content as Colin Wells explained in *On The Edge* magazine.

> Just in time for winter come two brand new guidebooks to Ben Nevis. And even better, both are refreshingly innovative, albeit very different in style and substance, but by a striking example of serendipitous coincidence, these two guides complement each other perfectly, despite their origins in two diverging traditions.[1]

After being limited to one dedicated guidebook for the previous decade, climbers were now spoilt for choice. The comprehensive SMC volume listed detailed summer and winter route descriptions while Perroux's excellent photographs providing pictorial back up of the ice climbs.[2] In a stroke, these two guides took away the uncertainty of where the majority of winter routes on the mountain lay, and the stage was set for dozens of repeats and a rise in standards.

As Richardson explained in his Introduction, the new SMC guidebook provided an opportunity to update many of the grades used in the 1994 edition, which was the first Scottish guidebook to use two-tier winter grades.

> Keen observers will also note several grade changes compared to the previous edition. Many of these involve upgrading of existing routes. Typically these are climbs that have only recently acquired enough ascents to reach a consensus grade and were undergraded at the time of their first ascent. More noticeable perhaps will be a number of pure ice routes that have been downgraded. Their technical difficulty remains unchanged, but advances in ice screw technology now allows steep ice to be readily protected. Furthermore, recent winters have been mild, which allows mid-level ice routes to consistently form with fatter ice.[3]

In contrast to the downgrading of some of the more modern ice routes, Tower Ridge was upgraded from its traditional Grade III to IV,3. This raised eyebrows amongst some traditionalists, but the revised rating was the result of a request by the Lochaber Mountain Rescue Team who were becoming over stretched by repeated rescues of parties who had underestimated the climb. The technical standard of Tower Ridge is reasonable, but it is a long expedition by Scottish standards and the major difficulties are high on the route.

After the hectic activity of the previous two seasons, the 2003 winter was a more subdued affair. Chris Cartwright and Simon Richardson continued to find more new mixed climbs in Coire na Ciste such as Pinncer (IV,4), the north ridge of Pinnacle Buttress, and The Borg Collective (V,6) on the front face of Goodeve's Buttress. The most significant event of the season however was the establishment of South Trident Buttress as a modern mixed venue. Andy Nisbet and Jonathan Preston had made the first winter ascent of The Slab Climb on the buttress two seasons before, but their climb had gone almost unnoticed. It turned out that Nisbet had been assessing the winter possibilities on this part of the mountain for several years.

> Looking at Jimmy Marshall's guide some time in the 1980s, it puzzled me that there was a Very Difficult on the buttress that hadn't had a winter ascent. Then I noticed that it was south facing, so not a good winter objective, but I never quite forgot about it.[4]

Andy Nisbet has been the most prolific of all Scottish winter pioneers, and has had a profound influence on the sport. From early experiments with torquing techniques on Carn Etchachan in the Cairngorms in the early 1980s through the development of modern mixed climbing and the first Grade VIII climbs, to the exploration of dozens of new cliffs in the Northern Highlands, Nisbet has been at the forefront of the winter game for over 30 years.

In September 2001, he was researching winter objectives for the forthcoming winter season, and remembering the possibilities on South Trident Buttress, he decided to pay Ben Nevis a visit.

> It was lovely weather, so soloing The Slab Climb was no hardship. I had always assumed that the rock on the Ben was all sloping, so I was amazed that the holds on South Trident Buttress were incut. Even so, the comfortable Very Difficult turned out to be anything but, and I chickened out of the summer finish and went left to finish up Spartacus.[5]

SCOTTISH MOUNTAINEERING CLUB CLIMBERS' GUIDE

The 2002 SMC guidebook to Ben Nevis by Simon Richardson. The carefully written route descriptions and detailed drawings by Mark Hudson revealed the mountain in greater detail than ever before and led to surge in new route activity

Andy Nisbet, Scotland's most prolific Scottish winter pioneer. His series of long and demanding mixed routes in the 1980s were a quantum leap in technical standards. On Ben Nevis, his key contribution was the establishment of South Trident Buttress as an important mixed climbing venue

Photo: Dave McGimpsey

The big slab on The Slab Climb has continuous cracks, so Nisbet realised that not only could the holds be hooked, but there would be good protection too. Here was a potential winter route where most of the moves would be on rock, rather than ice or frozen turf, making it an ideal objective for the first big snowfall of the season. Two months later in early November, Nisbet returned with Jonathan Preston, to put theory into practice. They climbed the complete summer line resulting in a superb VI,7 mixed outing, but Nisbet's winter exploration of the buttress was only just beginning.

> The start of The Slab Climb had been a bit wet during my summer recce, so I missed it out by going under the initial groove of Spartacus. It was full of grass, and therefore a fair assumption it could be climbed in winter. That only left a few metres of unknown terrain, since I had already climbed the finish of the route in summer. So again with the first major snowfall the following year, we were back.[6]

The winter ascent of Spartacus by Nisbet and Preston in November 2002 was another absorbing mixed climb, and despite the difference of two summer grades it was graded VI,7 – the same winter standard as The Slab Climb. (Based on his summer experience, Nisbet upgraded The Slab Climb from Very Difficult to Severe in the selected rock climbing guidebook *Scottish Rock Climbs* [SMC 2006] so the grade discrepancy is not so acute.) The noteworthy aspect of these two routes is that they were climbed at the very start of the season with just a heavy covering of snow. Unlike the classic Ben Nevis routes which require ice build up, or even the late 1990s mixed climbs that rely on frozen turf to some degree, here were a couple of reasonably graded winter climbs that were pure snowed up rock routes. Within a couple of years, both climbs had received several repeats, and it was realised that South Trident Buttress is one of the finest early season venues in the area. Ben Nevis, long shunned in the early winter months before the build up of any ice, was now becoming a venue of choice.

By the winter of 2004, other climbers were beginning to realise the mixed climbing possibilities on the mountain as James Edwards recalled.

> It was the efforts of folk like Cartwright and Richardson that opened my eyes to the possibility of the Ben as a venue where new mixed routes were there for the taking. Once dismissed as only a snow and ice venue, it had become apparent that there were high quality mixed lines staring you in the face if you just looked with the right eyes.

Gareth Hughes and Edwards were tired of the hustle and bustle of the Cairngorms over the New Year holiday, so they drove over to Ben Nevis and found that they had the mountain to themselves. On their first day they climbed Gargoyle Wall, but that night it snowed heavily, and next morning they thought better of wading up the avalanche prone slopes of Coire na Ciste or Observatory Gully to reach the established routes.

> A quick look out of the door of the hut in the morning showed lines for the taking on the closest bit of rock, the Douglas Boulder. We looked at the wealth of possibilities and decided on a line based on the crux pitch of Militant Chimney and five pitches later Turf War (VI,6) was born. The snow was still preventing access to the higher cliffs the next day and feeling lazy we visited

Bruce Poll on the first winter ascent of Arthur (VIII,8) on Number Three Gully Buttress. This route was the highlight of the 2004 season and one of the first Grade VIIIs in Scotland to receive an on-sight first ascent

Photo: Tony Shepherd

the Boulder again and plumped for an alternative start to Left-Hand Chimney (V,7). The thaw came on that night and the avalanches began so we went home. Upon tidying up the hut we managed to break the newly installed electricity main fuse box. However, we were spared the wrath of the hut custodian as he was more interested in getting the details of our new routes![7]

The first winter ascent of Arthur on Number Three Gully Buttress by Bruce Poll and Tony Shepherd was the highlight of the 2004 season. This steep, four-pitch HVS runs up the centre of the intimidating front face of the buttress and was first climbed by Klaus Schwartz and Gordon Webster in September 1971 with a point of aid on the third pitch. Lying high on the mountain Arthur was a likely candidate for a winter ascent, but it had thwarted several hopefuls, as the line rarely carries much snow. Poll and Shepherd timed their climb to perfection and nipped in to make a very smooth ascent just after New Year when the cliff was white with frost and the cracks free of ice. Two difficult entry pitches, that each weighed in at technical 7, led to the crux third pitch, as Poll recounted later.

> It was awesome. We followed the summer line exactly. The crux involved getting into a half Egyptian and then making a difficult dynamic move. Protection was there, but it was very committing.[8]

Gareth Hughes on the first winter ascent of Strident Edge (VI,7) on South Trident Buttress. Brunskill and Hughes timed their ascent to perfection and climbed this steep route the day after the great storm of January 2005

Photo: Erik Brunskill

Arthur was only the third Grade VIII to be climbed on Ben Nevis, joining a very small number of Scottish Grade VIIIs at the time which had received on-sight first winter ascents.

The following January, Andy Nisbet and Jonathan Preston continued their winter exploration of South Trident Buttress, with the first ascent of Rattling (V,5), a fine winter version of The Rattler. South Trident Buttress was also the scene for one of the highlights of the season later that month with the first winter ascent of Strident Edge by Erik Brunskill and Gareth Hughes. This steep VS rock climb on South Trident Buttress looks very imposing in summer, and its exposed location makes it seem a very unlikely winter objective. The Trident Buttresses face east and catch the sun first thing in the morning, and it is rare to see Strident Edge in condition, but Brunskill and Hughes made their ascent the day after the great storm that wreaked damage across Scotland in the middle of that January. The strong westerlies brought a huge amount of snow that swamped the mountain's easterly facing crags with powder. Routes like Strident Edge are rarely climbed on their first attempt, as Gareth Hughes later explained.

> We attempted the line in early December when it was plastered in just-freezing snow. I led off up the first hard pitch and ran out of steam so we abseiled off and vowed to return. The next time we had perfect conditions for the route. There was less snow sticking to the open faces, because the snow was colder and drier this time, but the grooves were choked with ice and powder, due to the previous day's westerly storm. On our first attempt I gained the groove by mono-pointing up a blank slab and hooking a flake, but Erik gained the groove from the bottom and made short work of it, belaying at 15m below the roof. I joined him and solved the blank roof problem, (made worse by

sloping ledges below it) by swinging out left via a tiny mono-point hold to gain a large spike, made more exciting by my crampon falling off due to the leverage! I could then see that the way was clear. There was a couple of balancy moves on tenuous hooks to reach the final steep groove, which revealed bomber hooks and a belay on an airy prow – a stunning pitch![9]

The first winter ascent of Strident Edge was a classic piece of Scottish mountaineering. Vision, tenacity and the ability to be in the right place at the right time were the main ingredients of Hughes and Brunskill's success. But the greatest surprise of all was the grade. The route came in at a reasonably amenable grade of VI,7, which goes to show that the most rewarding Scottish winter climbs, are not necessarily the hardest.

A couple of weeks later, in February, Chris Cartwright and Simon Richardson settled a long standing score with the first ascent of Archangel (VII,7), the line of impending corners to the right of Darth Vader on Creag Coire na Ciste. This major line was too obvious to ignore and was being openly talked about by other activists. Relieved to have bagged the first ascent, they graded the route VIII,7, but later downgraded it to VII,7 as Richardson explained three years later.

> It can be difficult for first ascensionists to be objective, especially after success on a long sought after line close to one's limit...The route looked so steep from the corrie floor that we ran away without attempting it on several occasions, and the initial grade was more a reflection on our own psychological battle rather than a true reflection of the actual difficulties on the climb itself.[10]

Three weeks later the pair returned to the same area and climbed The Madness of Crowds (VII,7), the steep corner system to the right of South Sea Bubble and their last major addition to the mountain. The following year, Cartwright decided to redirect the energy and commitment he had applied to winter climbing to progressing his career and raising a family. Cartwright's contribution to the development of winter climbing on Ben Nevis had been significant, and over a 20-year period he added over 40 new winter routes to the mountain.

In early March, the pace stepped up a notch during the International Winter Meet. These week-long events, which are held every two years, are jointly organised by the British Mountaineering Council and the Mountaineering Council of Scotland, and are based at Glenmore Lodge. Two climbers are invited from various countries around the world to climb with British hosts and experience Scottish winter climbing. Since the meet's inception in 1997, the event has proved very successful and attracted many of the world's finest mountaineers.

The 2005 meet was no exception, and when the Glenmore Lodge minibus arrived at the dam below Ben Nevis at around 8.30am on March 1, a dozen eager climbers jumped out, sprinted up the Allt a' Mhuilinn and set to work on some of the more challenging climbs on the mountain. Nine hours later, after rapid ascents of The Shield Direct, Gemini, Route I Direct, Route II Direct, Cornucopia and Orion Direct, everyone was back in the bus heading back for dinner at the Lodge. Other teams that day battled up waves of spindrift in Point Five Gully and Hadrian's Direct, whilst Ian Parnell and visiting US climber Kelly Cordes made the second ascent of Arthur on Number Three Gully Buttress.

Later in the week there was another ascent of Cornucopia by Parnell

Simon Richardson on the first ascent of The Madness of Crowds (VII,7). This steep groove-line on Creag Coire na Ciste was the last significant addition by the Cartwright-Richardson team. Over a ten year period, the pair added 35 new winter routes to Ben Nevis

Photo: Chris Cartwright

Kelly Cordes on the first ascent of Godspell (VII,8) on The Castle during the 2005 International Winter Meet. Cordes, one of North America's finest alpinists, commented afterwards that this one route more than justified his visit from the US

Photo: Simon Richardson

and Stanislav Hovanec from the Czech Republic and across on The Comb, Stan Halstead and John Kuzcera from Poland made the second ascent of The Good Groove. Kelly Cordes and Simon Richardson headed up to The Castle to try the ominous looking hanging chimney that slices through the headwall. This had been on Richardson's list for a long time, but is so steep that it rarely catches much snow. Conditions were perfect, and after Richardson had ground out the first difficult section, Cordes treated him to a virtuoso performance as he bridged up the overhanging second pitch. Cordes was so enthralled by the climbing that he grabbed the third pitch as well, and on top he enthused that this one route (Godspell VII,8) had more than justified his trip over from the United States.

A fierce cold snap in the middle of April brought the high Scottish mountains into good condition, and the final new route of the season was the first winter ascent of the summer HVS Sidewinder on South Trident Buttress, by Iain Small and Richardson. Small had been considering this objective for some time as he later explained.

> A friend had climbed Strident Edge in summer and said it was very cracked and flaky and would make a good winter route. I asked him about Sidewinder, and he said he'd looked down it and it had good cracks too. So when Brunskill and Hughes climbed Strident Edge in winter it got me thinking about Sidewinder, because the buttress comes into condition so readily after a heavy snowfall.

Small led the smooth crux groove on the second pitch and the route weighed in at VII,8. For Small the route was a revelation, and was to provide him with the confidence to climb at a higher standard in future years.

> It was the first time I'd used monopoints and fortunately they were really sharp for the crux pitch. It made me realise that there were more routes that I could climb at that level.[11]

The following season, the spotlight once again fell on first winter ascents of rock climbs in Coire na Ciste. High up on the front face of Number Three Gully Buttress on Ben Nevis is a vertical sheet of perfect cracked rock taken by the summer HVS Sioux Wall. First climbed in the summer of 1972 by Ian Nicolson and George Grassam, Sioux Wall is one of the finest rock climbs on the mountain and had entered climber's consciousness as a futuristic winter climbing target. With winter standards rising year on year, it was only a matter of time before it was climbed. After Ian Parnell made the second ascent of Arthur with Kelly Cordes during the International Meet in 2005, he set his eyes set on a new route on the front face of Number Three Gully Buttress.

> This wall harboured a triptych of summer lines: a groove, an arete and a crack, all as yet without a winter ascent. Unremittingly steep for a full 100 meters, any of the lines would represent a new level of difficulty for Ben Nevis winter climbing. But how hard would that level be?[12]

Parnell, a tall and articulate man, who has made a living as a mountain photographer, had the depth of experience to break down psychological barriers. Over the previous 10 years he had moved away from pioneering serious traditional rock climbs on the sea cliffs of South-

Ian Parnell applied a strong background in traditional rock climbing and high standard alpinism to Scottish winter climbing. His on-sight first winter ascent of Sioux Wall (VIII,8) in January 2006 took Nevis mixed climbing to a new level

Photo: John Varco

Iain Small on the first winter ascent of Sidewinder (VII,8) on South Trident Buttress. This route gave Small the confidence to open up a series of difficult mixed routes on Nevis

Photo: Simon Richardson

*Ian Parnell leading
the crux pitch on the
first winter ascent of
Sioux Wall (VIII,8)
on Number Three
Gully Buttress*

Photo: Olly Metherell

West of England through to high standard mountaineering, and had established a series of cutting edge alpine routes across the world in Patagonia, the Himalayas and Alaska. On the last day of 2005, Parnell visited Ben Nevis with Oliver Metherell, a young and enthusiastic climber from Edinburgh, and seized the opportunity to fulfil his dream.

> On the evening of the 31st we walked up towards the Ben and camped about two-thirds of the way to the CIC Hut. New Year's Day was warm and slushy so we walked up with little optimism into Coire na Ciste planning to have a go at Archangel. As we got higher we began to realise how white everything was, with soggy snow stuck to overhanging as well as vertical aspects, so I persuaded Olly to switch to an attempt on Sioux Wall.[13]

They took a slightly more direct line than the summer route to gain the square-cut niche below the steep central wall. The next pitch was the crux and Parnell took the lead.

> Where Sioux Wall differed from previous Scottish mixed routes I'd climbed was its unrelenting steepness. Devoid of any rests, the crux second pitch had me fighting a rising pump. I locked off, screaming, only to come up short on the final bulge, Slumped straight-armed on my axes, I fought to control my mind, which seemed to be filling with lactic acid rather than solutions. Camming the monopoint of my crampon an inch higher in the crack, I twisted every part of my body for that little extra reach. The first notch of my axe scratched into a sliver of semifrozen ice. Shouting seemed to keep it in place as I swapped hands and, crampons sparking, pedalled my feet up to make a final lunge for the turf of the next belay ledge.

The hardest technical climbing was now below them, but the route was not over yet. Metherell continued up the corner-groove above that turned out to be surprisingly well protected. Although the pitch had more places to rest than the previous one, it was still very strenuous. Metherell fell off, leaving his axes in the belay ledge, so he climbed up again to finish off the pitch. From here the summer pitch three continues up a steep crack, but with half an hour of daylight left Parnell chose a rightward trending line.

> As darkness descended, panic set in: the snow was becoming too deep to clear. I was forced to run out the final pitch, hooking up eggshell snow-ice. But as the angle eased back in my little pool of headlight, I was enveloped by a sense of euphoria. Our little gamble had coincided with a lucky break in the weather and a miraculous trick of conditions to give us the perfect Scottish day out[12].

With two pitches of 7 and two of 8, climbed on-sight in almost perfect style on one of the shortest days of the year, Sioux Wall (VIII,8) was a significant advance. Parnell and Metherell's ascent was met with general acclaim, and summed up by Scottish winter pioneer Andy Nisbet.

> This sort of route is moving up a grade from the 80s and 90s. It's the sort of route we couldn't quite do, and there's a lot of scope in Scotland for this type of climb. Really it's the new routeing future.[14]

Almost as if to prove Nisbet correct, a few days later, Andy Turner and Duncan Hodgson repeated the route and made a complete ascent of the summer line.

US climber Freddie
Wilkinson leading the
second pitch of Sioux
Wall during the 2007
International Winter
Meet

Photo: Viv Scott

*Es Tresidder, a
superb athlete and
accomplished
mountaineer added
several difficult
mixed routes to Ben
Nevis. He is best
known for his record-
breaking run of the
Skye Ridge in May
2007*

Photo: Ian Parnell

A month later, another very difficult mixed route was added to the mountain when Es Tresidder, Iain Small and Dan McManus added Red Right-Hand (VIII,8) to Minus Two Buttress. They started up Left-Hand Route, but the lack of ice forced them right into the hanging corner to the right. Small led out rightwards across the steep retaining wall of the corner onto a thinly iced slab, and continued up to a belay in the big, left trending, stepped overhanging corner. Tresidder, a talented climber and outstanding fell runner who would set a new record for running the Skye Ridge in May 2007, then headed up into the corner but soon ground to a halt finding little protection. He then traversed out from the belay and unearthed a pick-width crack, which he climbed level with

*I had a strong
sense that, heroic
as it may seem
writing about it
now, it was
something that I
shouldn't have
done – it was too
dangerous, too
scary, and it was
luck as much as
skill that had got
me out of trouble.
The route haunted
me for weeks
afterwards...*

the point he had previously reached from under the roof. From here the climbing appeared to get easier, but appearances were deceptive.

> I kept climbing as I kept thinking it was going to get easier. It never did get easier, and after a while I passed the point where the only way I was going to get out of it unhurt was to carry on climbing until I got to easy ground or a piece of gear I was happy to lower off. The pitch took all that I had – I placed pegs, tied them off and equalised and clipped them one handed in a position that when first arrived at seemed ludicrously strenuous. I torqued, stacked axes, fist jammed, knee barred, Egyptianed, stein-pulled and thrutched. Every desperate move was encouraged by what looked like a ledge or good runner above, every ledge turned out to be loose snow sticking to 70 degree smooth rock, every crack turned out to be flared or blind. The best rest was an icy fist jam combined with a knee lock. The good runner or easy ground took 60m to arrive. I found a good belay, and brought the others up. I had a strong sense that, heroic as it may seem writing about it now, it was something that I shouldn't have done – it was too dangerous, too scary, and it was luck as much as skill that had got me out of trouble. The route haunted me for weeks afterwards, and everything else I did that season seemed easy.[15]

Later in February, Dave MacLeod and Tim Emmett made a direct finish to Italian Climb. This well-known objective tackled the cave and overhang at the top of the initial gully, where the original Grade III route goes right. The crux was a steep cracked wall with long reaches, followed by a poorly protected groove-line leading onto the crest of Tower Ridge. The Italian Job (VIII,9) was climbed on-sight and became the highest graded winter route on the mountain, although it is possible that the top groove will become easier when iced.

Higher up in Coire na Ciste, Nick Bullock and Owen Samuels climbed a difficult route to the right of Darth Vader. Avenging Angel (VII,8) starts up the first three pitches of Archangel and then continues up the true line of the impending corner system. Bullock was on form, and a couple of weeks earlier, he had made the second ascent of Babylon (VII,8) on Number Three Gully Buttress with Matt Helliker. The final pitch, a desperate looking corner proved to be the crux. Bullock's description of his lead captures the uncertainty and excitement of pioneering difficult Nevis mixed climbs.

> Skipping feet buried beneath frost, I hoped the invisible rugosites holding me were more than rime. The crack on the left was perfect. Slotting a pick and twisting gave security. Pulling hard, feet high, the right hand crack was cleaned. A hook, good enough to hang and hold bodyweight was desperately sought and 'thank god' found. Feet, higher, placed, balanced. Laybacking, reaching, the pick missed. Barn-door, swinging, one front-point, one torque. Body tension saved me. Stinging, the wind and snow woke me from my cocoon. This was no bolted well-practiced sequence. Ten minutes passed, locking-off, twisting-tension-torquing, two pieces of gear gave the confidence to continue. More force, more commitment, confidence coursed through my body. Reaching high, slotting a pick into the left hand crack and twisting, leaning, stepping high, was it going to go, would the placements keep coming? Pulling, locking, don't shake, slot a pick, lean, clean, move. Look down at Samuels strapped into the corner below, the swirling snow spirals, I nod my head and smile. He gives me the thumbs up.[16]

Dave MacLeod on the first ascent of The Italian Job (VII,9), the true finish to Italian Climb. The complete route is the most difficult gully climb on Ben Nevis

Photo: Tim Emmett

At the end of April, Brian Davison and Simon Richardson fulfilled a long held dream by making a girdle traverse of the Ben Nevis cliffs. Richardson had noted the possibility of a winter version of Bell's 1941 girdle traverse since working on the 1994 edition of the SMC guide, and the project had weighed heavily on his mind ever since.

> …about ten years ago it struck me that a girdle traverse of the Ben Nevis cliffs would make a superb winter challenge. The technical difficulty would not be particularly high, but the 4km long expedition would probably be the longest winter route in the country and the logistical complexity would be immense. The more I thought about it, the more fascinated I became.

Clearly a winter version of Bell's girdle would need a very long day, which pointed to an April attempt. But the problem with April is that the east facing Trident Buttresses in Coire na Ciste strip of snow late in the winter and the traverse line quickly becomes exposed scree. Aside from the logistics, Richardson's major hurdle was finding a partner willing to commit to the route. Then by chance, Lancaster based Brian Davison mentioned on the telephone that he'd spotted the possibility of a winter girdle whilst editing the manuscript for the 2002 Ben Nevis

Highly individualistic and deeply talented, Brian Davison was at the forefront of winter climbing developments in Scotland for over 20 years. His finest contribution to Ben Nevis was the winter girdle traverse

Photo: Davison Collection

guide. Thinking fast, Richardson asked him whether he'd like to do the route together.

Brian immediately agreed and I excitedly talked about the difficulty of catching it in condition as the sun caught the second half of the route later in the day.

'Oh, I've thought all about that;' Brian said coolly. 'It's simple, we do it from right to left, the opposite way to summer. That way if we start early enough the sun will be following us around the route.'

Brian's logic was brilliant. Why hadn't I thought of that?[17]

Davison was the ideal partner for such a venture, and had a string of cutting edge winter routes across Scotland to his name, including the iconic first winter ascent of Mort (IX,9) on Lochnagar. For four seasons, they carefully watched the weather, but by March every year the snow had stripped and the route had disappeared. But March 2006 was different – it was cold and still very snowy and a date was set for the third week in April. The die was cast and they settled in for an anxious wait, watching the weather forecasts every day. It stayed cold and continued to snow. With three days to go climbers were still reporting massive avalanches and poor snow conditions all over the mountain. But snow consolidates fast in April so at 5.30am on April 21 they were gearing up in the gloom of dawn below North Castle Gully beside Castle Ridge. Although a lonely star twinkled overhead, the snow was soft and the entire mountain appeared to be running with water. Prospects looked bleak, but there was nothing to lose, so they set off kicking steps up the gully.

The snow was still unfrozen as they approached the steep bulge at half-height, but fortunately the temperature had dropped just a fraction to give a little structure to the snow, and as they gained height a slight frosting appeared on the sidewalls of the gully. At the top they tagged Castle Ridge, and then headed over The Castle, down across mixed ground into Castle Corrie, up Ledge Route, crossed the Trident Buttresses, descended Number Four Gully, climbed North Gully, traversed across Creag Coire na Ciste, up Thompson's Route, down Number Three Gully Buttress, up Green Gully, down Hesperides Ledge, across Comb Gully Buttress, up Raeburn's Easy Route and left into Glover's Chimney. They dropped down from the Tower Gap into Observatory Gully and had lunch at 12pm.

We'd covered half the route in six hours, but I knew what lay ahead looked more precarious, traverses along ledges with large drops below, not as friendly as the first section…As we headed across, the snow started to feel less secure under foot. It was time for the rope. Simon led off with me hoping he'd reach Point Five Gully in one pitch. My optimism was short-lived as he ran out of rope and direction and constructed a disintegrating belay by an outcrop. I could see the gully tantalisingly close. A careful traverse down and round some suspect rock took me into the gully above the Rogue Pitch and a poor belay above.[18]

The pair climbed the steep Left-Hand Finish to Point Five Gully and then very carefully made their way across Hadrian's Wall, Observatory Ridge and Zero Gully on poorly consolidated snow and thin slabs to finish up Slav Route to reach the crest of North-East Buttress at about 5.45pm. There was about 4000m climbing in all and they rated the expedition V,4. Grades are pretty irrelevant on a route like this, and the real crux was waiting several seasons for favourable snow conditions to allow fast travel over the easier sections. Rather surprisingly for the first ascensionists, the route attracted considerable interest, and accomplished Scottish winter activist Guy Robertson commented later that –

> For many Scottish winter climbers, the research, planning, preparation, conditions monitoring, route finding and sheer enthusiasm required to undertake this sort of nonsense are precisely what makes the sport so crazy yet so special. Let's hope that future seasons bring us all as much fun, uncertainty and madness.[19]

Robertson, did not have to wait long. The following two seasons, Ben Nevis was to be the stage for some of the finest winter climbing ever seen in Scotland.

Simon Richardson traversing across Observatory Buttress on the first winter ascent of The Girdle Traverse (V,4). The 4km route is the longest winter climb in the British Isles

Photo: Brian Davison

References

1. **Wells**, Colin, *The Benny Hill Show*. On The Edge 124, 67 – 68, February 2003.

2. **Perroux**, Godefroy, *Ben Nevis, Winter Climbs, Selected Routes*. (Les Houches, France: Alp Impression, 2002, ISBN 2951774907.) Perroux's guide went to press shortly before his untimely death in February 2002, and was published posthumously.

3. **Richardson**, Simon, *Ben Nevis, Rock & Ice Climbs*. (Glasgow: Scottish Mountaineering Trust, 2002, ISBN 0907521738.)

4. **Nisbet**, Andy, *Personal communication, October 2007*.

5. Ibid.

6. Ibid.

7. **Edwards**, James, *Personal communication, September 2006*.

8. **Poll**, Bruce, in: Richardson, Simon, *Four of the Best*. High Mountain Sports 258, 26 – 27, May 2004.

9. **Hughes**, Gareth, in: Richardson, Simon, *Scottish Winter Notes*. Climb 2, p14, April 2005.

10. **Richardson**, Simon, *Scottish Winter Notes*. Climb 37, 26 – 27, March 2008.

11. **Small**, Iain, *Interview, 9 March 2008*.

12. **Parnell**, Ian, *Sioux Wall*. Alpinist 22, p40, November 2007.

13. **Parnell**, Ian, in: Richardson, Simon, *Scottish Winter Notes*. Climb 14, 24 – 26, April 2006.

14. **Nisbet**, Andy, in: Richardson, Simon, *Ben Nevis Rock & Ice Climbs*. (Glasgow: Scottish Mountaineering Trust, 2002, ISBN 0907521738.)

15. **Tresidder**, Es, *Personal communication, September 2006*.

16. **Bullock**, Nick, *Personal communication, March 2006*.

17. **Richardson**, Simon, *Round The Ben*. Climb 25, 38 – 42, March 2007.

18. **Davison**, Brian, *Who Needs The Himalayas?*, SMCJ 198, 509 – 510, 2007.

19. **Robertson**, Guy, *Climb Scotland – Winter 05/06*. Scottish Mountaineer 33, 25 – 31, November 2006.

Situated directly below the summit, Indicator Wall lies at the highest altitude of all the cliffs on Ben Nevis. Its steep, slabby walls are home to many of the finest thin face routes in Scotland

Photo: Simon Richardson

The Petzl Nomic, a typical leashless tool. The acutely bent shaft places the pick at the optimum angle for climbing steep ice or hooking small holds. The comfortable grips allow the tool to be held in a variety of hand positions without rotating the pick. The lack of hammer and shaft spike limits the axe in a mountain environment

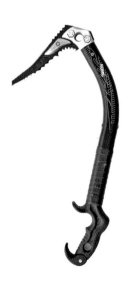

18: The New Generation (2007)

WINTER CLIMBING HAS UNDERGONE a remarkable evolution over the last 50 years. Scotland has often been at the forefront of world developments, from the step cutting mastery of Marshall and Smith, through to the introduction of the Terrordactyl and development of front pointing in the 1970s. During the 1980s, the emphasis in North America and Europe was on climbing steep frozen waterfalls, but in Scotland the focus switched towards mixed climbing. Aberdonian Andy Nisbet led the charge, and together with the strong and talented Colin MacLean, he created a string of difficult and challenging routes including the first Grade VIIIs.

Routes such as Unicorn in Glen Coe and The Needle on the Shelter Stone were undoubtedly amongst the hardest mixed climbs in the world at the time, and would ultimately transform the winter game. (Unicorn and The Needle were first climbed in the winter of 1985 with a little aid. A free ascent of Unicorn was made in February 1999, and it was not until February 2004 that The Needle was climbed free in a day. Both routes are still considered to be amongst the hardest Grade VIIIs in Scotland.) The Nisbet – MacLean era set the standard for the next 15 years, and it was only after the turn of the 21st Century that their greatest routes were considered realistic objectives for the strongest of teams.

Throughout the 1990s there was exploration in other venues away from the well-known winter cliffs in the Central Highlands and Cairngorms. The North-West in particular attracted an increasing number of pioneering climbers who soon realised that there were hundreds of little known cliffs that came into winter condition far more often than previously thought. More remote crags in the Central Highlands were also thoroughly explored such as the Aonachs and Ben Alder. The cliffs of Aonach Mòr quickly spawned some of the most popular winter climbs in Scotland, following the opening of the Nevis Range ski area in 1990. Across in the Cairngorms, the Northern Corries were developed, with a series of mixed climbs. A *cragging* atmosphere existed most weekends, and easily accessible and relatively short routes such as The Hoarmaster (V,6) and Deep Throat (V,6), introduced many winter climbers to the delights and intricacies of mixed climbing.

The confidence created by these developments gave climbers the impetus to leave behind the surety of following a summer route, and move on to harder, winter-only mixed lines. At best, these take steep, wet and vegetated terrain that invoke shudders in summer, but when frozen, provide winter climbs of the highest quality. At first sight, technical standards appeared to remain static throughout this period, and the big Grade VIII routes of the 1980s were not superseded in difficulty. The 1990s were a time of consolidation however, when a new generation of climbers was learning the new mixed techniques, and there was little incentive to repeat routes when so much new route potential existed elsewhere. But slowly the Grade VIII routes saw second ascents in good style. The one or two aid and rest points that were accepted on hard climbs in the 1980s as the norm, were shunned by a generation influenced by a purer rock-climbing ethic, and by the turn of the century, many of the big routes had been repeated and their aid points eliminated.

During the second half of the 1990s, the world of winter climbing was transformed with the development of M-climbing in North America and Continental Europe. M-climbing, a term used to describe technically extreme mixed climbing with bolt protection, is the winter equivalent of summer sport climbing, and grew out of waterfall ice climbing. Bored with the predictability of thick ice, climbers turned their attention to unformed ice lines, which typically entailed climbing long sections of pre-protected rock with axes and crampons (known as dry tooling) to reach hanging icicles. This was a radical departure from traditional snow and ice climbing, and it opened up a new dimension to the sport as accomplished Canadian mixed climber and alpinist Raphael Slawinski explained.

> Jeff Lowe's 1994 first ascent of Octopussy (M8) in Colorado's infamous Vail amphitheatre, threw mixed climbing into the limelight. With its pre-placed protection, red pointing tactics and exotic moves, this route signalled a radical departure in mixed climbing. Technically, it was certainly by far the hardest mixed climb yet made. The easy access, reliable protection, and lack of objective hazards freed climbers to pursue pure technical difficulty.[1]

The development of M-climbing was an almost exact parallel to what had happened in rock climbing ten years before. The acceptance of bolt protected sport climbs allowed climbers to tackle routes purely for their technical difficulty, without worrying about placing protection. In the same way that sport climbing allowed technical rock climbing grades to soar, during the ten years following Octopussy, M-climbing standards

Dave MacLeod, the finest Scottish climber of his generation. His focus, commitment and technical ability have led to first ascents of Scotland's most difficult routes in summer and winter

Photo: Michael Tweedley

Scott Muir climbing Reptile, M10+, Colorado. The techniques, equipment and fitness levels developed by M-climbing led to higher on-sight ability and ultimately a step change in Scottish mixed climbing standards

Photo: Scott Muir

across the world rocketed from M8 to M13.

As Scottish climbers wrestled with the explosion of M-climbing, and how to relate it to the Scottish game, the state of Scottish winter climbing was severely challenged. The most vocal criticism came from ex-pat English climber Stevie Haston, who had moved to Chamonix and adopted the pre-protected dry tooling approach. Haston's new routes in France and Italy often surmounted huge horizontal roofs, and made headlines in the climbing magazines of the day. Haston graded his routes Scottish 11, and he mocked the state of play in Scotland. *'Scottish climbs are not just off the pace, they're off the f...... planet!'*[2]

Haston's taunts rankled deep, but they contained an element of truth, because a huge technical gap had opened up between the hardest Scottish winter climbs and the top end, pre-protected mixed routes in Europe and North America. A simple grade comparison does not reveal the full story however, because Scottish climbers were focused on climbing winter routes in perfect style, preferably on-sight at the first attempt, whilst M-climbing disregarded traditional ethics and redefined the rules to make technical climbing easier. Attempts to reproduce M-climbs in Scotland, either by placing bolts or pre-protecting routes, were met with general disapproval, as it was realised that they undermined the essence of Scottish winter climbing and that there was a fierce desire to maintain the Scottish on-sight style. In effect, the difference in ethics was driven more by practicality rather than tradition. The ancient rocks that comprise the Highlands support on-sight climbing and leader placed protection, whilst the geologically younger rocks in the mixed climbing areas in the Alps and North America are made of poorer quality rock, typically requiring bolts to make them climbable.

M-climbing brought with it new equipment and new techniques. Leashless tools in particular allowed climbers to make moves that are not possible when the tools are connected by wrist loops, as Canadian mixed specialist Sean Isaac explained in his instruction book on the new mixed climbing techniques.

> Being unshackled provides incredible freedom of movement. It also exponentially increases your repertoire of moves. Instead of being forced to think and move with one tool fixed to each hand, leashless trickery offers the opportunity to explore an unlimited array of possibilities. The distinction between right tool and left tool, or even top of tool and bottom of tool becomes lost as one's perception of moving over winter terrain morphs. Many climbers who first realise the power of leashless climbing comment immediately on how it feels more fluid, like the flow of rock climbing instead of the choppy right-left, right-left stutter of ice climbing.[3]

British climbers slowly began to sample M-climbing abroad, and several Scottish climbers such as Scott Muir and Dave MacLeod became very proficient at the new discipline. Neil Gresham, a talented all-round English climber, best known for the second ascent of the iconic E9 route Indian Face on Clogwyn Du'r Arddu in North Wales, was one of the first to make a direct comparison with climbs in Scotland. He was clear that Scottish winter climbing was not *'dropping off the world pace'*.

> ...definitely not lagging behind in an overall sense, because it's wrong to compare the style of climbing. Of course the dry tooling routes are much harder

from a technical perspective but they lack the element of danger and adventure that so often feature highly in Scottish routes.[4]

As leashless tools became more widely available, they started to be used by the mainstream for all forms of technical mountaineering. Fears of dropping tools quickly vanished, as the benefits of unencumbered movement, particularly when placing protection, became apparent. The tools were lighter too, which enabled them to be held with outstretched arms more easily, enabling sequences of difficult moves. Several climbers noted that the new tools reduced the difficulty of hard mixed climbing by at least a grade and there was a surge in ascents of difficult routes across Scotland.

In February 2005, using leashless tools, Dave MacLeod made the first winter ascent of The Hurting, a 35m-high E4 climb in Coire an t-Sneachda in the Cairngorms. Graded XI,11, the route was claimed to be the 'hardest single pitch traditional mixed route in the world', but pre-inspection by abseil meant that it did not completely live up to its billing. The following winter, MacLeod upped the ante by making the first on-sight ascent of a Scottish Grade IX, when he climbed of Defenders of the Faith (IX,9) on Creag an Socach above Bridge of Orchy. This ascent attracted genuine acclaim as key activist and commentator Guy Robertson explained.

> MacLeod may well be remembered as the man who brought the levels of physical strength and stamina required to climb the world's hardest M-style routes down to bear on the ethically purist world of Scottish traditional winter climbing.[5]

Several days later, Robertson was in the headlines himself with the second winter ascent of The Steeple on the Shelter Stone with Pete Benson. The first ascent by Alan Mullin and Steve Paget over 24 hours in November 1999 had attracted intense criticsm due to the early season nature of their ascent. Robertson and Benson's climb was accomplished in a startlingly swift 12 hours in full winter conditions. The Hurting, Defenders of the Faith and The Steeple sent a clear message that Scottish winter standards had progressed. Psychological barriers came tumbling down, and no longer were Grade VII mixed routes the preserve of the elite.

Nothing better emphasised the renewed self-confidence in Scottish winter climbing than the difficult new routes climbed on Ben Nevis during the 2007 season. The first winter ascent of the prominent groove line of The Knuckleduster on the front face of Number Three Gully Buttress on February 12, was the first indication that a profound change was underway. This summer HVS was first climbed by Jimmy Marshall and his brother Ronnie in 1966, and had been admired by climbers for many years as a futuristic winter possibility. Over the previous three winter seasons, two other HVS routes on Number Three Gully Buttress, Sioux Wall and Arthur, had received winter ascents, and The Knuckleduster was the next obvious target. Other parties had been forced to retreat due to its steep and sustained terrain, and during one attempt in the winter of 2004, the leader fell off the second pitch, ending up hanging unconscious below his belayer after ripping out old in-situ gear.

The route was finally climbed by the very strong pairing of Steve

Dave MacLeod on the first ascent of Defenders of the Faith (IX,9) on Creag an Socach, Beinn Dorain, in the Southern Highlands. This was the first Grade IX new route to be climbed on-sight demonstrating that routes of this level did not have to be practised or prepared

Photo: Dave Brown

Blair Fyffe on the first winter ascent of The Knuckleduster (VIII,9). The completion of the triptych of challenging Grade VIII climbs in the front face of Number Three Gully Buttress signalled the arrival of a new generation of talented Scottish mixed climbers

Photo: Steve Ashworth

Ashworth and Blair Fyffe. Ashworth, tall and powerfully built, was passionate about winter climbing and had created a formidable reputation with a series of very difficult winter routes in the Lake District. He managed the National Trust campsite in Langdale, and when conditions were good, he would run up into the fells after work and solo winter routes by headtorch. Fyffe, a strong and talented all-round climber, was working as an observer with the Scottish Avalanche Information Service, and was able to keep track of conditions on a daily basis. As a result he was having an excellent season with a string of good new routes from Glen Coe to the North-West.

The temperature was just above zero as they reached the base of the climb, and a thick, damp mist reduced visibility and soaked their clothing and equipment. Despite the warm weather, conditions on the route were good. A dribble of ice plastered the back of the groove, while rime covered the rocks. The first pitch was steeper and trickier than it appeared from below, and a little way up the crucial second pitch a large roof forced Fyffe to traverse rightwards out of the groove onto a vertical wall. It steepened significantly above, and this section proved to be the crux.

> Steep moves, with little for the feet, allowed me to grab an obvious flake. It felt loose, but I had no option but to haul on it. Luckily it held.[6]

Above the belay, they diverged from the summer route to enter a steep and tricky groove. A little way up this Ashworth took an unexpected fall, ripping his top wire and colliding with a ledge. Luckily he held onto his leashless tools and was able to regain the groove. Their equipment began to freeze up as night set in. A 30-metre blank, steep wall stymied progress until they found a delicate traverse right that led to a wide crack and easier ground. They graded the route VIII,9 and Ashworth commented afterwards that it was harder than Unicorn in Glen Coe.

The completion of the triptych of Grade VIII mixed routes on Number Three Gully Buttress – Arthur, Sioux Wall and The Knuckleduster signalled the arrival of a new generation. All of these routes were climbed on-sight, on the first attempt without recourse to aid or rests. They represented a genuine advance in style from the hard Scottish winter routes of the 1980s that were often climbed after multiple attempts or used points of aid. Three weeks later, this advance was consolidated during a remarkable final day of the British Mountaineering Council's 2007 International Winter Meet, as Rob Jarvis reported on the internet.

> The biannual Meet gathers climbers from around the world to push their mixed on-sighting limits in the fickle Scottish climate. Although venues like Creag Meaghaidh and the North West were totally out of condition, and the Meet began with heavy thawing and windy conditions, the climbers turned the bleak situation into a send-fest. March 1 was probably the most active day, from a hard mixed climbing perspective, ever to take place on Ben Nevis.[7]

Steve Ashworth developed strong winter climbing skills in the Lake District. His focus on the mixed potential on Ben Nevis resulted in the first ascents of several important routes such as The Knuckleduster

Photo: Viv Scott

The pace truly was breathtaking. Steve Ashworth and Nils Nielsen from Norway climbed the 1990s test-piece Darth Vader, followed by The Sorcerer (VII,8), a new line up the front face of the buttress taken by Lost The Place, before racing up Thompson's Route on Number Three Gully Buttress to warm down. Fellow Norwegian Bjorn Artun and Tim Blakemore had a similarly impressive day by climbing Albatross, one of the most prized routes on Indicator Wall, followed by Darth Vader. Nearby, Stu McAleese and Tomaz Jakofcic from Slovenia climbed Cornucopia, while Es Tresidder and Paul Sab from Germany made an ascent of Stringfellow on Pinnacle Buttress of the Tower.

Two big ascents took place on Number Three Gully Buttress. US climber Freddie Wilkinson and Rok Zalokar from Slovenia made the third ascent of Sioux Wall, and Ian Parnell and Canadian Sean Isaac added the intricate line of Curly's Arete (VIII,8). This takes the blunt edge between The Knuckleduster and Sioux Wall and is based on the summer HVS Last Stand. The route was named after American climber Karen 'Curly' McNeil who had tragically disappeared on the Infinite Spur on Mount Foraker in Alaska the previous spring. Isaac, an athletic and enthusiastic mountain guide who had spearheaded the development of M-climbing in the Canadian Rockies, was captivated by the Scottish winter experience.

> After a moderate first pitch of snowy rock, Ian spent 2 hours unlocking the tenuous crux second pitch. It was technical and bold compounded by route finding difficulty. By the time I reached the belay, Ian was already shivering so he launched off on the next pitch which was still hard but had better gear. This deposited us at the Sioux Wall finish which was climbed in 2 more pitches to the top. I pulled over the cornice on top of the Ben just as it got dark... I already cannot wait to return to Scotland. The Haggis sucks (bad texture, no flavour, nasty ingredients) but the excellent single malt and classy climbing more than makes up for it. Scotland's no bolt ethic and ground-up on-sight style provides big adventure from little mountains. It is no wonder why some of the best alpinists in the world hail from the UK.[8]

Japanese climber Hiroyoshi Manome on the first ascent of Isami (VIII,8). This attractive hanging groove high on the front face of The Comb had been stared at by Nevis ice climbers for years but it was eventually climbed as an icy mixed route

Photo: Dave MacLeod

Young and enthusiastic, Viv Scott was a vibrant member of the new generation of Nevis mixed climbers

Photo: Ian Parnell

Next door on Creag Coire na Ciste, Viv Scott, a young and enthusiastic PhD student from Edinburgh University, and Domagoj Bojko from Croatia climbed the hanging chimney just left of the icicle of South Sea Bubble. The aptly named Salva Mea (VIII,8), which starts up the lower ramp of South Sea Bubble and continues up a hidden slot to reach the upper snow funnel, gave Scott a testing time.

> It's the hardest thing I've ever led. The protection was really poor and holds kept snapping under my feet but the position was really exciting![9]

Across on The Comb, Dave MacLeod and Hiroyoshi Manome and Katsutaka Yokoyama from Japan climbed Isami (VIII,8), the conspicuous hanging groove situated above The Good Groove. Several teams had stared longingly at this line over the years, waiting for the requisite amount of ice, but MacLeod circumvented the waiting game by treating it as a mixed climb.

> We headed into Coire na Ciste and almost every party was starting up routes of Grade VII or harder. I pointed to several unclimbed routes and left it up to Yoko and Mano to decide which looked the most fabulous. They are ice masters so opted for a potential new thin neve route I knew about from a picture in Ken's [Crocket's] Ben Nevis book.

After a long pitch of snaking between ramps, MacLeod took a belay at the base of the top ramp, which ran out into two ominous looking, overhanging corners to his right. They looked blank, but Manome worked his way carefully across the ramp, which was thinly plated with ice and appeared to be poorly protected.

But Mano was pretty hardcore, and dismissing the first blank corner he got established below the second one. An hour passed and me and Yoko agreed it was getting a little chilly as Mano scratched and grunted in the base of the corner before announcing it was too hard and devoid of hooks and reversing, ushering me to have a try.

It was cold, and MacLeod was all for abseiling off, but for the sake of his guests he felt obliged to have a look. After six attempts to climb the corner, he went up for one last go.

> I knew the time had come to either commit or admit the abseil was inevitable. I got really pumped and scared the higher I got and felt a little ill when a really bad hook broke and I almost took the fall. A bit of shouting to re-focus and accept I was committed and I flailed into the groove above, so pumped I had to shake out before I could even open the krabs on my harness to place a much needed runner. Soon I was hanging from a sound belay and thinking it had been a long time since I felt ill at the prospect of a likely bad peeler. The guys had a nasty time with the corner and tested my belay a few times each on the way up, but they still were beaming and proclaiming a great, great route. [10]

Iain Small added a series of demanding mixed routes on Ben Nevis. His precise and delicate style allowed him to climb thin fragile ice far above protection

Photo: Simon Richardson

Three new Grade VIIIs climbed the same day in the same corrie was an unprecedented event in Scottish winter climbing. Only a couple of years before, three new routes of this level climbed throughout an entire Scottish season would have been an indication of a bumper year. Rather than competing against each other, the traditional on-sight ethic and the M-climbing revolution had combined in a powerful and constructive way, allowing a new group of climbers to raise their game. There was a renewed and infectious self-confidence about Scottish climbing. Dave MacLeod's ascent of the E11 route Rhapsody on Dumbarton Rock the year before had put Scottish rock climbing on the world stage. Now, in winter a new generation, strong, bold and willing to lead on-sight with modern tools and techniques, had unlocked another dimension of possibilities, and Ben Nevis was their new playground.

Iain Small was typical of the new breed of Nevis winter climbers. Slim and quietly spoken, Small was an Environmental Science graduate, who preferred to work as a stonemason rather than pursue a professional career. He had climbed many of the established mountain rock routes across Scotland and had ascended many of the hard winter classics. He had a superb knowledge of Ben Nevis and had amassed a huge repertoire of climbs, many of them solo. Confident, supremely fit, and acutely aware of the remaining potential on the mountain, he was keen to start leaving his own mark. Small had made the first winter ascent of Sidewinder on South Trident Buttress with Simon Richardson in April 2005, and the pair agreed to team up for the 2007 season.

The season started poorly, but ice conditions briefly came good in January, and Small immediately had his eye on a new line high on the Little Brenva Face.

> I remember doing Isandhlwana and looking left across the big unclimbed vertical headwall to the left and wondering what it would be like. I climbed Galactic Hitchhiker with Chris Cartwright in March 2002 and as we went down the abseil posts I noticed the Little Brenva headwall looked very icy. We were all set to climb it next day, but there was a rescue that night and we helped

Mark 'Ed' Edwards and Andy Nisbet on the first ascent of Unleashed (VII,6) on Number Three Gully Buttress

Photo: Jana Edwards-Lihocka

stretcher off a casualty and only got back to the hut in the early hours. The weather was awful the next day anyway, but a few days later Hannah Burrows-Smith and Dave McGimpsey climbed the icefall of Super G. This was the obvious line on the wall, but I knew that there was a line of ramped corners to its right. It was all a matter of finding the right conditions to climb them.

The pair started up the broad rib between Slalom and Frostbite, then continued up to the base of the headwall and belayed right of Super G. They were expecting difficult mixed climbing above, but instead they found the wall was covered in a layer of squeaky plastic ice, and the eight-pitch Wall of the Winds went at the relatively amenable grade of VI,5.

The lower ground was icy and the ramps were smeared with ice. Late in the season the wall strips in the sun so I guess we were really lucky to find it in such good condition. It was a really wet day and raining most of the time, but the ice was plastic and gave great climbing.[11]

The pair could scarcely believe that a 300m-long route on Ben Nevis could have been overlooked for so long, but the next day it thawed and the climb collapsed as quickly as it had appeared. Several days later another freeze brought the higher cliffs briefly into condition again, and Steve Kennedy and Bob Hamilton had a good find with the icy Close to the Edge (IV,4) on the true right arete of Gardyloo Buttress. A few weeks later, Dave MacLeod and visiting US climber Alicia Hudelson made the first winter ascent of Steam Train at VI,7, a steep HVS on the lower section of North-East Buttress that had seen very few summer ascents.

We climbed it in pretty heavy conditions. What an excellent climb though – bold bits, safe bits, thank god cracks and difficult cruxes. Alicia missed her flight to London but.... thank god for the sleeper train which saved the day.[12]

Later in March ice-climbing conditions became good again when a couple of days after a brief thaw, a high-pressure system centred over Scandinavia began sucking in cool easterly winds. This is the weather scenario that Scottish ice climbers drool over, because the clear skies and frosty nights coupled with warm daytime temperatures are perfect for building ice on the higher Ben Nevis routes. Many teams were quick to take advantage of the superb conditions with ascents of Sickle, Orion Direct and Astral Highway. It was quickly realised that the ice conditions were very special indeed, and some of the mountain's most highly prized thin face routes such as Riders on the Storm on Indicator Wall and The Great Glen on Gardyloo Buttress saw ascents. The quality of the ice was superb, with first time placements every swing.

Andy Nisbet and Ed Edwards were first on the spot to take advantage of the new route potential with the first ascent of Unleashed (VII,6), the steep undercut ice smear to the left of Vulture on Number Three Gully Buttress. Further right on Creag Coire na Ciste, Roger Webb and Simon Richardson climbed Wall Street (VI,7), the ramp and steep mixed groove right of South Sea Bubble leading to a hanging ice tongue. The following week, Nisbet made a couple of visits to Raeburn's Wall and climbed Life on Mars (VI,6), the large hanging icy slab to the right of The Upper Cascade, and Chiquita (VI,5), a thinner icefall right of Adieu and Farewell.

Simon Richardson on the first ascent of Arctic Tern (VII,5) on Indicator Wall

Photo: Pete MacPherson

The most intense action centred on Indicator Wall. Iain Small and Blair Fyffe were first to venture onto new ground when they made a rare ascent of Stormy Petrel, and took a more direct variation up a thinly iced groove in the centre of the route. Just to the left, Ian Parnell and Viv Scott climbed a more direct version to Fyffe's Rhyme of the Ancient Mariner. Parnell quickly despatched the difficult South Wind Start (VII,7) that avoided the cunning detour on the original line, and then continued up the original line to make the second ascent. Next day, Andy Benson, Rich Cross and Dave Hollinger repeated Parnell and Scott's direct line and confirmed its superb quality. With three difficult and sustained pitches straight up the centre of the imposing Indicator Wall, this is one of the great modern mixed climbs on the mountain.

Whilst Benson, Cross and Hollinger were doing battle with the new addition, Small and Richardson climbed the thin overlapping grooves to the left of Albatross. Arctic Tern (VII,5) starts just left of Albatross, passes the smooth slab of Fascist Groove before climbing a spectacular

Iain Small above the crux overlap on the first ascent of Ship of Fools (VIII,7) on Indicator Wall

Photo: Simon Richardson

tiered ramp system on centimetre-thick ice before finishing up the upper rib. Other teams were eager to capitalise on the exceptional conditions, and the route saw two repeats within a week.

On the descent down Tower Gully, Small noticed a slender ribbon of vertical ice, little more than 20 centimetres wide, hanging down the unclimbed pillar between Riders of the Storm and Albatross. The thread bottomed out onto a thin discontinuous smear of ice running down a 75 degree overlapping slab. The line looked preposterous, but the pair decided to return the following weekend to attempt it. It was April 1 and a perfect spring day. Richardson started up the introductory rib, and belayed below the ice smear to the right of Riders on the Storm. Small's lead of the crux section, pulling through the overlapping slab on thin hollow ice was one of the most impressive leads Richardson had ever seen.

The ice smear has fractured at his feet, and a crack now extends diagonally across its two-metre width. A brief thaw two days before lifted the ice a few millimetres, detaching it from the rock below. Now, his monopoints only half penetrate the ice before they hit rock; his tools barely reach their first notch. There are no gear placements in sight. Iain commits to a meticulous dance. Every placement, each step, has to be perfectly executed the first time; a second kick, or another swing, and the delicate skein of ice will shatter.

Small was now in a very precarious position. He was climbing a vertical crazy paving of ice held in place by its weight and friction against the rock below. As he moved up and swung his axe, the ice split perpendicular to the last crack, and ran upwards from the line of his tools. At the top of the smear was a blob of ice, about the size of a loaf of bread, which was also detached from the rock below. Small planted his left axe deep in the blob and used its mass as a counterweight to ease his torso around the overlap. He reached up and found a one-notch placement in the thin hollow ice above.

> Iain steps higher on the smear. The thaw has worked in his favour: a runner placement appears on the upper slab. Delicately, he wiggles in a wire. The ice sheet vibrates as he makes his second placement, but it holds his weight as he manoeuvres himself over the roof and levers his right crampon onto a finger-width, sloping notch. Four moves later and he reaches the foot of a narrow ice ribbon. It is solid, ten centimetres thick – thick enough, even, for a stubby screw. Iain begins to relax, and on a surge of adrenaline floats past another roof to a large ledge. I breathe a sigh of relief. I've just witnessed one of the finest leads in Scottish ice climbing history...[13]

Difficult mixed climbing up the crest of the pillar led to a spectacular finish up the vertical ice arete left of the exit gully of Le Nid d'Aigle. Acutely aware of the date and marginal nature of their climb, the pair called the route Ship of Fools and graded it VIII,7, a rating rarely used and reserved for the most serious of undertakings.

Suddenly the winter was all over, and the snow and ice all but vanished during a rapid thaw in the first week of April. The 2007 season was a turning point. M-climbing was no longer a threat but an ally, and a new generation had embraced new techniques and attitudes and successfully merged them with traditional values. Scottish climbing had a new vibrancy and self-confidence, and Ben Nevis was at the very heart of it all.

References

1. **Slawinski**, Raphael, *Degrees of Freedom*. American Alpine Journal, Volume 44, 72 – 85, 2002.

2. **Haston**, Stevie, in: Douglas, Ed, *Fast Burn Fuse – Ed Douglas talks with Stevie Haston*. Climber, 18 – 27, February 1998.

3. **Isaac**, Sean, *Mixed Climbing*. (Connecticut, USA: Falcon, 2005, ISBN 0762729635.)

4. **Gresham**, Neil, in: Parnell, Ian, *Future Scottish*. Climber, 46 – 51, January 2002.

5 **Robertson**, Guy, *Climb Scotland – Winter 05/06*. Scottish Mountaineer 33, 25 – 31, November 2006.

6. *www.alpinist.com*

7. *Ibid.*

8. *www.seanisaacblog.blogspot.com*

9. **Scott**, Viv, in: Richardson, Simon, *Scottish Winter Notes*. Climb 29, 22 – 25, June 2007.

10. *www.davemacleod.blogspot.com*

11. **Small**, Iain, *Interview, 9 March 2008.*

12. *www.davemacleod.blogspot.com*

13. **Richardson**, Simon, *The Ben*. Alpinist 22, 24 – 41, November 2007.

Mark Garthwaite elegantly bridging up the first pitch of The Secret (VIII,9) on the second ascent

Photo: Guy Robertson

The Black Diamond Viper, an evolution of the pure leashless tools, incorporating a hammerhead and spike at the foot of the shaft. Although not as positive as pure leashless tools on the steepest ground, its versatility makes it more suited to the varied nature of Scottish winter climbing

19: Full Confidence (2007 – 2008)

FOLLOWING THE EXCITEMENT and successes of 2007, the 2008 winter season was eagerly anticipated. There were some outstanding early season performances, such as the fourth winter ascent of Sioux Wall by Steve Ashworth and Tim Blakemore, and Martin Moran and Rob Jarvis's early repeat of the excellent Strident Edge, where they found a more direct version at VII,7. Ben Nevis was now firmly established as an early season mixed climbing venue, and the hard mixed routes of the 1990s had become trade routes as Simon Richardson explained.

> Ben Nevis is undergoing something of a renaissance at present, with many of the harder mixed climbs rapidly acquiring modern classic status. Top of the popularity list is Darth Vader (VII,8) at the left end of Coire na Ciste, which has seen six or so ascents this winter. Now the hooks are getting cleaned out of it, the route is becoming easier and one party suggested it was an ideal route for a first Grade VII lead. Across on Number Three Gully, Babylon (VII,8) has also seen a number of ascents, and is taking over from Gargoyle Wall as one of the most travelled mixed routes on Number Three Gully Buttress. South Trident Buttress is now firmly established as an excellent early season venue and The Slab Climb (VI,7) has proved especially popular.[1]

The first big event of the season was the first ascent of The Secret on Creag Coire na Ciste on December 10. This steep crackline slicing the right wall of Number Three Gully was climbed by Andy Turner, Steve Ashworth and Viv Scott and news of its ascent electrified the winter climbing community. The line had been stared at by mixed climbers for a number of years, but its unremitting steepness and apparent lack of footholds meant that most looked at it in disbelief. Turner's three-hour lead of the 40-metre crux pitch was a Scottish winter climber's dream – an on-sight, first ascent of a cutting edge winter-only line at the first attempt.

Turner, a mountaineering instructor from Stockport, had amassed an impressive tally of all-round mountaineering experience, including an ascent of Cerro Torre in Patagonia. He first spotted the line of The Secret when climbing Thompson's Route on Number Three Gully Buttress several years before.

> Conditions were amazing as we made our way up the first pitch. We stopped to look around and inspect both Darth Vader (VII,8) and Cornucopia (VII,9) on the opposite side of the gully. None of us had climbed routes that hard before so they were inspiring to look at, although very daunting. This was when we noticed the soaring crack line to their left. Surely it must have been climbed? It looked a perfect winter line, steep and straight up.

The seed had been sown, and over the next few seasons Turner built on his winter experience. He learned M-climbing techniques from Scott Muir, practised them in Birnham Quarry near Dunkeld, and then made ascents of hard Cairngorms classics such as The Vicar and Citadel. In 2006 he repeated Sioux Wall with a harder and more direct finish, and in January 2007 he climbed the test-pieces Unicorn and Cornucopia. Turner was now ready to climb The Secret, but other climbers had spotted the crack line too, and 'The Secret was no longer a secret.' Turner was frustrated by poor conditions coinciding with his time off during the remainder of the 2007 season, and he held his breath during the International Winter Meet in March. There was a lot of talk about attempting the line during the meet, but it remained untouched. Turner trained hard with Steve Ashworth in the Lake District over the summer, and they resolved to attempt The Secret at the beginning of the following season.

They drove north to Fort William as the remnants of the first major cold front of the winter were blowing through, picking up Viv Scott from Edinburgh on the way. At first light they made their way up into Coire na Ciste as the weak winter sun lit up the white cliffs around them. Ashworth struggled with the awkward initial shallow chimney for an hour or so, before reluctantly handing over the lead. Turner was in an inspired mood. He found a different sequence of moves, and was soon belayed on a ramp alongside the soaring crack line. Gaining the impending foot of the crack was awkward, but Turner soon found himself battling with the deep, off-width crack above.

> Throwing in all sorts of axe placements across the width of the crack allowed a slow upwards progression until after about 10ft I reached a chockstone. This was the first decent piece of gear and proved to be a struggle to lasso. Rapidly running out of arm power and swopping hands frantically on my tools to get some sort of rest I managed to get a sling over the top of it and clip the rope in; the next problem was getting the axes out from underneath it. With loads of expletives flying through the brisk air, and aided by encouragement from Steve and Viv, I summoned the strength to mantel onto the chockstone and get a semi-rest. This proved to be the crux of the route or at least the strenuous crux.

Andy Turner combined a background of high standard alpine climbing with specific strength training to make the first ascent of The Secret in December 2007

Photo: James Thacker

Andy Turner's lead of the 40 metre crux pitch of The Secret was a Scottish winter climber's dream – an on-sight, first ascent of a cutting edge winter only line at the first attempt

Photo: Viv Scott

Turner was carrying a large rack of camming devices to protect the crack, but they proved useless in the icy conditions. It was now a matter of preserving the limited number of hexes he was carrying to protect the pitch. Situated high up in Coire na Ciste, the route is fully exposed to the blast of northerly winds, and the thick layer of hoar frost was causing Turner a problem.

> ...the rime was covering up any useful axe placements. With Scottish mixed routes relying generally on hooks and torques in thin cracks or turf this was no help in what we were climbing. With no obvious features on the side walls the crack had to be tackled head on. Making it up as I went along inch by inch, I kept looking up trying to convince myself the thing was possible. Thankfully the crack was now getting narrower and axe placements easier to find.[2]

They finished The Secret at dusk and graded the route X,10, making it the most difficult on-sight first ascent ever achieved in Scotland. News of their success travelled at lightning speed. Whilst descending the mountain that night, they phoned Rob Jarvis, a friend and mountaineering instructor based in Fort William. Jarvis immediately posted news of their ascent on the popular internet bulletin board <ukclimbing.com> and before the team had left the mountain the ascent of The Secret was flashing up on computer screens around the land. The following day Ashworth uploaded video footage of Turner's lead of the crux crack onto You Tube and the ascent was reported on the websites of the American magazines Alpinist and Climbing. The instant nature of the coverage was intense and exciting, and immediately inspired Ian Parnell to attempt the second ascent.

> Winter 2007/8 marked the moment Scottish mixed climbing came alive on the web. I was used to endless hype over three move boulder problems but now numerous snow-filled photos, videos and reports flashed across the screen seemingly before the boys had got back down to the CIC Hut. It was enough to make an old fart like me go sharpen his tools...

Parnell recruited experienced Scottish winter climbers Guy Robertson and Mark Garthwaite, and three weeks later they were uncoiling their ropes at the foot of the route on a crystal still December morning. Their ascent went smoothly with Garthwaite quickly despatching the difficult entry pitch and Parnell taking the honours with a forceful lead of the long crux crack.

> Luck had also spun us a favour: where Andy had to fight a deep crust of hoar, we found a layer of verglas and a more manageable coating of the white stuff. It was wintry enough for sure, but a notch easier than Andy had to battle through... My biggest helping of fate happened when two small flakes I was hooking ripped on consecutive moves. Somehow I was able to maintain contact and made the on-sight – on another day it could have been very different.[3]

Inevitably, the relative ease of the second ascent led to discussion about the grade. The second ascent trio's initial view was that The Secret was 'hard VIII' and they eventually agreed that VIII,9 was a reasonable rating. Grading new winter routes is never straightforward, partly because conditions can vary significantly, but mainly because climbing any new route on-sight involves huge psychological pressure. Second ascents of mixed routes inevitably feel easier because the burden of the unknown is removed, and the repeat climbers can focus on the technicalities of the climbing with the knowledge that the route links together and the moves are possible. The team was full of praise for Turner's lead, stating that The Secret was one of the finest winter routes they had ever climbed.

The Secret and its attendant publicity provided a superb insight into the world of Scottish mixed climbing, but it was not only British climbers that took notice. Across in Canada, Raphael Slawinski was exploring further mixed possibilities on the Stanley Headwall, the showpiece mixed climbing venue in the Canadian Rockies, when he noticed a sinuous crack splitting a clean vertical wall.

> I had just read about the hard new route The Secret on Ben Nevis. Could this be the Rockies' version of it? One thing was clear: I wanted to try the line on-sight, using only natural gear. In the end the on-sight attempt came to naught, as a combination of pump, thin ice, spindrift and frozen hands sent me for three increasingly long whippers. I had to be satisfied with coming back the next day and redpointing the line. But I did succeed in my other

Steve Ashworth on the attempting Storm Trooper (VIII,8) on Creag Coire na Ciste. He returned four weeks later with Andy Turner for the successful ascent

Photo: Andy Turner

Guy Robertson's fast repeats of many of Scotland's hardest mixed routes were made in exemplary style. These ascents injected a renewed self confidence into Scottish winter climbing that was struggling to come to terms with the world- wide development of M-climbing

Photo: Ian Parnell

goal: puzzling out the climbing and the protection from the ground-up. Given that the inspiration came from across the pond, Victoria's Secret Deviation (M7+ 50m) seemed like an appropriate name.

Slawinski had discovered a new found zeal for traditional mixed climb- ing, and during the course of the 2008 season he established four more first ascents resulting in the most concentrated series of new routes in the Headwall's history. Remarkably, for an area that many thought climbed out, they were accomplished without placing any bolts.

> Do not misunderstand me. I love sport climbing in both its summer and winter incarnations. Bolts can open up fantastic terrain, allowing us to play with gravity on big overhangs and big daggers. However, bolts should add to the adventure, not diminish it. If a line looks even remotely feasible without bolts, then before reaching for the gun we owe it to ourselves to simply walk up to it and start climbing.[4]

The influence of M-climbing had gone full circle, and the Scottish on-sight ethic was now reverberating around the world. In the same way that dry tooling techniques had resulted in a step change in Scottish standards, they had given climbers like Slawinski the strength and skill to venture onto steep terrain with no bolts in sight. But Ian Parnell, who sampled several of the more difficult Canadian ice and mixed climbs in April 2008, cautioned against any sense of triumph. He noted that Slawinski's grading was on the modest side, and that the continued appli- cation of M-climbing skills in Scotland will allow on-sight standards to develop considerably further.

Raphael's recent Victoria's Secret also at Stanley is probably M9, trad and climbed ground up and I guess would rate Scottish grade X. All good inspiration to see what we can do next year in Scotland.[5]

Back on Ben Nevis, Steve Ashworth and Andy Turner hit the headlines once again early in 2008, with the first ascent of the very impressive Storm Trooper, the wall and narrow, tapering ramp right of Darth Vader on Creag Coire na Ciste. They spotted the line the day they climbed The Secret, and attempted it the next day, but not surprisingly, after their exertions on The Secret they ran out of steam, and retreated after the first pitch. They returned at the next opportunity on January 8. It was a poor day with blowing snow and gale force winds, but the cliff was white with new snow and coated in a thick layer of hoar frost. This time Turner took a more direct line up a shallow groove to gain the ramp, which turned out to be harder and less well protected than the original way. Following the intense grading debate after their ascent of The Secret, they rather conservatively rated the climb VIII,8, but the route is undoubtedly at the upper end of its grade.

A heavy fall of snow at the end of the January, followed by exceptionally strong northerly winds, brought the lower cliffs across Scotland into superb condition. Unfortunately, the weather was too severe for difficult winter climbing, but late on the evening of Friday, February 1, the winds dropped, leaving the Highlands coated white with fresh powder. The route of the weekend was the second winter ascent of Centurion by Guy Robertson and Pete Benson. The pair had noticed that Càrn Dearg Buttress was looking unusually white on a photo posted on the Scottish Avalanche Information Service blog, so they had no hesitation in seizing a rare opportunity to attempt this challenging climb. Centurion was first climbed in winter by Kenny Spence and John (Spider) McKenzie during the superb winter of 1986. This was Spence's third attempt on the route, and the pair climbed it over two days with a bivouac, finishing along the Route II traverse. Conditions were unusually good that year as a long weep of ice ran down into the main corner and directed a plume of spindrift that kept the lower two pitches white with snow. Although Alan Mullin made a remarkable solo ascent in quasi-winter conditions in February 2001, the route had not been repeated in full winter conditions.

Robertson and Benson found that the strong northerlies had coated the cliff with a thin layer of ice and the route sparkled white with fresh snow and hoar frost. At first they were concerned that the route was too wintry and would be impossible to protect, but the consistency of the ice was perfect – enough to hold bodyweight, but easily cleared from cracks for placing protection. Robertson quickly led the awkward first pitch, and then Benson ground out the long and sustained second pitch. Above that the next three pitches went smoothly and by late afternoon the pair had reached the Route II traverse with the climb apparently in the bag.

The good ice conditions that had helped lower down on the route were replaced by difficult powder snow on the Route II traverse, and their progress became very slow. To make matters worse they were hit by a southerly storm that made it very difficult to climb in the fierce winds. They eventually finished the route at 9pm, but the rapidly rising temperature meant that descending the avalanche-prone Number Five

Guy Robertson at the top of the first pitch of Centurion during the second winter ascent. Twenty-two years after the first winter ascent, the talented duo of Robertson and Benson found once in a lifetime conditions to make the first bona fide winter repeat

Photo: Pete Benson

Gully was out of the question. They continued to the top of Càrn Dearg in the dark with the sinking feeling that they had left the compass in their rucksack at the foot of the route. After several false starts they finally found their way down from the summit after a 23-hour round trip.

> A lot of muted screaming, frustration, angst, and a vague knowledge of the topography of the mountain, combined with raw luck, saw us stumbling down the Red Burn, fording the Allt a' Mhuillin (in spate) and then finally arriving back at the car at the back of 4am.... The route was outstanding. It's worth four stars, and is as good as The Needle, and just as hard![6]

Four days after the Centurion ascent, Dave MacLeod and Mike Tweedley visited Ben Nevis with their eyes set on a steep unclimbed chimney line to the left of The Minge on South Trident Buttress. A large, icicle-fringed roof barred progress, and after bombarding Tweedley with several huge icicles, MacLeod pulled over the lip only to be stopped by an overhanging wall above. Fortunately, an exposed traverse led left into the upper corner of 1944 Route that made a good finish to the appropriately named Under Fire (VII,7).

After a dry, snowless and rather quiet February, March turned out to be a very active month with a superb series of ascents. Heavy early snowfalls brought several of the lower routes on Ben Nevis into condition, and the classic South-West Ridge of the Douglas Boulder saw well over a dozen ascents. This easily accessible mixed climb is a good choice in poor conditions although the traditional III grade in the current SMC guidebook is a little sporting and IV,5 may be a more realistic rating. Just to its left, Rich Bentley and Mark Davies made a winter ascent of the summer VS Walking Through Fire, resulting in a tricky VII,7.

A few days later, Iain Small and Simon Richardson climbed The Survivor (VII,8), the groove system on the left side of Number Three Gully Buttress. This prominent line had escaped the recent intense development elsewhere on the buttress, and is characterised by a large niche. This is so overhung that it rarely catches much snow, but the continuous bad weather in early March meant it was well hoared. Staring up at the niche after the first pitch, the pair were not sure the route was possible, because the capping roofs looked blank and the vertical back corner of the niche itself was lined with a wafer-thin, seven metre high flake. Small made a virtuoso lead, climbing protectionless up the flake to avoid disturbing it, before pulling left across the blank wall along a hidden horizontal crack. The pitch above provided more steep and sustained climbing, greatly assisted by sinker placements and hard neve on every ledge.

A week later, on March 16, Richardson was back on the mountain with Roger Webb to take advantage of more hard neve conditions. They set their sights on the unclimbed buttress between Abacus and Maelstrom on the West Face of Observatory Ridge, but unfortunately a short thaw had lifted the snow-ice from the rock resulting in a very tenuous expedition. The pair noted that in more amenable conditions, The Frozen Chosin would provide a good VI,6 icy mixed outing.

The climb of the day however, was the first free ascent of Don't Die of Ignorance by Dave MacLeod and Joe French on the front face of The Comb. Andy Cave and Simon Yates first climbed this route in February

Dave MacLeod on the first ascent of the appropriately named Under Fire (VII,7) on South Trident Buttress. When MacLeod pulled through the ice fringe he sent a cascade of huge icicles down on to his belayer below

Photo: Mike Tweedley

Dave MacLeod attempting a free ascent of Don't Die of Ignorance (XI,11) on The Comb. MacLeod finally succeeded on his sixth attempt resulting in the most technically difficult mixed route ever climbed in Scotland

Photo: Steven Gordon

1987, which is based on the great hanging groove to the right of the crest of the buttress. A huge overhanging wall prevents direct access the groove, so they used aid to traverse right along a wide break from the foot of Tower Face of the Comb. Their ascent was graded VI,6 and A2 and had not been climbed since, although in 2001 Andy Nisbet and Chris Dale repeated the traverse pitch to reach The Flying Groove, a second corner-line further right. MacLeod was clearly inspired by this part of the mountain. In 2005 he added the difficult summer climb Anubis (E8) to the crest of The Comb (see Chapter 15), and the next project on his agenda was a free ascent of the original line of Don't Die of Ignorance. MacLeod had failed to free the route for the fifth time just two days earlier.

Iain Small on the first ascent of Cold Play (VIII,8). This difficult mixed climb at the left end of Creag Coire na Ciste carries all the hallmarks of an Iain Small route with wafer thin ice and strenuous technical climbing

Photo: Simon Richardson

Ian Parnell arriving at the top of Number Three Gully Buttress out after the first ascent of Burning with Anxiety (VIII,8). Sustained climbing above poor protection prompted Parnell to comment afterwards that this was the boldest Scottish route he had ever climbed

Photo: Alastair Lee

I was back once again, staring at that grim undercut crack disappearing round the prow into no man's land. I desperately struggled to seat my axe in the crux tin opener. I screamed to Joe to expect a fall and released my left axe, cutting loose onto one arm. The axe slid and jerked a centimetre. My heart missed a beat and the jolt nearly made me fall, my hand sliding down the upside down axe to the head and rolling onto three fingers. A dynamic match and kung fu [move] allowed one foot to swing onto the wall to the right and up to the peg I got in on Friday. The vertical wall above was climbed in an utterly 'go for broke' style, axes ripping, dropping onto one hand and gasping with pump and shrieking for slack.[7]

With the crux completed, the rest of the route should have been a formality, but French took over two hours to second the traverse, and by the time he reached the belay MacLeod was suffering severely from the cold. Two pitches of rapid climbing up the hanging groove and then easier climbing up the upper crest of The Comb saw the pair reach the plateau well into the night, with the hardest technical winter climbing ever done on Ben Nevis below them. MacLeod graded their free version of the route XI,11, the same grade he gave to his winter ascent of The Hurting in Coire an Lochain in the Cairngorms, which he had climbed three seasons before.

At the time of writing, Don't Die of Ignorance stands as the most difficult technical winter route in Scotland. MacLeod's ascent fully embraced the Scottish ground up ethic, and was the result of a focused campaign involving six separate visits to the mountain. The effort involved was huge, and on a parallel to the commitment shown by Nisbet, MacLean, Spence and McKenzie on their multiple attempts on The Needle and Centurion in the 1980s. These routes consolidated a quantum leap in Scottish winter standards, and no doubt future cutting edge winter routes will require the same combination of talent and relentless determination displayed by MacLeod on his ascent of Don't Die of Ignorance.

Ian Parnell made the final new addition that month with the first ascent of the left wall of Winter Chimney on Number Three Gully Buttress. Several teams had previously probed this short, but very difficult line, so it was no surprise that it turned out to be a technical and tenuous climb. Parnell graded Burning with Anxiety a rather conservative VIII,8, modestly stating that better ice on the central section may make it a little less serious. He later commented that there was

> ...an extremely bold central section with lots of ground fall possibilities and almost no gear before a steep gymnastic finish. It turned out to be a very intense three hour lead, and the boldest winter route I've done so far.[8]

The first half of April was a magnificent time for climbing high on Ben Nevis. A long settled period of cool northerly winds brought the higher icy lines into good condition, and conditions were even good enough on the Minus Face to prompt Guy Robertson and Viv Scott to attempt a winter ascent of Subtraction. This summer E1 climbs grooves on the right side of Minus Two Buttress, before crossing Minus One Gully, to finish up a steep, impending groove on the left flank of Minus One Buttress. A winter ascent had been discussed for over twenty years, but since the lower section of the climb coincides approximately with the Grade V winter route Minus Two Buttress, the main challenge in winter was thought to centre on the difficulty of the final groove.

It had been several years since Minus Two buttress had been fully iced, and Robertson and Scott found this section to be in challenging mixed condition. Scott made a bold lead of the first pitch, which was very sustained and only marginally protected. The second pitch was technically harder, and a little steeper, although the gear was at least adequate. Unfortunately, by the time they had climbed these two pitches, the upper groove had stripped in the morning sun, so they escaped into Minus Two Gully.

Iain Small and Simon Richardson realised that the late March storms had lined some of the mountain's north-facing grooves with good ice. This crucial information allowed them to make the first ascent of Cold Play, the pronounced rib between Archangel and South Sea Bubble on Coire na Ciste. Only a centimetre-thick trickle of ice had formed on one side of the impending lower groove, but this was enough for Small to place his picks sideways between the rock and the ice. Above, a steep overhanging Y-shaped crack led to the very exposed upper rib with another overhanging crack to finish, resulting in a sustained and challenging VIII,8. The following weekend the pair returned, and Small made another thin ice lead up Last Tango (VII,8), the deep corner and hanging groove right of the icy slab of Quickstep on Number Three Gully Buttress. This appeared to be the end of the season, but incredibly the cool weather held on for another week, prompting Andy Cave and

Iain Small on the first ascent of Last Tango (VII,8) on Number Three Gully Buttress. The frozen rope to his left was left by a party unable to negotiate the cornice of Quickstep, which takes the icefall to the left

Photo: Simon Richardson

Andy Cave wraps up the 2008 winter season with the first ascent of Techno Wall (V,6) on Goodeve's Buttress. The route was named after the music carried on the wind from loudspeakers on the Nevis Range ski slopes on Aonach Mòr

Photo: Simon Richardson

Richardson to climb Techno Wall (V,6), a direct mixed line to the left of The Borg Collective on the front face of Goodeve's Buttress.

The 2008 summer was dominated by a single, extraordinary event. On the evening of July 28, belayed by Kevin Shields and filmed by his wife Claire, Dave MacLeod led the overhanging arete defining the centre of Echo Wall on the east side of Tower Ridge.

For MacLeod, it was the culmination of a two-year campaign preparing and practising for an ascent he knew was close to the limit of the possible, with the almost certainty of a ground fall from above the crux. The only line of weakness up the poorly protected, 70-metre sheet of rock, the route was immediately recognised as the most difficult mountain rock climb in the British Isles, if not the world, for its combination of technical difficulty, seriousness and situation. MacLeod wrote on his blog

> The air was so crisp but it was hot... time passed. I was waiting for the katabatic winds of the late evening rolling off the plateau and snowfields just above the route. At 8pm the chill wind gently got going. I waited and waited until the temperature and rock friction was perfect, and at 9pm exactly, the preparation over months crystallised and I led the route in a dream state of confident execution. It felt easy, as every hard route I've ever done has – the great paradox!

Many climbers and mountaineers will recognise the sensation of entering a 'dream state' when their bodies and minds work in absolute harmony when engaged on a route at their absolute limit. MacLeod continued

> The feeling of climbing on perfect rock, in perfect conditions in the company of Claire and Kev will stay with me all my life. It's hard for me to describe the feeling of freedom from experiencing something that had seemed so unreachable could feel so effortless, all that was required was to draw the right ingredients together, piece by piece over time.[9]

Few may repeat Echo Wall, but eventual success after the long struggle for a much sought-after route, will continue to evoke similar feelings of elation and fulfilment among climbers on Ben Nevis.

We pause here with this history of Britain's highest mountain at the end of the 2008 summer season. It is a remarkable story of courage and determination, vision and ambition. The mountain has influenced meteorologists and scientists, artists and writers, but above all, Ben Nevis has been a touchstone for mountaineers and climbers. As successive generations have explored the mountain and probed the intricacies of the extensive cliffs of this great peak, they have found more challenges to test and inspire them. Ben Nevis has a status in world mountaineering that belies its diminutive stature. The equipment, techniques and ethics developed on Ben Nevis have influenced alpinism across the globe, and without doubt the mountain will continue to inspire those that venture onto its flanks for many years to come.

References

1. **Richardson**, Simon, *Scottish Winter Notes*. Climb 37, 26 – 27, March 2008.

2. **Turner**, Andy, *Unlocking The Secret*. Climb 38, 48 – 51, April 2008.

3. **Parnell**, Ian, *Unlocking The Secret – The 2nd Ascent*. Climb 38, p51, April 2008.

4. **Slawinski**, Raphael, *Past the Bolt*. Canadian Alpine Journal, 42 – 45, Volume 91, 2008.

5. *ianparnellphotography.blogspot.com*

6. **Robertson**, Guy, in: Richardson, Simon, *Scottish Winter Notes*. Climb 39, 12 – 14, May 2008.

7. *www.davemacleod.blogspot.com*

8. **Parnell**, Ian, in: Richardson, Simon, *Late Season Action on The Ben*. Climb 40, 28 – 29, June 2008.

9. *www.davemacleod.blogspot.com*

Dave MacLeod on the first ascent of Echo Wall. Extreme technical difficulty combined with minimal protection qualifies the route as one of the most difficult mountain rock climbs in the world

Photo: Claire MacLeod

Gaelic Place Names

Each derivation or translation is followed by the suggested phonetic spelling (Ph.) In this, pronounce 'A' as in Apt. The sound of these place names as rendered by a native Gaelic speaker is usually completely different from most attempts commonly heard, and the reader is urged to try and hear the music of this language as spoken by a native. For further reading see References for Chapter 1 and below.

Achintee. Probably from the (Ga.) achadh an t-sithidh, or 'field of the shaped hill', the hill in this case being Meall an t-Suidhe. Sìthe, or sìthean in (Ga.) means 'mound shaped hill', and is often associated with fairies, or sithichean. Alternatively, according to MacMillan neither the topography nor the local pronunciation favour this derivation. Sitheadh in (Ga.) means 'quick onrush', which could refer to the wind, so 'field of the stormy blast' as suggested by MacMillan is not impossible. (Ph.) *Achu an cheehee*. Using 'ch' as in loch, 'u' as in up, achu an. Using 'ch' as in 'cheat', cheehee.

Allt a' Mhuilinn. (Ga.) for 'the mill burn'. It is also known to an older generation as Allt Domhnall an t-Siucair, (Ga.) for 'Donald of the sugar burn'. Mothers used to admonish their naughty children by telling them that 'Donald of the sugar' would come and get them. Another old name is the Allt a'phriosain, (Ga.) for 'the prison burn', after an old prison. (Ph.) *Owltt a vooleen*. Owltt, 'Owl' + 'tt'.

Allt na h-Urchaire. (Ga.) for 'burn of the shot'. Modern name is the Red Burn. As (Ga.) for red is dearg we might guess that at some time a story was connected with the burn, perhaps of hunting. (Ph.) *Owltt na Hoorichiru*. 'Ch' as in loch, 'u' as in up.

Ben Nevis. (Ga.) Nibheis or Nimheis. The late Professor Watson suggests an old Irish word 'neamhaise', meaning 'terrible', and also a (Ga.) word 'ni-mhaise', meaning 'no beauty'. W.C. MacKenzie has made an attempt to associate the Irish 'neamhaise' with the Scottish 'uamhais', or 'dread', thus drawing in the two Scottish mountains Nevis and Wyvis (both, interestingly, large shapeless masses from certain angles). The word 'neamh' in (Ga.) means 'a raw and bitingly keen atmosphere', and is sometimes confused with the (Ga.) word 'neimh', meaning 'poison, bitterness, and malice'. (Ph.) *Ben Neevish*.

The Gaelic scholar Alexander MacBain was the author of 'An Etymological Dictionary of the Gaelic Language'. (Gairm Publications, Glasgow, 1st Edition 1896, reprinted as a photolitho of the 2nd edition of 1911 in 1982.) Here he suggested that Nevis was from a European root-word neb, meaning cloud or water. The wits amongst us would immediately point out that the two are usually inextricably connected on Ben Nevis! There is no doubt that with its geographical position, Nevis inevitably acts as a meteorological magnet for bad weather, making this origin a good contender.

What makes pinning down the origin difficult is not only the lack of a coherent history, but the number of similar-sounding words which have different meanings. We have nimheil or nibheis (evil or venomous), neimheas, nimheas, or nimheis (all from neimh, poison or venom), nèamh (sky, or heaven), neimhidh (heavenly or divine), uamhais (dread), and even neimh (venom as above, or the sting of a cold frost). Failing new evidence, choose what feels right for the day.

Càrn Beag Dearg. The little red rock or mountain. (Ph.) *Carn Bayg Jerrag*. 'Carn' as in Carnivorous, 'Bay + G', 'G' as in good, 'Jerrag', 'G' as in good.

Càrn Dearg. The red rock or mountain. The mass of rock seen from the climber's point of view in the Allt a' Mhuilinn is andesite, and therefore dark grey, but from the Fort William side the flanks of Càrn Dearg are of the surrounding red granite. (Ph.) *Carn Jerrag*.

Càrn Dearg Meadhonach. The middle red rock or mountain. The intermediate point on the ridge between Càrn Mòr Dearg and Càrn Beag Dearg. (Ph.) *Carn Jerrag Me-an-och*. 'Och' as in 'Och Aye!'.

Càrn Mòr Dearg. The big red rock or mountain. The ochre-coloured granite screes of this mountain above the Allt a' Mhuilinn are an obvious contrast to the darker andesite of Ben Nevis. (Ph.) *Carn More Jerrag*.

Coire Eòghainn. There is some doubt as to whether this should be translated as John's coire or Ewen's coire. The (Ga.) for John is Iain or Eoin. (Ph.) *Corry Ee-o-in*. Said quickly with emphasis on the 'o'.

Coire Gaimhnean. Coire of the yearling deer or cows. One yearling is gamhainn, with the plural gaimhne. Grammatically it should be written Coire nan gaimhne. (Ph.) Corry Guynone. 'Guy' + 'none'.

Coire Giùbhsachain. Coire of the little pine forest. (Ph.) *Corry Geeoosachan*. G as in good, 'Ch' as in loch.

Coire Leis. The leeward or sheltered coire. (Ph.) Corry Laysh.

Coire na Ciste. The coire of the chest or casket. (Ph.) *Corry na Quichechu*. 'Quiche' as in 'Quiche Lorraine', 'Chu' as in 'Chugg'.

Corpach. (Ga.) A'Chorpaich. 'Ground under which there is decayed wood'. MacMillan states that this is descriptive of the peaty soil of Corpach Moss and is more feasible than the more popular derivation of 'body-place', where the illustrious dead are said to have rested before being shipped to Iona for burial. (Ph.) *A Chorpeech*. Both 'Ch' as in loch.

Lochaber. (Ga.) Lochabair, 'the confluence loch', named as the main rivers and burns flow into it, and giving the district its name. Now known as Loch Linnhe (see below). (Ph.) *Llochappir*.

Loch Laggan. (Ga.) for 'loch of the small hollow'.

Loch Linnhe. In (Ga.) known as An Linnhe Dhubh, 'the dark channel'. (Ph.) *An Lleena Ghoo*. (The 'h' is aspirated to soften the 'g' sound.)

Loch Trèig. Derivation uncertain. May be from Treig, (Ga.) for 'forsake', thus giving 'the forsaken loch'. (Ph.) *'trake'*, as in drake.

Meall an t-suidhe. (Ga.) for 'hill of the seat', with its associated lochan. This is the popular derivation, though MacMillan thinks that 'hill of the stormy blast' may be a contender. (See entry for Achintee). (Ph.) *Meowll an tooyee*. 'Meow' as in cats.

Meall Cumhann. 'Narrow-shaped hill'. (Ph.) *Meowll Cooven*.

Poldubh. (Ga.) Poll Dubh, 'the dark pool'.

Steall, An. 'The waterfall'. (Ph.) *Steowll*.

Further Reading

Drummond, Peter, *Scottish Hill Names – Their origin and meaning*. (Glasgow: Scottish Mountaineering Trust, 2007.)

Geology

by Noel Williams

BEN NEVIS IS NOT ONLY Britain's highest mountain it is also a spectacular example of a deeply eroded caldera volcano. The rocks now forming the summit of Ben Nevis would not have survived erosion but for a cataclysmic event which shook the whole Lochaber area some 410 million years ago.

Marine sediments: The story of the formation of Ben Nevis begins much earlier however – around 700 million years ago – when the original sediments which now form many of the rocks seen in neighbouring mountains, such as the Mamores and Grey Corries, were starting to be laid down. These sediments included silt, limy muds and clean quartz sand. They built up layer upon layer on the sea floor, sometimes in shallow coastal waters, and at others in deeper water bordering a developing ocean. Complex life forms had not evolved at this time and so these marine sediments did not contain any fossil remains.

Folding and mountain building: Around 500 million years ago the blocks of the Earth's crust that now make up Scotland lay south of the equator and formed the margin of a large tectonic plate called Laurentia which also included Greenland and North America. Over the next 70 million years, as the intervening Iapetus Ocean began to close, Laurentia moved towards two other plates – Baltica (Sweden, Finland and Russia) and Avalonia (England, Wales and southern Ireland). As these three plates started to collide the sedimentary rocks were squeezed, folded and heated. Such was the intensity of this squeezing that not only were huge mountains created, but the original rock layers were deeply buried and in places completely overturned. This treatment caused the rocks themselves to change in character in a process known as metamorphism. Siltstones changed to schist, quartz sandstones changed to quartzite, mudstones changed to slate, and limestones changed to marble.

The Caledonian Mountains formed an impressive chain several thousand kilometres long. The remaining roots of this chain can be traced today from eastern North America across northern Britain, Norway, Greenland and up into Spitzbergen. The mountains themselves must once have been at least as high as many Alpine peaks and were possibly similar in character to those seen today in parts of the Himalaya such as the Hindu Kush.

Some idea of the scale of folding can be appreciated by examining the metamorphic rocks in Glen Nevis. Normally younger rocks are found on top of older ones, but exactly the opposite is the case in the Mamores. The mica schist found at Polldubh in the floor of Glen Nevis is younger than the quartzite which overlies it and forms the summit of Sgùrr a' Mhaim on the south side of the glen.

The separate crustal blocks which Scotland is built from were slowly assembled together after the main phase of mountain building was complete. Around 425–400 million years ago several fragments of crust, which were originally widely separated, started to slide alongside each

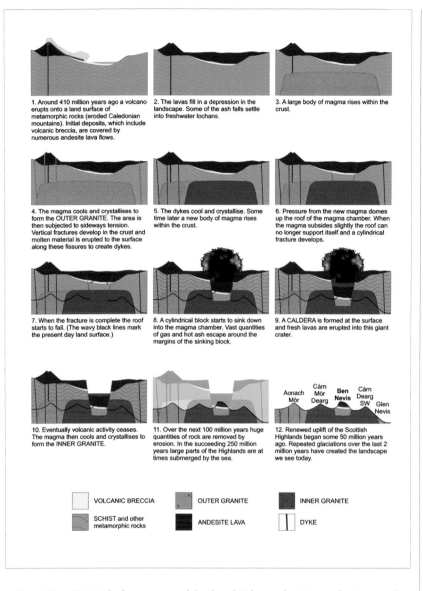

The various stages of formation of the Ben Nevis caldera and surrounding mountains

Diagrams: Noel Williams

1. Around 410 million years ago a volcano erupts onto a land surface of metamorphic rocks (eroded Caledonian mountains). Initial deposits, which include volcanic breccia, are covered by numerous andesite lava flows.

2. The lavas fill in a depression in the landscape. Some of the ash falls settle into freshwater lochans.

3. A large body of magma rises within the crust.

4. The magma cools and crystallises to form the OUTER GRANITE. The area is then subjected to sideways tension. Vertical fractures develop in the crust and molten material is erupted to the surface along these fissures to create dykes.

5. The dykes cool and crystallise. Some time later a new body of magma rises within the crust.

6. Pressure from the new magma domes up the roof of the magma chamber. When the magma subsides slightly the roof can no longer support itself and a cylindrical fracture develops.

7. When the fracture is complete the roof starts to fail. (The wavy black lines mark the present day land surface.)

8. A cylindrical block starts to sink down into the magma chamber. Vast quantities of gas and hot ash escape around the margins of the sinking block.

9. A CALDERA is formed at the surface and fresh lavas are erupted into this giant crater.

10. Eventually volcanic activity ceases. The magma then cools and crystallises to form the INNER GRANITE.

11. Over the next 100 million years huge quantities of rock are removed by erosion. In the succeeding 250 million years large parts of the Highlands are at times submerged by the sea.

12. Renewed uplift of the Scottish Highlands began some 50 million years ago. Repeated glaciations over the last 2 million years have created the landscape we see today.

VOLCANIC BRECCIA

SCHIST and other metamorphic rocks

OUTER GRANITE

ANDESITE LAVA

INNER GRANITE

DYKE

other. Ben Nevis belongs to a block which geologists refer to as the Grampian Terrane. It is bounded by the Great Glen Fault to the north-west and the Highland Boundary Fault to the south-east.

Volcanoes and magma chambers: At the same time as these blocks were sliding into place huge quantities of molten rock or magma began to form deep within the thickened crust beneath the rapidly eroding Caledonian mountains. Some of this magma erupted to the surface and poured out as lava; much remained within the crust and cooled more slowly to form intrusions of granite and diorite.

When geologists working for the Geological Survey first mapped the Ben Nevis area early in the 20th Century they made an astonishing discovery. They found that the summit of the mountain consists of a

Contact point near the Allt a' Mhuilinn, between the dark andesite lavas and the fine-grained pink inner granite

Photo: Noel Williams

cylindrical block of lavas and volcanic breccias completely surrounded by a large body of granite. These very different rocks would not normally be found alongside each other because lavas erupt at the Earth's surface and granite forms deep within the crust. They explained this juxtaposition by a process they termed 'cauldron subsidence'. The lavas had originally been at a much higher level, until the roof above a granite magma chamber gave way, possibly in a number of stages. A cylindrical block of the overlying rocks collapsed into the molten granite in a series of truly spectacular events which created a huge crater or caldera at the surface. Vast quantities of ash and lava escaped around the margins of the subsiding block. So much ash and dust would have been blasted high into the atmosphere that it may well have affected sunsets around the world for months afterwards – just as occurred when Krakatoa erupted in 1883 and Mount St Helens in spring 1980.

The down-faulted block of andesite lavas became trapped within the granite when it cooled. No trace remains of the lavas that erupted outside the caldera. So the rocks now forming the top half of the highest mountain in the country would have been eroded away a long time ago had they not been 'preserved' inside the granite. This also means that the rocks now forming the summit were once many hundreds of metres higher in the Earth's crust.

An extra baking and prolonged erosion: The great heat from the granite magma passed into the neighbouring rocks. This brought about further changes to the surrounding metamorphic rocks and also to the lavas within the collapsed block. The mica schist at Polldubh is particularly good for climbing on because the extra heating (or thermal metamorphism) it received from the granite magma caused new minerals to form within the schist up to two kilometres from the margin of the granite. These new minerals (such as cordierite and andalusite) make the schist sounder and rougher than normal mica schist.

Much of the remaining history of Ben Nevis involves prolonged periods of erosion. Indeed weathering processes over long periods of time were so effective that by 300 million years ago the mighty Caledonian mountains had been eroded back down almost to sea level.

Further uplift and final shaping by ice: So how come the mountains in the Highlands are as high as they are today? A fairly recent episode of uplift took place about 50 million years ago. This may have been part of the mountain building events associated with the creation of the Alps in southern Europe, or more likely a general tilting related to the opening of the North Atlantic. Either way it is remarkable that we can now enjoy a second version of the Caledonian mountains.

The finishing touches to the shape of Ben Nevis were made during the relatively recent Ice Age. Vast ice sheets built up and melted away again on several occasions over the last two million years. The classic U-shaped profile of Glen Nevis and the hollows of Coire na Ciste and Coire Leis as well as the spectacular arete linking Ben Nevis with Càrn Mòr Dearg were all sculpted by ice during the multiple glaciations that occurred in northern Britain, but particularly during the last glaciation that ended only 11,500 years ago. Large quantities of rock were removed and transported by the ice. Numerous erratics of Ben Nevis granite are found as far south as Loch Leven indicating that the ice moved in a

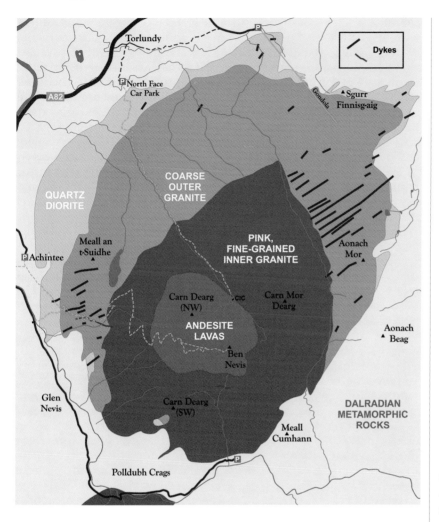

The geological map of the Ben Nevis caldera, with rock types indicated on the map. Rock boundaries after Burt 1994 (unpublished PhD thesis)

Diagram: Noel Williams

Quartz-diorite on the Achintee path

Photo: Noel Williams

south-westerly direction down Loch Linnhe. Smaller glaciers carried boulders from the volcanic pile northwards towards the Great Glen.

A walk into a cauldron: Some of the distinctive rock types that Ben Nevis is built from can be examined during an ascent of the mountain by the path from Achintee. The first part of the path crosses glacial moraine and no bedrock is exposed. However, a short distance after crossing a stile, some 600m from Achintee, there is a small outcrop of metamorphic rock on the east side of the path. It was originally an impure limestone but was strongly affected by heat from the Ben Nevis granite and was changed into a pale-green and white banded rock called hornfels; the pale green colour is due to the presence of a mineral called tremolite.

Soon after this the path crosses onto quartz-diorite – the outermost of the Ben Nevis intrusions. This rock is similar to granite, but is grey in colour and has rather less quartz. There are numerous exposures of it beside the path.

The next change in rock type occurs where the path from the Youth

Vertical dyke cutting through the coarse-grained outer granite on the Achintee path

Photo: Noel Williams

Younger basalt dyke between the bridges on the Achintee path, with distictive 'onion-skin' weathering

Photo: Noel Williams

Hostel joins the main path. Here the rock is a very coarse-grained granite known as the Ben Nevis Outer Granite. This rock also forms the summit of neighbouring Aonach Mòr. It has the largest vertical thickness (1200m) of any granitic rock exposed in the UK. As the path ascends through two sets of zigzags it is possible to see several dykes cutting through the granite. These narrow intrusions are finer-grained and slightly darker than the granite. They were formed when magma was injected into vertical fractures which formed in the granite after it had cooled. They trend in a NE–SW direction. These dykes are completely absent from the inner granite.

There is also a conspicuous dark-coloured dyke clearly visible in the path between the two aluminium bridges. However, this trends in a completely different direction to the others (WNW–ESE). This is because it is a much younger basalt dyke which can be linked to the volcanic activity that occurred on Skye around 60 million years ago. It shows very obvious spheroidal or 'onion-skin' weathering.

Shortly before the path zigzags towards Lochan Meall an t-Suidhe the rock changes again to the much redder Ben Nevis Inner Granite. This rock is easily seen where the path cuts southwards and crosses the 'Red Burn'. The rock is also obvious on the first three legs of the major zigzags which ascend the western flank of the mountain.

Then, just by the third corner of these zigzags, the path moves onto a very different dark grey coloured rock. This is the start of the great pile of volcanic rocks – mainly andesite lavas – which form all the upper section of the mountain. In some samples the rock is speckled with small light-coloured crystals of feldspar. Where separate angular blocks of various sizes can be distinguished within the rock it is known as volcanic breccia.

The most remarkable feature of the upper plateau of Ben Nevis is the blockfield which everywhere covers the ground. This coating of boulders was created by freeze-thaw action when the summit experienced periglacial conditions. This happened during the last glaciation when ice sheets were less extensive and the highest peaks remained exposed above the ice as nunataks. Previous coverings of blockfield would have been removed when the summits were completely buried by a major ice sheet.

If you descend the south-eastern flank from the summit you will notice that you leave andesite lavas behind and move back onto the red Inner Granite just where the ground flattens out at the start of the arete which leads round to Càrn Mòr Dearg.

The volcanic pile: The best place to see the full sequence of rocks inside the down-faulted block, is on the spectacular north-east side of the mountain. Here it can be seen that the rocks have a basin-like structure with steeply upturned margins. This suggests there was frictional dragging as the block subsided.

The lowest rocks in the sequence are phyllites. These metamorphic rocks were originally siltstones. They were not as strongly metamorphosed as the local schists because they had not been buried as deeply in the crust. They can be found on the west side of the Allt a' Mhuilinn about 300m south-east of the CIC Hut. Various sedimentary rocks, mainly mudstones and conglomerates, can also be found beside the phyllites. These much younger rocks are difficult to see, but they tell an important story of the environment preceding volcanic activity. A slightly more extensive area of sedimentary rocks occurs around the base of North-East Buttress by the lip of Coire Leis. These sedimentary rocks are similar to modern day playa lake deposits and indicate the existence of a freshwater lake.

The onset of volcanic activity is marked by the presence of volcanic breccia. This rock is particularly conspicuous in the slabs immediately west of the CIC Hut. Some of the blocks in it are an enormous size. The blocks consist of fragments of lava that were blasted apart by explosive volcanic eruptions. The jumbled and unsorted nature of the fragments suggests that this material probably moved downhill as a mass flow under gravity rather than being transported by flowing water.

All the units within the volcanic pile are of limited lateral extent. However one distinctive member of ash-fall deposit can be traced from Ledge Route above Càrn Dearg Buttress in a southerly direction towards Lochan Coire na Ciste. One of the best exposures of sedimentary rock within the volcanic pile can be seen at the base of this member in the rock band which surrounds the base of North Trident Buttress. The beds were deposited in a freshwater lake and the layers show evidence of disturbance presumably caused by earth tremors associated with volcanic eruptions.

Much of the upper part of the pile consists of andesite lavas but with some evidence of subaqueous block and ash flows. Some of the magma may have been erupted into water and some injected as sills.

There are several lines of weakness cutting through the volcanic pile that have eroded out to form gullies and gaps such as that behind the Douglas Boulder. Dykes of the local swarm are absent from the down-faulted block so these features probably mark the line of faults within the volcanic pile. The western flank of Càrn Mòr Dearg is fairly uniform in character because dykes are also absent from the Inner Granite. The western flank of Aonach Mòr on the other hand is seamed with gullies because the Outer Granite is riddled by a swarm of dykes which have eroded more quickly than the granite.

Ben Nevis remains a fascinating place to study a variety of igneous processes. It is the only location in Scotland where it is possible to examine in close proximity rocks that were erupted from a volcano at the Earth's surface, and rocks that formed in a magma chamber deep within the crust.

Further Reading

Stephenson, David and **Goodenough**, Kathryn, *Ben Nevis and Glencoe – A Landscape Fashioned by Geology.* (Inverness: Scottish Natural Heritage, 2007.)

McGarvie, D.W., *Ben Nevis and the Allt a' Mhuilinn*, in: Caledonian Igneous Rocks of Great Britain, Geological Conservation Review Series No. 17, 492 – 7, (Joint Nature Conservation Committee, 1999.)

A version of this document can be downloaded from http://www.jncc.gov.uk/pdf/gcrdb/GCRsiteaccount2073.pdf

British Mountain Maps – Ben Nevis & Glen Coe. (Harvey in conjunction with the BMC, MCofS and BGS, 2007.)

During the last glaciation, the summit of Ben Nevis stood proud of the ice, exposing the rock to freeze-thaw and creating the blockfield debris which still covers the summit

Photo: Noel Williams

Breccia formed from fragments of lava blasted apart by volcanic eruptions

Photo: Noel Williams

A section from the
Ordnance Survey six-
inch to the mile map
of 1875, showing the
summit and North-
east face of Ben Nevis

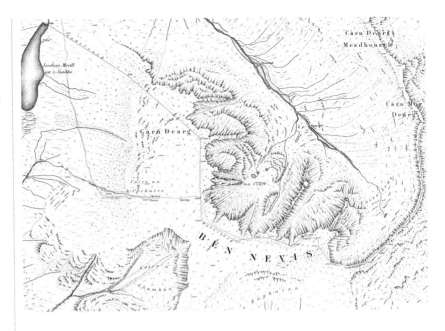

Mapping

by Graham E. Little

OF THE THOUSANDS of hillwalkers and climbers ascending Ben Nevis
every year the vast majority will be carrying a map, although few will
be aware that man's earliest cartographic interest in the mountain dates
back to the 16th Century.

The earliest maps of the Scottish mainland were concerned primarily with communication, whether by path, track or water. Mountains,
merely serving to hinder this process, were of relatively little interest
and were therefore depicted in a very stylised fashion with no individual identity. One of the most prolific of the early map makers was the
redoubtable Timothy Pont, who travelled throughout Scotland between
1583 and 1611 often suffering great privitations in pursuit of his chosen
task. He was probably the first cartographer to depict the name Ben Nevis
on a map. Robert Gordon, a graduate of the University of Aberdeen and
described at the time as 'doyen of geographers', revised Pont's maps
between 1636 and 1648. Thirty six of Pont's updated Regional maps were
published in Johan Blaeu's Novus Atlas in 1654.

By the middle of the 18th Century a military survey of Scotland was
in progress under the guidance of William Roy who by 1781 reached
the rank of Major General. Roy is often considered the founder of the
Ordnance Survey although he died before it formally came into being.
Using basic theodolites, without telescopes and fifty foot chains Roy
and his colleagues produced the 'Great Map' in less than ten years at
a scale of 1 inch:1000 yards. Ben Nevis is clearly depicted, although without a height. Roy said of this map that *'it is rather to be considered as a
magnificent military sketch than as a very accurate map.'* However it was

undoubtedly more accurate than anything yet produced.

Over the next century many Estate and County maps were produced, of varying scales and quality.

The next major cartographic development was the survey of Inverness-shire CLI (151), a 6 inch:1 mile map, published by the Ordnance Survey in 1875. This was the first map to delineate the complex form of Ben Nevis, although unlike its English counterparts, did not include contouring. This map was revised in 1899 to include the recently constructed 'pony track' and observatory and republished in 1902.

During the late 1950s the Ordnance Survey embarked upon a resurvey of the upland areas of Scotland, based upon aerial photography and in 1967 published a new and detailed 1:10,560 map, NN17SE, of Ben Nevis with 25 foot interval contouring. Rumour has it that the surveyor responsible for the ground completion of this sheet became totally lost in thick cloud on the summit plateau, eventually descending the mountain on the wrong side and returning to base only just in time to prevent the launch of a full scale rescue party! All subsequent smaller scale mapping has been based on NN17SE, which has been converted from 1:10,560 to the metric scale of 1:10,000.

In recent times two maps have been published with the mountaineer specifically in mind. In 1989 Ordnance Survey brought out a water resistant 1:25,000 Mountainmaster map of Ben Nevis with a 1:10,000 inset of the summit area. In 2007 Harvey, in conjunction with the BMC, MCofS and British Geological Survey, brought out a 1:40,000 map in their British Mountain Map series with a 1:15,000 inset of the summit area. The map is printed on polyethylene rather than paper, making it waterproof and tear-resistant.

TRIANGULATION AND PILLAR MAINTENANCE

The prominent white concrete Ordnance Survey pillar situated on the summit plateau of Ben Nevis, just to the south of the cliff edge, (code named PP323) is part of a network of similar pillars spread throughout the country. Contrary to popular opinion these pillars are not necessarily sited on the highest point of a mountain (although they often are) but are positioned to allow intervisibility with surrounding pillars. They were constructed to allow the instrumental observation of a rigid framework of triangles, braced quadrilaterals and polygons, known as triangulation, which forms the skeleton upon which the mapping of the country is based. This geodetic framework is related, via astronomical observation, to latitude and longitude, thus ensuring cartographic sympathy between adjacent countries.

William Roy had proposed a systematic triangulation of Britain in the 18th Century but his desire was not fulfilled until much later, being published as the 'Principal Triangulation' in 1858.

In its present form, the triangulation pillar was erected in August 1936 as part of the triangulation of Great Britain, on the site of an earlier triangulation station. PP323 is unusual, if not unique, in that it was built on the top of a man made cairn and not on 'living rock' as is the normal practice. However a flat, three metre wide, concrete platform was laid over the cairn and the foundation of the pillar extended well into its body and as such was considered stable and permanent.

*Triangulation figure
for Ben Nevis*

Diagram: Graham Little

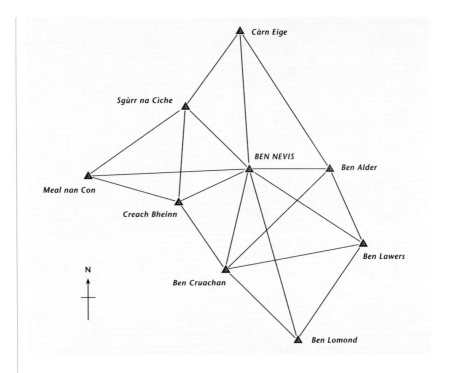

Despite the choice of May when weather is likely to be at its clearest for long-range triangulation observations, it took senior observers and their helpers 22 nights to complete the task. Senior observers Bert Smith and Bernard Willis had agreed to take turns with each other on the Tavistock theodolite, but the effort of climbing up and down the mountain so often proved such a strain they decided to take alternate spells on top. Much of the time was spent in the tent with the Primus going, in a temperature of -3.3° Celsius. Their first camp pitched on the snow in mist had to be moved at the first clearing, as they found they were camped dangerously close to the lip of the cornice overhanging the cliffs. Nevis proved to be one of the most exactingly rigorous stations of the whole Primary Triangulation. This triangulation began in 1936, but was suspended on the outbreak of war. Work resumed in 1949 and finished in 1952; the remarkable space of just seven Field Seasons.

Inevitably the ravages of the elements and the passage of countless thousands of feet have caused considerable damage to both cairn and pillar over the years. The first major repair work undertaken was in 1959 when two tons of material were lifted, by helicopter, to the plateau. Serious undermining of the concrete platform, threatening the stability of the pillar, was made good by the use of pit prop type timbers and stone infill. Despite continued maintenance by 1971 the removal of stone and thirty five years' exposure to the mountain's hostile climate had caused slight pillar movement and further cairn deterioration. In 1972 the cairn was again repaired and a new pillar cast and erected.

With the advent of Global Positioning System technology, the pillar now has a new role, a plaque on the side of the pillar explaining that 'This monument forms part of the Ordnance Survey National GPS

Network'. Maintaining the triangulation pillar on Britain's highest mountain is an ongoing process but one that is essential, not only as a matter of prestige but to retain an occupiable station for inevitable cartographic and scientific use in the future.

DEPICTION OF RELIEF

The relatively small scale of early mapping precluded a detailed survey of the complex form of Ben Nevis. Initially a very symbolic, hand drawn, hill denoted its approximate location. Early attempts to show its actual mountain form used brush strokes of grey wash (P. Sandby) or hachures (W. Johnson), often to great effect if not accuracy. (Hachures are short lines to indicate steepness of slope by their closeness.)

Not until 1870 were surveyors called upon to map out the steep and complicated rock features of the great north eastern precipice of Ben Nevis, which must have presented a difficult not to say dangerous undertaking. At this time the Ordnance Survey was still a military concern and visions of the commanding officer ordering his troops to measure distances over impossible terrain spring to mind! However it can reasonably be assumed that the surprisingly accurate depiction achieved of the major gullies and ridges on this 1:10,560 map was due more to the surveyor's eye and artistic talent than to the quality of his surveying equipment or the selflessness of his men! An attractive hand etched rock system was used, most effectively, to depict cliffs on this map, its presentation being an 'art form' quite unique to each individual area.

The use of aerial photography, in the mid-20th Century, revolutionised the survey of precipitous relief features and heralded an era of mapping excellence. The precise contouring derived from stereo photography was far superior to anything that had or could be achieved by ground methods. Although some may lament the passing of the cartographer's artistic skills the clarity and accuracy of relief depiction on current Ordnance Survey 1:10,560 and 1:25,000 mapping is beyond criticism. Not only can all the mountain features be clearly located but the trained eye may even identify climbing routes from the comfort of one's own home!

On small scale mapping, as an addition to contours, layer tinting (Bartholomew 1:1000,000) and hill shading (OS 1 inch:1 mile Tourist Map) have been used for relief enhancement. In fact various combinations of hachuring, hill shading, layer tinting and contouring have been used over the years often creating stunning three dimensional visual effects.

PLACE NAMES

The history of Ben Nevis mapping throws light not only on the development of topographic data depiction but also on the evolution of place and feature names. Ironically, perhaps, the change in spelling and usage over the centuries can frequently be attributed to cartographic misrepresentation. The early surveyors, rarely being Gaelic speakers or scholars, commonly transcribed phonetic versions of place names, sometimes at great variance to the pure ethnic version, which have subsequently become the accepted form.

The Gaelic root of Ben Nevis itself is open to considerable conjecture having appeared on mapping in variety of forms. Likewise Coire

Leis and Allt a' Mhuilinn have undergone numerous changes in spelling although, unlike their parent mountain, have remained close to their Gaelic roots. The earliest recognisable cartographic references to the name are Bin Novesh in c.1595 (T. Pont) and Bin Neves in c.1640 (R. Gordon). In the 18th Century a variety of versions occurred from Ben Nevish (M. Armstrong) to Ben Nivis (R. Campbell) with the first appearance of Ben Nevis (W. Roy) in c.1750. With the exception of Bein Nevis in 1830 (W. Johnson), in the 19th and 20th Centuries the version of Ben Nevis seems to have been widely accepted.

The incorrect application of feature names has occasionally occurred, most strikingly perhaps, Castle Ridge is positioned at the head of Number Four Gully on first edition of OS 1:10,560 mapping, over 750m south of its true location! Even more remarkably this error has been perpetrated on the current 1:10,560 map although on the 1:25,000 edition of 1980 it at last found its true location!

On the 1902 1:10,560 map only two rock feature names are shown, Tower Ridge and Castle Ridge, whereas the 1967 edition contains a dozen. The criteria for their inclusion seems a trifle inconsistent in that The Castle is named yet The Comb isn't, the vast and accessible Observatory Gully isn't named yet curiously Point Five Gully, definitely a pure climbing route, is.

Although the forces of erosion will inexorably if slowly alter the topography of Ben Nevis it seems likely that its name and the names of its myriad features have now entered into a long period of stability.

HEIGHTING

Scottish hill heights are a subject of great sensitivity and often controversy. The desire to establish a 'true' height value is inevitably at odds with an equally strong desire to maintain the status quo. This applies to Ben Nevis perhaps more than any other Scottish peak. Given the relatively level nature of the summit area of Ben Nevis, agreeing to the exact location of the highest point is another consideration.

'A New and Correct Map of Scotland or North Britain' published in 1794, in two sheets, boldly announced, *'Ben Nivis – 4370 feet High – The Highest Mountain in Great Britain'*. This map, at a scale of 7.5 miles:1 inch, was an updated version of a 1782 map and bears the name of an unknown cartographer Lt. R. Campbell. How this surprisingly good height value was calculated remains unclear and the assertion following it is equally surprising as at the time many authorities believed Britain's highest mountain to be Ben Macdui in the Cairngorms.

Between the publication of the 6 inch map in 1875 and the publication of the results of post war triangulation and levelling in 1964 a remarkable cartographic consistency reigned, the height of Ben Nevis being universally accepted at 4406ft. The new value announced of 4418ft caused much comment and confusion but in fact this value was to the flush bracket (No.81595), a brass levelling plate low down on the face of the pillar, and not to natural ground level. As the pillar is built upon a cairn nine feet and six inches high, the true ground level height is actually 4408ft 6in. This figure when converted gave a value, to the nearest metre, of 1344m and this height became standard on all Ordnance Survey maps for many years. Inexplicably, there was a blip in this

Harvey British Mountain Map of Ben Nevis (2007). This innovative 1:40,000 scale map is based on original photogram-metric and field surveys and uses colour shading for increased three dimensional effect. A more detailed 1:15,000 inset of the summit area shows the descent route to the Red Burn

Illustration courtesy HARVEY Maps © HARVEY 2009 www.harveymaps.co.uk

consistency in 2001 when a height of 1343m appeared on a revised edition of the 1:50,000 scale map. Hopefully this is just a temporary aberration. Other map and atlas publishers have used a variety of alternative height values over the years although the many Internet references now seem to have standardised on 1344m.

Thus the calculated height difference between the 19th and 20th Century observations was slightly under one metre, surely a great compliment to the expertise of the early Ordnance Survey cartographers.

Ben Nevis is indisputably Britain's highest mountain at 1344m and barring some major reactivation of the Great Glen fault, seems certain to maintain its status. With the continuing uplift of the Scottish landmass, due to the effect of isostatic readjustment, the 'true' height of Ben Nevis must remain a matter of speculation. However, with the wider availability of high order Global Positioning System (GPS) technology, it is only a matter of time before the height value of 1344m is either confirmed or challenged. No doubt the traditionalist will always require the height of Ben Nevis to be expressed in feet!

Bibliography:

The Early Maps of Scotland. Vol. 1. Royal Scottish Geographical Society.

Harley, J.B., *Ordnance Survey – A Descriptive Manual*. (Oxford: HMSO, 1975.)

The Mitchell Library Map Collection, Glasgow.

The National Map Library of Scotland, Edinburgh.

The NLS also has an excellent collection available on the web at www.nls.uk/maps/

Natural History

FLORA

AS THE ICE AGE drew to a close and bare ground gradually became exposed, so plants began to colonise the land. The first plants to move in were Arctic and Alpine types, such as may be seen at present adjacent to glaciers and snowfields. The plant cover was much as seen on Ben Nevis today, above a height of about 2400ft, or just above the CIC Hut, being an abundance of low-growing, cushion-like perennial forms. The low-growing habit resists drought; in addition the leaves of alpines are usually very small, with a coating or wax or perhaps a thick, leathery epidermis. The root system has to be well-developed, often more so than the visible part of the plant, while most alpines also possess an underground stem or rhizome in which food can be stored in the summer. With the arrival of milder weather, though before water absorption may be possible, such plants can begin growing almost immediately, therefore making use of the short growing season.

Such alpines may be found growing on the margins of the smaller streams, perhaps where a spring provides more reliable water, alpines

*Starry Saxifrage
(Saxifraga stellaris)*

Photo: Tom Prentice

such as the Yellow Mountain Saxifrage (*Saxifraga aizoides*), clusters of which may be mixed with denser white-flowered Mossy saxifrage (*Saxifraga hypnoides*). The shady spots on rock faces may harbour such rosette forms as the Starry saxifrage (*Saxifraga stellaris*), its short main stock crowned by a rosette of egg-shaped leaves. Each rosette sends up a flowering shoot topped by a panicle of small, white flowers, each one conspicuously star-shaped. The Starry saxifrage can attain considerable elevation.

More rarely, on the rock faces will be found the Alpine Saxifrage (*Saxifraga nivalis*). Its thick leaves are well adapted to conserve water, while it has four to 12 fairly large, white flowers. In early summer the drier rocks may exhibit sheets of the evergreen, purple-flowered Purple Saxifrage (*Saxifraga oppositifolia*), one of our most beautiful alpine flowers. It may be seen flowering on Nevis about May, when much of the snow may have cleared. The leaves of the Purple Saxifrage possess an interesting mechanism for drought control. Water pores are found at the apex of each leaf. The tissue around this pore can secrete chalk, supplied by the roots. Water leaving this pore will contain some dissolved chalk, which on a day of high evaporation will soon leave sufficient chalk to block the pore and thereby reduce water loss. At night, when evaporative losses are reduced, escaping water will dissolve this chalk barrier, permitting transpiration

Above: The yellow flowers of Bog Asphodel (Narthecium ossifragum) are a common sight throughout the summer

Left: Purple Saxifrage (Saxifraga oppositifolia)

Photos: Tom Prentice

Moss Campion
(Silene acaulis)

Photo: Tom Prentice

Heath Spotted
Orchid (Dactylorhiza
maculata) flowers
profusely in early
spring on wet upland

Photo: Tom Prentice

again. Even on rocks containing little or no chalk, the roots of this plant can selectively obtain sufficient minerals to continue this protective mechanism.

Accompanying the Purple Saxifrage may be found the Moss Campion (*Silene acaulis*), a typical Cushion Plant, with a proportionally much larger root system. Throughout the short summer the woody rhizome of this plant, and others like it, will be storing energy. In the four short months on Nevis in which average temperatures will be above freezing, these plants must go through the entire reproductive cycle.

The Cerastium family is represented on Ben Nevis by the Starwort Mouse-ear (*Cerastium cerastioides*), while another hairy-leaved plant is the Alpine Lady's Mantle (*Alchemilla alpina*), which has its stems and leaves covered with shining, silver hairs as a protection against excess water loss. The Scottish Sibbaldia (*Sibbaldia procumbens*) is a perennial forming a low growth well adapted for long periods under snow. Its small hairy leaves are, of course, to guard against drought. The flowers do not produce nectar and are probably usually self-fertilised.

Another plant which can coat a fair area of ground is the Dwarf Willow (*Salix herbacea*), sometimes known as 'the smallest tree in the world'. Its roots dive deep in this plant, while its very small leaves conserve moisture. The catkins are very short with very few flowers.

Of immense importance to climbers, but rarely noticed until the rocks are wet, are the algae, whose thin film on the rocks becomes very slimy when wet. And then there are the lichens, whose natural history fills books and occupies the lives of researchers full time. The algae and lichens are best left to the expert, but some introductory words can be said. The green algae (phylum *Chlorophyta*) are mostly small, simple plants, from which the land plants are believed to have evolved. Many are single celled, though others consist of thin sheets of cells.

The lichens arouse much interest. These strange plants have evolved through the combination, in the same tissue mass, of an alga and a fungus. The fungus, an *Ascomycete* or *Basidiomycete*, forms a dense mat of interwoven hyphae (a mass of long thread-like structures, which contain many nuclei unseparated by cell walls). Within this mat the algae grow. The relationship is a symbiotic one, as the fungus obtains its organic food from the algae, which in turn obtains dissolved salts and water which the fungus has extracted from the rock. Most of the algae and fungi are incapable of living independently, but together form a tough combination, one which can survive environmental conditions hostile in the extreme. The various patterns and colours formed by the lichens are beautifully subtle, though the andesite of Ben Nevis is not nearly so good a substrate as say the easily eroded mica schists of the Southern and Central Highlands.

The lichens have two especially interesting uses, despite their simplicity and small size. One is a use which dates back to prehistory, as a source of natural dyes. Their colours are mostly in the yellow to brown range, though some purples and reds are also available in some areas. The other use is the more contemporary one of being a pollution index, as they are very sensitive to atmospheric sulphur dioxide amongst other pollutants. Some work has been done on the effect of the pulp mill on local lichens. Generally, the western seaboard of Scotland will be a safe haven for the lichens, as here the atmosphere is almost free from pollution.

Another modest group of plants which must be mentioned in the passing are the numerous grasses, sedges and rushes. The Glaucous Meadow-grass (*Poa glauca*) is a slightly creeping plant with smooth, narrow leaves, sometimes of a bluish-green colour. Another species, the Wavy Meadow-grass (*Poa flexuosa*), is closely related to the Alpine Meadow-grass, though very hard to find. The Alpine Cat's-tail (*Phleum alpinum*) is to be found on wet, rocky ledges, as is the Alpine Fox-tail (Alopecurus alpinus). All of the above are real Alpine grasses, only to be found on the flanks of the high hills. The success of the grasses can be explained by their prolific seed production, their perennial habit, and their production of runners and offsets, by which the plants reproduce themselves.

Alpine Lady's Mantle (Alchemilla alpina)

Photo: Tom Prentice

Stiff Sedge
(Carex bigelowii)

Photo: Stuart Rae

The Sedge Family (*Cyperaceae*) belong mainly to the genus *Carex*, containing over 75 British species. The sedges have their flowers united into shapely conical or cylindrical spikes. The flowers are pollinated by the wind, no nectar being produced. The Stiff Sedge, (*Carex bigelowii*), is to be found on Nevis, as well as on most of the other high hills. It is barely six inches high, with flat and very rigid leaves. Besides the grasses and sedges there are the wood-rushes, represented on Ben Nevis by the Curved Wood-rush (*Luzula arcuata*). Its leaves are almost cylindrical with its flowers found in a panicle of small clusters.

As we approach the summit rocks of Nevis there appear the various mosses. These show two growth forms; the tightly packed, upright stems which form dense cushions, and the flattened, creeping sort. Like the lichens, this is not the place to go into these beautiful plants in detail. Also like the lichens, these plants are adapted to withstand conditions of drought.

Finally, for the plant world, Lochan Meall an t-Suidhe has various aquatic plants, such as the Water Awl-wort (*Subularia aquatica*). This interesting little plant may be seen in summer as a soft green carpet on the bottom of shallow parts of the lochan. It is unusual for a mountain plant in being an annual, the seed starting to germinate as soon as the temperature of the water rises sufficiently in the early summer. The leaves rarely rise above the surface of the water, while from the middle of the leaves rises a short, naked stalk which gives rise to a raceme of small white flowers.

The Water Lobelia (*Lobelia dortmanna*), is a common species, found around the shores of many a Highland loch, including Lochan Meall an t-Suidhe. It usually forms a carpet of green leaves beneath the surface of the water. The rootstock is topped with a tuft of bright green leaves, formed into two hollow tubes placed side-by-side. This structure allows the plant to withstand the strong wave action often caused by wind. Its flower is a bright blue.

This list of plants to be found on Ben Nevis is by no means exhaustive; we have not, for example, gone into the bog flora, nor the wooded areas lower down the hill. Readers will have no difficulty in finding a suitable reading list as a starter, though there is no substitute for a tour with an expert. The rocks of Ben Nevis may not be as rich in plants as hills nearby, but the eagle eye can still find much to interest from the plant kingdom.

FAUNA

In the autumn the hare moults into a new brown coat. The white coat then begins to appear, perhaps as early as October. The change to white is usually complete by about late November. A sudden thaw in mid-winter can result in an embarrassed looking hare, stark white against a dark background. In the snow, and unmoving, a passing climber is unlikely to notice. Tracks of hare criss-crossing with those of the fox are more often seen than the animals who make them.

Stoats (Mustela erminea) and Weasels (*Mustela nivalis*) were well known to the observatory staff. Likewise, the common Rat (*Rattus norvegicus*) and Mouse (*Mus musculus*), who were unwelcome occupants of the summit observatory. A humourous sighting of a large mammal was that of the Badger (*Meles meles*) who fell down Green Gully in the early 1970s. The animal rolled down to the bottom of the gully, shook the snow off its coat, and gamely tried to climb back up again.

The Field or Short-tailed vole (*Microtus agrestis*) is relatively common, below the cliffs and sometimes on top of the hill. It is a grass-eater notable for explosive rises in population, reaching a peak density about every four years, and suddenly collapsing then building up again. Shrews, (*Sorex araneus*), much smaller and darker than voles, were commonly caught by the Observatory cat.

The Golden Eagle (*Aquila chrysaetos*) gets mention as a common sight on the Nevis cliffs in the 1936 guide book. It is a less likely sight today, though it may be seen above upper Glen Nevis. Perhaps the most interesting bird of Ben Nevis is the Snow Bunting (*Plectrophenax nivalis*). This hardy sparrow-sized bird with the white wings is a true singer. Harold Raeburn describes his pleasure at hearing its song, (see Chapter 4 for this reference), a short, far-carrying musical phrase. Undoubted it breeds on Nevis some years, nesting usually in a rock niche or among the stones. In winter snow buntings may be met with on the summit, even in bad weather, or around the CIC Hut.

A family of Ravens (*Corvus corax*) is usually present on

Snow Bunting (Plectrophenax nivalis)

Photo: David Whitaker / www.highlandwildlife photography.com

Wheatear
(Plectrophenax
nivalis)

Photo: David Whitaker /
www.highlandwildlife
photography.com

Ben Nevis, their locality differing from year to year. Its aerial acrobatics have drawn applause from many a spectator, while its throaty croak is part of the mountain sound. The Ptarmigan (*Lagopus mutus*) is occasionally seen, though not often enough, and the author was delighted to see a pair in winter on top of the First Platform. It is the only mountain bird that moults three times a year, turning white in winter. Other small birds to be looked out for on Ben Nevis are the ubiquitous Meadow Pipit (*Anthus pratensis*), which arrive in Spring, followed by the Wheatear (*Oenanthe oenanthe*), which nests in convenient holes in the ground. The Ring Ouzel (*Turdus torquatus*) occurs on the lower slopes, a blackbird with a white collar, while the Wren (*Troglodytes troglodytes*) and the Dipper (*Cinclus cinclus*) may be spotted near the streams, on occasion moving upstream and underwater, head down looking for food.

The observant, and expert ornithologist, will no doubt spot other species of birds on Ben Nevis, though the above short list probably includes most of the birds that have been seen on the hillside above the tree line.

Untouched by this section so far are the insects, many of which are blown up by winds, sometimes to land in great numbers on the snow, where snow buntings find them. Of significance as an indicator of environmental changes mention must be made of the Mountain Ringlet butterfly (*Erebia epiphron*). This butterfly has a very limited range, surviving

Mountain Ringlet
(Erebia epiphron)
Photo: Keith Miller

*Common or
Viviparous Lizard
(Lacerta vivipara)*

Photo: Tom Prentice

in a small number of places in the Lake District and on Scottish mountains, including Ben Nevis. It is the only true alpine butterfly in the UK. The John Muir Trust organise volunteers for an annual count of this species, camping at altitude in Coire Giubhsachan. This small brown butterfly has been found as high as 875m on Aonach Beag. They appear to be most commonly found at altitudes of between 750 – 800m.

Also not mentioned so far are the amphibians. Small frogs are quite common on the lower slopes, the common frog (*Rana temporaria*) spawning in the Highlands to a height of over 1500ft. Lizards and snakes may be found too, on the lower slopes, with the Common or Viviparous Lizard (*Lacerta vivipara*) and the Adder (*Vipera berus*), its diamond markings distinguishing it from the Grass snake. Again, as with the birds, the patient and experienced observer will see far more than the casual walker or climber.

Bibliography:

Clapham, A.R., **Tutin**, T.G. and **Warburg**, E.F., *Flora of the British Isles*. 2nd Edition. (Cambridge: Cambridge University Press, 1962).

Darling, F.F. and **Boyd**, J.M., *The Highlands and Islands*. New Naturalist Series (London: Collins, 1969.)

Fitter, R.S.R., **Fitter**, A., and **Blamey**, M., *The wild flowers of Britain and Northern Europe*. (London: Collins, 1974.)

Fletcher, H.R. *Exploration of the Scottish Flora*. Trans. Bot. Soc. Edinb. 38, 30 – 47, 1959.

Holden, A.E., *Plant life in the Scottish Highlands*. (Edinburgh: Oliver & Boyd, 1952.)

Kempe, Nick and **Wrightham**, Mark (Eds.), *Hostile Habitats – Scotland's Mountain Environment*. This covers all aspects of the Scottish mountains and is profusely illustrated. (Glasgow: Scottish Mountaineering Trust, 2006.)

MacNally, L. *Highland Year*. (London: Pan Books, 1972.)

Peterson, R., **Mountfort**, G., and **Hollom**, P.A.D. *Birds of Britain and Europe*. (London & Glasgow: Collins, 1974.)

SCOTTISH MOUNTAINEERING CLUB
SCOTTISH MOUNTAINEERING TRUST
Prices were correct at time of publication, but are subject to change

HILLWALKERS' GUIDES

The Munros	£22.00
Munros GPS data sets – from SMC website	£10.50
The Corbetts and Other Scottish Hills	£22.00
The Cairngorms	£18.00
Central Highlands	£18.00
Islands of Scotland Including Skye	£20.00
North-West Highlands	£22.00
Southern Highlands	£17.00

SCRAMBLERS' GUIDES

Skye Scrambles	£18.00
Highland Scrambles North	£18.00

CLIMBERS' GUIDES

Scottish Winter Climbs	£24.00
Scottish Rock Climbs	£24.00
Ben Nevis	£21.00
Glen Coe	£21.00
North-East Outcrops	£21.00
Arran, Arrochar and Southern Highlands	£15.00
The Cairngorms	£24.00
Highland Outcrops	£17.50
Lowland Outcrops	£21.00
Northern Highlands North	£21.00
Northern Highlands Central	£24.00
Northern Highlands South	£24.00
Skye	£24.00
The Islands	£24.00

OTHER PUBLICATIONS

Hostile Habitats – Scotland's Mountain Environment	£16.00
Scottish Hill Names – Their origin and meaning	£15.00
A Chance in a Million? Avalanches in Scotland	£15.00
The Munroist's Companion	£16.00

Visit our website for more details and to purchase on line:
www.smc.org.uk

Distributed by:
Cordee Ltd, Leicestershire, UK
(t) 0116 254 3579 (e) sales@cordee.co.uk
www.cordee.co.uk

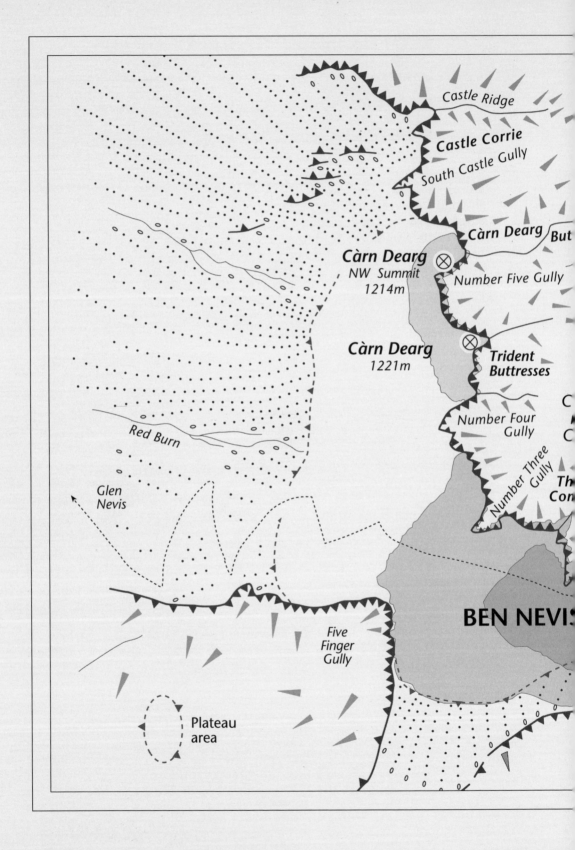

Castle Ridge

Castle Corrie

South Castle Gully

Càrn Dearg But

Càrn Dearg
NW Summit
1214m

Number Five Gully

Càrn Dearg
1221m

**Trident
Buttresses**

Number Four
Gully

Number Three Gully

Th
Co

BEN NEVIS

Red Burn

Glen
Nevis

Five
Finger
Gully

Plateau
area